TRIAL PRACTICE SERIES

Jury Selection

The Law, Art, and Science of Selecting a Jury

Second Edition

James J. Gobert
Professor of Law
University of Essex

Walter E. Jordan
Author of First Edition

CBC
CLARK
BOARDMAN
CALLAGHAN®

DEERFIELD, IL • NEW YORK, NY • ROCHESTER, NY
Customer Service: 1-800-323-1336

Revised edition of *Jury Selection* by Walter E. Jordan (Shepard's/McGraw-Hill 1980)

2345678910 SHHA 9987654321

Library of Congress Cataloging-in-Publication Data

Jordon, Walter E., 1918-
Jury selection : the law, art, and science / Walter E. Jordon,
James J. Gobert. — 2nd ed.
p. cm.—(Trial practice series)
Includes index.
ISBN 0-07-172235-1
1. Jury selection—United States. I. Gobert, James J. II. Title. III. Series.
KF8979.J67 1990
347.73'0752—dc20
[347.307752] 90-40578
CIP

ISBN 0-07-172235-1

JSO

The sponsoring editor for this book was Margaret Makar and the editor was Frear Simons.

This book is dedicated to my parents, who showed me the way, although it was decades before I was able to see it. My father, unfortunately, did not live to see the publication of this book, but I hope that it would have made him proud.

James J. Gobert

Shepard's Trial Practice Series

Advocacy: The Art of Pleading a Cause, Second Edition
Attorney Fee Awards
Constitutional Limitations on Criminal Procedure
Cross-Examination of Witnesses: The Litigator's Puzzle
Defense of Equal Employment Claims
Determining Economic Loss in Injury and Death Cases
Eyewitness Testimony: Strategies and Tactics
Federal Appeals: Jurisdiction and Practice
Guide to Multistate Litigation
Head and Neck Injury Handbook
Hearsay Handbook, Second Edition
How to Prepare Witnesses for Trial
Manual of Federal Practice, Third Edition
Newberg on Class Actions, Second Edition
Questioning Techniques and Tactics
Statistics in Litigation: Practical Applications for Lawyers
Structuring Settlements
Successful Trial Techniques of Expert Practitioners
Testimonial Privileges
Toxic Torts: Litigation of Hazardous Substance Cases
Trial Communication Skills

Our civilization has decided, and very justly decided, that determining the guilt or innocence of men is a thing too important to be trusted to trained men. If it wishes for light upon that awful matter, it asks men who know no more law than I know, but who can feel the things that I felt in the jury box. When it wants a library catalogued, or the solar system discovered, or any trifle of that kind, it uses up its specialists. But when it wishes anything done which is really serious, it collects twelve of the ordinary men standing round.

G. K. Chesterton
"The Twelve Men,"
Tremendous Trifles 86 (1920)

Preface

For better or for worse, the American legal system has made a commitment to the use of juries in the adjudication of legal disputes. Many are the criticisms of the jury: it is time-consuming and expensive; its members are unqualified by training, education, or experience, and are often swayed more by emotion than logic; its deliberations are conducted in secret, with no degree of accountability; and its verdicts may be irrational. All of these criticisms, and more, may be valid.

One may respond, however, in a paraphrase of Winston Churchill's classic remark about democracies, that the jury may be the worst form of dispute resolution ever invented except for all other forms which have been tried from time to time. Judges, like jurors, may be biased by experience, education, or upbringing; but they act alone, without the benefit of eleven others to serve as a counterweight to their prejudices. If a judge dozes during a witness's testimony, there are not eleven others to assure that the witness's testimony is taken into account. Moreover, judges quickly become habituated to trials and lack the freshness of perspective that jurors can bring to a case. Is it irrational to prefer the common sense judgment of lay persons, with their ability to inject community values into the adjudicational process, to the technical methods of a legal logician?

The debate over the merits of the jury is, in any event, moot. Lawyers and their clients are saddled with the jury system, like it or not. The challenge is to make the system work for, rather than against, the litigant. The first and most critical step in meeting this challenge lies in the selection of the jury.

The process of jury selection is a relativistic one. The lawyer's task is to select not the best possible jury but the best jury possible. The term *jury selection* is a misnomer. Lawyers can reject jurors but they cannot select jurors. Further, to a large extent they are limited in this process by the community from which the jury is drawn and the members of that community summoned for jury duty. A lawyer must find from the summoned jurors of the community the best mix to serve on the jury of the actual case, recognizing that whatever choices the lawyer might prefer are constrained by the rights of the opposing party.

Several basic premises regarding jury selection underlie this book. The first is that who serves on a jury does make a difference: the same case, consisting of the same evidence, conducted pursuant to the same trial strategy, but tried before different juries can result in different verdicts. This is particularly true of cases in which strong arguments on the facts and the merits are available to both sides. These are the bulk of the cases which are litigated, most noncontroversial cases having been settled. While it may be going too far to say, as some have, that jury selection is the trial, it is certainly one of its most critical phases. A lawyer who can pack the jury with persons whose life experiences, values, and personality incline them to the lawyer's position has won a significant battle in the overall war. Attorneys on each side thus vie to choose jurors favorably disposed to their clients and/or witnesses, their legal position, or the attorneys themselves. The key is to identify subconscious partiality, since blatantly partial jurors will in effect identify themselves and can be challenged for cause.

A second premise underlying this book is that identifying juror bias, even subconscious bias, is a skill which can be learned. While a fortunate few intuitively possess this ability, for most attorneys it will be the product of a systematic approach to jury selection. A combination of pretrial surveys, juror investigations, and mock trials can be used to construct profiles of favorable and unfavorable jurors. Information about jurors can be obtained through pre-voir dire questionnaires. Voir dire can be structured to reveal aspects of juror personalities of which the jurors themselves may be unaware or which they may try to conceal.

A third premise is that it is in the lawyer's interest to have as sophisticated an insight into the personality of the jurors chosen to serve in a particular case as is possible. Trial strategy is often dictated by the composition of the jury. Different jurors respond to different presentations and different arguments. It is better to make a theoretically less persuasive argument to which a jury will respond than a theoretically more persuasive argument to which it will not.

Jury selection is both an art and a science. The successful jury selector must be able to relate to people—to know, for example, how to delicately probe during voir dire, when to press forward and when to back off. The successful jury selector must be attuned to the vibrations which emanate from the jurors; one must feel the beat as well as hear the music. The successful jury selector must have a sense of what constitutes the right mix of jurors for any particular case, without being tied to any rigid formula.

Many would suggest that these kinds of sensitivities make jury selection an art, which may well be true, and one which cannot be taught, which is definitely not true. Instincts can be honed and refined. They can benefit from a study of human personality. They can be informed by social science research. One can sift through juror investigations and demographic analyses, incorporating what is valuable, discarding what is not.

It would probably be impossible to remove the "art" from jury selection. It would be foolish to try. The computer within our brain may comprehend matters which our rational selves do not. In the final analysis, jury selection decisions are often matters of judgment—two jurors whose ratings on an objective scale are similar may "feel" quite different to the lawyer who is about to try the case. The lawyer should not ignore those feelings, if for no other reason than that the lawyer will be more effective performing before an audience with whom he or she feels comfortable.

To say that jury selection is an art is not to deny that it is a science. Even if ultimate decisions are matters of judgment, it would be sheer obstinacy to refuse to allow one's judgment to be informed by science. Increasingly, scientific methodologies are being used to assist, not replace, lawyers. Social science studies (such as those on the authoritarian personality), pretrial demographic surveys and analyses of the community, and mock trials can help identify those qualities that make for a desirable juror. Scientifically conducted investigations of members of the jury pool can tell the lawyer the extent to which these qualities can be found in each of the potential jurors. Socio-psychological analysis of body language and paralinguistic cues during voir dire can indicate the extent to which the juror's responses reflect the juror's true feelings, regardless of whether the juror is consciously lying or subconsciously ambivalent.

To put into effect information geared about the jurors, whether from intuition or scientific research, requires a knowledge of the law. Without an understanding of the law of challenges, a lawyer would not be able to remove undesirable jurors from a panel. More fundamentally still, without an understanding of when one has a legal right to a jury and when one may waive that right, it is impossible to make even the most basic decision of whether to opt for a jury. A knowledge of the law of venue and vicinage is necessary to identify the community from which the jurors are to be drawn, and the options available when that community is likely to produce a hostile jury. A knowledge of legal rulings relating to features of the jury, such as size and verdict unanimity, also informs the decision whether to opt for a jury, as well as one's jury selection strategy.

An understanding of the history and function of the jury is useful. Particularly important is an understanding of the concept of impartiality. *First and foremost, jury selection involves the search for impartial jurors.* That lawyers approach this task by eliminating those jurors whom they perceive to be partial to the opposition, that they understandably prefer and search for jurors partial to their side rather than neutral jurors, does not detract from the importance of impartiality. Impartial juries, who engage in impartial decision making and reach impartial verdicts, are essential for assuring society of the fairness and justice of its legal system. Without this public confidence, the legal system would collapse, and likely the state soon after.

The people to whom I am indebted in the preparation of this book are many. A special tribute needs to be paid to Judge Walter Jordan, the author of the predecessor edition. The seeds for much of what appears in this book were planted in the first edition. Unfortunately, Judge Jordan died before work on the present volume could be begun, but I would hope that his spirit lives on in this book. I express this hope with some trepidation, however. Careful readers of Judge Jordan's writings may have gathered that the Judge was not particularly enamored of "scientific" jury selection techniques, that he believed that the skill and experience of a lifetime in the courtroom was the best teacher. Perhaps Judge Jordan would have blanched at the amount of space devoted in this successor volume to social science methodologies. These methodologies, however, have become more refined and sophisticated since publication of the original work, and I would like to think that Judge Jordan was a sufficiently, open, flexible, and fair man that he would have recognized the value of including this material.

Numerous other persons have contributed to the development of this book. Among the lawyers who have provided me with the benefit of their experience are Bob Ritchie and J.D. Lee of Knoxville, Tennessee; Jim Sanders of Nashville, Tennessee; and Stanley Arkin, Mark Arisonn, and Leonard Marks of New York City. Racehorse Haynes and Joe Shannon provided invaluable assistance to Judge Jordan in the preparation of the first edition, and the instructive voir dire of Racehorse Haynes in the trial of Thomas Cullen Davis, which appeared in the earlier volume, is preserved in this edition. In respect to social science methodologies, the pioneering work of the National Jury Project needs to be acknowledged.

Judge Jordan enjoyed a warm and positive relationship with Lawyers Co-operative Publishing Company, of Rochester, New York and Bancroft-Whitney Company, of San Francisco, California. In the predecessor volume Judge Jordan, with the permission of these two companies, used materials that had first appeared in their publications, particularly *American Jurisprudence,* 2d and *American Jurisprudence Trials.* Some of that material remains in this new edition, and I can only echo Judge Jordan's acknowledgment and thanks.

Law student assistants have also been helpful. In particular I have in mind Amy Spencer, Greg Gundlach, Mark Hooten, and Andrew Walsh of the University of Tennessee; and Karen Swenson and Matt Painter of Vanderbilt University. Sandy Selvage and Missy Williams, secretaries at the University of Tennessee, displayed admirable patience in typing drafts of this manuscript.

Finally, Carolyn Yates, my wife and professional colleague at the University of Essex, read the final draft with an eye toward separating that which made sense from that which did not. To the extent that she succeeded, credit is due her. What errors remain are the responsibility of the author.

This book was written during a period that spanned teaching posts at the University of Tennessee and the University of Essex. Both institutions were supportive of my research. I am particularly grateful to the University of Tennessee for granting me study leave for a term.

James J. Gobert
Colchester, England
March 13, 1990

Contents

Detailed Preface

PART I The History, Functions, and Features of the Jury

Overview

1 The Right to a Jury Trial

PART II Laying the Groundwork

Overview

PART IV Voir Dire

Overview

9 Voir Dire Generally

10 Voir Dire in Civil Cases

11 Voir Dire in Criminal Cases

Part I

The History, Functions, and Features of the Jury

Overview

Enlightened jury selection should be informed by an understanding of the history, functions, and purposes of the jury. The critical distinctions between the jury system in England and America stem largely from the fact that in America the right to a jury is enshrined in both federal and state constitution. The federal constitutional right to jury trial in criminal cases has been extended by the United States Supreme Court to state criminal prosecutions. A comparable extension, however, has not occurred in respect to the federal constitutional right to jury trial in civil cases. Chapter 1 explores the reasons behind these developments, the limitations on them, and the status of state law as a result of them. It also provides an overview of the historical development of the jury as an institution.

Chapter 1 ends with a discussion of the most basic jury selection decision—the decision to waive a jury. By waiving a jury, whether by opting for a nonjudicial method of dispute resolution or by choosing to have the case decided by a judge, a party in effect rejects all potential jurors. The legal standards governing waiver, as well as the tactical considerations informing it, are explored in the final four sections of Chapter 1.

Jury selection strategy is also dictated by the characteristics and features of the jury. A different strategy may be employed, for example, where the jury's verdict does not have to be unanimous than when it does; or where the size of the jury is six rather than twelve. Chapter 2 of Part I examines many of the key features of the American jury, how they have changed over time, and the implications of these changes for jury selection strategy. The decisions of the United States Supreme Court on these matters are analyzed in some depth.

Particular attention is paid in Chapter 2 to the constitutional requirement that the jury be impartial. Jury selection involves, first and foremost, the search for impartial jurors. In practice this search may take the form of eliminating those jurors perceived to be partial to the opposition, a perhaps inevitable consequence of the Anglo-American adversary system. Nonetheless, it is instructive to examine the generally ignored questions of what the law means by "impartial" and what the characteristics of the impartial juror are.

Finally, Chapter 2 looks at some of the antinomies, inconsistencies, and contradictions within the legal system in respect to the jury. These effects are doubtless the product of the piecemeal development of the relevant law. At the same time, they argue for a more integrated and cohesive perception of the jury and its role in the Anglo-American legal system.

1 The Right to a Jury Trial

§1.01 Introduction

The right to jury trial is one of the unique features of the Anglo-American legal system. In much of the civilized world, lawsuits are tried by judges. In England, the birthplace of the jury, the twentieth century has witnessed a drastic cutback on the cases and issues which a jury can hear.[1] In the United States, on the other hand, the jury retains its vitality and place of prominence. Indeed, the United States Supreme Court in recent years has reaffirmed and strengthened the jury's role in dispute resolution, particularly in criminal cases. It is probably not unfair to say that America has made a firmer commitment to the jury system than has any other country in the world.[2]

Why should this be so? Over the years, the jury system has not been without its critics.[3] The lack of uniformity, and therefore predictability, in verdicts is greater in cases tried before juries than in cases tried before judges. In civil suits, wide variation in damages can occur in factually similar tort cases as a consequence of the composition of the jury. Juries, it is also claimed, are time-consuming, expensive, and inefficient. The selection of a jury can in some cases take months.[4]

Attorneys believe that jurors are swayed by emotion, and often play to that perceived aspect of their character. Good theater may result, but not necessarily justice. Whether an injustice occurs, moreover, is difficult to ascertain, for jurors are not accountable for their decisions—they deliberate in secret and provide no reasons for their verdicts.

The lay persons who serve on juries are not trained in the law,[5] and rules of evidence have had to be devised lest they give evidence more weight than its due. The hearsay rules and the exceptions to them are a prime example. Because of a fear that jurors will unduly credit hearsay testimony, the legal system deprives them of much of this evidence altogether. Despite rules of evidence, many jurors still experience difficulty comprehending complex or technical testimony and judicial instructions.

---

[1] Except for cases involving libel, slander, malicious prosecution, fraud, and false imprisonment, English juries try virtually no civil cases. In the criminal arena, the situation is not very different. Many offenses are triable summarily by a magistrate, many defendants plead guilty, and many who go to trial opt not to have a jury. *See generally* J. Spencer, Jackson's Machinery of Justice ch 32 (1989).

[2] One author reports that approximately 80% of all jury trials in criminal cases occur in the United States. W. Cornish, The Jury 16 (1968).

[3] *See, e.g.*, J. Frank, Courts on Trial (1949).

[4] In Press-Enterprise Co v Superior Court, 464 US 501 (1984), the voir dire had lasted over six weeks. Chief Justice Burger observed that such lengthy voir dire undermined public confidence in the courts and the legal profession. *Id* 510 n 9. The Chief Justice also noted that in response to a question counsel had indicated that it was not unknown in California for jury selection to take six months.

[5] This lack of legal training is sometimes cited as an advantage of the jury system, for jurors may be more inclined to do "justice" than to apply a mechanistic legal formula to the controversy. *See, e.g.*, Wigmore, *A Program for the Trial of a Jury*, 12 Am Jud Socy 166 (1929).

An irrational juror can derail the course of justice, and a corrupt juror can sabotage it. The odds of an irrational or corrupt juror are mathematically twelve times that of an irrational or corrupt judge[6]—greater still, perhaps, because judges are chosen with an eye towards their integrity, and are constantly subject to press and public scrutiny. The risk and consequences of exposure may have more of a deterrent effect on a judge than on a juror.

Why, then, does the American legal system entrust the decision in important matters, indeed in matters of life and death, to a group of ordinary citizens drawn from the community? In one sense the jury represents a commitment to democracy. Verdicts are rendered by the people, or at least a microcosm of the people. Jurors are expected to, and do, bring community values to the decision making process. When appropriate, jurors can temper the rigor of the law with the compassion of the community.

In criminal cases the jury provides a buffer zone between the state and its citizens. It can by its verdict protect individuals from abuses of government power. If a state charges a citizen with a crime, a judge appointed and paid by that state should not decide the defendant's guilt; it may give the unseemly appearance of a conflict of interest.

The government too has a vested interest in the jury system. A verdict is more likely to be accepted by litigants who are allowed a say in the choice of decision maker. Similarly, a verdict is more likely to be accepted in a community whose members are responsible for that verdict. Confidence in the state and its legal system is thus bolstered by the use of juries.

Jurors also benefit from service. For many it is their only first-hand exposure to the inner workings of the legal system. A judge's instructions are a practical lesson in law. Jurors not only see how the legal system operates, but also participate in its operation. The fact that the state entrusts jurors with such important decisions enhances the jurors' self-esteem. Doubtless satisfied with their own performance, jurors are more likely to accept verdicts of other juries.

Jurors, although not as conversant with the law as judges, bring a greater diversity of backgrounds to their task. This collective experience is an invaluable aid in the assessment of witness credibility. Furthermore, although a juror's life experiences may affect his or her objectivity, at least there are jurors with different values and prejudices who will serve as a counterpoint; there may be nobody to challenge a judge's biases. Because they are twelve, jurors collectively can better remember testimony than can a single judge. And unlike a judge, who quickly becomes habituated to the routine of trials, jurors bring a freshness of purpose to the few cases for which they are selected.

America's commitment to the jury system is not mere rhetoric. The right to jury trial is guaranteed both by the federal Constitution[7] and by state

---

[6] On the other hand, those odds may drop considerably if the jury is permitted to return a nonunanimous verdict. *See* **§§2.17-2.19.** The bribed or corrupt juror will not by force of his or her one vote be able to affect the outcome.

[7] *See* **§§1.04-1.17.**

constitutions.[8] That commitment is often reinforced by statute.[9]

On the other hand, it is not the purpose of the government to force a jury upon an unwilling litigant. The right to jury trial can be waived. This book is concerned with jury selection. The most fundamental selection decision is the decision whether to be tried by a jury. By waiving a jury, a party elects to be tried by a judge. In order to make this decision intelligently, a party must assess the relative advantages of trial by judge and trial by jury.

This chapter describes the development of the jury at common law[10] and in American history.[11] The constitutional provisions, both state and federal, guaranteeing the right to a jury are examined, along with exceptions to that right.[12] Finally, the chapter concludes with an inquiry into the circumstances when one is permitted to and one might choose to waive a jury.[13]

§1.02 The Jury at Common Law

The roots of the jury system can be traced to several practices which existed in medieval England and on the European continent.[14] Out of these the jury system gradually evolved. It has never stopped evolving.[15]

Prior to the development of jury trial, there were three primary forms of dispute resolution in England: trial by battle, trial by ordeal, and trial by compurgation.[16] In trial by battle, the protagonists fought to determine the merits of their dispute, the theory being that God would enable the righteous to prevail. It was not only atheists and agnostics, however, who had misgivings about the theory. Litigants who were able to recruit "champions" were permitted to have them fight in their stead. In a crude sense, an attorney may be thought of as the modern day champion of the litigant.[17]

Trial by ordeal was also premised on the idea of divine intervention: God would allow the innocent to survive the ordeal. There were three forms of

---

[8] *See* **§1.19.**

[9] *See, e.g.,* 28 USC §1861 *et seq.*

[10] *See* **§1.02.**

[11] *See* **§1.03.**

[12] *See* **§§1.04-1.19.**

[13] *See* **§§1.21-1.23.**

[14] *See generally* W. Forsyth, The History of the Jury (1852); L. Moore, The Jury: Tool of Kings, Palladium of Liberty (1973). *See also* Eastman, *The History of Trial by Jury,* 3 Natl BJ 87 (1945); Thayer, *The Jury and its Development,* 5 Harv L Rev 249 (1892).

[15] In recent decades, for instance, the Supreme Court has decided that jury verdicts need not be unanimous (*see* **§§2.17-2.19**) and that juries of fewer than twelve are permissible (*see* **§§2.13-2.16**). Both of these developments constitute a marked change from the historical conception of the jury.

[16] Virtually all suits, even criminal actions, were between private parties.

[17] One critical difference is that champions at common law who lost a battle were punished for having in effect borne false witness. *See* M. Bloomstein, Verdict: The Jury System 15 (1968). The consequences of a lost case in modern America befall the client, not the attorney.

ordeal. In one, the ordeal of the hot iron, a person accused of crime had to carry hot iron for a set distance. The accused's hands were then wrapped in bandages. After three days the bandages were removed. If the wounds had healed, the accused was pronounced innocent. A related ordeal based on the same healing principle required the accused to remove a stone from boiling water.

In a second form of ordeal, the defendant was immersed in water. A defendant whose body floated was deemed guilty (the water had rejected the body), while one whose body sank beyond a certain point was adjudged innocent. Although drowning conclusively established innocence, many no doubt would consider it a pyrrhic victory. In most instances, the body of the defendant was rescued in time.

A third form of ordeal was the ordeal of the accursed morsel. In this ordeal, available primarily to clergy, the defendant had only to swallow a morsel of bread. The defendant was supposed to pray to choke on the bread if guilty. If he or she in fact choked on the bread or was unable to swallow it cleanly, it was taken as a sign of having borne false witness.

The religious underpinnings of trial by ordeal were removed in 1215 when Pope Innocent III forbade clergy from further involvement.[18] With the loss of its religious sanction, trial by ordeal, already a somewhat suspect method of fair dispute resolution, fell into disfavor.

In addition to trial by battle and trial by ordeal, there was trial by compurgation. Compurgators were citizens who swore to a party's credibility. If a sufficient number of compurgators, usually twelve,[19] so swore, the party prevailed, unless more swore to the contrary.[20] The dangers of perjury were omnipresent despite the oath taken by the compurgators.

Out of these primitive and questionable modes of decision making evolved the jury. Jurors were originally chosen because of their knowledge of the controversy. Like compurgators, they gave testimony under oath. Unlike compurgators, they swore not to a party's trustworthiness, but to the facts of the case as they understood them. Jurors were witnesses. Their firsthand knowledge of the events giving rise to the dispute put them in the best position to adjudicate the dispute on its merits. The jury as an institution was formally recognized in 1215 in the Magna Carta.[21]

The metamorphosis of the jury from a body of persons with knowledge of the facts to a body of persons ignorant of the facts occurred gradually over time. In some cases, sufficient witnesses to the facts could not be found to comprise a jury. The jury had to be augmented with persons not familiar with the controversy and the jurors had to base their decision in part on the testimony of the litigants. In other cases, a twelve person jury was inadequate to encompass all who possessed relevant information bearing on the case. If the size

---

[18] *See* F. Heller, The Sixth Amendment to the Constitution 5 (1969).

[19] The number of compurgators varied with the rank of the defendant and the seriousness of the charge. *See* L. Moore, *supra* note 14, at 29.

[20] *See* M. Bloomstein, *supra* note 17, at 12-13.

[21] *See* L. Moore, *supra* note 14, at 49-51.

of the jury was not to be expanded, these additional witnesses had to be separately questioned in order that their testimony could be received and considered. As the approach of questioning at least some witnesses became accepted, it no longer made sense to divide witnesses into those who were subject to cross-examination and those (the jurors) who were not. Nor did it make much sense to have some jurors who knew the facts and others who did not. The logical solution was to separate the two camps. Those knowledgeable about the facts testified as witnesses while those ignorant of the facts served on the jury.

Although English jurors were independent citizens, the Crown was still able to exert considerable influence over the jury. One reason was that jurors were chosen by state officials. It was no doubt relatively easy to select individuals who could be expected to be sympathetic to the state's position. Another factor was that where the Crown was dissatisfied with a verdict, it could present its case to a second jury, known as the jury of attaint. This second jury could decide that the initial verdict was false, in which case the original jurors could be imprisoned and their land seized by the state. Doubtless these risks had a considerable chilling effect on juror independence.

The landmark decision which abolished the attaint and established the jury's independence was handed down in 1670. Two Quaker activists, William Penn[22] and William Mead, had been charged with unlawful assembly. Several jurors, led by Edward Bushell, refused to convict. The court, after chastising the jurors, ordered them to resume their deliberations without food or drink. When the jurors persisted in their refusal to find the defendants guilty, the court fined them and committed them to prison until the fines were paid. On appeal the Court of Common Pleas ordered the jurors' release. The court declared that jurors could not be punished for their verdict.[23] From this decision was born the modern concept of the independent, impartial jury.

§1.03 American Developments

The colonists who emigrated to the United States from England had ambivalent feelings about their motherland. They abhorred the religious persecution which drove them into exile. At the same time, they admired much of the British legal system. Indeed, the colonists had little law other than that of England upon which to model their own legal systems. One of the hallmarks of British justice which particularly appealed was trial by jury, since its democratic underpinnings reflected ideals held dear by the colonists. Thus it was not surprising to find the right to trial by jury included in many of the constitutions and charters of the colonies, albeit sometimes in a more populistic and less technical form than found in England.[24]

---

[22] Penn was subsequently the founder of the colony of Pennsylvania.

[23] Bushell's Case, 124 Eng Rep 1006 (CP 1670).

[24] *See* F. Heller, The Sixth Amendment to the Constitution 16-24 (1969). *See generally* L. Moore, The Jury: Tool of Kings, Palladium of Liberty (1973).

In 1774, the first Continental Congress was convened. Among the rights recognized was the citizens' "great and inestimable privilege of being tried by their peers."[25] Similarly, among the grievances against the Crown listed in the Declaration of Independence were those instances where individuals had been denied the benefit of trial by jury. The product of these concerns was the incorporation into the Constitution in not one, but several places, of the right of trial by jury. In *Duncan v Louisiana*[26] the United States Supreme Court captured the functional significance of the jury in the American political system:

> The guarantees of jury trial in the Federal and State Constitutions reflect a profound judgment about the way in which law should be enforced and justice administered. A right to jury trial is granted to criminal defendants in order to prevent oppression by the Government. Those who wrote our constitutions knew from history and experience that it was necessary to protect against unfounded criminal charges brought to eliminate enemies and against judges too responsive to the voice of higher authority. The framers of the constitutions strove to create an independent judiciary but insisted upon further protection against such arbitrary action. Providing an accused with the right to be tried by a jury of his peers gave him an inestimable safeguard against the corrupt or overzealous prosecutor and against the compliant, biased or eccentric judge. If the defendant preferred the commonsense judgement of a jury to the more tutored but perhaps less sympathetic reaction of a single judge, he was to have it. Beyond this, the jury trial provisions in the Federal and State Constitutions reflect a fundamental decision about the exercise of official power—a reluctance to entrust plenary powers over the life and liberty of the citizen to one judge or to a group of judges. Fear of unchecked power, so typical of our State and Federal Government in other respects, found expression in the criminal law in this insistence upon community participation in the determination of guilt or innocence.[27]

The jury's independence in England was established following the criminal prosecution in *Bushell's Case.*[28] Similarly, a dramatic criminal trial in America helped secure the jury's independence. In 1735 John Peter Zenger, the publisher of a New York newspaper reknown for its trenchant criticisms of the British governor, was prosecuted for seditious libel. He was defended by Alexander Hamilton, the leading attorney of the day. Under the controlling English law of libel, the role of the jury was to determine whether Zenger published the newspaper; the role of the judge was to decide whether the articles were libelous as a matter of law. Hamilton argued that the legal and factual questions were inextricably intertwined, and urged the jury to reject the English law. Further, he argued that the jury had the right to acquit where the government

---

[25] *See* R. Perry, Sources of Our Liberties 288 (1959).

[26] 391 US 145 (1968).

[27] *Id* 155-56 (footnotes omitted).

[28] *See* **§1.02.**

had abused its power, as he maintained it had in Zenger's case, in order to curb individual liberties. The jury returned a verdict of not guilty.[29]

The principles established in Zenger's case received a mixed reception. Although juries continued to adjudicate issues of law late into the eighteenth century,[30] the Supreme Court ultimately ruled that the jury did not have this authority.[31] On the other hand, while it remains controversial, juries in criminal cases are still said to retain the power to nullify, i.e., to return a verdict of acquittal despite evidence which clearly establishes factual guilt. Jurors tend to exercise this power primarily in two class of cases: when they are not persuaded that the defendant is morally blameworthy and when they deem the law under which the defendant has been prosecuted to be overly oppressive.[32]

Although the American love affair with the jury may have waned somewhat over time, the jury's preeminent role in the legal system continues. Even a casual comparison with the practice in England reveals the greater confidence that Americans place in the jury. A far greater percentage of cases, both civil and criminal, are tried by juries in America than in England. In England judges routinely comment on the facts of a case, and often in a way that leaves the jurors little doubt as to the verdict that they are expected to return; in the United States judges are often forbidden to comment on the evidence or refrain from doing so. In common law England the Crown could convene a second jury if it was dissatisfied with the verdict of the first; in the United States, the constitutional guaranty against double jeopardy rendered the jury's verdict virtually sacrosanct.[33] In England, sentencing is the sole prerogative of the judge; in many American states, the jury plays a significant role in sentencing, particularly in cases involving the death penalty. The jury is expected to be the conscience of the community.

§1.04 Constitutional Protection for the Right to a Jury Trial: Overview

The right to jury trial in America is not simply a part of the common law tradition; it is enshrined in three distinct provisions of the United States Constitution. Article III provides: "The trial of all crimes, except in Cases of Impeachment, shall be by jury."[34]

---

[29] For a fuller account of Zenger's trial, see J. Alexander, A Brief Narration of the Case and Trial of John Peter Zenger (1963).

[30] *See* Georgia v Brailsford, 3 US 1 (1794).

[31] *See* Sparf & Hansen v United States, 156 US 51 (1895). *See generally* Howe, *Juries as Judges of Criminal Law*, 52 Harv L Rev 582 (1939). In a few states, jurors retain the right to decide questions of law by virtue of statute.

[32] The subject of jury nullification is examined in greater depth in **§§2.20-2.21.**

[33] US Const amend V. The guarantee against double jeopardy has also been incorporated into the fourteenth amendment and made binding on the states. Benton v Maryland, 395 US 784 (1969).

[34] US Const art III, §2(3).

The language of Article III was thought by many to be too enigmatic. In response to this concern, the guarantee of jury trial was made more explicit in the Bill of Rights. The sixth amendment addresses juries in criminal cases: "In all criminal prosecutions, the accused shall enjoy the right to a speedy and public trial, by an impartial jury of the State and District wherein the crime shall have been committed."[35]

The seventh amendment focuses on juries in civil cases: "In Suits at common law, where the value in controversy shall exceed twenty dollars, the right of trial by jury shall be preserved, and no fact tried by a jury, shall be otherwise re-examined in any Court of the United States, than according to the rules of the common law."[36]

The Bill of Rights applied only to the federal government.[37] Therefore, the sixth amendment could not provide a basis for a right to a jury trial in a state criminal prosecution. The fourteenth amendment, however, applies to the states. In *Duncan v Louisiana,*[38] the United States Supreme Court held that the due process clause of the fourteenth amendment incorporated the sixth amendment's guarantee of the right to a jury trial. By incorporating the sixth amendment into the fourteenth, the Court in *Duncan* extended the right to jury trial to state criminal prosecutions.

In truth, the decision was unnecessary. Every state constitution already provided for the right to jury trial in criminal prosecutions.[39] The significance of *Duncan* is that it provides a defendant in a state criminal prosecution with alternative bases for asserting a right to a jury. The federal Constitution provides a floor. A state must grant at a minimum whatever features of a jury trial are held to be required under the Supreme Court's interpretation of the sixth amendment. On the other hand, where the Court has decided that the sixth amendment right is inapplicable (as in the case of petty offenses), or a particular feature of the jury, such as a unanimous verdict, is not mandated by the sixth amendment, the accused can still argue that the right to a jury trial or the particular feature in question is guaranteed under the state constitution. A state constitutional provision can be interpreted more liberally, but not more narrowly, than a comparable federal constitutional provision.

By incorporating the sixth amendment into the due process clause, the Supreme Court in *Duncan* extended the right to trial by jury to state criminal proceedings. A corresponding incorporation for the seventh amendment has never occurred. Thus, while a litigant is constitutionally entitled to a jury in a *federal* civil trial involving more than twenty dollars if a jury would have been available at common law, no comparable right is available in a *state* civil trial by virtue of the federal Constitution. Of course, a state constitution or statute may provide such a right.

---

[35] *Id* amend VI.

[36] *Id* amend VII.

[37] *See* Twitchell v Pennsylvania, 74 US (7 Wall) 321 (1868); Barron v Baltimore, 32 US (7 Pet) 243 (1833).

[38] 391 US 145 (1968).

[39] *See id* 153.

§1.05 The Sixth Amendment Right to a Jury Trial in a Federal Criminal Case

The sixth amendment to the United States Constitution provides, inter alia: "In all criminal prosecutions, the accused shall enjoy the right to a speedy and Public Trial, by an impartial jury of the State and District wherein the crime shall have been committed."[40]

There are several noteworthy aspects of this provision as it relates to trial by jury. First, the jury must be drawn from the "State and District wherein the crime shall have been committed." This codification of the common law requirement of vicinage will be examined in the next chapter.[41] Second, the jury is to be impartial. In a very real sense, impartiality lies at the philosophical heart of any discourse on jury selection. Yet what precisely the term means is rarely articulated. This issue will also be addressed in Chapter 2.[42] Finally, the amendment implies that jury trial is available in "all criminal prosecutions." This is not true, and the circumstances in which jury trial is not available will be explored in the subsequent three sections of this chapter. Whether jury trial is available is critical for jury selection; if a defendant is not entitled to a jury trial, the question of jury selection becomes moot.

In addition to the questions raised by the language of the amendment, there are several others which arise which are not apparent on the face of the amendment. For one, is there a constitutional requirement that the jury be of a particular size? The tradition has been juries of twelve, but is a lesser (or greater) number constitutionally acceptable? This issue is discussed in Chapter 2. Also, must the jury's verdict be unanimous? Again, history suggests an affirmative answer, but the Constitution itself is silent. This question too is considered in Chapter 2.

§1.06 —Petty Offenses

The sixth amendment purports to be applicable to "all criminal prosecutions," but in a thoroughly researched article written in 1926, Felix Frankfurter and Thomas Corcoran documented a "petty offense" exception.[43] In both common law England and colonial America petty offenses were not subject to jury trial. They identified three characteristics which distinguished a petty offense: (1) the offense did not seriously outrage the moral sense of the community; (2) the danger to society was not great; and (3) the punishment allotted to the crime was light. This historical background, presumably known by the drafters of the Constitution, informed subsequent judicial analysis as to what was meant by the term *jury* in the sixth amendment.

---

[40] US Const amend VI.

[41] *See* **§§2.02-2.06.**

[42] *See* **§§2.09-2.12.**

[43] Frankfurter & Corcoran, *Petty Federal Offenses and the Constitutional Guaranty of Trial by Jury,* 39 Harv L Rev 917 (1926).

In *Schick v United States*[44] the United States Supreme Court addressed the question whether under article III a jury trial was constitutionally mandated for a crime carrying a fifty dollar penalty. The Court, noting the small amount of the fine and the lack of moral delinquency involved, held that the charge did not require a jury trial. The Court pointed out that the constitutional wording of article III had been amended from "the trial of all criminal offenses" to "the trial of all crimes." The term *crimes,* said the Court, was meant to be understood in its historical and popular context, which did not include petty offenses. The Court added that "the nature of the offense, and the amount of punishment prescribed, rather than its place in the statute . . . " determined whether an offense was petty.[45]

In a subsequent decision, *District of Columbia v Colts,*[46] the Court seemed to deemphasize the second prong of the *Schick* test. The issue in *Colts* was whether a jury was required where the charge was reckless driving. The Court said that the defendant's act was "of such obvious moral depravity that to characterize it as a petty offense would be to shock the general moral sense."[47] The Court also observed that the defendant's crime was malum in se rather than malum prohibitum.[48]

In *Duncan v Louisiana,*[49] the Court shifted the emphasis to the punishment attached to the offense. The penalty authorized by the law of the locality, stated the Court, "may be taken as a gauge of its social and ethical judgments."[50] What is critical under this test is not the actual punishment imposed but the potential punishment for the crime charged. Accordingly, the defendant in *Duncan* was held entitled to a jury trial for an offense (battery) punishable by up to two years in prison, even though his actual sentence was only sixty days in jail. Although the Court declined to draw a firm boundary between petty and serious offenses, it hinted that incarceration for six months might well be an apt dividing line.

In *Baldwin v New York* [51] the Supreme Court again examined the petty offense exception. The appellant had been convicted of a crime carrying a maximum penalty of one year. Making explicit what was implicit in *Duncan,* the Court concluded that "no offense can be deemed 'petty' for purposes of the right to trial

---

[44] 195 US 65 (1904).

[45] *Id* 68.

[46] 282 US 63 (1930).

[47] *Id* 73.

[48] A *malum in se* offense is one that would be considered wrong by its very nature. A *malum prohibitum* offense is wrong because the legislature says that it is wrong. Murder, for example, is malum in se; driving on the left side of the road is malum prohibitum. Malum in se offenses generally carry a higher penalty, in large part due to the moral turpitude deemed inherent in the offense. *See generally* W. LaFave & A. Scott, Criminal Law §1.6b (2d ed 1986).

[49] 391 US 145 (1968).

[50] *Id* 160 (quoting District of Columbia v Clawans, 300 US 617 (1937)).

[51] 399 US 66 (1970).

by jury where imprisonment for more than six months is authorized."[52] The Court specifically declined to draw the line between petty and serious offenses at the point which separated misdemeanors from felonies.

Baldwin mandated a right to jury trial in cases where the potential punishment was more than six months, regardless of the actual punishment imposed. By the phrasing of its holding, however, the Court left open the possibility that some offenses carrying a penalty of less than six months might also be deemed sufficiently serious to require a jury trial.

In *Blanton v City of North Las Vegas,*[53] the Supreme Court returned to this issue. The Court reiterated that crimes carrying a penalty of less than six months imprisonment were to be presumed to be petty, the punishment being taken as the legislature's judgment of the seriousness of the offense.[54] However, continued the Court, it was open to a defendant to rebut this presumption by pointing to additional statutory penalties which, taken in conjunction with the maximum authorized period of incarceration, indicated that the legislature in fact deemed the offense to be serious, and deserving of a jury trial.[55] In *Blanton,* the defendant argued that the crime of driving under the influence of alcohol (DUI) with which he was charged was sufficiently serious to require a jury trial. He pointed to a range of potential penalties which included 48 hours of community work while identifiably dressed as a DUI offender, a fine of up to $1,000, attendance at an alcohol abuse education course, and loss of one's driving license for 90 days. The Supreme Court, however, was not persuaded. The Court again stressed that the most relevant criterion for determining the seriousness of an offense was the maximum period of imprisonment fixed by the state legislature, which, for DUI in Nevada, was six months. That other states might impose more severe penalties for the same offense was deemed irrelevant,[56] as was the fact that non-statutory penalties might also attach to a conviction.[57]

§1.07 —Fines Only Offenses

The line between petty and serious offenses drawn by the Court in *Baldwin v New York*[58] turned on the potential imprisonment to which the accused could be subjected. But what of crimes punishable by a fine rather than incarceration? Many citizens might, for instance, prefer twenty days in jail to a $20,000 fine. One of the problems, however, is that while a jail sentence is roughly of the

---

[52] *Id* 69.

[53] 109 S Ct 1289 (1989).

[54] *Id* 1292. This inference regarding legislative intent is important for it is generally inappropriate for a court to substitute its view of the seriousness of an offense for that of the legislature. *Id.*

[55] *Id* 1293.

[56] *Id* 1294 n 11.

[57] *Id* 1293 n 8.

[58] 399 US 66 (1970).

same onerousness to everyone, a fine is not; a $20,000 fine might bankrupt a member of the middle class but constitute pocket change to a multimillionaire. Perhaps because of this consideration the Supreme Court has yet to fix a financial line above which an offense will be deemed serious.[59]

A federal statute, since repealed, defined a *petty offense* as one for which a maximum penalty of $500 could be imposed.[60] Although Congress no longer characterizes offenses as petty,[61] a defendant in federal court facing a maximum prison sentence of 6 months also faces a maximum fine of $5,000.[62] In *Blanton v City of North Las Vegas,* the Supreme Court referred to this $5,000 figure in determining whether a maximum fine of $1,000 (among other penalties) rendered a state offense not carrying a greater than six-month prison sentence sufficiently serious to require a jury trial.[63] The Court concluded it did not.

As did the Supreme Court in *Blanton,* lower courts have used the federal statute as a guide in determining whether a defendant was entitled to a jury trial.[64] Other factors which might induce a court to hold that a jury trial is available even though the maximum punishment is less than six months in prison include the moral blameworthiness of the offense, the danger posed by the offense, and the status of the offense at common law. Although decided on state statutory grounds, the California court in *Tracy v Municipal Court*[65] extended the right to jury trial to a fines only offense.

§1.08 —Contempt and Quasi-Criminal Offenses

The *Baldwin* test for petty offenses is problematic in cases where a defendant has been jailed for contempt, as a contempt sentence may be indefinite. Faced with this situation, the United States Supreme Court has held that prosecutions for criminal contempt are within the sixth amendment,[66] and are also subject to the petty offense exception. Whether a particular contempt offense is petty is to be determined by the actual penalty imposed.[67] A judge, however, cannot circumvent the six-month dividing line by imposing cumulative sentences, each of which is less than six months but whose aggregate exceeds six months, for

---

[59] *See* Muniz v Hoffman, 422 US 454 (1975).

[60] 18 USC §1(3).

[61] 98 Stat 2027, 2031, 99 Stat 1728 (repealing 18 USC §1).

[62] Blanton v City of North Las Vegas, 109 S Ct 1289, 1294 n 11 (1989).

[63] *Id* 1294.

[64] *See, e.g.,* United States v McAlister, 630 F2d 772 (10th Cir 1980); United States v Hamdan, 552 F2d 276, 279-80 (9th Cir 1977); Douglass v First Natl Realty Corp, 543 F2d 894 (DC Cir 1976). *Compare* Muniz v Hoffman, 442 US 454 (1975) (refusing to establish a $500 petty offense limit in the case of a fine of a labor union). The courts which have accepted the $500 boundary line generally fail to consider the effect of inflation.

[65] 22 Cal 3d 760, 597 P2d 227, 150 Cal Rptr 785 (1978).

[66] Bloom v Illinois, 391 US 194 (1968).

[67] Frank v United States, 395 US 147, 149 (1969); Dyke v Taylor Implement Mfg Co, 391 US 216 (1968).

a series of contempts occurring in a single trial.[68] Where the conduct constituting the contempt also constitutes a federal or state crime, a jury trial may also be available as of right.[69]

In cases involving offenses that have not traditionally been classified as criminal, the courts have trodden warily in extending the right to jury trial. In *McKiever v Pennsylvania,*[70] for example, the Supreme Court held that there was no right to jury trial in juvenile proceedings. Similarly, courts have rejected a right to jury trial in paternity suits[71] and sexual psychopath proceedings.[72]

§1.09 The Fourteenth Amendment Right to a Jury Trial in a State Criminal Case

The provisions of the Bill of Rights apply only to the federal government.[73] In *Twitchell v Pennsylvania*[74] the Supreme Court made explicit in regard to the sixth amendment what was implicit in its earlier decisions: the right to trial by jury guaranteed by the sixth amendment is available only in a *federal* criminal prosecution.

In contrast to the sixth amendment, the fourteenth amendment applies specifically to the states. Thus, in order to secure a constitutionally guaranteed right to jury trial in state cases, it was necessary to find a doctrinal basis for jury trial within the rights established by the fourteenth amendment:

> No state shall make or enforce any law which shall abridge the privileges and immunities of citizens of the United States; nor shall any state deprive any person of life, liberty or property, without due process of law; nor deny to any person within its jurisdiction the equal protection of the laws.[75]

The initial efforts to extend the right of jury trial to the States centered on the privilege and immunities clause, with attorneys arguing that one of the privileges and immunities enjoyed by citizens was the right to jury trial in a criminal prosecution.[76] This contention, however, was rejected by the Supreme Court in *Maxwell v Dow.*[77] The holding was hardly surprising, for the Court had

---

[68] Codispoti v Pennsylvania, 418 US 506 (1979).

[69] *See* United States v Pyle, 518 F Supp 139 (ED Pa 1981).

[70] 403 US 528 (1971).

[71] *See, e.g.,* People v Marshall, 82 Mich App 92, 266 NW2d 678 (1971).

[72] *See, e.g.,* State v Wilmoth, 22 Wash App 419, 589 P2d 1270 (1979).

[73] Barron v Baltimore, 32 US (7 Pet) 243 (1833).

[74] 74 US (7 Wall) 321 (1868).

[75] US Const amend XIV, §1.

[76] *See, e.g.,* the argument of John Randolph Tucker in *Spies v Illinois,* 123 US 131 (1887), *reprinted in part in* F. Heller, The Sixth Amendment to the Constitution at 39-40 (1969).

[77] 176 US 581, 595 (1900).

previously rejected the argument that the seventh amendment right to a jury trial falls within the privileges and immunities clause.[78]

The focus subsequently shifted to the due process clause of the fourteenth amendment. Since one convicted of crime can be deprived of life, liberty, or property, the question was whether a sentence inflicted without the benefit of a jury trial violated the process due a defendant in a state criminal case. Unfortunately, the phrase *due process* is not self-explanatory. Three major views of its meaning have emerged, each concerned with the relationship between due process and the rights guaranteed by the Bill of Rights.

§1.10 —The Fundamental Fairness Approach to Due Process

One theory, espoused by, among others, Justices Cardozo, Frankfurter, and Harlan, called for a flexible approach. This view found its roots in principles most often associated with natural law theory. According to its judicial exponents, only those rights which could be characterized as "fundamental"[79] or "of the essence of ordered liberty"[80] were entitled to due process protection. That a particular right was within the Bill of Rights did not, by virtue of that fact alone, make it fundamental. Thus, there was no necessary correlation between those rights guaranteed by the Bill of Rights and those included within due process. Some guarantees contained in the Bill of Rights might not be deemed fundamental; others not specifically mentioned in the Bill of Rights might be found to be fundamental, as "privacy" was subsequently determined to be.[81]

Critics of this *fundamental fairness* approach charged that it failed to give citizens fair notice of the rights to which they were entitled. States found themselves in a similarly uncomfortable position; a state might try an accused under procedures it considered fair, only to see the conviction overturned because the procedures failed to comply with the Supreme Court's conception of fundamental fairness. Uncertainty was prevalent, and federal appellate judges had little to guide them in their decisions. As a consequence, some judges may have looked to personal value systems to determine what requirements the Constitution deemed fundamental. Appeals by convicted defendants were inevitable, for attorneys also had no way of knowing whether their clients had been denied due process until the Supreme Court provided a definitive answer.

---

[78] Walker v Savinet, 92 US 90 (1876).

[79] *See* Snyder v Massachusetts, 291 US 97, 105 (1934), *quoted in* Palko v Connecticut, 302 US 319, 325 (1937). *See also* Hurtado v California, 110 US 516 (1884).

[80] Palko v Connecticut, 302 US 319, 325 (1937).

[81] *See* Roe v Wade, 410 US 113 (1973).

§1.11 —The Total Incorporation Approach to Due Process

The principal alternative to the fundamental fairness approach to due process was offered by those Justices, most notably Black and Douglas, who maintained that all the provisions of the Bill of Rights should be incorporated into the due process clause.[82] They reasoned that if a right was sufficiently important to be protected against infringement by the federal government, it was sufficiently important to be protected against infringement by a state government. Total incorporation would, they maintained, give specific content to the due process clause to the benefit of lawyers, judges, and citizens. It would guarantee to the citizens of one state the same basic rights enjoyed by citizens of another state.

It was difficult, however, to reconcile total incorporation with the language of the fourteenth amendment. If the drafters had wanted the provisions of the Bill of Rights to apply to the states, why had they not said so? A pragmatic criticism of total incorporation held that it would have a stultifying effect, denying states the flexibility to address primarily local problems in innovative or experimental ways. Further, if due process were restricted to safeguards specified in the Bill of Rights, there would be no possibility of expanding the rights to which a citizen was entitled in a state court.

Justice Murphy responded to the latter point by advocating an approach which melded fundamental fairness and total incorporationist theories. Under this "incorporation plus" approach, all rights contained in the Bill of Rights would be incorporated into the fourteenth amendment but the fourteenth amendment would not be limited to those rights contained in the Bill of Rights; other rights deemed fundamental could also be included.[83]

§1.12 —The Selective Incorporation Approach to Due Process

Neither the proponents of fundamental fairness nor those of total incorporation were able to muster a majority on the Supreme Court. A compromise was inevitable. Generally referred to as "selective incorporation," the compromise drew on the two competing positions. Certain provisions, but not all, of the Bill of Rights would be incorporated into the due process clause. The test of whether a particular provision would be incorporated would depend on whether the provision was "fundamental" to the "Anglo-American regime of ordered liberty."[84]

The use of an "Anglo-American" sphere of reference is not without significance. One can hypothesize a fair adjudication system that did not use juries. Indeed, in much of the civilized world, cases are tried by judges, not juries.

---

[82] *See* Adamson v California, 332 US 46 (1947) (Black, J, joined by Douglas, J, dissenting).

[83] *See id* (Murphy, J. dissenting).

[84] Duncan v Louisiana, 391 US 145, 149-50 n 14 (1968).

Under a "fundamental fairness" test which looked to the practice of civilized nations, this fact would have been sufficient to defeat an argument for incorporation. Under a test which looked to whether jury trial is fundamental to the "Anglo-American regime of ordered liberty," this fact would not be determinative.

Selective incorporation has the advantage of providing judges, lawyers, and citizens with greater guidance than was available under fundamental fairness. At the same time the test does not saddle states with provisions of the Bill of Rights which are not essential to a scheme of ordered liberty. Selective incorporation also leaves the door open for due process recognition of rights not contained in the original Bill of Rights.

§1.13 —The Right to Jury Trial Under a Selective Incorporation Approach to Due Process

In *Duncan v Louisiana*[85] the Supreme Court held that the sixth amendment right to a jury trial in a criminal prosecution was fundamental to the Anglo-American justice system and, as such, was incorporated into the due process clause. Justice White, speaking for the majority, further stated that the right to jury trial guaranteed by due process was coextensive with that contained in the sixth amendment: "[W]e hold that the fourteenth amendment guarantees a right of jury trial in all criminal cases which—were they to be tried in a federal court—would come within the sixth amendment's guarantee."[86]

Not all the Justices subscribed to this "jot for jot" view of incorporation.[87] The dissenters argued that the states should be allowed greater flexibility to shape their jury procedures to respond to local conditions. In rebuttal, it was maintained that citizens should not be subjected to a watered down version of jury trial in state courts. This philosophical split on the Court was potentially significant, and turned out to be so when the Court considered whether juries in criminal cases were required to reach a unanimous verdict.[88]

It has been observed that the Court's incorporation of the right to jury trial into the fourteenth amendment has had the beneficial effect of forcing the Court to develop its sixth amendment jurisprudence more than it would otherwise likely have done. The reason is that there are far more state criminal prosecutions than federal criminal prosecutions and a far wider variety of state procedures. Appeals from state court convictions have generated a wide range of knotty constitutional issues for the Court's consideration.

---

85 391 US 145 (1968).

86 *Id* 149.

87 *See* Fortas, J, concurring in *Duncan* at 213; Harlan, J, dissenting at 215.

88 *See* **§2.17.**

§1.14 The Seventh Amendment Right to a Jury Trial in a Federal Civil Case

The seventh amendment provides:

> In Suits at common law, where the value in controversy shall exceed twenty dollars, the right of jury trial shall be preserved, and no fact tried by a jury, shall be otherwise re-examined in any Court of the United States, than according to the rules of the common law.[89]

On the face of the amendment, there are two requirements that must be satisfied in order for a party to be entitled to a jury trial: first, the amount in controversy must exceed twenty dollars, not a particularly large amount given inflation; and second, the suit must be one that would have been tried by a jury at common law in England. In respect to the latter requirement, the courts look to the English practice as of 1791, the date of the seventh amendment's adoption.[90] The common law practices in the United States prior to the adoption of the seventh amendment are deemed irrelevant,[91] perhaps because of the wide variety of such practices among the colonies. A court should look to the substance of the pleadings, and not the labels used by the parties, in determining whether a jury trial is available.[92]

Tull v United States[93] is instructive. The government sued a real estate developer for violations of the Clean Water Act. The district court rejected the defendant's demands for a jury trial. It subsequently granted injunctive relief and fined the defendant. The Supreme Court reversed, holding that the seventh amendment entitled the petitioner to a jury trial on the issue of liability.

In reaching this conclusion, the Court asked whether the suit in question was more like those triable in an English law court, where litigants were entitled to a jury trial, or more like those which would be heard by a court of equity, where a jury was not available. Thus the Court looked to how the action would have been treated in an 18th-century English court prior to the merger of law and equity. The Court examined both the nature of the action and the remedy sought. The civil penalty, the Court reasoned, likened the action to one of debt, where a jury trial was available at common law. The fact that the purpose of the fine was to punish reinforced the Court's thinking. While the issue of liability therefore required honoring the petitioner's request for a jury, the Court

---

[89] US Const amend VII. *See also* Fed R Civ P 38(a) (right of jury trial in seventh amendment preserved inviolate). For a discussion of the historical background of this amendment, see Wolfram, *The Constitutional History of the Seventh Amendment,* 57 Minn L Rev 639 (1973).

[90] Dimick v Schiedt, 293 US 474, 476 (1935). *See also* Curtis v Loether, 415 US 189, 193 (1974).

[91] United States v Wonson, 28 F Cas 745 (CCD Mass 1812) (No 16,750).

[92] *See* Owens-Illinois, Inc v Lake Shore Land Co, 610 F2d 1185, 1189 (3d Cir 1979). *Cf* Granfinanciera v Nordberg, 109 S Ct 2782, 2800 (1989) (Congress may not eliminate seventh amendment right to jury by mere relabelling of a cause of action).

[93] 481 US 412 (1983).

also held that a jury was not required to determine the amount of the penalty. The Court's rationale was that the seventh amendment only preserved elements of a jury trial which could be deemed fundamental, of which the amount of the penalty was not.

The difficulty with the historical test is that no common law analogue to a modern action may exist, or if it does exist, the action may have so dramatically changed in nature that application of the historical test could be misleading. This point was recognized in *Ross v Bernhard,*[94] a shareholder's derivative suit. Although paying lip service to the historical test, the Supreme Court acknowledged the need for flexibility, albeit in a cryptic footnote:

> As our cases indicate, the "legal" nature of an issue is determined by considering, first, the pre-merger [of law and equity] custom with reference to such questions; second, the remedy sought; and third, the practical abilities and limitations of juries. Of these factors, the first, requiring extensive and possibly abstruse historical inquiry, is obviously the most difficult to apply.[95]

The issue becomes more complicated when it is Congress that purports to assign an action to a court that does not employ a jury as a fact finder. In *Atlas Roofing Co v Occupational Safety & Health Review Commission,*[96] the United States Supreme Court stated that when Congress creates a new statutory "public right" it can assign its adjudication to an administrative agency without violating the seventh amendment.[97] The term "public right" was not precisely defined, but apparently referred to suits between the government and its citizens arising out of the performance of either the government's legislative or executive functions.[98] Public rights have also been held to include what might be thought to be private rights that are "so closely integrated into a public regulatory scheme" as to be appropriate for agency resolution.[99] However, when it comes to purely "private rights," those which are at issue between individuals, Congress cannot deprive litigants of their right of jury trial by assigning the action to a court of equity or an administrative agency.[100] In sum, in order to be able to claim a right to a jury trial under the seventh amendment, a party must show that the cause of action is legal in nature (or analogous to a common law action which was triable in the English law courts), *and,* in the case where Congress has attempted to assign the action to a non-jury tribunal or court,

---

[94] 396 US 531 (1970).

[95] *Id* 538 n 10.

[96] 430 US 442 (1977).

[97] *Id* 455.

[98] *See* Granfinanciera v Nordberg, 109 S Ct 2782, 2795, n 8 (1989), citing the reference in *Atlas Roofing* 430 US at 450 to Crowell v Benson, 285 US 22 (1932).

[99] *See* Thomas v Union Carbide Agric Prods Co, 473 US 568, 593-94 (1985) (Brennan, J, concurring).

[100] Granfinanciera v Nordberg, 109 S Ct 2782 (1989).

that the action involves a matter of private as opposed to public right.[101] The label which Congress chooses to attach to the action (legal or equitable; public or private) is not decisive.[102]

§1.15 —Mixed Law and Equity Actions

At common law there were separate courts of law and equity. A litigant had a right to a jury trial in a court of law, but not in a court of equity. The United States Supreme Court has consistently interpreted the phrase "suits at common law" within the seventh amendment as referring to "suits in which *legal* rights were to be ascertained and determined, in contradistinction to those where equitable rights alone were recognized, and equitable remedies were administered."[103] The Federal Rules of Civil Procedure, however, adopted in 1938, permitted legal and equitable claims to be merged in a single civil action. The inevitable question was whether the seventh amendment entitled a litigant to a jury trial in a case involving both issues of law and equity.

In *Beacon Theatres, Inc v Westover,*[104] and *Dairy Queen, Inc v Wood,*[105] the United States Supreme Court attempted to provide guidance. *Beacon Theatres* was an antitrust action. There were claims and counterclaims, and both money damages and declaratory relief were sought. The case thus raised issues of both law and equity. The trial court, focusing on the equitable issues, ordered that these be decided by the judge before the legal issues were submitted to the jury.

The Supreme Court disagreed. In effect it reversed the order of the proceedings in order to preserve the right to trial by jury. Rather than having the trial judge first hear the equitable issues, with the potential collateral estoppel effect on issues otherwise triable by the jury, the jury would first hear the legal issues. After the jury returned its verdict, the trial judge could grant equitable relief as appropriate. The Court said that in exceptional cases the order of hearings might be reversed.

In *Dairy Queen, Inc v Wood*[106] the Supreme Court expanded its holding in *Beacon Theatres.* The plaintiff in the case had sought both injunctive relief and damages (which the plaintiff referred to as an "accounting"). Labeling the legal claims as "incidental" to the primary equitable relief being sought, the trial court denied the defendant's demand for a jury.

The Supreme Court again reversed. It held that as long as there were *any* legal issues triable by a jury and a jury was properly demanded, the seventh amendment required that the jury be permitted to hear the case first. It did

---

[101] *Id* 2790, n 4.

[102] *Id* 2800.

[103] Parsons v Bedford, 26 US (3 Pet) 433, 447 (1830) (emphasis in original), *quoted in* Granfinanciera v Nordberg, 109 S Ct 2782, 2790 (1989).

[104] 359 US 500 (1959).

[105] 369 US 469 (1962).

[106] *Id.*

not matter that the legal issues were secondary or incidental to the equitable issues.

§1.16 —Complex Litigation

In *Ross v Bernhard* [107] the Supreme Court in a footnote raised the possibility that it might be permissible to deny the right of jury trial in a complex civil case of long duration.[108] Some commentators claimed historical precedent for such an exception.[109] Others disagreed.[110] The *Ross* footnote, indicating that "the practical abilities and limitations of juries" were relevant considerations, provided support for the exception. Moreover, there was a constitutional dimension to the controversy—for a jury to decide issues which it was incapable of understanding could constitute a denial of due process.[111] The latter argument is intriguing for it pits the fifth amendment right to due process against the seventh amendment right to trial by jury. So far the circuit courts of appeals have split on the issue,[112] and the Supreme Court has yet to settle the controversy.

§1.17 —Written Demand

Either party to a civil case may request a jury trial,[113] and the objection of the opposing party will not defeat the request.

In order to obtain a jury in a federal civil case, a party must make a timely written demand.[114] The same is generally true in state court.[115] A failure to

---

[107] 396 US 531 (1970).

[108] *Id* 538 n 10.

[109] *See, e.g.*, Comment, *Constitutional Law: The Complexity Exception and the Seventh Amendment*, 20 Washburn LJ 153 (1980).

[110] *See, e.g.*, Lempert, *Civil Juries and Complex Cases: Let's Not Rush to Judgment*, 80 Mich L Rev 68 (1981); Sperlich, *The Case for Preserving Trial by Jury in Complex Civil Litigation*, 65 Judicature 397 (1982).

[111] Note that the argument is not simply that having the judge as decision maker would be preferable; rather, it is that the issues are so complex as to be beyond the understanding of a reasonable person.

[112] *Compare In re* Japanese Elec Prods Antitrust Litig, 631 F2d 1069, 1088 (3d Cir 1980) (recognizing a complexity exception) *with In re* United States Fin Sec Litig, 609 F2d 411 (9th Cir 1979), *cert denied*, 446 US 929 (1980). *See generally* Arnold, *A Historical Inquiry into the Right to Trial by Jury in Complex Civil Litigation*, 128 U Pa L Rev 829 (1980); Campbell & Le Poidwin, *Complex Cases and Jury Trials: A Reply to Professor Arnold*, 128 U Pa L Rev 965 (1980); Lempert, *Civil Juries and Complex Cases: Let's Not Rush to Judgment*, 80 Mich L Rev 68 (1981).

[113] Fed R Civ P 38(b).

[114] Id 38(b), (c).

[115] *E.g.*, State v Berg, 237 Iowa 356, 21 NW2d 777 (1946).

make a timely demand will usually constitute a waiver of the right.[116] The courts take quite seriously this requirement of a timely written demand, and a party who experiences a subsequent change of mind is unlikely to obtain relief. This rule cuts both ways: a party who fails to demand a jury within the prescribed time limits will not subsequently be allowed as a matter of right to demand a jury;[117] and a party who demands a jury but then thinks better of the decision will not be allowed to withdraw the demand unless the consent of all parties is obtained.[118]

This approach to waiver stands in sharp contrast to that taken in regard to juries in criminal cases. In criminal cases a jury will be impaneled unless the defendant waives a jury. The waiver must be in writing, and will not be presumed from a silent record.

§1.18 —State Civil Trials

The seventh amendment applies only to the federal government. It does not guarantee a right to jury trial in a state civil case even if the controversy involves more than twenty dollars and would have been the subject of a jury trial at common law.[119] Unlike the sixth amendment right to a jury in criminal cases,[120] the seventh amendment has not been incorporated into the due process clause of the fourteenth amendment. Nor has the argument that the right to a jury trial falls within the privileges and immunities guaranteed by the fourteenth amendment succeeded.[121] No doubt the Supreme Court is sensitive to the potentially enormous financial costs which could be imposed on states as a result of a decision in favor of incorporation. As a result, litigants desirous of a jury trial in a state civil case will need to look to state statutes and constitutions.

§1.19 State Constitutions and Statutes

The availability of a right to a jury in state criminal trials is controlled by both state and federal law. As discussed in **§1.13,** the right to jury trial in state criminal proceedings is, for most serious crimes, guaranteed as part of the process due the citizen under the fourteenth amendment. This right of jury trial is, moreover, generally reinforced by a *state* constitutional provision guaranteeing a right to jury trial in criminal cases, or stating that the right to jury trial shall remain inviolate. As in the federal Constitution, the state constitutional

---

116 Fed R Civ P 38(d).

117 *See e.g.,* Olund v Swarthout, 459 F2d 999 (6th Cir), *cert denied,* 409 US 1008 (1972); Ligouri v New York, NH & HR Co, 26 FRD 565, 568 (1961). *See also* Houston N Hosp Properties v Telco Leasing, Inc, 688 F2d 408 (5th Cir 1982).

118 *See e.g.,* Leng Wing Chaw v Nagai, 44 Hawaii 290, 353 P2d 998 (1960).

119 *See* Livingston v Moore, 32 US (7 Pet) 469, 551-52 (1883).

120 *See* **§1.13.**

121 Walker v Sauvinet, 92 US 90 (1876).

guarantee of jury trial is worded as a broad statement of principle, with the specifics of the right then being spelled out in statute.

Although it might seem that these statutes and constitutional provisions are redundant in light of the fourteenth amendment decisions of the United States Supreme Court, this is not so. Indeed, the criminal lawyer who disregards state constitutional law in formulating overall trial strategy does the client a disservice. A state supreme court may interpret its state constitutional provision to provide greater protection to its citizenry than does the federal Constitution. Thus the conscientious lawyer frustrated by an adverse (or anticipated adverse) United States Supreme Court decision delineating the contours of jury trial should carefully consider raising the same challenge under the state constitutional provision. While a United States Supreme Court interpretation of a federal constitutional right to jury trial is a binding interpretation of the federal constitutional right, a state Supreme Court remains free to interpret its state constitutional right to jury trial more liberally, even though both constitutional provisions may be identically worded.

State statutory and constitutional provisions relating to jury trial in civil cases are of even greater importance. Unlike the sixth amendment right to jury trial in criminal cases, its seventh amendment counterpart in civil cases has not been incorporated into the fourteenth amendment and is not therefore binding on the states. Accordingly, there is no *federal* constitutional right to a jury trial in a *state* civil case. Whatever right to jury trial in a state civil case that exists must perforce be the product of state statute or constitution. Such a right to jury trial in civil cases exists to a large but varying degree in every state, and the attorney has to consult the specific law of the state in which the trial is to be held. State statutes and judicial decisions will often fill in the interstices of a more general constitutional provision,[122] particularly where the cause of action postdated the adoption of the state constitution.[123] Needless to add, regardless of the law of the state, actual jury practices may vary considerably from district to district, depending on local rule and judicial disposition.

§1.20 Waiver of the Right to a Jury

Although the federal Constitution, state constitutions, and various federal and state statutes guarantee the right to a jury, they do not compel parties to submit to a jury trial. Implicit and sometimes explicit in a statute or constitutional provision that creates a right is a corresponding right to forgo, or waive, that right.

The argument has been advanced that the language of Article III §2(3), that "The trial of all crimes, except in cases of Impeachment, shall be by

---

[122] *See, e.g.,* Graham v Stillman, 100 AD2d 893, 474 NYS2d 580 (1984) (no right to jury in medical malpractice cases).

[123] *See* Rankin v Frebank Co, 47 Cal App 3d 75, 121 Cal Rptr 348 (1975) (stockholder derivative action).

Jury . . . ,"[124] requires a jury in all criminal cases and therefore bars waiver.[125] The United States Supreme Court, however, has rejected that argument. Article III must be read in pari materia with the sixth amendment, which states that "in all criminal prosecutions, the accused shall enjoy the right to . . . trial, by an impartial jury. . . ." Reading the two clauses in pari materia, the Supreme Court concluded that a defendant in a criminal case could waive the right to a jury.[126]

Waiver in a civil case has been less controversial. It is provided for by federal statute.[127] The Supreme Court has also recognized the right to waive a jury in a civil case.[128]

Waiver of the right to jury can be said to have occurred in two distinct contexts. Parties to a civil case or a defendant in a criminal case may choose to resolve the pending controversy without resort to a trial. By waiving trial, the parties also waive a jury. Such a disposition could be termed an indirect waiver of a jury; it follows from the basic decision to waive trial. A direct waiver of a jury occurs when a case goes to trial, but the choice is made to have the case heard by a judge rather than by a jury.

§1.21 —Indirect Waiver of Jury by Waiver of Trial

In civil cases the waiver of trial, and indirect waiver of a jury, usually results from the parties' settlement of their dispute by negotiated agreement. Sometimes a third-party mediator or conciliator is enlisted to facilitate the settlement process. Other times the parties agree to submit the dispute to arbitration; an arbitration clause may be written into a contract, or the parties may agree to submit their claim to an arbitrator after a dispute has arisen. In any event, where negotiations, mediation, or arbitration (the three are often collectively referred to as alternative dispute resolution) are successful, the case never comes to trial. The parties have as a consequence waived their right to have the dispute adjudicated by a jury. Because resort to alternative dispute resolution has the advantage of avoiding the time, cost, and uncertainties associated with litigation, it has become an increasingly attractive means of dispute resolution.

The counterpart in the criminal arena to a negotiated settlement is a plea bargain. The defendant agrees to plead guilty. In exchange, the defendant will typically receive a reduction in the charge, an agreement to dismiss other charges, a recommendation for a lenient sentence (or an agreement not to recommend a sentence), or some combination of these considerations. The defendant saves the government the time and expense of a jury trial, and the

---

[124] US Const, art III, §2(3) (emphasis added).

[125] At early common law, a criminal defendant was not permitted to waive a jury. *See* M. Bloomstein, Verdict: The Jury System 19 (1968).

[126] Patton v United States, 281 US 276, 298 (1930); Callan v Wilson, 127 US 540 (1888).

[127] Fed R Civ P 38(d).

[128] Kearney v Case, 79 US (12 Wall) 395, 396 (1871).

government saves the defendant from the risk of a harsh sentence imposed as a result of facts brought out at a jury trial. At the same time the defendant forgoes certain rights, including the right to a jury. Because fundamental constitutional rights are being waived, the Supreme Court requires that the waiver be knowing, voluntary, and intelligent.[129]

As a result of alternative dispute resolution and plea bargaining, cases that go to trial are the exception. It is estimated that between eighty per cent and ninety five per cent of all criminal prosecutions are plea bargained. Figures are more difficult to ascertain in civil cases, for many are settled before any formal filings are entered, but the pattern appears to be similar. The clear trend is away from trial as the primary mechanism of dispute resolution. Whether this trend is the product of a desire to save time and expense, a concern about the vagaries of jury trial, or a sincere doubt regarding the ability of a jury to reach a fair and just result, is unclear.

§1.22 —Direct Waiver of Jury: The Legal Standard

Assuming that a case does go to trial, and assuming there is a right to a jury, the decision must be made whether to exercise or waive that right. At common law a criminal accused was not permitted to waive trial by jury. In part this was because convictions worked an attaint as well as a forfeiture of official titles of inheritance.[130]

The language of article III of the Constitution can be construed as not permitting waiver: "The trial of all crimes, except in Cases of Impeachment, *shall* be by jury. . . ."[131] Indeed, several early cases seem to have proceeded on this assumption.[132] Theoretical arguments can also be advanced in support of not allowing waiver. To the extent that jury service benefits the public and the jurors, to allow a defendant to waive a jury infringes upon the public's right, exercised through those members of its community chosen to serve, to know. Jurors are also deprived of their right to serve. Finally, just as does the defendant, the state has an interest in the impartial decision making provided by the jury which will be defeated by a defendant's waiver of a jury.

These views of waiver did not prevail. In *Patton v United States,*[133] a verdict was returned by a jury of eleven, the reduction from twelve being necessitated by the illness of one of the jurors during the trial. Although at the time the defendants consented to the jury of eleven, they subsequently argued that they lacked the power to waive their constitutional right to a jury of twelve.

The United States Supreme Court proceeded on the assumption that the

---

[129] *See* Henderson v Morgan, 426 US 637 (1976); North Carolina v Alford, 400 US 25 (1970); Boykin v Alabama, 395 US 238 (1969). *See also* Fed R Crim P 11(c), (d).

[130] *See* Patton v United States, 281 US 276, 306 (1930).

[131] US Const amend III, §2(3) (emphasis added).

[132] *See, e.g.,* Schick v United States, 195 US 65 (1904).

[133] 281 US 276 (1930).

right to a jury was the right to a jury of twelve;[134] the question was whether the defendants could waive that right by agreeing to be tried by a lesser number. Having rejected any distinction between a partial and complete waiver as constitutionally indefensible,[135] the Court held that the defendants were entitled to waive their right to a jury. The Court reasoned that a jury trial was intended to be a privilege of the accused, a protection against the power of the government and the arbitrariness of the judge. Seemingly mandatory language to the contrary in Article III had to be construed in pari materia with the language of the sixth amendment that "the accused shall enjoy the right to . . . an impartial jury." Since the right to a jury trial was the prerogative of the defendant, it followed that the defendant had the right to waive a jury trial. To have ruled otherwise would have created an anomaly in the law: an accused could plead guilty, thereby waiving a right to trial and with it, the right to a jury; but an accused could not elect a trial but waive the right to a jury. Furthermore, the common law conditions which initially justified not allowing waiver no longer existed. For a waiver to be effective, added the Court, it had to be made expressly and intelligently.[136] Under the Federal Rules of Criminal Procedure, the waiver must now also be in writing.[137]

Given the language of the sixth amendment, which accords the right to a jury trial to an "accused," and the Court's reasoning in *Patton,* one might think that it was *solely* defendant's choice whether to submit to a jury trial. This is not correct. The court must consent, and in some jurisdictions the prosecutor as well. In *Patton* the Supreme Court stated:

> [T]he value and appropriateness of jury trial have been established by long experience, and are not now to be denied. Not only must the right of the accused to a trial by a constitutional jury be jealously preserved, but the maintenance of the jury as a fact-finding body in criminal cases is of such importance and has such a place in our traditions, that, before any waiver can become effective, *the consent of government counsel and the sanction of the court must be had. . . .*[138]

In *Singer v United States*[139] the Court reaffirmed that there was no constitutional barrier to conditioning waiver of a jury trial on the consent of the court and the prosecutor. The Supreme Court reasoned that if either refused, the defendant would be denied no constitutional right, since he would be tried by the impartial jury which the Constitution envisioned. The *Singer* Court, however, recognized that a situation might arise where not to allow a defendant to waive a jury trial could itself raise constitutional questions:

---

134 *Id* 288. For subsequent developments regarding this issue see **§§2.13-2.17.**

135 *Id* 290-91.

136 *Id* 312.

137 Fed R Crim P 23(a).

138 281 US at 312 (emphasis added). *See also* Fed R Crim P 23(a).

139 380 US 24 (1965).

> We need not determine in this case whether there might be some circumstances where a defendant's reason for wanting to be tried by a judge alone are so compelling that the Government's insistence on trial by jury would result in the denial to a defendant of an impartial trial. Petitioner argues that there might arise situations where "passion, prejudice . . . public feeling" or some other factor may render impossible or unlikely an impartial trial by jury. However, since petitioner gave no reason for wanting to forego trial other than to save time, this is not such a case, and petitioner does not claim that it is.[140]

The right to waive a jury trial in a civil case has been less controversial. One reason is that lesser interests are at stake. Neither litigant is faced with loss of life or liberty as a result of an adverse verdict. Another reason is that the government and public interest in the outcome is significantly less than in a criminal case. It is primarily only the parties to the civil suit who are affected by the result. Finally, the language of the seventh amendment, which speaks of the right to trial by jury being "preserved," does not lend itself to a literal interpretation that would require the parties to have their suit tried by a jury. Thus it is not surprising that the Supreme Court early recognized the parties' right to waive jury trial:

> Undoubtedly both the Judiciary Act and the amendment to the Constitution served the right to either party in a suit at common law to a trial by jury, and we are also of opinion that the statute of 1789 intended to point out this as the mode of trial in issues of fact in such cases. Numerous decisions, however, had settled that this right to a jury trial might be waived by the parties, and that the judgment of the court in such cases should be valid.[141]

As the quotation indicates, the right to a jury may be asserted by either plaintiff or defendant. Under federal rules of civil procedure, however, the right to a jury in a civil case must be formally requested in writing.[142] The failure to request a jury trial constitutes a waiver.[143] In criminal cases the opposite is true: jury trial is automatic unless there is a waiver, which must be in writing.[144]

§1.23 —Waiver of Jury: Strategic Considerations

Waiver of a jury in a criminal or civil case is a jury selection decision. It is a decision to reject all potential jurors and to have the case decided by a judge. On the basis of what considerations should this decision be made?

---

[140] *Id* 37-38.

[141] Kearney v Case, 79 US (12 Wall) 395, 396 (1871).

[142] Fed R Civ P 38(b), (c).

[143] *Id* 38(d).

[144] *Id* 23(a).

Preliminarily, it might be observed that in a criminal case, if one knew nothing about the judge, jury, or facts, a defendant would be ill-advised to waive a jury. In their classic study of the American jury, Kalven and Zeisel examined judge-jury disagreements.[145] Judges who had presided over a criminal trial were asked whether they agreed with the verdict of the jury. The researchers found that judges and juries disagreed in over twenty per cent of the cases. Juries were six times more likely to acquit where the judge would have convicted than they were to convict where the judge would have acquitted. Where there was agreement regarding guilt but not degree of guilt, the jury was more prone than the judge to convict for a lesser offense.

Therefore, assuming no other information is available, it would appear, as an a priori matter, that a criminal defendant should not choose to waive a jury. But more information is almost always available or can be obtained. From the defendant's vantage point, the basic question to be answered is who will be more receptive to the defendant's case: the judge or the jury. The answer may turn on the background and values of the judge, the nature of the crime, the defendant's criminal record (and whether that will be introduced if the defendant testifies), the demographic makeup of the community from which the jurors will be drawn, and the attitude of that community toward the accused, the victim, and the crime. Depending upon the nature of the case, other variables may enter the picture. Further, the possibility of substituting judges (e.g., by seeking recusal of the assigned judge[146]) as well as the possibility of substituting juries (e.g., by moving for a change in venue or venire) must also be factored into the equation. Much pretrial investigation will be required if these matters are to be accurately assessed.

Several types of cases prima facie caution against a jury trial. Where there is strong community sentiment against a defendant, whether engendered by the nature of the crime, the defendant's record or some other characteristic of the defendant, or the sympathy in the community for the victim, a jury trial may not be to a defendant's advantage. Even if a change in venue or vicinage were to be granted, the revulsion of a typical jury for the defendant's crime may argue in favor of having the case decided by a judge. A related situation is where a client who intends to testify is likely to make a poor impression on the jury, perhaps because of personal appearance, language difficulties, or a speech defect.

A second class of case where a jury trial may be inadvisable is where a party's best chance of success is to secure a favorable ruling on a point of law or the party actively desires the judge to rule on a key issue, perhaps so that it can be taken to a higher court. While a judge should and most will rule on the relevant point in a jury trial, there may be others who are inclined to let the case go to the jury on the facts, hoping that the jury's verdict will relieve them

---

[145] H. Kalven & H. Zeisel, The American Jury (1966).

[146] Judges should recuse themselves not only in cases where bias is present but also in cases where the appearance of bias may be present. *See* 1 ABA Standards for Criminal Justice 6-20 (2d ed 1980). Some jurisdictions permit attorneys to peremptorily challenge judges. *See generally* 2 W. LaFave & J. Israel, Criminal Procedure §21.4(d) (1984).

from having to decide what may be a difficult legal question. By waiving jury trial, the lawyer forces the judge to face up to the legal issue.

A third class of case where a party might decide to waive a jury is where the attorney plans to present evidence and testimony which may be difficult to comprehend. A judge is less likely than a jury to be confused by complex evidence.

Other tactical considerations may argue in favor of waiving a jury. The trial will be speedier (for no time need be spent in jury selection), the likelihood for a need for a second trial will be less (for the possibility of some types of reversible errors will be eliminated), and the result of the trial may be more predictable.[147]

In order to make a meaningful comparison between the likely quality of a trial before a judge and that before a jury, the attorney must learn as much as possible about the judge's values, tendencies, and past rulings. Often the lawyer will be familiar with the judge from personal experience. If not, other lawyers in the jurisdiction may be able to supply the necessary information.

Similarly, the attorney must attempt to assess the likely result of a jury trial. There are numerous pretrial methodologies which will assist the attorney in making this assessment. Community/demographic surveys and analyses, investigations of the venire, and mock trials all provide insight into the likely response of jurors to a case. These topics will be examined in detail in Part II of this book.

Only after a thorough analysis of all the variables can a true "knowing and intelligent" waiver of the right to trial by jury be made. In the real world, the world where parties win or lose lawsuits, a "knowing and intelligent" waiver refers not to a technical legal knowledge and understanding of the rights being waived, but to an enlightened strategic evaluation of whether it is in a party's best interests to be tried by a jury. The decision whether to waive a jury trial should of course be fully discussed with the client, as it is the client who will have to live with the jury's decision.

---

[147] R. Keeton, Trial Tactics and Methods 237 (1954).

2 Characteristics and Features of the Jury

§2.01 Introduction

Any study of jury selection presupposes a jury trial. The previous chapter examined when the right to a jury trial was available and when it might be advisable to waive that right. As indicated, the right may be granted by the federal constitution, a state constitution, or a state or federal statute.

Although the term *jury* is employed as if it had a settled meaning, this is not the case. Were Blackstone to be reincarnated, the jury he would see today would differ from that with which he was familiar in common law England. Some features, it is true, have remained constant. The jury has always consisted of lay members of the community. They are brought together for a limited time and for a limited purpose, that of hearing and deciding a legal dispute. When they have completed their service, they melt back into the community from which they came.

Other features of the jury have not remained static. Jurors were once selected because of their personal knowledge of the facts of the case; now such knowledge is more likely to disqualify one from being a juror. While once it may have been heretical to suggest that a jury could consist of some number other than twelve, the United States Supreme Court has held that juries of half that size are acceptable.[1] The Supreme Court has also held that the traditional requirement of a unanimous verdict in a criminal case is not constitutionally required.[2] Moreover, the social, sexual, and economic composition of the typical jury has changed dramatically over time. Barriers to jury service have been found unconstitutional by the Supreme Court and states have moved to liberalize juror eligibility rules.

Surprisingly, many of the Supreme Court decisions giving content to the right to a jury are of relatively recent vintage. Questions relating to the jury persist because the Constitution itself provides few answers. What, for example, is an acceptable number of jurors? Who is eligible to be a juror? Does a jury's verdict have to be unanimous? The drafters of the Constitution provided little specific guidance. They were more concerned with preserving the basic right of jury trial than with giving it content.

The fact that most Supreme Court jury decisions are of recent vintage also reflects a more pervasive development relating to constitutional adjudication. Prior to the latter half of the twentieth century the sixth amendment right to trial by jury, like most other constitutional rights, applied only to the federal government. Federal statutes filled in the interstices of that right. Most criminal prosecutions, however, were brought not in federal court but in state court. After the United States Supreme Court decided in 1968 that the right to jury trial in a criminal case was part of the process due a citizen in a state criminal court,[3] it was confronted with constitutional challenges to a wide array of differing state jury practices. In deciding these cases, the Court reshaped the concept of the jury.

---

1 *See* **§§2.13-2.14.**

2 *See* **§2.17.**

3 *See* Duncan v Louisiana, 391 US 145 (1968). *See generally* **§§1.09-1.13.**

As the state legislatures restructured jury trial, both in reaction to and in anticipation of Supreme Court decisions, litigants had to reevaluate the desirability of opting for a jury trial, as well as rethinking what qualities made for a desirable juror. A criminal defendant who might have demanded a jury when the verdict had to be unanimous might reconsider where a less than unanimous verdict was permitted.[4] Characteristics in a juror which might have been favorable if unanimity was required might be unfavorable if unanimity is not required.[5] The right to a jury trial has remained, but the nature of the right has changed.

This chapter will examine some of the more important features of the jury and the decisions of the Supreme Court which have given them content. The implications of these decisions for questions relating to waiver and jury selection will also be considered.

The term *jury selection* is used in its broadest sense. Just as a decision to waive a jury trial is a jury selection decision (a decision to reject all potential jurors in favor of a judge), so too are other legal maneuvers not ordinarily conceived of in jury selection terms. For instance, the decision to move for a change in venue or venire,[6] considered in the next five sections, is a jury selection decision. It is a decision to reject the jury pool of one district in favor of the pool of a different district.

§2.02 Venue and Vicinage

At common law a party was entitled to a jury of the *vicinage.* The term referred to the neighborhood in which the dispute arose.[7] In light of the historical fact jurors were chosen because of their personal knowledge of the controversy, the vicinage requirement was logical. Those in the community were most likely to know the parties and the events giving rise to trial.

The rationale for maintaining a vicinage requirement for the modern jury whose members are supposed to be ignorant of the facts and parties is less clear. Community members are more likely to know the facts and parties, and more likely to have heard something of the case. Convenience to jurors may be the explanation. If dislocation were added to the low compensation provided jurors, many would be reluctant to serve. The pressure to reach a quick decision would increase. While these considerations may justify continuation of the vicinage requirement, more likely its survival is attributable to tradition and inertia.

Historical injustices fueled the demand for a right to a jury trial in the locality where the crime occurred. Wary that colonial juries would not protect the Crown's interest in court, the British Parliament had enacted statutes permitting trial in England of colonists charged with the commission of criminal acts

---

[4] *See* **§2.16.**

[5] *Id.*

[6] *See* **§§2.02-2.06.**

[7] *See* Williams v Florida, 399 US 78, 93 n 35 (1970).

in America.[8] Colonial legislatures protested, and one of the itemized grievances in the Declaration of Independence was "transporting us beyond Seas to be tried for pretended offenses."[9]

The constitutional response was the creation of both a venue and a vicinage guaranty in criminal cases. Venue is concerned with the place where the trial is held. Article III of the United States Constitution states: The trial of all crimes, except in Cases of Impeachment, shall be by jury; and *such trial shall be held in the state where the said crime shall have been committed. . . .*[10]

In contrast to venue, vicinage refers to the geographical area from which the jurors are drawn. The sixth amendment to the Constitution, although often misread as a reiteration of the venue requirement, in fact establishes a separate vicinage requirement. It provides: In all criminal prosecutions, the accused shall enjoy the right to a speedy and public trial, *by an impartial jury of the State and district wherein the crime shall have been committed,* which district shall have been previously ascertained by law.[11]

When the British transported colonists to England for trial for offenses committed in America, they violated a venue interest; when they impaneled English jurors to hear these cases, they violated a vicinage interest.

Together venue and vicinage increase the probability that an accused will be tried in a familiar locale, near friends and family who can provide support. The accused is more likely to know the jurors, and be able to exercise challenges intelligently; and the jurors are more likely to know the accused, as well as the victim, and be better able to evaluate their respective actions in light of community standards. A local attorney, one presumably in whom the defendant has confidence, can be retained. There will be less inconvenience to witnesses, particularly character witnesses; and the local jurors will be better able to judge the credibility of those witnesses.

The underlying assumption, of course, is that a crime is most often committed near where the defendant resides. The potential benefits of venue and vicinage will not be available where the defendant is charged with a crime in a locality far from home. In these circumstances, venue and vicinage operate to ensure: (1) that witnesses and evidence, most likely located near the scene of the crime, are readily available; and (2) that members of the community, in the form of jurors, will be able to inject community values into the adjudication process. In state prosecutions, venue and vicinage constitute a recognition that each state has the sovereign power to determine what conduct should be criminal within that state.

---

[8] *See generally* Blume, *The Place of Trial of Criminal Cases: Constitutional Vicinage and Venue,* 43 Mich L Rev 59 (1944); Kershen, *Vicinage,* 29 Okla L Rev 803 (1976), 30 Okla L Rev 1 (1977).

[9] *See* Kershen, *supra* note 8, at 807.

[10] US Const art III, §2 (emphasis added).

[11] *Id* amend VI (emphasis added). One might note that the drafters substituted the word *district* for *vicinage* in order to provide greater clarity and uniformity.

§2.03 —Motions for a Change in Venue or Venire

The constitutional rights of venue and vicinage, like other constitutional rights, can be waived by a defendant who believes it is in his or her interest to do so.[12] A defendant may therefore seek, although a court is not required to grant, a change in venue or venire. If a judge orders a change in venue, the trial is transferred to another district. Jurors from the new district hear the case. A defendant who seeks a change in venire is asking that the case be tried in the district in which the crime occurred, consistent with article III's concept of venue, but by jurors imported from another jurisdiction. Defendant is waiving the right to a jury of the vicinage.

It is debatable whether the government should be able to obtain a change in venue. The sixth amendment grants to an accused the right to a jury of the vicinage. This right might be defeated if a government motion for a change in venue were to be granted. The Federal Rule of Criminal Procedure which governs transfers of trials likewise speaks only in terms of motions by the defense.[13] A government motion for a change in venue would be desirable, however, where government witnesses and jurors were being threatened. The government could argue that its interest in due process and an impartial jury was at risk.[14]

A governmental request for a change in the venire is even more dubious. One traditional function of the jury is to serve as the conscience of the community. If the community believes an accused is not morally blameworthy or the acts charged should not have been made criminal, it has the power to acquit, despite evidence of guilt.[15] Arguably a defendant is entitled to a local jury's consideration of whether to exercise this nullification power.[16] Allowing the government to obtain jurors from another vicinage by way of a motion for a change of venire would frustrate this entitlement.

It might appear that the government could defeat the defendant's interest in a trial of the vicinage by obtaining a change in venue. This is not necessarily so, however. A court may have the authority to order a change in venue while still requiring the use of jurors from the original vicinage. This mode of proceeding might be appropriate where the jurors were being subjected to abuse or threats, or where prejudicial local news coverage of the trial was anticipated.

---

[12] *See, e.g.,* Oborn v State, 143 Wis 249, 126 NW 737 (1910). *See generally* **§§1.20-1.22.**

[13] Fed R Crim P 21. *See generally* Note, *Validity of a Statute Granting the State Change of Venue in a Criminal Trial,* 17 Iowa L Rev 399 (1932).

[14] *See* ABA Standards for Criminal Justice, Standard 8-3.3(a) (2d ed 1980) (advocating giving prosecutor the right to seek a change in venue). The government's interest in a fair trial and impartial jury is recognized in Chicago Council of Lawyers v Bauer, 371 F Supp 689, 691 (CD Ill 1974) ("The right to a fair and impartial adjudication extends not only to criminal defendants but also to the government and through it to society"), *revd on other grounds,* 522 F2d 242 (7th Cir 1975), *cert denied,* 427 US 912 (1976).

[15] *See* **§2.21.** Conversely, in opposing a motion for a change in venue or venire, the government can argue that the local community has an interest in expressing its views about local crimes, an interest which will be defeated if the motion for change in venue or venire is granted.

[16] *See generally* **§§2.20-2.21.**

An accused can in theory waive venue and/or a jury of the vicinage. Several permutations are possible. The defendant might seek a change in venue while insisting on a jury of the vicinage. In this situation the request, if granted, would lead to a trial in a district other than that in which the crime was committed but before jurors from the district in which the crime was committed. Alternatively, the defendant might waive both venue and vicinage. Trial would then be in a district other than that in which the crime was committed before jurors of the district to which the trial was transferred. A final possibility is that a defendant might waive a jury of the vicinage but not venue. The result, if granted, would be the importation of a jury pool from another district to the district where the crime was committed and where trial would be held. As indicated previously, this importation of foreign jurors is known as a change of venire.[17]

Although venue and vicinage are analytically distinct concepts, courts tend to confuse the two. In part this tendency may be attributable to a failure of attorneys to appreciate the differences involved. It is extremely rare to find a defense motion in respect to one but not the other. Often the same reasons which prompt a motion for a change in venue argue in favor of a change in vicinage. As a practical matter, a defense attorney may not want to risk alienating jurors by requiring them to serve in a venue which takes them away from their homes. A judge may also be reluctant to incur the costs of transporting jurors to another city and providing them with food and lodging.

Confusion is also generated by the relevant Federal Rule of Criminal Procedure, entitled "Transfer from the District for Trial."[18] In relevant part the Rule provides:

> (a) **For Prejudice in the District.** The court upon motion of the defendant shall transfer the proceeding as to him to another district whether or not such district is specified in the defendant's motion if the court is satisfied that there exists in the district where the prosecution is pending so great a prejudice against the defendant that he cannot obtain a fair and impartial trial at any place fixed by law for holding court in that district.
>
> (b) **Transfer in Other Cases.** For the convenience of parties and witnesses, and in the interest of justice, the court upon motion of the defendant may transfer the proceeding as to him or any one or more of the counts thereof to another district. . . .[19]

The rule does not specifically allude to the possibility of a change in venue but not vicinage, or vice versa. These are separate options, however, which the conscientious attorney should consider. For instance, a defense attorney who believes that past articles in the local press have inflamed the community

---

[17] *See generally* Note, *Community Hostility and the Right to an Impartial Jury,* 60 Colum L Rev 349 (1960).

[18] Fed R Crim P 21.

[19] *Id.*

against the defendant may desire to waive the right to a jury of the vicinage. Waiver of venue, however, may not be desirable—the defendant may want to remain near friends and family. Further, a change in venue would impede consultation with local counsel, and would inconvenience defense witnesses. In such a case a motion for a change of venire but not venue would be appropriate.

Conversely, a defense attorney may be satisfied with a jury of the vicinage but fear inflammatory articles by a hostile local press. Under these circumstances sound trial strategy may dictate a change in venue but not vicinage. Jurors, however, may resent being transported to another district away from their homes, and may become subconsciously biased against the party responsible for the inconvenience. The more common alternative of sequestration, on the other hand, may be equally resented.

An intriguing theoretical argument merits consideration. Under the sixth amendment an accused is entitled to both an impartial jury and a jury of the district in which the crime is committed. What if an impartial jury cannot be obtained in that district? Presumably a court would order a change in venue or venire. But what if the defendant insists on both an impartial jury and the right to be tried in the district in which the crime occurred by jurors of that district. A defendant should not have to waive one constitutional right in order to enjoy another. If both cannot be granted, is the defendant not entitled to dismissal of the charges? While it is doubtful that a court would be receptive to an argument that would allow a potentially guilty defendant to escape trial altogether, there does appear to be at least a theoretical basis for the argument.[20]

§2.04 —Legal Standards

In *Groppi v Wisconsin*[21] the United States Supreme Court held unconstitutional a state statute which prevented a change in venue in misdemeanor cases, regardless of the extent of local prejudice. The Court recognized that a change in venue is often the most effective means for assuring the impartial jury to which an accused is entitled under the sixth amendment.[22]

The Constitution does not specify under what circumstances a change in venue or venire should be granted. Both the due process right to a fair trial and the sixth amendment right to an impartial jury (binding on the states as

---

[20] This argument was accepted in United States v Cotton, No 68-CR-113 (ED Wis Sept 9, 1969). an unreported Wisconsin decision. The court's opinion is reported in A. Ginger, 1 Jury Selection in Civil & Criminal Trials 375-79 (2d ed 1984).

[21] 400 US 505 (1971).

[22] Possible alternatives might include the grant of a continuance or simple reliance upon effective use of challenges. A continuance, however, would work against the defendant's right to a speedy trial. Voir dire, with the subsequent exercise of challenges, is often an ineffective method of identifying bias. *See* **§12.14.**

a result of its incorporation into the fourteenth amendment[23]), however, inform the appropriate standard. A court must be sensitive to the ability of the government and the accused to receive a fair trial before an impartial jury in the district in which trial is scheduled.[24] The inability need not be absolute; the Supreme Court has stated that a "reasonable likelihood" of prejudice is sufficient.[25] Mere knowledge about the case on the part of jurors, on the other hand, will not necessarily warrant a change in either venue or venire.[26]

In some instances a court will presume prejudice sufficient to justify a change in venue. In *Rideau v Louisiana,*[27] a local television station had on several occasions broadcast the defendant's confession. The Supreme Court held that it was a denial of due process for the trial court to have refused the defendant's request for a change in venue. Significantly, the Court declined to inquire whether any individual juror's impartiality had been compromised:

> [W]e do not hesitate to hold, without pausing to examine a particularized transcript of the voir dire examination of the members of the jury, that due process of law in this case required a trial before a jury drawn from a community of people who had not seen and heard Rideau's televised "interview."[28]

The Court's reasoning, although directed to the motion for change in venue, would apply with equal force to a motion for a change of venire.

If prejudice cannot be presumed, the party seeking a change of venue or venire will have to demonstrate sufficient community bias to warrant the granting of the motion. Pretrial community surveys may prove helpful.[29] A trial court's decision will not be reversed except for an abuse of discretion or manifest error.[30]

The most common ground of prejudice is pretrial publicity. The moving party will generally need to show publicity which is hostile, inflammatory, and of wide circulation. Another justification for a change of venue or venire is significant community animosity, because of either a negative perception of the defendant or a positive perception of the victim. The courts are particularly sensitive to claims of racial prejudice against the accused. In the final analysis, however, there are no constitutional limitations on the grounds upon which a motion for a change in venue or venire can be premised.

Under the Federal Rules of Criminal Procedure a federal judge *must,* upon motion of the defendant, transfer trial when "there exists in the district where

---

[23] *See* Duncan v Louisiana, 391 US 145 (1968).

[24] *See* Sheppard v Maxwell, 384 US 333 (1966); Estes v Texas, 381 US 532 (1965); Rideau v Louisiana, 373 US 723 (1963). *See also* Fed R Crim P 21(a).

[25] *See* Sheppard v Maxwell, 384 US 333, 363 (1966).

[26] *See* Irvin v Dowd, 366 US 717, 722-23 (1961).

[27] 373 US 723 (1963).

[28] *Id* 727.

[29] *See* **§3.07.**

[30] *See* Irvin v Dowd, 366 US 717, 733 (1961).

the prosecution is pending so great a prejudice against the defendant that he cannot obtain a fair and impartial jury at any place fixed by law for holding court in that district."[31] Where a federal crime is committed in more than one district, a defendant may also be able to secure a change in venue as of right.[32] In addition, the federal rules permit a court to transfer a trial for "the convenience of parties and witnesses, and in the interest of justice" upon motion of the defendant.[33]

§2.05 —Strategic Considerations

The attorney attempting to decide whether to seek a change in venue or venire should compare the quality of the trial the defendant can expect to receive in the jurisdiction where the crime was committed with the quality of the trial the defendant can expect to receive in another district. In which district will the jurors be more receptive to defendant's case? In order to make these comparisons, the lawyer should investigate all possible locations where trial can be held. Community surveys need to be conducted.[34] Mock trials held in each of the potential districts can also help answer the question.[35] The lawyer may discover that even though prejudice against the defendant may exist in the district where the crime was committed, similar or greater prejudice will be encountered in other districts.

Complicating the inquiry is the fact that different time frames come into play. Consider a defendant on trial for murder. The local press coverage has been both extensive and inflammatory. The story, however, has been ignored in most other state newspapers. Community analysis and mock trials may indicate, not surprisingly, that local jurors will be prejudiced against the defendant because of the newspaper articles. Comparable research may indicate that jurors in other districts are more likely to be impartial because they have not been exposed to the adverse publicity. The difficulty is that if there is a change in venue, the murder may become a popular news item in the district to which the case is transferred. By the date of trial the potential jurors in the new district may be as biased as those in the old.

In comparing the desirability of venues, the lawyer needs to weigh a number of strategic considerations. One is the effect of the change in venue on the ability to prepare for trial. Witnesses, particularly character witnesses, may find appearing at a remote district inconvenient. The defendant may also lose the psychological support of friends and family who might otherwise attend the trial. Greater expenses may be incurred if the defendant's attorney has to secure temporary office space and secretarial assistance. Food and lodging may also be more expensive. Finally, one should take into account the respective

---

[31] Fed R Crim P 21(a).

[32] *See id,* note 4 of Notes of Advisory Committee on Rules.

[33] *Id* 21(d).

[34] *See* **§§3.01-3.10.**

[35] *See* **§§5.02-5.06.**

judges and prosecutor who will be involved in the trial. To move for a change in venue in order to obtain a marginally more sympathetic jury makes little sense if in the process one acquires a significantly less sympathetic judge. The judge will be responsible for critical evidentiary rulings as well as sentencing, should the defendant be convicted.[36] Similarly, an attorney should consider the skill and aggressiveness of the respective prosecutors.

Another variable relates to the specific district to which the case will be transferred if the motion for a change in venue is successful. Districts vary, some being more advantageous to the defendant than others. The right to a change in venue is not a right to be tried in a district of one's choice.[37] On the other hand, arguments that a particular district will produce the most fair trial are certainly permissible, and an attorney should feel no compunction on proposing transfer to a particular venue. Supporting documentation would include affidavits and community surveys indicating the degree of prejudice in the respective districts.

In some states a statute or local rule may specify that transfer be to a contiguous district. The rule may be mandatory or advisory, and a rule apparently mandatory on its face may be advisory in practice. In the murder trial of Joan Little,[38] the court was persuaded that the prejudice that would be encountered in contiguous counties as well as in the one in which the crime was committed justified nonadherence to a contiguous county rule. Well documented demographic surveys prepared by social scientists were instrumental in persuading the judge.[39] A judge might also allow a defendant considerable input as to the district to which the case will be transferred if it is apparent that a transfer to a contiguous county will eventually be the subject of an appeal.

Other considerations come into play in regard to a motion to seek a change of venire or to transfer jurors of the vicinage to a different venue. If a lengthy trial is contemplated, jurors forced to spend time in a strange city away from their homes, families, and friends may resent the attorney responsible for their inconvenience. This resentment may translate into a subconscious bias against the moving party.

---

[36] A defense attorney should discover whether in a given district the original judge is still permitted to preside, in effect moving with the case, and whether a retransfer for sentencing is possible (or mandatory) after a conviction. Similarly, the attorney should ascertain whether the prosecutor from the district in which the crime occurred will try the case if there is a change in venue.

[37] *See, e.g.*, United States v Marcello, 280 F Supp 510, 523 (ED La 1968), *affd*, 423 F2d 983 (5th Cir), *cert denied*, 398 US 959 (1970). *But see* Note, *Change of Venue in Criminal Cases: The Defendant's Right to Specify the County of Transfer*, 26 Stan L Rev 131 (1973).

[38] Joan Little was a black woman charged with murdering her white jailer in Beaufort County, North Carolina. A demographic survey indicated that the case had received considerable publicity and had inflamed racial prejudice in all of eastern North Carolina. The case had to be transferred to a central, more urban county in order to find jurors who could be impartial. *See generally* McConahy, Mullin & Frederick, *The Uses of Social Science in Trials with Political Overtones: The Trial of Joan Little*, 41 Law & Contemp Probs 205 (Autumn 1977).

[39] *Id* 209-13. *See also* People v Remiro, 89 Cal App 3d 809, 153 Cal Rptr 89 (1979).

The optimal time for moving for a change in venue or venire is before trial. Rule 22 of the Federal Rules of Criminal Procedure permits a transfer motion to be made at or before arraignment or at such time as the court prescribes.[40] Many judges, however, prefer to await the results of voir dire in order to see if an impartial jury can be impaneled. The difficulty is that voir dire may not reveal subconscious prejudices of which jurors are unaware, or biases which jurors are unwilling to admit publicly.[41] Attorneys should request the maximum latitude in conducting voir dire. Mock voir dires, using a sample of the jury pool, can be conducted to demonstrate the difficulties in impaneling an impartial jury,[42] but these are subject to many of the same problems as actual voir dires.

In any event, pretrial motions for a change of venue or venire may sensitize a judge to the potential problems of prejudice involved in a case. Even if the motion is denied, the judge may become more receptive to expanding the length and scope of voir dire, more willing to grant challenges for cause or allow additional peremptory challenges, and more open to a renewed motion for a change in venue or venire after voir dire is completed.

Pretrial motions for a change in venue or venire may be necessary in order to preserve the issue for a subsequent appeal. In rejecting a defendant's claim of denial of a fair trial because of pretrial publicity, the United States Supreme Court in *Strobles v California*[43] specifically noted that the defense had not requested a change in venue.[44] A failure to exhaust all peremptory challenges may give rise to a similar inference, regardless of whether such exhaustion is required as a matter of law.

§2.06 —Civil Cases

The discussion of venue and vicinage in the preceding sections has focused on criminal trials. Article III and the sixth amendment, when read together, provide guaranties in respect to both venue and vicinage. The seventh amendment, on the other hand, is silent on both issues. Civil litigants are, however, entitled to due process under the fifth and fourteenth amendments.[45] This guaranty arguably includes the right to both impartial jurors and a fair trial. To achieve these, a change in venue or venire may be necessary.

A change in venue in a civil case may be permitted by rule or statute. The relevant federal statute, 28 USC §1404(2), allows for transfers to any other district in which the case might have been brought for "the convenience of

---

[40] Fed R Crim P 22.

[41] *See* **§12.14.**

[42] *See* National Jury Project, Jurywork 7-37 to 7-40 (2d ed 1987).

[43] 343 US 181 (1952).

[44] *Id* 193.

[45] US Const amends V, XIV. The fifth amendment's due process clause applies to the federal government; the fourteenth amendment's to the states.

parties and witnesses, in the interest of justice."[46] The decision to order a transfer is a matter of discretion for the trial judge.[47]

The same kinds of considerations which will support a transfer in a criminal case will support a transfer in a civil case. Likewise, the same kinds of evidence will be relevant. Unlike in a criminal case, however, a community *financial* interest is more likely to result in a change in venue in a civil case, as where the defendant in the civil suit is the primary employer of most members of the community or their families.[48] Conversely, prejudicial publicity is less likely to be a factor. Because no litigant's life or liberty is at stake in a civil trial, the likelihood of a court's ordering a change of venue or venire may also be less.

The doctrine of forum non conveniens vests a court with discretion to transfer a case to a more convenient district where jurisdiction also lies. A court will balance the interests of the party seeking the transfer against the hardship to the opposing party which will result from the transfer. In *Gulf Oil Corp v Gilbert,*[49] a case decided before the adoption of 28 USC §1404(2), the Supreme Court listed the general factors to be weighed:

> Important considerations are the relative ease of access to sources of proof; availability of compulsory process for attendance of unwilling, and the cost of obtaining attendance of willing, witnesses; possibility of view of premises, if view would be appropriate to the action; and all other practical problems that make trial of a case easy, expeditious and inexpensive. There may also be questions as to the enforcibility of a judgment if one is obtained. The court will weigh relative advantages and obstacles to a fair trial. It is often said that the plaintiff may not, by choice of an inconvenient forum, "vex," "harass," or "oppress" the defendant by inflicting upon him expense or trouble not necessary to his own right to pursue his remedy.[50]

The Court, however, sounded an ominous warning to defendants seeking a change in venue: "[U]nless the balance is strongly in favor of the defendant, the plaintiff's choice of forum should rarely be disturbed."[51] The policy considerations articulated by the Supreme Court in *Gilbert* are still likely to be relevant, even though the Court's holding has been to a significant extent superseded by the 1948 adoption of 28 USC §1404(a). A change in venue will not affect the law to be applied.[52]

---

[46] 28 USC §1404(a).

[47] *See* 28 USC §1404(b).

[48] *See, e.g.,* Arctic Enter v Plastics, Inc, 292 Minn 16, 192 NW2d 822 (1971).

[49] 330 US 501 (1947).

[50] *Id* 508.

[51] *Id.*

[52] *See* Van Dusen v Barrack, 376 US 612 (1964).

§2.07 A Jury of One's Peers

In referring to the jury in a criminal case, courts often speak in terms of a jury of one's peers. The apparent source of this concept is the reference to judicum parium in the Magna Carta.[53]

In common law England an alien was entitled to jury de mediatate linguae.[54] Such a jury was composed in part of persons of the defendant's background. The jury de mediatate linguae appears to have been recognized in at least some American courts through the first half of the nineteenth century,[55] although there is no explicit reference to it in the Constitution. The concept is specifically rejected in a 1936 Supreme Court case, *United States v Wood.*[56]

In England the right to a jury of one's peers seems to have meant that an accused should not be judged by those of inferior status. As such, it was a one-way street: the upper classes could judge the lower but not vice versa. This objective was to an extent achieved by making land ownership a qualification for jury service.[57] In the less class-conscious "New World," peers were defined as persons of the same legal status as the defendant.[58] There is, perhaps significantly, no specific reference to a right to a jury of one's peers in the Constitution.

The concept of peers has never been taken literally in the American legal system. A youthful offender is not entitled to a jury composed of citizens all below a certain age. Nor is a black defendant entitled to an all black jury, despite occasional arguments to the contrary.[59] Even the less extreme position that a black defendant is entitled to *some* blacks on the jury has been rejected by the Supreme Court.[60]

Of what significance, then, is the concept of a jury of one's peers? The answer that the legal system appears to offer is that a defendant is entitled to a jury drawn from a pool from which the defendant's peers, assuming they are not disqualified by law from jury service, have not been systematically excluded. Thus the Supreme Court has overturned the conviction of a black when a state

---

[53] *See* Marshall, *The Judgment of One's Peers: Some Aims and Ideals of Jury Trial, in* N. Walker, The British Jury System 1, 5 (1974). Forsyth, however, maintains that judicum parium was not intended to refer to the jury. W. Forsyth, History of Trial by Jury 108-14 (1852). *See also* B. Keeney, Judgment by Peers (1952).

[54] *See* Larue, *A Jury of One's Peers,* 33 Wash & Lee L Rev 841, 848-50 (1976).

[55] *Id* 850-63.

[56] 299 US 123, 145 (1936).

[57] The property requirement for jury service in England was not formally abolished until the Criminal Justice Act of 1972.

[58] *See* Strauder v West Virginia, 100 US 303 (1880):

> The very idea of a jury is a body of men composed of the peers or equals of the person whose rights it is selected or summoned to determine; that is, of his neighbors, fellows, associates, persons having the same legal status in society as that which he holds.
> *Id* 308.

[59] *See* Note, *The Case for Black Juries,* 79 Yale LJ 531 (1970).

[60] *See* Virginia v Rives, 100 US 313 (1879) (black defendants have no right to have blacks on either petit jury which tried them or grand jury which indicted them).

statute prohibited blacks from jury service.[61] A like result was reached where persons of Mexican descent were excluded by law from serving on the jury that convicted a Mexican-American defendant of murder.[62]

The Supreme Court's focus in these cases, however, seems to be more on the rights of those excluded from jury service than on the right of the defendant to a jury of his or her peers. Support for this hypothesis can be drawn from decisions where the Court has permitted challenges to exclusionary jury statutes despite the fact that the defendant was not a member of the excluded class.[63] Further support comes from these cases where the Court has permitted the excluded group itself to bring suit.[64] Moreover, if the Court were concerned that a defendant have peers on his or her jury, it presumably would have required *inclusion* rather than limiting its decisions to discriminatory *exclusion.* The Court has, to the contrary, repeatedly stated that there is no right to have persons of the same race, sex, or class as the defendant serve on the jury.[65]

§2.08 —The Concept of Peers as It Relates to Jury Selection

Whether or not there is a right to a jury of one's peers, it is usually in a defendant's interest to have members of his or her peer group on the jury. The reason is not that nonpeers are incapable of being fair or impartial, or even that they are incapable of empathy. Rather, the reason is that peers are much more apt to have had life experiences similar to those of the accused.[66] They are more likely to be understanding of the defendant's actions, and perhaps more willing to exercise their power of nullification.[67] They will also be better able to judge the credibility of the defendant's testimony, as well as that of witnesses who are of the same race, class, or ethnic background as the defendant. An illustration of this process at work is provided by a black juror from Los Angeles:

> It seemed like the only reason that they arrested the [black] defendant [who was charged with auto theft] was that someone in the gas station across the street looking out into the light in the dark could identify the run-of-the-mill black man from 90 to 100 feet away. They arrested him in the area of York Boulevard [a white neighborhood near Occidental College and Pasadena]. Well, we all know what being black is on York

---

61 Strauder v West Virginia, 100 US 303 (1880).

62 Hernandez v Texas, 347 US 475 (1954).

63 *See, e.g.,* Taylor v Louisiana, 419 US 522 (1975) (male defendant permitted to challenge the exclusion of women); Peters v Kiff, 407 US 493 (1972) (white defendant permitted to challenge the exclusion of blacks).

64 *See, e.g.,* Turner v Fouche, 396 US 346 (1970); Carter v Jury Commn, 396 US 320 (1970).

65 *See, e.g.,* Virginia v Rives, 100 US 313 (1879).

66 *See also* **§12.07.**

67 *See* **§§2.20-2.21.**

> Boulevard. I was raised and born in Los Angeles so it is nothing new to me. If you are black and you're on York Boulevard at four o'clock in the morning, they are going to pick you up. They will pick me up on York Boulevard walking at four o'clock in the morning. This was the only thing that they seemed to have against the man, so we acquitted him.[68]

Jurors who are peers of an accused may be able to dispel or counteract whatever prejudices may exist on the part of other jurors. At the very least, the presence of the defendant's peers may inhibit overt expressions of racism, sexism, or other prejudice.

It might finally be observed that the legal system has an interest in having peers of the defendant on the jury. Peers serve a legitimating function. Both the defendant, and the class of which defendant is a member, will be more likely to accept a verdict from a jury which included the defendant's peers than from one which did not.

§2.09 Impartiality

The sixth amendment guarantees an accused the right to an impartial jury in a federal criminal trial.[69] The sixth amendment right to jury trial, with its requirement of impartiality, has been incorporated into the due process clause of the fourteenth amendment and is therefore binding on the states.[70] Although the sixth amendment speaks in terms of the rights of an accused, courts have recognized that both the government and society also have an interest in an impartial jury.[71]

The seventh amendment provides for a jury trial in civil cases involving more than twenty dollars when it would have been available at common law. Unlike the sixth, the seventh amendment fails to specifically mention impartiality. This striking change of language might seem to suggest, as a matter of construction, that there is no constitutional right to an impartial jury in a civil trial. Such an interpretation, however, was probably not intended. The drafters envisioned a civil jury as it existed at common law, which has been held to have included impartiality.[72]

---

[68] Davis, *Black Juror,* 30 Guild Prac 112-13 *quoted in* V. Hans & N. Vidmar, Judging the Jury 50 (1986).

[69] US Const amend VI.

[70] Duncan v Louisiana, 391 US 145 (1968).

[71] *See, e.g.,* Chicago Council of Lawyers v Bauer, 371 F Supp 689, 691 (CD Ill 1974), *revd on other grounds,* 522 F2d 242 (7th Cir 1975), *cert denied,* 427 US 912 (1976).

[72] *See* McDonough Power Equip, Inc v Greenwood, 464 US 548 (1984); Thiel v Southern Pac Co, 328 US 217, 220 (1945); Kiernan v Van Schaik, 347 F2d 775, 778 (3d Cir 1975).

The requirement of impartiality relates to the jury which actually hears the case and not to the venire or the jury pool. In *Ross v Oklahoma,*[73] the trial judge incorrectly refused to excuse a juror for cause. The defendant, as required by state law, used a peremptory challenge to remove the improperly seated juror. Although the United States Supreme Court agreed that the trial court had erred in not excusing the juror, it found no violation of the defendant's right to an impartial jury. The Court reasoned that, as a result of the defendant's required rectification of the trial judge's error, the jury which had heard the case was impartial.

The guaranty of impartiality may be the most important safeguard of justice in an individual case. Juror deliberations are conducted in secret. Jurors do not have to provide reasons for their verdict, either at the time they deliver the verdict or after the fact. They are not allowed to impeach their verdict, and are not held legally accountable for their decisions. Taking this structure as a given, the requirement of impartiality provides one of the few and one of the prime safeguards that the verdict is fair and just.

But what is meant by impartiality? Platitudes about its value abound, but giving content to the concept has proven more difficult and challenging. The difficulty springs from the fact that all adults have beliefs, values, and prejudices which make impartiality in the tabula rasa sense impossible. The challenge is to define impartiality in a way both that is acceptable to the legal system and that takes into account the moral, political, economic, and psychological baggage that prospective jurors bring with them.[74]

§2.10 —Common Law Origins

With the transition of the common law jury from a group of fact-knowers to fact-finders came a corresponding concern that jurors be impartial. Otherwise, there was the danger that their verdict might be based on personal favoritism rather than on the evidence. The ideal juror was thought to be one who was not acquainted with the parties or their witnesses and who had no knowledge of the facts and no interest, financial or otherwise, in the outcome of the case. To a significant extent, this same approach to impartiality continues today.

The concept of impartiality as an a priori lack of knowledge about or interest in the case was summed up in Lord Coke's oft-quoted equating of it with "indifference."[75] The term, however, was ill-chosen. Jurors should not be indifferent in the sense of not caring, of being satisfied to reach a verdict by a flip of the coin or roll of the dice. They should not be indifferent to the demands of justice. More accurately, Coke was concerned with neutrality: prior to hearing the evidence, jurors should not be inclined to either side.

---

[73] 487 US 81 (1988).

[74] Many of the themes in respect to this issue and those raised in the subsequent sections on impartiality are examined more fully in Gobert, *In Search of the Impartial Jury,* 79 J Crim L & Criminology 269 (1988).

[75] E. Coke, Commentary Upon Littleton Section 1556 (9th ed London 1832), *quoted in* Reynolds v United States, 98 US 145, 154 (1879).

Even as so reformulated, "indifference" should not be overrated. More critical than an initial indifference is the willingness and ability to set aside any pretrial partiality and listen to the evidence with an open mind. Detachment, open-mindedness, and objectivity in fact evaluation are the roads to neutrality. In their deliberations, impartial jurors must resolve not to let their pretrial lack of indifference affect the fairness of their verdict. This standard of impartiality is reflected in practice as well as in theory. Judges routinely ask jurors against whom a prima facie case of bias has been made whether they can set aside their bias and decide the case on the merits. An affirmative response will, if believed by the judge, qualify the juror as impartial.[76]

Coke's full statement required an impartial juror to be "indifferent as he stands unsworn." In terms of this temporal vantage point, Coke's maxim was a correct statement of the law in civil cases but an incorrect statement of the law in criminal cases. At the outset of a criminal prosecution jurors are not supposed to be impartial. The presumption of innocence demands that they be biased in favor of the accused. It is the state's obligation to overcome this *institutionally created bias* in favor of the accused by proof beyond a reasonable doubt.[77] If it fails to do so, the jury must acquit. In both criminal and civil cases the legal system commands that the jury convert any lingering indifference into a partiality against the party having the burden of proof.

§2.11 —Supreme Court Development

The United States Supreme Court has recognized the link between impartiality and jury selection. In *McDonough Power Equipment, Inc v Greenwood*[78] the Court acknowledged that a juror's dishonest answer to a voir dire question could undermine the impartiality of the jury. The Court held, however, that in order to justify a new trial, an attorney had to establish both that a juror failed to answer honestly a material question on voir dire and that a correct response would have created a basis for a challenge for cause.

The Supreme Court's examination of impartiality has occurred primarily in criminal cases involving pretrial publicity. Unfortunately, the Court does not appear clear in its own mind on the relationship between a juror's knowledge of a case and the juror's impartiality. In *Irvin v Dowd*[79] the Court appeared to adopt a middle of the road approach:

> It is not required . . . that the jurors be totally ignorant of the facts and issues involved. In these days of swift, widespread and diverse methods of communication, an important case can be expected to arouse the interest of the public in the vicinity, and scarcely any of those best qualified to serve as jurors will not have formed some impression or opinion as

---

[76] *See* Patton v Yount, 467 US 1025 (1984).

[77] *See In re* Winship, 397 US 358 (1970).

[78] 464 US 548 (1984).

[79] 366 US 717 (1961).

> to the merits of the case. This is particularly true in criminal cases. To hold that the mere existence of any preconceived notion as to the guilt or innocence of an accused, without more, is sufficient to rebut the presumption of a prospective juror's impartiality would be to establish an impossible standard. It is sufficient if the juror can lay aside his impression or opinion and render a verdict based on the evidence presented in court.[80]

The Court presumed impartiality, placing the burden of rebuttal on the challenging party: "Unless he shows the actual existence of such an opinion in the mind of the juror as will raise the presumption of partiality, the juror need not necessarily be set aside. . . ."[81] In applying this test to the facts of the case, however, the Court seemed to do a somersault. It found that persistent and prejudicial news coverage had so permeated the community as to make impartiality impossible. The Court chose to disbelieve the declarations of some impaneled jurors that they could render an impartial verdict, tendering its own analysis of the psychological processes at work:

> The influence that lurks in an opinion once formed is so persistent that it unconsciously fights detachment from the mental processes of the average man. . . . No doubt each juror was sincere when he said that he would be fair and impartial to petitioner, but psychological impact requiring such a declaration before one's fellows is often its father.[82]

Thus the Court in effect presumed partiality, and adopted a theory of opinion formation that made the rebuttal of this presumption extremely difficult. The Court may well have been correct, but it failed to provide empirical evidence to support its reasoning.

The Court tilted even more toward the position that knowledge per se is unacceptable in *Rideau v Louisiana*.[83] A local television station had on several occasions broadcast the defendant's confession to the crimes with which he was charged. Given the circumstances, the Supreme Court held that it was a denial of due process to refuse the defense's request for a change of venue. This unremarkable holding was supplemented by reflections on the more general question of the desirability of "knowledgeable" jurors. Justice Stewart, speaking for the majority, observed:

> For anyone who has ever watched television the conclusion cannot be avoided that this spectacle, to the tens of thousands of people who saw it, in a very real sense *was* Rideau's trial—at which he pleaded guilty of

---

[80] *Id* 722-23.

[81] *Id* 723 (quoting Reynolds v United States, 98 US 145, 157 (1878)).

[82] 366 US 717, 727-28 (1961).

[83] 373 US 723 (1963).

> murder. Any subsequent court proceedings in a community so pervasively exposed to such a spectacle could be but a hollow formality.[84]

Furthermore, the Court did not find it necessary to inquire whether any individual juror's impartiality had been affected:

> [W]e do not hesitate to hold, without pausing to examine a particularized transcript of the voir dire examination of the members of the jury, that due process of law in this case required a trial before a jury drawn from a community of people who had not seen and heard Rideau's televised "interview."[85]

While the decision may have turned on the extreme facts of the case, the Court's language, besides suggesting the extraordinary proposition that a change in venue should have been granted even if none of the jurors had seen or were aware of the television broadcast, appeared to indicate that impartiality presumes a complete or limited lack of knowledge about the critical facts of a case.

The Court appeared to soften its position in *Murphy v Florida*,[86] where it held that the mere exposure of some jurors to adverse publicity did not presumptively deny the defendant due process. Significantly, the Court did what it had declined to do in *Rideau:* it examined the transcript of the voir dire to determine whether any of the jurors were in fact biased against the accused.[87] Previous cases were distinguished as involving widespread community bias.[88]

The per se linking of impartiality with knowledge is questionable. One effect is to penalize well-read citizens. The better informed a person is about current events, the less likely that person is to satisfy a conception of impartiality which views advance knowledge as undesirable. Individuals who in most respects would be considered model citizens will be deemed unfit for jury duty. The seemingly inevitable result will be juries representative of the "average stupidity."[89] Regardless of whether such stupidity is reflective of the community, it is doubtful that this is what the Supreme Court had in mind when it called for a jury drawn from a fair cross-section of the community.[90] A blue ribbon panel composed only of the best informed and most intelligent members of society

---

[84] *Id* 726 (emphasis in original).

[85] *Id* 727.

[86] 421 US 794 (1975).

[87] *Id* 800-02.

[88] *Id* 802-03.

[89] H. Spencer, *Representative Government,* in Essays: Moral, Political, and Aesthetic 182 (1968), *quoted in* Hassett, *A Jury's Pretrial Knowledge in Historical Perspective: The Distinction between Pre-Trial Publicity and "Prejudicial" Publicity,* 43 Law & Contemp Probs 155 (Autumn 1980).

[90] *See* **§6.13.**

may not be the objective,[91] but neither is its opposite. Furthermore, in an era in which news coverage is constantly expanding and where information in a wide variety of forms is readily available, finding a nonknowledgeable juror in a highly publicized case may be no mean task.

Can a potential juror be both knowledgeable and impartial? The Supreme Court appeared at one time to be drifting toward the position that knowledge is inconsistent with impartiality. The more pertinent inquiry is the extent to which knowledge has affected impartiality. The focus should be on the animus of the individual juror. Only when a juror's ability to decide the case fairly and justly has been compromised by the information or knowledge to which he or she has been exposed should the juror be disqualified. This standard is not a concession to the pervasiveness of the modern media's coverage of news but a return to principles enunciated at an early stage of United States history. In the treason trial of Aaron Burr,[92] Chief Justice Marshall discussed juror knowledge and impartiality against the backdrop of a series of inflammatory articles published by the local press:

> Were it possible to obtain a jury without any prepossessions whatever respecting the guilt or innocence of the accused, it would be extremely desirable to obtain such a jury, but this is perhaps impossible; and therefore will not be required. The opinion which has been avowed by the court is, that light impressions which may fairly be supposed to yield to the testimony that may be offered, which may leave the mind open to a fair consideration of that testimony, constitute no sufficient objection to a juror; but that those strong and deep impressions which will close the mind against the testimony that may be offered in opposition to them, which will combat that testimony, and resist its force, do constitute a sufficient objection to him.[93]

The vulnerable point in the analysis is the assumption that faint impressions can be set aside. Psychologically this may not be so, and must in any event be explored on an individual basis. Even a faint impression may make an indelible, albeit unappreciated, impact on a particular juror's psyche. Expert evaluation may be needed to make this determination. Although this may be time-consuming, expensive, and difficult, the alternative of disqualifying all knowledgeable jurors may be worse. To again quote Chief Justice Marshall:

> It would seem to the court that to say that any man who had formed an opinion on any fact conducive to the final decision of the case would therefore be considered as disqualified from serving on the jury, would

[91] *See* Thiel v Southern Pac Co, 328 US 217, 224 (1946) (jury is not the "province of the economically and socially privileged").

[92] United States v Burr, 25 F Cas 49 (CD Va 1807) (No 14,692g).

[93] *Id* 50-51.

> exclude intelligent and observing men, whose minds were really in a situation to decide upon the whole case according to the testimony, and would perhaps be applying the letter of the rule requiring an impartial jury with a strictness which is not necessary for the preservation of the rule itself.[94]

Chief Justice Marshall's opinion points the way to the relevant considerations in analyzing the proper relationship between knowledge and impartiality: (1) knowledge on the part of the jurors is more or less inevitable; (2) the more intelligent and well-informed the potential juror, the more likely he or she is to know something about the case; (3) persons generally knowledgeable about public affairs will, because of the intellectual curiosity reflected in their reading, in most instances be more discerning jurors than those who are generally ignorant about public affairs; (4) a juror's impartiality is compromised only to the extent that the juror's knowledge impedes a decision on the merits; and (5) whether a juror's impartiality has in fact been compromised by knowledge must be determined on an individual basis. In short, recognition that a juror possesses information relating to a case must be the start, not the end, of the inquiry.

§2.12 —The Myth of the Impartial Juror

For legal purposes impartiality is more than the absence of partiality. If partiality is viewed as a negative state and its absence a neutral state, impartiality is a positive state encompassing a constellation of juror traits. Impartial jurors must, of course, have no financial or personal interest in the outcome of a case. They must also be prepared to detach themselves from pretrial prejudices and suspend judgment until after hearing the proof presented by both sides. They must accept the institutional biases of the legal system, such as, in a criminal trial, the presumption of innocence and the requirement of proof beyond a reasonable doubt. They must be open to persuasion and be willing to consider the arguments of counsel and the views of other jurors. They must strive to follow the instructions of the judge. They must be willing to base their verdict on the evidence and the inferences to be drawn therefrom, while at the same time prepared to temper their decisions, when appropriate, with a principled sense of justice.

The legal system's ultimate interest is arguably not impartiality but impartial decision making. Selection of impartial jurors is only a means to achieving this end. The need to focus on a priori juror impartiality stems from the inability in the Anglo-American legal system to examine the impartiality of the decision making process. It is a part of the price the system pays for its reluctance to expose juror deliberations to critical scrutiny or to require jurors to provide reasons for their verdict. The decision to concentrate on juror impartiality rather than on the impartiality of the deliberation process may, however, have been an enlightened one. One of the intriguing findings of Kalven and Zeisel in their classic study of the American jury is that jurors often make up their

---

[94] *Id* 51.

minds *before* they retire; deliberations serve only to solidify initial inclinations and to bring about unanimity.[95] If so, impartial decisions are critically dependent on individual juror impartiality.

But is there such a creature as a truly impartial juror? The concept of the impartial juror as one without discernible bias or private interest in the outcome of the case developed at a time when society had a relatively unsophisticated understanding of the human mind. The effects of childhood training and experiences, as well as the role of subconscious motivations, were not fully appreciated. The processes by which biases and prejudices come into being were not well understood. It is these more subtle, hidden biases which were to a large extent ignored in early conceptions of impartiality. It is at these biases that the social science jury selection techniques discussed in Part II are largely directed.

Modern psychological studies have contributed greatly to our understanding of human nature. Freud and his followers have made us aware that subconscious factors may affect everyday activity.[96] It would be remarkable if persons acting in the capacity of jurors were somehow immune from these subconscious influences.[97] Long-standing opinions, values, and beliefs cannot be checked like a hat at the jury room door. The Supreme Court was probably correct in *Irvin v Dowd*[98] when it observed that "[t]he influence that lurks in an opinion once formed is so persistent that it unconsciously fights detachment from the mental processes of the average man."[99] Although the Court was referring to the effects of pretrial publicity, its point can be extended to all life experiences.[100]

Kalven and Zeisel, for example, found that one significant factor leading to judge-jury verdict disagreements was the defendant's attractiveness.[101] Sympathetic defendants elicited greater juror leniency.[102] But what causes a defendant to evoke sympathy? Kalven and Zeisel did not probe the issue, but in part jurors may be responding to characteristics in a defendant which remind them of sympathetic persons with whom they have had contact. Similarly, Kalven

---

[95] H. Kalven & H. Zeisel, The American Jury 488-89 (1966).

[96] *See* S. Freud, The Psychotherapy of Everyday Life (Brill ed 1948); C. Jung, Psychology of the Unconscious (1950). *See also* H. Ellenberger, The Discovery of the Unconscious (1970); L. Frey-Robin, From Freud to Jung: A Comparative Study of the Psychology of the Unconscious (1974); G. Groddick, Exploring the Unconscious (1950).

[97] One argument that persons may not be as affected by their biases in their capacity as jurors is that the judge admonishes them to act impartially. In their everyday affairs jurors do not receive such admonitions, and when they do, it is not from someone with the stature of a judge. The formality of the trial setting further contributes to the seriousness with which jurors approach their task.

[98] 366 US 717 (1961).

[99] *Id* 727.

[100] One study reported that jurors spend slightly over one-fifth of deliberation time discussing their own experiences. James, *Status and Competence of Jurors,* 64 Am J Soc 563 (1959).

[101] H. Kalven & H. Zeisel, *supra* note 95, at ch 15.

[102] *Id.*

and Zeisel discovered that jurors were less inclined to convict for an activity, such as gambling or reckless driving, in which they themselves had engaged.[103]

A juror's values and life experiences may affect the juror's perception of the parties and their witnesses, the issues, and the facts. A juror is in effect a witness to the events of a trial, with all the shortcomings of a witness.[104] If the mannerisms of a party, witness, or attorney remind the juror of a disfavored relative, the juror may have a subconscious negative reaction.[105] Bias may seep in despite the juror's lack of personal acquaintance with any of the principals.

Jurors also tend to have general philosophical predispositions concerning the issues of a case. An unhappy sexual encounter, long forgotten or long remembered, may surface in a pornography or sodomy prosecution. The particular occurrence which leads to the juror's attitude may be undiscoverable. Often one's attitudes are the product of a series of minor incidents, the cumulative effect of which may be devastating. There now exists, for instance, fairly convincing evidence that "authoritarian" personalities are prone to favor the state in a criminal trial.[106] Identification of the totality of experiences which result in the formation of an "authoritarian" personality may be impossible.

Even the facts of a case, seemingly subject to objective ascertainment, are filtered through a juror's life history. A juror is likely to disbelieve a factual scenario which conflicts with the juror's personal experiences.[107] Evidence may not be as much an intrinsic entity as a reflection of the personality and values of the jurors.[108] In this regard juror diversity may enhance accurate fact finding. Since human perception tends to be selective, facts which contradict one's beliefs may be ignored. A homogeneous jury, whose members share a common background, values, and attitudes, will tend to ignore the same facts. A heterogeneous jury, where different jurors see different parts of the picture, is more likely to come up with a better sense of the whole.[109] It is in the interests of justice as well as in the interests of the parties to have a heterogeneous jury.

The vagueness of controlling legal principles also allows for personal factors to enter a juror's deliberations. In a criminal case the prosecutor must establish

---

[103] *Id* 291, 326.

[104] *See* J. Frank, Courts on Trial 153 (1949).

[105] *Id* ch 10.

[106] *See* **§§12.15, 12.16;** *see also* Boehm, *Mr. Prejudice, Miss Sympathy and the Authoritarian Personality: An Application of Psychological Measuring Techniques to the Problem of Jury Bias,* 1968 Wis L Rev 734; Buckhout, Licker, Alexander, Gambardella, Eugenio, & Kakoullis, *Discretion in Jury Selection, in* L. Abt & I. Stuart, Social Psychology and Discretionary Law 176 (1979); Note, *Juror Bias—A Practical Screening Device and the Case for Permitting its Use,* 64 Minn L Rev 987 (1980).

[107] *See* Hovey v Superior Court, 28 Cal 3d 1, 616 P2d 1301, 1313, 168 Cal Rptr 128, 140 (1980).

[108] *See* Hepburn, *The Objective Reality of Evidence and the Utility of Systematic Jury Selection,* 4 Law & Hum Behav 89 (1980).

[109] *See* Hovey v Superior Court, 28 Cal 3d 1, 616 P2d 1301, 1312-13, 168 Cal Rptr 128, 139-40 (1980).

the guilt of the accused beyond a reasonable doubt. While all jurors may accept this standard, the amount of proof required to create a "reasonable doubt" in an individual juror's mind may differ.[110]

Numerous studies now suggest a correlation between juror attitudes and such variables as occupation,[111] sex,[112] race,[113] and socio-economic status.[114] In addition, a juror's family, social, political, and personal associations may all affect the juror's decision making. The juror's mood at the time of trial may also be relevant. For instance, a juror who has recently received a parking ticket thought to be undeserved may be less sympathetic to the state's case than a juror who has recently received an unexpected tax refund. These observations about opinion formation and personality dynamics may be neither original nor profound, but their relevance to the concept of the impartial juror is rarely articulated or seemingly fully appreciated. The psychological baggage that human beings bring to the jury room may render illusory any talk of a truly impartial juror.

§2.13 Size of the Jury—Criminal Trials

Historically, the jury has consisted of twelve members, although Forsyth, in his authoritative history, reports instances of juries of more than twelve, and others of less than twelve.[115] Why twelve came to be viewed as the appropriate number is somewhat obscure but the fact remains that by the beginning of the fifteenth century it had.[116] In *Thompson v Utah* [117] the United States Supreme Court added its imprimatur:

> Assuming, then, that the provisions of the constitution relating to trials for crimes and to criminal prosecutions apply to the territories of the

---

[110] *See* People v Carmichael, 198 Cal 534, 545, 246 P 62, 67 (1926).

[111] *See, e.g.*, Broeder, *Occupational Expertise and Bias as Affecting Juror Behavior: A Preliminary Look*, 40 NYU L Rev 1079 (1965); Hermann, *Occupations of Jurors as an Influence on Their Verdict*, 5 Forum 150 (1970).

[112] *See, e.g.*, Snyder, *Sex Role Differential and Juror Decisions*, 55 Soc & Soc Res 442 (1971); Stephan, *Sex Prejudice in Jury Simulation*, 88 J Psychology 305 (1974); Strodtbeck, James & Hawkins, *Social Status in Jury Deliberations*, 22 Am Soc Rev 713 (1957); Strodtbeck & Mann, *Sex Role Differentiations in Jury Deliberations*, 19 Sociometry 3 (1956).

[113] *See, e.g.*, R. Simon, The Jury and the Defense of Insanity 111 (1956); Broeder, *The Negro in Court*, 1965 Duke LJ (1965). The race of the juror, the defendant, and the victim may all be relevant.

[114] *See, e.g.*, R. Simon, *supra* note 113, at ch 6; Adler, *Socioeconomic Factors Influencing Jury Verdicts*, 3 NYU Rev of L & Soc Change 1 (1973); Rose & Prell, *Does the Punishment Fit the Crime? A Study in Social Valuation*, 61 Am J Soc 247 (1955); Strodtbeck, James, & Hawkins, *supra* note 112. *See generally* Stephan, *Selective Characteristics of Jurors and Litigants: Their Influence on Juries' Verdicts*, *in* R. Simon, The Jury System in America: A Critical Overview (1975).

[115] W. Forsyth, History of Trial by Jury 131-32 (1852).

[116] *See* Williams v Florida, 399 US 78, 89 (1970).

[117] 170 US 343 (1898).

> United States, the next inquiry is whether the jury referred to in the original constitution and in the sixth amendment is a jury constituted, as it was at common law, of twelve persons, neither more nor less. This question must be answered in the affirmative.[118]

The Court proceeded to strike down a Utah statute permitting juries of eight in noncapital cases. Thirty-two years later, in *Patton v United States,*[119] the Court reaffirmed its understanding of the Constitution:

> [W]e first inquire what is embraced by the phrase "trial by jury". That it means a trial by jury as understood and applied at common law, and includes all the essential elements as they were recognized in this country and England when the Constitution was adopted, is not open to question. Those elements were: (1) *that the jury should consist of twelve men, neither more nor less;* (2) that the trial should be in the presence and under the superintendence of a judge having power to instruct them as to the law and advise them in respect of the facts; and (3) that the verdict should be unanimous.[120]

This unbroken line of precedent continued until the 1970 case of *Williams v Florida.*[121] At issue was Florida's use of six-person juries. Despite its previous seemingly unequivocal pronouncements, the Supreme Court in *Williams* held that the federal Constitution did not require any particular number of jurors and that Florida's six-person jury system was acceptable.

The Court's reasoning in *Williams* is instructive. Looking first to history, the Court saw the fixing of the size of the jury at twelve as little more than "a historical accident, unrelated to the great purposes which gave rise to the jury in the first place."[122] Second, the Court examined the background surrounding the adoption of the Constitution and found that there was no conclusive evidence of an intent on the part of the drafters to equate the constitutional and common law characteristics of the jury. Thus the Court freed itself to view the critical question as a functional one—whether a given feature of the jury was relevant to the fulfillment of its purpose.[123]

The primary purpose of the jury, as seen by the Supreme Court, is to prevent governmental oppression. It does so by interposing between the accused, on the one hand, and the corrupt or overzealous prosecutor or the compliant, biased, or eccentric judge, on the other, the common sense judgment of laypersons drawn from the community. This function, reasoned the *Williams* Court, was not related to the size of the jury. The jury should be sufficiently large to promote group deliberation, insulate itself from outside intimidation, and

---

[118] *Id* 349.

[119] 281 US 276 (1930).

[120] *Id* 288 (emphasis added).

[121] 399 US 78 (1970).

[122] *Id* 89-90.

[123] *Id* 99-100.

provide a reasonable opportunity to obtain a representative cross-section of the community.[124] To achieve these purposes, however, the Court saw no meaningful distinction between six- and twelve-person juries. Nor did the Court see any relationship between verdict reliability and jury size. The possibility of a holdout juror who would cause a deadlock was obviously greater on a twelve-person jury but, parried the Court, that juror could as easily frustrate a verdict of acquittal as a verdict of guilt.

As a result of *Williams* six-person juries became constitutionally permissible in state criminal trials. They are, of course, not required; indeed they may be forbidden by state statute or constitution. Because the court in *Williams* was interpreting the sixth amendment as incorporated in the fourteenth amendment's due process clause, moreover, six-person juries are in theory *constitutionally* acceptable in federal criminal trials. In practice, however, the Federal Rules of Criminal Procedure generally require a jury of twelve.[125]

Is there a limit below six which would be constitutionally impermissible? The issue arose in *Ballew v Georgia,*[126] where the accused had been convicted by a five-person jury. The Supreme Court reversed. In reaching its decision the Court cited the results of numerous post-*Williams* studies that attempted to evaluate the effect of reducing the size of the jury.[127] Among the conclusions of the studies were: (1) smaller juries were less likely to foster effective group deliberation; (2) smaller juries were not as able to determine facts accurately or to apply community values correctly; (3) smaller juries were not as able to counterbalance or overcome biases of individual members; (4) the risk of convicting innocent individuals increased as the size of the jury decreased below six; (5) the likelihood of inconsistent verdicts increased with a reduction in the size of the jury; (6) smaller juries were less likely to result in a hung jury, to the detriment of the defendant; (7) the likelihood of minorities and other identifiable community groups serving on juries decreased as the size of the jury was reduced; and (8) previous studies had masked differences in the operation of larger and smaller juries. Based on this empirical evidence the Court, while not overruling *Williams,* concluded that "the purpose and functioning of the jury in a criminal trial is seriously impaired, and to a constitutional degree, by a reduction in size to below six members."[128] The Court could find no counterbalancing cost- or time-saving justification for the reduction of juries from six to five, as it had for the reduction from twelve to six.

The Court's extensive reliance in *Ballew* on social science research was ironic. The aim of many of the cited studies was to show that the Court's conclusions in *Williams* were neither empirically valid nor sociologically enlightened. Although it is unlikely to happen, the same studies relied upon in *Ballew* could be cited to justify the overruling of *Williams.*

---

[124] *Id* 100.

[125] Fed R Crim P 23(b). A smaller jury may be permissible in necessitous circumstances or if the parties concur and the court approves.

[126] 435 US 223 (1978).

[127] The studies are cited at 435 US at 231, n 10.

[128] *Id* 239.

Perhaps the long-term significance of *Ballew* lies in the Supreme Court's willingness to be informed by social science research.[129] Many of the legal arguments favoring modification of the methods of jury selection have as their underpinning the results of social science studies.

§2.14 —Civil Trials

In *Williams v Florida*[130] the Supreme Court held that six-person juries were constitutionally permissible in state criminal trials. In *Colgrove v Battin,*[131] decided three years after *Williams,* the Supreme Court considered whether six-person juries were constitutionally permissible in civil cases as well. As it had done in *Williams,* the Court initially found that as a historical matter the drafters of the Constitution were more concerned with preserving the right to jury trial than with defining its contours. The seventh amendment, however, unlike the sixth, specifically referred to "suits at common law." The court reasoned that this reference was intended to delineate the class of cases in which a jury trial would be available rather than to incorporate the features of a common law jury.

Proceeding from that premise, the Court, again as it had in *Williams,* took a functional approach. It concluded that jury performance and verdict reliability would not be adversely affected by a reduction in the size of the jury to six. References in earlier cases suggesting that civil juries were to be composed of twelve[132] were dismissed as dicta. Legislative references to preserving the civil jury as it existed at common law[133] were construed not to establish unalterable jury characteristics.

The seventh amendment has not been incorporated into the fourteenth amendment's due process clause. Therefore, the Court's holding in *Colgrove,* unlike its holding in *Williams,* applies *only* to civil trials in *federal* court. The size of the civil jury in state cases must be determined in accord with state constitutions and statutes. The reasoning of the Court in *Colgrove,* however, does indicate that the Court is not likely to be receptive to an argument that a six-person jury in a state civil trial violates the state's due process obligations under the fourteenth amendment.

---

[129] Not too much significance should be read into this point. If *Ballew* is a high water mark in the Court's receptivity to social science research, its subsequent decision in Lockhart v McCree, 476 US 162 (1986), in which it rejected an impressive body of empirical research relating to jury decisions in death penalty cases, signals that the Court has not been completely persuaded as to the value of such studies.

[130] 399 US 78 (1970).

[131] 413 US 149 (1973).

[132] *See* Maxwell v Dow, 176 US 581 (1900); Capital Traction Co v Hof, 174 US 1, 13 (1899).

[133] *See* 28 USC §2072; Fed R Civ P 48.

§2.15 —Statutes and State Constitutions

Since there is no federal constitutional bar to reducing the size of juries to six, only those constraints imposed by state and federal statute and state constitutions remain. A defendant in a federal criminal case has, as a general matter, a statutory right to a jury of twelve.[134] In addition, a few states have interpreted their constitutions to require juries of twelve.[135] The emerging statutory pattern among the states is to require juries of twelve in capital cases and major felonies while permitting juries of six in misdemeanor and civil cases. The rationale for these distinctions is an understandable concern that the greater the interests that are at stake, the more the protection of the jury is needed. A jury of twelve is likely to be more reliable and more representative of the community than a jury of six. It is also better able to protect an accused against governmental oppression.

§2.16 —Jury Selection as a Function of Jury Size: Strategic Considerations

The size of the jury has implications for jury selection. The natural leader(s) of the jury will assume an even more dominant role in a jury of six than in a jury of twelve.[136] Special care must be taken in determining which person(s) are likely to assume this role and in assessing in which directions these jurors are likely to lead the jury.[137]

It is difficult for jurors in the minority to hold out against those in the majority without the support of others.[138] These allies are less likely to be found in the smaller jury. Thus if the best that an attorney can realistically hope for is a hung jury, the attorney must attempt to evaluate a prospective holdout candidate with an eye toward whether that person has the psychological fortitude to hold out against five other jurors. On the other hand, jurors who find themselves in the minority may be less inhibited in expressing an opinion before a group of six than before a group of twelve.

The dynamics of group interaction may also be altered by the reduction in size of the jury. As is true in regard to many jury issues, consultation with a

---

[134] Fed R Crim P 24(b).

[135] *See, e.g.,* People v Feagley, 14 Cal 3d 346, 350, 14 P2d 373, 380, 121 Cal Rptr 509, 516 (1975); Gilbreath v Wallace, 292 Ala 267, 292 So 2d 651 (1974).

[136] *See* P. DiPerna, Juries on Trial 62 (1984).

[137] *See also* **§12.02.**

[138] *See* H. Kalvin & H. Zeisel, The American Jury 462-63 (1966). *See also* P. DiPerna, *supra* note 136, at 61. In an instructive experiment, Asch asked groups to judge the length of lines. All but one of the participants were instructed to deliberately misjudge the length. Each of these confederates expressed in turn the same incorrect opinion. Finally, the true subject was asked his opinion. Fully 37% of the critical subjects concurred in the incorrect judgment. Members of a control group, not subject to group pressure, made virtually no mistakes. Asch, *Effects of Group Pressure Upon the Modification and Distortion of Judgments, reprinted in* Groups, Leadership, and Men 177 (H. Guetzkow ed 1951).

knowledgable social scientist may prove invaluable in predicting the interaction patterns which may develop. In some instances, an attorney may prefer a jury of six, even though a jury of twelve is available.

It is obvious that a jury of six is less likely than a jury of twelve to contain minority representatives or to reflect a fair cross-section of the community. This may work to the disadvantage of an attorney representing a minority defendant or a prosecutor in a case in which the victim is a member of a minority. In such situations the judge should examine challenges for cause of minority jurors even more critically than usual. The judge should also carefully scrutinize peremptory challenges to ensure compliance with the Supreme Court's holding in *Batson v Kentucky* that such challenges not be exercised on a racially discriminatory basis.[139] Indeed, a defense attorney representing a minority defendant should carefully consider waiving a jury[140] if the jury will consist of six members and the attorney envisions a racially biased panel without a minority representative capable of offsetting that bias.

§2.17 Verdict Unanimity—Criminal Trials

The evolution of the law with respect to unanimous verdicts in criminal cases followed a similar path to that taken with respect to the size of the jury. Just as the common law practice was to have juries of twelve, so too was the practice to require unanimity. The precise justification for either of these traditions is today somewhat unclear.[141] The United States Constitution does not directly address the question of either size or unanimity. An early draft of the Bill of Rights did contain a unanimity requirement but it was deleted because it was thought to be implicit in the right of trial by jury. This understanding was reflected by the Supreme Court in *Patton v United States:*[142]

> [W]e first inquire what is embraced by the phrase "trial by jury." That it means a trial by jury as understood and applied at common law, and includes all the essential elements as they were recognized in this country and England when the Constitution was adopted, is not open to question. Those elements were: (1) that the jury should consist of twelve men, neither more nor less; (2) that the trial should be in the presence and under the superintendence of a judge having power to instruct them as to the

---

[139] 476 US 79 (1986), *discussed in* **§§8.05-8.11.**

[140] *See generally* **§1.23.**

[141] Professor Van Dyke offers several different hypotheses to explain the unanimity requirement. J. Van Dyke, Jury Selection Procedures: Our Uncertain Commitment to Representative Panels 204(f) (1977). Among these are that the unanimity rule developed as a protection for defendants at a time when evidentiary rules were not fully developed, that it was a mere historical accident, that it was a method to relieve judges from governmental pressure to convict, that it was a counterbalance to the harsh penalties imposed following a conviction, that it was a means of implementing the requirement that the community consent to the verdict, and that it was a way to protect jurors from being punished for erroneous verdicts.

[142] 281 US 276 (1930).

law and advise them in respect of the facts; and (3) *that the verdict should be unanimous.*[143]

In the early 1970s, however, as it had done in regard to the issue of jury size, the United States Supreme Court decided that it was appropriate to consider the constitutionality of less than unanimous verdicts. The companion cases in which the Court addressed the issue were *Johnson v Louisiana*[144] and *Apodaca v Oregon.*[145] In both the Court upheld a state statute permitting less than unanimous verdicts. Because the Court's rationale is different in the two cases, however, each must be examined separately. Together the two decisions reject both due process and sixth amendment objections to less than unanimous verdicts in state criminal trials.

The facts which gave rise to *Johnson v Louisiana*[146] occurred prior to the Supreme Court's decision in *Duncan v Louisiana,*[147] in which the Court had incorporated the sixth amendment into the fourteenth amendment and thereby made it binding on the states.[148] As a result, the defendant's challenge to the Louisiana law which permitted convictions by a nine-to-three vote had to be judged under the pre-*Duncan* standards, i.e., whether such verdicts violated the defendant's fourteenth amendment right of due process.[149]

Johnson contended that a unanimous verdict was required in order to give effect to the constitutional requirement that guilt be proven beyond a reasonable doubt.[150] That three jurors voted to acquit arguably indicated such a doubt. A majority of the Supreme Court was not persuaded. It reasoned that the mere fact that three jurors were unable to vote to convict did not prevent the remaining nine from honestly concluding that guilt had been established beyond a reasonable doubt. But did the fact that three jurors were not so convinced in itself establish a reasonable doubt? The Court held that it did not, finding that disagreement was not equivalent to a failure of proof. In support of its position the Court noted that in the federal system, where unanimity is required, an inability to reach a unanimous verdict results not in an acquittal (which it logically should if the presence of jurors not willing to convict is sufficient to create a reasonable doubt) but in a mistrial.

---

143 *Id* 288 (emphasis added).

144 406 US 356 (1972).

145 406 US 404 (1972).

146 406 US 356 (1972).

147 391 US 145 (1968).

148 *See* **§1.13.**

149 The defendant also raised an equal protection argument based on the fact that both in capital cases and in cases where the state used a five-person jury, the verdict had to be unanimous. The Court saw nothing invidious in treating capital cases differently. Nor did it seem to the Court unreasonable to reduce the size of the jury while concomitantly requiring a greater percentage vote to convict.

150 *See In re* Winship, 397 US 358, 363-64 (1970).

In *Apodaca v Oregon*[151] the Court considered whether the sixth amendment's right to jury trial as incorporated in the due process clause of the fourteenth amendment required unanimity. A fractured Court split four to four, with Justice Powell casting the deciding vote.

The plurality, in an opinion by Justice White, took the same tack that it had in regard to the issue of the size of the jury.[152] It found no conclusive evidence that the drafters of the Constitution had intended to preserve the unanimity requirement which had existed at common law.[153] The absence of a historical mooring allowed Justice White to apply a functional test. Under it the question became whether the unanimity requirement was necessary to fulfill the jury's historic role of preventing governmental oppression by interposing a group of lay decision makers between the state and the accused.

The plurality claimed not to see a meaningful difference between requiring twelve votes to convict and allowing conviction by a vote of ten to two, as permitted by Oregon law. In either case, the defendant would still receive the benefit of the judgment of the community as represented by the jury. In response to defendant's argument that the lack of unanimity indicated the existence of a reasonable doubt, the plurality answered that the Court had never held that the sixth amendment contained a reasonable doubt requirement and that the due process reasonable doubt argument had been disposed of in *Johnson.*

The plurality was also not persuaded that the less than unanimous verdict would defeat the requirement of cross-section representation.[154] The petitioner had maintained that the effect of not requiring a unanimous verdict would be to allow the majority to ignore the views of minorities. Justice White responded that there was no reason to believe that the majority would be so crass or that they would base their verdict on prejudice rather than principle.[155]

The plurality in *Apodaca* had proceeded on the assumption that the fourteenth amendment guaranteed a defendant the same right to jury trial in state court as did the sixth amendment in federal court. The dissent agreed with the plurality's premise, but not its conclusions. The dissenters asserted that nonunanimity diminished both the reliability of the verdict and the respect it would receive. Without a requirement of unanimity, jurors in the majority would not have to make the effort to convince holdouts of their position. Likewise, the majority would have to neither listen to nor respond to the arguments

---

[151] 406 US 404 (1972).

[152] *See* Williams v Florida, 399 US 78 (1970). *See generally* **§2.13.**

[153] On the one hand, it was arguable that a unanimity requirement was omitted because it was thought unnecessary; on the other, it was arguable that the omission was deliberate.

[154] *See* **§6.13.**

[155] England has adopted a rule allowing conviction by a ten-to-two vote. However, to ensure full deliberation, the rule does not go into effect until the jury has deliberated for two hours. *See* Criminal Justice Act 1967. In *Apodaca* the jury deliberated for only 41 minutes.

of the minority.[156] Deliberation as a consequence might not be as full or extensive. The defendant would lose the opportunity for a compromise verdict on a lesser included offense, as well as the possibility of a hung jury. (Although theoretically a hung jury could disadvantage the state as easily as the accused, Kalven and Zeisel had found that when there was a deadlock the majority were over three times more likely to favor conviction than acquittal.[157]) Disagreeing strongly with the plurality, the dissenters also thought that lack of unanimity did indicate the existence of a reasonable doubt.

The critical vote in *Apodaca* belonged to Justice Powell. He agreed with the dissent that, as a historical matter, the *sixth amendment* required a unanimous vote to convict. However, he disagreed with both the plurality and the dissent that the due process right to jury trial was coextensive with the sixth amendment right to jury trial. He rejected the "jot for jot" approach to incorporation, and concluded that unanimity was not a "fundamental" aspect of the right to jury trial. Therefore it was not part of the "process" due under the fourteenth amendment.

Justice Powell's opinion leaves the constitutional law of trial by jury in a state of asymmetry. A consensus exists on the Court that constitutional rights incorporated into the fourteenth amendment apply to the state to the same extent that they apply to the federal government. In a federal criminal trial an accused has a sixth amendment right not to be convicted except by the vote of a unanimous jury. There is, on the other hand, no corresponding constitutional right under due process in a state criminal trial; majority verdicts are permissible.

Given *Johnson* and *Apodaca,* what percentage vote of a jury should be sufficient to convict? *Johnson* permitted conviction by a nine to three margin. In a concurring opinion, Justice Blackmun indicated that he would have "great difficulty" with a system permitting conviction by a seven-to-five vote.[158] In his plurality opinion, Justice White characterized the three-fourths vote needed to convict as a "substantial majority."[159] The implication may be that a state statute permitting conviction by a bare majority would not be upheld. The unanswered question is what percentage of the jury will be deemed to constitute a "substantial majority." Although the Supreme Court has not provided further guidance on this issue, it has indicated that the substantiality of the vote required to convict may be related to the size of the jury. In *Burch v Louisiana*[160] the Court held that when the jury is reduced to six, the vote to convict must be unanimous.

Johnson and *Apodaca* established that as a matter of *federal* constitutional law, less than unanimous verdicts are permissible in state but not federal criminal trials. In fact, few state legislatures have accepted the invitation to rewrite their laws to allow less than unanimous verdicts. Perhaps they agree with Justice Blackmun that while less than unanimous verdicts are acceptable as a matter

---

156 Kalven and Zeisel found that in one out of ten cases the minority was able to persuade the majority. H. Kalven & H. Zeisel, The American Jury 490 (1966).

157 *Id* 460.

158 406 US 356, 366 (1972) (Blackmun, J, concurring).

159 *Id* 362.

160 441 US 130 (1979).

of constitutional law, they are not desirable as a matter of social policy. Although Justice Blackmun did not elaborate, others have maintained that nonunanimity does not save time and expense, does not negate the effect of a bribed, corrupt, or irrational juror, and is not justifiable in light of the social costs.[161] If a state were to enact a statute permitting nonunanimous verdicts, the statute, despite *Johnson* and *Apodaca,* might still be found in violation of a *state* right to jury trial. All states have constitutional provisions guaranteeing jury trial. It is for the state supreme court to determine whether such a provision requires jury unanimity. A state supreme court may interpret its own constitution to provide more stringent safeguards for an accused than does an even identically worded federal constitutional provision.

§2.18 —Civil Trials

In an 1897 case, *American Publishing Co v Fisher,*[162] the United States Supreme Court held that a Utah statute permitting less than unanimous verdicts in federal civil cases was unconstitutional. The Court found that the statute conflicted with the right of jury trial guaranteed in the seventh amendment. The continuing authority of this decision, however, is problematic. Similar pronouncements relating to unanimity in criminal trials had been made in contemporaneous cases; these decisions did not prevent the Court from reexamining that issue in *Johnson* and *Apodaca.* Also, because the seventh amendment has never been incorporated into the fourteenth, the authority of *Fisher* is limited to civil cases in *federal* court.

Johnson and *Apodaca* involved criminal trials. They did not address whether the Constitution required that jury verdicts in civil cases be unanimous. It is unlikely, however, were the Supreme Court to address the issue, that the result would be different. First, the interests at stake in a civil case are generally considered to be less weighty than in a criminal case. If the possible loss of life or liberty does not justify a unanimity requirement, it is doubtful that the mere loss of money or property will. Second, the arguments in both *Apodaca* and *Johnson* hinged to some extent on the requirement that guilt in criminal cases had to be established beyond a reasonable doubt. Lack of unanimity, it was argued, indicated the existence of such a doubt. In civil cases the burden of proof is the far less onerous preponderance of the evidence standard. Third, the Court in *Johnson* and *Apodaca* rejected the due process contention that lack of a unanimity requirement impaired the jury's ability to return rational, fair verdicts. A like conclusion could be expected in regard to civil cases.

---

[161] *See* J. Van Dyke, Jury Selection Procedures: Our Uncertain Commitment to Representative Panels 209-10 (1977).

[162] 166 US 464 (1897).

§2.19 —Jury Selection as a Function of Verdict Unanimity: Strategic Considerations

Lawyers in jurisdictions that permit less than unanimous verdicts may need to reconsider their jury selection strategy. Some criminal defense attorneys, as a matter of tactics, particularly in cases where they despair of prevailing on the merits, will seek a jury of fractious individuals. They reason that such individuals will probably be unable to agree on anything, including a verdict, and the result will be a hung jury. This strategy is less likely to succeed when nonunanimous verdicts are permitted.

Similarly, to identify the iconoclasts who will hold out in the face of ten or eleven others will not serve the same purpose that it does where unanimity is required. Stubborn jurors will no longer be able to hang the jury. Indeed, their presence on the jury may be counterproductive: they may alienate other jurors, who may in turn ignore their arguments.

Attorneys will need to learn to think more in terms of group dynamics than in terms of representative viewpoints.[163] To include a minority member of the community on a jury in order to provide a different perspective will do little good if the majority can ignore that perspective. Although there may be little basis to believe that this will occur, the possibility must be considered. If only one minority representative will be on the jury, care must be taken to choose one who will be able to influence others. Likewise, it is even more important than usual to challenge close-minded jurors who will be unwilling to listen to opposing viewpoints.

The permissibility of nonunanimous verdicts may have implications for a constitutional claim that a jury pool is not representative of a cross-section of the community.[164] While the presence of a minority juror may tend to refute such a claim when unanimity is required, token representation should be viewed differently when nonunanimous verdicts are permitted. If there remain sufficient other jurors to return a verdict without having to listen to the arguments of the minority juror, part of the purpose of cross-section representation is defeated. This consideration may have particular force in cases where a prosecutor has exercised peremptory challenges so as to exclude all but one or two blacks. The Supreme Court has held that a prosecutor cannot exercise peremptory challenges to exclude all blacks merely because of their race.[165] In a jurisdiction permitting a nonunanimous verdict, an attorney should be sensitive to the possible prosecutorial tactic of permitting blacks on the jury but in insufficient numbers to defeat the requisite majority required to convict in the jurisdiction. As the Massachusetts Supreme Judicial Court aptly observed in *Commonwealth v Soares:*[166]

---

[163] *See* **§12.02.**

[164] *See* Taylor v Louisiana, 419 US 522 (1975). *See generally* **§6.13.**

[165] Batson v Kentucky, 476 US 79 (1986) *discussed in* **§§8.05-8.11.**

[166] 377 Mass 461, 387 NE2d 499, *cert denied,* 444 US 881 (1979).

> One need not eliminate 100 percent of minority jurors to achieve an impermissible purpose. If the minority's representation is reduced to impotence, as, for example, by the disproportionate challenge of minority members, and the failure to challenge a minority member who can be reasonably relied on as safe, the majority . . . biases are likely to meet little resistance.[167]

§2.20 Jury Nullification

The term *jury nullification* refers to the power of a jury to acquit a defendant in a criminal case even though a strict application of legal principles to the evidence would logically require a conviction. The source of the nullification power is often traced to the English decision in *Bushell's Case.*[168] In that case several jurors, led by Edward Bushell, refused to convict two Quaker activists charged with unlawful assembly. The judge refused to accept a verdict other than guilty, and ordered the jurors to resume their deliberations without food or drink. When the jurors persisted in their refusal to convict, the court fined them and committed them to prison until the fines were paid. On appeal the Court of Common Pleas ordered the jurors' release, holding that they could not be punished for their verdict. Thus the jury's independence was established in England.

The American counterpart to *Bushell's Case* was the 1735 trial of John Peter Zenger.[169] Zenger was charged with seditious libel. In his closing remarks to the jury, Alexander Hamilton, his attorney, argued among other points that the jury had the right to acquit when the government had abused its powers. The jury returned a verdict of not guilty.

In a 1952 decision, *Morissette v United States*[170] the United States Supreme Court recognized the power of juries to engage in nullification:

> Had the jury convicted on proper instructions it would be the end of the matter. But juries are not bound by what seems inescapable logic to judges. . . . They might have refused to brand Morissette as a thief. Had they done so, that too would have been the end of the matter.[171]

Likewise, the Supreme Court in *Duncan v Louisiana*[172] implicitly endorsed the policies behind nullification when it stated: "If the defendant preferred the common-sense judgment of the jury to the more tutored but less sympathetic reaction of the single judge, he was to have it."[173]

---

[167] *Id* n 32.

[168] 124 Eng Rep 1006 (CP 1670), *discussed in* **§1.02.**

[169] *See generally* J. Alexander, A Brief Narration of the Case and Trial of John Peter Zenger (1963). The case is discussed in **§1.03.**

[170] 342 US 246 (1952).

[171] *Id* 276.

[172] 391 US 145 (1968).

[173] *Id* 156.

It is sometimes debated whether jury nullification is a right or a power. Most regard it as the latter. As early as 1784, in the English case of *R v Shipley*,[174] Justice Ashurst stated: "I admit the jury have the *power* of finding a verdict against the law and so they have of finding a verdict against the evidence, but I deny they have the *right* to do so."[175] As a practical matter, whether a jury has engaged in nullification is virtually impossible to establish. Jurors are not required to disclose the basis of their verdict or the substance of their deliberations.

Nullification is a one-way street. The jury's verdict in favor of a defendant in a criminal case is subject to neither review nor reversal, even if illogical. An equally illogical verdict in favor of the prosecution would be reversed.[176] The rationale for this dichotomy is that community values should be allowed to temper the rigor of the law and that the government not be allowed to wear down the defendant through repeated trials.[177] Compassion and empathy are worthy virtues; vindictiveness and vengeance are not.

Nullification occurs primarily in two types of cases. The first is where a defendant, though technically guilty of a crime, is not deemed to be morally blameworthy. A classic example is the defendant charged with the murder of a terminally ill relative who begged the defendant to put him out of his misery. Neither mercy killing nor the victim's consent is a recognized defense to homicide. By accepting a jury acquittal, the legal system allows for leniency without compromising the system's professed objectivity.[178]

The second common situation where a jury is likely to engage in nullification is when the law no longer accords with community values. When, for example, juries declined to convict for violation of prohibition laws, they expressed their attitude toward prohibition as surely as if they had voted in a referendum. Laws routinely broken by all citizens, including jurors, may also result in nullification. Gambling laws fall into this category. Sometimes the community's dissatisfaction lies not with the law, but with the penalty for its violation. In nineteenth century England, countless crimes carried an automatic death penalty. Jury acquittals often reflected not the defendant's innocence, but the jury's belief that the penalty was disproportionate to the offense.[179]

---

[174] 99 Eng Rep 774 (KB 1784).

[175] *Id* 828 (emphasis added).

[176] *See* McCleskey v Kemp, 481 US 279, 311 (1987).

[177] *See* United States v Scott, 437 US 82, 91 (1978).

[178] Related instances where juries may exercise their nullification power are when they believe the victim has unduly contributed to the commission of the crime, the defendant has already suffered sufficiently, or the police have abused their authority. Cases involving civil disobedience are also prime candidates for nullification. It should not be automatically assumed, as civil libertarians are wont to do, that all exercises of jury nullification are benign. History is replete with examples of racially motivated crimes against minority victims where a not guilty verdict has been returned because the jury apparently shared the racial prejudices of the defendants.

[179] Ironically, in the death penalty context, the Supreme Court has held that the constitutional guaranty of an impartial jury is not offended by the somewhat greater proneness toward conviction of a jury from whose membership have been removed those

Although nullification has long been an accepted power of the jury, the legal system remains ambivalent toward it. That a judge may direct a verdict in favor of, but not against, an accused is a clear acknowledgment of the jury's inalienable power to acquit, regardless of the strength of the state's case. It is a systemic recognition of the jury's power to apply its own values rather than those dictated to it by the court or inherent in the law. The failure to require juries to give reasons for their verdicts reinforces this latitude. On the other hand, the idea that jurors in an individual case in effect can undo the work of the popularly elected legislature causes discomfort. Nullification is a threat to the fundamental tenet that the law applies equally to all. Indeed, to a cynic it suggests that there is no such entity as the law except to the extent that a jury is willing to recognize it.

The fact that judges rarely, if ever, inform jurors of their power of nullification may attest to this ambivalence. The United States Supreme Court has indicated that a judge has no duty to inform a jury of its nullification power.[180] Some jurors may be aware of this prerogative, but no doubt many more believe that their responsibility is to apply the letter of the law.[181] So they are generally instructed by a judge.[182] As a consequence, while the legal system tacitly recognizes that nullification in some situations is acceptable, it believes that informing jurors that they may so act is not. The seemingly inevitable result is that jury nullification will be exercised haphazardly depending in part on jurors' personal knowledge of its availability. Worse still, since jurors receive no instructions from trial judges as to when nullification is appropriate, they may act out of caprice or prejudice rather than principle.

§2.21 —Jury Selection as a Function of the Nullification Power: Strategic Considerations

An attorney in a case where nullification may be appropriate has several ways to suggest this possibility to a jury. Optimally, the attorney would prefer that the judge instruct the jury on its power to nullify, leaving the attorney in closing argument to explain why this power should be exercised in the particular case.

---

persons whose ability to judge a case might be affected by their compunctions about capital punishment. Lockhart v McCree, 476 US 162 (1986). Such a jury is obviously less likely to exercise its power of nullification.

[180] *See* Sparf & Hansen v United States, 156 US 51 (1985). *See also* United States v Dougherty, 473 F2d 1113 (DC Cir 1972).

[181] Some state constitutions entitle the jury to determine questions of law as well as fact. *See, e.g.*, Ind Const art 1, §19; Md Const art 115, §5. Where such is the law, it would seem that judges would have to inform jurors of their nullification power. *See* J. Van Dyke, Jury Selection Procedures: Our Uncertain Commitment to Representative Panels 234-35 (1977).

[182] *See* **§9.02.**

Thus the first step is to request appropriate instructions from the judge.[183] Such instructions are necessary to inform jurors that nullification is proper. Jurors will also need guidance in order to exercise their nullification power in a rational manner, which may require consideration of evidence not technically relevant to guilt or innocence. They will have to evaluate the evidence in light of generalized principles of justice and fairness regarding which they might otherwise receive no instruction.[184] Nor can the principles simplistically be equated with community values. Community values may be the irrational product of majoritarian prejudices; principles of justice and fairness relate to basic and widely accepted ideals, such as equality, dignity, liberty, and compassion.

Even if a judge refuses to instruct regarding nullification, an attorney might attempt to appeal to a jury's nullification instincts in closing argument.[185] A judge who will not instruct the jury on nullification, however, may not permit such an appeal. In any event, an appeal to nullification in closing argument may have little impact on jurors who are not aware that nullification is an acceptable option.

Even a judicial instruction that informs the jury of their nullification prerogative backed up by a closing argument directed towards nullification will have little effect if the jurors are not psychologically receptive to the concept. This consideration suggests the desirability of identifying potential nullifiers at the jury selection stage. Judges may be willing to permit some leeway in voir dire for an attorney to inquire about the values held by prospective jurors. Questions might focus on juror views of civil disobedience and the belief in a "higher law" than that imposed by the state. Jurors who place a greater premium on "justice" than on "law" may also be more inclined to exercise their nullification power. Conversely, authoritarian personalities—those who tend to be submissive to authority, hostile to nonconformists and persons of inferior status, and conventional in their scheme of values—are poor candidates to be nullifiers.[186]

---

[183] An illustrative nullification instruction given in an actual case is reprinted in 2 A. Ginger, Jury Selection in Civil and Criminal Cases 1245 (2d ed 1984).

[184] One difficulty at present with judges giving instructions on nullification is that trial judges also receive little in the way of guidance. Appellate courts rarely discuss the issue. This is not surprising, for a defendant cannot appeal a jury decision not to nullify while nullification results in an unappealable acquittal.

[185] For examples of attorney discussion of nullification in closing argument, see J. Van Dyke, Jury Selection Procedures: Our Uncertain Commitment to Representative Panels 238-40 (1977); 2 A. Ginger, *supra* note 183, at ch 22.

[186] The concept of the authoritarian personality has been long recognized in the social science literature. *See generally* J. Kirscht & R. Dillehay, Dimensions of Authoritarianism: A Review of Research and Theory (1967). For discussion of the juror with an authoritarian personality, see Boehm, *Mr. Prejudice, Miss Sympathy and the Authoritarian Personality: An Application of Psychological Measuring Techniques to the Problem of Jury Bias,* 1968 Wis L Rev 734; Buckhout, Licker, Alexander, Gambardella, Eugenio & Kakoullis, *Discretion in Jury Selection,* in L. Abt & I. Stuart, Social Psychology and Discretionary Law 176 (1979); Note, *Juror Bias—A Practical Screening Device and the Case for Permitting its Use,* 64 Minn L Rev 987 (1980). *See also* **§§12.15-12.16.**

The existence of potential nullifiers on a jury may affect an attorney's trial strategy. Greater emphasis may be placed on the defendant's character and the motivations behind the crime. Nullifiers may be receptive to this type of testimony. Similar testimony may not persuade jurors who believe the letter of the law should be applied to all.

§2.22 Antinomies and Realities

The law as it relates to juries is rife with antinomies, inconsistencies, and contradictions. This chapter has examined several of the more important features of the jury system. Reflection shows that many of these features are in tension if not outright conflict with one another.

The law prefers jurors who know nothing of the facts or the participants, yet it selects jurors from the locality which is most likely to yield persons who are directly or indirectly acquainted with these. In a civil case the law wants jurors who will not be financially affected by the verdict. But the ripple effects of a judgment for or against an insurance company, a local corporation, or the city or state in which the jurors reside may be felt by the entire community, not simply the defendants.

The law speaks in a criminal case of a jury of a defendant's peers. In the same breath it says that jurors are to be impartial. To the extent that an accused's peers can be expected to empathize with his or her acts, the result will be a favorably disposed jury, rather than one which is impartial. Prosecutors are not unaware of this problem, and routinely exercise peremptory challenges against defendants' peers.

The law's position on jury nullification is itself replete with antinomies. The jury's power to nullify has long been recognized. Yet few courts instruct jurors regarding the nullification prerogative. If lawyers are also not permitted to explain this concept to the jury, its exercise will depend on the fortuity that one of the jurors happens to know of its availability. Furthermore, the very concept of nullification is in tension with the notion of impartiality.

The Supreme Court has not alleviated but has added to the problems. The Court has held on numerous occasions that jurors in a criminal case are to be drawn from a cross-section of the community.[187] If the entire community, however, is prejudiced against a party, cross-section representation must take a back seat to impartiality. Moreover, while the law may not exclude a particular group or groups[188] from the jury pool, the jury in an individual case does not have to include any particular group or mirror a cross-section of the community. In such a case, the parties lose the benefit of different viewpoints, which is the prime reason for the cross-section requirement. Furthermore, there will be an inevitable tension between having a defendant's peers on the jury and cross-section representation, unless the community is remarkably homogeneous or the defendant embodies all the values and characteristics of the

---

[187] *See* **§6.13.**

[188] *See* **ch 6.**

community. In the death penalty context, the Court has implicitly sanctioned juries from which a segment of the community, those with a sufficiently serious reservation about capital punishment that it would interfere with their ability to decide the case objectively, have been effectively eliminated.[189] In so ruling, the Court may have in effect nullified the jury's power of nullification.

Whether cross-section representation, nondiscriminatory jury selection, or a jury of peers is the goal, the achievement has been impaired by Supreme Court decisions dealing with jury size and unanimity. In the now permissible six-person jury it will be far more difficult to include all segments of the community. The likelihood of minority representation will be diminished. There will be less chance that the jury will include *any* of a defendant's peers.

Even if peers and minorities are included on the jury, they will have a reduced voice if the jury need not reach a unanimous verdict, as the Supreme Court has held is constitutionally permissible in state court prosecutions. Part of the rationale for inclusion of both minorities and a defendant's peers is that they can often provide perspectives not available to other jurors. This benefit, however, will be lost if jurors are unwilling to and do not have to listen to the arguments of those who do not share their perspectives. Although one would hope that jurors would be sufficiently open-minded to listen to all views, the possibility of this not happening is created by Supreme Court decisions permitting nonunanimous verdicts.

Perhaps the greatest contradiction between theory and reality relates to impartiality. Jurors are supposed to be impartial. The sixth amendment, which has been incorporated into the fourteenth, guarantees an impartial jury. In real life, however, attorneys do not seek impartial jurors, self-serving public pronouncements notwithstanding. Certainly attorneys seek to eliminate jurors partial to the opposition. Equally certainly they prefer jurors who favor their client's position. Lawyers would do their clients a not easily explained disservice if they rejected a juror believed to be disposed to their side in favor of one thought to be totally neutral or impartial. It is each attorney's responsibility to discover and to challenge, either for cause or peremptorily, jurors who are biased toward the opposition. There is no obligation, however, to excuse jurors believed to favor one's own side. By the adroit use of challenges each side strikes those jurors thought to be most partial to the opposition. But after this subtraction, is the remainder an impartial jury? If so, it is the result of fortuity rather than the conscious search for impartial jurors.

An attorney is under an ethical obligation not to commit a fraud upon the court. It would be improper for counsel to fail to disclose certain clearly disqualifying characteristics, such as that a juror was related to a party or had a strong enough financial interest in the case to justify disqualification for

---

[189] *See* Lockhart v McCree, 476 US 162 (1986); Wainwright v Witt, 469 US 412 (1985). It might also be noted that there is considerable tension between the Court's decisions in the death penalty context regarding qualifications for jury service and the concept of nullification. *See generally* Gobert, *In Search of the Impartial Jury,* 79 J Crim L & Criminology 269, 298-306 (1988).

cause.[190] But an attorney has no duty to help the opposition by revealing that there is some personality characteristic in a juror that will incline him or her to favor a particular side.

For better or for worse, the Anglo-American legal system, unlike its continental counterpart, has opted for an adverserial approach to dispute resolution. An attorney is supposed to be an advocate. An attorney is supposed to present the client's position in its most favorable light. The various and often inconsistent features of the jury system allow attorneys to choose to emphasize those aspects which will be most advantageous to their clients while minimizing those features which will have the opposite effect.

---

[190] *See In re* Shon, 262 AD 225, 28 NYS2d 872 (1941) (upholding disbarment of an attorney for, inter alia, permitting two men with whom he was personally acquainted to sit on a jury without advising the court or opposing counsel of the relationship).

Part II

Laying the Groundwork

Overview

Experienced trial attorneys know that cases are not won and lost in the courtroom. Events in the courtroom are but a reflection of an attorney's pretrial preparation. Well before trial the lawyer must thoroughly investigate the facts and interview the witnesses. Opening statements, lines of direct and cross-examination, and closing arguments must be prepared. Objections to evidence must be anticipated and supporting legal authority must be found. Ideally, there should no surprises. Although the ideal may not always be realized, few trial attorneys would dispute the relationship between the thoroughness of pretrial investigation and the likelihood of success at trial.

These same attorneys would concede the critical importance of selecting a sympathetic and responsive jury. In contrast to their pretrial preparation of other phases of the case, however, they rely solely or primarily on in-court voir dire as their primary basis for jury selection. Yet voir dire is not a particularly effective method of picking a jury. The judge may limit the scope of voir dire or the time allotted to it. Many judges will not allow the attorneys to personally question prospective jurors. Those judges that permit attorneys to conduct voir dire may require that questions be addressed to the panel collectively. Even when permitted to address jurors individually, an attorney must take care not to alienate a prospective juror by asking probing or embarrassing questions. Conversely, eliciting admissions that a juror's sympathies lie with the attorney's client may serve only to alert opposing counsel to the need to challenge the juror.

Compounding the problem in using voir dire as the primary basis for choosing a jury is the fact that juror responses to voir dire questions are not very reliable. Persons not aware of their subconscious biases will deny them when questioned. Those who are aware may not admit to bias, either because of an unwillingness to confess publicly a perceived character fault or because of an overriding desire to serve on a jury. There are also jurors whose objective seems to be to please the attorney by giving the response they believe the attorney wants to hear.

These aspects of voir dire will be explored in greater depth in Chapter 9. Suggestions for overcoming or minimizing the shortcomings of voir dire will be offered. The important point for purposes of the present discussion, however, is that it is naive to expect to be able to make informed and intelligent jury selection decisions solely or primarily on the basis of voir dire. The groundwork for effective jury selection, like the groundwork for effective case presentation, must be laid prior to entering the courtroom. The less time and scope given to voir dire by the trial judge, the more important this groundwork becomes.

The chapters in Part II advocate a systematic pretrial approach to jury selection integrated with continuing analysis of the jury during and following trial. There are six stages in the process: (1) community/demographic analysis; (2) mock trials; (3) investigations of members of the venire; (4) voir dire; (5) shadow juries; and (6) post-trial interviews of jurors. Contrary to popular belief, even among attorneys, voir dire is not the first but one of the last stages of the jury selection process.

The jury selection process begins with surveys and interviews designed to ascertain community attitudes toward the pending litigation. Analysis of the results may lead to a decision to seek a continuance or a change in venue, or to waive a jury and allow the case to be tried by a judge. Sometimes the lawyer becomes convinced of the advisability of seeking a negotiated settlement. If a trial is to be held, the lawyer, by correlating the views of survey respondents toward the case with demographic, attitudinal, and sociopsychological data about the respondents, can construct profiles of favorable and unfavorable jurors.

Pretrial investigation continues after the publication of the jury list. The focus then shifts from the community in the abstract to that finite group of persons from whom the jury will actually be selected. These individuals should be discreetly investigated. The results of the investigations can be matched against juror profiles to make a preliminary prediction of which jurors will be receptive to the client's case. Investigation of jurors, however, raises ethical and legal considerations which need to be addressed.

Another valuable aid in jury selection is the mock trial. Mock trials provide a lay reaction to the case, indicate which attorney arguments are persuasive and which are not, and help to sharpen the attorney's presentation. A series of mock trials may establish the futility of the lawyer's original theory of the case while suggesting an alternate theory to which a jury may be more receptive. Mock trials allow witnesses to experience direct and cross-examination under trial conditions. By obtaining demographic, personality, and attitudinal information from the mock jurors and correlating this data with the views expressed by the mock jurors in their deliberations, the attorney can refine the previously constructed juror profiles.

Related to yet different from a mock jury is a shadow jury. Unlike a mock jury, to whom the case is presented prior to the trial, a shadow jury is used during the course of trial. Shadow jurors are persons, optimally with the same characteristics as the actual jurors, who sit in the gallery and provide feedback to the attorney on the day's events. If well selected, shadow jurors should have the same reactions to the day's events as the actual jurors. Shadow jurors can also be profitably used to preview the effect of anticipated direct and cross-examination, objections, and closing arguments. Used in the latter way, the shadow jury becomes a mock jury.

Post-trial interviews of jurors, where permitted, provide valuable feedback to the attorney about his or her performance and that of the witnesses. This feedback may be useful on appeal or in future cases. Post-trial interviews also allow the attorney to empirically validate the accuracy of pretrial predictions.

The cost of pretrial, trial, and post-trial investigation may appear beyond the reach of the ordinary litigant in the ordinary case. If, however, the opposing side has engaged in such investigations, it may be possible to discover the results. Where opposing counsel has not engaged in such investigations, a lawyer can apply for court-appointed expert assistance. In any event, there may be relatively low-cost ways to finance these investigations.

3 Community Analysis: Goals and Methodologies

§3.01 Introduction

There is probably no such creature as an impartial juror, at least in the tabula rasa sense of the term.[1] Jurors are the product of their experiences, values, and beliefs. Although no two persons may hold identical values and beliefs, members of the same community are likely to have more in common than members of different communities. Members of the same community may have

[1] *See* **§2.12.**

many shared experiences: they may have been educated in the same school system, perhaps even by the same teachers; they may be influenced by a common circle of friends; they may attend the same church or synagogue; and they may have voted for and been represented by the same elected officials. Community economic perspectives may be influenced by local major employers and social perspectives by local events or incidents. Although it may be impossible to identify the totality of these experiences, an attorney should attempt to construct a psychological profile of the community. It is critical to understand which aspects of a case the community will respond to and which it is less likely to respond to, and why. It is through an understanding of the community that the lawyer gains insight into the minds of prospective jurors.

Within a community are persons of different backgrounds, races, religions, and socio-economic status. The lawyer needs to know how each of these variables can affect a community member's attitude toward the issues in the pending litigation. By correlating personality, demographic, and sociopsychological data about members of the community with their attitude toward the case the lawyer can make a preliminary prediction of what characteristics make for a favorable juror and for an unfavorable juror. Juror profiles can be constructed and later matched against the characteristics of those called to hear the case.

The most simple way to learn about the attitudes of persons in a community is to talk with them. It would obviously be impractical to talk to all members of a community. The attorney must instead rely on information gathered from a random sample of the community.

Some information may be available as a matter of public record. Census data provide a rough sketch of the demographic characteristics of a community. Political party registrations and the officials who have been elected to public office reveal the political leanings of the community. Similar information may be gleaned from the results of local elections. Local newspapers may reflect the character of their readers, or vice versa. The major employers will have an economic influence on the community, and the nature of their business will indicate whether the work force is predominantly blue- or white-collar. Church membership and attendance figures may disclose the religiosity of community members. Police records will shed light on the crime rate in the community; and court records of past verdicts on the legal attitudes of the community.

Lawyers who have practiced for many years in a community may believe that they have an intuitive sense of this information. However, the attorney's own values, beliefs, and experiences may make this impressionistic judgment inaccurate. Objective data can disclose such errors. Similarly, it is unsound to rely on general psychological studies indicating a correlation between a certain personality variable, or variables, and juror behavior. As a general proposition these studies may be accurate, but they may not hold true for the particular community in which the trial will be held or for the particular constellation of issues, witnesses, attorneys, and parties involved in a given case.

Community surveys can be particularly useful to an attorney trying a case in unfamiliar territory. The attorney here does not even have an intuitive sense of the community on which to rely. Often in this situation local counsel will be retained to assist in jury selection, but community surveys will still prove helpful.

§3.02 Questionnaires, Surveys, and Interviews

There are several steps which must be taken before formal interviews can be conducted or surveys administered.[2] First, the lawyer must determine what information is to be sought. The lawyer needs to thoroughly analyze the case, identifying the key legal and factual issues involved. These issues must be examined objectively. It would be misleading to obtain opinions about a version of the facts that is skewed to favor the client. The respondents may be sympathetic, but not representative of the attitudes of a jury that would be exposed to both sides' strongest arguments. The goal is not to convince the survey respondents of the merits of the client's position, but to obtain an accurate gauge of community sentiment. A candid presentation of each side's strongest arguments will elicit more informative feedback. Similarly, any factual description of the case which included evidence likely to be ruled inadmissible would not yield results likely to be duplicated at trial.

The next step is to construct a survey or questionnaire which will elicit community views on the key issues. A trained social scientist experienced in constructing questionnaires and conducting surveys should be employed or consulted. Alternatively, attorneys may become their own social science experts through private study or a course at a local university. The key point to bear in mind, however, is that the results of the surveys and/or questionnaires will be no better than the quality of their design and administration. Greater methodological rigor will be necessary if the attorney plans to introduce the results of the survey in court (for example, in support of a motion for a change in venue) than if the attorney is seeking the information for his or her own elucidation.

§3.03 —Designing a Questionnaire

A questionnaire will seek both general and case-specific information. It will usually begin with an introduction which explains the purpose of the survey or interview.[3] Honesty is preferable although it may be neither desirable nor necessary to identify the party who has commissioned the questionnaire. Thus, respondents might be informed that the goal is to learn about general community attitudes toward the legal system and a particular pending case.[4] Respondents should be thanked in advance (as well as at the completion of the

---

[2] An excellent discussion of this topic also appears in National Jury Project, Jurywork ch 9 (2d ed 1987).

[3] The problem with identifying the party who commissioned the questionnaire is that this fact may skew the interviewees' answers to questions. Many respondents will give the answers that they think the interviewer wants to hear.

[4] For a sample introduction, see National Jury Project, Jurywork app E (2d ed 1987).

interview) for their time. They should be assured that their answers will be kept confidential.

Second, it is necessary to obtain some general background information about each respondent. Place of residence, age, ethnic background, sex, education, employment, political affiliations, marital status, hobbies, and organization memberships are but a few examples of the data which may be collected. Social, political, and religious attitudes may also be inquired into, but in a discrete way. This background information will help insure that the sample is random. It will also provide factors which can be correlated with case-specific attitudes in order to determine the characteristics of jurors who are likely to be favorable or unfavorable to the client's cause. If the background information reveals that the respondent is not eligible for jury service (or has already been summoned) the interview can be gracefully terminated.

Third, the questionnaire should probe the respondent's general attitudes toward legal issues. In a criminal case one might inquire about the crime problem in the jurisdiction, the presumption of innocence, the burden of proof and who bears it, the accused's right not to testify, and the harshness or leniency of sentencing by local judges. In a civil case the questions might focus on the respondents' perceptions of the incidence of frivolous suits, individual responsibility for life's misfortunes, the role of insurance, and the extent to which verdicts in the district have exceeded reasonable bounds. By correlating this information with responses to questions about issues in the pending case, the lawyer can learn whether these general attitudes are likely to be transposed to the specific litigation. In both civil and criminal cases, respondents might be asked about the comprehensibility and effect of instructions which the attorney plans to request from the judge.

Finally, the lawyer should seek case-specific information. The starting point may be to ask whether the respondent has heard about the case and, if so, the source of the information and what the respondent has heard. A respondent who is aware of the litigation should be asked whether he or she has formed an opinion in regard to the case. An affirmative answer should then trigger an interviewer inquiry into the nature of and the reasons for the opinion.

If the respondent is not familiar with the litigation, the interviewer will want to provide a brief objective summary of it. Following this presentation, specific questions can be asked. These questions will necessarily vary with the facts of the case. In a suit where a plaintiff is suing for wrongful discharge because of union activities, for example, the questions may focus on the respondent's attitude toward unions, management, and the right to work. In a criminal prosecution of a long-haired youth for cocaine possession, the questions may probe the respondent's attitudes towards drugs, nonconformists, and law enforcement policies.

The questions in the survey may be either open or closed-ended,[5] or a mixture of both. Closed-ended questions call for a yes-no answer. The range of responses can be expanded (e.g., strongly agree, mildly agree, mildly disagree,

---

[5] For a discussion of open- and closed-ended questions in the voir dire context, see **§9.15.**

strongly disagree, no opinion), but the characteristic of a closed-ended question is that the response is short, specific, and capable of being checked in a designated box. Such responses are easy to code, tabulate, and analyze statistically.

More difficult to code and tabulate, but potentially more revealing, are answers to open-ended questions. Respondents are encouraged to explain their responses and the reasons for them. Follow-up questions can be used to clarify ambiguous responses. Attorneys thus gain insight into those issues which are troubling the respondents, insights which might not be revealed by a yes or no answer. For open-ended questions to be effective, however, a verbatim transcription of the responses is desirable; but, to record answers verbatim, may be difficult and time-consuming.

Although open-ended responses may be more revealing than closed-ended responses, they may still be misleading unless the questions are carefully framed. Answers to questions designed to determine the degree of racism in the community may be particularly unrevealing as few respondents will openly admit to bigotry. However, a general question asking about the respondent's experiences with persons of different races may shed light on the issue.

The respondent's demeanor and body language in answering the question is also important. Interviewers need to be trained to be sensitive to and to record these dimensions of the response.

§3.04 —Choosing a Sample

Having designed a questionnaire, the attorney must next decide to whom to administer it. Since the ultimate goal is to obtain insight into how potential jurors will perceive the issues in the pending litigation, the sample should be limited to persons who are eligible for jury duty. In like vein, the attorney needs to ascertain the geographic boundaries of the district from which the jury will be drawn. It is the views of the community in which the case is to be tried which are essential, not those of some other community. The views of other communities may be important, however, if the lawyer contemplates a motion for a change of venue. If some segments of the population, such as physicians, attorneys, police, and the elderly, are allowed to exempt themselves from jury duty and routinely do so, this too should be taken into account in constructing the target sample.

After the group to which the questionnaire is to be administered is identified, a methodology must be devised to allow for a random sampling of that group. Interviewing all members will rarely be feasible. Nor is it necessary; public opinion polls regularly sample only a small percentage of the population to yield statistically significant results. A social scientist can tell an attorney how large the sample must be. The social scientist can also devise a methodology for choosing the sample to ensure that it is random. Persons who are on the jury list for the trial should be excluded from the sample.

The size of the sample will, to some extent, depend on the nature of the questionnaire and the method of administering it. Individual interviews with open-ended questions, while extremely informative, are also extremely time-consuming. Practical constraints may dictate a smaller sample than when a telephone survey asking closed-ended questions is employed. The size of the district in which the trial will be held will also be relevant; the larger the district, the greater the sample may have to be in order to obtain results which are statistically significant.

§3.05 —Administering the Questionnaire

There are several possible methods of administering a survey and collecting data. One is random mailing of questionnaires. The results may be suspect, however, as those who respond in effect select themselves for inclusion in the survey. These persons may not constitute a representative sample. Face-to-face interviews with persons selected at random are preferable. Interviewers can adjust the content of the interview to reflect responses to previous questions, and can also record nonverbal responses. Face-to-face interviews, however, are costly and time-consuming. An often-used compromise is the telephone survey. The flexibility of the interpersonal interview is preserved. Since the interviewer is stationary, large numbers of interviews are possible. In the Harrisburg 7 trial, for example, where anti-Vietnam war protesters were charged with, among other offenses, plotting to kidnap Henry Kissinger and to blow up heating tunnels in Washington, D.C., over *800* telephone interviews were conducted.[6] One drawback to telephone interviews, however, is the inability to observe many nonverbal responses.[7]

A worthwhile format is to hold small group interviews. In addition to obviating the need to repeat the same questions to each interviewee, this approach allows the interviewer to observe the interaction patterns which develop among group members. Understanding and predicting how potential jurors will interact is a vital part of jury selection[8] and group interviews provide insight into this phenomenon. The lawyer who is to try the case can conduct some of the interviews, thereby obtaining feedback as to the community reaction to him or her as a person.

Whether a group, individual, or telephone interview method is selected, interviewers need to be carefully trained. They must be both courteous and competent. They should be able to put the respondents at ease. They should never argue with respondents and should not put words in their mouths. They need to learn to deal with unexpected questions, and must be sensitized to pick up on nonverbal responses. Their recording of responses, both verbal and nonverbal, must be efficient and accurate. They need to know how to draw

---

[6] *See* Schulman, Shaver, Colman, Emrich & Christie, *Recipe for a Jury, Psychology Today* May 1973, at 37, 40. In comparison, the reserachers were able to conduct only 252 face-to-face interviews. *Id.*

[7] *See generally* **§§12.09-12.12.** Paralinguistic cues, such as pauses or changes in pitch, can still be recorded.

[8] *See* **§12.02.**

out a respondent who is reticent and how to cut off a respondent who is garrulous. An experienced social scientist may be the most qualified person to provide training in these skills.[9]

In an ideal world, the interviewers would embody the characteristics of the attorney who will be trying the case. One variable that can influence interpersonal questionnaire responses is the psychological interaction between the person doing the questioning and the person being questioned. The latter may be trying to please the former for any number of reasons. Researchers usually attempt to control this variable, but it can be turned to an advantage. If the interviewers share the personality characteristics of the attorney who will be trying the case (or better yet, if the attorney who will be trying the case conducts the interviews[10]) the responses, though perhaps less scientifically accurate, will more likely correspond to the responses of the actual jurors at trial.

§3.06 —Analyzing the Results

The degree of sophistication of the analysis of the results of a questionnaire will depend on the purposes to which the attorney intends to put the results. If the results are to be presented in court, the data need to be rigorously analyzed by a person qualified to testify in court as an expert witness. The attorney should consider the expert's communicative abilities as well as his or her technical expertise. Among other matters, the witness must be able to speak to the reliability and validity of the study.[11]

Less precision may be acceptable if the results are solely for the benefit of counsel. Even then, it is necessary to determine whether the results are statistically significant. For an attorney to rely on survey results which have been misanalyzed or which are invalid is more dangerous than not to have conducted the surveys in the first place.

The types of analysis to which the raw data will be subjected will be determined by the attorney's goals. If, for instance, the attorney intends to seek a change in venue, the most important statistic may be the percentage of respondents who have heard of and have formed a fixed opinion about the case. If, on the other hand, the attorney has commissioned the survey as an aid in jury selection, the most useful analysis will be one that shows which demographic, attitudinal, and socio-psychological variables correlate with a favorable or unfavorable view of the case.

---

[9] An extremely helpful list of instructions for interviewers can be found in National Jury Project, Jurywork app F (2d ed 1987).

[10] Having the attorney conduct the interview is most beneficial but probably only feasible when group interviews are used.

[11] *Validity* refers to whether a test measures what it is designed to measure. *Reliability* refers to the achievement of consistent results over a series of trials. If one determined a person's weight by measuring his height, the results would be reliable but not valid. To persuade a judge, the results of a study probably need to be both reliable and valid.

§3.07 —Utilizing the Results in Pretrial Motions

In cases where a litigant has a choice of districts in which to file, community and demographic analyses may indicate which district will be most favorable. The results of the survey may support a pretrial motion for a change in venue or venire,[11] or a motion for a continuance. They may be used as an aid in jury selection or for arguing for improved voir dire conditions. Finally, they may be used to help the attorney in formulating trial strategy. In this subsection the use of the surveys to support pretrial motions will be explored; in subsequent subsections, other uses will be considered.

Attitudinal surveys may demonstrate such a high degree of prejudice against a party within a community that obtaining a fair trial and impartial jury becomes problematic. If convinced, the judge may grant a motion for a continuance or a change in venue or venire. In support of such a motion, the attorney should be prepared to present expert testimony demonstrating the degree of prejudice within the community. Community surveys and affidavits of persons interviewed can be introduced in support of the motion.[12]

As a practical matter, an attorney needs to learn whether jurors in other districts will be less biased. It accomplishes little to transfer a case from one biased district to one equally or more biased. Thus the attitudinal surveys conducted in the district in which the trial is scheduled need to be replicated in other districts. An expert witness should be prepared to present a comparative analysis of the degree of prejudice in several different districts. If, in a criminal case, there is no district in which an impartial jury can be seated, the attorney may have a basis for arguing that due process requires dismissal of all charges.[13]

Even a judge not persuaded that there is sufficient prejudice in the community to justify a change in venue or venire may become sensitized by the survey results to the difficulty in impaneling an impartial jury. As a consequence, the judge may become more inclined to rule in favor of motions for attorney-conducted voir dire, an expanded scope to voir dire, and an increase in the number of peremptory challenges. The judge may also become more receptive to challenges for cause.

In an appropriate case, the results of community surveys can be used to demonstrate that the jury pool does not reflect a fair cross-section of the community.[14] The comparison will be between the demographic characteristics of that segment of the community which is eligible for jury service and the demo-

---

[11] *See generally* **§§2.02-2.05.**

[12] For a sample affidavit, see National Jury Project, Jurywork 8-13 to 8-15 (2d ed 1987).

[13] It is, of course, highly unlikely that a judge will take such a drastic step, particularly before voir dire is conducted. The theoretical argument is that a defendant should not have to forfeit the constitutional right to a trial of the vicinage in order to enjoy the constitutional right to a fair trial and impartial jury. This argument was accepted in United States v Cotton, No 68-CR-113, (ED Wis Sept 9, 1969) an unreported Wisconsin case, *discussed in* 1 A. Ginger, Jury Selection in Civil and Criminal Trials 375-79 (2d ed 1984).

[14] *See* **§6.13.**

graphic characteristics of those persons who have been summoned for jury service. If, for example, the community survey indicates that 50 per cent of the community is black but only a small percentage of blacks are on the jury list, a prima facie case of a violation of the fair cross-section requirement may be established. The substantive law relating to these challenges will be examined in a subsequent chapter.[15]

§3.08 —Utilizing the Results in Constructing Juror Profiles

Apart from pretrial motions, the results of community surveys and questionnaires will still be invaluable in jury selection. The attorney needs to correlate demographic, attitudinal, and socio-psychological data with respondents' views toward the issues in the case. A profile of both desirable and undesirable jurors can be constructed. The profile will allow a meaningful comparison between jurors. Peremptory challenges can then be efficiently exercised. At trial an attorney might, for example, discover that all the jurors who have, to a particular point, been seated are more favorable than those who can be expected to be called if a juror is excused. In that case the attorney may decide not to exercise any peremptory challenges.

The characteristics of a favorable jury will obviously vary with the facts, witnesses, and principals of a case. A law of inverse relationships is no doubt at work. Jurors in a case who are favorable for one side will in all likelihood (although not necessarily) be unfavorable for the other. In a criminal case, for example, it is likely that the more pro-prosecution the juror, the less acceptable to the defendant the juror is.

The characteristics which make for a favorable juror are difficult to predict. In the Harrisburg 7 trial,[16] where anti-Vietnam war protesters were charged with a variety of serious offenses, the community survey indicated that a female Democrat with no religious preference, sympathetic to anti-Vietnam views, holding a white-collar or skilled blue-collar job, would be the ideal juror for the defense.[17] To the surprise of the attorneys, college-educated persons, usually predicted liberals, were not so in Harrisburg.[18] Liberal college graduates apparently preferred not to live in Harrisburg. In contrast, the most favorable jurors for the defense in the New York trial of John Mitchell (former Attorney General of the United States) and Maurice Stans (former Secretary of Commerce) for conspiracy, obstruction of justice, and perjury were determined to be working-class Catholics earning between $8,000 and $10,000 per year, who read the *New York News.*[19]

---

[15] *See* **ch 6.**

[16] *See* Schulman, Shaver, Colman, Emrich, & Christie, *Recipe for a Jury,* Psychology Today, May 1973, at 37.

[17] *Id.*

[18] *Id.*

[19] *See* Note, *The Constitutional Need for Discovery of Pre-Voir Dire Juror Studies,* 49 So Cal L Rev 597, 605 (1976).

Utilizing juror profiles in jury selection has several advantages over traditional voir dire. For one thing, it avoids the risk of incurring a juror's resentment stemming from probing and embarrassing questions. Further, it permits reasonably accurate predictions to be made from relatively little information. Sufficient information to make educated guesses about juror leanings can be gathered prior to trial, through observation in court, and by asking jurors neutral questions about their background during voir dire. By inferring juror attitudes from demographic, attitudinal, and socio-psychological profiles a lawyer circumvents restrictions on the scope of voir dire imposed by judges; the fact that a judge will not permit detailed inquiry into juror attitudes and values has less adverse effect, since the judge will virtually always permit general background questions. Finally, the use of juror profiles helps avoid errors in jury selection resulting from jurors who misrepresent their biases, whether because of an unawareness, an unwillingness to publicly admit them, or an overriding desire to serve on the jury.[20] While a juror may lie about his or her prejudices, it is less likely that the juror will appreciate the need to lie or be able to lie about basic demographic characteristics.

Preliminary decisions as to whether to challenge a juror based on demographic, attitudinal, and socio-psychological profiles can be incorporated into a voir dire strategy. Searching and potentially alienating questions need not be put to jurors predicted to be favorable. Opposing counsel will not be alerted to the need to exercise a challenge against the juror. Conversely, more rigorous questioning of jurors predicted to be hostile can be employed in an attempt to lay the basis for a challenge for cause. If the attorney succeeds, a peremptory challenge is saved; if not, the attorney uses a peremptory challenge that had already been allocated.[21]

It would be naive to assume that because persons with particular characteristics respond favorably or unfavorably to the client's case in pretrial surveys, all jurors with like characteristics will respond similarly. Not all persons within a class share identical views. Even if most liberals will, for example, be sympathetic to defendants prosecuted for civil rights violations, some jurors who would be characterized as liberals might hold a contrary view. The use of jury profiles should not become an exercise in stereotyping. Juror profiles provide an attorney with probabilities, not certainties. Favorable and unfavorable juror profiles based on community surveys are a tool which can help the attorney identify fertile areas for voir dire examination, as well as provide objective criteria that can tip the jury selection scales in close cases. It is a tool, however, that needs to be supplemented with information about the actual jurors gained through pretrial investigation[22] and voir dire.[23] It is also a tool which should

---

[20] *See also* **§12.14.**

[21] Attorneys who opt for this approach should occasionally vary their tactics so as to disguise their overall strategy. Otherwise opposing counsel will discern the need to peremptorily challenge those jurors who are not asked probing questions.

[22] *See* **ch 4.**

[23] *See* **pt IV.**

not be employed at the expense of the lawyer's judgment.[24]

§3.09 —Other Uses

Other benefits can be derived from pretrial surveys and questionnaires, although they do not relate directly to jury selection, the focus of this book. In some instances, the survey results may be introduced as substantive evidence in a given case. For example, a survey that demonstrated significant racism in a community may have evidentiary significance in a suit alleging discriminatory refusal to sell a home to blacks.

More significantly, the results of pretrial surveys may affect trial strategy. An attorney may discover that the theory on which he or she intended to try the case is not persuasive to members of the community. The theory may need to be abandoned or restructured. Conversely, a theory originally thought to be weak might strike a responsive chord in the survey respondents. Questions that the respondents raise sua sponte about the case may identify issues about which more information will need to be gathered. Along with mock trials,[25] which provide similar feedback, survey responses can assist the attorney in formulating trial strategy.

§3.10 —Evaluating Community/Demographic Analysis

Community/demographic surveys and questionnaires are a critical first step in trial preparation and the development of a jury selection strategy. They are indispensable in laying the foundation for a request for a continuance, a change in venue or venire, or a challenge to the representational composition of the jury pool. They provide the raw data on which juror profiles are constructed, profiles which can prove invaluable in jury selection, particularly in those jurisdictions where judges do not permit wide-ranging voir dire and the attorney lacks familiarity with the local population.

Community/demographic surveys do, however, have their limits. Respondents are generally questioned in the privacy of their homes, where the tension

---

[24] Perhaps the soundest approach is one that allows for the interaction of juror profiles and attorney judgment. The more negative the profile of a juror, the stronger the attorney should have to feel toward that juror in order to retain the juror. If, in comparison, the profile indicates the juror will be neither strongly favorable nor unfavorable, the more the attorney should rely on judgment and experience. If the profile indicates the juror will be highly favorable, the attorney should not strike the juror unless the attorney has very strong negative feelings.

It should be noted that a strong case can be made for relying *solely* on juror profiles, much as it might offend lawyer confidence in their ability to evaluate jurors. In numerous clinical studies matching human decision making against decisions made in accord with a mathematical model, the mathematical model proved more accurate and reliable. *See* Saks, *Social Scientists Can't Rig Juries*, Psychology Today, (1976), *reprinted in* L. Wrightsman, S. Kassin & C. Willis, In the Jury Box 48, 52 (1987).

[25] *See* **ch 5.**

of the courtroom is not present. Their responses may lack reflection. They have not heard the testimony of witnesses, but at best to a summarized version of the facts. They have not been exposed to either arguments of counsel or the instructions of a judge. They have not had the benefit of the type of deliberation that occurs in a jury room. Any or all of these variables may distort the responses made in the surveys and interviews. Nor do community/demographic surveys provide feedback to an attorney about the credibility of witnesses or the quality of the attorney's courtroom presentation.

The above points are not intended to denigrate the value of pretrial surveys and community/demographic analyses. They are a critical first step, but to achieve full effectiveness they need to be supplemented with investigation of members of the venire,[26] mock trials,[27] and voir dire.[28]

§3.11 Post-trial Interviews of Jurors

At the polar opposite end of the proceedings, many conscientious attorneys, where permitted, will conduct interviews with jurors after a trial is completed. They have several goals in mind. One is simply to satisfy their own curiosity as to what happened in the jury room. Beyond that, counsel can receive valuable feedback from these interviews. The foundation for a challenge to the verdict can be laid. Post-trial interviews may also be the first *pre*trial attitudinal surveys for a future case.

On a very basic level, lawyers are concerned about how well they performed. Were they perceived by the jurors as too strident, or not sufficiently aggressive? Did they fail to manifest conviction in their client's cause? Did their arguments go over the heads of the jurors or, conversely, did the jurors feel that the lawyer was condescending? What did the jurors think of the lawyer's tactics generally? Although this feedback cannot alter the verdict in a case, it can improve the attorney's performance in future cases. If, on the other hand, a mistrial, hung jury, or successful appeal results, the post-trial interviews will allow the attorney to strengthen the presentation of the client's case on retrial.

Post-trial interviews also can provide feedback as to the jurors' perception of witnesses. In one case, for example, an attorney was granted a directed verdict after all the evidence had been presented. The attorney, however, had another pending case in which the chief witness in the first case was again to testify. Post-trial interviews with jurors indicated that they did not find the witness credible. As rehabilitation of the witness appeared unlikely, the attorney decided to settle the second case. Although the specific situation may be uncommon, many attorneys, particularly those in the medical malpractice and products liability fields, repeatedly employ the same expert witness. It is critical to learn whether the expert is effectively communicating with the jurors, and in what ways the expert can better serve the jury.

---

[26] *See* **ch 4.**

[27] *See* **ch 5.**

[28] *See* **pt IV.**

Post-trial interviews provide valuable empirical data for use in future cases. Whether based on a community/demographic analysis, pretrial investigation of jurors, mock trials; voir dire, or hunches, attorneys are in the business of making predictions of how particular jurors will react to the evidence. The verdict provides a gross feedback on the accuracy of these predictions. More refined feedback, however, can be gained by talking to individual jurors. It may turn out, for instance, that although an unfavorable verdict was returned, the attorney's estimate of the jurors was correct save for one strong-willed individual who persuaded the others to accede to his views. If, on the other hand, the attorney has misread most of the jurors, it is imperative for future cases that the attorney improve his or her accuracy in predicting juror behavior. The starting point is often a frank post-trial interview with the jurors.

Post-trial interviews of jurors will be of especial value if some or all of the jurors are likely to appear in another case involving that same attorney. Often jurors sit for a set period, and hear a number of cases. Many attorneys compile a "jury book" based in part on the answers to post-trial questioning of jurors. In a small town a jury book may obviate the need for juror investigations whenever interviewed jurors are again summoned for jury duty.[29] In larger cities, lawyers may choose to pool their jury books, a practice not uncommon among government attorneys. A computer bank containing juror information is no longer technically or financially unfeasible.

Finally, post-trial interviews can be used to compare the thought processes of the actual jurors with those of shadow jurors[30] and mock jurors.[31] The lawyer may discover, for example, that a mock trial lacked sufficient verisimilitude to be an effective predictor of jury behavior. Shadow jurors, the attorney may learn, did not take their responsibility as seriously as the real jurors.

§3.12 —Post-trial Interviews as a Basis for Impeaching the Verdict

Perhaps the most common, although potentially the most troublesome, use of post-trial interviews is to lay the basis for an appeal.[32] As far back as the 1785 English case of *Vaise v Delaval*[33] jurors have been forbidden to impeach their verdict.[34] The policy justifications for the rule were articulated by the United States Supreme Court in *McDonald v Pless*:[35]

---

[29] The possibility must, of course, be recognized that intervening events between the first and second trial may have altered the juror's perspectives.

[30] *See* **§§5.07-5.10.**

[31] *See* **§§5.02-5.06.**

[32] *See generally* Annotation, Propriety of Attorney's Communications with Jurors after Trial, 19 ALR4th 1209 (1983).

[33] 99 Eng Rep 944 (KB 1785).

[34] Nonjurors, however, may give testimony to impeach the jury's verdict.

[35] 238 US 264 (1915).

> The rule is based upon controlling considerations of a public policy which in these cases chooses the lesser of two evils. When the affidavit of a juror, as to the misconduct of himself or the other members of the jury, is made the basis of a motion for a new trial, the court must choose between redressing the injury of the private litigant and inflicting the public injury which would result if jurors were permitted to testify as to what had happened in the jury room.
>
> These two conflicting considerations are illustrated in the present case. If the facts were as stated in the affidavit, the jury adopted an arbitrary and unjust method in arriving at their verdict, and the defendant ought to have had relief, if the facts could have been proved by witnesses who were competent to testify in a proceeding to set aside the verdict. But let it once be established that verdicts solemnly made and publicly returned into court can be attacked and set aside on the testimony of those who took part in their publication and all verdicts could be, and many would be, followed by an inquiry in the hope of discovering something which might invalidate the finding. Jurors would be harassed and beset by the defeated party in an effort to secure from them evidence of facts which might establish misconduct sufficient to set aside a verdict. If evidence thus secured could be thus used, the result would be to make what was intended to be a private deliberation, the constant subject of public investigation to the destruction of all frankness and freedom of discussion and conference.[36]

McDonald involved an allegation that the jurors had reached a quotient verdict, which would have been improper. Nonetheless, the Supreme Court held that the rule against juror impeachment of verdicts prevented the introduction of proof of what the jury had done. Similarly, in *Hyde v United States,*[37] jurors were not allowed to testify that there had been an agreement to exchange votes on some issues for concessions on others.

That the Supreme Court has not softened its position on juror impeachment of verdicts is illustrated by its 1987 decision in *Tanner v United States.*[38] Petitioners sought a new trial based on a juror's unsolicited statement that several jurors had consumed alcohol during lunch breaks and had dozed off during the afternoon sessions. Another juror told of marijuana and cocaine use by jurors. The district court declined to hold an evidentiary hearing at which jurors could testify and the Supreme Court affirmed. The Court cited the common law rule against impeachment of verdicts, now codified in Federal Rule of Evidence 606(b). The Court again refered to the policy considerations

---

[36] *Id* at 267-68. *See also* United States v Homer, 411 F Supp 972, 980 (WD Pa 1976), *affd,* 545 F2d 864 (3d Cir), *cert denied,* 431 US 954 (1977); United States v Miller, 284 F Supp 220 (D Conn), *appeal dismissed,* 403 F2d 77 (2d Cir 1968); United States v Driscoll, 276 F Supp 333 (SDNY 1967).

[37] 225 US 347 (1912).

[38] 483 US 107 (1987) *discussed in* Alschuler, *The Supreme Court and the Jury: Voir dire, Peremptory Challenges, and the Review of Jury Verdicts,* 56 U Chi L Rev 153, 218-29 (1989).

involved, including the encouragement of full and frank discussion in the jury room, the prevention of harassment of jurors by losing parties or their attorneys, and the preservation of public trust in a system that relies on the decisions of laypersons. The Court further found that the constitutional right to a competent, unimpaired, and impartial jury had not been violated.

As the Court in *Tanner* noted, both the common law[39] and Federal Rule of Evidence 606(b) contain an exception for cases where jurors have been exposed to extraneous prejudicial influences. Rule 606(b) provides:

> Upon an inquiry into the validity of a verdict or indictment, a juror may not testify as to any matter or statement occurring during the course of the jury's deliberations or to the effect of anything upon his or any other juror's mind or emotions as influencing him to assent to or dissent from the verdict or indictment or concerning his mental processes in connection therewith, except that a juror may testify on the question whether extraneous prejudicial information was improperly brought to the jury's attention or whether any outside influence was improperly brought to bear upon any juror. Nor may his affidavit or evidence of any statement by him concerning a matter about which he would be precluded from testifying be received for these purposes.[40]

The rule permits interviews with jurors to ascertain whether they have been subjected to external influences.[41] The exception is a narrow one, however, and a court will carefully scrutinize lawyer conduct to insure that legitimate inquiry does not turn into harassment.[42]

§3.13 —Ethical Restrictions

Attorneys who interview jurors after trial in order to obtain feedback concerning their courtroom performance, the accuracy of their jury selection decisions, and the effectiveness of witnesses are not likely to be as adversarial in approaching jurors as attorneys whose goal is to impeach the jury's verdict. Nevertheless, a juror is under no legal obligation to talk to a lawyer. Counsel, bearing this in mind, should approach jurors with courtesy and respect. This dictate of common sense is reinforced in the Code of Professional Responsibility:

> After the trial, communication by a lawyer with jurors is permitted so long as he refrains from asking questions or making comments that tend to harass the juror or to influence actions of the juror in future cases. . . . When an extrajudicial communication by a lawyer is permitted by law,

---

[39] *See* Parker v Gladden, 385 US 363 (1966); Remmer v United States, 347 US 227, 228-30 (1954); Mattox v United States, 146 US 140, 149 (1892).

[40] Fed R Evid 606(b).

[41] *See also* ABA Model Code of Professional Responsibility EC 7-29 (1980).

[42] *See* State v LaFera, 42 NJ 97, 107, 199 A2d 630, 636 (1964).

> it should be made considerately and with deference to the personal feelings of the juror.[43]

A juror is most likely to cooperate with the attorney who explains that he or she is seeking the juror's help in order to become a more effective lawyer, as well as one who can better assist jurors in fulfilling their responsibility.

Attorneys should be sensitive to even the appearance of impropriety. For example, having a drink with a juror whom the attorney seeks to interview might suggest to the losing side an inappropriate relationship. Accordingly, a more neutral situs for interviews should be sought.

§3.14 —Court-Imposed Restrictions on Post-Trial Interviews

In some jurisdictions local rules of practice or individual judges forbid post-trial interviews of jurors without court permission. Such restrictions are usually aimed at newspaper, television, and radio reporters, but can apply to attorneys as well. The wisdom of the restrictions as they pertain to attorneys is questionable.

Prior to and during trial, courts are understandably concerned that attorney contact with jurors could compromise juror impartiality, as well as the fairness or the appearance of fairness of the trial. There is also an understandable desire to protect the privacy of jurors. These interests are arguably sufficient to outweigh whatever first amendment rights an attorney may have in communicating with jurors.

After trial the calculus changes. There is no need to be concerned with the effect of contact with jurors on the fairness of the trial. The verdict will already have been delivered. While protection of juror privacy remains a concern, the ethical restraints on attorneys previously discussed[44] are arguably sufficient to protect against juror harassment. It is possible that some future jurors may be intimidated in their deliberations by knowledge that their positions will be revealed by other jurors. This risk, however, is ever present, as after trial jurors are generally free to discuss the case with third parties.

In sum, in the inevitable balancing which arises in respect to first amendment rights, the attorney's right to speak to jurors is outweighed before and during trial by the court's legitimate concern about juror privacy and impartiality, and the possibly adverse effects on the fairness of the proceedings. After trial, however, the balance shifts in favor of the attorney's first amendment interests, because of the reduced possibility of affecting the fairness of the proceedings and the sufficient protection against harassment contained in ethical rules governing attorney conduct.

---

[43] ABA Model Code of Professional Responsibility, EC 7-29 (1980).

[44] *See* **§3.13.**

Despite these policy considerations, restrictions on post-trial questioning of jurors have been sustained.[45] The matter falls within the court's supervisory power. Accordingly, the authority to permit or deny the right to interview jurors lies in the sound discretion of the court. The attorney who respectfully explains to the judge that the goal is not to impeach the jury's verdict but to obtain educational feedback is more likely to receive a sympathetic hearing.

§3.15 Financing Pretrial, Trial, and Post-Trial Jury Analyses

The case is made in this and the following two chapters for a systematic pretrial approach to jury selection combined with continuing jury analysis during and even following trial. There are six stages in the process.

The first stage consists of a community/demographic analysis. This analysis is critical for motions for a continuance or a change in venue or venire. It is also the first step in the development of juror profiles, which allow the attorney to make reasonably accurate predictions about the likely voting patterns of jurors.

The second stage consists of attorney-conducted mock trials (discussed in Chapter 5). These help the attorney to sharpen his or her presentation and formulate trial strategy. They allow the attorney's client and witnesses to experience direct and cross-examination under trial conditions. They permit the jury selection team to further refine their juror profiles by correlating demographic, attitudinal, and socio-psychological data obtained from the mock jurors with their views expressed in the deliberations.

The third stage, investigation of the venire, (discussed in Chapter 4), is designed to provide the attorney with more than just general demographic data about the community. The goal is to acquire as much information as possible about the persons who will actually serve on the jury. This information can be compared with the juror profiles developed from community/demographic surveys and mock trials to allow meaningful exercise of peremptory challenges. The collected data will obviate the need for potentially embarrassing voir dire questions, will lessen the impact of a restricted scope of voir dire, and will frustrate attempts by jurors to misrepresent their attitudes.

The fourth stage of the process is voir dire. This is the stage with which attorneys have the greatest familiarity. For many, if not most, attorneys, it is the sole basis for jury selection. It is a topic deserving of extended discussion, and in depth. Part IV of this book addresses it.

The fifth stage entails the creation of a shadow jury (discussed in Chapter 5). The shadow jurors sit in the gallery, listen to the evidence and follow whatever instructions are given to the jurors by the judge. By meeting with the shadow jurors during recesses and overnight breaks, the attorney receives

---

[45] *E.g.*, United States v Franks, 511 F2d 25, 38 (6th Cir), *cert denied,* 422 US 1042 (1975); Bryson v United States, 238 F2d 657, 665 (9th Cir 1956); United States v Miller, 284 F Supp 220 (D Conn 1968).

feedback on how the case is progressing. Closing arguments, anticipated objections, and lines of direct and cross-examination also can be previewed before the shadow jury for its reactions.

The final stage of the process consists of post-trial interviews with jurors. If approached respectfully, most jurors will cooperate, even though they are under no legal obligation to do so. Post-trial interviews provide feedback on the trial performance of the attorney and the witnesses. They also permit the attorney to empirically validate the accuracy of the attorney's juror selection techniques and predictions. In some cases, post-trial interviews can lay a foundation for a challenge to the verdict.

The above-described jury analysis and selection methods can be quite expensive. It may be necessary to compensate those who administer and conduct the community surveys and questionnaires. Social scientists may have to be employed to design a questionnaire, assemble a sample, train interviewers, analyze the results, construct juror profiles for use at trial, and in some instances testify in court with regard to their conclusions. They also may be needed to analyze kinesic and paralinguistic cues of jurors during voir dire. Professional investigators may have to be hired to conduct the pretrial investigation of the venire.

The costs mount in the mock trial stage. The mock jurors, the attorneys used to represent opposing counsel and the judge, and the witnesses may all expect to be compensated for their time. Social scientists may again be needed both to integrate the information obtained from the mock trial into the previously constructed juror profiles and to analyze the interaction patterns which developed among the mock jurors.

If a shadow jury is used at trial, its members may expect to be compensated for both in-court time and the time, usually in the evenings, spent in discussing the case with the attorney. In a lengthy trial of several months or more, these expenses can be considerable.

Finally, the lawyer may want to employ interviewers to talk to jurors after the trial is completed. Since the individuals who gathered the raw data at the community analysis stage will have already been trained in interviewing techniques, these persons might also be used to conduct the post-trial interviews.

The costs involved can be staggering. In some cases they can run as high as six figures. But can the conscientious attorney afford not to use these techniques? Where significant damages, say, a million dollars or more, are at stake, or where the client has unlimited resources and is committed to winning the case, expense may be no obstacle.

But what of the more common case which does not fit into these categories? It would be a pyrrhic victory if the damages recovered or saved at trial were less than the expenses incurred in jury selection and analysis. And what of the indigent criminal defendant, represented by court-appointed counsel, who cannot afford any of these services?

The following sections will explore ways to minimize the costs involved in the various stages of juror selection and community analysis. There are two primary ways of reducing expenses. The first is to persuade the court that as a matter of constitutional or statutory law, a party is entitled to have the government pay for the costs of acquiring the necessary information. The second is to enlist volunteers to do the necessary legwork.

§3.16 —Court-Appointed Experts: Constitutional Analysis

Considerable costs can be saved if an attorney can convince a court to appoint experts to assist in jury selection. Both statutory and constitutional arguments can be mustered in support of this position. Despite whatever merit these arguments may have, one must appreciate that courts will be hesitant to open a Pandora's Box of potentially unlimited aid. The normal fiscal restraints which might operate on a client who must pay the bills are not present when the services are being borne by the government. Other social needs, such as education, health care, and services for the elderly and handicapped, have a legitimate claim for a fair share of government revenues. Looking more closely at only the criminal justice system, successful prisoner rights' suits have necessitated a greater expenditure of public funds. The courts are not unaware of these competing economic claims. Perhaps as a result, they tend to take a minimalist approach in regard to the assistance that they will require the government to subsidize in legal disputes. They will generally only make such aid available to persons who are truly indigent and then primarily in criminal cases where the loss of life or liberty is threatened.

There are two interrelated constitutional arguments that can be advanced in favor of court-appointed experts. The first is based on a combination of due process and equal protection considerations. The second hinges on the right to effective assistance of counsel.

Due Process–Equal Protection

Due process guarantees the right to a fair trial. Equal protection mandates that no person be discriminated against on bases unrelated to the merits of the cause. Both due process and equal protection are guaranteed to citizens in federal and state court by, respectively, the fifth and fourteenth amendments to the United States Constitution.[46]

In *Griffin v Illinois,*[47] state law permitted a defendant to appeal a criminal conviction as a matter of right. In order to obtain an appeal, however, the defendant had to submit a trial record. In order to prepare a trial record, the defendant required access to a stenographic transcript. The state, however, refused to supply indigent defendants with a free transcript. The United States Supreme Court held that although a state was under no obligation to provide an appeal, once it had chosen to do so, it could not structure its appellate system

---

[46] The fourteenth amendment, which applies to the states, explicitly mentions both rights. US Const amend XIV. The fifth amendment, which applies to the federal government, explicitly guarantees due process. US Const amend V. It has been held to implicitly guarantee equal protection. *See, e.g.,* Bolling v Sharpe, 347 US 497 (1954).

[47] 351 US 12 (1956).

in a way which discriminated against the poor. In an often quoted passage, Justice Black declared: "There can be no equal justice where the kind of trial a man gets depends on the amount of money he has."[48]

The *Griffin* principle was extended to a right to counsel on appeal in *Douglas v California.*[49] More recently, in *Ake v Oklahoma,*[50] the Supreme Court held that due process required that a state provide access to a psychiatrist to an indigent defendant who had made a preliminary showing that insanity would be a major issue at trial. The Court cautioned that an indigent did not have a right to all the assistance that a wealthier person could afford, but rather just those basic tools necessary to present a defense. Lower courts in appropriate cases have been willing to fund court-appointed handwriting analysts,[51] fingerprint experts,[52] forensic pathologists,[53] ballistics experts,[54] and general investigators.[55]

Based on this line of cases, one can argue that the right to an impartial jury[56] and, with it, the due process right to a fair trial will be frustrated if a party is unable to conduct pretrial investigations to determine whether either the community or the venire is biased. If the inability to conduct these investigations is due to the party's indigency, due process and equal protection require that the funding be supplied by the government.

It should be acknowledged that the cases in which expert assistance has been ordered arguably are distinguishable from the claim for expert assistance in jury selection. In the former, virtually all criminal prosecutions, the accuseds would have been unable to present a substantive defense central to the case without expert assistance. Without jury experts, a defendant could still present a full array of defenses. Thus counsel seeking experts to assist in jury selection should be prepared for an initially hostile response by the court. The attorney will most likely have to establish particularized need for the expert assistance and demonstrate its relevance to a fair trial in the case at hand. Unfortunately, courts tend to ask whether a reasonable attorney representing a client of independent financial means would utilize the services sought.[57] Since few attorneys currently employ jury experts, it is difficult to maintain that it is something

---

[48] *Id* 19.

[49] 372 US 353 (1963). A right to counsel at trial was established in Gideon v Wainwright, 372 US 335 (1963). *Gideon,* however, was based on the sixth amendment right to counsel as incorporated in the fourteenth amendment's due process clause rather than due process–equal protection principles.

[50] 470 US 68 (1985).

[51] *See, e.g.,* Bandy v United States, 296 F2d 882 (8th Cir 1961).

[52] *See, e.g.,* United States v Durant, 545 F2d 823 (2d Cir 1976).

[53] *See, e.g.,* Williams v Martin, 618 F2d 1021 (4th Cir 1980).

[54] *See, e.g.,* United States v Pope, 251 F Supp 234 (D Neb 1966).

[55] *See, e.g.,* Mason v Arizona, 504 F2d 1345 (9th Cir 1974), *cert denied,* 420 US 936 (1975). *See generally* Margolin, *The Indigent Criminal Defendant and Defense Services: A Search for Constitutional Standards,* 24 Hastings LJ 647 (1973).

[56] US Const amend VI. *See generally* **§§2.09-2.12.**

[57] *See, e.g.,* United States v Armstrong, 621 F2d 951 (9th Cir 1980).

which reasonable attorneys do. Counsel will have to educate the court as to the subconscious biases of jurors and how they can undermine the search for a fair and impartial jury; and why voir dire is inadequate to detect these biases. Nonetheless, some attorneys have apparently been successful in convincing courts of the need for experts to assist in community analysis and jury selection.[58]

Effective Assistance of Counsel

The sixth and fourteenth amendments to the United States Constitution guarantee the effective assistance of counsel in criminal prosecutions.[59] This right establishes an independent basis for seeking court-appointed jury experts, as well as buttressing the previously discussed due process—equal protection argument.[60]

Counsel's position will be that without expert assistance it will be difficult, if not impossible, to fulfill the duty owed the client to select a fair and impartial jury. A court will most likely answer that voir dire provides an adequate opportunity to eliminate biased jurors. In response, counsel will need to show that voir dire is an inadequate screening tool.[61] The success of this argument in part depends on the latitude the court allows counsel in conducting voir dire.

It is extremely difficult to establish ineffective assistance of counsel. Courts presume that attorneys are competent.[62] Moreover, only reasonably effective assistance is required.[63] In order to establish ineffectiveness, counsel's performance must be so deficient as to call into question the correctness of the verdict.[64] Furthermore, a defendant must show a reasonable probability that but for counsel's incompetence, the verdict would have been different.[65]

These strict standards will confound an attorney seeking to argue ineffective assistance of counsel based on a court's failure to provide jury selection experts. Counsel will likely have to demonstrate affirmatively that the jury was not impartial, that voir dire was inadequate to demonstrate prejudice, and that an impartial jury would have reached a different verdict. Each prong will be difficult to establish. Thus, the attorney may prefer to rely on a due

---

[58] Relevant cases, most unreported, are collected in National Jury Project, Jurywork app A (2d ed 1987).

[59] US Const amends VI, XIV. The sixth amendment right to counsel was incorporated into the fourteenth amendment and made binding on the states in Gideon v Wainwright, 372 US 335 (1963). The right to effective assistance of counsel was first articulated in Powell v Alabama, 287 US 45 (1932). *See also* United States v Cronic, 466 US 648 (1984); McMann v Richardson, 397 US 759, 771 n 14 (1970).

[60] Indeed, in United States v Cronic, 466 US 648, 658 (1984) the Supreme Court stated that the right to the effective assistance of counsel is recognized not for its own sake, but because it affects the ability of the accused to receive a fair trial.

[61] *See* **§12.14.**

[62] United States v Cronic, 466 US 648, 658 (1984).

[63] Strickland v Washington, 466 US 668 (1984).

[64] *Id.*

[65] *Id.*

process–equal protection analysis, with ineffective assistance of counsel used merely to bolster the basic arguments.

Conclusion

Two further observations: First, the constitutional arguments will almost surely be available only to indigents. Courts will be extremely reluctant to expend scarce resources on middle-class defendants who are unwilling to spend their own money. Second, the case law has developed virtually exclusively in the criminal law field, where a defendant's life or liberty is at stake. A court will be even less inclined to accept due process–equal protection or ineffective assistance of counsel arguments in civil cases, where the stakes are less and attorneys are often hired on a contingent fee basis.

§3.17 —Court-Appointed Experts: Statutory Analysis

The Criminal Justice Act, 18 USC §3006A(e), provides expert services for persons who would otherwise be unable to afford them. The section states in relevant part:

> **(e) Services other than counsel.—**
>
> **(1) Upon request.—**Counsel for a person who is financially unable to obtain investigative, expert, or other services necessary for adequate representation may request them in an ex parte application. Upon finding, after appropriate inquiry in an ex parte proceeding, that the services are necessary and that the person is financially unable to obtain them, the court, or the United States magistrate if the services are required in connection with a matter over which he has jurisdiction, shall authorize counsel to obtain the services.
>
> **(2) Without prior request.—(A)** Counsel appointed under this section may obtain, subject to later review, investigative, expert, and other services without prior authorization if necessary for adequate representation. Except as provided in subparagraph (B) of this paragraph, the total cost of services obtained without prior authorization may not exceed $300 and expenses reasonably incurred.
>
> **(B)** The court of the United States magistrate (if the services were rendered in a case disposed of entirely before the United States magistrate), may, in the interest of justice, and upon the finding that timely procurement of necessary services could not await prior authorization, approve payment for such services after they have been obtained, even if the cost of such services exceeds $300.

The statute permits payment to the expert of up to $1,000, exclusive of reimbursement for expenses reasonably incurred.[66] A higher payment is authorized for services of an unusual character or duration. Payment must be approved by the trial judge (or United States magistrate) *and* the chief judge of the circuit (or the delegate of the chief judge). The federal act has filled a major gap in the law, and many states, recognizing this, have enacted comparable statutory provisions modeled after it.[67]

To secure assistance under the federal statute requires a showing that the defendant is indigent and that the services are necessary. The federal statute, as well as most state statutes, are generally limited to criminal prosecutions.

In several cases the Criminal Justice Act provision has been invoked to obtain jury experts.[68] This is a promising avenue, for the standards governing assistance appear to be less stringent than those applied in a constitutional context. Nevertheless, even when proceeding under the Act, an attorney should highlight the constitutional dimensions of the request, stressing the need for jury experts to obtain an impartial jury and a fair trial. The attorney also should be prepared to demonstrate why voir dire is inadequate for these purposes.[69]

§3.18 Juror Investigations and Analyses on a Limited Budget

Where a court has rejected constitutional and statutory arguments for jury experts, the attorney needs to devise a strategy for obtaining these services which minimizes the cost to the client. Often there is a fertile source of inexpensive labor available. In many of the leading cases, community and juror investigations have been done by volunteers.

A starting place to search for volunteers is a local university. While attorneys and clients may have a paramount economic interest in a case, university faculty may be interested in it for its academic and educational value. Many social science researchers will be delighted to seize the opportunity to empirically validate hypotheses about group behavior in general or juror behavior in particular. If properly approached, they may be willing to volunteer their services. They may even be able to obtain university funding or a government grant to defray expenses.

University faculty may also be willing to enlist student volunteers. Students are generally excited about academic projects with real world implications, particularly if they will also receive academic credit for participation. Students can

---

[66] 18 USC §3006A(e)(3). The cost represents not a total for all expert assistance, but maximum payment for *each* expert.

[67] *See* N. Lefstein, Criminal Defense Services for the Poor, app B (1982); *Recent Development—Equal Protection—Refusal to Provide Expert Witness for Indigent Defendant Denies Equal Protection—Williams v Martin, 618 F2d 1021 (4th Cir 1980),* 59 Wash U LQ 317, 320-21 n 18 (1981) (collecting statutes).

[68] The cases, mostly unreported, are collected in National Jury Project, Jurywork app A, A-3 (2d ed 1987).

[69] *See* **§12.14.**

be taught how to conduct telephone surveys and interviews, as well as how to conduct discreet investigations. Students can also be used as jurors or witnesses in mock trials.

Even when a faculty sponsor is unavailable, many students, particularly those who aspire to a career in law, will be willing to volunteer their time. The payoff for them is the experience. They may also be pleased to develop a contact with a practicing attorney. Such concerns carry particular weight with law students. A strategically placed notice on a campus bulletin board may attract these students' attention. Even if students are unwilling to work for free, lawyers will discover that they constitute a relatively inexpensive yet competent labor force.

In addition to university faculty and students, volunteers may be found within the ranks of those philosophically in sympathy with the client's position. In many of the politically charged trials of the past decades, volunteers emerged from groups who felt the defendants were being prosecuted for their political beliefs. Although the highly publicized cases which attract volunteers without recruitment may be infrequent, there are often individuals who have a vested interest in seeing a similarly situated litigant's position vindicated. In a sexual harassment suit, for instance, nonworking women may identify with the complainant. In a wrongful discharge suit, union members may have an active stake in the outcome. In an antitrust action, small businesses may see their companies being squeezed out of the market if a large corporate defendant prevails. With a little imagination, an attorney can identify persons or groups who share common interests with the client and seek to recruit their assistance in the litigation.

More simply, a client may be able to persuade friends or relatives to volunteer their services. Those temporarily out of work or nonworking spouses may welcome the opportunity to become involved in a trial. Even parents with young children may be able to conduct telephone interviews from their home. A network of friends can often learn more about potential jurors than a professional investigator.[70] Friends and relatives can also serve as mock or shadow jurors, although in such circumstances the attorney must impress upon them the importance of not letting their friendship with the client affect their objective analysis of the case.

To like end, an attorney may recruit professional colleagues and personal friends to assist in interviewing, investigating, serving in the mock trial, or taking turns as shadow jurors. Being involved in the drama of a trial will appeal to many. Others may simply be willing to help a friend in need. The assistance can be obtained on a highly informal level. The attorney, for example, can invite a diverse group of friends to dinner. Afterwards, the attorney might casually ask their thoughts on a case on which the attorney "just happens to be working". The lawyer, however, should not indicate which side he or she represents. The resulting discussion may be as fruitful as a community survey, even though the group has not been randomly selected. Similarly, many attorneys will use persons with whom they come in casual contact as sounding boards for jury arguments. Barbers, hairdressers, taxi drivers, clerks, bartenders, and

---

[70] This networking approach is discussed in greater depth in **§4.03.**

travelling companions can provide useful feedback even though they may not constitute a randomly selected sample.

A reciprocal arrangement may be entered into with legal colleagues to serve as mock or shadow jurors. Even though their legal training and experience distinguish them from actual jurors, this can be both a blessing and a curse. Lawyers may be more sensitive to gaps in the attorney's case and/or weaknesses in the presentation. On the other hand, they may not appreciate when the evidence is being presented in a way which is likely to confuse lay persons. The attorney may therefore prefer to recruit secretaries, messengers, and other non-law trained firm personnel to serve as mock and shadow jurors.

Law and non-law trained members of a firm can also help in telephone surveys, questionnaire administration, and juror investigation. A few well-placed phone calls by an attorney or the attorney's associates to friends who live in the same neighborhood as a juror may reveal the same information that would be discovered by a professional investigator.

Finally, an attorney should not ignore the possibility of becoming his or her own expert. A course at the local university or a few treatises read during spare time can render the attorney sufficiently proficient to design questionnaires, perform basic statistical analyses, and construct juror profiles. In a middle-sized or large law firm, one member may become the designated jury expert available to assist other firm members in jury selection.

The rigor of the attorney's pretrial, trial, and post-trial jury analysis depends to an extent on the attorney's goals. If the goal is to convince a court to grant a motion, a mistrial, or a directed verdict, use of the results obtained from a homogeneous group, such as students, friends, or members of one's law firm, may lack the methodological rigor required to prevail. Experts need to be involved, if for no other reason than to testify in court. But if the objective, as is more common, is to gather information to help in jury selection and trial preparation and to provide attorneys with a variety of perspectives reflective of those likely to be found among jurors, methodological rigor becomes less important. Even if not optimally done, community/demographic analyses, juror investigation, mock trials, shadow juries, and post-trial interviews will improve the attorney's jury selection and trial performance.

4 Investigation of the Venire

§4.01 Introduction

Community/demographic surveys, discussed in the previous chapter, provide the attorney with information about the locality in which the trial is to be held and the individuals within it—their values, their perceptions of the legal system, and their attitudes toward the pending case. These surveys are essential in laying the foundation for a motion for a change in venue or venire, or for a challenge to the array based on a failure of the jury pool to reflect a fair cross-section of the community. Analysis of the data collected from the surveys enables the attorney to identify those demographic, attitudinal, and socio-psychological variables which will incline persons toward or against a client's case. Profiles of desirable and undesirable jurors can be constructed.

Community/demographic surveys, while extremely valuable, provide information only in the abstract. They do not tell the lawyer anything about the prospective jurors who will actually hear the pending case. The lawyer wants as much information as possible about these individuals. Armed with this information the lawyer can match the jurors against the previously constructed profiles of favorable and unfavorable jurors.

An investigation of prospective jurors is needed. In some instances the investigation will reveal that those actually summoned for jury duty do not constitute a random sample of the community, as indicated by the community survey. If so, the lawyer may want to challenge the array.[1]

By comparing the results of juror investigations with previously constructed juror profiles, the attorney can make a preliminary determination of which persons on the jury list are likely to be sympathetic to the client's cause. Prospective jurors can be rank ordered in terms of their degree of desirability. This rank ordering breathes life into abstract juror profiles, allowing the attorney to know, for example, whether to challenge a juror whose profile is neutral and nondescript; the lawyer would want to retain the juror if the remaining jurors in the pool were more unfavorable but might strike the juror if the remaining jurors in the pool were more favorable.

Investigation of the venire also serves to counteract the dangers of stereotyping. A juror profile tells an attorney that an individual with a particular demographic background and personality characteristics, and holding certain beliefs and attitudes, is likely to respond to the pending case in a particular manner. It is naive and simplistic, however, to assume that because a racial or ethnic group favors a particular position, each member of the class shares that view. Common sense and statistical theory say that this is not so. Juror investigations can inform an attorney whether a particular prospective juror in fact shares the attitudes of persons with similar demographic and socio-psychological characteristics.

Traditionally, attorneys have relied on voir dire to learn about a juror's background and beliefs. Voir dire, however, may reveal far less than juror investigations. One reason is that judges often restrict the scope and time allotted to voir dire. A second is that lawyers in voir dire are understandably reluctant to probe sensitive issues or ask embarrassing questions lest they alienate jurors. In the case of a juror likely to be sympathetic to the client's cause, it is preferable to discover this fact in a pretrial investigation rather than during voir dire; if sympathetic leanings are revealed in voir dire, the opposing side will most likely challenge the juror. Finally, many jurors will not admit their prejudices when asked, either because of an unwillingness to admit publicly what are generally perceived as character faults or because of an overriding desire to serve on the jury. Pretrial investigation can unearth such prejudices.

The Supreme Court has held that a new trial is justified when a juror responds dishonestly to a material question on voir dire if a true answer would have served as a basis for a challenge for cause.[2] Without independent investigation of the jurors, however, dishonesty is difficult to discover. Thus some juror investigations may be necessary in any event. It is logical to conduct the investigations prior to trial so that the information discovered can also be used in jury selection. Investigations before trial can be discreet, selective, and thorough. The results can be evaluated at leisure rather than under the press of

---

[1] *See* **ch 6.**

[2] McDonough Power Equip, Inc v Greenwood, 464 US 548 (1984).

trial, as is the case with voir dire. Even for attorneys who find voir dire an effective jury selection technique, the information revealed by pretrial investigation can be used to supplement that uncovered in voir dire in making challenges.

The legality of pretrial juror investigation is problematic. Ethical rules appear to permit the practice.[3] United States Supreme Court decisions, on the other hand, have disapproved shadowing jurors[4] or talking to them.[5] These cases, however, have involved sitting jurors. In a recent decision, the Supreme Court referred offhandedly but uncritically to the pretrial investigation of jurors.[6] As long as jurors are not intimidated, harassed, or contacted directly, such investigations are probably permissible.[7]

§4.02 Conducting the Investigation—Professional Investigators

Many commercial firms will, for a fee, investigate jurors.[8] They have considerable experience in conducting background checks. Where the state is a party, as in a criminal case, it may use police or federal agents to conduct its investigation.[9] Often the state has access to sources of information, such as tax and police files, not generally available to private parties or their investigators.

A typical private investigation will be based on public records relating to the prospective juror and talks with the juror's friends, neighbors, and coworkers. The scope of inquiry and depth of questioning will depend on the information sought. Among items typically included in an investigator's report are the prospective juror's age, marital history, and status; children; present and previous employment; religion; political affiliation; criminal record; property (including home); leisure interests; and previous involvement with the court system, either as a juror or party.[10] Some reports, however, have been known to deal with more private and sensitive material, such as the juror's extracurricular activities and sexual relations.

The hiring of a commercial investigation firm can be expensive.[11] The size

---

[3] *See* **§4.04.**

[4] *See* Sinclair v United States, 279 US 749 (1929).

[5] *See* Gold v United States, 352 US 985 (1957); Remser v United States, 350 US 377 (1956).

[6] Batson v Kentucky, 476 US 79, 89 n 12 (1986).

[7] *See* Dow v Carnegie-Illinois Steel Corp, 224 F2d 414, 430-31 (3d Cir 1955).

[8] Apparently some investigatory firms routinely collect information about jurors which they later sell to lawyers. *See* Newsweek, Aug 26, 1974, at 49.

[9] *See generally* Okun, *Investigation of Jurors by Counsel: Its Impact on the Decisional Process,* 56 Geo LJ 839 (1968).

[10] *Id* 851.

[11] This is obviously not a problem for the government, which can use local police or the FBI to conduct its investigations.

of the venire can range from twenty to two hundred.[12] To investigate every juror will be time-consuming and costly. It may make more economic sense to invest limited resources in other phases of the case (*e.g.*, factual investigation and expert witnesses). In any event, as ethical restrictions forbid contacting persons on the jury list directly, the results of the investigation will be based in large part on hearsay and rumor.[13]

There is the danger that an investigation conducted by a commercial firm will backfire. Consider, for example, the interviewing of neighbors. Those who do not like the person under investigation may well be forthcoming in revealing all manner of gossip about the target of their dislike. This information may be titillating, but it may also be unreliable. On the other hand, close friends of the person under investigation may be cautious or noncooperative. Worse, they may inform the prospective juror about the investigation.[14] If the detective has revealed that the investigation relates to a pending case, the potential juror may report the matter to the court, with potentially embarrassing repercussions. Even if the court is not informed, the juror may become disaffected with the side perceived to have employed the investigators. While such backlash can be avoided if the investigator is less honest or even deceptive in talking with sources of information, the ethical propriety of proceeding in this fashion is questionable. Moreover, if brought to light, the repercussions to the attorney and the client may be greater still.

§4.03 —Amateur Investigators

It is not generally necessary to employ professionals to investigate jurors. Working together, the attorney, the client, and a network of their friends and associates can conduct an effective investigation of the venire.

The jury list itself will usually disclose the jurors' names, addresses, and occupations. Similar information may be included about the jurors' spouses. Some jurisdictions also require prospective jurors to answer a more detailed questionnaire distributed by the court. Counsel should examine these questionnaires. Other public records may yield information about criminal records, home ownership, and involvement in lawsuits (as well as the result of such suits). Credit reports may be obtainable. In some jurisdictions there exists, as a matter of either public or private record, a jury book which will indicate previous cases on which the juror has sat and the verdicts in those cases.

The client's assistance should be enlisted. The client should be shown the jury list to see if he or she is personally acquainted with anyone on it. If the client is a corporation, or if the client is self-employed or employed by a corporation, business records should be checked to determine if any of the jurors

---

[12] Often when a large venire is summoned, its members will be divided among several courts in the jurisdiction. It may, however, be possible to learn which jurors will be assigned to the courtroom in which the attorney's case is to be heard.

[13] *See* **§4.04.**

[14] *See* Dow v Carnegie-Illinois Steel Corp, 224 F2d 414, 430 (3d Cir 1955). *See also* Allen v Snow, 635 F2d 12 (1st Cir 1980) (prosecutor informed of investigation).

work for a competitor. Business records will also reveal whether a juror is a customer, and, if so, whether the juror has ever filed a complaint against the client or been involved in a dispute with the client's company.

A drive through the juror's neighborhood may reveal a juror's socioeconomic status. The lawyer should note the juror's automobile(s). Bumper stickers on automobiles may provide a glimpse into the juror's political and social leanings (and often whether the juror has a sense of humor). Whether the juror's home, yard, and automobiles are well kept or neglected may also be significant.

A network approach can be used to learn more about the prospective jurors.[15] The attorney and client begin by drawing up a list of friends and associates who are active in the community. Persons who have extensive social and business contacts are most valuable. Each member of the group can recruit a friend and each friend, another, until the group achieves a workable size. The group should be large enough to accomplish the goal of investigating all persons on the jury list but not so large as to be unwieldy.

The group should be assembled to examine the jury list to identify those prospective jurors with whom members of the network are personally acquainted. The address of a prospective juror with whom nobody is familiar should be noted. At least one group member is likely to have acquaintances who live in the neighborhood. These acquaintances can be contacted, preferably by the group member with whom the neighbor is friendly. To this end, group members should be provided some basic training in interviewing techniques. Persons contacted should be told that their answers will be kept confidential and in turn asked to keep confidential the fact of the interview.

A similar process may be used to arrange interviews with the juror's coworkers or employers. The jury list or a juror questionnaire will usually disclose juror occupations. If not already indicated on the official form, a trade directory can be used to identify the juror's employer. Once the employer is known, the group can contact personal acquaintances who work for that employer. These persons can again then be interviewed, with the same cautions regarding confidentiality.

In some instances a check of public records, a jury book, or a juror information sheet will indicate previous jury service by a member of the venire. It will then be useful to speak to the attorneys who tried the case on which the juror sat. Besides being able to provide information about the verdict in the case, the attorneys may have notes on the juror based on their own pretrial investigation, or post-verdict interview of the juror. The attorneys may have an independent recollection of the juror's performance on voir dire.

Although conducted by amateurs, a networking approach has several advantages over professional investigations. Besides the cost savings, which may be considerable, the group members are more likely to know the persons whom they contact for information. As a result, they will be in a better position to assess the reliability of the information received. Without conducting an inde-

---

[15] *See* 1 A. Ginger, Jury Selection in Civil and Criminal Trials §5.8 (2d ed 1984).

pendent investigation of their sources, professional investigators may be uncertain about the reliability of the information they receive. Furthermore, it is less likely that persons interviewed by members of the network will disclose the contact to the court or the juror. They will be reluctant to betray the confidence of the friend who approached them; when the interviewer is a private investigator with whom the respondent has no acquaintance, there are no competing loyalties.

In raw form, the information collected about each member of the venire can be read and analyzed by the attorney. In addition, a social scientist can interpret and code the data into a form in which it can be matched against the juror profiles previously constructed.[16] The result will be a statistical profile of the juror's leanings. The attorney can then rank order the members of the venire in terms of their degree of desirability. The numerical ranking can indicate not only whether one juror is more desirable than another, but by how much. These profiles and rankings, supplemented with information gleaned from voir dire, will provide the attorney with an informed basis for exercising peremptory challenges.

§4.04 Ethical Restrictions

The legal system is concerned, and rightly so, with protecting members of the venire from outside influence prior to trial. Attempts by parties or their associates to contact prospective jurors in pending litigation may compromise jurors' impartiality, as well as invade their privacy. Public confidence in the jury system could be undermined. To safeguard jurors from extraneous influences, the Canons of Professional Responsibility and Disciplinary Rules of the American Bar Association explicitly forbid pretrial communication with members of the venire:

> EC 7-29 . . . There should be no extrajudicial communication with veniremen prior to trial . . . by or on behalf of a lawyer connected with the case. Furthermore, a lawyer who is not connected with the case should not communicate with or cause another to communicate with a venireman or a juror about the case. . . .[17]
>
> DR 7-108(A): Before the trial of a case a lawyer connected therewith shall not communicate with or cause another to communicate with anyone he knows to be a member of the venire from which the jury will be selected for the trial of the case.[18]

The restrictions apply to both lawyers and those working on "behalf of a lawyer connected with the case." Thus both professional investigators and

---

[16] *See* **§3.08.**

[17] ABA Model Code of Professional Responsibility EC 7-29 (1980).

[18] ABA Model Code of Professional Responsibility DR 7-108 (1980). *See also* ABA Model Rules of Professional Conduct Rule 3.5 (1989).

those persons comprising the lawyer-assembled network of amateur juror investigators would fall within the prohibitions.

Nonlawyers, of course, would not be subject to professional sanctions for violations of these rules, as the rules are directed to attorneys. Attorneys, on the other hand, may be vicariously responsible for the actions of those working under them or liable for negligent supervision. While responsibility was only obliquely suggested in the American Bar Association's Model Code of Professional Responsibility, it is made explicit in the more recently promulgated Rules of Professional Conduct:

> RULE 5.3 Responsibilities Regarding Nonlawyer Assistants
>
> With respect to a nonlawyer employed or retained by or associated with a lawyer:
>
> (a) a partner in a law firm shall make reasonable efforts to ensure that the firm has in effect measures giving reasonable assurance that the person's conduct is compatible with the professional obligations of the lawyer;
>
> (b) a lawyer having direct supervisory authority over the nonlawyer shall make reasonable efforts to ensure that the person's conduct is compatible with the professional obligations of the lawyer; and
>
> (c) a lawyer shall be responsible for conduct of such a person that would be a violation of the rules of professional conduct if engaged in by a lawyer if:
>
> (1) the lawyer orders or, with the knowledge of the specific conduct, ratifies the conduct involved; or
>
> (2) the lawyer is a partner in the law firm in which the person is employed, or has direct supervisory authority over the person, and knows of the conduct at a time when its consequences can be avoided or mitigated but fails to take reasonable remedial action.[19]

On the other hand, the American Bar Association rules implicitly recognize that discreet investigations of members of the venire are permissible:

> EC 7-30. Vexatious or harassing investigations of veniremen or jurors seriously impair the effectiveness of our jury system. For this reason, a lawyer or anyone on his behalf who conducts an investigation of veniremen or jurors should act with circumspection and restraint.[20]

Although, on the one hand, circumspect and restrained investigations are permissible, and, on the other, vexatious or harassing investigations are not, many in-between cases will arise where the category into which the investiga-

---

[19] ABA Model Rules of Professional Conduct Rule 5.3 (1989). *See also* United States v Warlick, 742 F2d 113 (4th Cir 1984).

[20] ABA Model Code of Professional Responsibility EC 7-30 (1980).

tion falls is not clear. In questionable cases, lawyers should proceed cautiously. At stake is their personal and professional reputation and standing, as well as that of the profession. That the American Bar Association takes this matter seriously is indicated by the reporting duties imposed on attorneys:

> EC 7-32. Because of his duty to aid in preserving the integrity of the jury system, a lawyer who learns of improper conduct by or towards a venireman, a juror, or a member of the family of either should make a prompt report to the court regarding such conduct.[21]

It should be noted that the restrictions imposed on contact with and investigation of members of the venire extend to members of their families:

> EC 7-31. Communications with or investigations of members of families of veniremen or jurors by a lawyer or by anyone on his behalf are subject to the restrictions imposed upon the lawyer with respect to his communications with or investigations of veniremen and jurors.[22]

An attorney should be aware that there may be an ethical duty to reveal information discovered in an investigation which would justify the disqualification of a juror for cause, if the information is not brought out on voir dire. In *In re Shon,*[23] a lawyer was disbarred for permitting two men with whom he was personally acquainted to sit on the jury without informing the court or opposing counsel of the relationship. In *United States v Kyle,*[24] a prosecutor was held to be under an obligation to disclose to defense counsel that several jurors had previously served on a case where the judge had berated the jury for returning a verdict of acquittal.

§4.05 Juror Privacy

In addition to ethical limitations on juror investigation, a court may impose its own restrictions. The judge may wish to protect juror privacy and safety. In order to be able to investigate jurors, an attorney needs to know their names.[25] By withholding juror names and information which would allow unnamed jurors to be identified, a judge can effectively frustrate lawyer efforts at investigation. The issue arose in *United States v Barnes.*[26]

---

[21] ABA Model Code of Professional Responsibility EC 7-32 (1980).

[22] ABA Model Code of Professional Responsibility EC 7-31 (1980).

[23] 262 AD 225, 28 NYS2d 872 (1941). *Compare* State v Kitto, 373 NW2d 307 (Minn 1985) (prosecutor not required to disclose fact prospective juror was acquaintance of prosecutor).

[24] 469 F2d 547 (DC Cir 1972), *cert denied,* 409 US 1117 (1973).

[25] Many state statutes provide for a defendant's receipt of the names of prospective jurors in advance of trial. *See* W. LaFave v J. Israel, Criminal Procedure 723 (1984), *see* also 3 American Bar Association Standards for Criminal Justice 15-47 (2d ed 1980).

[26] 604 F2d 121 (2d Cir 1979), *cert denied,* 446 US 907 (1980).

The defendants in *Barnes* were charged with narcotics-related offenses. The case had generated considerable pretrial publicity. Previous narcotics trials in the district had been marred by attempts to influence witnesses and jurors. To avoid a repetition of such occurrences, the trial judge sua sponte decided not to disclose jurors' names or addresses. The court cited the need to safeguard the privacy of jurors and their families, and the importance of preserving the jury's impartiality.

The appellate court upheld the trial judge's order. The appellate court, however, preferred to stress the need to protect the safety of jurors rather than the more nebulous privacy concerns. Anonymity, reasoned the court, furthered the goal of impartiality:

> If the giving of names and addresses had been required so that investigation could have been made in the neighborhood or from their families as to their characteristics, any semblance of an impartial jury could have been destroyed. Fear of retaliation against themselves or members of their family would inevitably have been uppermost in their minds during their deliberations.[27]

The problem with the appellate court's reasoning is that it sweeps too broadly. The same concern with retaliation and intimidation could be cited in every case. *Barnes* differs from the routine case in degree. If *Barnes* were to be routinely followed, juror anonymity could become the norm. Jury selection would then be based solely on responses to voir dire. But without being able to conduct background investigations of jurors, attorneys would be unable to verify the truth of responses to voir dire questions. Intelligent exercise of peremptory challenges would be frustrated. The United States Supreme Court has held that a juror's failure to honestly answer a material question on voir dire can justify a new trial if the response would have provided a valid basis for a challenge for cause;[28] but establishing dishonesty under the *Barnes* conditions would be difficult at best.

By refusing to disclose the names of jurors even to the attorneys, the *Barnes* court impliedly impugned the attorneys' integrity. The assumption appears to have been that the lawyers could not be trusted to obey a judicial directive not to reveal juror identity. As an officer of the court, an attorney is obliged to obey such a court order.

The *Barnes* court did indicate that its intention was not to sanction anonymity in every case. The court specifically noted the extensive pretrial publicity in the case, the allegations of dangerousness and unscrupulousness attributed to the defendants, and the past incidences of violence in narcotics cases in the district. Comparable exceptional circumstances may be necessary before anonymity will be ordered, and in only a small percentage of cases either before or after *Barnes* has such a constellation of circumstances been found.

---

[27] 604 F2d at 141.

[28] McDonough Power Equip v Greenwood, 464 US 548 (1984).

The argument can be made that in becoming jurors citizens forfeit rights of privacy that they otherwise enjoy. Jurors in effect become akin to public figures. A recent Supreme Court decision, however, lends support to the position that jurors do not waive all rights of privacy.

In *Press-Enterprise Co v Superior Court*[29] the trial court had barred the press from being present during voir dire. Citing the jurors' right of privacy, the trial court has also refused to release a transcript of the voir dire. The United States Supreme Court reversed. It reasoned that voir dire proceedings were a public process requiring a presumption of openness, a presumption which had not been rebutted in the case.

The Supreme Court, however, recognized the legitimacy of the jurors' privacy interest. Where specific voir dire questions of a sensitive nature threatened to invade that interest, the Court advised that a juror be permitted to make an in camera showing (but with counsel present and on the record) for limited closure of the hearing. Furthermore, the Court stated that a valid juror privacy interest could justify the sealing of the transcript, or even the withholding of the name of a juror from the press.

The privacy of prospective jurors should be respected. Jurors serve a vital public function for minimal compensation. The government has summoned them to perform this duty; they did not volunteer. Beyond the sacrifice in time and money which jurors must incur, they should not be asked to sacrifice their privacy. Protecting juror privacy will also lessen the reluctance of many to serve.[30] These interests, however, need to be balanced against the right to an impartial jury and the extent to which it is impaired by restrictions on lawyers' ability to gather information about jurors.[31]

In *Press-Enterprise Co v Superior Court*[32] the Supreme Court countenanced a less restrictive approach than that taken in *United States v Barnes.*[33] Attorneys in *Press-Enterprise Co* were at least aware of jurors' identities and therefore in a position to conduct pretrial investigations. Nonetheless, the Supreme Court's discussion may harbinger an increasing judicial solicitude for juror privacy. Protection of juror privacy appears to fall within the sound discretion of the trial judge. In an exceptional case, such as *Barnes,* protection of juror privacy and safety may override a party's constitutional interest in an impartial jury to the extent that it is impaired by the court's order.

Federal law permits a district to adopt a jury plan which allows the chief judge (or a designee) to keep juror names confidential "in any case where the inter-

---

[29] 464 US 501 (1984).

[30] *See* Sinclair v United States, 279 US 749, 765 (1929). This argument was rejected as "far-fetched" in United States v Costello, 255 F2d 876 (2d Cir 1958).

[31] *See generally* Note, *The Right of Privacy of Prospective Jurors During Voir Dire,* 70 Cal L Rev 708 (1982).

[32] 464 US 501 (1984), discussed earlier in this section.

[33] 604 F2d 121 (2d Cir 1979), *cert denied,* 446 US 907 (1980) discussed earlier in this section.

ests of justice so require."[34] Indeed, the relevant statutory section begins "[i]f the [jury] plan permits these names to be made public".[35] This language can be read to suggest that a jury plan can bar disclosure of juror names in all circumstances. A more narrow reading of the statute, however, is that juror names can be withheld from the general public, but not from the attorneys and/or parties in the litigation.

As a practical matter, the issue may be moot in federal court. A federal statute permits the inspection of jury lists for the purpose of preparing motions challenging jury selection procedures.[36] Interpreting this provision, the United States Supreme Court has stated that a litigant has "essentially an unqualified right to inspect jury lists."[37] By exercising this right in order to determine whether there is a viable challenge to jury selection procedures, the attorney also learns the names of members of the venire.

There are indirect methods by which judges can effectively prevent juror investigation. Augmenting the size of the venire, where that is permitted, will decrease the feasibility of juror investigations; it is one thing to investigate 30 persons and quite another to investigate 300. Alternatively, the judge may decline to release the juror list until immediately before trial. Federal law does not specify when jurors' names need to be revealed, but generally leaves the matter to individual districts.[38] Even when a disclosure date is specified by Congress, the period for study may be quite short; in cases of treason or other capital offenses, for example, the jury list does not have to be disclosed until three days prior to trial.[39] An attorney who does not learn the identity of jurors until three days before trial will lack adequate time to investigate the jurors unless the trial judge is willing to grant a continuance for this purpose. Such a continuance appears to lie within the judge's discretion.[40] By restricting the time available for jury investigation while expanding the size of the venire, the trial judge can safeguard juror privacy by undermining the feasibility of juror investigation.

---

[34] 28 USC §1863(b)(7).

[35] *Id.*

[36] 28 USC §1867(f).

[37] Test v United States, 420 US 28, 30 (1975).

[38] *See* 28 USC §1863(b)(7). *See also* United States v Whiting, 538 F2d 220 (8th Cir 1976) (granting of continuance to allow for further inspection of jury lists for purpose of preparing challenge to selection procedures lies within a court's discretion).

[39] 18 USC §3432. This section has been construed not to apply to other types of cases. Hamer v United States, 259 F2d 274 (9th Cir 1958). A 1427 English statute granted litigants a list of the jury six days before trial so that the parties could inform the jurors of their positions. *See* L. Moore, The Jury: Tool of Kings, Palladium of Liberty 70 (1973).

[40] *See* United States v Whiting, 538 F2d 220 (8th Cir 1976). If a lengthy voir dire is contemplated, the attorney's investigation team may have time to conduct their investigations while the voir dire is proceeding.

§4.06 The Pros and Cons of Juror Investigation

There are numerous advantages to pretrial investigations of members of the venire. Combined with community/demographic analyses, the results may provide the basis for challenging the nonrepresentative character of the venire. Further, the investigations will often yield information critical to informed jury selection which cannot be obtained on voir dire. By matching the information learned about the juror with the juror profiles constructed on the basis of community/demographic surveys and mock trials, the attorney can make an informed judgment about the juror's likely leanings in the case.

The results of pretrial juror investigations can alert a lawyer to the possibility that a juror is being untruthful or less than candid in answering voir dire questions. Moreover, the need to ask potentially embarrassing voir dire questions will be obviated if the answers are already known because of the pretrial investigation. Where the investigation indicates that a juror will be receptive to the client's position, the lawyer need not ask questions of the juror on voir dire the answers to which might prompt opposing counsel to challenge the juror.

Because a significant amount of information about the jurors will already be known as a result of pretrial investigation, voir dire should require less time. The trend to lengthier voir dire has been a matter of concern to many judges.[41] Pretrial juror investigation reduces the need to turn voir dire into a fishing expedition.

While some pretrial investigation of the venire is desirable and inevitable (even if it consists of nothing more than the attorney's reading the names of the jurors and mentally noting the information contained on the jury list), the scope of the investigation will depend on many variables. The larger the venire, the less cost-efficient will be the investigation. Whether the attorney must hire a commercial firm to conduct the investigation is another important financial consideration, particularly if the client is not wealthy. As previously suggested, however, investigations can often be effectively undertaken by the attorney, the client, and a network of friends and associates.[42] But even a fully financed or staffed investigatory team will not succeed if there is inadequate time to investigate; the release date of the jury list will be critical in determining the feasibility and scope of an investigation.

The judge's attitude toward pretrial investigation of jurors should also be weighed. If the judge frowns on the practice, the attorney may prefer not to risk the loss of the judge's good will,[43] especially if the trial will raise critical evidentiary rulings which lie within the judge's discretion. Likewise, the judge's approach to voir dire needs to be considered. The less leeway allowed attorneys in voir dire, the greater the need for pretrial juror investigations to make intelligent selection decisions.

---

[41] *See* Press-Enterprise Co v Supreme Court, 464 US 501, 510 n 9 (1984) (lengthy voir dire undermines public confidence in the courts and the legal profession).

[42] *See* **§4.03.**

[43] *See* Allen v Snow, 635 F2d 12 (1st Cir 1980), where counsel voluntarily curtailed juror investigations because of fear of being held in contempt.

An investigation of the venire is both in itself important in jury selection and a valuable tool in preparing for voir dire. Nevertheless, even assuming adequate time and resources to conduct a thorough investigation, the limitations of this approach should be noted. Ethical restrictions forbid contact with prospective jurors or their families. As a consequence, much of the information collected may be based on rumor and hearsay. The accuracy of the information will be suspect, depending on the reliability and personal knowledge of the providers of the information. Even if accurate, the investigation is unlikely to directly reveal the most critical piece of information which the attorney desires—the views of the prospective jurors on the issues, parties, and witnesses involved in the pending case. This knowledge will generally have to await the voir dire stage, which will be the first opportunity the lawyer has to discuss these matters directly with the jurors.

§4.07 Discovery of the Results of Juror Investigations and Analyses

Despite the suggestions previously offered for juror investigations which are relatively low-cost,[44] less wealthy and indigent litigants may still find themselves at a disadvantage. Many of the suggested alternatives depend on the goodwill and cooperation of volunteers. Those who can afford to hire social scientists, jury investigators, consultants, and other assistants are not dependent on volunteers.

If community/demographic analyses, juror profiles, and jury investigation are effective in identifying jurors with subtle and subconscious predispositions for or against a party, the side which lacks access to this information is at a disadvantage in selecting a jury. Greater reliance will have to be placed on voir dire. The effectiveness of voir dire as a jury selection tool will depend on the time and scope allotted to it by the trial judge and the truthfulness of jurors in responding to questions. But the lawyer will still be at a disadvantage. The size of the disadvantage will depend on the thoroughness and accuracy of the opposing side's pretrial investigations, and the sophistication of their analyses. Even a slight disadvantage, however, can be significant. Most cases which go to trial are close on the merits. If they were not, the two sides most likely would have reached a settlement. In a case likely to be closely contested, any advantage, no matter how slight, will be magnified.

The American legal system prides itself on providing (at least in theory) equal justice for all. If so, it needs to examine ways of addressing the problem of resource imbalance. In addition to concerns regarding equality, a jury subconsciously predisposed to one side is a threat to the constitutional guaranty of an impartial jury. The danger is that the jury's verdict will reflect more the psychological predispositions of the jurors than the strength of the evidence. On the other hand, pretrial jury analyses and investigations arguably further the seating of an impartial jury by identifying persons with hidden biases which

---

[44] *See* **§3.18.**

would otherwise escape detection. This point may be valid as a matter of theory but in order for it to be so as a matter of practice requires that both sides have an equal opportunity to uncover these biases. The most straightforward way of addressing the problem of resource imbalance is to allow the disadvantaged side to discover the results of the juror investigations and analyses conducted by the opposition.

§4.08 —Civil Cases: Statutory Bases for Discovery

The Federal Rules of Civil Procedure govern civil trials in federal court. They have also served as the model for state laws of civil procedure. The federal rules do not directly address the issue of discovery of the results of juror investigations and analyses, nor is it clear that discovery of such information fits within any of the categories covered by the relevant Federal Rule:

> **Rule 26. General Provisions Governing Discovery**
>
> . . .
>
> (b) **Discovery Scope and Limits.** Unless otherwise limited by order of the court in accordance with these rules, the scope of discovery is as follows:
>
> (1) In General. Parties may obtain discovery regarding any matter, not privileged, which is relevant to the subject matter involved in the pending action, whether it relates to the claim or defense of the party seeking discovery or to the claim or defense of any other party, including the existence, description, nature, custody, condition and location of any books, documents, or other tangible things and the identity and location of persons having knowledge of any discoverable matter. It is not ground for objection that the information sought will be inadmissible at the trial if the information sought appears reasonably calculated to lead to the discovery of admissible evidence.
>
> . . .
>
> (3) Trial Preparation: materials. Subject to the provisions of subdivision (b)(4) of this rule, a party may obtain discovery of documents and tangible things otherwise discoverable under subdivision (b)(1) of this rule and prepared in anticipation of litigation or for trial by or for another party or by or for that other party's representative (including the other party's attorney, consultant, surety, indemnitor, insurer, or agent) only upon a showing that the party seeking discovery has substantial need of the materials in the preparation of the party's case and that the party is unable without undue hardship to obtain the substantial equivalent of the materials by other means. In ordering discovery of such materials when the required showing has been made, the court shall protect against disclosure of the mental impressions, conclusions, opinions, or legal theories of an attorney or other representative of a party concerning the litigation.
>
> . . .
>
> (4) Trial Preparation: Experts. Discovery of facts known and opinions held by experts, otherwise discoverable under the provisions of subdivi-

sion (b)(1) of this rule and acquired or developed in anticipation of litigation or for trial, may be obtained only as follows:

(A)(i) A party may through interrogatories require any other party to identify each person whom the other party expects to call as an expert witness at trial, to state the subject matter on which the expert is expected to testify, and to state the substance of the facts and opinions to which the expert is expected to testify and a summary of the grounds for each opinion. (ii) Upon motion, the court may order further discovery by other means, subject to such restrictions as to scope and such provisions, pursuant to subdivision (b)(4)(C) of this rule, concerning fees and expenses as the court may deem appropriate.

(B) A party may discover facts known or opinions held by an expert who has been retained or specially employed by another party in anticipation of litigation or preparation for trial and who is not expected to be called as a witness at trial, only as provided in Rule 35(b) or upon a showing of exceptional circumstances under which it is impracticable for the party seeking discovery to obtain facts or opinions on the same subject by other means.

(C) Unless manifest injustice would result, (i) the court shall require that the party seeking discovery pay the expert a reasonable fee for time spent in responding to discovery under subdivisions (b)(4)(A)(ii) and (b)(4)(B) of this rule; and (ii) with respect to discovery obtained under subdivision (b)(4)(A)(ii) of this rule the court may require, and with respect to discovery obtained under subdivision (b)(4)(B) of this rule the court shall require, the party seeking discovery to pay the other party a fair portion of the fees and expenses reasonably incurred by the latter party in obtaining facts and opinions from the expert . . .[45]

Under Rule 26(b)(1), whose general provisions regarding discoverability control subsequent sections, the results of juror investigations would arguably not be relevant to the subject matter of the litigation or the claim or defense of the party seeking discovery, or that of any other party. Nor would discovery of information relating to jurors seem calculated to lead to the discovery of admissible evidence.

Even if these hurdles were to be surmounted, Rule 26(b)(3) raises further requirements that the party seeking discovery have "substantial need" of the materials being sought and be "unable without undue hardship to obtain the substantial equivalent of the materials by other means." Although a relatively indigent litigant may be unable to afford the juror investigators and expert analysts of a wealthier opposing party, a judge who had read **§4.03** of this chapter might maintain that a "substantially equivalent" investigation and analysis could be accomplished through the use of amateur networks. A court might also deem the opportunity to engage in voir dire to be a "substantial equivalent" to pretrial juror investigation. On the same reasoning, the court might conclude there was not "substantial need" for the information being sought.

[45] Fed R Civ P 26.

A further hurdle under Rule 26(b)(3) is posed by the provision which allows the court to protect against disclosure of the "mental impressions, conclusions, opinions, or legal theories of an attorney or other representative of a party concerning the litigation." This is a codification of the work product doctrine first formulated by the United States Supreme Court in *Hickman v Taylor.*[46] Under this doctrine, the mental impressions, conclusions, opinions, and legal theories of the lawyer *and the social scientists and jury consultants employed by the lawyer* would arguably be protected against discovery. It is extremely doubtful that the juror profiles constructed on the basis of analysis of community/demographic surveys, juror investigations, and mock trials would not be considered work product. The design of the questionnaire used in the surveys, the preparation of interviewers, and the analysis of the results might also be protected. Likewise, the staging of a mock trial, the arguments advanced during it, and the analysis of the deliberations of the mock jury would appear to be the product of the attorney's thought processes and consequently nondiscoverable. Perhaps all that might escape the work product exception would be the raw data relating to jurors uncovered by investigators. But even here, the questions asked by the investigators might reflect the work product of the attorney or the investigator. Routine information about jurors, while it might fall outside the work product exception, would fall within the exception which bars discovery of information which can be obtained through other means without undue hardship.

Rule 26(b)(4) addresses discovery of facts known and opinions held by expert witnesses. The experts referred to in subsection (A), however, are those whom the other party plans to call at trial. Jury consultants, investigators, and social science experts would rarely testify at trial.

Subsection (B) of Rule 26(b)(4) is perhaps the most promising basis for seeking discovery. It relates to experts (other than examining physicians) retained by the opposing side who are not expected to be called at trial. The party seeking discovery, however, must demonstrate "exceptional circumstances under which it is impracticable . . . to obtain facts or opinions on the same subject by other means." It would not be surprising for a court to rule that "facts and opinions" relating to juror fitness and impartiality can be discovered at voir dire. An attorney seeking discovery should be prepared to argue that voir dire examination is an ineffective means for discovering juror bias.[47] The degree to which the judge restricts the scope of voir dire and the time allotted to it should be relevant considerations.

Finally, it should be observed that a party who succeeds in obtaining discovery under Fed R Civ P 24(b)(4) may be required to contribute to the fees and expenses of the experts employed by the opposing side. While such contribution may be less expensive than hiring one's own jury expert, it may still tax the limited resources of a client.

---

[46] 329 US 495 (1947).

[47] *See* **§12.14.**

§4.09 —Criminal Cases: Statutory Bases for Discovery

Obtaining discovery of juror investigations and analyses is even less likely under the Federal Rules of Criminal Procedure, and its state counterparts, than under the Federal Rules of Civil Procedure. Liberalized discovery has long been accepted in civil procedure. A similar philosophy has been slow to develop in the criminal arena. Although discovery in both civil and criminal cases helps eliminate surprise, equalizes investigative resources, and facilitates the search for truth, the importance of these concerns in criminal trials has been overshadowed by a fear that discovery will lead to perjury and the intimidation of jurors. There is also a feeling that the already heavy burden on the prosecutor to prove guilt beyond a reasonable doubt should be counterbalanced by restricting discovery of the state's case prior to trial. Protection of informers is yet another consideration not present in civil cases.

Reflecting these concerns, Federal Rule of Criminal Procedure 16 permits only limited discovery.[48] The defense, upon request, may inspect or obtain a copy of a statement made by the defendant.[49] The defense may also obtain a copy of the defendant's criminal record,[50] documents and tangible objects,[51] and reports of physical examinations, mental examinations, scientific tests, and experiments.[52] Except for these identified items, the rule does not "authorize the discovery or inspection of reports, memoranda, or other internal government documents made by the attorney for the government or other government agents in connection with the investigation or prosecution of the case. . . ."[53]

The government's scope of discovery is reciprocal and similar.[54] The government's power to compel discovery under Rule 16, furthermore, hinges on a defense request to discover information within the control of the government. When such a request is not forthcoming, the government has no independent right of discovery. Again the rule seems to indicate that it is to be read narrowly:

> Except as to scientific or medical reports, this subdivision does not authorize the discovery or inspection of reports, memoranda, or other internal defense documents made by the defendant, or the defendant's attorneys or agents in connection with the investigation or defense of the case. . . .[55]

---

[48] Fed R Crim P 16. A separate rule, not relevant in the jury context, covers the discovery of alibi witnesses as well as governmental witnesses who will be called to place the defendant at the scene of the offense. *Id* 12.1.

[49] *Id* 16(a)(1)(A).

[50] *Id* 16(a)(1)(B).

[51] *Id* 16(a)(1)(C).

[52] *Id* 16(a)(1)(D).

[53] *Id* 16(a)(2).

[54] *Id* 16(b)(1)(A), (B).

[55] *Id* 16(b)(2).

One could argue that community/demographic analyses, the construction of jury profiles, and mock trials constitute "scientific tests" within the meaning of Rule 16. The Advisory Committee notes to the Rule, however, indicate that the provision was directed toward scientific tests that were themselves to be introduced in evidence or were designed to lead to admissible evidence.[56] Community analyses and juror investigations whose purpose is to aid in jury selection would not qualify.

Rule 16 prescribes only the minimum discovery to which the parties are entitled.[57] It does not limit the judge's discretion to order broader discovery in an appropriate case.[58] Therefore, it may lie within a judge's discretion to order the disclosure of the results of juror investigations and analyses.

In support of such a motion, a petitioner could point to the importance of discovery in order to impanel a fair and impartial jury, as constitutionally required.[59] An indigent defendant might emphasize the gross disparity in resources available to the defense as compared to those available to the government. A state prosecutor can in effect commandeer the state's police force and a federal prosecutor the Federal Bureau of Investigation to help in the investigation of jurors.[60] Neighbors and coworkers of jurors are more likely to cooperate with state and federal officers than with private investigators, be they professional or amateur. In some instances, information available to the government, such as tax and police records, cannot be obtained by a defendant with even unlimited funds.

These arguments notwithstanding, it is unlikely that a court will permit discovery. As indicated previously, there is not the same tradition of liberal discovery as in civil cases. Many judges will be concerned that the release of information about jurors could lead to their being threatened, bribed, or intimidated. This possibility is of greater concern than in civil cases because the record of many criminal defendants does not inspire confidence as to their willingness to obey legal restrictions, particularly when their life or liberty is at stake. Furthermore, judges will be as sensitive to the need to protect an attorney's work product as they are in civil cases.[61] They may also, as in civil cases, believe that voir dire is adequate to allow an assessment of a juror's impartiality. On the other hand, in the criminal area there is greater scope for constitutionally based arguments in favor of discovery. These will be examined in the next section.

---

[56] *See* Notes of Advisory Committee on Rules, 1974 Amendments.

[57] *Id.*

[58] *Id.*

[59] US Const amend VI. *See generally* **§§2.09-2.12.**

[60] *See* Okun, *Investigation of Jurors by Counsel: Its Impact on the Decisional Process,* 56 Geo LJ 839 (1968).

[61] The 1974 Advisory Committee Notes indicate that the work product exception is retained under Rule 16.

§4.10 —Constitutional Arguments in Favor of Discovery

In the past several decades the United States Supreme Court has developed a body of constitutional jurisprudence respecting discovery in criminal cases. The fountainhead decision was *Brady v Maryland*,[62] holding that the prosecutor's suppression of evidence favorable to an accused, following a request, where the evidence is material to either guilt or punishment, violates due process.[63] The Court has also upheld discovery in favor of the prosecution.[64] These decisions have turned primarily on fair trial–due process considerations.

It must be conceded that the cases decided by the Supreme Court are distinguishable from those seeking discovery of juror-related information. Without discovery of evidence material to guilt or innocence, a defendant would be unfairly handicapped in presenting a defense; without discovery of juror-related information, a defendant could still present a full array of defenses. The defendant's rejoinder would be that the right to present a full array of defenses to jurors selected because of their psychological nonreceptivity to such defenses is meaningless. The underlying right at stake, a fair and just trial, requires an impartial jury. Juror investigations, if not discoverable, threaten to allow the seating of a jury that is less than impartial. The side lacking the ability to conduct juror investigations and community analyses and lacking access to the results of the other side's research may be at a significant disadvantage in its ability to select an impartial jury.

Judicial nonreceptivity to this argument stems in part from a seemingly absolutist conception of impartiality: either a jury is impartial or it is not. There is no recognition that degrees of impartiality may exist, that some juries may be more impartial than others. The jury which results when only one side has access to jury consultants may not be as impartial as the jury where each side has access to such experts. In some instances the diminution in impartiality may make no difference; in others it may alter the verdict. Unfortunately, it is extremely difficult, if not impossible, to determine which of these effects has occurred. Thus it would seem that the preferable practice, to avoid potential unfairness as well as the appearance of unfairness, would be to provide each side with equal access to that information necessary to select an impartial jury.

Most of the decided cases involving jury-related information have been brought by defendants in criminal cases. There would appear no reason, however, why a prosecutor could not seek to discover the jury data in the possession of the defendant. The government as well as the accused is constitutionally entitled to a fair trial and an impartial jury,[65] and the defendant's priviledge against self-incrimination could not be invoked, for the information sought would not pertain to either guilt or innocence.

---

[62] 373 US 83 (1963).

[63] *See also* United States v Bagley, 473 US 667 (1985); United States v Agurs, 427 US 97 (1976).

[64] *See, e.g.,* Williams v Florida, 399 US 78 (1970).

[65] *See, e.g.,* Chicago Council of Lawyers v Bauer, 371 F Supp 689, 691 (CD Ill 1974) ("The right to a fair and impartial adjudication extends not only to criminal defendants

The overwhelming majority of courts have rejected a constitutional right to discover the results of juror investigations.[66] Often, however, their reasoning is cursory.[67] Some courts appear concerned with the unfairness of requiring the government to do the defendant's investigatory work.[68] A related rationale is that the juror studies are protected by the work product doctrine.[69] Some courts reason that the fact that the prosecution may have been in a better position to exercise its peremptory challenges does not mean that the jury which was impaneled was not impartial.[70] Voir dire, say these courts, provides an adequate opportunity to uncover a juror's prejudices.[71]

A few decisions have permitted the discovery of juror-related data.[72] Illustrative is *Losavio v Mayber*,[73] where the police department had for years provided the district attorney with the criminal and traffic records of prospective jurors. The district attorney had consulted these records in making jury selection decisions. As those were not public records, the public defender's office sought but was denied access to them.

The Colorado Supreme Court en banc ruled that fundamental fairness and justice required that the records be discoverable: "[T]he request of the petitioners is eminently reasonable, just and fair. In our view, the reasons advanced for denying these annotated lists of prospective jurors to the public defender's office, or, for that matter, to any defense attorney, are completely devoid of merit."[74] The court rejected the argument that the records in question were

---

but also to the government and through it to society"), *revd on other grounds*, 522 F2d 242 (7th Cir 1975), *cert denied*, 427 US 912 (1976). *See generally* **§§2.09-2.11.**

[66] *See, e.g.*, United States v Harris, 542 F2d 1283 (7th Cir 1976); United States v Falange, 426 F2d 930, 932-33 (2d Cir), *cert denied*, 400 US 906 (1970); United States v Costello, 255 F2d 876, 884 (2d Cir), *cert denied*, 375 US 937 (1958); Best v United States, 184 F2d 131 (1st Cir 1950), *cert denied*, 340 US 939 (1951); Spranger v Indiana, 498 NE2d 931 (Ind 1986). Further cases are collected in Note, *The Constitutional Need for Discovery of Pre-Voir Dire Juror Studies*, 49 S Cal L Rev 569, 602 n 34 (1976).

[67] *See, e.g.*, Commonwealth v Galloway, 231 Pa Super 69, 352 A2d 518 (1975); Enriquez v Texas, 429 SW2d 141 (Tex Crim App 1968).

[68] *See, e.g.*, Florida v Crawford, 257 So 2d 898 (Fla 1972).

[69] *See, e.g.*, Slinker v State, 344 So 2d 1264 (Ala Crim App 1977); People v Heard, 58 Mich App 312, 227 NW2d 331 (1975).

[70] United States v Costello, 255 F2d 876 (2d Cir), *cert denied*, 400 US 906 (1970); Hamer v United States, 259 F2d 274 (9th Cir 1958). *See also* People v Brawley, 1 Cal 3d 277, 461 P2d 361, 82 Cal Rptr 161 (1969) (no error in refusing discovery where prosecutor's information on jurors would not have furnished basis for challenge for cause).

[71] *See, e.g.*, Hamer v United States, 259 F2d 274, 280 (9th Cir 1958); People *ex rel* Keller v Superior Court, 175 Cal App 2d 830, 1 Cal Rptr 55 (1959). *See also* State v Holmes, 347 So 2d 221 (La 1977).

[72] *E.g.*, Losavio v Mayber, 178 Colo 184, 496 P2d 1032 (1972); People v Aldridge, 47 Mich App 639, 209 NW2d 796 (1973). *See also* California v Murtishaw, 29 Cal 3d 733, 631 P2d 446, 176 Cal Rptr 738 (1981), *cert denied*, 455 US 922 (1982).

[73] 178 Colo 184, 496 P2d 1032 (1972).

[74] *Id* at 188, 496 P2d at 1034. *Accord* People v Aldridge, 47 Mich App 639, 209 NW2d

"internal matters" as well as that they were protected "work products." The court also refused to credit the unspoken assumption of the state that the public defender's office could not be trusted with the information; the court was unwilling to presume that members of the bar, who were officers of the court, would act illegally or unethically.

Losavio highlights why defendants seek discovery of juror information used by prosecutors in making selection decisions. The police records available to the district attorney were not public records and were therefore not readily available to the defense. It was therefore not a case of a defendant sitting idly by while the prosecutor did all the work and then obtaining the fruits of the prosecutor's labors; the defendant lacked access to the raw materials to perform his own labors.

Nor were the police records which were sought the product of the prosecutor's thought processes or opinions. They contained neutral data compiled by state officials. The situation is quite different from one in which the defendant seeks the district attorney's ratings of jurors based on an evaluation of police records; in such a case a work product argument would have more merit.

The due process–fair trial analysis of the *Losavio* court draws further support from the constitutional right to an impartial jury.[75] The right to an impartial jury has been incorporated into the fourteenth amendment and is thereby binding on the states.[76] A jury composed of persons subconsciously biased toward the state is arguably not impartial. Indeed, the Supreme Court has maintained that one of the vital functions of the jury in a criminal case is to protect the defendant against the "overzealous or mistaken prosecutor."[77] Pro-prosecution jurors will find it more difficult to perform this function. They may also find it more difficult to exercise their power of nullification[78] when it is appropriate to do so. But without discovery of the juror information available to the prosecutor, the defense will be unable to determine a juror's subconscious biases. This argument, of course, depends on convincing the court that voir dire is inadequate to reveal juror bias and that alternative methods of discovering bias are not feasible. As indicated previously, most courts are not convinced of either point.

If discovery of juror-related information is to be allowed, two qualifications seem appropriate. The first is a requirement of mutuality. Each side should have equal access to the research results of the other. Both prosecutors and accuseds in criminal cases, and plaintiffs and defendants in civil cases, have a right to a fair trial and an impartial jury. Stated another way, nobody has an interest in the seating of a biased jury.

The second qualification relates to the work product doctrine, whose purpose is to protect the thought processes of the lawyer. One side should not

---

796, 798 (1973) ("Our evaluation is formed upon the concept of fundamental fairness rather than upon the current underpinnings of criminal discovery").

[75] US Const, amend VI. *See generally* **§§2.09-2.12.**

[76] Duncan v Louisiana, 391 US 145 (1968).

[77] *Id* 530.

[78] See **§2.20.** for a discussion of jury nullification in criminal cases.

be able to stand by and thereafter discover the research and analysis of a more diligent opposing counsel.[79] As applied to juror-related information, the work product doctrine arguably would permit discovery of the raw data but not the analyses of the data made by either the investigators or the attorney who hired them.[80] This is a sensible and reasonable compromise, for it is the compilation of the data which is time-consuming and expensive, and which cannot be duplicated by the side with meager resources. On the other hand, the data can be analyzed by an attorney, even if some self-education or consultation may be required.

Allowance of discovery of the raw data generated by social scientists and jury investigators is the most straightforward way to neutralize any disadvantage in jury selection which would result from a disparity of resources. Discovery might, of course, have an inhibitory effect on the trend toward use of jury consultants, since the advantage to be gained might not be worth the expense. Such a development would not necessarily be salutary, for, if properly used, juror investigations and analyses provide the best hope for seating a truly impartial jury.

One advantage to authorizing discovery of juror-related information is that it allows the court to sidestep thorny legal questions, such as whether a court has the authority to bar juror investigations or whether a jury selected by the use of social science methodology comports with the constitutional requirement of impartiality. The most serious legal issue, the equal protection ramifications of the disparate access to social scientists, also disappears. And at least in theory both sides will be best positioned to select an impartial jury.

---

[79] *See* People v Aldridge, 47 Mich App 639, 209 NW2d 796 (1973).

[80] *See* People v Heard, 58 Mich App 312, 227 NW2d 331 (1975).

5 Mock and Shadow Juries

§5.01 Introduction

Community/demographic surveys[1] are designed to provide insight into the thinking of community members. Pretrial investigations of the venire[2] do the same in respect to prospective jurors. The weakness in both approaches, however, is that neither those sampled in the survey nor the members of the venire have been exposed to the case in a meaningful way: not to the evidence; not to the witnesses; not to the arguments of counsel; and not to the instructions of the judge. At best, and this applies only to those in the community survey, they have been exposed to a summarized version of the facts. How these more particularized variables will affect respondents is inferred from general knowledge of their values, attitudes, and personality characteristics. In the case of community interviews there are also respondents' reactions to questions about the case.

---

[1] *See generally* **ch 3.**

[2] *See generally* **ch 4.**

The most effective means of discovering prior to trial how an actual jury will respond to the case when exposed to the full panoply of variables which will emerge at trial is to hold a mock trial. A mock trial serves a function similar to the testing of a product on a local level before its introduction on a national scale. Both provide feedback at a time when changes in marketing strategy are still possible.

In a mock trial persons drawn from the community are exposed to a preview of the trial. The mock jurors listen to the same opening statements, evidence, and arguments that will be presented in court. They are instructed by a person playing the role of the judge. They deliberate to verdict as would an actual jury. The major difference is that the opposition's side, both its witnesses and attorney, will be presented through actors representing the principals rather than, for obvious reasons, the principals themselves. In order to gain the maximum benefit from the mock trial, however, the opposition's case should be presented as vigorously and persuasively as possible.

The deliberations of the mock jurors can be videotaped for future review. The lawyer wants to identify those issues which caused the mock jurors concern and generated debate. Interaction patterns which developed among the mock jurors can be profitably analyzed. In addition to videotaping, it is useful for the lawyer to discuss the case with the mock jurors after their deliberations. Mock jurors can provide a consumer perspective as to how the client's case can be strengthened. By correlating demographic, personality, and attitudinal data obtained from mock jurors with their views during deliberations, the lawyer can refine previously constructed juror profiles.

Although it will be more time-consuming and expensive, a series of mock trials will produce more reliable results than a single such trial. Different arguments and approaches can be tried to determine which will be the most effective.

A mock trial allows an attorney to ascertain the reactions to the case of a representative sample of the community prior to trial. The attorney obtains direct feedback from the mock jurors about the strength of the client's case, the effectiveness of the witnesses, and the persuasiveness of the attorney's presentation at a point when trial strategy can still be altered; at trial it is usually too late. Nonetheless, the attorney during trial would welcome the kind of feedback provided by the mock jury. While wholesale redefinition of the theory of the case may be impossible, strategic refinements, changes in emphasis, and modulation in style may not.

How to obtain such feedback? A lawyer is ethically barred from contacting the jurors. If it were scientifically possible, the lawyer would discuss the case with clones of the jurors. The closest approximation in the real world to clones is the shadow jury. Shadow jurors are persons recruited because of their similarity, in terms of values, demographics, and personal characteristics, to the actual jurors. The shadow jurors sit in the gallery and listen to the evidence. They follow whatever instructions the judge gives to the actual jury. The critical difference between the actual and shadow jury is that during recesses and overnight breaks the lawyer is free to meet with the shadow jurors and ascertain their reactions to the events of the trial. This information can prove invaluable in shaping trial strategy. The present chapter examines the use of mock and shadow juries.

§5.02 Mock Trials—Selecting the Jurors

Choosing jurors for a mock trial presents problems similar to those encountered in choosing a sample for a community survey.[3] As the goal is to approximate trial conditions as closely as possible, the mock jurors should be from the jurisdiction in which the case is to be tried and have the qualifications required for jury service in that jurisdiction. Those disqualified from jury service should not be selected for the mock jury. If certain groups in the community, such as doctors, lawyers, and police, are allowed to and routinely do exempt themselves from jury duty, these groups, too, should not be included on the mock jury. Nor, obviously, should members of the venire, if known. If the attorney has already investigated the venire, mock jurors should be sought who share common characteristics with its members.[4]

The mock jury should include persons predicted to be hostile to the client's case, as well as those expected to be receptive. Some hostile jurors may, unknown, slip onto the jury; or the lawyer may lack sufficient peremptory challenges to remove all jurors predicted to be hostile. The mock trial allows the lawyer to explore potential lines of argument that might appeal to jurors predicted to be hostile.

The mock jury should be the size of the jury which will hear the case, as the group dynamics of juror interaction may vary with size. Thus, depending on the law in the jurisdiction, the mock jury may have between six and twelve members.[5]

The lawyer should obtain demographic, attitudinal, and socio-psychological data from the mock jurors through either a questionnaire or interview. The data can be correlated with views expressed by individual mock jurors in their deliberations. Using this information the lawyer can refine the juror profiles developed from the community/demographic survey.[6]

The mock jurors should not be told which side has recruited them; such knowledge might impair their objectivity. The mock jurors should also be required to sign a pledge of confidentiality. It would not be helpful if a mock juror disclosed counsel's arguments and strategies to the opposing side.

In choosing a jury for a mock trial, an attorney must decide whether to conduct a mock voir dire. Voir dire furthers the goal of duplicating trial conditions

---

[3] *See* **§3.04.**

[4] Some attorneys have recruited mock jurors by calling unemployment offices and specifying the characteristics they seek in the mock jurors. Although at first blush this approach might seem to exclude those in the higher socio-economic strata, the latter often successfully evade jury duty anyway. In major cities a jury consultant firm may be available to assemble a mock jury. *See* Gidmark, *The Verdict on Surrogate Jury Research,* 74 ABAJ 82 (Mar 1, 1988).

[5] For a discussion of jury size, see **§§2.13-2.16.**

[6] *See* **§3.08.**

as much as possible, but is time-consuming. Failure to conduct voir dire, on the other hand, risks including persons on the mock jury who would be challenged peremptorily or for cause at the actual trial. The attorney also loses the opportunity to test reactions to the planned voir dire. A possible compromise is to make a few general inquiries designed to reveal clearly disqualifying characteristics while not engaging in the searching voir dire one might employ at trial.

§5.03 —Conducting the Mock Trial

It is important to create a trial atmosphere. Mock jurors begin with the handicap that they know that their decision will not actually affect other human beings. Their "verdict" will not cost a defendant life, liberty, or property. As a result they may not take their task as seriously as will the actual panel. Fortunately, the drama of a trial, even a mock trial, is usually sufficiently absorbing that the jurors soon forget the artificiality of the circumstances. Nevertheless, attempting to duplicate trial conditions is important in order that the mock jurors be exposed to the same stimuli as the actual jury.

The goal of verisimilitude has important implications for the conduct of the mock trial. The physical environment should resemble a courtroom. Some attorneys have been known to construct their own mock courtroom; others have arranged to use actual courtrooms after hours. The party represented by the attorney should be present, and an individual should be conscripted to play the role of the opposing party. There should be an attorney for each side rather than one attorney who represents both sides. The attorney for the opposition might be another member of the firm who is familiar with the case. A person knowledgable about law should be recruited to play the role of judge, so as to allow evidentiary objections to be entertained, as they would at the actual trial.

Some attorneys who conduct mock trials present a summary of each side's evidence or a videotape. These approaches have several disadvantages compared to the presentation of actual witnesses. First, the goal of duplicating trial conditions is defeated. Attorney summaries or videotapes may smooth over what would be rough edges in a witness's testimony. The mock jury is deprived of the opportunity to judge the credibility of the witnesses. Summaries and videotapes also lack the immediacy of live testimony.[7]

The attorney who does not present witnesses to the mock jury also loses a unique opportunity to see how the witnesses will perform under courtroom conditions. Most attorneys will go over a witness's testimony with the witness before trial and perhaps conduct a simulated direct and cross-examination. But this simulation, often in the calm of the attorney's office, may lack the tension

---

[7] An exception from this approach may be taken with the witness whose testimony will be presented at trial by deposition or videotape. If more than one mock trial is to be held the lawyer might use the opportunity to compare the effectiveness of live testimony by the witness with the use of a deposition or videotaped testimony.

of the courtroom environment.[8] By having the witnesses testify in the mock trial, where they are subjected to direct and cross-examination before jurors and a judge, the lawyer can observe how effective the witnesses are likely to be in court. This pretrial preview is particularly important for the criminal accused. One of the most critical decisions in a criminal trial is whether to have the defendant testify, and it is vital to determine whether the he or she will be an effective witness.

To save time, a summary of the testimony of nonessential witnesses can be read. Other information not likely to be the subject of cross-examination at trial can also be presented in summary form. If the attorney plans to introduce physical or demonstrative evidence at trial, however, this evidence should be presented at the mock trial.

It would, of course, be tactically inadvisable, even if it were possible, to enlist the opposing side's witnesses in the mock trial. An attorney rarely wants to reveal cross-examination strategy prior to trial. The advantage of surprise would be lost, and the witness would be afforded the opportunity to consult with opposing counsel as to how most effectively to respond to the cross-examination. Nor could the witness's testimony in the mock trial be introduced at the trial for impeachment purposes, for it would not have been given under oath. To use the other side's witnesses in a mock trial without informing opposing counsel might also be deemed improper or sharp practice. Thus, while there are significant advantages to using one's own witnesses in a mock trial, the opposite is true in regard to the opposing side's witnesses. Actors, not necessarily professional, can be recruited to play the role of the opposition's witnesses.

Care must be taken to fairly and vigorously present the opposing side's case. A weak and unconvincing presentation may yield a favorable verdict from the mock jury but will not further the goal of trial preparation and, worse, may induce a false sense of confidence. It is therefore critical to fully analyze the opposition's arguments and to present its case in the most persuasive light possible.

Following presentation of the evidence, each side should make a closing argument to the mock jury. The mock judge should then instruct the jury. In most cases an attorney will know or have a fairly good idea of what the content of those instructions will be.

§5.04 —Observing the Deliberations of the Mock Jury

A mock trial helps attorneys and witnesses prepare for trial. It also allows an attorney to ascertain third-party reactions to the merits of the case. To achieve this objective, the mock jurors should deliberate as would a trial jury.

---

[8] Some attorneys do attempt to simulate the courtroom environment during witness preparation by, for example, taking the witness to the courthouse when it is not in use, sitting the juror in the witness box, and then conducting a sample direct and cross-examination.

The attorney should not be physically present during the deliberations but should observe them, if at all possible, through a one-way mirror.[9] Rooms equipped with one-way mirrors can often be found at a local university, where they are used in social science experiments. A law firm which makes extensive use of mock trials may want to construct such a room for the deliberations of its mock juries.

The mock jury's deliberations should also be videotaped. The videotape can be reviewed at the attorney's convenience. Social scientists can be asked to examine the videotape and give their analysis, particularly with respect to the group dynamics which develop during the deliberations.

In reviewing the videotape, there are several features to be noted. What were the key issues for the jurors? As to these issues, what evidence swayed the jurors; what did not? What additional information would the jurors have liked to have been provided? Which witnesses impressed the jurors and which did not? Which arguments of the lawyers did the jurors find persuasive and which were unconvincing? What were the critical influences that led to the verdict?

In analyzing the deliberations, a lawyer needs to proceed on two levels. First, the attorney should identify the views of individual jurors. Second, the attorney needs to be sensitive to the group dynamics of the jury. The individual views of the mock jurors can be correlated with demographic, attitudinal, and socio-psychological data obtained from them. This information will allow the lawyer to refine the profiles of favorable and unfavorable jurors constructed on the basis of community surveys. These refinements are quite valuable for in few community surveys do the respondents receive firsthand exposure to the parties, witnesses, and attorneys.

The group dynamics analysis of the mock jury is important to inform the lawyer as to what mix of jurors is desirable.[10] A trained social scientist will best be able to analyze the interaction patterns which developed on the mock jury.

Following the mock jury's deliberations, counsel should meet with the jurors to debrief them. At the debriefings, the lawyer can further probe their reactions to the case. Issues which may not have been discussed in the deliberations can be identified and explored. It is particularly important to ask the jurors what they felt were the "holes" in the case and what further information they would have found helpful. Finally, the attorney should remind the mock jurors of their pledge of confidentiality and thank them for their assistance.

§5.05 —Utilizing the Results of the Mock Trial

Most of the advantages of the mock trial have already been mentioned in passing. In this section they will be briefly summarized and illustrated with examples from actual cases. There are four primary benefits to be derived from the mock trial.

---

[9] A one-way mirror permits an outside observer to watch events within a room without those within the room being able to see the outside observer.

[10] *See* **§12.02.**

First, the mock trial helps the attorney to formulate trial strategy. Arguments which are well received by the mock jury can be emphasized at trial; those which are unpersuasive can be restructured or abandoned. In one case, for example, a large northern corporation defended a tort suit in a small southern town. Attorneys for the corporation planned to expose the plaintiff's wild and reckless lifestyle, which may have contributed to his injuries. Mock trials, however, indicated that community members would resent an attack on a local resident by an outsider, no matter how justified. The attorneys, switched their emphasis to a more straightforward legal argument and went on to prevail at trial.[11] Sometimes mock jurors will suggest meritorious arguments not previously considered by the attorney.

To explore alternative approaches to the case, some of which may be contradictory or inconsistent, may require more than one mock trial. In its suit against American Telephone and Telegraph Company, attorneys for MCI Communications Corporation conducted several mock trials. In the first, the jurors responded negatively to the argument that AT&T should have to share its telephone lines with its competitors. In a second, the attorneys emphasized AT&T's legal obligations. The second jury had less difficulty in finding AT&T liable. Also, the MCI attorneys discovered through several mock trials that jurors returned higher verdicts when a specific damage figure was not suggested to them. The awards were as high as $900 million when no figure was mentioned, compared to only $100 million when there were allusions to a specific amount of lost profit. The lawyers incorporated these lessons into their trial strategy. The jury returned a verdict of $600 million which, because a violation of the antitrust laws was involved, was trebled.[12]

The average verdict in a series of mock trials is more likely to reflect the verdict at trial than the verdict in a single mock trial. If each of the mock juries returns a low or adverse verdict, the attorney should consider waiving a jury or negotiating a settlement. Verdicts in mock trials often provide an indication of a reasonable settlement figure.[13]

The second benefit of a mock trial is to help the attorney sharpen his or her courtroom presentation. Is this a case where an aggressive posture is required? Is a low-key approach likely to be more effective? These questions can be answered by identifying the approach to which the mock jurors responded most favorably. Many attorneys cannot, and should not, change their natural style. That style, however, can often be modulated in response to the reactions of the mock jurors.

Examining and cross-examining witnesses before mock jurors also helps lawyers. Nonproductive lines of questioning, such as character attacks on the plain-

---

[11] *See* Hunt, *Putting Juries on the Couch,* NY Times, Nov 28, 1982, (Magazine), at 70, 85.

[12] The use of the mock trials in the MCI litigation is discussed in *id* 70.

[13] Opposing lawyers may sometimes agree to present their respective cases to a mock jury and use the mock jury's verdict as the basis for settlement.

tiff in the tort case discussed previously,[14] can be discarded. Nonessential witnesses whose testimony was unconvincing can be dropped.

Third, mock trials can benefit witnesses who will have to testify at trial. The mock trial allows them to experience the pressures of direct and cross-examination under trial conditions. As a result, the witnesses's performance at trial may be improved. Ineffective testimony will alert the attorney of the need to develop ways to strengthen the witness's testimony at trial. One of the most critical decisions in a criminal case is whether to allow an accused with a criminal record to testify; the accused's performance at the mock trial may help resolve this question.

Finally, the mock trial is an invaluable aid in devising a strategy of jury selection. The demographic, attitudinal, and socio-psychological data supplied by the mock jurors can be correlated with their views expressed during the deliberations and used to refine the profiles of favorable and unfavorable jurors. The interactions of the mock jurors give the attorney a glimpse into the group dynamics likely to develop in the jury room.

A case described in the treatise *Jurywork* nicely illustrates many of the benefits of mock trials.[15] A contract between a family-owned local package pick-up/delivery service (the plaintiffs) and a national air freight company (the defendant) had been terminated by the latter. Plaintiffs maintained that the termination was without cause or notice and in violation of the terms of the contract. After terminating the contract, the defendant had locked officials of the local company out of its office, and had seized client lists and company records. The local owners were forced to start over. The defense claimed that their actions were justified by the plaintiffs' lack of diligence in the joint enterprise, to a large extent the result of plaintiffs' efforts to branch into another business. According to the national company, desperate measures were necessary to protect their investment.

Four mock trials were held. Plaintiffs' attorneys originally believed that their strongest argument was that defendants were unjustified in terminating the contract. Mock jurors were not persuaded. They were, however, offended by the lockout, which they thought disproportionate to the plaintiffs' fault. As a result, plaintiffs' attorneys modified their trial strategy. They still sought to show that the defendant's actions were unjustified in light of plaintiffs' management practices, but the emphasis shifted to the egregiousness of the defendant's response and the human costs incurred by the plaintiffs in starting over.

The image of one of plaintiffs' chief witnesses changed as a result of the mock trial. His flashy lifestyle, epitomized by a heavy gold necklace, did not appeal to the mock jurors. He appreciated the need to moderate his image for trial.

The mock trials also altered the plaintiffs' thinking in regard to jury selection. Originally they had assumed that persons who prized an entrepreneurial spirit and individual initiative would be sympathetic to the plaintiffs' position. Analysis of the mock jury's deliberations, however, revealed that persons holding

---

[14] *See* Hunt, *supra* note 11, and accompanying text.

[15] National Jury Project, Jurywork 13-48 to 13-58 (2d ed 1987).

these values were accepting of the cutthroat competition of the business world and were consequently less troubled by the lockout. On the other hand, jurors who placed a high value on ethics, honesty, and fairness in business were upset by the defendant's conduct, which they saw as an abuse of power. Mock jurors who had favorable experiences with small businesses also tended to be sympathetic to the plaintiffs; those that were impressed by the size, status, and superior efficiency of national companies tended to side with the defendant. Furthermore, mock jurors who believed in personal responsibility for life's misfortunes felt that plaintiffs had received their just desserts; those who believed that one could be a victim of circumstances beyond one's control were more sympathetic to the plaintiffs' plight.

At the trial voir dire, plaintiffs' attorneys focused on juror attitudes toward large and small companies, as well as ethics and honesty in business. The emphasis in the case presentation was on the defendant's excessive and unjustifiable retaliation in locking out plaintiffs from their business and the hardships suffered by the plaintiffs as a consequence. The jury returned a verdict in favor of the plaintiffs for 4.7 million dollars, several million of which constituted punitive damages.

§5.06 —The Pros and Cons of Mock Trials

Mock trials benefit attorneys in formulating trial strategy and sharpening their presentations, witnesses by preparing them for the rigors of direct and cross-examination at trial, and social scientists assisting in jury selection by indicating how jurors with varying personalities and attitudes react to the evidence and interact with each other. For these reasons, the mock trial is among the most effective forms of pretrial preparation.

Mock trials do have their limitations, however. Most significantly, they can be extremely time-consuming and costly. Savings can be achieved by not having all witnesses testify or by presenting a summarized version of each side's position,[16] but at the expense of verisimilitude. The less the mock trial resembles the actual trial, the less reliable are the results. Time and costs multiply if more than one mock trial is held. Yet several mock trials may be desirable in order to try out different theories of the case, as well as to avoid a possibly aberrant mock jury. The more mock trials that are held, the more reliable are the results, but the greater the expense.

Favorable mock trial results should not engender overconfidence. Often it is impossible to duplicate the opposition's best case. Not all of its witnesses and their testimony may be known. Its strongest arguments and trial strategy may not be appreciated. Despite the best efforts of the attorney representing the opposing side in the mock trial, it may be difficult to manifest the same degree of zeal as will the actual opposing counsel. Moreover, the person selected to play the role of opposing counsel may simply lack the latter's skill.

---

[16] The use of summaries may be unavoidable in a trial likely to last for weeks or months.

Similarly, since the opposing side's witnesses should not be solicited to participate in the mock trial,[17] those selected to portray them may not be as effective as the actual witnesses.

Subjecting the mock jurors to voir dire is time-consuming and expensive. Unless the attorney does so, however, the composition of the mock jury may differ from that of the actual panel. At a minimum, mock jurors will not have experienced the "conditioning" of voir dire. Many attorneys also use voir dire to establish rapport with jurors and to indoctrinate them; without voir dire, these parameters of the trial will be missing from the mock trial.

Nonetheless, despite these qualifications, mock trials are one of the most valuable aids in trial preparation. When combined with the results of community/demographic surveys and juror investigations, the attorney will be in an excellent position to conduct voir dire, select an impartial and receptive jury, and successfully try the case.

§5.07 Shadow Juries

Mock trials are a useful tool at the pretrial stage. They are less useful at trial. At trial an attorney would ideally like to discuss with the jurors their reactions to the case as it unfolds. Ethical rules, however, forbid extrajudicial communication with jurors.[18] These rules extend to the attorneys in the case, third parties whose actions are under the direction of counsel, and other lawyers.[19]

As a substitute for speaking to the jurors, a few attorneys, often with the assistance of social scientists, have constructed shadow juries. A shadow jury consists of laypersons who sit in the gallery and listen to the evidence. They abide by the rulings of the judge as they pertain to the jury. Thus, if the judge forbids the jurors to read newspaper accounts of the case, or watch television news, or discuss the case among themselves or with third parties, the shadow jurors place themselves under like restrictions. The objective is to create a group of persons who are undergoing the same experience as the jurors.

The critical difference between the actual jury and the shadow jury is that counsel is free to discuss the case with the shadow jury. Following the day's proceedings or during recesses, the attorney can meet with the shadow jurors to ascertain their reactions to trial events. Have the witnesses been persuasive—why or why not? What about the lawyers—has their searching cross-examination destroyed the opposition's witness or induced sympathy for the witness? Have their explanations clarified or confused the issues?

On the not unreasonable assumption that the shadow jurors will react similarly to the impaneled jurors, the feedback obtained from the shadow jury can be used to plot future strategy. An attempt can be made to rehabilitate the witness who did not come across as credible. Complex evidence that may have

---

[17] *See* **§5.03.**

[18] ABA Model Code of Professional Responsibility EC 7-29, DR 7-108 (1980).

[19] *Id.*

confused the jurors can be clarified through additional testimony. The lawyer may be able to modify behavior or demeanor which offends the shadow jurors.

The shadow jury can be used not only to evaluate what has happened to a particular point in the trial, but also to plan future tactics. Lines of direct and cross-examination can be previewed by the shadow jury. Whether the shadow jurors will resent an objection that will deprive them of access to evidence can be discussed. Possible closing arguments can be tried out on the shadow jury for its reactions.

§5.08 —Selecting Shadow Jurors

In order to maximize the value of the shadow jury, its members should resemble members of the actual panel as much as possible. In a science fiction world, the shadow jurors would be clones of the jurors. In the real world, they should share the socio-economic background, demographic profile, and personality characteristics of the impaneled jurors. The assumption is that persons who are similar are most likely to react similarly to the events of trial.

Voir dire and pretrial investigations should provide the attorney with a fairly accurate attitudinal, demographic, and socio-psychological profile of each juror. The attorney then may be able to identify persons interviewed in the community survey who share common profiles with particular jurors and who therefore would make excellent shadow jurors. If this is not possible, such individuals need to be recruited.

§5.09 —An Illustrative Case

The use of a shadow jury in a major antitrust suit against IBM illustrates its potential.[20] A shadow jury which mirrored the demographic and psychological composition of the actual jury was recruited by a social scientist. The shadow jurors were not permitted to ask, and were not told, the source of funding for this project. Each evening the social scientist discussed with the jurors in a neutral, nonpartisan fashion the events which had occurred in the courtroom. The social scientist reported back to the attorney.

Some intriguing insights emerged from the IBM experience. One was that the shadow jurors (and presumably the actual jurors) reached a decision on the merits of the case early in the trial.[21] Thereafter they were most receptive to evidence which supported this decision. Evidence which conflicted with this decision tended to be rationalized away. Thus, as lawyers have long suspected, first impressions are extremely important.[22]

---

[20] *See* Vinson, *The Shadow Jury: An Experiment in Litigation Science,* 68 ABAJ 1242 (Oct 1982).

[21] *Id* 1244.

[22] Many trial attorneys believe that, after jury selection, opening statements are the most critical part of the trial. The experience of the shadow jury gives credence to this position.

A second finding was that jurors, even without discussing their positions on the case, rapidly learned where each other stood.[23] Unspoken and nonverbal cues aided in the process. In a related development, subgroups formed among jurors based on common background and interests. Each subgroup had its own "safe" topics of conversation. Members of the subgroups, however, also tended to influence each other's thinking. Whether this influence was a matter of cause or effect is unclear; one might hypothesize that members of subgroups chose each other in part because of a subconscious awareness of their common positions on the case. An alternative theory suggests that it was simply a case of persons with similar backgrounds and attitudes reacting similarly to the evidence.

The shadow jury experience highlights the importance in jury selection of determining the social groupings which are likely to form on a jury, as well as the views of individual jurors.[24] It is critical to be aware of subgroup formation, for members of subgroups will influence and reinforce each other before and during deliberations. A skilled social scientist may need to be recruited to shed light on potential interaction patterns in a given case.

§5.10 —The Pros and Cons of Shadow Juries

The advantages of a shadow jury have been pointed out in the preceding sections. There are, however, limitations of which a lawyer should be aware; overreliance on a shadow jury at the expense of the lawyer's experience and judgment would be ill-advised.

Shadow jurors may demographically, psychologically, and economically resemble the actual jurors, but they are not the actual jurors. First there is the obvious point that two persons with similar backgrounds, although *more likely* to respond similarly to witnesses, evidence, and arguments, may nonetheless react differently. Second, shadow jurors, unlike their impaneled counterparts, are employed by one side. Even if not told which side that is, perceptive shadow jurors will very likely be able to make an educated guess. This awareness may induce a conscious or subconscious bias which affects their perceptions of the case. Third, shadow jurors are periodically debriefed and questioned by the attorney or a representative, an experience not shared by the impaneled jurors. As a consequence, they have insight into both their own developing views and the attorney's strategy which is not available to the impaneled jurors. Fourth, if the actual jurors suspect the presence of a shadow jury (*e.g.*, because the same twelve persons in the gallery leave the courtroom each time the jury does), they may resent what they perceive as a manipulation of the system and react negatively to the side which they think is responsible. Finally, the shadow jury is not faced with the same often awesome responsibility as the panel; thus they may not take their task as seriously. Despite these qualifications, and the fact

---

[23] Vinson, supra note 20, at 1244.

[24] *See also* **§12.02.**

that they can be very expensive as shadow jurors will expect to be compensated for their time and effort, a well-selected shadow jury can provide a lawyer with better feedback at trial than can be obtained from any other source.

Part III

The Law Relating to Challenges

Overview

The goal of jury selection is to remove from the jury those persons whom the attorney has reason to believe will not be impartial. The term *jury selection* is, however, a misnomer. Parties and their attorneys are not permitted to select the persons whom they want to serve on the jury; they are only permitted to reject (or *de*select) persons whom they do not want to serve.

The legal system allows this process of rejection to occur through the grant to the parties of the right to challenge jurors. Three types of challenge are permitted. In the sequential order in which they are most likely to occur, they are: challenges to the array; challenges for cause; and peremptory challenges. All three types of challenge are recognized in both federal and state court.

In England, where the law of challenges finds its roots, challenges for cause are rare and peremptory challenges have been abolished. Not so in the United States, where the grounds for challenge for cause are fairly wide-ranging and challenges are liberally granted. Although peremptory challenges are not as sacrosanct as they once were, they continue to exist in all American jurisdictions. There is much to be said for these policies—a jury's verdict is more likely to be accepted by both the parties and the public when those most directly affected by the decision have been given a strong voice in the choice of decision maker.

To effectively exercise challenges, an attorney needs to be able to identify those jurors whom it is desirable to have serve on the jury, as well as those whom it is not desirable to have serve. Part II of this book focused on pretrial techniques for identifying into which of these two categories a juror falls. Part IV will address voir dire, in which jurors are questioned about their background and impartiality. The information disclosed should assist the attorney in exercising challenges. The following three chapters, which make up Part III, are concerned with the substantive and procedural law which permits lawyers to remove jurors from the panel. A knowledge of this law is essential. Without it, a lawyer would be hard pressed to prevent jurors who are not impartial or who are otherwise undesirable from serving.

As indicated, there are three types of challenges: challenges to the array, challenges for cause, and peremptory challenges. A challenge to the array (or a motion to quash the venire, as it is also known) is directed not to any individual juror but to all the jurors summoned for service. Often the challenge will find its basis in a violation of the relevant state or federal statute governing jury selection. Statutory criteria may not have been followed, or improper procedures may have been employed. Using the Federal Jury Selection and Service Act of 1968, 28 USC §1861 *et seq,* as a model, the first part of Chapter 6 will examine statutory challenges to the array.

Other challenges to the array are grounded in an alleged violation of the Constitution. The federal Constitution forbids discrimination in jury selection and guarantees a venire which is drawn from a fair cross-section of the community. The courts are concerned with both the rights of the parties to a fair and impartial jury and the rights of the persons wrongfully excluded from jury service. Chapter 6 will also examine constitutional challenges to the array.

Next in chronological order are challenges for cause. Challenges for cause are made to individual jurors. The contention is that something in the juror's background, character, or experience will impair the juror's ability to decide the case impartially. The grant of a challenge for cause lies in the discretion of the trial judge. The law that guides the trial judge may be either statutory, common law, or constitutional. The grounds on which a challenge for cause can be made vary from state to state, and a lawyer should be familiar with local statutes, rules, and judicial decisions. Chapter 7 will analyze many of the more common grounds of challenge for cause.

Peremptory challenges constitute the final stage of the jury rejection process. Peremptory challenges can be made on any basis that a party thinks fitting. Ordinarily, they need not be justified to nor approved by the court. This statement, however, must be qualified in light of a United States Supreme Court decision, *Batson v Kentucky,* which indicates that under certain circumstances the discriminatory exercise of peremptory challenges on racial grounds will run afoul of the United States Constitution. *Batson* will be examined in depth in Chapter 8, dealing with peremptory challenges. Apart from this case and its progeny, there are, in keeping with the basic concept of the peremptory challenge, virtually no legal restrictions on its exercise.

6 Challenges to the Array

§6.01 Introduction

The original English jurors were witnesses. They were selected because of their knowledge of the facts. Accordingly, it was a fairly straightforward matter to determine who should serve on a jury: those familiar with the facts which gave rise to the dispute. As the jury evolved toward a body of citizens not familiar with the facts, new questions confronted the legal system: What qualifications, if any, should be placed on jury service; and how, in a given case, should the legal system choose from among those persons who were qualified for service?

In common law England, after the jury ceased to be composed of witnesses, jurors were chosen by the Crown. Those selected were usually respected members of the community. Property ownership was a prerequisite for service. As a result, juries contained a disproportionately high percentage of members of the upper classes. This disproportionality occurred even if the jurors were chosen at random from those eligible to serve.

The United States was founded on the principle that "all men were created equal" and that merit was not to be equated with class. This democratic commitment was in theory to be reflected in eligibility for jury service. In fact, this commitment was more myth than reality. It was not uncommon to find jury pools that excluded certain classes and were not representative of the community.

Discrimination could be either de jure or de facto. Among the most iniquitous of the de jure restrictions were state statutes which excluded racial minorities, usually blacks, from jury service. More subtle were laws which permitted certain cognizable groups, such as women, to serve, but only if conditions not applicable to other jurors, such as a specific request to serve, were satisfied. These and other discriminatory practices in jury selection have been challenged on federal constitutional grounds which will be examined in this chapter. Where discrimination is established, reversal is automatic.[1]

Even where the criteria for jury eligibility are nondiscriminatory, the potential to skew the composition of the jury may inhere in the procedures used to select the jury pool. Those charged with the actual selection may have the practical, although not the legal, power to exclude classes of persons from jury service. Illustrative is the "key man" system, under which selected community leaders are asked to nominate persons for jury service. From this list a venire will be chosen. The key men may strive to be objective in their selection criteria, but their choices may be limited by their circle of acquaintances. The consequent underrepresentation of poor persons and minorities is hardly surprising. The courts, however, have been more hesitant to invalidate such jury selection practices than they have been to strike down those laws which are discriminatory on their face.[2]

In addition to the courts, Congress and state legislatures have contributed to the democratization of jury selection. It is they, for instance, who have been said to be largely responsible for the decline in the use of "key man" systems.[3] The Federal Jury Selection and Service Act of 1968, 28 USC §1861 *et seq,* pro-

---

[1] *See* Vasquez v Hillery, 474 US 254 (1986); Rose v Mitchell, 443 US 545 (1979).

[2] *See generally* **§6.09.**

[3] *See* United States v Gometz, 730 F2d 475 (7th Cir 1984), *cert denied,* 475 1124 (1986); United States v Hanson, 472 F Supp 1049, 1055 (D Minn 1979); United States v Armsbury, 408 F Supp 1130, 1131 n 1 (D Or 1976).

vides for random, nondiscriminatory selection of jurors. Because it has served as a model for state legislative reform, it will be examined in some depth in this chapter.[4] Individual state systems will not be examined.

Nonetheless, problems remain. Most commonly, the names of jurors have been drawn from the electoral rolls. Voter registration, however, has historically yielded an underrepresentation of minority jurors. Whether this underrepresentation is attributable to racially discriminatory voter registration laws, or discriminatory application of laws neutral on their face, or a failure of minority voters to register is unimportant as far as jury selection is concerned. The end result is that juries do not include minority members in numbers commensurate with their presence in the community. The response of the courts to exclusive reliance on voter lists will be examined in **§6.08.**

Other approaches to jury selection have also proven problematic. Telephone directory listings are, in the case of a married couple, often only in the name of the husband; their use as a source of juror names would discriminate against married women. Furthermore, the use of telephone directories, like the use of driver's license registrations (another possible source of juror names), passively discriminates against those too poor to afford these services. City directories may be limited to householders and, in any event, may not be regularly updated. The continued reliance on the electoral rolls for juror names may be more the product of a lack of a suitable alternative than of a belief in its fitness for the purpose.[5]

Increasingly, officials are using multiple sources to compile their lists of prospective jurors.[6] The utilization of multiple sources, however, gives rise to a new concern: the possibility that an individual's name will appear on more than one list, with the result that the person in question will have a disproportionate chance of being summoned for jury duty. Those in charge of the process will need to take care to eliminate duplicate names.[7]

Improper creation or selection of a jury pool can give rise to a challenge to the array. This chapter will examine the statutory and constitutional standards which inform such a challenge. At common law, where the sheriff was responsible for the selection and summoning of the jury, the sole ground for a challenge to the array was the sheriff's "indifferency."[8] While bias of the person charged with compiling the jury pool or summoning the venire remains a viable basis for a challenge to the array, statutory and constitutional bases of challenge have taken over center stage. It is the latter challenges with which the courts have increasingly been confronted. Many of the relevant cases arise in the context of selection of members of a grand jury. The United States

---

[4] *See* **§§6.02-6.11.**

[5] *See* United States v Kronke, 321 F Supp 913 (D Minn 1970).

[6] *See generally* Kairys, Kadane, & Lehoczky, *Jury Representativeness: A Mandate for Multiple Source Lists,* 65 Cal L Rev 776 (1977).

[7] *See* State v Long, 204 NJ Super 469 499 A2d 264 (1985).

[8] *See* F. Busch, Trial Procedure Materials 41 (1961).

Supreme Court has indicated, however, that the same constitutional standards apply to the selection of grand and petit jurors.[9]

§6.02 The Federal Jury Selection and Service Act of 1968—Goals and Policies

The Federal Jury Selection and Service Act[10] governs jury selection in federal courts. In 28 USC §1861, the major philosophical premises underlying the Act are set forth:

> It is the policy of the United States that all litigants in Federal courts entitled to trial by jury shall have the right to grand and petit juries selected at random from a fair cross-section of the community in the district or division wherein the court convenes. It is further the policy of the United States that all citizens shall have the opportunity to be considered for service on grand and petit juries in the district courts of the United States, and shall have an obligation to serve as jurors when summoned for that purpose.[11]

There are several features of this section worth noting. First, juries are to be selected at random. This requirement of randomness applies to the jury pool and venire, but not to the actual jury that hears the case. Exemptions, disqualifications, excuses, challenges for cause, and peremptory challenges may lead to a jury which is not random in the statistical sense of the term. Moreover, the randomness requirement relates to those who are eligible for jury service, and not the population at large. In 28 USC §1865, to be examined in subsequent sections, Congress has identified certain classes of individuals who are either exempt or disqualified, or who can be excused, from jury service.[12]

Second, juries are to be drawn from a fair cross-section of the community. One court described it this way: The purpose is to provide litigants with juries which are "microcosms of the community."[13] This may be the aspiration, but it is recognized that precise proportional representation is realistically unlikely to be achieved.[14] Only a *fair* cross-section representation is required, and this requirement is deemed to be satisfied so long as no cognizable group is systematically excluded from jury service. This statutory mandate is also a constitu-

---

[9] *See* Vasquez v Hillery, 474 US 254 (1986); Alexander v Louisiana, 405 US 625, 626 n 3 (1972).

[10] 28 USC §1861 *et seq.*

[11] *Id* §1861.

[12] *See* **§§6.04-6.06.**

[13] United States v Perez-Hernandez, 672 F2d 1380, 1385 (11th Cir 1982).

[14] *See* United States v Test, 550 F2d 577 (10th Cir 1976). *See also* Swain v Alabama, 380 US 202 (1965); Thiel v Southern Pac Co, 328 US 217, 220 (1946).

tional requirement.[15] It is within the constitutional context that the cross-section requirement has been judicially analyzed. For this reason discussion of its parameters will be deferred to the sections focusing on the constitutional right.[16] At this juncture it might simply be observed that there is no statutory or constitutional requirement that petit juries actually mirror the community and the various subgroups in it.[17]

Third, the jury is to be drawn from the district or division wherein the court convenes. This is a codification of the common law rule that jurors be from the vicinage.[18] It also echoes the constitutional guaranty that the jury be drawn from "the state and district wherein the crime shall have been committed."[19]

Fourth, all citizens are to have an equal opportunity to be considered for jury duty. This policy should not be taken literally. Certain classes of citizens are in fact disqualified from service.[20] Nonetheless, 28 USC §1861 makes clear that it is not solely the rights of the litigants which are at stake; there is also the right of a citizen to be considered for jury service. Not everyone has the right to serve on a jury, but everyone does have the right to be considered for service. Thus, even though no party may have been injured by improper jury selection, there is injury to those denied the opportunity for service, as well as injury to the system itself.[21]

Fifth, 28 USC §1861 indicates that citizens have an obligation to serve as jurors. Excuses from jury service, however, particularly for hardship, are commonplace. Nevertheless, this express statutory policy suggests that requests for excuses should be carefully screened and sparingly granted.

Although 28 USC §1861 may be thought to represent only a statement of policy, such a crimped reading is not warranted. As discussed in a subsequent section, nonsubstantial violations of the Act do not result in redress.[22] Congress has left to the courts the determination of whether a violation is substantial. In determining the substantiality of a violation, a court will balance the seriousness of the violation against the goals set out in §1861.[23]

The statutory requirement of random selection is designed in part to eliminate discrimination in jury selection. Nevertheless, in a separate statutory section, 28 USC §1862, a congressional policy against discrimination in jury

---

[15] *See* Taylor v Louisiana, 419 US 522 (1975).

[16] *See* **§§6.13-6.19.**

[17] Taylor v Louisiana, 419 US 522, 538 (1975); Swain v Alabama, 380 US 202, 208 (1965).

[18] Vicinage is discussed in §2.02.

[19] US Const amend VI.

[20] These are identified in 28 USC §1865 and are discussed in **§6.04.**

[21] Abbott v Mines, 411 F2d 353 (6th Cir 1969). *See also* Carter v Jury Commn, 396 US 320 (1970) (class action by members of group allegedly discriminated against in regard to jury selection). *See generally* **§§6.11, 6.14.**

[22] *See* **§6.11**

[23] *See* United States v Savides, 787 F2d 751 (1st Cir 1986); United States v Brummitt, 665 F2d 521 (5th Cir 1981), *cert denied,* 456 US 977 (1982); United States v Jenison, 485 F Supp 655 (SD Fla 1979).

selection is explicitly set out: "No citizen shall be excluded from service as a grand or petit juror in the district courts of the United States or in the Court of International Trade on account of race, color, religion, sex, national origin, or economic status."[24]

§6.03 —Jury Plans under the Federal Act

Each federal district court is charged with the implementation of the policies set out in 28 USC §§1861 and 1862. Congress opted not to impose a uniform plan, but left to each district court the responsibility for devising and putting into operation its own written plan for complying with the congressional mandate.[25] The plan had to be approved by a reviewing panel.[26] The reviewing panel could reject the plan if it determined that it failed to comply with the congressional mandate.[27] If so, the panel had to state the perceived deficiencies in the plan. The district court then had to present an alternative plan which would rectify those deficiencies.[28] The district court at all times retained the power to modify the plan.[29]

Although Congress declined to impose a uniform plan, it did provide for mandatory guidelines. 28 USC §1863(b) required that the district plan *shall:*

> (1) either establish a jury commission, or authorize the clerk of the court, to manage the jury selection process. If the plan establishes a jury commission, the district court shall appoint one citizen to serve with the clerk of the court as the jury commissioner: *Provided, however,* that the plan for the District of Columbia may establish a jury commission consisting of three citizens. The citizen jury commissioner shall not belong to the same political party as the clerk serving with him. The clerk or the jury commission, as the case may be, shall act under the supervision and control of the chief judge of the district court or such other judge of the district court as the plan may provide. Each jury commissioner shall, during his tenure in office, reside in the judicial district or division for which he is appointed. Each citizen jury commissioner shall receive compensation to be fixed by the district court plan at a rate not to exceed $50 per day for each day necessarily employed in the performance of his duties, plus reimbursement for travel, subsistence, and other necessary expenses incurred by him in the performance of such duties. The Judicial Conference of the United States may establish standards for allowance of travel, subsistence, and other necessary expenses incurred by jury commissioners.

---

[24] 28 USC §1862.

[25] 28 USC §1863(a).

[26] *Id.* The panel consisted of the judicial council of the circuit and the chief judge of the district or his or her designee.

[27] *Id.*

[28] *Id.*

[29] *Id.*

(2) specify whether the names of prospective jurors shall be selected from the voter registration lists or the lists of actual voters of the political subdivisions within the district or division. The plan shall prescribe some other source or sources of names in addition to voter lists where necessary to foster the policy and protect the rights secured by sections 1861 and 1862 of this title. The plan for the District of Columbia may require the names of prospective jurors to be selected from the city directory rather than from voter lists. The plans for the districts of Puerto Rico and the Canal Zone may prescribe some other source or sources of names of prospective jurors in lieu of voter lists, the use of which shall be consistent with the policies declared and rights secured by sections 1861 and 1862 of this title.

(3) specify detailed procedures to be followed by the jury commission or clerk in selecting names from the sources specified in paragraph (2) of this subsection. These procedures shall be designed to ensure the random selection of a fair cross section of the persons residing in the community in the district or division wherein the court convenes. They shall ensure that names of persons residing in each of the counties, parishes, or similar political subdivisions within the judicial district or division are placed in a master jury wheel; and shall ensure that each county, parish, or similar political subdivision within the district or division is substantially proportionally represented in the master jury wheel for the judicial district, division, or combination of divisions. For the purpose of determining proportional representation in the master jury wheel, either the number of actual voters at the last general election in each county, parish, or similar political subdivisions, or the number of registered voters if registration of voters is uniformly required throughout the district or division, may be used.

(4) provide for a master jury wheel (or a device similar in purpose and function) into which the names of those randomly selected shall be placed. The plan shall fix a minimum number of names to be placed initially on the master jury wheel, which shall be at least one-half of 1 per centum of the total number of persons on the lists used as a source of names for the district or division; but if this number of names is believed to be cumbersome and unnecessary, the plan may fix a smaller number of names to be placed on the master wheel, but in no event less than one thousand. The chief judge of the district court, or such other district judge as the plan may provide, may order additional names to be placed on the master jury wheel from time to time as necessary. The plan shall provide for periodic emptying and refilling of the master jury wheel at specified times, the interval for which shall not exceed four years.

(5) Specify those groups or occupational classes whose members shall, on individual request therefor, be excused from jury service. Such groups or classes shall be excused only if the district court finds, and the plan states, that jury service by such class or group would entail undue hardship or extreme inconvenience to the members thereof, and excuse of

members thereof would not be inconsistent with sections 1861 and 1862 of this title.

(6) specify those groups of persons or occupational classes whose members shall be barred from jury service on the ground that they are exempt. Such groups or classes shall be exempt only if the district court finds, and the plan states, that their exemption is in the public interest and would not be inconsistent with sections 1861 and 1862 of this title. The plan shall provide exemption of the following persons: (i) members in active service in the Armed Forces of the United States; (ii) members of the fire or police departments of any State, district, territory, possession, or subdivision thereof; (iii) public officers in the executive, legislative, or judicial branches of the Government of the United States, or any State, district, territory, or possession or subdivision thereof, who are actively engaged in the performance of official duties.

(7) fix the time when the names drawn from the qualified jury wheel shall be disclosed to parties and to the public. If the plan permits these names to be made public, it may nevertheless permit the chief judge of the district court, or such other district court judge as the plan may provide, to keep these names confidential in any case where the interests of justice so require.

(8) specify the procedures to be followed by the clerk or jury commission in assigning persons whose names have been drawn from the qualified jury wheel to grand and petit jury panels.[30]

To summarize, the statutory guidelines provided for a mechanism for the selection of jurors (the jury commission or the clerk of court), a source from which juror names were to be drawn (voter registration lists or the lists of actual voters), procedures for selecting and assigning jurors, and a general description of those persons who would be excused or exempt from jury service. Voter registration lists (state, local, and federal) must be made available to the jury commission or clerk of the court for the purpose of discharging the responsibilities of the statute.[31]

§6.04 —Disqualifications under the Federal Act

The ideal of 28 USC §1861 envisions a jury drawn at random. Congress, however, recognized that it would be inadvisable for certain classes of individuals to serve. Accordingly, it granted to the chief judge of the district court (or such other district court judge as provided by the district's jury plan) the authority to declare a person unqualified for jury duty.[32] The determination

---

[30] *Id* §1863(b).

[31] *Id* §1863(d).

[32] 28 USC §1865.

of whether a person is qualified to serve is to be based on the information provided on the juror qualification form and other "competent evidence."[33]

The criteria which disqualify individuals from jury service eligibility are set forth in 28 USC §1865(b):

> In making such determination the chief judge of the district court, or such other district court judge as the plan may provide, shall deem any person qualified to serve on grand and petit juries in the district court unless he-
>
> (1) is not a citizen of the United States eighteen years old who has resided for a period of one year within the judicial district;
>
> (2) is unable to read, write, and understand the English language with a degree of proficiency sufficient to fill out satisfactorily the juror qualification form;
>
> (3) is unable to speak the English language;
>
> (4) is incapable, by reason of mental or physical infirmity, to render satisfactory jury service; or
>
> (5) has a charge pending against him for the commission of, or has been convicted in a State or Federal court of record of, a crime punishable by imprisonment for more than one year and his civil rights have not been restored.[34]

The first subsection requires that a juror be eighteen years of age, a citizen, and a resident of the judicial district for a period of one year. Although discrimination on the basis of alienage is generally suspect,[35] the requirement that jurors be citizens has been upheld against constitutional challenge.[36] The requirement in the jury context is said to be justified by the fact that aliens are less likely to be committed to the proper application and enforcement of the laws of the United States.[37]

More problematic is the residence requirement. In the nonjury context, some residence requirements have been sustained,[38] but others have been held to discriminate against persons who have exercised their constitutional right to

---

[33] *Id* §1865(a).

[34] *Id* §1865(b).

[35] *See, e.g.*, Plyer v Doe, 457 US 202 (1982); Graham v Richardson, 403 US 365 (1971).

[36] *See, e.g.*, United States v Gordon-Nikkar, 518 F2d 972 (5th Cir 1975); United States v Armsbury, 408 F Supp 1130 (D Or 1976); Perkins v Smith, 370 F Supp 134 (D Md 1974), *affd*, 426 US 913 (1976).

[37] United States v Gordon-Nikkar, 518 F2d 972, 976 (5th Cir 1975) (quoting Perkins v Smith, 370 F Supp 134, 142 (D Md 1974) (Winter, J, concurring), *affd*, 426 US 913 (1976).

[38] *See, e.g.*, Sosna v Iowa, 419 US 393 (1975) (upholding Iowa one-year residency requirement before filing for divorce).

travel.[39] Significantly, the latter group includes a Supreme Court decision which invalidated a state residency requirement for voting.[40] Since the federal statute contemplates jury panels drawn from the ranks of eligible voters, it would seem that a residence requirement which would be unconstitutional for voting purposes would also be unconstitutional for jury selection purposes. Nonetheless, the one-year residence requirement of 28 USC §1865(b)(1) has withstood constitutional challenge.[41] In criminal cases courts see the residency requirement as furthering the sixth amendment's command that jurors be from the state and district wherein the crime was committed.[42] The requirement also serves to assure a "substantial nexus between a juror and a community whose sense of justice the jury as a whole is expected to reflect."[43]

The second class of persons disqualified from jury service consists of those not proficient in the English language. If the trial is to be conducted in English, a juror who does not understand the language will be significantly handicapped in rendering an informed verdict. Subsection (2) of 28 USC §1865(b) provides a ready test for measuring a juror's comprehension of English: those persons who are unable to read, write, and understand English sufficiently to satisfactorily complete the juror qualification form presumably will not be able to follow a trial conducted in English. Where a jury has included persons who do not understand English, reversal has been ordered without a showing of prejudice.[44] The mere inability to read and write English, however, should not be disqualifying if the juror can understand spoken English and all the evidence will be oral.[45]

The third class of persons disqualified from jury service consists of those who, because of mental or physical infirmity, are incapable of rendering satisfactory jury service. Mental infirmity is not to be equated with a lack of education or a low level of intelligence. Something more disabling is contemplated. Indeed, a declaration of insanity has been said not to be sufficient to reverse a verdict in which an insane juror participated unless the insanity impaired the juror's ability to understand the issues or fairly deliberate in regard to the verdict.[46]

The test for a physical infirmity justifying disqualification is likewise a functional one. Deafness will be disqualifying if it prevents a juror from hearing

---

[39] *See, e.g.*, Shapiro v Thompson, 394 US 618 (1969).

[40] Dunn v Blumstein, 405 US 330 (1972).

[41] United States v Perry, 480 F2d 147 (5th Cir 1973); United States v Ross, 468 F2d 1213 (9th Cir 1972), *cert denied,* 410 US 989 (1973); United States v Armsbury, 408 F Supp 1130 (D Or 1976).

[42] *See* United States v Duncan, 456 F2d 1401, 1406 (9th Cir 1972).

[43] United States v Armsbury, 408 F Supp 1130, 1134 (D Or 1976) (quoting HR 1076, 1968 US Code Cong & Admin News vol 2, at 1976).

[44] *See* United States v Okiyama, 521 F2d 601 (9th Cir 1975).

[45] *See* Bumpus v Uniroyal Tire Co, 392 F Supp 1405 (ED Pa 1975).

[46] *See* United States v Dioguardi, 492 F2d 70, 78 (2d Cir), *cert denied,* 419 US 873 (1974).

the evidence. Blindness will not prevent a juror from hearing the evidence, but may be disqualifying in a case requiring examination of documents. Other physical disabilities similarly need to be examined on a case-by-case basis.[47]

In contrast, there are some disabilities, such as those which impair physical mobility, which create difficulties in appearing in court. Such cases are more appropriately treated under the head of hardship excuse rather than disqualification.[48] If a disabled juror is able to attend court sessions, and desires to serve, there is little justification for disqualifying the juror.

The final class of persons disqualified from jury service consists of those who have charges pending against them for crimes punishable by imprisonment for more than one year or who have been convicted of such crimes and have not had their civil rights restored. The theory is that such persons cannot be trusted to render fair verdicts. Even if this were not so, it is said that they need to be disqualified in order to preserve public confidence in the "probity" of the jury.[49] While the theory may be valid for a person convicted of a crime involving moral turpitude, it makes less sense in the case of an individual convicted of a crime committed out of principle, such as the draft resister convicted of refusing induction because of a conscientious objection to a particular war.

It has been held that the disqualifications enumerated in 28 USC §1865 are exclusive.[50]

§6.05 —Exemptions under the Federal Act

In addition to those persons disqualified from jury service, the Federal act identifies classes of persons who are exempt from jury service. 28 USC §1863(b)(6) states in relevant part:

> The [jury] plan shall provide for the exemption of the following persons: (i) members in active service in the Armed Forces of the United States; (ii) members of the fire or police departments of any State, district, territory, possession, or subdivision thereof; (iii) public officers in the executive, legislative, or judicial branches of the Government of the United States, or any State, district, territory, or possession or subdivision thereof, who are actively engaged in the performance of official duties.[51]

Although the practical effect of an exemption may be the same as a disqualification, the rationale is quite different. Persons who are disqualified are thought not to be sufficiently competent to discharge the obligations of jury service.

---

[47] For cases and further discussion, see §7.50.

[48] *See* **§6.06.**

[49] *See* United States v Foxworth, 599 F2d 1 (1st Cir 1979). *See also* United States v Armsbury, 408 F Supp 1130, 1134 (D Or 1976) (rejecting the argument that exclusion of felons denied defendant a jury of his peers).

[50] United States v Pellegrini, 441 F Supp 1367 (ED Pa 1977), *affd,* 586 F2d 836 (3d Cir), *cert denied,* 439 US 1050 (1978).

[51] 28 USC §1863(b)(6).

The competence of those who are exempt from jury service is not suspect. Rather, it is felt that the service which they provide to the community is so important that they should be allowed not to have to take time from it to serve on a jury.

The legal status of the person who is exempt from jury service also differs from that of the person who is disqualified. Those who are disqualified are forbidden from serving, regardless of their desire to serve; those who are exempt from service are allowed to serve if they choose to waive their exemption. Furthermore, a disqualification provides a valid basis for a challenge for cause; an exemption does not. An exemption creates a personal privilege in the juror to serve if he or she so desires; it creates no right in either party, or the court, to prevent that person from serving.

It should be noted that 28 USC §1863(b)(5)'s list of exemptions is nonexclusive. It states that a district plan *shall* exempt members of the police and fire departments, members of the Armed Forces, and officers in the executive, legislative, and judicial branches of government. The first sentence of the subsection, however, allows the district plan to identify other groups of persons or occupational classes who will be exempt from jury service. Doctors and lawyers constitute two occupational groups who are commonly exempted: doctors, because their services are believed to be too vital to be spared for jury duty; lawyers and judges, because it is thought that their position and training will enable them to unduly influence the jury. Other groups which have been granted exemptions include accountants, teachers, pharmacists, nurses, dentists, prison employees, and clergy. Some might see ministerial exemptions as violative of the constitutional separation of church and state, but these have been upheld.[52] Child care exemptions have also been upheld,[53] but should be written in gender neutral terms.[54]

In creating categories of exemptions, a district must balance the justification for an exemption against the damage that all exemptions do to the general policy that jurors be drawn from a fair cross-section of the community.[55] This point was underscored by the United States Supreme Court in *Duren v Missouri*:[56]

> [T]he constitutional guarantee to a jury drawn from a fair cross-section of the community requires that States exercise proper caution in exempting broad categories of persons from jury service. Although most occupational and other reasonable exemptions may inevitably involve some degree of overinclusiveness or underinclusiveness, any category

---

[52] United States v Butler, 611 F2d 1066 (5th Cir), *cert denied,* 449 US 830 (1980); United States v Maskeny, 609 F2d 183 (5th Cir 1980).

[53] *E.g.,* United States v Manbeck, 514 F Supp 141 (DSC 1981).

[54] *See* United States v Goodlow, 597 F2d 159 (9th Cir), *cert denied,* 442 US 913 (1979). *See also* Duren v Missouri, 439 US 357 (1979).

[55] 28 USC §1861. *See* Rabinowitz v United States, 366 F2d 34, 55 (5th Cir 1966). *See also* **§6.13.**

[56] 439 US 357 (1979).

> expressly limited to a group in the community of sufficient magnitude and distinctiveness so as to be within the fair cross-section requirement—such as women—runs the danger of resulting in underrepresentation sufficient to constitute a prima facie violation of the constitutional requirement. We also repeat the observation made in *Taylor* that it is unlikely that reasonable exemptions, such as those based on special hardship, incapacity, or community needs, would pose substantial threat that the remaining pool of jurors would not be representative of the community.[57]

§6.06 —Excuses under the Federal Act

The grounds for exemptions and disqualifications from jury service are set forth with some degree of specificity in the federal act. Excuses, on the other hand, are authorized only in the most general of terms. Section (b)(5) of 28 USC §1863 provides that a district plan shall:

> specify those groups or occupational classes whose members shall, on individual request therefor, be excused from jury service. Such groups or classes shall be excused only if the district court finds, and the plan states, that jury service by such class or group would entail undue hardship or extreme inconvenience to the members thereof, and excuse of members thereof would not be inconsistent with sections 1861 and 1862 of this title.[58]

Several aspects of this section are worth noting. First, a group or occupational class needs to be recognized in the district's jury plan as appropriate for excusal from jury service before an excuse can be granted to an individual juror. This limitation, however, has to be read in conjunction with 28 USC §1866(c) which permits a court to excuse a prospective juror upon a showing that jury service would cause undue hardship or extreme inconvenience. The excusal is not permanent, but only for as long a period as the court deems appropriate. At the end of the period, the excused individual again becomes eligible for jury duty. Because each district is permitted to establish its own category of excuses, different districts may, because of the individual needs of the district, establish different categories.

Second, the request to be excused must be made by the eligible juror. 28 USC §1863 does not create a basis for a challenge for cause, and neither the judge nor a party may invoke it in order to remove a prospective juror from the panel. A corollary is that a juror, although falling into one of the groups or occupational classes eligible to be excused, is not under any obligation to request to be excused.

Third, mere membership in a recognized class or occupation is not in itself sufficient to warrant excusal. The trial judge must in addition find that jury service would entail undue hardship or extreme inconvenience. Some members of the designated class may suffer no hardship from jury duty.

---

[57] *Id* 370 (citations omitted).

[58] 28 USC §1863(b)(5).

Finally, excusal must not be inconsistent with the policies of the act favoring random selection, fair cross-section representation, and nondiscrimination. The implication is that requests for excuses should be carefully screened and sparingly granted.

Challenges to grounds for excuses have generally not succeeded. The court in *United States v Eskew,*[59] for example, held that a district plan permitting all persons over 70 and all women with children under 12 to request to be excused did not violate the statute.[60] Hardship excuses based on the distance a juror lives from the courthouse have been upheld,[61] as have excusals to small business proprietors.[62] Students, too, have been held properly excused.[63] A few courts, however, have observed that hardship excuses are likely to result in significant underrepresentation of poor persons on juries, in conflict with the general policies of the act.[64]

If a juror falls within an eligible class or occupational group, the responsibility for determining whether jury duty will entail undue hardship or extreme inconvenience lies within the discretion of the trial judge. Each case must be considered on its merits. The grant of an excuse will be reversed only for an abuse of discretion. Such reversals are rare, as illustrated by *United States v Barnette.*[65] In *Barnette,* the district court granted 245 excusals due to hardship out of 249 requests. Despite the inference to be drawn from these statistics that an overly liberal or even perfunctory standard for granting excuses may have been employed, the appellate court found no error. It specifically noted that the trial judge had evaluated each request on its individual merits.

§6.07 Random Selection of Jurors

The federal act prescribes that jurors be "selected at random from a fair cross-section of the community."[66] Randomness in a statistical sense is not con-

---

[59] 460 F2d 1028 (9th Cir 1972).

[60] *See also* United States v Goodlow, 597 F2d 159 (9th Cir), *cert denied,* 442 US 913 (1979); United States v Briggs, 366 F Supp 1356 (ND Fla 1973); United States v Grey, 355 F Supp 529 (D Okla 1973). Arguably a plan such as that in *Eskew,* permitting those with responsibility for young children to be excused, should be written in gender neutral terms.

[61] *E.g.,* United States v Lewis, 504 F2d 92 (6th Cir 1974), *cert denied,* 421 US 975 (1975); United States v Valentine, 472 F2d 164 (9th Cir 1973).

[62] *See, e.g.,* United States v Blair, 493 F Supp 398 (D Md 1980), *affd,* 665 F2d 500 (4th Cir 1981); United States v Horton, 526 F2d 884 (5th Cir), *cert denied,* 429 US 820 (1976).

[63] United States v Ross, 468 F2d 1213 (9th Cir 1972), *cert denied,* 410 US 989 (1973).

[64] *See, e.g.,* United States v Leonetti, 291 F Supp 461 (SDNY 1968).

[65] 800 F2d 1558 (11th Cir 1986).

[66] 28 USC §1861.

templated.[67] Rather, the concern is twofold: that no identifiable group in the community be systematically excluded from the jury pool; and that every individual in the jury pool have an equal chance of being called for service.[68] In conjunction with the requirement that disqualifications, excuses, and exemptions be based on objective criteria, the requirement of randomness aims at eliminating arbitrariness and discrimination. A summons for jury duty should be the result of chance rather than design. A self-selected sample is not a random sample.[69]

The right to a jury drawn at random is a statutory creation rather than a constitutional command.[70] As such, it is governed by procedures prescribed by the legislature.[71] When these procedures are not followed, a party forfeits whatever statutory right he or she might otherwise have. Thus, the court in *United States v Hawkins*[72] held that although a venire on which preselected names had been placed may have violated the randomness requirement, the defendant's failure to follow the prescribed statutory procedures left him without remedy.[73]

Under the federal act each district court is responsible for generating its own plan for random jury selection.[74] There are two critical stages. First, a pool from which to select jurors must be randomly generated. Second, a procedure that will result in every person in the pool having an equal chance of being called for jury duty must be devised.

Unlike in some countries, in the United States there is no form of universal registration from which a list of all persons eligible for jury duty can be compiled. The most commonly used source for juror names is the rolls of persons who vote or register to vote. Indeed, subsection (b)(2) of 28 USC §1863 provides that a district plan shall "specify whether the names of prospective jurors shall be selected from the voter registration lists or the lists of actual voters

---

[67] *See* United States v Gometz, 730 F2d 475 (7th Cir 1984), *cert denied,* 475 US 1124 (1986); United States v Cabrera-Sarmiento, 533 F Supp 799 (SD Fla 1982); United States v Marcano, 508 F Supp 462 (D PR 1980).

[68] *See* United States v Nelson, 718 F2d 315 (9th Cir 1983); McClendon v United States, 587 F2d 384 (8th Cir 1978), *cert denied,* 440 US 983 (1979).

[69] *See* United States v Gometz, 730 F2d 475 (7th Cir 1984), *cert denied,* 475 US 1124 (1986); United States v Kennedy, 548 F2d 608 (5th Cir), *cert denied,* 434 US 865 (1977). *But compare* United States v Anderson, 509 F2d 312 (DC Cir 1974), *cert denied,* 420 US 991 (1975) (absent showing jury pool was not representative of fair cross-section of community, judge committed no error in asking jurors to volunteer for service beyond period for which they had been summoned).

[70] United States v Hawkins, 566 F2d 1006 (5th Cir), *cert denied,* 439 US 848 (1978).

[71] *Id.*

[72] *Id.*

[73] *See also* United States v Kennedy, 548 F2d 608 (5th Cir), *cert denied,* 434 US 865 (1977).

[74] 28 USC §1863.

of the political subdivisions within the district or division."[75] The use of voter lists is justified on the basis that it will yield a comprehensive list of qualified jurors, or at least a list as comprehensive as could be reasonably expected from any other source. Whether in fact voter lists do so has been a bone of contention, and will be examined in the next section.

Recognition that no one source is likely to include all who are eligible to serve as jurors has led to increasing use of multiple sources. The federal act provides for this possibility, allowing the district plan to "prescribe some other source of names in addition to voter lists where necessary to foster the policy and protect the rights secured by sections 1861 and 1862 of this title."[76] Telephone and city directories, driver license registrations, and membership in civic and other organizations are but some of the supplementary sources of names now used. Care must be taken when multiple sources are utilized, of course, to weed out duplicates lest an individual's chances of being summoned exceed the likelihood to be expected by chance.[77]

Once a jury pool is generated, a method must be devised to ensure that every person in the pool has an equal opportunity for being selected for service. Federal law provides that the names of prospective jurors be placed in a master jury wheel,[78] from which names are selected at random.[79] No doubt the future will see increasing selection by computer.[80] Nonrandom selection of a venire from an initially randomly selected jury wheel constitutes a violation of the randomization requirement.[81] Names may be drawn on a case-by-case basis; or a large pool of jurors may be summoned, with jurors later assigned to particular cases.

The requirement of randomness is a means to obtain a jury pool which is representative of a fair cross-section of the community. It is that, but it may also have independent significance. As stated by the Court of Appeals in *United States v Kennedy,* "otherwise technical violations of the statute constitute 'substantial failure to comply' when they affect the random nature or objectivity of the selection process. . . . A litigant need not show prejudice . . . [or] that the violation tended to exclude some cognizable group. . . ."[82] Although the defendant in *Kennedy,* lost on procedural grounds, the court condemned the use of volunteers to fill in the gaps in the month's jury pool.

---

[75] *Id* §1863(b)(2).

[76] *Id.*

[77] *See generally* Kairys, Kadane & Lehoczky, *Jury Representativeness: A Mandate for Multiple Source Lists,* 65 Cal L Rev 776 (1977).

[78] 28 USC §1863(b)(4).

[79] *Id* §1864(a).

[80] *See* United States v Davis, 546 F2d 583 (5th Cir), *cert denied,* 431 US 906 (1977).

[81] United States v Kennedy, 548 F2d 608 (5th Cir), *cert denied,* 434 US 865 (1977).

[82] *Id* 612.

§6.08 Selection of a Jury Pool—Voter Registration

The federal act indicates that the names of potential jurors should be selected from either the voter registration lists or the lists of actual voters of the political subdivisions within the district or division.[83] The clear implication is that voter rolls are a legitimate and appropriate, if not the optimal, means of compiling a list of prospective jurors. However, Congress recognized that exclusive reliance on voter registration might in some instances be inadvisable. Some groups in a community may not register to vote or may register at a lower rate than would be suggested by their incidence in the community. Congress therefore provided, "The plan shall prescribe some other source or sources of names in addition to voter lists where necessary to foster the policy and protect the rights secured by sections 1861 and 1862 of this title."[84]

It is in the context of this proviso that much of the litigation has arisen. Those who believe that reliance on voter registration fails to yield a representative cross-section of the community have contended that the failure to supplement the voter lists with additional sources of names constitutes a violation of the federal act.[85] Few challenges have been successful.

The logic of the cases finding no violation of the federal act in the exclusive reliance on voter rolls is often questionable. Typically it is stated that citizens who choose not to vote do not constitute a cognizable class.[86] That may be so, but no explanation is provided why a cognizable class should be required if the exclusion of nonvoters yields a jury pool which is unrepresentative of a cross-section of the community. The concept of cognizability comes from the test for determining whether there has been a violation of the *constitutional* requirement that jurors be drawn from a fair cross-section of the community.[87] Some courts have openly stated that the test for a statutory violation is the same as that for a constitutional violation,[88] but such an equating renders the question of a statutory violation redundant.

An alternative rationale based on forfeiture was advanced by the court in

---

[83] 28 USC §1863(b)(2). The District of Columbia, as well as the districts of Puerto Rico and the Canal Zone, are permitted to prescribe other sources of names for jury duty. While the use of either actual voting lists or registration lists is permitted by the statute, use of the former will generally yield significantly fewer jurors than the latter. *See* United States v Coats, 611 F2d 37 (4th Cir 1979), *cert denied,* 446 US 909 (1980).

[84] 28 USC §1863(b)(2).

[85] It has been observed that while additional sources can be used to supplement voter lists, they cannot be used to supplant them. United States v Brady, 579 F2d 1121 (9th Cir 1978), *cert denied,* 439 US 1074 (1979).

[86] *See, e.g.,* United States v Freeman, 514 F2d 171 (8th Cir 1975); United States v Dangler, 422 F2d 344 (5th Cir 1970); Grimes v United States, 371 F2d 709 (5th Cir), *cert denied,* 393 US 825 (1968).

[87] *See generally* **§6.13.**

[88] *E.g.,* United States v Brady, 579 F2d 1121 (9th Cir 1978), *cert denied,* 439 US 1074 (1979); United States v Test, 550 F2d 577 (10th Cir 1976); Foster v Sparks, 506 F2d 805 (5th Cir 1975).

United States v Kronke:[89] "Those who wish to disassociate themselves from the political process by not voting forfeit the right to be selected for jury duty. . . ."[90] The reasoning seems specious: an individual may be so disaffected by the choices offered by the major political parties and the relative impotence of a single vote as to decide not to register; that same individual may see jury duty as an opportunity to become involved in the democratic process in a meaningful way.

The groups alleged to have been excluded from jury service as a result of exclusive reliance on voter lists are as diverse as their reasons for not registering. Blacks and other ethnic minorities are often the focus of the judicial inquiry.[91] Their nonregistration to vote may be attributable to a disaffection with the political process.

Many young persons choose not to register to vote or are unable to register immediately upon reaching voting age; they, too, will be excluded from juror pools based exclusively on voter rolls.[92] Most courts have not found a violation of the federal statute based on the underrepresentation of young persons.[93] The Seventh Circuit Court of Appeals in *United States v Dellinger,*[94] however, recognized the problem and suggested that voter rolls be supplemented in order to redress it.[95]

Some groups will not register to vote on religious grounds. In *Camp v United States,*[96] a Jehovah's Witness maintained that his coreligionists fell into this category. The court responded that those who choose not to vote are not a cognizable class for purposes of the statute.[97]

Somewhat similar are cases involving American Indians. Indians are often more concerned with tribal than popular elections. The courts, however, have rejected proposals to supplement voter registration rolls with tribal rolls.[98] The

---

[89] 321 F Supp 913 (D Minn 1970).

[90] *Id* 914.

[91] *See, e.g.,* Berry v Cooper, 577 F2d 322 (5th Cir 1978) (blacks); United States v Bennett, 445 F2d 638 (9th Cir 1971), *cert denied,* 404 US 1023 (1972) (blacks); United States v Wesivich, 666 F2d 984 (5th Cir 1982) (Hispanics); United States v Brummitt, 665 F2d 521 (5th Cir 1981), *cert denied,* 456 US 977 (1982) (Hispanics).

[92] *See, e.g.,* United States v King, 492 F2d 895 (8th Cir 1974); United States v Ross, 468 F2d 1213 (9th Cir 1972), *cert denied,* 411 US 908 (1973); United States v Kuhn, 441 F2d 179 (5th Cir 1971).

[93] See cases cited at preceding footnote.

[94] 472 F2d 340 (7th Cir 1972), *cert denied,* 410 US 970 (1973).

[95] *Id* 365-66.

[96] 413 F2d 419 (5th Cir), *cert denied,* 396 US 968 (1969).

[97] *See also* United States v Dangler, 422 F2d 344 (5th Cir 1970) (the reason that Jehovah's Witnesses do not serve as jurors is not because they are deliberately excluded but because they are excused at their own request).

[98] *See, e.g.,* United States v Hanson, 618 F2d 1261 (8th Cir), *cert denied,* 449 US 854 (1980); United States v Freeman, 514 F2d 171 (8th Cir 1975).

court in *United States v Freeman*[99] said that supplementation was not required absent a showing that obstacles had been placed in the paths of Indians who desired to vote.

It is difficult to extract from the cases a precise statement of the elements of a prima facie case of a statutory violation. The burden of proof is on the party arguing for supplementation.[100] The more of the following elements which the challenging party can establish, the greater the likelihood of success:

1. A cognizable class other than that of nonvoters (although nonvoters do not become a distinct class simply by virtue of not voting, an otherwise cognizable class, such as blacks, does should not lose its cognizability because its underrepresentation on jury rolls is attributable to a failure to register to vote[101])
2. A jury wheel which is not representative of a cross-section of the community (established by showing a *significant* disparity between a group's presence in the community and its presence in the voter rolls; such a showing is usually a necessary but not a sufficient condition of prevailing)
3. Intentional discrimination, systematic exclusion, or bad faith on the part of officials in registering persons to vote (while the statute does not explicitly require such a showing,[102] it will obviously strengthen a challenger's claim)
4. A history of discrimination in the district, either in regard to jury selection or voter registration
5. Artificial barriers to voter registration, particularly when they have a disproportionate impact on a particular group

Two other factors should also be mentioned. First, the federal statute imposes a general requirement that the alleged violation be "substantial."[103] Thus a nonsubstantial disparity between a group's demographic representation in the community and its representation on voter lists will not lead to a finding of a violation.

Second, a party alleging a violation should be prepared to show an economically viable method of supplementation which will significantly increase the representativeness of the jury pool. As one court observed, state policy is not fostered where excessive costs are required to obtain minimal increases in representativeness.[104] This latter point may provide insight into why such heavy

---

[99] 514 F2d 171 (8th Cir 1975).

[100] United States v Parker, 428 F2d 488 (9th Cir), *cert denied,* 400 US 910 (1970).

[101] *See* United States v Facchiano, 500 F Supp 896 (SD Fla 1980).

[102] *See* United States v Armsbury, 408 F Supp 1130 (D Or 1976).

[103] 28 USC §1867. What constitutes *substantial* is left to the courts. *See* United States v Kennedy, 548 F2d 608 (5th Cir), *cert denied,* 434 US 865 (1977). *See generally* **§6.11.**

[104] United States v Facchiano, 500 F Supp 896 (SD Fla 1980).

reliance is put on voter lists in the first place: It is not because they are perfect by any means, but because they are both the most effective and the most cost-effective means available to achieve representativeness.[105]

While almost all legal challenges to exclusive reliance on voter lists have failed, there have been some notable exceptions. *Broadway v Culpepper*[106] was a class action brought by blacks. Statistics introduced at trial showed that 52 per cent of the community but only 39 per cent of the voter list was black. Evidence was also introduced that when questionnaires were sent to those on the voter list requesting information about their qualifications and willingness to serve as jurors, 40 per cent of the questionnaires were returned as undeliverable. Citing these figures, the court said that absent a showing that the missing 40 per cent were comparable to the 60 per cent who had responded to the questionnaire, the list would not yield a jury pool which was representative of a fair cross-section of the community. The court concluded that supplementation was justified.[107]

§6.09 —"Key Man" Systems

Whereas the use of a voter registration list is the most common method of juror selection, the use of a "key men" system is the most controversial. Certain "key" persons in the community are asked to nominate jurors. From these nominations the juror rolls are composed. While once not uncommon in the federal system, the Federal Jury Selection and Service Act has led, apparently intentionally, to a significant decline in their use.[108] Nevertheless, "key man systems" continue to operate in both federal and state jurisdictions.

The basic criticism of key man systems is that they yield juries which are not representative of a cross-section of the community. The reasoning is as follows: The key men asked to make juror nominations are usually drawn from the ranks of the middle and upper classes. Their task is to identify persons whom they believe will be competent jurors. In doing so, they will tend to nominate persons with whom they are personally acquainted. Their range of acquaintances tends to be skewed toward persons of the some social background as themselves, i.e., persons of the middle and upper classes. As a consequence, poor persons and members of minority groups will not be nominated for jury duty

---

[105] Telephone listings, in contrast, may be in the name of the male member of a married couple and thereby result in the underinclusion of women. Both telephone directories and driver's license registration may discriminate against those too poor to afford these services. City directories may be infrequently updated or inaccurate, and may discriminate against nonhouseholders. *See* United States v Kronke, 321 F Supp 913 (D Minn 1970).

[106] 439 F2d 1253 (5th Cir 1971).

[107] *See also* Berry v Cooper, 577 F2d 322 (5th Cir 1978); United States v Burkett, 342 F Supp 1264 (D Mass 1972); People v Harris, 36 Cal 3d 36, 679 P2d 433, 201 Cal Rptr 782, *cert denied,* 469 US 965 (1984).

[108] *See* United States v Gometz, 730 F2d 475 (7th Cir 1984), *cert denied,* 475 US 1124 (1986); United States v Hanson, 472 F Supp 1049, 1055 (D Minn 1979); United States v Armsbury, 408 F Supp 1130, 1133, n 1 (D Or 1976).

in proportion to their incidence in the population. The resulting juries will not reflect a cross-section of the community.

"Key man" systems of juror selection have generally withstood constitutional challenge.[109] The courts tend to state that they are not per se unlawful, but only so if they fail to meet legal or constitutional standards.[110] Often the issue is one of proof.

There are several focal points in the judicial analysis of key man systems. First, courts will look to see how the key men are chosen.[111] Neutral criteria must be used.[112] The broader the base from which key men are selected, the more likely the key man system will be upheld. In one case where the court found no violation, the key men included religious leaders (ministers, priests, and rabbis), state officials, county court clerks, registers of wills, election supervisors, and labor leaders.[113] A "key man" system is also more likely to be sustained if the key men include members of the group allegedly discriminated against.[114]

A second focal point is the criteria used by the key men in making juror nominations. The criteria must be neutral and consistent with statutory requirements. *Rabinowitz v United States,*[115] although not involving a key man system, is informative. In *Rabinowitz* the jury commissioners supplemented the federal statutory criteria with their own standards of character, intelligence, and ability to understand legal issues. More blacks than whites failed to meet these enhanced standards, and the resultant jury rolls were not representative of a cross-section of the community. Although an intent to exclude blacks was denied, the court said that the jury commissioners must be held to have intended the natural consequence of their actions. The court held the jury selection system invalid.[116] Similarly, a key man system is more likely to be invalidated where the "key men" use inappropriate criteria or criteria which result in the underrepresentation of a cognizable group in the community.

---

[109] *E.g.,* United States v Butera, 420 F2d 564 (1st Cir 1970); United States v Tropiano, 418 F2d 1069 (2d Cir 1969), *cert denied,* 397 US 1021 (1970); United States v DiTommaso, 405 F2d 385 (4th Cir 1968), *cert denied,* 394 US 934 (1969); United States v Duke, 263 F Supp 828 (SD Ind 1967). *See also* Castaneda v Partida, 430 US 482 (1977).

[110] United States v Butera, 420 F2d 564 (1st Cir 1970); United States v DiTommaso, 405 F2d 385 (4th Cir 1968), *cert denied,* 394 US 934 (1969); United States v Valentine, 285 F Supp 957 (DPR 1968). *See also* Castaneda v Partida, 430 US 482 (1977).

[111] *See, e.g.,* United States v Butera, 420 F2d 564 (1st Cir 1970).

[112] *Id.*

[113] United States v DiTommaso, 405 F2d 385 (4th Cir 1968), *cert denied,* 394 US 934 (1969).

[114] *See, e.g.,* United States v Hyde, 448 F2d 815 (5th Cir 1971), *cert denied,* 404 US 1058 (1972) (blacks). *But see* Castaneda v Partida, 430 US 482 (1977) (mere fact members of underrepresented group included among key men not dispositive).

[115] 366 F2d 34 (5th Cir 1966).

[116] *But compare* United States v Duke, 263 F Supp 828 (SD Ind 1967) (fact juror suggesters considered intelligence, common horse sense, and other personal qualities did not render illegal grand jury which returned indictment).

The bottom line is that the key man system must yield a venire which is representative of a cross-section of the community. Precise proportional representation is not required; it will suffice if there is *substantial* representation of all the various groups in the community.[117] Mere token representation, however, may not be enough.[118]

The burden of proof is on those who seek to challenge the "key man" system. Often introduced into evidence are statistical analyses showing that identifiable groups in the community are not proportionally represented in the jury pool. The burden of proof notwithstanding, courts will look critically at key man systems because of their potential for abuse. In addition to those factors already mentioned, others may tip the balance in favor of invalidation in close cases. One is a showing of bad faith. Any indication that there has been an attempt to intentionally or systematically exclude an identifiable group may be fatal.

Another relevant consideration is whether the key men are the sole source of juror names. In *United States v Tropiano,*[119] the recommendations of the key men were supplemented with names obtained from voting lists, as well as city and telephone directories. Likewise, in *United States v DiTommaso,*[120] telephone, city, and county directories and the rosters of various clubs and civic groups provided additional sources of juror names. In both cases the courts upheld the use of the key man recommendations. Summing up, the court in *Tropiano* said that a "key man" system is a practical and reasonable method of jury selection, at least absent a showing that the selection procedure is not a random one or does not produce a jury pool which is a fair cross-section of the community or from which cognizable groups have been excluded.[121]

§6.10 The Qualification Process

The pool of prospective jurors, whether the product of voter rolls, key man recommendations, or other sources, must be winnowed down in practice. Some persons on the original list may be disqualified or exempt from jury service. Others may be able to claim an excuse.

The winnowing process begins with a pretrial questionnaire. A federal statute requires that a juror qualification form be sent to all prospective jurors.[122] The form must be completed, signed and sworn, within ten days.[123] The ques-

---

[117] United States v DiTommaso, 405 F2d 385 (4th Cir 1968), *cert denied,* 394 US 934 (1969).

[118] *Id.*

[119] 418 F2d 1069 (2d Cir 1969), *cert denied,* 397 US 1021 (1970).

[120] 405 F2d 385 (4th Cir 1968), *cert denied,* 394 US 934 (1969).

[121] 418 F2d at 1078-79.

[122] 28 USC §1864(a).

[123] *Id.* A person unable to fill out the form may have another do so.

tionnaire may be followed by a personal interview.[124] The goal is to determine whether a juror is willing to serve, and, if willing, is not subject to disqualification, exemption, or excuse.

Questionnaires can serve a useful function in theory, but in practice they often exacerbate the tendency for poor people and minorities to be underrepresented in jury pools. The same groups which are disinclined to register to vote may also be disinclined to return questionnaires. They also may be more transient than persons in the general population, with the consequence that the questionnaire is less likely to be delivered to them. In *Broadway v Culpepper,*[125] the court, in ordering supplementation of voting lists to select prospective jurors, noted that 40 per cent of the questionnaires that had been sent to potential jurors had been returned as undeliverable. The inference of a nonrepresentative jury pool was strengthened by the fact that blacks were significantly underrepresented in the jury pool relative to their presence in the community.

Broadway v Culpepper can be instructively compared with *United States v Gometz.*[126] In *Gometz* 70 per cent of those who were sent jury questionnaires did not respond. Although this nonresponse rate was far higher than that in *Broadway,* the court found no statutory violation, in part because the defendant had failed to show that any particular group was underrepresented in the jury pool.[127]

The defendant in *Gometz* also challenged the failure to follow up on those who did not respond to the questionnaire. The court said that the issue was not

> whether it would be a good thing to follow up on persons who do not respond to a jury questionnaire or to conduct an investigation of the effect of nonresponse on the representativeness of the jury wheel, or to place jury service on a basis of true conscription, but only whether the act imposes any duty on the clerk or judges of the district court to follow up on the nonresponders.[128]

The court gave a negative answer, at least so long as the response rate was sufficient to generate the number of jurors required for service. The court noted that while the federal act empowered clerks to pursue those who failed to return their jury questionnaires,[129] it did not require them to do so.[130]

---

[124] In the federal system, a person may be questioned at the time he or she appears for jury service, but questioning is limited to matters contained in the questionnaire. 28 USC §1864(a).

[125] 439 F2d 1253 (5th Cir 1971).

[126] 730 F2d 475 (7th Cir 1984), *cert denied,* 475 US 1124 (1986).

[127] *See also* United States v Hyde, 448 F2d 815 (5th Cir 1971), *cert denied,* 404 US 1058 (1972).

[128] 730 F2d at 479.

[129] *See* 28 USC §1864(a).

[130] *See also* United States v Santos, 588 F2d 1300 (9th Cir), *cert denied,* 441 US 906 (1979).

Qualification for jury service may be determined by reference to either subjective or objective criteria. Objective criteria, such as whether a juror is a citizen or has a criminal record, lead to nondiscretionary ministerial decisions on the part of those charged with weeding out persons not qualified for jury service. Subjective criteria, on the other hand, such as being of "good character," allow the decision maker substantial discretion in determining whether a person is fit for jury duty. Courts are more inclined to look with suspicion on a disparity between a group's presence in the community and its presence in the jury pool when subjective criteria susceptible to discriminatory application are employed.[131]

§6.11 Procedural Issues Relating to a Statutory Challenge to the Array

Where rights relating to jury selection are created by statute, the legislature can prescribe procedures which must be followed before a claim of an alleged violation can be heard by a court.[132] In the federal system, key procedures include a showing of standing, the filing of a timely objection, and proof of a *substantial* violation. State laws contain similar, as well as other, procedural requirements which need to be checked by counsel. Noncompliance may constitute a waiver or forfeiture of what would otherwise be a viable claim.

Standing

A party seeking to establish a failure to comply with statutory requirements must initially show that he or she is a proper person to bring the suit in question or, in legal parlance, that he or she has standing. A two-step inquiry is called for: the petitioner must demonstrate a personal injury stemming from the statutory violation; and the petitioner must show that the interest sought to be vindicated falls within the zone of interests protected by the statute.[133] In practice, this standard seems to be fairly liberally construed. One court went so far as to say that "no specialized showing of standing is necessary for a defendant to challenge jury composition as illegal under the federal jury statutes."[134] The federal statute specifically grants standing in a criminal case to both the defendant and the Attorney General,[135] and, in a civil case, to any party to the suit.[136]

---

[131] *See, e.g.,* Rabinowitz v United States, 366 F2d 34 (5th Cir 1966); Sanford v Hutto, 394 F Supp 1278 (ED Ark), *affd,* 523 F2d 1383 (8th Cir 1975); Bonaparte v Smith, 362 F Supp 1315 (SD Ga), *affd,* 484 F2d 956 (5th Cir 1973), *cert denied,* 415 US 981 (1974). *See also* **§6.18.**

[132] *See* United States v Hawkins, 566 F2d 1006 (5th Cir), *cert denied,* 439 US 848 (1978).

[133] United States v Musto, 540 F Supp 346 (DNJ 1982), *affd,* 715 F2d 822 (3d Cir 1983), *cert denied,* 468 US 1217 (1984).

[134] United States v Hyde, 448 F2d 815, 822 N 1 (5th Cir 1971), *cert denied,* 404 US 1058 (1972).

[135] 28 USC §1867(a).

[136] *Id* §1867(c).

The two most troublesome issues relating to standing are first, whether the challenging party must be a member of the group alleged to have been excluded; and second, whether a member of the excluded group may challenge the statutory violation although not party to the litigation. Following the decision of the United States Supreme Court in *Peters v Kiff*,[137] in which the Court permitted a white defendant to raise a constitutional claim that blacks had been excluded from the jury which had convicted him,[138] courts have permitted defendants to raise statutory violations without requiring them to show that they belonged to the groups excluded by the violations.[139] Similarly, United States Supreme Court decisions permitting class actions by representatives of groups excluded as a result of constitutional violations[140] led to comparable lower court decisions in respect to statutory violations.[141]

Not everyone has been granted standing to allege a violation of the federal act. Witnesses before a grand jury have not been allowed to challenge the composition of the grand jury which summoned them.[142] Nor does a defendant have standing to challenge a grand jury other than the one that indicted him or in some other way took action against him.[143]

Timely Objection

In both civil and criminal cases, a motion to stay the proceedings[144] because of an alleged violation of the federal act must be filed "before the voir dire examination begins, or within seven days after the party discovered or could have discovered, by the exercise of diligence, the grounds therefor, whichever is earlier. . . ."[145] The motion must contain a "sworn statement of facts" which, if proved, would make out a "substantial" failure to comply with the act.[146]

The statute on its face appears somewhat ambiguous about the applicable time limits, in particular when the violation is not discovered until after voir dire. There is judicial authority, however, that voir dire constitutes the outer

---

[137] 407 US 493 (1972).

[138] *See also* Taylor v Louisiana, 419 US 522 (1975) (permitting male defendant to challenge exclusion of women). *See generally* **§6.15.**

[139] *See, e.g.*, United States v Hafon, 726 F2d 21 (1st Cir), *cert denied*, 466 US 962 (1984); United States v Test, 550 F2d 577, 581 n 2 (10th Cir 1976); United States v Musto, 540 F Supp 346 (DNJ 1982), *affd*, 715 F2d 822 (3d Cir 1983), *cert denied*, 468 US 1217 (1984); United States v Marcano, 508 F Supp 462 (DPR 1980).

[140] Turner v Fouche, 396 US 346 (1970); Carter v Jury Commn, 396 US 320 (1970).

[141] *See, e.g.*, Broadway v Culpepper, 439 F2d 1253 (5th Cir 1971).

[142] *E.g.*, *In re* Archuletta, 432 F Supp 583 (SDNY 1977).

[143] *See, e.g.*, United States v Caron, 552 F Supp 662 (ED Va 1982), *affd*, 722 F2d 739 (4th Cir 1983), *cert denied*, 465 US 1103 (1984).

[144] In United States v Raineri, 670 F2d 702 (7th Cir), *cert denied*, 450 US 1035 (1982), the court said that a motion to stay proceedings was the exclusive procedure for challenging the selection of petit jurors.

[145] 28 USC §1867(a), (b), (c).

[146] 28 USC §1867(d). An oral objection is not sufficient. *See* United States v Green, 742 F2d 918 (11th Cir 1984).

limit for raising an objection.[147] This construction of the statute draws support from legislative history. The relevant House Report states that "challenges must be offered before voir dire begins. And if the challenging party discovered, or in the exercise of diligence could have discovered the grounds for the challenge earlier, the challenging motion must be made within seven days of the earlier date."[148]

The requirement of a timely objection is strictly construed.[149] Courts are concerned that objections not be used as a dilatory tactic. In criminal cases delayed objection can threaten a defendant's right to a speedy trial. After trial, the concern is that jury composition objections provide a "too-ready impeachment of jury verdicts on the basis of . . . afterthoughts suggested by a disappointed litigant."[150] The longer the delay in filing a motion, the less receptive is a court likely to be to it.[151]

United States v Kennedy[152] illustrates the draconian consequences which can flow from a failure to make a timely objection. The court found that the use of volunteer jurors constituted a clear violation of the federal act, but held that counsel's failure to comply with the timeliness requirements of the act resulted in the claim's being forfeited.

A delay in making an objection may be excused if the basis for the motion was not known or could not have been discovered with the exercise of due diligence. This standard has proven quite difficult to meet in practice.[153] As jury plans are a matter of public record, a party's delayed objection to a jury plan is virtually never justifiable.[154] In other instances, a review of the available records would have indicated the basis for an objection, again rendering a tardy motion inexcusable.

In *United States v Silverman,*[155] for example, the jury which convicted the defendant contained a juror who could neither read nor write English. This fact did not come to light until the jury foreman asked the judge what to do about the vote of this juror. Six days later, the defendant moved to dismiss

---

[147] *See* United States v Jones, 687 F2d 1265 (8th Cir 1982); United States v De Alba-Conrado, 481 F2d 1266 (5th Cir 1973); McGinnis v ML Harris, Inc, 486 F Supp 750 (ND Tex 1980).

[148] House Report on the Jury Selection and Service Act of 1968, Pub L No 90-274, §101, 82 Stat 591.

[149] United States v Wellington, 754 F2d 1457 (9th Cir 1985); United States v Bearden, 659 F2d 590 (5th Cir 1981), *cert denied,* 456 US 936 (1982); United States v Hawkins, 556 F2d 1006 (5th Cir), *cert denied,* 439 US 848 (1978); United States v Foxworth, 599 F2d 1 (1st Cir 1979).

[150] Thornburg v United States, 574 F2d 33, 35 (1st Cir 1978) (quoting from Paterman v Indian Motorcycle Co, 216 F2d 289, 293 (1st Cir 1954)).

[151] *See* Thornburg v United States, 574 F2d 33 (1st Cir 1978).

[152] 548 F2d 608 (5th Cir), *cert denied,* 434 US 865 (1977).

[153] *But see* United States v Santos, 588 F2d 1300 (9th Cir), *cert denied,* 441 US 906 (1979) (permitting motion filed after 25 days).

[154] *See* United States v Layton, 519 F Supp 946 (ND Cal 1981) (parties are chargeable with constructive knowledge of the contents of the district's jury plan).

[155] 449 F2d 1341 (2d Cir 1971), *cert denied,* 405 US 918 (1972).

the indictment on the ground that the inclusion of the non-English speaking juror constituted a violation of the federal act. The court acknowledged a possible violation, but held that the defendant's motion was not timely. The court noted that on the juror qualification form the juror had indicated a deficiency in English. Although neither the court clerk nor the judge had caught the problem, the defendant was in effect penalized for not having done so.

A party filing a late motion should explain to the court why the motion could not have been filed earlier.[156] Sometimes the delay results from the need to conduct demographic surveys and statistical analyses to support the claim of a violation. In such circumstances, the better practice may be to inform the court of the forthcoming challenge and the reason for the delay in filing, and to seek an extension of the filing period.[157]

The timeliness requirement imposed by 28 USC §1867 relates only to alleged violations of the federal act. Many grounds for challenge, particularly those relating to the failure of the jury pool to reflect a fair cross-section of the community, also form the basis of a constitutional claim. While a claim of a statutory violation may be foreclosed by a failure to object within the time limits imposed by the act, a claim of the constitutional violation may not.[158]

Substantial Violation

Not all violations of the federal act warrant judicial relief. The statute specifically requires that there be a "substantial" violation.[159] Mere technical violations will not suffice.[160]

Whether a violation is substantial is a matter for the court to decide.[161] Courts tend to read the requirement of substantiality in light of the policies of the act, specifically those favoring nondiscrimination, a fair cross-section representation, and the determination of disqualifications, exemptions, and excuses on the basis of objective criteria.[162] Substantiality has both a quantitative and qualitative dimension: quantitative, turning on the number of potential jurors affected by the violation; and qualitative, turning on the degree to which

---

[156] *See* United States v Layton, 519 F Supp 946 (ND Cal 1981).

[157] *See* United States v Percival, 756 F2d 600 (7th Cir 1985).

[158] *See* United States v Kennedy, 548 F2d 608 (5th Cir), *cert denied,* 434 US 865 (1977); United States v De Alba-Conrado, 481 F2d 1266 (5th Cir 1973); United States v Arnett, 342 F Supp 1255 (D Mass 1970).

[159] 28 USC §1867(d).

[160] *See* United States v La Chance, 788 F2d 856 (5th Cir 1986); United States v Savides, 787 F2d 751 (1st Cir 1986). *But see* United States v Kennedy, 548 F2d 608 (5th Cir), *cert denied,* 434 US 865 (1977) ("Otherwise technical violations of the statute constitute 'substantial failure to comply' when they affect the random nature of the selection process . . .").

[161] United States v Nelson, 718 F2d 318 (9th Cir 1983). *See also* 1968 US Code Cong & Admin News 1794.

[162] *E.g.,* United States v Savides, 787 F2d 751 (1st Cir 1986); United States v Brummitt, 665 F2d 521 (5th Cir 1981), *cert denied,* 456 US 977 (1982); United States v Jenison, 485 F Supp 655 (SD Fla 1979); United States v Tarnowski, 429 F Supp 783 (ED Mich 1977), *affd,* 583 F2d 903 (6th Cir 1978), *cert denied,* 440 US 918 (1979).

the violation frustrates the policies of the act.[163] It is, however, generally held unnecessary for those alleging a violation of the act to show actual prejudice.[164]

Some insight into what constitutes a substantial violation can be gleaned from cases in which the courts have found that a claimed violation was *not* substantial. In *United States v Bearden,*[165] the court held that the use of an improper method for choosing starting numbers, the failure to post a public notice of the selection of starting numbers, the grant of permanent rather than temporary excusals, and some erroneous disqualifications, excusals, and exemptions did not, either individually or in combination, amount to a substantial violation.[166] In *United States v Savides*[167] the use of commercial mailing firms to select juror names, with only sporadic supervision by the clerk, was held not to constitute a substantial violation. The defendant had failed either to identify a specific group which had been systematically excluded or to demonstrate that the result was a jury pool which did not reflect a fair cross-section of the community. In *United States v Davis*[168] the court held that the lack of public access to computerized drawing of juror names, coupled with the delegation of part of the responsibility for juror selection to General Services Administration computer personnel, was not a substantial violation of the act.

Discovery

It is often difficult to establish that a substantial violation of the federal act has occurred. In a case alleging either discriminatory selection or a jury pool which does not reflect a fair cross-section of the community, demographic surveys may be necessary to determine the racial or ethnic composition of the community. The results of the surveys need to be compared with the racial or ethnic composition of the jury pool. In order to show a *substantial* violation, complex statistical analyses may be required.

The starting point is to discover the composition of the jury pool. Federal law permits government records to be inspected for this purpose: "The parties in a case shall be allowed to inspect, reproduce, and copy such records or papers at all reasonable times during the preparation and pendency of such

---

[163] United States v Bearden, 659 F2d 590 (5th Cir 1981), *cert denied,* 456 US 936 (1982). *See also* United States v La Chance, 788 F2d 856 (2d Cir 1986).

[164] *See* United States v Nelson, 718 F2d 315 (9th Cir 1983); United States v Kennedy, 548 F2d 608 (5th Cir), *cert denied,* 434 US 865 (1977); United States v Tarnowski, 429 F Supp 783 (ED Mich 1977), *affd,* 583 F2d 903 (6th Cir), *cert denied,* 440 US 918 (1978); United States v Armsbury, 408 F Supp 1130 (D Or 1976). *Contra* United States v Silverman, 449 F2d 1341 (2d Cir 1971), *cert denied,* 405 US 918 (1972).

[165] 659 F2d 590 (5th Cir 1981), *cert denied,* 456 US 936 (1982).

[166] *See also* United States v Haley, 521 F Supp 290 (ND Ga 1981) (infrequent, simple, and inadvertent deviations in random selection of starting numbers); United States v Matthews, 350 F Supp 1103 (D Del 1972) (erroneous excusals, exemptions, and disqualifications).

[167] 787 F2d 751 (1st Cir 1986).

[168] 546 F2d 583 (5th Cir), *cert denied,* 431 US 906 (1977).

a motion. . . ."[169] In *United States v Test*[170] the United States Supreme Court held that the right to inspect and copy jury lists was absolute.

Although 28 USC §1867(f) provides counsel with the raw data needed for a statistical analysis, the data will not be meaningful without the statistical analysis. Unfortunately, courts have held that there is no right, statutory or constitutional, to the assistance of an expert statistician to help interpret the data.[171] Lawyers whose clients are unable to afford such experts will either have to educate themselves as to the necessary analytic techniques or recruit volunteer statisticians, perhaps from a local university.[172]

§6.12 Challenges to the Array Based on Equal Protection

The fourteenth amendment to the United States Constitution guarantees the equal protection of the laws to all persons.[173] Although the fourteenth amendment protects only against actions by a state, the United States Supreme Court has held that the fifth amendment contains a comparable protection against actions by the federal government.[174]

In *Strauder v West Virginia,*[175] the United States Supreme Court considered the applicability of the equal protection clause in the context of jury selection. A state statute provided that jurors be drawn from the ranks of "all white male persons who are twenty-one years of age who are citizens of this State. . . ." The defendant was a black male convicted of murder by an all-white jury. He argued that his right to equal protection had been violated by the exclusion of members of his race from jury service. The Supreme Court agreed, and found the statute in violation of the fourteenth amendment. The Court reasoned that the purpose of the equal protection clause was to eliminate discrimination against blacks:

> The very fact that colored people are singled out and expressly denied by a statute all right to participate in the administration of the law, as jurors, because of their color, though they are citizens and may be in other respects fully qualified, is practically a brand upon them, affixed by law; an assertion of their inferiority, and a stimulant to that race prejudice which is an impediment to securing to individuals of the race that equal justice which the law aims to secure to all others.[176]

---

[169] 28 USC §1867(f).

[170] 420 US 28 (1975).

[171] *E.g.*, United States v Armstrong, 621 F2d 951 (9th Cir 1980). *See generally* **§§3.16-3.17.**

[172] *See generally* **§3.18.**

[173] US Const amend XIV.

[174] *See* Bolling v Sharpe, 347 US 497 (1954).

[175] 100 US 303 (1880).

[176] *Id* 308.

The Court's opinion was not intended to foreclose all discrimination in the selection of jurors, however. In language which it was later to have cause to reconsider, the Court said:

> We do not say that within the limits from which it is not excluded by the [Fourteenth] Amendment a State may not prescribe the qualifications of its jurors, and in so doing make discriminations. It may confine the selection to males, to freeholders, to citizens, to persons within certain ages, or to persons having educational qualifications. We do not believe the Fourteenth Amendment was ever intended to prohibit this.[177]

Strauder involved a statute which was discriminatory on its face. One year after *Strauder,* the Court considered the case of a statute, not discriminatory on its face, which had allegedly been applied in a discriminatory manner. In *Neal v Delaware,*[178] the state claimed, and the Supreme Court accepted, that Delaware jury statutes were interpreted in light of the fourteenth and fifteenth amendments' proscriptions against discrimination. The evidence, however, showed that no black had ever been summoned for jury duty in Delaware. The chief justice of the state Supreme Court explained this statistical anomaly by stating that it was common knowledge that "the great body of black men residing in this State are utterly unqualified by want of intelligence, experience or moral integrity, to sit on juries."[179] The Supreme Court again found a violation of equal protection. The exclusion of blacks from jury service, whether the result of discriminatory laws or the discriminatory administration of nondiscriminatory laws, is forbidden. Ostensibly objective selection criteria, which when applied consistently yield all-white juries, are as invidious as discriminatory criteria. Nor does it matter whether the state action which results in discrimination is effected by the legislative, executive, or judicial branches of government.[180]

The Supreme Court's decisions gave rise to what became known as the "rule of exclusion." In *Castaneda v Partida,*[181] the Supreme Court delineated the two key elements of this rule. First, a defendant has to show that he or she belongs to an identifiable class singled out for different treatment under the applicable law, as written or as applied.[182] Second, the defendant has to show that the class has been substantially underrepresented in jury venires over a significant

---

[177] *Id* 310. More recently, in Carter v Jury Commn, 396 US 320 (1970), the Court said that states "remain free to confine the selection to citizens, to persons meeting specified qualifications of age and educational attainment, and to those possessing good intelligence, sound judgment, and fair character." *Id* 321.

[178] 103 US 370 (1881).

[179] *Id* 393-94.

[180] *Id* 397. *See also* Norris v Alabama, 294 US 587 (1935); Carter v Texas, 177 US 422 (1900).

[181] 430 US 482.

[182] *Id* 494.

period of time.[183] Underrepresentation is shown by comparing the proportion of the class in the area from which the jury is drawn with its proportion in the jury rolls.[184] If there is a significant disparity a court will infer a discriminatory selection policy. The inference is particularly strong where jury selection procedures provide the opportunity to discriminate.[185] Of course, the need to draw an inference of discriminatory intent is unnecessary where the jury selection laws are discriminatory on their face.

There are several points to note about the Supreme Court's decisions. The first is that they relate not to the jury but to the pool or venire from which the jury is drawn. Second, the right is to a jury pool from which persons have not been excluded on the basis of race or other discriminatory criteria; there is no right to a jury composed in whole or in part of persons of any particular race, including the defendant's own.[186] Third, it does not matter whether the discrimination occurs at the grand or petit jury stage; discrimination in jury selection is unconstitutional at either stage.[187] Fourth, the exclusion need not be total.[188] On the other hand, a minor disparity between a group's presence in the community and its presence in the jury pool will not lead to a finding of a constitutional violation.[189] The key lies in determining what constitutes a minor disparity.[190] Finally, not all groups are protected by the equal protection clause;[191] a statute, for instance, that excluded convicted felons from jury service might discriminate against the class of convicted felons, but this would not be a discrimination subject to constitutional redress.[192]

§6.13 Challenges to the Array Based on the Fair Cross-Section Requirement

The sixth amendment to the United States Constitution guarantees to a defendant a jury drawn from "the State and district wherein the crime shall have been committed, which district shall have been previously ascertained by law."[193] In the past half-century, the United States Supreme Court has apparently transformed this provision into a mandate that jurors be drawn from a

---

[183] *Id.*

[184] *Id. See generally* **§6.17.**

[185] *See* Turner v Fouche, 396 US 346 (1970).

[186] *See* Strauder v West Virginia, 100 US 303, 305 (1880).

[187] *See* Vasquez v Hillery, 474 US 254 (1986); Castaneda v Partida, 430 US 482 (1977); Alexander v Louisiana, 405 US 625, 626, n 3 (1972).

[188] *See* Alexander v Louisiana, 405 US 625 (1972); Cassell v Texas, 339 US 282 (1950).

[189] *See* Swain v Alabama, 380 US 202 (1965).

[190] *See generally* **§6.17.**

[191] *See* **§6.16.**

[192] *See, e.g.,* United States v Foxworth, 599 F2d 1 (1st Cir 1979).

[193] US Const, Amend VI. The right to a jury trial has been incorporated into the due process clause of the fourteenth amendment and thereby been made binding on the states. Duncan v Louisiana, 391 US 145 (1968). *See also* **§§1.09-113.**

fair cross-section of the community or else found that a fair cross-section requirement is implicit in the sixth amendment.

The philosophical underpinning of the fair cross-section requirement was set forth by the Supreme Court in *Smith v Texas:*[194] "It is part of the established tradition in the use of juries as instruments of public justice that the jury be a body truly representative of the community."[195] The "cross-section" terminology first appeared in *Glasser v United States,*[196] where, indicating the importance of the concept, the Court stated that jury officials "must not allow the desire for competent jurors to lead them into selections which do not comport with the concept of the jury as a cross-section of the community."[197] In *Thiel v Southern Pacific Co,*[198] the Court observed that the "American tradition of trial by jury, considered in connection with either criminal or civil proceedings, necessarily contemplates an impartial jury drawn from a cross-section of the community."[199] By 1975, in *Taylor v Louisiana,*[200] the Court had reached the stage where it could unequivocally state: "We accept the fair cross-section requirement as fundamental to the jury trial guaranteed by the sixth amendment. . . ."[201]

The fair cross-section requirement serves several important functions. Cross-section representation facilitates the introduction of the common sense judgment of the community into the decision-making process. This common sense judgment helps protect defendants against overzealous prosecutors, as well as biased or legalistically technical judges.[202] In broadening the base of the jury, cross-section representation reduces the possibility that a jury's verdict will be distorted by the biases of a narrow group.

By diversifying the range of backgrounds and experiences among the jurors, cross-section representation also contributes to accurate fact finding. Different jurors, as a result of their own life experiences, may be able to provide enlightening perspectives on the credibility of a witness's testimony. Furthermore, because human perception tends to be selective, facts which contradict one's beliefs may be ignored. A homogeneous jury, whose members share a common background, values, and attitudes, will tend to ignore the same facts or interpret evidence in the same way; a heterogeneous jury, where different jurors, because of their individualistic perspectives, highlight different parts of the evidence, is more likely to come up with a more accurate sense of the "big pic-

---

[194] 311 US 128 (1940).

[195] *Id* 130.

[196] 315 US 60 (1942).

[197] *Id* 86.

[198] 328 US 217 (1946).

[199] *Id* 220.

[200] 419 US 522 (1975).

[201] *Id* 530.

[202] *See* Taylor v Louisiana, 419 US 522, 530 (1975).

ture."[203] The requirement of cross-section representation contributes to the heterogeneity of the jury; the heterogeneity of the jury contributes to accurate fact finding; and accurate fact finding contributes to fair decision making.

Sometimes a legal standard, such as the one for pornography, is defined in terms of community values.[204] To the extent that the jury does not include all segments of the community, it will be handicapped in implementing this standard. More generally, one function of the jury is to serve as the conscience of the community, tempering technical legal doctrine with a community sense of justice. This sense of community justice will not be reflected if the jury does not reflect the community. The cross-section requirement helps to ensure that the jury does reflect the community.

Finally, cross-section representation, like the principle of nondiscrimination, promotes democratic values: both advance the goal of full citizen participation in the legal process; both help avoid the feelings of inferiority which might be suggested by exclusion from jury service; and both contribute to the acceptance of verdicts by the parties and the public.

The concept of cross-section representation should not be taken literally. First, it is important to observe that the description of the cross-section requirement is qualified by the adjective "fair." Mathematical precision is not required. Indeed, as the law has developed, all that is required is that no cognizable group be systematically excluded from the opportunity to participate in the jury system.[205] If jurors are selected on a random basis, the fact that a particular group in the community finds itself excluded by chance will not result in a finding of a constitutional violation. Conversely, and equally significantly, not all members of a group need be excluded in order for a court to find a violation of the fair cross-section requirement.

Second, not all groups in a community are eligible for jury service; some are disqualified or exempt. The fact that the class of convicted felons, for instance, may by statute be ineligible for jury duty does not mean that their absence constitutes a violation of the fair cross-section requirement.[206] Not all groups are deemed "cognizable"[207] for purposes of the fair cross-section requirement.

Third, like the principle of nondiscrimination, the fair cross-section requirement does not apply to individual juries, but only to the jury pool or venire.[208] The Supreme Court has repeatedly said that there is "no requirement that petit juries actually chosen must mirror the community and reflect the various

---

[203] *See* Hovey v Superior Court, 28 Cal 3d 1, 23-25, 616 P2d 1301, 1312-13, 168 Cal Rptr 128, 139-40 (1980).

[204] *See* Miller v California, 413 US 15 (1973).

[205] *See* Thiel v Southern Pac Co, 328 US 217, 220 (1946).

[206] *See* United States v Foxworth, 599 F2d 1 (1st Cir 1979).

[207] *See* **§6.16.**

[208] *See* Duren v Missouri, 439 US 357, 363-64 (1979).

distinctive groups in the population."[209] This surrender to reality (it would be impossible to include on a jury of 12 all groups in the community)[210] was doubtless inevitable, but it means that many juries will not contain that diversity of viewpoints at which the fair cross-section requirement is aimed.

Fourth, the Supreme Court has upheld the use of so-called blue ribbon juries whose members are chosen because of some special qualification.[211] Because it excludes those otherwise eligible for jury service who do not possess the particular qualification, a blue ribbon jury may well not reflect a fair cross-section of the community.

The elements necessary to establish a prima facie case of a violation of the fair cross-section requirement are set out by the Supreme Court in *Duren v Missouri*:[212]

> [T]he defendant must show (1) that the group alleged to be excluded is a "distinctive" group in the community; (2) that the representation of this group in venires from which juries are selected is not fair and reasonable in relation to the number of such persons in the community; and (3) that this underrepresentation is due to systematic exclusion of the group in the jury selection process.[213]

These elements will be examined in the succeeding sections.

§6.14 Establishing a Prima Facie Case of a Constitutional Violation

There are many similarities between those jury claims based on a violation of the equal protection clause and those based on a violation of the fair cross-section requirement. Often a party will be able to prevail on either theory. Conversely, either theory may founder on the same defect of proof. Among the elements common to both types of claim are that the party alleging a constitutional violation: (1) establish standing to bring the challenge; (2) show that a cognizable or distinct group has been adversely affected by the actions of state officials; (3) demonstrate a significant disparity between the group's incidence in the community and its incidence in the jury pool. Conversely, in regard to neither claim does the party alleging the constitutional violation have to show prejudice.[214]

Although discriminatory intent may technically have to be shown in cases alleging a violation of equal protection, as a practical matter this element may

---

209 *See, e.g.*, Batson v Kentucky, 476 US 79, 85 (1986); Taylor v Louisiana, 419 US 522, 538 (1975).

210 *See* Thiel v Southern Pac Co, 328 US 217, 220 (1946).

211 Fay v New York, 332 US 261 (1947).

212 439 US 357 (1979).

213 *Id* 364.

214 *See* Peters v Kiff, 407 US 493, 504 (1972); Avery v Georgia, 345 US 559 (1953). *See also* Taylor v Louisiana, 419 US 522, 538 (1975) (Rehnquist, J, dissenting).

be no more an obstacle than in the fair cross-section cases, where it need not be proven.[215] Rather than discriminatory intent, a litigant alleging a violation of the fair cross-section requirement must show "systematic exclusion" of the group in question.[216] In both cases, however, the courts have been willing to infer the critical element (discriminatory intent or systematic exclusion) from evidence of a significant unexplained disparity between a group's presence in the community and its presence in the jury pool.

The next four sections will examine the elements of a prima facie case of both a claim of discrimination in jury selection and a claim of failure to satisfy the fair cross-section requirement. Common ground predominates over differences, but where the paths of the two classes of cases part, this will be noted.

§6.15 —Standing

To raise a claim of a constitutional violation, a petitioner must make a preliminary showing of standing. Three key questions have had to be addressed by the courts. First, are blacks the only group which has standing to claim wrongful exclusion from jury service? Second, must the defendant be a member of the group alleged to have been excluded from jury service in order to claim a violation? Third, can a claim of a constitutional violation be raised by members of the excluded class who are not involved in the litigation?

As to the first issue, the right to a jury drawn from a fair cross-section of the community contemplates that all distinctive groups in the community will be included in the jury pool. By definition the Court is not concerned solely with the exclusion of blacks. A similar conclusion cannot be so readily drawn with regard to claims under the equal protection clause. In *Strauder v West Virginia,*[217] its seminal decision on the applicability of the equal protection clause to jury selection, the Supreme Court had indicated that the purpose of the fourteenth amendment was to extend to blacks the rights of all citizens. The Court opined that a strong case would have to be made before the amendment would be applied to another race. The Court, however, has since cut the amendment adrift from its historical moorings.

That the Court's concern is not limited to discrimination against blacks is illustrated by *Hernandez v Texas.*[218] The defendant in *Hernandez* alleged that persons of Mexican descent had been excluded from service as jury commissioners, grand jurors, and petit jurors. The state argued that the equal protection clause was restricted to the prevention of discrimination against Negroes. Disagreeing, the Court held that the systematic exclusion of any identifiable segment of the community violated the fourteenth amendment:

> Throughout our history differences in race and color have defined easily identifiable groups which have at times required the aid of the courts in

---

[215] *See* **§6.18.**

[216] *See* Duren v Missouri, 439 US 357, 364 (1979).

[217] 100 US 303 (1880).

[218] 347 US 475 (1954).

> securing equal treatment under the laws. But community prejudices are not static and from time to time other differences from the community norm may define other groups which need the same protection. Whether such a group exists within a community is a question of fact. When the existence of a distinct class is demonstrated, and it is further shown that the laws, as written or as applied, single out that class for different treatment not based on some reasonable classification, the guarantees of the Constitution have been violated.[219]

As a matter of theory, it is questionable whether a defendant not belonging to the class whose members have been wrongfully excluded from jury service should have standing to challenge the composition of the jury. Part of the concern is that a jury composed, for example, of all whites might be biased against a non-white defendant. The possibility of racial prejudice, however, disappears if the defendant is also white. Furthermore, there is concern about the absence of a defendant's peers on a jury from which members of the defendant's peer group have been excluded. While the sometimes proclaimed right to a jury of one's peers finds little support in the case law,[220] including peers of the defendant on the jury is desirable as a matter of policy: they may prevent or at least help allay fears of discriminatory action by the jury; and they may be able to place a defendant's action in a culturally explicable light. But where the class of which the defendant is a member is not excluded and the defendant's complaint relates to a class of which he or she is not a member, the concern regarding peer group representation is no longer present.

Ultimately, the Supreme Court was not convinced. Rather, it was persuaded that the advantages to be gained from extending the right to challenge improprieties in jury selection to non-members of the excluded class outweighed the disadvantages. In *Peters v Kiff,*[221] the Supreme Court permitted a white defendant to challenge his conviction on the grounds that blacks had been excluded from jury service. In *Taylor v Louisiana,*[222] it allowed a male defendant to challenge restrictions on jury service by women. The focus of these decisions is as much on the harm to the jury as an institution as on the harm to the defendant as an individual. As the Court explained in *Peters:*

> When any large and identifiable segment of the community is excluded from jury service, the effect is to remove from the jury room qualities of human nature and varieties of human experience, the range of which is unknown and perhaps unknowable. It is not necessary to assume that the excluded group will consistently vote as a class in order to conclude, as we do, that its exclusion deprives the jury of a perspective on human

---

[219] *Id* 478.

[220] *See* **§2.07.**

[221] 407 US 493 (1972).

[222] 419 US 522 (1975).

> events that may have unsuspected importance in any case that may be presented.[223]

In *Ballard v United States,*[224] the Court emphasized the interaction on the jury among different segments of the community:

> It is said, however, that an all male panel drawn from the various groups within a community will be as truly representative as if women were included. The thought is that the factors which tend to influence the action of women are the same as those which influence the action of men—personality, background, economic status—and not sex. Yet it is not enough to say that women when sitting as jurors neither act nor tend to act as a class. Men likewise do not act as a class. But if the shoe were on the other foot, who would claim that a jury was truly representative of the community if all men were intentionally and systematically excluded from the panel? The truth is that the two sexes are not fungible; a community made up exclusively of one is different from a community composed of both; the subtle interplay of influence one on the other is among the imponderables. To insulate the courtroom from either may not in a given case make an iota of difference. Yet a flavor, a distinct quality is lost if either sex is excluded.[225]

It is the threat to the intangible decision making processes of the jury which is implicated by the exclusion of any particular group from service.[226] In order to allow the courts to redress the constitutional violation, standing is granted to nonmembers of the excluded group. Indirectly, the challengers may benefit from the superior decision making processes of a fully integrated jury drawn from a fair cross-section of the community, although the converse is also possible.

The decisions permitting standing to a nonmember of the excluded class also constitute a recognition of the need to vindicate the rights of those excluded from jury service. Such exclusion stigmatizes members of the excluded group by implying that they are not fit to serve as jurors.[227] It denies them their right to participate in the state-created legal decision making process. If only defendants who were members of the excluded group were allowed

---

[223] 407 US at 503-04.

[224] 329 US 187 (1946).

[225] *Id* 193-94.

[226] It is, of course, difficult to reconcile the Supreme Court's pronouncements in this regard with its insistence that it is sufficient that no group be excluded from jury service and it is not necessary that any group, be it of defendant's peers or otherwise, be specifically included on a particular jury. The benefits to be attained from having a variety of perspectives on a jury will seemingly be lost if any group does not in fact serve. Of course, the Court is sensitive to the practical difficulties of including on a panel of twelve all community groups. *See* Akins v Texas, 325 US 398, 403 (1945).

[227] *See* Norris v Alabama, 294 US 587, 599 (1935); Strauder v West Virginia, 100 US 303, 308 (1880).

standing to challenge the exclusion, it could be perpetuated in cases involving nonmembers of that group. Yet the harm suffered by members of the class excluded from service would be no less.

For the same reason, the overriding need to vindicate the rights of those excluded from jury service, the Supreme Court has permitted class action suits by members of the excluded class. In *Carter v Jury Commission*[228] black citizens brought a class action to obtain declaratory and injunctive relief to prevent discrimination against blacks in jury selection.[229] Plaintiffs alleged that, although qualified, they had never been summoned for jury duty. On the question of standing, the Supreme Court said that there was no jurisdictional or procedural bar to the plaintiffs' suit: "Defendants in criminal cases do not have the only cognizable legal interest in nondiscriminatory jury selection. People excluded from juries because of their race are as much aggrieved as those indicted and tried by juries chosen under a system of racial exclusion."[230]

Class action suits, however, are expensive and time-consuming, and their paucity attests to their inefficacy in vindicating the rights of the excluded class. It is more practical to allow the challenge to be brought by the defendant convicted by a jury from which an identifiable class has been improperly excluded, even if the defendant is not a member of that class.[231]

§6.16 —Cognizability

In order to establish a prima facie case of a constitutional violation, a petitioner must show that a cognizable group has been excluded from jury service. Cognizability is an elusive concept. In his dissenting opinion in *Thiel v Southern Pacific Co,*[232] Justice Frankfurter identified some of the relevant considerations: whether the group in question has "a different outlook, psychologically and economically," whether it has adopted "a different social outlook," and whether it has "a different sense of justice and a different conception of a juror's responsibility."[233]

A lawyer should be prepared to define and limit the group allegedly excluded. The lawyer needs to demonstrate that the group has cohesive elements which distinguish it from other groups, and that its perspective cannot be adequately represented by members of other groups. The attitude of the community to the group, whether it regards and treats the group as distinct, is also relevant to the issue of cognizability.[234]

---

[228] 396 US 320 (1970).

[229] *See also* Turner v Fouche, 396 US 346 (1970).

[230] *Id* 329.

[231] One disadvantage of this approach, of course, is that the issue of discrimination will not come to the appellate court's attention when the defendant is not convicted. The constrictions of double jeopardy will generally prevent an appeal by the prosecutor.

[232] 328 US 217 (1946).

[233] *Id* 230.

[234] *See* Hernandez v Texas, 347 US 475, 479 (1954).

The Supreme Court has never attempted to compile a list of all groups who are included within the fair cross-section requirement or who come under the umbrella of the equal protection clause. Indeed, such a compilation would not be advisable; some flexibility is desirable. Different groups may be excluded or discriminated against in different districts. Further, the passage of time, changing social attitudes, and remedial legislation may lead to a group's becoming so accepted that the need for constitutional protection disappears. Another group may, in contrast, become ostracized to the point where it requires constitutional protection. As the Supreme Court said, referring to the fair cross-section requirement: "What is a fair cross section at one time or place is not necessarily a fair cross section at another time or a different place."[235] Whether a group is cognizable is thus a question of fact.[236]

The test of cognizability tends to be functional. The implications of a functional test of cognizability in the jury context were examined by the Supreme Court in *Lockhart v McCree.*[237] The Court's comments were directed to the question of what groups would be included in determining whether a jury venire reflected a fair cross-section of the community, but the Court also indicated that its analysis was pertinent to equal protection claims:

> We have never attempted to precisely define the term "distinctive group," and we do not undertake to do so today. But we think it obvious that the concept of "distinctiveness" must be linked to the purposes of the fair cross-section requirement. In *Taylor* we identified those purposes as (1) guard[ing] against the exercise of arbitrary power and ensuring that the "commonsense judgment of the community" will act as a "hedge against the overzealous or mistaken prosecutor," (2) preserving "public confidence in the fairness of the criminal justice system", and (3) implementing our belief that "sharing in the administration of justice is a phase of civic responsibility."
>
> Our prior jury cases, whether based on the fair cross-section component of the Sixth Amendment or the Equal Protection Clause of the Fourteenth Amendment, have involved such groups as blacks, women, and Mexican-Americans. The wholesale exclusion of these large groups from jury service clearly contravened all three of the aforementioned purposes. . . . Because these groups were excluded for reasons completely unrelated to the ability of members of the group to serve as jurors in a particular case, the exclusion raised at least the possibility that the composition of juries would be arbitrarily skewed in such a way as to deny criminal defendants the benefit of the common-sense judgment of the community. In addition, the exclusion from jury service of large groups of individuals not on the basis of their inability to serve as jurors, but on the basis of some immutable characteristic such as race, gender, or ethnic background, undeniably gave rise to an "appearance of unfairness". Finally,

[235] Taylor v Louisiana, 419 US 522, 537 (1975).

[236] Hernandez v Texas, 347 US 475, 478 (1954).

[237] 476 US 162 (1986).

> such exclusion improperly deprived members of these often historically disadvantaged groups of their right as citizens to serve on juries in criminal cases.[238]

The functional test articulated by the Court might seem quite broad, but the Court's reference to "large," "historically disadvantaged" groups and "immutable characteristics" should sound a cautionary note. A group may not be sufficiently large, sufficiently distinct, or sufficiently disadvantaged to qualify as cognizable. As indicated in the above quotation, the Supreme Court has recognized the cognizability of blacks,[239] women,[240] and Mexican-Americans.[241] In *McCree,* however, the Court held that those philosophically opposed to the death penalty were not a distinct group for constitutional purposes. Indeed, the Court intimated that any group defined solely in terms of shared attitudes that rendered members of the group unable to carry out their responsibilities as jurors would not be considered "distinct" for the purposes of the fair cross-section requirement.[242] Among the groups whose cognizability has *not* been recognized by lower courts are youths,[243] the elderly,[244] and newly arrived residents of a community.[245] The Supreme Court, although recognizing the class of daily wage earners as cognizable,[246] has yet to hold that either the poor or the unemployed are a cognizable class.[247]

§6.17 —Disparity

As part of a prima facie case, a petitioner must prove that a cognizable group[248] has been significantly or substantially underrepresented in the jury pool. Typically, underrepresentation is established by showing a disparity

---

[238] *Id* 174-75 (citations omitted).

[239] *E.g.,* Norris v Alabama, 294 US 587 (1935); Strauder v West Virginia, 100 US 303 (1880).

[240] *E.g.,* Duren v Missouri, 439 US 357 (1979); Taylor v Louisiana, 419 US 522 (1975).

[241] *E.g.,* Castaneda v Partida, 430 US 482 (1977); Hernandez v Texas, 347 US 475 (1954).

[242] 476 US at 176-77.

[243] *E.g.,* Barber v Ponte, 772 F2d 982 (1st Cir 1985), *cert denied,* 475 US 1050 (1986); Brown v Harris, 666 F2d 782 (2d Cir 1981), *cert denied,* 456 US 948 (1982); United States v Olson, 473 F2d 686 (8th Cir), *cert denied,* 412 US 905 (1973); United States v McVean, 436 F2d 1120 (5th Cir), *cert denied,* 404 US 822 (1971).

[244] *See* State v Brewer, 247 NW2d 205 (Iowa 1976) (persons over 65).

[245] *See* United States v Owen, 492 F2d 1100 (5th Cir), *cert denied,* 419 US 965 (1974); United States v Perry, 480 F2d 147 (5th Cir 1973).

[246] *See* Thiel v Southern Pac Co, 328 US 217 (1946).

[247] Some lower courts, however, have not felt a similar compunction. *See, e.g.,* United States v Andrews, 342 F Supp 1261 (D Mass) (paupers a cognizable group), *revd on other grounds,* 462 F2d 914 (1st Cir 1972).

[248] *See* **§6.16.**

between a group's presence in the community[249] and its presence in the jury pool. The longer the period of time for which the disparity can be shown, the stronger the inference that the disparity is "systematic" or the result of conscious design rather than the product of chance.[250]

Whether a petitioner will be able to satisfy a court that there is underrepresentation sufficient to make out a prima facie case will depend on the size of the disparity which the court requires to be shown and the basis on which the court calculates the disparity. Judges are not chosen for their mathematical prowess, and the methods which some judges, including some Supreme Court Justices, have used to calculate disparities might make a mathematician cringe.[251] The two most commonly used methods focus, respectively, on absolute disparity and comparative disparity.

The absolute disparity is obtained by subtracting a group's percentage incidence in the jury pool from its percentage incidence in the community. If, for example, a group constituted 50 per cent of the community but only 25 per cent of the jury pool, the absolute disparity would be 25 per cent (50 per cent minus 25 per cent). In *Swain v Alabama,*[252] the United States Supreme Court concluded that where blacks constituted 26 per cent of the population but between 10 and 15 per cent of the jury pools, the underrepresentation was 10 per cent. The Court's subtraction was, of course, faculty, but the intent appears to have been to use an absolute disparity standard. Likewise, in *Castaneda v Partida,*[253] where Mexican-Americans constituted 79 per cent of the population of the county but only 39 per cent of those summoned for grand jury duty, the Supreme Court referred to a disparity of 40 per cent.

An example of the potentially absurd results which can flow from an absolute disparity test can be found in *United States v Whitely.*[254] Blacks made up 2.33 per cent of the population but only .28 per cent of the jury venire. The court, subtracting the latter figure from the former, concluded that a "deviation of 2.05 per cent standing alone is simply too slight to establish a prima facie case of knowing or intentional discrimination." The court would presumably have reached the same conclusion if blacks had been excluded entirely, for the mathematical difference between 2.05 per cent and 2.33 per cent is insignificant. As *Whitely* well illustrates, the lurking danger in the absolute disparity test is that a group whose percentage share of the community is small can never be sufficiently underrepresented to satisfy the test.

Under a comparative disparity test a court will compare the mathematical ratio of a group's percentage incidence in the jury pool with its percentage

---

[249] This is generally established by demographic surveys or census data.

[250] The Supreme Court's opinion in Castaneda v Partida, 430 US 482 (1977) suggests that if a petitioner's claim is based on equal protection, discrimination over a "significant period" of time must be shown. *Id* 494.

[251] *See generally* Finklestein, *The Application of Statistical Decision Theory to the Jury Discrimination Cases,* 80 Harv L Rev 338 (1966).

[252] 380 US 202 (1965).

[253] 430 US 482 (1977).

[254] 491 F2d 1248 (8th Cir), *cert denied,* 416 US 990 (1974).

incidence in the community. If, for example, a group were to constitute 50 per cent of the community but only 25 per cent of the jury pool, the comparative disparity would be 50 per cent. Under an absolute disparity test the disparity would be 25 per cent. In *Swain,* where the Supreme Court calculated a disparity of 10 per cent using an absolute disparity test, the comparative disparity would have been 50 per cent (calculating the black incidence in the jury pool as 13 per cent, roughly the midpoint of the range of figures given by the Court). The comparative disparity in *Partida* would also have been around 50 per cent (the ratio between the 79 per cent of the population which was Mexican-American and the 39 per cent of Mexican-Americans on the grand jury rolls). A comparative disparity test was employed by the Supreme Court in *Alexander v Louisiana,*[255] and its use has become increasingly common among lower courts.

Neither the absolute nor the comparative disparity test works well when the group allegedly excluded from jury service is relatively small. Consider, to take a simple example, a community of 200 with a black population of 12 (6 per cent). If a venire of 50 jurors were to be summoned, it would be expected that there would be three blacks in the pool. Suppose the venire included only one black. Under the comparative disparity approach, the disparity would be 66⅔ per cent (one juror instead of the expected three). Arguably this figure overstates the extent of the disparity. On the other hand, under the absolute disparity approach, the disparity would be 4 per cent (the difference between the black incidence in the community, 6 per cent, and its incidence in the jury pool, 2 per cent). This figure may understate the extent of the disparity. In a situation such as this, some courts will look at the number of potential jurors actually affected (in the hypothesized case, two) rather than either percentage figure.[256] Other courts, arguably more appropriately, will look to the likelihood that the disparity is due to chance.[257]

Some government attorneys have argued that, regardless of whether an absolute or comparative disparity standard is used, the appropriate point of comparison is not the percentage incidence of the group in question in the community but the percentage incidence of *jury-eligible* members of the group in the community. An exceptionally high illiteracy rate, for example, could lead to the disqualification from jury service of many of a group's members. If so, there could be a significant difference between the percentage of the group in the community and the percentage of its jury-eligible members in the community. In *Castaneda v Partida,*[258] however, the Supreme Court, over a dissent by Chief Justice Burger raising this precise point, looked to the percentage of Mexican-Americans in the community unadjusted for illiteracy and other jury-disqualifying characteristics as the appropriate figure for constitutional comparisons. The majority supported its position by reference to state law,

---

[255] 405 US 625 (1972). *See also* Duren v Missouri, 439 US 357 (1979).

[256] *See, e.g.,* United States v Jenkins, 496 F2d 57 (2d Cir 1974), *cert denied,* 420 US 925 (1975). *But see* Alston v Manson, 791 F2d 255, 259 (2d Cir 1986) (disapproving of *Jenkins*).

[257] *See* Castaneda v Partida, 430 US 482, 496 n 17 (1977).

[258] 430 US 482 (1977).

under which it was for the judge to determine competency *after* the jurors had been summoned rather than for the jury commissioners to do so *before* the jurors were summoned.

As a court will not find a violation of either equal protection or the fair cross-section requirement absent a substantial disparity, the method utilized to calculate the disparity assumes obvious significance. Equally important, however, is the size of the disparity required to establish a prima facie case. In *Swain v Alabama,*[259] the Supreme Court held that a 10 per cent absolute disparity (actually 11 per cent to 16 per cent, even using the absolute disparity method of calculation, as the difference was between a 26 per cent black incidence in the population and a 10 to 15 per cent incidence in the jury pool), albeit roughly a 50 per cent comparative disparity, was insufficient to make out a constitutional violation. In *Alexander v Louisiana,*[260] on the other hand, a 33⅓ per cent comparative disparity (the ratio between a 21 per cent incidence of blacks in the community and a 14 per cent incidence in the jury pools), albeit a 7 per cent absolute disparity, led to a finding of a constitutional violation.

Rather than looking at the size of either the absolute or comparative disparity, a court should consider the likelihood that the disparity is the result of chance. In fact, the Supreme Court, although never formally abandoning the absolute or comparative disparity standard, has increasingly paid attention to this figure. In *Castaneda v Partida,*[261] the Court noted that the probability of the disparity in the case being the product of chance was 1 in 10 to the 140th power.[262] In *Alexander v Louisiana,*[263] the Court put the likelihood of the disparity being the result of chance at 1 in 20,000.[264] In both cases the Court found a constitutional violation.[265]

The Supreme Court's reasoning in *Alexander* highlights another dimension of the problem. In *Alexander* the jury questionnaire provided a space for respondents to indicate their race. Knowledge of race facilitated discrimination by officials who were so inclined. In such circumstances a court will be less indulgent to a disparity, no matter how measured, than it will be if the method of jury selection is more objective and less arbitrary.

§6.18 —Discriminatory Intent and Systematic Exclusion

Part of a claimant's burden in traditional equal protection cases is to prove discriminatory intent. Proof of such intent is not required to establish a viola-

---

[259] 380 US 202 (1965).

[260] 405 US 625 (1972).

[261] 430 US 482 (1977).

[262] *Id* 496 n 17.

[263] 405 US 625 (1972).

[264] *Id* 630, n 9.

[265] *See also* Alston v Manson, 791 F2d 255 (2d Cir 1986). *See generally* Finklestein, *The Application of Statistical Decision Theory to the Jury Discrimination Cases,* 80 Harv L Rev 338 (1966).

tion of the fair cross-section requirement.[266] The defendant must instead prove "systematic exclusion."[267] Systematic exclusion is established by showing that the underrepresentation is "inherent in the particular jury selection process utilized."[268]

Courts have been willing to infer both discriminatory intent and systematic exclusion from proof of a significant and unexplained disparity between a group's presence in the community and its presence in the jury pool. The inference becomes stronger still when non-neutral selection procedures provide the opportunity to discriminate.[269] The converse is also true: the clearer the discriminatory intent, the less of a disparity a court will require to be established before finding a constitutional violation.

The cases, mostly involving equal protection, have run the gamut from those in which a jury selection statute is discriminatory on its face to those where there is no evidence of discrimination but the selection procedures provide the opportunity to discriminate to those who are of a mind to do so. Into the former class of cases falls *Strauder v West Virginia,*[270] where a state statute provided that jurors be drawn from the ranks of "all white male persons who are twenty-one years of age who are citizens of this State. . . ." The defendant, a black male convicted of murder by an all-white jury, argued that his right to equal protection had been violated by the exclusion of blacks from jury service. As the statute on its face was discriminatory against blacks, there could be no quarrel regarding discriminatory intent, and the United States Supreme Court had no difficulty in finding a violation of equal protection.

Because *Strauder* involved a statute which was discriminatory on its face, the Court did not require direct proof of discriminatory intent. The year after *Strauder,* the Court was confronted with a case involving a statute neutral on its face but allegedly applied in a discriminatory manner.[271] The evidence in support of this claim was that no blacks had been called for jury service in the state. Beyond whatever inference of discrimination was to be drawn from this fact, the chief justice of the state supreme court stated that it was common knowledge that "the great body of black men residing in this State are utterly unqualified by want of intelligence, experience or moral integrity, to sit on juries."[272] This sterotypic characterization of blacks doubtless contributed to the Supreme Court's finding of discriminatory intent.

Similar statements by jury commissioners, judges, or clerks charged with the selection of jurors will be strong evidence of discriminatory intent. *Norris v Alabama*[273] provides another example. One of the jury commissioners testified that he

---

[266] *See* Castaneda v Partida, 430 US 482, 509-10 (1977) (Powell, J, dissenting).

[267] Duren v Missouri, 439 US 357, 364 (1979).

[268] *Id* 366.

[269] *See* Castaneda v Partida, 430 US 482, 493-94 (1977).

[270] 100 US 303 (1880).

[271] Neal v Delaware, 103 US 370 (1881).

[272] *Id* 393-94.

[273] 294 US 587 (1935).

> did not know of any Negro in Morgan County over twenty-one and under sixty-five who is generally reputed to be honest and intelligent and who is esteemed in the community for his integrity, good character, and sound judgment, who is not an habitual drunkard, who isn't afflicted with a permanent disease or physical weakness which would render him unfit to discharge the duties of a juror, and who can read English, and who has never been convicted of a crime involving moral turpitude.

This testimony, said the Supreme Court, belied the commissioner's assertion that he had not taken race into account in jury selection.[274]

Most officials, however, are too smart to make such damaging admissions. To the contrary, they will assert good faith. In many cases discriminatory intent has to be inferred from a selection scheme that provides officials with the opportunity to discriminate coupled with a significant disparity between the incidence of a cognizable group in the community and its incidence in the jury pool.

In *Avery v Georgia,*[275] for example, color-coded jury cards were kept for white and black jurors. The cards of white jurors were printed on white tickets, those of black jurors on yellow tickets. Although discriminatory intent was denied and although there was no evidence of conscious selection of jurors by race, there were no blacks on the jury panel of sixty. The Supreme Court found that a prima facie case of discrimination had been made out, and that it was for the state to rebut it. The Court commented that the cards made it easier for those of a mind to discriminate to discriminate.[276]

A like result had previously been reached in *Norris v Alabama*[277] where the designation "col." had been placed beside the names of prospective black jurors. This fact, combined with evidence of the availability of qualified blacks and the absence of blacks on grand juries, led to the Supreme Court's finding of discrimination. The disclaimer by jury commissioners of an intent to discriminate was given short shrift and held insufficient to rebut the prima facie case which had been made out.[278]

Some cases are more subtle. In *Castaneda v Partida*[279] the group alleged to have been discriminated against was Mexican-Americans. Unlike in *Avery* and *Norris,* no identifying mark had been placed by the names of members of the class. This was unnecessary, observed the Supreme Court, because the Spanish surnames themselves provided a ready form of identification. This potential for discrimination, when coupled with a discretionary selection system which

---

[274] *Id* 598-99.

[275] 345 US 559 (1953).

[276] *Id* 562.

[277] 294 US 587 (1935).

[278] *See also* Alexander v Louisiana, 405 US 625 (1972); Whitus v Georgia, 385 US 545 (1967) (prima facie case of discrimination established where tax return files from which jury list was compiled indicated race).

[279] 430 US 482 (1977).

resulted in significant underrepresentation of Mexican-Americans on jury rolls, persuaded the Court that there had been a constitutional violation.

§6.19 Rebutting a Prima Facie Case of a Constitutional Violation

After a petitioner establishes a prima facie case of a constitutional violation, the burden shifts to the government to rebut the claim of unconstitutionality.[280] A prima facie case is *not* rebutted by a claim of good faith or nondiscriminatory intent on the part of selection officials.[281] Nor is a prima facie case rebutted by showing that the petitioner was not prejudiced.[282] Furthermore, a rebuttal based on the fact that the members of the group allegedly discriminated against constituted the "governing majority" in the district has been rejected by the Supreme Court.[283]

In *Vasquez v Hillery*[284] the government argued that discrimination in the selection of the grand jury should be deemed harmless error where the defendant was convicted by a lawfully constituted petit jury. The Supreme Court disagreed, citing an unbroken line of authority stretching over a century.[285] To rule otherwise, reasoned the Court, would be to remove the only effective deterrent to discrimination in the selection of grand jurors.[286] Reversal had to be automatic. On the same reasoning, the government will not be able to rebut a prima facie case by reference to the overwhelming nature of the evidence supporting the verdict.

What must be shown to rebut a prima facie case is that neutral selection criteria and procedures have produced the "monochromatic result."[287] A detailed statement of the methods used by selection officials is virtually indispensable to a successful rebuttal. Where jury selection procedures facilitate discrimination in jury selection, the burden on those seeking to justify the selection procedures will be greater still.[288]

The government may also be able to rebut a prima facie case by showing that an exclusion is necessary to achieve a significant government interest, and

---

280 Alexander v Louisiana, 405 US 625 (1972).

281 *See* Alexander v Louisiana, 405 US 625 (1972); Turner v Fouche, 396 US 346 (1970); Whitus v Georgia, 385 US 545 (1967); Hernandez v Texas, 347 US 475 (1954). *But compare* Swain v Alabama, 380 US 202 (1965) (Court's finding of no constitutional violation rested in part on denial by jury commissioners that race had entered into their selection decisions).

282 *See* Peters v Kiff, 407 US 493, 504 (1972); Avery v Georgia, 345 US 559 (1953). *See also* Taylor v Louisiana, 419 US 522, 538 (1975) (Rehnquist, J, dissenting).

283 Castaneda v Partida, 430 US 482 (1977).

284 474 US 254 (1986).

285 *Id* 261.

286 *Id* 262.

287 Alexander v Louisiana, 405 US 625, 632 (1972).

288 *See* Castaneda v Partida, 430 US 482 (1977); Alexander v Louisiana, 405 US 625 (1972); Avery v Georgia, 345 US 559 (1953).

that the restriction is no greater than necessary to achieve that interest. In *Duren v Missouri,*[289] the Supreme Court held that a state provision which granted women an automatic exemption from jury service at their request violated the fair cross-section requirement. The Court, however, added: "[A] state may have an important interest in assuring that those members of the family responsible for the care of children are available to do so" and that an exemption "appropriately tailored to this interest would . . . survive a cross-section challenge."[290]

The quantum of evidence required in order for a state to rebut a prima facie case is not quite clear. In *Taylor v Louisiana*[291] the Supreme Court said: "The right to a proper jury cannot be overcome on merely rational grounds. There must be weightier reasons."[292] How much weightier the reasons must be has not been spelled out with precision, although the Court in *Duren* referred to a required showing of a "significant" state interest.[293] To some extent, the significance of the state interest required may depend on the degree to which the group in question is excluded from jury service: total exclusion will require more in the way of a governmental justification than partial exclusion.

---

[289] 439 US 357 (1979).

[290] *Id* 370.

[291] 419 US 522 (1975).

[292] *Id* 534.

[293] Duren v Missouri, 439 US 357, 367 (1979).

7 Challenges for Cause

§7.01 Introduction

As the jury evolved from fact knowers to fact finders, it became increasingly important to exclude from service individuals who were biased or prejudiced against either side in a case, for whatever reason. It was also recognized that parties should not be penalized for insisting upon the right to a jury free from prejudiced jurors. It was within this context that the law of challenges for cause developed.

Challenges for cause are unlimited in number, and virtually unlimited in scope. *Cause,* in this context, refers to any reason which will prevent a prospective juror from being fair and impartial. It is the lack of impartiality, and not the reason for the lack of impartiality, which is critical.

The United States Supreme Court has stated that the challenge for cause permits "rejection of jurors on a narrowly specified, provable and legally cognizable basis of partiality."[1] Specific grounds for challenge can be found in statute, court rule, and judicial precedent. Moreover, a trial judge is generally said to retain a residual power to disqualify any prospective jurors whose prejudice will prevent them from deciding the case on the merits.[2] This power is essential in order that each party receive its constitutional right to a fair and impartial jury.[3]

The art of jury selection consists not only in identifying prospective jurors who are unlikely to be impartial, but also in being able to demonstrate to the court, through voir dire questioning, their lack of impartiality. If successful, the jurors will be excused for cause. In this way the lawyer removes partial jurors without the necessity of expending scarce peremptory challenges.

Some attorneys are of the view that it is tactically unwise either to question jurors closely about their biases or to challenge jurors for cause. In part it is because these attorneys do not expect the judge to grant many challenges for cause. If the judge is disinclined to grant challenges for cause, the lawyer risks a jury which contains members who may have been alienated by the lawyer's questions.

There is some truth to these views. A few judges, sensitive to a juror's feelings, are reluctant to grant challenges for cause out of a concern that the jurors will be upset that the legal system has found them "unfit." Far more commonly, however, judges do not grant challenges for cause because the attorney has failed to lay an adequate foundation for the challenge. Establishing a basis for a challenge for cause often requires careful questioning, and in the hands of the unskilled such questioning does carry the potential for alienating some jurors.

Alienation can be avoided or minimized with appropriate introductory remarks. The lawyer should educate the jurors as to the purposes of voir dire. The lawyer should emphasize the ethical and constitutional responsibility to the client to seek a fair and impartial jury. The lawyer should acknowledge the possibility of a misconceived or mistaken challenge, and explain that a challenge represents only a guess on the part of the lawyer that something in the juror's experience or background will prevent the juror from being impartial in that particular case. The lawyer should make clear that the person challenged may well be an exemplary juror in a different case, and that the challenge should not be taken as a general condemnation of the juror.

These introductory remarks, coupled with tactful voir dire questioning, should help prevent juror alienation. Even if they did not, however, the failure to probe for biases on voir dire risks a jury which will contain persons who are predisposed to find against the attorney's client. This risk is simply not

---

[1] Swain v Alabama, 380 US 202, 220 (1965).

[2] Johnson v Missouri-K-T RR, 374 SW2d 1 (Mo 1964); Mount v Welsh, 118 Or 568, 247 P 815 (1926); Redwine v Fitzhugh, 78 Wyo 107, 329 P2d 257 (1958).

[3] US Const amend VI. *See generally* **§§2.09-2.12.** *See also* United States v Liddy, 509 F2d 428 (DC Cir 1974), *cert denied,* 420 US 911 (1975); State v Leonard, 296 NC 58, 248 SE2d 853 (1978).

acceptable. If there are jurors whom the attorney has unduly alienated during voir dire, they can be removed through the exercise of peremptory challenges.

As can thus be seen, challenges for cause and peremptory challenges work in tandem. Challenges for cause allow the attorney to save peremptory challenges for jurors whom the attorney suspects, but cannot establish to the court's satisfaction, are biased. Peremptory challenges allow the attorney to carefully question jurors about their biases without fear of being saddled with jurors who have been alienated by the lawyer's unsuccessful attempt to establish a challenge for cause. Both forms of challenge have their unique advantages. Challenges for cause are unlimited in number, and peremptory challenges generally need not be explained or defended.[4]

This chapter will examine the more common grounds for challenges for cause. It is impossible in a text of this size to examine all such grounds, and the attorney needs to consult the law of the local jurisdiction.

The legal issues relating to challenges for cause often arise in the context of whether a line of questioning on voir dire is permissible. Questioning is generally permitted when it will lead to a proper challenge for cause.[5] The Missouri appellate court in *State v Reed*[6] put it well: "Questions on voir dire calculated to expose prejudice should be liberally permitted; those designed to induce prejudice should be vigorously denied."[7]

In many jurisdictions voir dire questions are also permitted to facilitate an intelligent exercise of peremptory challenges.[8] To the extent that these decisions, too, will find their way into this chapter, the chapter overlaps with the one on peremptory challenges.

§7.02 —At Common Law

At common law jurors could be challenged because of a high status (propter honoris respectum), a suspect status (propter defectum), or an infamous status (propter delictum).[9] A juror could also be challenged for suspicion of bias or partiality (propter affectum).[10] The latter challenge was either for principal cause or to the favor. A challenge to the favor was based on a juror's actual bias in favor of one of the parties. Where established, it rendered the juror unfit to determine the truth of the matter in question. In contrast, a challenge for principal cause arose from circumstances which implied bias as a matter

---

[4] Peremptory challenges in a criminal prosecution apparently used to exclude members of defendant's race are the exception which may require an explanation. *See* **§§8.05-8.11.**

[5] *See* United States v Lewin, 467 F2d 1132 (7th Cir 1972) (sufficient voir dire questioning should be permitted to allow for a reasonably knowledgeable exercise of the right of challenge).

[6] 629 SW2d 424 (Mo Ct App 1981).

[7] *Id* 426.

[8] *See* Alabama Power Co v Bonner, 459 So 2d 827 (Ala 1984); People v Williams, 29 Cal 3d 392, 628 P2d 869, 174 Cal Rptr 317 (1981).

[9] 47 Am Jur 2d *Jury* §265 (1969).

[10] *Id.*

of law. The grant of a challenge to the favor lay in a court's discretion, but a challenge for principal cause was said to leave nothing for the discretion of the court.[11]

Various principal causes of challenge were recognized at common law. Among these were that the juror was related by consanguinity or affinity to either of the parties within the ninth degree; that the juror was godfather to the child of either party, or vice versa; that the juror was of the same society or corporation with, or was a tenant, or within the distress, of either party; that the juror had an action implying malice with either party; that the juror was master, servant, counselor, steward, or attorney for either party; or that the juror, after being returned, ate and drank at the expense of either party, or had been chosen as arbitrator by either party.[12] Furthermore, it was a valid ground of challenge that the juror had formed and declared an opinion on the matter in controversy.[13]

A nonspecific bias, such as ill-feeling toward a litigant's class or religion, could not be the basis for a challenge for cause. Thus, no questioning on such matters was allowed at common law.

§7.03 —American Development

The law of challenge under the common law became the prevailing practice in the American colonies. In the many political trials of the period, however, revolutionaries demanded a broader right to question jurors about their prejudices. Matters came to a head in the treason trial of Aaron Burr. Burr, vice president under Thomas Jefferson from 1801 to 1805, had killed Alexander Hamilton in a duel in 1804, and shortly thereafter had assembled a small army in Kentucky. Treason charges were brought against him.

During the impaneling of the jury, Chief Justice Marshall enunciated many of the principles of law which govern jury service. Chief Justice Marshall's opinion remains in most respects as authoritative today as the day it was delivered, and it is still widely quoted. Among the numerous points that he made were the following:

> The great value of the trial by jury, certainly consists in its fairness and impartiality. . . .
>
> . . . This is not to be expected, certainly the law does not expect it, where the jurors, before they hear the testimony, have deliberately formed and delivered an opinion that the person whom they are to try is guilty or innocent of the charge alleged against him. . . .
>
> Relatives
>
> . . . Why is it that the most distant relatives of a party can not serve

---

[11] Brown v Woolverton, 219 Ala 112, 121 So 404 (1928); Hagans v State, 77 Ga App 513, 48 SE2d 700 (1948).

[12] *See* Coughlin v People, 144 Ill 140, 33 NE 1, 8 (1893).

[13] *Id.*

upon his jury? Certainly the single circumstance of relationship, taken in itself, unconnected with its consequences, would furnish no objection. The real reason of the rule is that the law suspects the relative of partiality; suspects his mind to be under a bias which will prevent his fairly hearing and fairly deciding on the testimony which may be offered to him. The end to be obtained is an impartial jury; to secure this end, a man is prohibited from serving on it whose connection with a party is such as to induce a suspicion of partiality. . . .

Personal Prejudices

Why do personal prejudices constitute a just cause of challenge? Solely because the individual who is under their influence is presumed to have a bias on his mind which will prevent an impartial decision of the case according to the testimony. . . .

Is there less reason to suspect him who has prejudged the case, and has deliberately formed and delivered an opinion upon it? . . . He will listen with more favor to that testimony which confirms, than to that which would change his opinion; it is not to be expected that he will weigh evidence or argument as fairly as a man whose judgment is not made up in the case.

Light Impressions

. . .The opinion which has been avowed by the court is, that light impressions which may fairly be supposed to yield to the testimony that may be offered; which may leave the mind open to a fair consideration of that testimony, constitute no sufficient objection to a juror; but that those strong and deep impressions, which will close the mind against the testimony that may be offered in opposition to them—which will combat that testimony and resist its force, do constitute a sufficient objection to him. . . . The court has considered those who have deliberately formed and delivered an opinion on the guilt of the prisoner, as not being in a state of mind fairly to weigh the testimony, and therefore as being disqualified to serve as jurors in the case. . . .

Opinions

The question now to be decided is, whether an opinion formed and delivered, not upon the full case, but upon an essential part of it, not that the prisoner is absolutely guilty of the whole crime charged in the indictment, but that he is guilty in some of those great points which constitute it, do also disqualify a man in the sense of the law and of the constitution from being an impartial juror? . . .

. . . [I]f the opinion formed be on a point so essential as to go far towards a decision of the whole case, and to have a real influence on the verdict to be rendered, the distinction between a person who has formed such an opinion, and one who has in his mind decided the whole case, appears too slight to furnish the court with solid ground for distinguishing between them. . . .

> In the case now under consideration the court would perhaps not consider it as a sufficient objection to a juror that he did believe and had said that the prisoner at a time considerably anterior to the fact charged in the indictment, entertained treasonable designs against the United States. . . . But if the juror has made up and declared the opinion that to the time when the fact laid in the indictment is said to have been committed, the prisoner was prosecuting the treasonable design with which he is charged, the court considers the opinion as furnishing just cause of challenge, and can not view the juror who has formed and delivered it as impartial, in the legal and constitutional sense of that term. . . .
>
> Fair to Both Sides
>
> . . . If, instead of a panel composed of gentlemen who had almost unanimously formed, and publicly delivered an opinion that the prisoner was guilty, the marshal had returned one composed of persons who had openly and publicly maintained his innocence, who had insisted, that notwithstanding all the testimony in possession of the public, they had no doubt that his designs were perfectly innocent; who had been engaged in repeated, open, and animated altercation to prove him innocent, and that his objects were entirely opposite to those with which he was charged; would such men be proper and impartial jurors? . . . I can not declare a juror to be impartial who has advanced opinions against the prisoner which would be cause of challenge if advanced in his favor.[14]
>
> The opinion of the court is, that to have made up and delivered the opinion that the prisoner entertained the treasonable designs with which he is charged, and that he retained those designs, and was prosecuting them when the act charged in the indictment is alleged to have been committed is good cause of challenge.[15]

§7.04 —American Jurisdictions Today: An Overview

The various grounds of challenge for cause are generally set out in a statute. Some jurisdictions purport to limit challenges to those grounds identified in the statute.[16] Others, however, hold that where there is no statutory provision

---

[14] As an accused is entitled to a presumption of innocence, while the state is not entitled to a presumption of guilt, the fact that a prospective juror comes to court believing in defendant's innocence is no basis for disqualification; the same cannot be said of the juror who comes to court believing in defendant's guilt. Chief Justice Marshall's concern was with jurors whose opinion of defendant's innocence was not susceptible to change by the evidence.

[15] United States v Burr, 25 F Cas 49 (CCD Va 1807) (No 14, 692g).

[16] *See, e.g.,* Jones v Ford, 154 Iowa 549, 134 NW 569 (1912), (excluding a certain ground of challenge on the theory that it was not listed under a statute); State v Morse, 35 SD 18, 150 NW 293 (1914). *See generally* Annotation, *Statutory Grounds for Challenge of Jurors for Cause as Exclusive of Common-Law Grounds,* 64 ALR 645 (1929).

to the contrary, challenges for cause existing at common law may also be asserted.[17]

Courts have also held that statutes which enumerate particular grounds of challenge do not deprive a trial judge of the inherent authority to dismiss a prospective juror in order to insure a fair trial.[18] The *federal* constitutional guarantee of an impartial jury cannot be nullified simply because the state legislature has omitted a ground that clearly renders a juror unfit.[19] *State* constitutional provisions to the effect that the right of trial by jury is to remain inviolate also necessarily imply a jury which is fair, impartial, and unbiased. The machinery for obtaining such a jury must be adequate for the purpose, and restrictions which frustrate achievement of this purpose infringe both the federal and state constitutional guarantees.[20]

Most statutes specify particular grounds for challenge. In addition, there is often a catchall provision which permits the disqualification of jurors who have a state of mind that will prevent them from acting with impartiality and without prejudice to the rights of the parties.

Among the more common grounds for challenge for cause are the following:

1. Relationship by blood or marriage to a party
2. Relationship by blood or marriage to an attorney or a member of the attorney's firm
3. Friendship or acquaintance with a party, a party's business associates, or a party's family
4. Friendship or acquaintance with an attorney, the attorney's family, or a member of the attorney's firm
5. Business relations with an attorney or party in the relationships of (a) employer or employee; (b) client; (c) customer or salesperson; (d) landlord or tenant; or (e) indebtedness
6. Social relations with an attorney or a party through (a) club, society, or association; (b) church; (c) fraternal order; (d) school; (e) politics; or (f) participation in sports
7. Relationship to, or friendship or acquaintance with, any prospective witness

---

[17] *E.g.*, Lewis v State, 260 Ala 368, 70 So 2d 790 (1954); Johnson v Missouri-K-T RR, 374 SW2d 1 (Mo 1963); State v Gates, 131 Mont 78, 307 P2d 248 (1957); Moss v Fidelity & Cas Co, 439 SW2d 734 (Tex Civ App 1969); Nolan v Venus Motors, Inc, 64 Wis 2d 215, 218 NW2d 507 (1974). *See generally* Annotation, *supra* note 16.

[18] *See* Johnson v Missouri-K-T RR, 374 SW2d 1 (Mo 1964); Mount v Welsh, 118 Or 568, 247 P 815 (1926); Redwine v Fitzhugh, 78 Wyo 107, 329 P2d 257 (1958); Black v State, 100 Ind 357 (1884).

[19] Klinck v State, 203 Ind 647, 179 NE 549, 551 (1932); Black v State, 100 Ind 357 (1884). *See also* Redwine v Fitzhugh, 78 Wyo 407, 329 P2d 257 (1958).

[20] *See, e.g.*, Beyer v City of Dubuque, 258 Iowa 476, 139 NW2d 428, 433 (1966) (quoting from Schwickerath v Maas, 230 Iowa 329, 336-37, 297 NW 248, 251 (1941)).

8. A preconceived opinion about the merits of a case arising from (a) reading about it in the newspaper or hearing about it on radio or television; (b) discussing it or hearing it discussed; or (c) participation in a similar case as a party, witness, or juror
9. Stockholder, officer, agent, or employee of a corporate party
10. Stockholder, officer, agent, or employee, or otherwise having an interest in an insurance company insuring against liability or injury to person or property
11. Direct or indirect financial interest in the outcome of the case
12. Prejudice, including (a) racial prejudice; (b) religious prejudice; (c) prejudice against particular type of action or defense; (d) prejudice against prosecution of case on a contingency basis; or (e) prejudice against certain classes of witnesses
13. Sympathy
14. Prior personal experience or prior jury service on the same or a related case
15. Prior knowledge of the facts

The case law relating to these challenges for cause will be examined in greater depth in subsequent sections. In general terms, the juror who falls into one of these categories is unlikely to be able to judge the case with an open mind. While this conclusion may not be a mathematical certainty, the probability is sufficiently great that it makes more sense to excuse the juror than to run the risk of a verdict tainted by bias. The appearance of justice is important, and litigants should feel that they have been treated fairly. Permitting challenges for cause to persons who are likely to be biased promotes this sense of being treated fairly.

§7.05 Procedures

The trial judge is charged with protecting the constitutional right to a fair and impartial jury. When a juror is challenged for cause, the judge must determine whether to excuse the juror. This is a question of fact,[21] and one which falls within the discretion of the judge. On appeal, the judge's ruling will be reversed only for an abuse of that discretion or the misapplication of well-settled principles of law.[22] The "abuse of discretion" standard is justified in part by the fact that, unlike the appellate court, the trial judge has had the opportunity to observe the juror during voir dire; often the demeanor of a juror

---

[21] *See* Patton v Yount, 487 US 1025, 1036 (1984); Davis v State, 594 SW2d (Ark Ct App 1980).

[22] Malvo v JC Penney Co, 512 P2d 575 (Alaska 1973); Davis v State, 594 SW2d 47 (Ark Ct App 1980); State v Allen, 380 So 2d 28 (La 1980); State v Woods, 662 SW2d 527 (Mo Ct App 1983); Paper Mach Corp v Nelson Foundry Co, 108 Wis 2d 614, 323 NW2d 160 (1982).

in responding to questions is more telling than the juror's actual words.[23] Even an erroneous ruling on a challenge for cause will generally not result in a reversal absent a showing of prejudice.[24]

A trial judge should permit counsel the leeway to fully probe possible grounds of bias which come to light during the voir dire.[25] If doubt as to the impartiality of a juror remains, the judge should personally question the juror.[26] The judge needs to be satisfied that the juror can set aside any possible bias and decide the case in accord with the evidence and the instructions of the court.[27] If so convinced, then the judge will most likely deny the challenge for cause.[28]

The law presumes impartiality, and the burden is on the party seeking to challenge a juror to show a basis for disqualification.[29] Unlike in the case of peremptory challenges, counsel will, unless it is obvious, have to articulate the basis of a challenge for cause.[30] It is tactically advisable to make the challenge in chambers or at the bench, but in any event out of the hearing of the other jurors. The purpose is to avoid possible prejudice stemming from the challenge—on the part of the juror, if the challenge is rejected, or on the part of the juror's friends on the jury, if it is accepted.[31] Many judges, however, require the challenge to be made in open court.

In criminal cases, it has been said that any reasonable doubt as to a juror's impartiality should be resolved in favor of the accused.[32] This approach has much to recommend it in all cases: if a judge erroneously grants a challenge for cause, the effect at worst is to substitute one impartial juror for another; if a judge erroneously rejects a challenge for cause, the effect is to seat a partial juror rather than an impartial one.

The law's ultimate concern is with the impartiality of the jury which decides the case. Accordingly, the removal of a biased juror through a peremptory

---

[23] *See* Reynolds v United States, 98 US 145, 156-57 (1878). *See also* Patton v Yount, 467 US 1025 (1984).

[24] Stroud v United States, 251 US 380 (1920); Hopt v Utah, 120 US 430 (1887).

[25] *See* United States v Corey, 625 F2d 704 (5th Cir 1980); Perillo v State, 656 SW2d 78 (Tex Crim App 1983).

[26] *See* State v Deaner, 334 SE2d 627 (W Va 1985).

[27] *Id;* Caldwell v Commonwealth, 634 SW2d 405 (Ky 1982).

[28] Caldwell v Commonwealth, 634 SW2d 405 (Ky 1982). *See also* State v Molasky, 655 SW2d 663 (Mo Ct App 1983); State v Corbett, 309 NC 382, 307 SE2d 139 (1983); State v Sammons, 656 SW2d 862 (Tenn Crim App 1982). Juror assertions of impartiality are, of course, relevant but not dispositive. State v Hohman, 138 Vt 502, 420 A2d 852 (1980).

[29] Montgomery v State, 277 Ark 95, 640 SW2d 108 (1982).

[30] State v Forsha, 190 Mo 296, 88 SW 746 (1905).

[31] In many courts, attorneys can submit a written list of the jurors whom they seek to challenge.

[32] People v Harris, 84 AD2d 63, 445 NYS2d 520 (1981), *affd,* 57 NY2d 335, 442 NE2d 1205, 456 NYS2d 694 (1982), *cert denied,* 460 US 1047 (1983); Justus v Commonwealth, 266 SE2d 87 (Va 1980); State v West, 200 SE2d 859 (W Va 1973). *See also* Burke v McKenzie, 313 P2d 1090 (Okla 1957) (civil case).

challenge has been held to cure an erroneous ruling by the trial court on a challenge for cause to that juror.[33] In like vein, parties who fail to exhaust their full complement of peremptory challenges may not be permitted to complain about the denial of a challenge for cause.[34] Thus, a lawyer who plans to appeal a trial court's ruling on a challenge for cause should exhaust all peremptory challenges. Even then, there is no error unless an incompetent juror hears the case.[35] Arguably the requirement that peremptory challenges be used to cure erroneous challenge for cause rulings denies litigants their full complement of peremptory challenges allowed by law. This argument, however, has been specifically rejected by the United States Supreme Court.[36]

The fact that peremptory challenges can cure erroneous rulings on challenges for cause reinforces the wisdom of moving for additional peremptory challenges.[37] A trial judge who harbors some doubt about the rejection of a challenge for cause may be receptive to such a motion. It provides a graceful retreat for the judge, allowing the party to remove the unwanted juror, while obviating the basis for an appeal of the judge's ruling on the challenge for cause.[38]

Trial courts are understandably reluctant to entertain a challenge for cause after evidence has been presented to the jury. To do so would be time-consuming and inefficient. Therefore the general rule is that a challenge for cause must be made before the juror is sworn or at least before evidence is presented; otherwise, the challenge will be deemed waived.[39] This rule can work a grave injustice if, despite counsel's diligence, the ground for challenge does not come to light until after the juror is sworn. Under these circumstances some courts appear willing to consider a delayed challenge to the juror.[40]

§7.06 Preconceived Opinions

Litigants are entitled to a fair trial by a jury free of preconceived opinions about the parties, facts, or issues of the case. A juror who admits, whether voluntarily or under questioning, to an opinion about a case which it would take

---

[33] *See* Ross v Oklahoma, 487 US 81 (1988); Hopt v Utah, 120 US 430 (1887); Mellinger v Prudential Ins Co, 322 Mich 596, 34 NW2d 450 (1948).

[34] *See* Ross v Oklahoma, 487 US 81 (1988); Mount v Welsh, 118 Or 568, 247 P 815 (1926). *But see* State v Reynolds, 619 SW2d 741 (Mo 1981). Exhaustion of peremptory challenges may not be required when it would be futile, as where the remaining members of the venire are as biased as the jurors already excused. Delaney v United States, 199 F2d 107 (1st Cir 1952).

[35] Ross v Oklahoma, 487 US 81 (1988).

[36] *Id.*

[37] *See* Pierce v State, 696 SW2d 899 (Tex Crim App 1985); Williams v State, 682 SW2d 538 (Tex Crim App 1984). *See also* **§8.02.**

[38] *See* Pierce v State, 696 SW2d 899 (Tex Crim App 1985); Williams v State, 682 SW2d 538 (Tex Crim App 1984).

[39] Petcosky v Bowman, 197 Va 240, 89 SE2d 4 (1955).

[40] *See, e.g.*, State v Jackson, 43 NJ 148, 203 A2d 1 (1964), *cert denied*, 379 US 982 (1965).

substantial evidence to dislodge is subject to challenge. Unless the juror can convince the court that he or she will be guided by the instructions of the court and not by the preconceived opinion, the juror must be excused.

It is simple enough to eliminate prejudiced jurors who will admit to having formed an opinion that cannot be changed by the evidence. It is obvious that such a juror must be excused, and the failure of the trial court to do so will constitute reversible error. The hard case involves the juror who admits to having formed an opinion, but maintains that the opinion is not so strong that it could not be changed by the evidence. When this occurs, counsel and the court must independently decide whether to believe the juror. If the trial judge is convinced that the juror will be guided by the evidence and not by the preconceived opinion, the judge will not excuse the juror for cause. If not similarly convinced, counsel will have to use a peremptory challenge to remove the juror.

A common judicial practice in this situation is to explain to the juror that the facts of the case will be developed by evidence during trial and then ask the juror if the already formed opinion is so strong that it cannot be changed by that evidence. Most jurors are conscientious. Once it is explained to them that their verdict is to be based on the evidence and not on preconceived ideas, they are willing to proceed on that premise. If the juror, sworn to tell the truth, agrees to listen to the evidence and be guided by it, the judge will generally reject the challenge for cause. In cases of doubt, however, there is much to be said for erring on the side of caution and excusing the juror.

Mere formation or expression of an opinion about a case is not in itself sufficient to disqualify a juror. It is generally held that the right to a trial by a fair and impartial jury does not require jurors who have never read or heard of the case.[41] If such knowledge were automatically disqualifying, it would be difficult to procure jurors of sufficient intelligence to understand a case. It would tend to put the trial of jury cases in the hands of the most ignorant and least discriminating of persons.

Even an expression of an opinion adverse to a defendant accused of crime will not necessarily render a juror incompetent. If the remark does not show ill-will or a fixed opinion as to guilt, the juror will not be disqualified.[42]

§7.07 —Relevance

Before a prospective juror will be disqualified for having a preconceived opinion, the opinion must be shown to relate to a material issue in the case. The opinion need not relate to all the material issues in the case; it is sufficient if the opinion relates to any of them.

---

[41] Irvin v Dowd, 366 US 717, 722-23 (1961); United States v Burr, 25 F Cas 47 (CCD Va 1807) (No 14,692g); Kujawa v Baltimore Transit Co, 224 Md 195, 167 A2d 96 (1961); Herring v State, 302 SW2d 428 (Tex Crim App 1957).

[42] *See, e.g.*, State v Butler, 221 SW2d 160 (Mo 1949); State v Grillo, 16 NJ 103, 106 A2d 294 (1954); Perdue v State, 225 Ga 814, 171 SE2d 563 (1969); State v Thorne, 41 Utah 414, 126 P 286 (1912).

An opinion on an issue which is not material, on the other hand, will not be disqualifying. In a Utah case, for example, a challenge for cause was held properly denied where a juror had stated that if a petition relating to the crime with which the defendant was charged had been presented to him, he "possibly would have signed it." The appellate court said that it appeared from the examination as a whole that the juror did not mean that he approved of the sentiments in the petition, but only that he might, without giving the matter any particular thought, have signed it. Thus the willingness to sign the petition was deemed irrelevant.[43] Similarly, it has been held that prospective jurors with an opinion on the adequacies or inadequacies of jury verdicts in negligence cases are not disqualified by virtue of that opinion alone.[44]

§7.08 —Subject to Change by Proof

Whether a preconceived opinion on a material issue in a case will disqualify a juror depends on the strength and firmness of that opinion. Tests laid down by Chief Justice Marshall in the trial of Aaron Burr have generally been accepted as striking the appropriate balance:

> [That] light impressions, which may fairly be presumed to yield to the testimony that may be offered, which may leave the mind open to a fair consideration of the testimony, constitute no sufficient objection to a juror; but . . . those strong and deep impressions which close the mind against the testimony that may be offered in opposition to them, which will combat that testimony and resist its force, do constitute a sufficient objection to him.[45]

If a prospective juror admits to an opinion as to the guilt or innocence of a defendant in a criminal case, or an opinion on the material facts adverse to or favorable to either party in a civil case, the trial judge must be convinced that the opinion is subject to change by the evidence before denying a challenge for cause. The trial judge must carefully assess the credibility of the juror who claims that the opinion is not so strong that it could not be changed by the evidence.

Unfortunately, some jurors, are not completely candid, and their answers to questions about the strength of their opinions may be misleading or inaccu-

---

[43] State v Thorne, 41 Utah 414, 126 P 286 (1912). Viewed in isolation, the court's reasoning seems strained, and its conclusion questionable. The better practice would have been to excuse the juror at the time. After the jury's verdict has been returned, however, an appellate court's reluctance to order a new trial on somewhat speculative grounds is understandable.

[44] *E.g.*, Kujawa v Baltimore Transit Co, 224 Md 195, 167 A2d 96 (1961).

[45] Burr's Trial 416, *quoted in* Reynolds v United States, 98 US 145, 155 (1878). *See also* Irvin v Dowd, 366 US 717, 722-23 (1961).

rate.[46] The task facing the attorney is twofold: first, to discern such disingenuousness; and second, to expose it through skilled voir dire questioning. The attorney needs to be given the opportunity to rebut the presumption of impartiality.[47]

Whether a criminal defendant has been denied due process because of a juror's preconceived opinion is a question of mixed law and fact.[48] A declaration of impartiality, after a juror has admitted to an opinion on a material fact, must be unequivocal and absolute.

A juror who admits to an opinion but asserts that it will be possible to fairly and impartially try the case according to the law and the evidence, is generally held competent to serve, assuming, of course, that the judge believes the juror.[49] Jurors need not be totally ignorant of the facts and issues involved; it is sufficient if they can lay aside an impression or opinion and render a verdict based on the evidence presented.[50]

Juror disqualification because of a preconceived opinion is decided in the first instance by the trial court. The trial court's decision is subject to review on appeal.[51] The appellate court is under a duty to independently evaluate the voir dire testimony of the juror to determine partiality.[52]

A juror will generally be disqualified by an admission that an opinion will require strong and positive evidence to overcome it, especially where the juror, in response to a not uncommon question, concedes hesitance to be tried by someone in the juror's own frame of mind.[53] Some courts go further, taking the position that a criminal accused should not have to take a chance on a juror who has a preconceived opinion, regardless of how impartially the juror pledges to act.[54]

§7.09 —Opinion of the Law

A juror is not disqualified for having an opinion on the law. However, the juror will be disqualified if he or she indicates an intention to follow that personal opinion rather than the instructions of the court. This is a proper subject of inquiry, and it has been held to be reversible error for a trial court to refuse

---

[46] *See generally* **§12.14.**

[47] *See* Murphy v Florida, 421 US 794, 800 (1975).

[48] Irvin v Dowd, 366 US 717, 723 (1961).

[49] Spies v Illinois, 123 US 131 (1887); Hopt v Utah, 120 US 430 (1887); Reynolds v United States, 98 US 145 (1878); Seals v Snow, 123 Kan 88, 254 P 348 (1927); State v Beck, 286 SE2d 234 (W Va 1981).

[50] Murphy v Florida, 421 US 794 (1975); Irvin v Dowd, 366 US 717 (1961).

[51] Coughlin v People, 144 Ill 140, 33 NE 1 (1893).

[52] Irvin v Dowd, 366 US 717, 723 (1961). *See also* Murphy v Florida, 421 US 794 (1975).

[53] Fitts v Southern Pac Co, 149 Cal 310, 86 P 710 (1906).

[54] *See, e.g.,* Scribner v State, 3 Okla Crim 601, 108 P 422 (1910); Burns v State, 145 Wis 373, 128 NW 987 (1910).

to question jurors as to their willingness to accept the presumption of innocence and the requirement of proof beyond a reasonable doubt.[55]

Illustrative of both the general rule and its application is *State v Rowe.*[56] The court stated that a juror who could not subordinate her personal opinion on an issue of law and obey the law set forth in the court's instructions must be excused for cause. However, the court questioned the juror and concluded that her views were not so fixed that she would be unable to follow its instructions as to the law.

§7.10 The Problem of Pretrial Publicity

Pretrial publicity is probably the most common source of preconceived opinions among jurors. This is particularly true in sensational cases which are covered in great detail, sometimes for weeks or months, by the media.

There are several ways of combating the effects of pretrial publicity. If the media coverage has been so pervasive and prejudicial as to prevent a fair trial, a judge can dismiss the case.[57] Most trial judges, however, will be understandably reluctant to embrace so drastic a remedy. A more likely resolution is the granting of a continuance until such time as the publicity subsides,[58] or a change in venue to a community in which the publicity has been less pervasive.[59] These options are unlikely to resolve the problem completely and it usually will be necessary to closely examine jurors on voir dire to determine what publicity they have been exposed to and what effect that publicity has had on them.

Mere exposure to pretrial publicity will not necessarily lead to disqualification. A juror who can convince the court that he or she can still be impartial will be allowed to serve.[60] A landmark case decided by the United States Supreme Court in 1887 held that a trial court did not commit error in allowing such a juror to sit where the juror indicated a willingness to decide the case on the proof presented.[61]

Holt v United States[62] presented the Supreme Court with a similar fact situation. The juror in *Holt* admitted to an opinion about the case formed on the

---

[55] United States v Hill, 738 F2d 152 (6th Cir 1984). *See also* Harvey v State, 341 So 2d 187 (Ala Ct Crim App 1977).

[56] 210 Neb 419, 315 NW2d 250 (1982).

[57] *See* United States v Cotton, No 68-CR-113 (ED Wis Sept 9, 1969) an unreported Wisconsin opinion *discussed in* 1 A. Ginger, Jury Selection in Civil and Criminal Trials 375-79 (2d ed 1984).

[58] *See* Patton v Young, 467 US 1025 (1984).

[59] *See* **§§2.02-2.06.**

[60] Murphy v Florida, 421 US 794 (1975); Irvin v Dowd, 366 US 717, 723 (1961); Gadd v Commonwealth, 305 Ky 318, 204 SW2d 215 (Ct App 1947); Commonwealth v McGrew, 375 Pa 518, 100 A2d 467 (1953); Chatterton v State, 221 Ga 424, 144 SE2d 726, *cert denied,* 384 US 1015 (1965).

[61] Spies v Illinois, 123 US 131 (1887).

[62] 218 US 245 (1910).

basis of newspaper accounts, which the juror accepted as accurate. The juror stated that evidence would change his opinion, although it would take some evidence to remove it. He further stated that if the evidence failed to substantiate the factual allegations in the newspapers, he would decide the case in accord with the evidence. The Supreme Court declined to overturn the trial court's refusal to sustain a challenge for cause to the juror.

A trial judge must carefully evaluate the words, attitude, and demeanor of a juror who asserts an impartial mind which is free from prejudice despite exposure to pretrial publicity. If the judge has any lingering doubt about the juror's capacity for total fairness and impartiality, the juror should be excused. In one case the fact that a juror knew and had confidence in the author of a newspaper article which was the basis for the juror's opinion tipped the balance in favor of disqualification.[63]

The modern media age, where news is available to potential jurors in an ever-expanding variety of forms, has exacerbated the problem of pretrial publicity. In the past several decades the United States Supreme Court has had to address what constitutes an impartial jury, as well as a fair trial, in this context. The results have not always been consistent.

In *Irvin v Dowd*[64] the defendant was convicted of murder in an Indiana state court and sentenced to death. Six murders had occurred in the area where trial was held. The murders had received extensive news coverage in the local press. Of the 430-person jury panel, 268 were excused for cause as having fixed opinions on the guilt of the accused. Eight of the twelve who finally served on the jury admitted that they thought he was guilty, but each indicated an intent to render an impartial verdict notwithstanding such opinion.

The United States Supreme Court held that Irvin did not receive the fair and impartial trial to which he was entitled under the due process clause of the fourteenth amendment. The Court began by noting the complexity of the problem:

> It is not required . . . that the jurors be totally ignorant of the facts and issues involved. In these days of swift, widespread and diverse methods of communication, an important case can be expected to arouse the interest of the public in the vicinity, and scarcely any of those best qualified to serve as jurors will not have formed some impression or opinion as to the merits of the case. This is particularly true in criminal cases. To hold that the mere existence of any preconceived notion as to the guilt or innocence of an accused, without more, is sufficient to rebut the presumption of a prospective juror's impartiality would be to establish an impossible standard. It is sufficient if the juror can lay aside his impression or opinion and render a verdict based on the evidence presented in court.[65]

---

[63] Sullins v State, 79 Ark 127, 95 SW 159 (1906).

[64] 366 US 717 (1961).

[65] *Id* 722-23.

The Court thus appeared to presume impartiality. It placed the burden of rebuttal on the challenging party: "Unless he shows the actual existence of such an opinion in the mind of the juror as will raise the presumption of partiality, the juror need not necessarily be set aside. . . ."[66]

In applying this test to the facts of the case, however, the Court seemed to do a somersault. It found that persistent and prejudicial news coverage had so permeated the community as to make impartiality impossible.[67] The Court chose to disbelieve the declarations of some impaneled jurors that they could render an impartial verdict, tendering its own analysis of the psychological processes at work:

> The influence that lurks in an opinion once formed is so persistent that it unconsciously fights detachment from the mental processes of the average man. . . . No doubt each juror was sincere when he said that he would be fair and impartial to petitioner, but psychological impact requiring such a declaration before one's fellows is often its father.[68]

Thus, the Court in fact may have presumed partiality rather than impartiality and adopted a theory of opinion formation that made rebutting this presumption virtually impossible.

The Court tilted even more toward the position that knowledge per se is unacceptable in *Rideau v Louisiana.*[69] A local television station had on several occasions broadcast the defendant's confession to the crimes with which he was charged. Given the circumstances, the Supreme Court held that the refusal of the defense's request for a change of venue denied the defendant due process.[70] This unremarkable holding was supplemented by reflections on the more general question of the desirability of "knowledgeable" jurors. Justice Stewart, writing for the majority, observed:

> For anyone who has ever watched television the conclusion cannot be avoided that this spectacle, to the tens of thousands of people who saw

---

66 *Id* 723 (quoting Reynolds v United States, 98 US 145, 157 (1878)). *See also* Marshall v United States, 360 US 310 (1959) (presuming prejudice on the part of prospective jurors who knew of the defendant's record).

67 *Irvin,* 366 US at 725.

68 *Id* 728. *See also* ABA Advisory Comm on Fair Trial and Free Press, Standards Relating to Fair Trial and Free Press (1968):

> [S]tudies indicate that people tend to form beliefs on a minimum of information and that because of the desire for social approval, they often attempt to reflect the opinions and beliefs of others. Available data also suggest that once formed, an impression or belief is extremely difficult to change, even when the individual is confronted with objective facts that tend to refute it. . . . In other words, the individual is likely to select those elements of observed phenomena which reinforce his preexisting beliefs and to neglect others or even to distort his perceptions so that they will confirm his beliefs.

Id 62.

69 373 US 723 (1963).

70 *Id* 726.

> and heard it, in a very real sense *was* Rideau's trial—at which he pleaded guilty to murder. Any subsequent court proceedings in a community so pervasively exposed to such a spectacle could be but a hollow formality.[71]

Furthermore, the Court did not find it necessary to inquire whether any individual juror's impartiality had been affected:

> [W]e do not hesitate to hold, without pausing to examine a particularized transcript of the voir dire examination of the members of the jury, that due process of law in this case required a trial before a jury drawn from a community of people who had not seen and heard Rideau's televised "interview."[72]

While the decision may have turned on the extreme facts of the case, the Court's language, besides suggesting the extraordinary proposition that the lower court should have granted a change in venue even if none of the jurors had seen or were aware of the television broadcast, appeared to indicate that impartiality presumes lack of knowledge about the facts of a case.

The Court retreated from its *Rideau* position in *Murphy v Florida.*[73] It stated that the mere exposure of some jurors to adverse publicity about the defendant did not presumptively deny him due process.[74] Significantly, the Court did what it had declined to do in *Rideau:* it examined the transcript of the voir dire to determine whether any of the jurors were in fact biased against the accused.[75] Although previous cases were distinguished as involving widespread community bias,[76] the Court provided no empirical support for its inference that widespread community bias rendered individual jurors' assertions of impartiality less reliable.

Any per se linking of impartiality with knowledge is questionable. One effect is to penalize well-read citizens. The better informed a person is on current events, the less likely that person is to satisfy a conception of impartiality which views advance knowledge as undesirable.[77] Individuals who, in most respects, would be considered model citizens will be deemed unfit for jury duty. The seemingly inevitable result will be juries representative of the "average stupid-

---

[71] *Id* (emphasis in original).

[72] *Id* 727.

[73] 421 US 794 (1975).

[74] *Id* 796.

[75] *Id* 800-02.

[76] *Id* 802-03.

[77] There is a subtle irony between the common practice of drawing jury panels from voting lists, thereby selecting persons with an interest in public affairs, while at the same time seeking petit jurors not knowledgeable about the case because they do not keep up with current events.

ity."[78] Regardless of whether such stupidity is reflective of the community, it is doubtful that this is what the Supreme Court had in mind when it called for a jury drawn from a fair cross-section of the community.[79] Indeed, it would seem that eliminating the more knowledgeable portion of the population from jury duty would be in tension with the fair cross-section requirement. A blue ribbon panel composed only of the best informed and most intelligent members of society may not be the objective,[80] but neither is its opposite. Furthermore, in an era in which news coverage is constantly expanding and in which information in a wide variety of forms is readily available, finding an unknowledgeable juror in a highly publicized case may not be an easy task.[81]

While the Supreme Court appeared at one time to be drifting toward the position that knowledge is inconsistent with impartiality, the more pertinent inquiry is the extent to which knowledge has affected impartiality. The focus should be on the "animus" of the individual juror. Only when a juror's ability to decide the case fairly and justly has been compromised by the information or knowledge to which he or she has been exposed should the juror be disqualified. This is not a concession to the pervasiveness of the modern media's coverage of news but a return to the principles enunciated by Chief Justice Marshall in *United States v Burr*:[82]

> Were it possible to obtain a jury without any prepossessions whatever respecting the guilt or innocence of the accused, it would be extremely desirable to obtain such a jury, but this is perhaps impossible; and therefore will not be required. The opinion which has been avowed by the court is, that light impressions which may fairly be supposed to yield to the testimony that may be offered, which may leave the mind open to a fair consid-

---

[78] H. Spencer, *Representative Government,* in Essays: Moral Political and Aesthetic 182 (1868). *See also* United States v Mesarosh, 116 F Supp 345, 348 (WD Pa 1953), *affd,* 223 F2d 449 (3d Cir 1955), *revd,* 352 US 1 (1956) ("to obtain a juror who would make the right answer (from defendants' point of view) to the question propounded, he or she would have to be a person who had lived in a vacuum, or was an imbecile, or a communist"); M. Twain, Roughing It 341-43 (1872) ("when the peremptory challenges were all exhausted, a jury of twelve men was impaneled—a jury who swore that they had neither heard, read, talked about nor expressed an opinion concerning a murder which the very cattle . . . were cognizant of.").

[79] *See generally* **§6.13.**

[80] *Compare* Thiel v Southern Pac Co, 328 US 217, 224 (1946) (jury is not "the province of the economically and socially privileged") *and* Glasser v United States, 315 US 60, 86 (1942) (jury is not to be "the organ of any special group or class") *with* Fay v New York, 332 US 261 (1947) (approving use of blue ribbon jury). *See generally* Dubois, *Desirability of Blue Ribbon Juries,* 13 Hastings LJ 479 (1962); Note, *The Blue Ribbon Jury,* 60 Harv L Rev 613 (1947).

[81] In Nebraska Press Assn v Stuart, 427 US 539, 549 n 3 (1976), the Supreme Court questioned whether a fair trial was even possible in a highly publicized national crime, such as the killings of President Kennedy and Lee Harvey Oswald. *See generally* Padawer, Singer & Barton, *Impact of Pretrial Publicity on Juror's Verdicts,* in The Jury System In America: A Critical Overview (R. Simon ed 1975).

[82] 25 F Cas 49 (CCD Va 1807) (No 14,692g), discussed in **§7.03.**

> eration of that testimony, constitute no sufficient objection to a juror; but that those strong and deep impressions which will close the mind against the testimony that may be offered in opposition to them, which will combat that testimony, and resist its force, do constitute a sufficient objection to him.[83]

The vulnerable point in this analysis is the assumption that faint impressions[84] can be set aside. Psychologically this may not be so, and in any event the hypothesis must be explored on an individual basis. Even a faint impression may make an indelible, albeit unappreciated, impact on a particular juror's psyche. Expert evaluation may be needed to make this determination. Although this may be time-consuming and difficult, the alternative of disqualifying all knowledgeable jurors may be worse. To again quote Chief Justice Marshall:

> It would seem to the court that to say that any man who had formed an opinion on any fact conducive to the final decision of the case would therefore be considered as disqualified from serving on the jury, would exclude intelligent and observing men, whose minds were really in a situation to decide upon the whole case according to the testimony, and would perhaps be applying the letter of the rule requiring an impartial jury with a strictness which is not necessary for the preservation of the rule itself.[85]

Chief Justice Marshall's opinion points the way to the relevant considerations in analyzing the proper relationship between knowledge and impartiality: (1) knowledge on the part of the jurors is more or less inevitable; (2) the more intelligent and well informed the potential juror, the more likely he or she is to know something about the case; (3) persons generally knowledgeable about public affairs will in most instances be more discerning jurors than those who are generally ignorant about public affairs; (4) a juror's impartiality is compromised only to the extent that the juror's knowledge impedes a decision on the merits; and (5) whether a juror's impartiality has in fact been compromised by knowledge must be determined on an individual basis. In short, recognition that a particular juror possesses information relating to a case must be the start, not the end, of the inquiry.

§7.11 —Examination of Juror

A prospective juror who admits to a preconceived opinion on a material issue in a case should be fully examined as to the extent of that opinion. It is proper to question the juror about the strength of the opinion, as well as the juror's ability to render a verdict based on the evidence.

---

[83] 25 F Cas at 50-51.

[84] Part of the problem, of course, lies in defining what constitutes a "faint impression." A "faint impression" for one juror may cause another to faint.

[85] *Burr,* 25 F Cas at 51.

Consider the issue which has arisen in many jurisdictions in recent years of the propriety of questioning prospective jurors as to their exposure to advertising by the insurance industry on the effects of personal injury jury verdicts on insurance premiums, and whether such exposure has caused them to form an opinion about the appropriate amount of damages in personal injury cases. Questioning jurors on this topic may be proper, but care must be taken to frame questions so that they are directed to the proposed juror's fairness and impartiality.[86] In one case the trial court refused to permit this question: "Have you read any article or literature or have you heard any discussion recently on amounts of verdicts in negligence cases, and if so, have you formed any ideas with reference to the amount of jury verdicts?" The denial was held not an abuse of the court's wide discretion in the matter.[87] Even if the subject of the inquiry was proper, said the court, the question was not framed so as to probe for the existence of a cause for disqualification, the sole purpose of voir dire examination in the jurisdiction. The court characterized the questions as being in the nature of an impermissible "fishing expedition."[88]

The court's decision is questionable. Although the lawyer's compound question may have been objectionable in form, it does seem to have been designed to lay a foundation for further inquiry as to bias. Arguably a lawyer must be given a fairly wide leeway to ensure an impartial jury.

§7.12 Prior Personal Experiences

Persons are the products of their environment, training, and experiences. These influences affect not only a prospective juror's personality and general character, but also the juror's attitudes toward other people and toward issues which arise in lawsuits. Often personal experience lies at the root of prejudice. The effect can vary from a slight leaning toward a side to a deep-rooted and unshakable conviction which will make a juror incapable of objectivity. Thus, relevant past experiences of prospective jurors are the proper subject of voir dire questioning.

Take the example of a personal injury case in which the plaintiff plans to call a chiropractor to testify. It is obviously important that jurors not be prejudiced against chiropractors. There are many people who have received, or who have close friends or family who have received, successful treatment from chiropractors and who as a result have a high opinion of them. Such jurors would not hesitate to accept the testimony of a chiropractor. Conversely, many people consider chiropractors to be quacks, and would give no credence whatever to their testimony.

The plaintiff's attorney should face the issue squarely. The attorney might begin with an open-ended question to the juror about their experiences or

---

[86] *See* **§7.34.**

[87] Kujawa v Baltimore Transit Co, 224 Md 195, 167 A2d 96 (1961). *See generally* Annotation, *Voir Dire Inquiry, in Personal Injury or Death Case, as to Prospective Jurors' Acquaintance with Literature Dealing with Amounts of Verdicts,* 89 ALR2d 1177 (1963).

[88] Kujawa v Baltimore Transit Co, 224 Md 195, 167 A2d 96, 98 (1961).

those of close friends and relatives with chiropractors. Each juror should then be asked first, whether, based on these or any other experiences, the juror has an opinion about chiropractors; second, what that opinion is; and finally, whether in light of that opinion the juror would be able to listen to the testimony of a chiropractor and evaluate it on the same basis as that of any other medical witness. If the juror admits to an inability to accept the testimony of a chiropractor, the lawyer should challenge the juror for cause. After hopefully eliminating those jurors who have a low opinion of chiropractors, the lawyer should extract a promise from the remaining jurors that they will fairly and impartially weigh the testimony of the chiropractor.

In criminal cases, too, lawyers are concerned about the past experiences of jurors. It is routine to ask jurors whether any of them has ever been the victim of a crime. Jurors who respond affirmatively can be expected to consciously or subconsciously identify with the victim. This identification is likely to be particularly strong where the crime committed on the juror is similar to the one with which the defendant in the case is charged. Such jurors have been held properly subject to challenge for cause.[89] Where a juror, rather than being a victim, has been convicted of or indicted for an offense similar to that charged against the defendant, a challenge for cause has again been held proper.[90]

§7.13 —Prior Experiences of Family Members

Jurors are influenced not only by their own personal experiences, but also by those of family members. Assume, for example, a personal injury case where the defendant is protected by insurance. The plaintiff's lawyer is questioning a Mrs. Johnson, who would appear to be an excellent juror. However, Mrs. Johnson's daughter, Karen, has worked in the claims department of an insurance company for some 10 years. There is a strong possibility that Karen has developed a cynical attitude toward claimants in general. It is also quite possible that Karen has conveyed this attitude to her mother. As a result, Mrs. Johnson might view the plaintiff's case with suspicion. Plaintiff's attorney would want to closely examine Mrs. Johnson as to her relationship with her daughter, and her daughter's experiences with insurance claimants.

Suppose, on the other hand, that Mrs. Johnson's daughter, Karen, is engaged to a lawyer who regularly represents plaintiffs in personal injury cases. It is now very possible that Karen's fiancé will be distrustful of insurance companies. He has probably conveyed his skepticism to Karen and she to her mother. The result will be that Mrs. Johnson would make a most desirable juror for the plaintiff, but not for the defendant. In this situation it would be the defense attorney

---

[89] Leon v State, 396 So 2d 203 (Fla Dist Ct App 1981); Nailor v People, 612 P2d 79 (Colo 1980). *But compare* People v Abbott, 690 P2d 1263 (Colo 1984) (not all crime victims, by virtue of that fact alone, subject to challenge). As to cases where a prospective juror and the crime victim share a common occupation, see Annotation, *Similarity of Occupation Between Proposed Juror and Alleged Victim of Crime as Affecting Juror's Competency,* 71 ALR3d 974 (1976).

[90] Lollar v State, 422 So 2d 809 (Ala Crim App 1982).

who would want to closely question Mrs. Johnson about the attitudes and experiences of her daughter and her daughter's fiancé.

The experiences of a family member will not necessarily disqualify a juror; only when they cause the juror to be biased. Both the past experience and its effect on the juror need to be explored on voir dire. *State v Young*[91] is illustrative. A juror in a rape case admitted that two of his cousins had been raped several years previous. The juror, however, denied that these events would affect him and stated that he would be fair to both sides. The trial judge believed the juror and denied the defense challenge for cause. The appellate court found no abuse of discretion.

Often the issue arises in a criminal case where a juror has a close family member who is a police officer. In *State v Sylvester,*[92] the court held that the refusal to grant a challenge for cause was an abuse of discretion and a basis for reversal where the juror had a long association of employment with the city police, as well as other connections with police and law enforcement officers, including a son who was a police detective. The court reached this result despite the juror's claims of being able to be impartial.[93] In comparison, in *State v Heald*[94] the court held that a personal, social, or familial relationship with a law enforcement officer would not justify a challenge for cause absent a showing of bias.[95]

§7.14 —Personal Injuries

In a personal injury case, both the plaintiff's and the defendant's lawyers will want to question a juror about all tortious injuries received by the juror or a member of the juror's family. Such an experience is very likely to color a juror's objectivity. If, for instance, a juror has been seriously injured as a result of an automobile collision firmly believed to have been caused by another party's fault, such juror's thinking in an automobile collision case in particular and tort cases in general is likely to be affected. The juror should be closely questioned about the accident, the nature and seriousness of the injury, and the effect that the experience might have on the juror's approach to the case.

The influence of such an experience may depend on the disposition of any claim the juror may have filed as a result of the injury. For example, suppose the juror sued the other driver's insurance company and the insurance company refused to settle. The insurance company's intransigence may have induced in the juror an extremely hostile attitude to tort defendants and insurance companies. The juror's personal, perhaps atypical, experience will have become generalized. On the other hand, another juror seriously injured by

---

[91] 643 SW2d 28 (Mo Ct App 1982).

[92] 400 So 2d 640 (La 1981).

[93] *Id* 646. *See also* State v Kohler, 434 So 2d 1110 (La Ct App 1983).

[94] 443 A2d 954 (Me 1982).

[95] *See also* Sudds v Maggio, 696 F2d 415 (5th Cir 1983); State v Hall, 612 SW2d 782 (Mo 1981); State v Harrell, 637 SW2d 752 (Mo Ct App 1982); Montgomery v State, 277 Ark 95, 640 SW2d 108 (1982). The subject of a juror's connection with law enforcement as a basis of disqualification is examined further in **§7.52.**

an uninsured motorist may have had to bear the full cost of his medical expenses. This juror's hostility may manifest itself in an unwillingness to award damages to plaintiffs under similar circumstances.

The thinking of a juror who has sustained personal injuries in an accident may also be affected by the amount of damages recovered. If a juror suffered similar or more serious injuries than the plaintiff and received a sum of money in settlement of this injury, the likelihood is that this sum will become the benchmark figure used by the juror in assessing damages. The juror will also probably inform other members of the jury of the previous settlement, thereby influencing their thinking on the damage issue as well.

It should be determined whether the juror employed a lawyer in resolving any claim that arose from the juror's injury. If not, then the juror should be asked if the case was settled satisfactorily. If the juror answers yes to this question, it is likely that the other driver's insurance company entered into direct settlement with the juror. In all probability the juror received a modest amount, and will think in those terms on the present jury. If, on the other hand, the juror did hire a lawyer and received a satisfactory settlement, the juror is likely to be favorable to the plaintiff's case.

The case law relating to the challenge of jurors who have received injuries similar to the plaintiff's is not uniform. In a maintenance worker's action against a refinery for injuries resulting from exposure to allegedly dangerous chemicals, it was held that the trial court did not abuse its discretion in excusing for cause a juror who suffered from the same ailment as the plaintiff.[96] In contrast, an Oklahoma court found that a juror who admitted that he had been suffering for years from the results of an accident but who said he could nevertheless be fair and impartial had been improperly excused.[97] The court proffered the opinion that a juror who had "experienced a good deal of pain" would help the jury reach a just result, and, indeed, conceivably could be "the only one to fully understand and properly evaluate the pain element of plaintiff's damages."[98]

§7.15 —Litigation

Another type of experience which can justify a challenge for cause is past involvement in litigation as a party, witness, or juror.[99] A juror who has filed one or more lawsuits as a plaintiff is likely to be a poor juror for the defense. A juror who has had to defend against one or more lawsuits is likely to be a poor juror for the plaintiff.

Such generalizations should not be accepted without careful inquiry, however. For example, the juror who has been sued may be of the view: (1) that the plaintiff in the previous case attempted to take advantage of the juror's

---

[96] Williams v Texas City Ref, Inc, 617 SW2d 823 (Tex Civ App 1981).

[97] Brown v Oklahoma Transp Co, 588 P2d 595 (Okla Ct App 1978).

[98] *Id* 598.

[99] Prior jury service as a ground of disqualification is examined in **§§7.17-7.20.**

insurance company by filing a false or exaggerated claim; or (2), that the insurance company made a settlement which was excessive in order to avoid a lawsuit; or (3) that the insurance company refused to settle a bona fide accident claim regarding which the juror felt himself to be at fault. While the first scenario may induce a pro-defendant bias, the third may lead to an anti-insurance company bias, and the second may precipitate ambivalent feelings. Inquiry into the nature and disposition of the juror's case, as well as the juror's reaction to that disposition, is required.

§7.16 Prior Knowledge of Facts

At common law, jurors were selected because of their personal knowledge of the facts of a case. Today, jurors familiar with the facts of a case are subject to challenge for cause. Whether such knowledge will be disqualifying lies within the trial judge's discretion.[100]

Many courts have declined to allow a challenge for cause to a juror who has knowledge of the facts of the case on trial. In most of these cases the court concluded that the juror would base his or her verdict on the facts shown by the evidence, uninfluenced by the previous knowledge. Thus, in *Kunk v Howell*[101] the court said that while a juror should be excused for having prior knowledge that would raise a strong inference of bias, knowledge of undisputed facts or of facts merely collateral or incidental would not render the juror incompetent, particularly where the juror disclaimed an opinion on the merits. In *Kunk,* an automobile collision case, the appellate court upheld the trial judge's refusal to declare a mistrial where, after two of the plaintiff's witnesses had testified, a juror announced that their testimony reminded him that he had passed the scene of the accident before the cars had been moved. On questioning by the court, the juror stated unequivocally that he had no impression as to who was at fault, that he would accept the proof at trial as to location of the cars at the time, and that he knew nothing material about the case.

A like result was reached in *Genova v Kansas City,*[102] a suit for damages resulting from a fall on a sidewalk. It was there held that the trial court had not abused its discretion in rejecting the defendant's challenge for cause of two jurors. One had stated that he had walked over the sidewalk in question for about three years since the time of the accident, but that he was unacquainted with the place prior to that time, and that this circumstance would in no way affect his verdict. The other had said that he had walked over the sidewalk nearly every day for six years, but that he would experience no problem rendering a verdict on the evidence and in accord with the instructions of the court.

---

[100] *See, e.g.,* Genova v Kansas City, 254 SW2d 38 (Mo Ct App 1953); Kunk v Howell, 40 Tenn App 183, 289 SW2d 874 (1956). *See generally* Annotation, *Juror's Previous Knowledge of Facts of Civil Case as Disqualification,* 73 ALR2d 1312 (1960).

[101] 40 Tenn App 183, 289 SW2d 874 (1956).

[102] 254 SW2d 38 (Mo Ct App 1953).

On the other hand, some courts have held a prospective juror disqualified for previous knowledge of the facts. *Lewis v State*[103] involved a quo warranto proceeding to exclude the defendant from the practice of veterinary medicine. Six prospective jurors had indicated that the defendant veterinarian had treated animals for them, but that they would not be influenced by that fact. It was held that there was no reversible error or abuse of discretion in excusing these jurors, because they did have some personal knowledge of the facts. Similarly, in *People v Taylor,*[104] a criminal prosecution, it was held to be an abuse of discretion for the trial judge to fail to excuse for cause jurors who were aware that a codefendant had been released after passing a lie detector test.

Even if a juror would be disqualified by personal knowledge, failure to challenge the juror for cause will constitute a waiver of the objection. Thus, in a case involving a suit for damages caused by blasting, a juror disclosed on the second day of the trial that he had knowledge of the blasting but had not recalled it until that time. It was held on appeal that the knowledge disqualified the juror. However, since the parties, after being informed of the situation, consented to continuation of the trial with the juror in the box, objection to the juror had been waived.[105]

§7.17 Prior Jury Service—Statutes

Prior jury service as a basis for disqualification arises occasionally, primarily in criminal cases. In two situations prior jury service can result in the disqualification of a juror: (1) where a state statute disqualifies a person from jury service within a prescribed time after earlier jury service; and (2) where the prior service has resulted in some bias or opinion in the juror affecting service in the subsequent case.

State statutes governing prior jury service differ. Some make jury service within a particular period of time a basis for a juror to request to be excused from subsequent service; others designate prior jury service as a grounds for challenge for cause; still others provide that a person who has served as a juror is not to be called again or be eligible for jury service within a specified time period.

The latter statutes have given rise to the question of the appropriate remedy when a violation occurs. One view holds that, since the statute is for the benefit of the juror, disqualification is not automatic.[106] There are, however, decisions to the contrary.[107] In the federal courts, the provision for challenge of a juror based on previous jury service formerly found at 18 USC §1869 has been rewritten. It now provides that in any two-year period, no person is required

---

[103] 260 Ala 368, 70 So 2d 790 (1954).

[104] 101 Ill 2d 377, 462 NE2d 478 (1984).

[105] Cook v Kansas City, 358 Mo 296, 214 SW2d 430 (1948).

[106] *E.g.,* Commonwealth v Di Stasio, 297 Mass 347, 8 NE2d 923 (1937). *See also* Harris v People, 113 Colo 511, 160 P2d 372 (1945).

[107] *E.g.,* Coca Cola Bottling Co v Jones, 74 Ariz 393, 250 P2d 586 (1952); City of Goshen v England, 119 Ind 368, 21 NE 977 (1889).

to serve as a petit juror for a total of more than thirty days (except when necessary to complete service in a particular case), or to serve on more than one grand jury, or to serve as both a grand and petit juror.[108]

The failure of a juror to disclose previous jury service within the statutory period is generally held not a ground for reversal or a new trial unless there has been prejudice.[109] The fact of conviction does not per se establish prejudice.

§7.18 —Basis for Challenge for Cause

A member of a jury which returned a verdict in a previous trial in the same case, or a juror in the same case in which a mistrial was declared, will be disqualified from subsequent service in the case.[110] This was the common law rule and is now generally embodied in statute. Denial of a challenge based on this ground would most likely also constitute a deprivation of the constitutional right to an impartial jury.

The underlying concern is that a juror who has already been exposed to the evidence in a case is likely to have formed an opinion which would prevent the juror from being fair and impartial in a subsequent trial where the parties and issues are the same.[111] The trial of the same defendant but on an unrelated charge raises similar problems involving the juror's being influenced by the evidence and outcome of the previous case; this, too, may serve as a basis of challenge for cause.[112] Prior jury service on a case involving the same witnesses however, has been held not disqualifying.[113]

---

[108] 28 USC §1866(e).

[109] *E.g.*, Harris v People, 113 Colo 511, 160 P2d 372 (1945). *Contra* Nuchols v Commonwealth, 312 Ky 171, 226 SW2d 796 (1950). *See generally* Annotation, *Failure of Juror in Criminal Case to Disclose His Previous Jury Service Within Disqualifying Period As Ground For Reversal or New Trial,* 13 ALR2d 1482 (1950).

[110] *See* Government of the Virgin Islands v Parrott, 551 F2d 553 (3d Cir 1977); Mottram v Murch, 458 F2d 626 (1st Cir), *revd on other grounds,* 409 US 41 (1972). *See generally* Annotation, *Juror's Presence at or Participation in Trial of Criminal Case (or Related Hearing) as Ground for Disqualification in Subsequent Criminal Case Involving Same Defendant,* 6 ALR3d 519 (1966). The same rule applies when the juror sat on the indicting grand jury. *E.g.*, Moya v State, 691 SW2d (Tex Crim App 1985). *See generally* Annotation, *Prior Jury Service on Grand Jury Which Considered Indictment Against Accused as Disqualification For Service on Petit Jury,* 24 ALR3d 1236 (1969).

[111] Burke v McKenzie, 313 P2d 1090 (Okla 1957); *see generally* Annotation, *supra* note 110, 6 ALR3d 519. While one might expect the same reasoning to apply where jurors at the second trial were physically present at the first trial, albeit not as jurors, the contrary has been held where the jurors claimed not to have formed an opinion as to defendants' guilt or innocence. Warden v State, 214 Tenn 398, 381 SW2d 247 (1964).

[112] Donavon v Davis, 558 F2d 201 (4th Cir 1977). *See also* Kelly v State, 371 So 2d 162 (Fla Dist Ct App 1979). *Contra* State v Riley, 151 W Va 364, 151 SE2d 308 (1966). *See also* Smith v State, 651 P2d 1067 (Okla Crim App 1982) (juror excused at defendant's earlier trial not disqualified).

[113] People v McCarver, 87 Mich App 12, 273 NW2d 570 (1978) (defense witnesses); State v Alvarez, 93 NM 761, 605 P2d 1160 (1978) (prosecution witnesses).

On a less case-specific level, prior jury service, like other experiences in a juror's life, may influence the juror's thinking in a subsequent action. Jurors who indicate prior jury service, particularly in a case similar to the one on trial, should be questioned about the verdict in the previous case and whether anything in the previous service would make it difficult for them to sit on the present case, or affect their verdict in the present case. Counsel should impress on jurors the fact that every case is different. The facts and law in an earlier case have no bearing on the facts and law of a later case. Sometimes, however, unusual or unpleasant experiences connected with prior jury service leave jurors with feelings about jury service, litigants, or lawyers that will affect their ability to be fair and impartial in a later case. Questioning jurors about past jury service can itself have a salutary effect, serving to call the juror's attention to the possibility of bias resulting from the previous jury experience.

§7.19 —Criminal Cases

Whether a juror may be challenged for cause for partiality resulting from previous jury experience in a similar criminal case will primarily depend on two factors: first, the extent of the juror's participation in the prior case; and second, the relationship between that case and the one in which the objection is being made. Individuals who have served on a jury which convicted a defendant have been held not competent to serve on a later case involving a codefendant or a defendant charged with commission of the same offense.[114] This rule has been applied despite a juror's assurance on voir dire that he or she can be fair and impartial.[115] The reasoning is that where the issues and facts in the two trials are virtually identical, the defendant in the second trial would be deprived of a fair and impartial jury if the case were to be decided by jurors who had heard the evidence in the first trial. If, however, the first trial did not reach the point of actual presentation of evidence, or if the juror was not exposed to evidence, the reasoning would not apply.[116]

---

[114] *See* United States v McIver, 688 F2d 726 (11th Cir 1982); Zartman v State, 667 P2d 1256 (Alaska Ct App 1983); Miracle v Commonwealth, 646 SW2d 720 (Ky 1983); Farrar v Commonwealth, 201 Va 5, 109 SE2d 112 (1959). *See generally* Annotation, *Effect Upon Accused's Sixth Amendment Right to Impartial Jury of Jurors Having Served on Jury Hearing Matter Arising Out of Same Transaction or Series of Transactions,* 68 ALR Fed 919 (1984).

[115] Langston v State, 129 Miss 394, 92 So 554 (1922); Helber v State, 37 Ohio App 333, 174 NE 804 (1930).

[116] *See, e.g.,* United States v Phillips, 577 F2d 688 (10th Cir 1978); Bonner v State, 180 Ga App 239, 348 SE2d 903 (1986). This result, however, should not ensue if the first trial ends with defendant pleading guilty. *See* Miracle v Commonwealth, 646 SW2d 720 (Ky 1983).

The general rule is demonstrated in *Lett v United States.*[117] The defendant and his wife were separately tried, although charged with participating in the same criminal events. A verdict of guilty was returned against the wife on the day the husband went to trial. It was held that the latter's challenge to eight jurors who sat on the trial of his wife should have been sustained. The language of the court is instructive:

> While we do not think the course of justice in all cases should be delayed because of the unavoidable presence in court of jurors during the trial of cases thus related, unless the prejudice claimed is sufficiently apparent, nevertheless, under the circumstances here existing, we cannot feel that the retention of these eight jurors, who had just previously sat upon the case of the wife, and had returned a verdict of guilty therein, was consistent with the requirements of a fair and impartial trial before an open-minded and unprejudiced jury. Especially is this true where, under the testimony, both husband and wife are said to have participated in the offense under consideration. The presumption of prejudice is too great to be ignored.[118]

A different approach is taken where the second trial is of a defendant for a similar offense which, however, arose out of a transaction separate and distinct from the one in the first case. In this situation the only real similarity is in the nature of the crime charged. A juror who served in the first trial is usually held not to be disqualified from serving in the second.[119]

A Washington rape prosecution illustrates the point.[120] Several jurors on the panel had served on a jury which had convicted another defendant of raping the same prosecutrix on a different occasion. The court held that these jurors were not disqualified in the subsequent case, saying:

> There are cases which hold that a person who has sat as a juror on the trial of a defendant is disqualified to sit on the trial of his codefendant. The rule is founded on the principle that the second trial is but a retrial of the same offense, and that a juror who has heard and rendered a verdict in the first trial must necessarily have an opinion as to the guilt or innocence of the accused. But no such condition appears in the case before us. There were two distinct and separate crimes, committed at different times, having no relation one with the other save that they were of the same character and were committed on the same person. A juror who had been convinced of the guilt of the defendant in the first could not

[117] 15 F2d 690 (8th Cir 1926).

[118] *Id* 691.

[119] Wilkes v United States, 291 F 988 (6th Cir 1923), *cert denied,* 263 US 719 (1924); State v Conner, 59 Idaho 695, 89 P2d 197 (1939); State v Hutchens, 604 SW2d 26 (Mo Ct App 1980).

[120] State v Van Waters, 36 Wash 358, 78 P 897 (1904).

from that fact alone have any knowledge or opinion as to the guilt or innocence of the defendant in the second, and, of course, would not be disqualified for that reason.[121]

The rule that a juror in a trial of a similar but distinct offense is not automatically disqualified because of prior jury service has particular force where the juror testifies that the prior experience will not affect his or her ability to give the second defendant a fair trial according to the law and the evidence.[122] The rule is otherwise, of course, if it can be demonstrated that the prior service has engendered bias in regard to the subsequent case.[123]

Some statutes permit a challenge for cause to jurors who served on a jury of a different defendant for the same offense. These statutes have been held not applicable where the prior case arose out of a separate transaction and had no connection with the pending case.[124]

§7.20 —Civil Cases

The competence of a juror to sit on a civil jury in a case similar to one in which the juror has already served arises infrequently. What few cases there are follow the same general principles which control the decisions in criminal cases. Thus, it has been held that a juror will be disqualified in a civil action for previous service on a jury in a criminal or civil action which arose out of the same transaction involved in the pending case.[125]

A juror is not incompetent to serve on a civil jury because of previous jury service in a similar action arising out of a separate and distinct transaction.[126] This rule parallels that in criminal cases. Of course, if the prior jury service has induced a prejudice which may be reflected in the subsequent case, the juror is subject to challenge.

§7.21 Acquaintance with Parties, Witnesses, or Attorneys

A juror who is friendly with a party, witness, or attorney in a case may experience a conflict of interest between loyalty to a friend and justice to the parties.

---

[121] *Id* at 363, 78 P at 898.

[122] Ramos v United States, 12 F2d 761 (1st Cir 1926); Ladner v State, 148 Miss 243, 114 So 341 (1927); State v Russell, 73 Mont 240, 235 P 712 (1925). *But see* Tubb v State, 109 Tex Crim 455, 5 SW2d 152 (1928) (attorney should be allowed to examine juror regarding service in previous case for purpose of exercising peremptory challenges).

[123] *See* United States v Franklin, 700 F2d 1241 (10th Cir 1983).

[124] *E.g.*, Johnson v State, 1 Okla Crim 321, 97 P 1059 (1908). *See generally* Annotation, *Juror's Presence or Participation in Trial of Criminal Case (or Related Hearing) as Ground for Disqualification in Subsequent Case Involving Same Defendant,* 6 ALR3d 519 (1986).

[125] Morris v McClellan, 169 Ala 90, 53 So 155 (1910).

[126] St. John v Commercial Union Ins Co, 719 F2d 374 (11th Cir 1983); United States v 662.44 Acres of Land, More or Less, 45 F Supp 895 (DDC 1942).

The right to an impartial jury may be placed in jeopardy. One objective of the attorneys in any case, therefore, is to remove from the jury all close acquaintances of the opposing party, its witnesses, or its attorney.

The next several sections will examine the legal effect of social, business, personal, and professional relationships between a prospective juror and a party (and, in a criminal case, a victim), a witness, or an attorney.

§7.22 —Personal or Social Relationships Generally

Persons who have had past or present business or social relations with any of the principals in a case should generally be excluded from the jury.[127] This is true even though the relationship in question may not be specifically included in the statute setting forth qualifications of jurors and grounds for challenge.[128] Logic suggests that a prospective juror who is a close personal friend of one of the parties, witnesses, or attorneys in the case will find it difficult to be completely fair and unprejudiced. It is very likely that, because of their relationship, the juror will tend to favor the friend's cause or credit the friend's version of the facts. The same is true of friends of the victim in a criminal case.[129]

Whether acquaintance with a party, witness, or attorney will disqualify a juror depends largely on the nature of the relationship. A casual acquaintance will rarely be disqualifying.[130] Disqualification also depends on the likely effect of the relationship on the juror's ability to be impartial. If the juror insists that, despite the relationship, he or she can be fair to all parties, the trial judge must decide whether the juror is to be believed.[131]

This is a difficult determination, for a judge can never be completely certain that the juror will not be affected by the relationship, albeit perhaps only on a subconscious level. If the relationship is close and of long standing, it is highly unlikely not to influence the juror.[132] If there is any doubt in the judge's mind, the better practice would seem to be to excuse the juror.[133]

The state of the law is well summarized in *Commonwealth v Johnson.*[134] The court identified two distinct situations where a prospective juror should be excused for cause: first, when the juror indicates or admits bias; second, when

---

[127] *See* Gray v Sherwood, 436 So 2d 836 (Ala 1983).

[128] *See* Sherman v Southern Pac Co, 33 Nev 385, 111 P 416 (1910); Preston v Ohio Oil Co, 121 SW2d 1039 (Tex Civ App 1938).

[129] Plair v State, 453 So 2d 917 (Fla Dist Ct App 1984). *Compare* State v Wilcox, 286 SE2d 257 (W Va 1982) (not abuse of discretion to fail to disqualify jurors who were employees of victim's brother).

[130] *See, e.g.,* Hurst v State, 469 So 2d 720 (Ala App 1985); Johnson v State, 311 A2d 873 (Del 1973); People v Kirkpatrick, 70 Ill App 3d 166, 387 NE2d 1284 (1979).

[131] *See* State v Martin, 643 SW2d 63 (Mo Ct App 1982); Words v State, 367 So 2d 974, *revd,* 367 So 2d 982 (Ala 1978).

[132] *See, e.g.,* Stokes v Delcambre, 710 F2d 1120 (5th Cir 1983) (challenge for cause of juror who had relationship of 20 years' duration with defendant sustained).

[133] Sydleman v Benson, 463 So 2d 533 (Fla Dist Ct App 1985).

[134] 299 Pa Super 172, 445 A2d 509 (1982).

the relationship with a party, attorney, victim, or witness is so close that the law, in accord with common sense, should presume bias. In the first situation, because demeanor and manner of the juror are so critical, an appellate court should reverse only for a clear abuse of discretion. In the second situation, the issue is virtually one of law and therefore subject to ordinary review.[135]

§7.23 —Relationship with Witness

A juror may be disqualified because of a relationship with a witness expected to testify in a case. Whether the relationship will disqualify the juror depends on the role of the witness in the case, and the nature and extent of the relationship.[136]

Those cases declining to disturb a decision not to disqualify a juror have generally rested on the fact that there is no prejudice shown from the failure to disqualify. In *Swallow v United States,*[137] for example, a juror indicated a casual acquaintance with a probable witness. The court held that there was no basis for a post-trial hearing on the issue of the juror's qualification, especially in light of the fact that the witness did not in fact testify at the trial.[138]

In *State v Sommer*[139] a prospective juror not only knew both the defendant and the prosecuting witness, but also stated that he had formed an opinion of the case. He averred, however, that if selected, he would give both sides a fair hearing, and would decide the case solely on the evidence presented in court. On appeal it was held that the trial court did not abuse its discretion in denying a challenge for cause to the juror. The result is questionable, and it would certainly have seemed wiser to have excused the juror, if for no other reason than to preserve the appearance of impartiality.

Sometimes the relationship does not become known until during or after trial. Reversal will usually not be ordered if the juror's failure to disclose the relationship was inadvertent or unintentional. In *Zein v Pickel Stone Co,*[140] for example, it was revealed during trial that a juror was acquainted with the plaintiff's chief medical witness and had served on a board with the witness. The defendant moved unsuccessfully to discharge the jury. On appeal, the appellate court noted that failure of the juror to disclose his acquaintance with the witness was an honest mistake, and that the acquaintance was a casual one. It held that to justify discharge of the jury, the defendant would have had to demonstrate substantial prejudice as a result of the failure to disclose.[141]

The fact that a juror's acquaintance with a witness might make it awkward to return a particular verdict will not in itself disqualify the juror. In a Texas

---

[135] *Id* at 177, 445 A2d at 512.

[136] *See generally* Annotation, *Social or Business Relationship Between Proposed Juror and Nonparty Witness as Affecting Former's Qualification as Juror,* 11 ALR3d 859 (1967).

[137] 307 F2d 81 (10th Cir 1962), *cert denied,* 371 US 950 (1963).

[138] *See also* State v Williams, 650 SW2d 642 (Mo Ct App 1983).

[139] 249 Iowa 160, 86 NW2d 115 (1957).

[140] 273 SW 165 (Mo Ct App 1925).

[141] *See also* Leach v State, 47 Md App 611, 425 A2d 234 (1981).

case the defendant appealed the denial of his challenge for cause to a juror who stated on voir dire that he knew the plaintiff's doctor and that it would be embarrassing for him to render a verdict contrary to the doctor's testimony.[142] The ruling was affirmed. The appellate court pointed to the fact that the juror, although admitting that reaching a verdict contrary to the doctor's testimony would be embarrassing, declared that he thought that he could be fair and impartial. This decision can be profitably contrasted with that in *Elder v Metropolitan Atlanta Rapid Transit Authority*,[143] where it was held that the trial court did not abuse its discretion in disqualifying a juror who was the son of a physician who was to testify at trial. The range of discretion allowed a trial judge is sufficiently broad to allow the results in the two cases.

Some courts have held that disqualification of a juror is required because of a social relationship between the juror and a witness. These cases illustrate that the courts will not ignore the dictates of common sense in determining the effect of a social relationship. In *State v Joiner*,[144] for example, a juror admitted on voir dire that he was an intimate friend of the deceased. He also was friendly with the chief witness for the state, who had informed him of the facts of the case. Furthermore, the juror admitted that he had formed an opinion which it would take evidence to change. The juror nevertheless asserted that he could be impartial and that he would not necessarily believe the testimony of his friend over that of a witness whose testimony was in conflict with that of his friend. It was held error to allow this juror to sit because, in the appellate court's terms, it was not humanly possible for a person in such circumstances to be indifferent as between the state and the accused.[145]

Similarly, a conviction of first-degree murder was reversed where the appellate court found that prejudicial error had been committed in the trial judge's refusal to excuse a juror who was friendly with members of the local police.[146] The juror in question had at first denied knowing any members of the police department. Later in voir dire he admitted that he had grown up with, had gone to church with, and was a neighbor of members of the department. He admitted having known for twenty years a detective who was a key state witness and whose credibility was under direct attack. The juror maintained, however, that he would not give credit to the detective's testimony if it were contradicted by testimony from another witness. The court in reversing stated that the juror's close relationship with members of the police department suggested an inability to deal with the evidence with the impartiality required by the law. It added that while the juror may have been sincere in stating that his long

---

[142] Kiel v Mahan, 214 SW2d 865 (Tex Civ App 1948). *See also* Stevens v Burnhart, 412 A2d 1292 (Md Ct App 1980); Sydleman v Benson, 463 So 2d 533 (Fla Dist Ct App 1985).

[143] 160 Ga App 78, 286 SE2d 315 (1981).

[144] 163 La 609, 112 So 503 (1927).

[145] *Id* at 615, 112 So at 505-06.

[146] State v Jackson, 43 NJ 148, 203 A2d 1 (1964), *cert denied*, 379 US 982 (1965).

and close friendship with the detective-witness would not have had an influence, such an assertion ran contrary to human nature, and should not have been accepted at face value.[147]

§7.24 —Membership in Same Organization as Party

Membership of a prospective juror and a party in the same association or fraternal order may be grounds for disqualification. The general rule is that a member of an organization is not disqualified from sitting as a juror in a case merely because another member is a party; however, if the organization itself has an interest in the case, the juror should be disqualified.[148]

The fact that a prospective juror and a party to an action are members of the same fraternal organization, standing alone, will usually not disqualify the juror.[149] The oaths of some organizations, however, such as that of the Masons, bind a member to help fellow members regardless of who is right or wrong. In *People v Horton,*[150] the court found that this oath was not intended to apply to lawsuits. It held that Masons were therefore not automatically disqualified as jurors simply because another member of the same order was a party. The *Horton* court's approach makes particularly good sense where the juror and the party belong to different local lodges and the lodge itself has no interest in the litigation.[151]

Membership in secret orders or lodges is, however, a proper matter of inquiry to permit counsel to effectively exercise peremptory challenges. The trial court must exercise sound discretion in ruling on the propriety of such examination. Among other factors, it should consider the good faith of counsel who seeks to inquire into these matters.[152]

The appropriateness of asking jurors about their affiliations with social or secret organizations has been an issue in only a few cases. Most challenges have been unsuccessful. In one case, for instance, the court held that it was not error to overrule the defendant's challenge for cause to a juror who admitted that he belonged to the same church and lodge as the plaintiff, when the juror maintained that this fact would not influence his verdict and that he would try the case impartially.[153] In another case, *Jackson v Prestage,*[154] the court's refusal to even allow voir dire on juror membership in social clubs was upheld.

---

[147] *Accord* Wilburn v United States, 340 A2d 810 (DC 1975). *See also* State v McIntyre, 365 So 2d 1348 (La 1979).

[148] Tayloe v Commonwealth, 335 SW2d 556 (Ky Ct App 1960).

[149] *E.g.,* American Creosote Works v Harp, 215 Miss 5, 60 So 2d 514 (1952).

[150] 13 Wend 9 (NY 1834), *noted in* Annotation, *Racial, Religious, Economic, Social, or Political Prejudice of Proposed Juror as Proper Subject of Inquiry or Ground of Challenge on Voir Dire in Civil Case,* 72 ALR2d 905, 916, §8(a) (1960).

[151] *See* Reed v Peacock, 123 Mich 244, 82 NW 53 (1900).

[152] *See* Bethel v State, 162 Ark 76, 257 SW 740 (1924).

[153] American Creosote Works v Harp, 215 Miss 5, 60 So 2d 514 (1952).

[154] 204 Va 481, 132 SE2d 501 (1963).

§7.25 —Business or Professional Relationship with Party

Voir dire examination often will reveal some business or professional relationship between a prospective juror and a party. Business relationships, like social relationships, take many forms. A juror may be an employer or employee of one of the parties or may work for the same company as a party. The juror may be or have been a partner of a party. The juror may have been involved in real estate deals or other business transactions with a party. A juror may be a stockholder in a corporation which is a party to the suit or which has a direct interest in it. The critical question, as always, is whether the relationship is such as to call into question the juror's impartiality.

A stockholder of a corporation which is a party to the suit or which has a direct pecuniary interest in the outcome is ordinarily incompetent to sit as a juror in the action.[155] Also disqualified are employees and agents of a company which is party to the suit or which is otherwise financially interested in the outcome of the suit.[156]

Existence of an employment or master-servant relationship between a party and a prospective juror is usually sufficient to support a challenge for cause. In some states this is a statutory ground;[157] otherwise, the matter lies within the trial judge's discretion.[158] In *Stephens v Smith,*[159] for example, an action was brought to recover damages to the plaintiff's cedar yard caused by a fire which allegedly originated at the defendant's ranch. It was held error to overrule a challenge for cause to a juror who, at the time of the fire, was employed by the defendant and was working on the ranch where the alleged negligence occurred. Where the relationship between juror and party is less direct, and in criminal prosecutions where a juror is an employee of the victim, the results are mixed.[160]

Not all employment relationships result in disqualification. In *Kuhnke v*

---

[155] *E.g.*, Noey v Ukpeagvik Inupiat Corp, 683 P2d 260 (Alaska 1984); Thompson v Sawnee Elec Membership Corp, 157 Ga App 561, 278 SE2d 143 (1981).

[156] *E.g.*, Ozark Border Elec Coop v Stacy, 348 SW2d 586 (Mo Ct App 1961).

[157] *See, e.g.*, Washington v City of Seattle, 170 Wash 371, 16 P2d 597 (1932) (master-servant relationship between juror and adverse party, being a statutory ground of challenge, also justified disqualification in community property state of spouse of person in such relationship). *But see* Basin Elec Power Coop v Miller, 310 NW2d 715 (ND 1981) (statute providing that challenge for cause may be based on employer-employee relationship did not require employee to be disqualified as a matter of law, particularly in the absence of a challenge for cause).

[158] *E.g.*, Welch v City of Birmingham, 389 So 2d 521 (Ala Crim App 1980); Lockhart v State, 145 Md 602, 125 A 829 (1924).

[159] 208 SW2d 689 (Tex Civ App 1948).

[160] *Compare* United States v Allsup, 566 F2d 68 (9th Cir 1977) (bank employees disqualified from service as jurors in trial of bank robbers) *with* United States v Brown, 644 F2d 101 (2d Cir), *cert denied,* 454 US 881 (1981) (bank employees not excusable for cause in trial of bank robbers).

Fisher,[161] the trial court's refusal to dismiss the personal physician of the defendant physician was held not to be an abuse of discretion. The juror had maintained that he could be impartial. Although the court's decision may have been technically correct, the arguably wiser course would have been to excuse the juror. The relationship was such as to inevitably cast a cloud over a verdict for the defendant.

It is often argued that former and present law enforcement officers are in a professional relationship with the prosecutor in a criminal case, even where the officer has never had any direct dealings with the prosecutor or the officers who are to testify in the case. Mere employment by a police force, however, is generally held not in itself to be disqualifying.[162]

Similarly, government employees have been held not disqualified from jury service in civil or criminal cases where the government is a party.[163] Under federal law, a juror is not to be presumed biased against a criminal defendant merely because the juror is a government employee.[164] Even where the government is the titular victim of the crime, as when items are stolen from a government office, government employees are not automatically disqualified from jury service.[165]

Prospective employees among jurors may also give rise to problems. In *Smith v Phillips,*[166] a juror had applied for a job as an investigator in the prosecutor's office. The prosecutor discovered this fact during the trial but failed to reveal it to either the court or defense counsel. The United States Supreme Court affirmed the conviction, finding that the defendant was not denied due process as a result of either the juror's or the prosecutor's conduct. The Court said that absent a showing of actual bias, it would not impute bias. Justice Rehnquist, writing for the majority, declared that "due process does not require a new trial every time a juror has been placed in a potentially compromising situation."[167]

§7.26 —Business or Professional Relationship with Witness

Challenges to jurors who have a business relationship with a witness have led to mixed results. Cases upholding a refusal by the trial court to disqualify

---

[161] 210 Mont 114, 683 P2d 916 (1984).

[162] *E.g.,* United States v Daly, 716 F2d 1499 (9th Cir 1983); State v Clark, 164 Conn 224, 319 A2d 398 (1973); State v McClain, 256 Iowa 175, 125 NW2d 764 (1964). *See generally* Annotation, *Former Law Enforcement Officers as Qualified Jurors in Criminal Cases,* 72 ALR3d 958 (1976). *See also* **§7.52.**

[163] Dennis v United States, 339 US 162 (1950); United States v Boyd, 446 F2d 1267 (5th Cir 1971); Goldsby v State, 240 Miss 647, 123 So 2d 429 (1960), *cert denied,* 365 US 861 (1961).

[164] Frazier v United States, 335 US 497 (1948).

[165] *See, e.g.,* United States v Boyd, 446 F2d 1267 (5th Cir 1971).

[166] 455 US 209 (1982).

[167] *Id* 217.

the juror are frequently premised on a finding of no prejudice. Absent a controlling statute, the matter lies within the discretion of the trial judge.[168]

In a New York case, the trial court declined to excuse a juror who informed the court, after the defendant's medical expert had testified, that he had taken a course some years earlier from the doctor and had purchased one of the doctor's books. The trial judge thoroughly questioned the juror in chambers, as did plaintiff's counsel. On the basis of this questioning the trial judge concluded that no prejudice to either party would result if the juror remained. The Second Circuit upheld the ruling as within the trial court's discretion.[169] The appellate court also found no prejudice to the plaintiff, reasoning that the juror's relationship with the witness could only have affected the issue of damages, and this issue was never reached because the verdict on liability was for the defendant.[170] The latter point is questionable, since the juror's obvious respect for the doctor could have affected the juror's vote on the issue of liability in favor of the side for which the doctor testified.

Another illustrative case is *Tomlin v State.*[171] During the trial, a juror informed the secretary in the district attorney's office that she had worked with one of the prospective witnesses. It was held that the trial judge's finding of no prejudice to the defendants, after questioning the juror and obtaining her assurance of impartiality, was proper.[172]

On the other hand, there are cases holding that a business relationship between a prospective juror and a witness requires the juror's disqualification. In one California case, trial had been in progress for some eleven days when it was discovered that one of the jurors worked in the same office as the defendant's brother, at a desk only 25 feet from that of the brother. The brother was a witness in the case. The juror stated that he had never talked to the brother and did not know him. He further maintained that he did not want to be excused and could render an impartial verdict. The trial court, however, perhaps finding the juror's assertions somewhat hard to believe, discharged the juror and seated a qualified alternate. The appellate court held that the trial court acted within its discretion in determining that there was good cause for discharging the juror.[173]

In *State v Dickens*[174] a conviction for theft of a calf was reversed because one of the jurors had formerly worked for the complaining witness. The juror had discussed the case with the witness, and had agreed with his assessment of it.

---

[168] *See, e.g.,* Kelly v Gulf Oil Corp, 28 F Supp 205 (ED Pa 1938), *affd,* 105 F2d 1018 (3d Cir 1939). *See generally* Annotation, *Social or Business Relationship Between Proposed Juror and Nonparty Witness as Affecting Former's Qualification as Juror,* 11 ALR3d 859, 865-72 §§5-7 (1967).

[169] Cisneros v Cities Serv Oil Co, 334 F2d 232 (2d Cir 1964).

[170] *Id* 234.

[171] 81 Nev 620, 407 P2d 1020 (1965).

[172] *See also* United States v Parisi, 365 F2d 601 (6th Cir 1966), *vacated on other grounds,* 386 US 345 (1967); State v Hollingsworth, 11 NC App 674, 182 SE2d 26 (1971).

[173] People v Abbott, 47 Cal 2d 362, 303 P2d 730 (1956).

[174] 68 Idaho 173, 191 P2d 364 (1948).

The Idaho Supreme Court ruled that these circumstances indicated actual bias. The juror simply could not be expected to be fair and impartial. A defendant in a criminal action, added the court, should not have to use a peremptory challenge when it clearly appears that a prospective juror is disqualified.[175]

Where a prospective juror is a deputy sheriff, and either the sheriff or some member of the sheriff's staff is to be a witness, the courts have generally held that the juror is disqualified. In *Tate v People,*[176] for example, one of the jurors was a special deputy sheriff, employed on a part-time basis. The sheriff was the prosecuting witness in the case. The trial court's denial of the defendant's request for discharge of the juror was reversed on appeal. The appellate court reasoned that the juror, as a deputy sheriff, could be expected to owe allegiance to the sheriff. Furthermore, his remuneration as a deputy sheriff was dependent on services he performed at the request of the sheriff. Disqualification of the juror, the court said, was not even a "debatable question."[177]

In *People v Boorman,*[178] on the other hand, the court said by way of dictum that the mere fact that a prospective juror was a deputy sheriff would not of itself support a challenge for cause. The court added, however, that where the sheriff's office had investigated the alleged crime and the complaint was sworn to by a deputy sheriff, the defendant should have been permitted to ask whether a prospective juror was a deputy sheriff.

The position of the *Boorman* court stands for a more general proposition. If an employment relationship on the part of a juror is a possible basis of challenge or may suggest bias, attorneys should be allowed to question the juror as to the employment relationship. For a trial judge not to permit such questioning is error.[179]

A relationship between a juror and a former employer is a more tenuous basis of disqualification. The danger of retaliation is significantly reduced. Nevertheless, the juror's perception of the witness may be colored by the employment and the circumstances under which it ended. Future references by the former employer may concern the juror. Exploration of this relationship should therefore be permitted.

§7.27 —Business or Professional Relationship with Attorney Where Regulated by Statute

A juror is sometimes challenged because of a past or present attorney-client relationship with one of the lawyers in the case. Sometimes the relationship

---

[175] *Id* at 177, 191 P2d at 365-66.

[176] 125 Colo 527, 247 P2d 665 (1952).

[177] *Id* at 540, 247 P2d at 671. *See also* State v Golubski, 45 SW2d 873 (Mo Ct App 1932); State v Guynn, 87 Utah 320, 48 P2d 902 (1935).

[178] 142 Cal App 2d 85, 297 P2d 741 (1956).

[179] United States v Lewin, 467 F2d 1132 (7th Cir 1972).

constitutes a statutory ground of disqualification;[180] otherwise, the question of disqualification is held to lie in the discretion of the trial court.[181] The attorney-client relationship need not be directly between the juror and the attorney. In a Missouri case the court held that a juror employed by a company represented by one of the attorneys in the case was disqualified.[182]

Statutes which provide generally that certain business or professional relationships will result in disqualification, but which do not explicitly proscribe a juror-attorney relationship, will not necessarily result in the disqualification of a juror who is the client of an attorney in the case.[183] Some courts in criminal cases have interpreted such statutes to refer to relations with defendants, prosecuting witnesses, and victims, but not attorneys.[184] Although the holdings in these cases could be construed to mean that a state's statutory grounds of disqualification are exclusive, and that a relationship with an attorney in a case is not disqualifying unless specified by statute, decisions to the contrary can be found. In *Black v State*,[185] for instance, the court held that a statute enumerating certain grounds for challenge in criminal cases and excluding all others would not prevent a challenge to a juror because he was a deputy to the prosecuting attorney. The court reasoned that any attempt to collect all grounds of possible challenge in a statute would be only partially successful, and that the statute could not displace a court's duty to provide a person accused of crime with an impartial jury.[186]

A few older civil cases held that statutes providing for challenges based on implied bias referred only to relationships between a juror and a party. Jurors who were clients of a party's attorney were therefore not disqualified.[187] In *Redwine v Fitzhugh*[188] the court held that a juror was qualified under a statute which did not include existence of an attorney-client relationship between juror and attorney as a ground for challenge. The court stated that statutes which enumerated certain causes as disqualifying were not exclusive and did not deprive courts of their inherent power to declare that other causes also required disqualification in order to insure a fair and impartial trial. However,

---

[180] *E.g.*, State v McGraw, 6 Idaho 635, 59 P 178 (1899). *See generally* Annotation, *Professional or Business Relations Between Proposed Juror and Attorney as Ground for Challenge for Cause*, 52 ALR4th 965 (1987).

[181] Bailey v McLeod, 143 Kan 638, 56 P2d 460 (1936). *See generally* Annotation, *Juror's Voir Dire Denial or Nondisclosure of Acquaintance or Relationship With Attorney in Case, or With Partner or Associate of Such Attorney, as Ground for New Trial or Mistrial*, 64 ALR3d 126 (1975); Annotation, *Professional or Business Relations Between Proposed Juror and Attorney as Ground for Challenge for Cause*, 72 ALR2d 673 (1960).

[182] Privett v St Louis-San Francisco Ry Co, 300 SW 726 (Mo 1927).

[183] *E.g.*, State v Carter, 121 Iowa 135, 96 NW 710 (1903).

[184] *E.g.*, People v Wilkes, 44 Cal 2d 679, 284 P2d 481 (1955). *See also* People v McQuade, 110 NY 284, 18 NE 156 (1888).

[185] 100 Ind 357 (1884).

[186] *Id* 361.

[187] Sorseleil v Red Lake Milling Co, 111 Minn 275, 126 NW 903 (1910); McCorkle v Mallory, 30 Wash 632, 71 P 186 (1903).

[188] 78 Wyo 407, 329 P2d 257 (1958).

the court continued, existence of a relationship not mentioned in the statute raised at most a rebuttable presumption of bias; the determination of whether a juror was qualified lay in the discretion of the judge.[189]

§7.28 —Business or Professional Relationship with Attorney in Absence of Statute

The constitutional guarantee of an impartial jury may not be impaired by a legislature's omission of a ground for challenge that would render a juror incompetent. Even absent a statutory disqualification, therefore, an attorney-client relationship between a juror and an attorney for one of the parties may be the basis of a challenge for cause. The relationship must exist at the time of trial. A past lawyer-client relationship between juror and attorney has been held not good cause for challenge.[190] Likewise the mere fact of having served on a case previously tried by one of the attorneys will not result in a juror's disqualification.[191]

Some courts take the view that the only grounds for challenge for cause are those stated in the controlling statute or those existing at common law which import absolute bias or favor. Thus one court held that, absent a statute, the fact that a prospective juror employed a party as an attorney in another case was not ground for challenge for principal cause, but that favor or bias had to be proved.[192] Where such proof is made to the satisfaction of the court, its exercise of discretion will not be reversed on appeal except for abuse.[193]

The majority of courts which have considered the question have agreed that, in the absence of controlling statute, a juror is not automatically disqualified for past or present professional or business relations with an attorney in the case.[194] In civil cases, a number of appellate courts have noted that a trial judge has considerable discretion in ruling on a challenge for cause based on an attorney-client relationship.[195]

In criminal cases, courts have held that a juror is not disqualified merely for being the client of one of the attorneys in the trial.[196] There is, however, significant contrary authority. In *Christiancy v State*,[197] for example, the court sustained the state's challenge to a proposed juror in a rape prosecution who had a case pending in which the defendant's counsel were his attorneys. The court stated

---

[189] *Id* at 421, 329 P2d at 261.

[190] Klinck v State, 203 Ind 647, 179 NE 549 (1932).

[191] *E.g.*, United States v Graham, 739 F2d 351 (8th Cir 1984).

[192] Brown v Wolverton, 219 Ala 112, 121 So 404 (1928).

[193] *Id.*

[194] *See, e.g.*, Herron v State, 409 So 2d 991 (Ala Crim App 1982).

[195] *E.g.*, Bailey v McLeod, 143 Kan 638, 56 P2d 460 (1936); Whitney v Louisville & NR Co, 296 Ky 381, 177 SW2d 139 (1944); Redwine v Fitzhugh, 78 Wyo 407, 329 P2d 257 (1958).

[196] *E.g.*, People v Wilkes, 44 Cal 2d 679, 284 P2d 481 (1955); State v Glover, 41 SD 465, 113 NW 625 (1907). *See also* State v Eastin, 419 So 2d 933 (La 1982).

[197] 106 Neb 822, 184 NW 948 (1921).

that the juror was so closely connected with the attorneys that his ability to act impartially was open to serious question.[198]

Business relationships other than the professional relationship of attorney and client have also been raised as the basis of a challenge for cause. The nature and closeness of the business relationship is the key. In most of these cases, courts have concluded that the particular relationship was not a ground for disqualification.[199] In a New York case to the contrary, the appellate court held that the trial judge should have excused a juror associated with the prosecutor in his campaign for office, even though the juror claimed she could be fair.[200]

The rule for business relationships tends to be the same as the one governing professional relationships. Each case rests on its own facts. The question of whether a particular juror should be disqualified therefore falls within the discretion of the trial judge.

Arguably the wiser course is to excuse a juror who is a client of an attorney in the trial. A juror with enough confidence in a particular lawyer to employ the lawyer will very likely be inclined toward whatever position the lawyer advocates. The juror may also fear that the lawyer will resent an adverse verdict and as a consequence be less zealous in representing the juror. This is not to deny that there are jurors who could be completely fair and unbiased in this situation. Rather, it is to say that, if nothing else, the appearance of justice and fair play would be served by not allowing jurors to sit on cases where their own attorneys are involved.

§7.29 —Family Relationship to Party

Family relationship between a prospective juror and a party either by consanguinity or affinity is a valid basis for a challenge for cause.[201] The natural tendency of the relationship is to create a partiality toward the related party. Of course, in some instances a family relationship will result in a bias against the relative, but the law proceeds on the assumption that that is the exception. The proscribed degree of relationship required for disqualification varies among the jurisdictions. At common law the rule has been stated to include relationships within the ninth degree, by consanguinity or affinity.[202]

As is the case with other challenges for cause, an objection on the ground of the relationship of a juror with a party should be timely, or else it may be

---

[198] *See also* Price v State, 383 So 2d 884 (Ala Crim App 1980).

[199] Billington v United States, 15 F2d 359 (6th Cir 1926); Montgomery v State, 277 Ark 95, 640 SW2d 108 (1982) Klinck v State, 203 Ind 647, 179 NE 549 (1932); Jones v Ford, 154 Iowa 549, 134 NW 569 (1912).

[200] People v Provenzano, 70 AD2d 960, 417 NYS2d 317 (1979).

[201] *E.g.*, Lewis v State, 469 So 2d 1291 (Ala Crim App 1984), *affd*, 469 So 2d 1301 (Ala 1985); Crawley v State, 151 Ga 818, 108 SE 238 (1921); Zimmerer v Prudential Ins Co, 150 Neb 351, 34 NW2d 750 (1948).

[202] *See* State *ex rel* Perez v Wall, 41 Fla 463, 26 So 1020 (1899); Zimmerer v Prudential Ins Co, 150 Neb 351, 34 NW2d 750 (1948).

deemed waived.[203] It has been held, however, that no waiver results by failure to raise the objection until after verdict where the relationship was not discovered until that time.[204] Due diligence on the part of counsel in discovering the ground of disqualification is, of course, required. However, if the relationship is not a distant one, and the party-relative is aware of it, there may be an ethical duty on the part of the attorney of the relative to bring the matter to the court's attention.[205]

§7.30 —Family Relationship to Attorney or Witness

At common law a juror related to an attorney in a case was not disqualified by the relationship.[206] The arguably better view, however, is that the relationship of a juror with an attorney in a case should be a ground for challenge. This is especially so where the attorney's fee is on a contingent basis.[207] Most jurors would naturally prefer to see a relative prevail over a stranger.

The closeness and the degree of the relationship is relevant. In *Ward v Commonwealth*[208] the court held that the prosecutor's uncle should have been excused despite his claim of impartiality. It was held not error, however, not to excuse a distant cousin of the prosecutor or his ex-brother-in-law.

The relationship of a prospective juror to a witness, either by affinity or consanguinity, will usually not be grounds for disqualification.[209] Relationship to the prosecuting witness in a criminal case, however, is more likely to be held a proper basis of disqualification.[210] Jurors in civil actions, on the other hand are rarely disqualified by relationship to a witness.[211]

In order for an attorney to be able to question jurors about a possible family relationship (or, indeed any relationship) with a witness, it is obviously necessary that jurors be aware of the witnesses who are to testify. In *United States v*

---

203 *See, e.g.,* State v Andrews, 29 Conn 100 (1860).

204 Crawley v State, 151 Ga 818, 108 SE 238 (1921); Johnston v State, 239 Ind 77, 155 NE2d 129 (1958).

205 *See In re* Shon, 262 AD 225, 28 NYS2d 872 (1941).

206 *See* Petcosky v Bowman, 197 Va 240, 89 SE2d 4 (1955).

207 *See* Roberts v Roberts, 115 Ga 259, 41 SE 616 (1902). *But see* Howard v State, 420 So 2d 828 (Ala Crim App 1982) (relative of counsel not disqualified).

208 695 SW2d 404 (Ky 1985).

209 Scott v State, 473 So 2d 1167 (Ala Crim App 1985); Taylor v State, 243 Ga 222, 253 SE2d 191 (1979); Jones v State, 230 Ark 18, 320 SW2d 645 (1959). *See generally* Annotation, *Juror's Relationship to Witness, in Civil Case, as Ground of Disqualification or for Reversal or New Trial,* 85 ALR2d 851 (1962).

210 United States v Baldwin, 607 F2d 1295 (9th Cir 1979); State v Kuster, 353 NW2d 428 (Iowa 1984).

211 Tidmore v Mills, 33 Ala App 243, 32 So 2d 769, *cert denied,* 249 Ala 648, 32 So 2d 782 (1947); Atlantic Coast R Co v Mead, 22 Ga App 70, 95 SE 476 (1918). *Contra* Arkansas State Highway Commn v Young, 241 Ark 765, 410 SW2d 120 (1967). *See generally* Annotation, *supra* note 209.

Brown[212] it was held to be reversible error for the trial court, upon request, to refuse to read the list of witnesses to the jury.

§7.31 —Family Relationship to Interested or Biased Person

The rule generally disqualifying a juror because of a family relationship with a party can extend to jurors related to nonparties who have an interest in the outcome of the case.[213] Thus, in a Texas case, the court held that the rule governing jurors who were related to a party was equally applicable to a juror related to a nonparty who had a house, built with the permission of one of the defendants, on the land involved in the suit.[214] In stark contrast is *State v Sonnier,*[215] where the court upheld the refusal of the trial court to excuse a juror whose niece was married to the brother of one of the victims, whose parents were friends of the other victim's family, whose brother was the victim's employer, and whose other brother was the sheriff of the county in which the crime occurred. The result in the latter case is, to say the least, questionable.

A California court held that its state statute was sufficiently broad to disqualify a person related to an interested person, though that person was not a party to the action.[216] The court explained its rationale:

> Section 602, (2), Code of Civ. Proc., makes consanguinity or affinity within the fourth degree of any party to a cause a ground of challenge. This provision has received, and should receive a liberal construction. It is not necessary that the party in interest should be in name a party to the litigation. It is sufficient if it be shown that he is immediately, directly, and beneficially interested in the result of the litigation.[217]

A relationship within the prohibited degree to members of or stockholders in a corporation which is a party or which is substantially interested in the litigation has also been held to be ground for disqualification of a prospective juror.[218]

---

[212] 799 F2d 134 (4th Cir 1986).

[213] *See, e.g.,* Thomas v State, 133 Ala 139, 32 So 250 (1902); Mono County v Flanigan, 130 Cal 105, 62 P 293 (1900); Melbourne v State, 51 Fla 69, 40 So 189 (1906).

[214] Zarate v Villareal, 155 SW 328 (Tex Civ App 1913).

[215] 379 So 2d 1336 (La 1979).

[216] Mono County v Flanigan, 130 Cal 105, 62 P 293 (1900).

[217] *Id* at 107-08, 62 Pat 293.

[218] *E.g.,* National Bank v Ragland, 51 SW 661 (Tex Civ App 1889), *affd,* 181 US 45 (1901).

§7.32 Pecuniary Interest

A juror with a direct financial interest in the outcome of a case will generally be disqualified for cause. In *M&A Electric Power Cooperative v Georger,*[219] for example, the Missouri Supreme Court held it error for the trial judge to refuse to disqualify members of the consumer electric cooperatives served by the plaintiff, even though the jurors maintained that they could be impartial.[220] Similarly subject to challenge are stockholders in a corporation involved in the suit.[221]

In some instances jurors have made a wager on the outcome of the case. The wager may justify disqualification on either of two theories. First, the wager may indicate a preconceived opinion of the merits of the case. Even if not, the wager may compromise the juror's impartiality by creating a conflict of interest between loss of a pecuniary advantage and justice in the case. On either rationale the juror should be excused.[222]

More difficult are cases in which a juror will be indirectly affected by the outcome of the case. Often the issue arises in the context of a suit against a state, city, or municipality of which the juror is a resident. If the defendant loses the suit, the juror may be faced with a tax or rate increase in order to defray the cost of the judgment. It is generally held in these circumstances that taxpayers are not automatically disqualified.[223] There are, however, a few decisions to the contrary.[224]

It is easy to understand a court's reluctance to disqualify jurors because of their indirect interest as taxpayers. The problem of impaneling a jury might be insurmountable. The more reasonable solution would seem to be to order, on appropriate motion, a change in venue.[225]

§7.33 Connection with Insurance Company

A question of concern to most civil litigants is a juror's connection with or financial interest in indemnity or liability insurance companies, or the insurance industry generally. Jurors are aware without being told that defendants are often protected by insurance. Both plaintiffs' and defense attorneys agree

---

[219] 480 SW2d 868 (Mo 1972).

[220] *See also* Ozark Border Elec Coop v Stacy, 348 SW2d 586 (Mo Ct App 1961).

[221] *See, e.g.,* Noey v Ukpeagvik Inupiat Corp, 683 P2d 260 (Alaska 1984); Thompson v Sawnee Elec Membership Corp, 157 Ga App 561, 278 SE2d 143 (1981).

[222] State v Warm, 92 Vt 447, 105 A 244 (1918). *But see* Fugate v State, 169 Neb 420, 99 NW2d 868 (1959) (rights of defendant not violated where bet made by juror before selection did not affect verdict, which was in fact contrary to juror's betting interest).

[223] *E.g.,* Ridglea v Unified School Dist No 305, Saline County, 206 Kan 111, 476 P2d 601 (1970); Smith v German Ins Co, 107 Mich 270, 65 NW 236 (1895); Nichols v Oklahoma City, 195 Okla 305, 157 P2d 174 (1945); State *ex rel* Douglas County v Sanders, 655 P2d 175 (Or 1982).

[224] *E.g.,* Beyer v City of Dubuque, 258 Iowa 476, 139 NW2d 428 (1966); Broadway Mfg Co v Leavenworth Terminal Ry & Bridge Co, 81 Kan 616, 106 P 1034 (1910).

[225] *See* **§§2.02-2.06.**

that knowledge by jurors that insurance is available can affect the verdict on liability, amount of recovery, or both. Where they disagree is on what that effect will be. Defense attorneys believe that jurors are more apt to return a verdict for an injured plaintiff, and for a large amount, if they know that the loss will be borne by an insurance company rather than by an individual defendant.[226] Plaintiffs' attorneys believe that some jurors may be inclined against a plaintiff when an insurance company is involved because the jurors fear that an adverse verdict will result in an increase in their own insurance premiums, a perspective encouraged by insurance company advertisements.[227]

Both the plaintiffs' and defense bars make persuasive cases. The plaintiff quite properly claims a right to a verdict unaffected by interests which a juror may have in the defendant's insurance company. Plaintiffs' attorneys argue that voir dire questioning must be permitted as to the existence and extent of a juror's connection with the insurance industry or an insurance company. On the other hand, the defendant is also entitled to an impartial jury, one which will return a verdict based on the evidence and not on the fact that the defendant is covered by insurance. Some jurors may be inclined, out of sympathy, to return a verdict for a severely injured plaintiff, even where they do not believe the defendant to have been negligent, if the judgement will be paid by an insurance company. Accordingly, defendants want knowledge of insurance to be kept from the jury. The dilemma is compounded by the fact that it is virtually impossible to question jurors about their interests in or connections with insurance companies without strongly implying that the defendant is covered by insurance.

The issue has been presented to appellate courts on many occasions; out of their decisions a compromise seems to have evolved. The plaintiff's counsel, acting in good faith, may question prospective jurors regarding interests in or connections with liability insurance companies generally. This is the rule in the majority of the states and also seems to be the rule in the federal courts.[228] Where, however, there is nothing to indicate that either party is insured, questioning that implies that an insurance company will pay the judgment is not permissible.[229]

Some courts have cautioned that counsel must not ask questions about insurance company connections in a way that suggests to the jury that an insurance company has an interest in the case or that the defendant is insured. One might

---

[226] *See* Kuntz v Spence, 67 SW2d 254, 256 (Tex Comm App 1934).

[227] *See* **§7.34.**

[228] *See,* Braman v Wiley, 119 F2d 991 (7th Cir 1941); Bass v Dehner, 103 F2d 28 (10th Cir), *cert denied,* 308 US 580 (1939); Loda v Raines, 193 Ark 513, 100 SW2d 973 (1937); Salazar v Ehmann, 505 P2d 387 (Colo Ct App 1972); Haymes v Catholic Bishop, 41 Ill 2d 236, 243 NE2d 203 (1968); Haynes v County of Missoula, 163 Mont 270, 517 P2d 370 (1973). *But compare* McCroskey v Proctor, 332 SE2d 646 (W Va 1985) (absent explanation to trial court as to why such questioning should be permitted, questioning relating to insurance company not permitted).

[229] *See, e.g.,* Miller Trucking Co v Wood, 474 SW2d 763 (Tex Civ App 1971); Green v Ligon, 190 SW2d 742 (Tex 1945). *See also* Cox v Roberts, 248 Ala 372, 27 So 2d 617 (1946); Skinner v Sisters of St Mary's, 686 SW2d 858 (Mo Ct App 1985).

genuinely question whether this is realistic, as any mention of insurance to a jury is likely to convey the impression that the defendant's losses will be covered by insurance. "If not, why ask," will be the thinking of the typical juror.

Cases often turn on the good faith of counsel;[230] bad faith may be inferred where counsel had no reason to believe that the defendant was insured.[231] Today such an approach is less useful as modern discovery rules, such as those operative in the federal courts, permit a plaintiff to discover whether a defendant is insured.[232] Only an inept attorney would not know if there was insurance available to pay off a judgment.

If a defendant is insured, or if there is strong indication that a defendant is insured, and the panel includes persons who might be stockholders of or otherwise interested in an insurance company, voir dire examination on this issue will be permitted.[233] However, if it is apparent that counsel's only purpose is to improperly suggest that the defendant is insured, questioning may not be permitted.[234] A bad faith effort to unduly stress insurance may be inferred by repetition of the same insurance-related questions to each juror.[235] In those states which permit both examination of jurors about their connection with insurance companies and examination to allow intelligent exercise of peremptory challenges, it does not matter whether the insurance-related information is sought for purposes of challenging for cause or peremptorily.[236]

The precise form of questions related to insurance company connections has also provoked controversy. Some jurisdictions limit inquiry to the interests of jurors in "any" insurance company issuing policies protecting against liability for negligence.[237] Others allow questions related to a juror's connections with the particular insurance company involved in the case.[238]

---

[230] *See, e.g.*, Skinner v Sisters of St Mary's, 686 SW2d 858 (Mo Ct App 1985).

[231] Jenkins v Chase, 53 SW2d 21 (Mo 1932); Glick v Arink, 58 SW2d 714 (Mo 1932). *See also* Miller v Kooker, 208 Iowa 687, 224 NW 46 (1929); Witt v Roper, 150 Kan 722, 96 P2d 643 (1939); Kennedy v Raby, 174 Okla 332, 50 P2d 716 (1935).

[232] Fed R Civ P 26(b)(2).

[233] *See, e.g.*, Hoffman v Royer, 359 NW2d 387 (SD 1984). *See also* cases cited note 228.

[234] *See* cases cited note 229. *But see* Santee v Haggart Constr Co, 202 Minn 361, 278 NW 520 (1938) (merely asking jurors whether they were interested as stockholders, directors, or policyholders in a particular insurance company is not in itself evidence of bad faith).

[235] Witt v Roper, 150 Kan 722, 96 P2d 643 (1939); Ryan v Simeons, 209 Iowa 1090, 229 NW 667 (1930).

[236] Missouri Pac Transp Co v Talley, 199 Ark 835, 136 SW2d 688 (1940); Schwickerath v Maas, 230 Iowa 329, 297 NW 248 (1941); Fedorinchik v Stewart, 289 Mich 436, 286 NW 673 (1939).

[237] *See* Braman v Wiley, 119 F2d 991 (7th Cir 1941); Loda v Raines, 193 Ark 513, 100 SW2d 973 (1937); Williams v Layne, 53 Cal App 2d 81, 127 P2d 582 (1942).

[238] *See* Wagner Elec Corp v Snowden, 38 F2d 599 (8th Cir 1930); Cox v Roberts, 248 Ala 372, 27 So 2d 617 (1946); Williams v Layne, 53 Cal App 2d 81, 127 P2d 582 (1942); Raines v Raines, 97 Colo 19, 46 P2d 740 (1935); Montanick v McMillin, 225 Iowa 442, 280 NW 608 (1938); Kalley v Huntley, 88 SW2d 200 (Mo 1935).

§7.34 Insurance Company Advertising

The insurance industry has periodically conducted aggressive publicity campaigns against what are in their estimation overly large verdicts. Insurance companies have taken out advertisements in national magazines and elsewhere which without much subtlety have sought to link a rise in the premiums charged policy holders to large jury verdicts. The message to prospective jurors is clear: a judgment in favor of a plaintiff can result in an increase in your insurance.

This advertising campaign has caused great consternation among plaintiffs' lawyers. It has also presented courts with the question of whether plaintiffs' attorneys should be allowed to inquire whether prospective jurors have seen the advertisements in question, and, if so, what effect such advertisements might have on their thinking and on their verdicts. Plaintiffs' lawyers contend that national publication of these ads has opened the door to voir dire examination about them, even in states where voir dire questions pertaining to insurance are prohibited.[239]

The courts do not always agree. In jurisdictions with a strict policy against voir dire examination of jurors about any interest in or connection with insurance companies, questions addressed to the relationship between verdicts and insurance premiums have also been prohibited.[240] In *Brockett v Tice,*[241] for example, plaintiff's counsel had asked whether any juror had any connection with any insurance company. Although admonished by the court to stop questioning along those lines, the attorney inquired whether any jurors "thought the verdict in the case would affect their insurance rates."[242] The questions were deemed prejudicial, and the judgment for the plaintiff was reversed. Whether the inquiry as to the effect of a verdict on jurors' insurance rates would by itself have led to reversal is unclear. It might well have, because the court's decision was based in large part on the intent of counsel to inject insurance into the case: "[T]he necessary effect of this [questioning] was to infer that appellant had insurance because a verdict could not possibly affect [the juror's] rates unless he had insurance."[243]

Similar advertising by insurance companies in the 1950s prompted a suit in federal court to enjoin the advertising campaign.[244] It was held that the advertising fell within the constitutional protection of freedom of speech. The court further noted that the plaintiff would have "an opportunity to question the prospective jurors concerning the possible effect such advertisements may have on any award of damages which they may render."[245] Giving a legal impri-

---

[239] *Compare* Kronzer, *A View from the Plaintiff's Bar: Jury Tampering—1978 Style,* 10 St Mary's LJ 399 (1979), *with* Hatchell, *A View from the Defense Bar: Insurance Advertising—Much Ado About Nothing,* 10 St Mary's LJ 427 (1979).

[240] *E.g.,* McCroskey v Proctor, 332 SE2d 646 (W Va 1985).

[241] 445 SW2d 20 (Tex 1969).

[242] Id __.

[243] *Id* 22.

[244] Hoffman v Perrucci, 117 F Supp 38 (ED Pa 1953), *appeal dismissed,* 222 F2d 709 (3d Cir 1955).

[245] *Id* 40.

matur to the latter suggestion, a New York appellate court set aside an order prohibiting inquiry on the jury verdict/insurance premium issue.[246]

Other courts have frowned on such examination. The Kentucky Court of Appeals held unnecessary a question asking if jurors had "read articles, periodicals, editorials, any material, pertaining to automobile accident jury verdicts?"[247] The Connecticut Supreme Court found a voir dire question asking, "Would you feel that you have any financial interest in this lawsuit, or might in any way be affected by awarding damages to the Plaintiffs?," to be "vague and ambiguous," but added that the plaintiff could have asked whether jurors had seen the specific article in question.[248] A Maryland case approved the trial court's prohibition against a plaintiff's voir dire inquiry as to whether jurors had "read any article or literature or . . . heard any discussion recently on accounts of verdicts in negligence cases, and, if so . . . formed any ideas with reference to amounts of jury verdicts.[249] In a North Carolina case the court held that it was a prejudicial injection of insurance to ask: "Is there any member of the jury who feels that his liability insurance rates will go up if he returns a verdict against the defendants in this case?[250]

In a well-reasoned opinion, the Montana Supreme Court began with the assumption that the advertising was "calculated to produce bias upon the part of jurors against awarding large amounts of damages to personal injury plaintiffs."[251] To counter this bias, and to secure a plaintiff's right to an impartial jury, the court ruled that liberal voir dire should be permitted.[252] The court indicated the proper balance to be struck:

> We . . . hold that, upon a proper showing of possible prejudice, an attorney may inquire whether a prospective juror has heard or read anything to indicate that jury verdicts for plaintiffs in personal injury cases result in higher insurance premiums for everyone; if so, whether that belief will interfere with the juror's ability to render a fair and impartial verdict. Depending upon the responses received to these inquiries and subject to the discretion of the trial court, limited follow-up inquiries may be made. We decline to hypothesize as to the permissible nature or extent of these follow-up questions at this time. We do conclude, however, that the alleged plan of Borkoski's attorney to circulate among the jury panel copies of the insurance companies' advertisements would have been improper and would have led to the very prejudice against which Borkoski is now arguing.[253]

---

[246] Graham v Waite, 23 AD2d 628, 257 NYS2d 629 (1965).

[247] Farmer v Pearl, 415 SW2d 358 (Ky 1967).

[248] Lowell v Daly, 148 Conn 266, 169 A2d 888, 889 (1961).

[249] Kujawa v Baltimore Transit Co, 224 Md 195, 167 A2d 96 (1961).

[250] Maness v Bullins, 19 NC App 386, 198 SE2d 752 (1973).

[251] Borkoski v Yost, 182 Mont 28, 594 P2d 688 (1979).

[252] *Id* at 39, 594 P2d at 694.

[253] *Id* at 40, 594 P2d at 694-95.

The court was not oblivious to the fact that the defendant's right to a fair and impartial jury was also at stake. It required the plaintiff's attorney to approach the issue with general introductory questions as to whether the jurors had read anything that might affect their ability to be impartial or whether they regularly read any of the periodicals in which the advertising had appeared. Absent a positive response, no further inquiry was to be permitted. The court stated that counsel must proceed in good faith and not simply for the purpose of impressing the jury with the fact that the defendant was covered by insurance.[254]

The Montana court cited with approval the Arkansas Supreme Court decision in *King v Westlake,*[255] and recommended for trial court guidance the voir dire examination approved in that case. In *Westlake,* the defendant in a rear-end collision case complained that the trial judge had erred in permitting counsel for the plaintiff to ask jurors whether they had liability insurance, and whether they believed that the size of jury verdicts in personal injury cases affected automobile liability insurance premiums. All but two of the jurors had seen one or more insurance company advertisements decrying the amount of jury verdicts. The advertisements indicated that the costs of such verdicts were ultimately paid by the jurors in the form of increased premiums. The plaintiff's attorney had stated:

> It is improper for either side to imply or suggest that the defendant does or does not have insurance, and the questions I will now direct to you have nothing to do with whether or not the defendant has insurance. The questions I will ask concern your insurance premiums, not insurance in this case. How many of you believe that jury verdicts affect insurance premiums?
>
> Your insurance premiums may not be affected greatly one way or the other, but will not the verdicts that you render have some effect on your insurance rates?

After one juror replied "yes" to that question, the plaintiff's lawyer continued:

> The question I have been building up to is this: Assuming that the verdict you render could cost you a little more or less money on your insurance premium, can you listen to the testimony, the statements of counsel, and the instructions and then put aside the financial interest you have in this case because of your insurance premiums and render a verdict? (All jurors raised their hands.)[256]

The Arkansas Supreme Court affirmed, holding that the voir dire was in good faith and was proper.

---

[254] *Id* at 40-41, 594 P2d at 695.

[255] 264 Ark 555, 572 SW2d 841 (1978).

[256] 572 SW2d at 844.

There is considerable merit to the views of the courts in the last two cited cases. Advertisements of the type at issue are placed by insurance companies for the clear purpose of influencing prospective jurors. They are thus distinguishable from articles written by journalists. Continuation of this type of national advertising could sway jurors to the point that they will either avoid plaintiffs' verdicts altogether or decrease the amount of recovery, simply on account of such advertising, *and regardless of the merits of the individual case.* While a ban on such advertisements might infringe free speech rights, questioning jurors about possible bias induced by the articles, when done in good faith, would seem to be a reasonable response. If the insurance industry objects, it can avoid the problem by voluntarily curtailing the advertisements.

§7.35 Sympathy

Sympathy is a natural human emotion, and there are few who do not feel for others' misfortunes and troubles. Jurors who swear that they will render a verdict based on the evidence, however, are expected to ignore natural feelings of sympathy. This is easier said than done, of course, and the juror who admits sympathy for a party must be questioned thoroughly.

In neither civil nor criminal cases will expressions of sympathy, standing alone, disqualify a juror. In a criminal prosecution an expressed sympathy for the accused will not disqualify a prospective juror if the juror can state that, despite the feeling of sympathy, it will still be possible to be impartial.[257] Indeed, to the extent that jury nullification[258] is recognized either explicitly or implicitly, some degree of sympathy must be not only expected, but tolerated. In a civil case it is natural that jurors will have sympathy for a severely injured plaintiff. This alone will not disqualify a juror, as long as he or she commits to decide the case on the evidence and in accord with the court's instructions.[259]

In certain cases, the facts are so aggravated that it would be impossible to entirely avoid sympathetic jurors. In such a case, a lawyer should attempt on voir dire examination to extract a commitment from the jurors to not let sympathy distort their verdict. Then, on final argument the lawyer should remind the jurors of their promise. The following two sections will examine closely the problem of the sympathetic juror from the tactical vantage point of each side.

§7.36 —Eliciting Admissions

The challenge for the lawyer trying a case where sympathy for the victim is likely to be a factor is to elicit from jurors an admission that the sympathy may affect their verdict. Most jurors willing to admit to sympathy will at the

---

[257] Commonwealth v Webster, 59 Mass (5 Cush) 295 (1850).

[258] *See* **§§2.20-2.21.**

[259] Burch v Southern Pac Co, 32 Nev 75, 104 P 225 (1909).

same time say that they are prepared to return a verdict based solely on the evidence. Sometimes that assurance is justified; other times it is not. Counsel's task is to have as many jurors sympathetic to the opposing side excused for cause as possible in order to save peremptory challenges.

Consider, for example, a case where the plaintiff is a severely injured child. A defense lawyer almost always must induce the more sympathetic jurors to disqualify themselves. Otherwise, the lawyer will quickly use up all peremptory challenges on those persons who have an understandable inclination to award some money to the injured child regardless of liability. Sometimes a juror will have had a relative or close friend who experienced a similar tragedy involving a child; that juror can be expected to have great sympathy because of the suffering of the relative or friend. The defense voir dire in such a case might take the following lines:

Q. Mr. Smith, you have told me, and I appreciate your honesty, that your brother's child suffered serious injuries similar to that of the plaintiff in this case. Do you recall what you felt at the time about the person that caused those injuries to your brother's child?

Q. And what is your feeling today about persons who are in some way responsible for injuries to young children?

Q. Mr. Smith, I realize that because of the experience of your brother when his child was injured, you have a great deal of sympathy for the child and his parents. That is perfectly natural. On the other hand I am certain that you understand, don't you, that a juror, when he accepts the responsibility to serve, must not let sympathy interfere with his decision?

Q. You agree, do you not, that my client, Harry Jones, is entitled to have a jury hear his case and decide it only on the facts presented in this courtroom, regardless of any natural feelings of sympathy for the plaintiff in this case?

Q. You are not alone in feeling sympathy for this little girl and her parents. We all do. But if that sympathy were to interfere with the jury decision in this case, then Harry Jones would not be getting the fair trial to which he is entitled under our Constitution and laws, would he?

Q. Now, if you felt that your natural feelings of sympathy for this little girl and her parents would be so strong as to affect your verdict, you would tell us about that, wouldn't you?

Q. Do you feel that because of this other tragic experience that you have related to us and the sympathies for this family which you naturally have, you would find it difficult to decide this case on cold, hard facts?

The lawyer begins with open-ended questions to acquire some sense of the juror's feelings. Then a series of closed-ended questions allows the juror who has any doubt about the effect of those feelings to admit to their likely influence and to ask to be excused. Even if the juror cannot be successfully challenged for cause, the voir dire will have left the attorney well-placed to make an intelligent decision as to whether to exercise a peremptory challenge against the juror.

§7.37 —Avoiding Disqualification

On the other side, plaintiffs' lawyers do not want to lose sympathetic jurors. In voir dire they seek to defuse the sympathy issue and avoid a challenge of those jurors who admit to sympathy. Some of the best plaintiffs' jurors will be siphoned off immediately if the first prospective juror states that feelings of sympathy for the victim make it better for her not to sit. If both lawyers and the trial judge praise the juror's candor, other jurors may be encouraged to make the same statement. A plaintiff's lawyer who recognizes the juror likely to be favorable can make it difficult for that juror to disqualify himself or herself. Voir dire might proceed along these lines:

Q. Mrs. Bark, there will be considerable evidence in this case showing that this little girl I represent was rather severely injured. I am sure that you will agree that all of us have a natural sympathy for this little girl, or for any other child who is injured.

Q. I am sure that you will also agree that both sides in this lawsuit are entitled to a fair trial.

Q. As a juror, I am sure that you will want to discharge your duties in such a way that both sides to this lawsuit will receive fair treatment at your hands.

Q. Do you feel that you can discharge your duties as a juror properly? By that I mean that you appreciate that the defendant is entitled to the same fairness and impartiality as the plaintiff; don't you agree?

Q. Do you have any disagreement with the proposition that a lawsuit must be tried free from any sympathy, passion, or prejudice?

Q. Do you have any prejudice against either side of this lawsuit as you sit there now?

Q. Do you know of any reason why you could not give both sides to this lawsuit a fair trial?

Q. As you sit there now, if there were any reason at all why you could not give the defendant, as well as the plaintiff, a fair trial, you would tell us about it, wouldn't you?

Q. I take it, then, that you are not withholding or hiding anything from us that would cause you to have any undue sympathy or prejudice for either side?

Q. I assume that as you sit there you feel that it is a duty and privilege to serve on a jury. I also assume that since you are an adult person, you will not be influenced by either sympathy or prejudice, and you will determine the facts in this case exactly as they may be shown from the evidence introduced.

Q. If you had any undue sympathy or prejudice, either one, am I correct in assuming that you would have volunteered such information by this time?

Q. Will you assure me, the defendant, and the court, that you will give both sides of this lawsuit a fair trial?

The purpose of this carefully structured, closed-ended questioning, in which the juror is limited to yes or no answers, is to put the juror believed to be sympathetic on record as impartial. The juror, by virtue of having made an open, express, and sworn commitment to judge the facts fairly, has made it extremely difficult for the opposing side to successfully challenge her for cause. The attorney has in effect educated that juror and others as to what to say to avoid challenge.

§7.38 Prejudice—Labor Unions

Where a labor union is a party, or where the case involves a labor dispute, questions concerning juror bias for or against unions are proper.[260] Conversely, where a labor dispute is not part of the case or where a labor union is not directly interested in its outcome, courts have held that examination of jurors as to their union affiliations is improper. Thus in a suit for injuries allegedly inflicted by a deputy sheriff, an Alabama court upheld the trial judge's refusal to permit defendants to ask jurors about their membership in the CIO.[261]

Another Alabama case held that union members were not disqualified to act as jurors, even though the rights of a wife, child, and personal representative of a union member were the subject of the trial.[262] The court stated that the right of unions to organize for lawful purposes was well recognized, and found no abuse of the trial judge's discretion in declining to allow examination of jurors as to their union affiliations.[263]

It is not union membership per se that is the problem. A common bond among workers can induce partiality. In a case against a mining company for on-the-job injuries, the Colorado Supreme Court held that the trial judge committed reversible error in denying the defendant's challenge for cause to a juror who stated on voir dire that he had a natural sympathy for the laboring man, was a miner himself, and would find for the plaintiff if the evidence were at

---

[260] Birmingham Elec Co v Driver, 323 Ala 36, 166 So 701 (1936); Gatzow v Buening, 106 Wis 1, 81 NW 1003 (1900); *see also* Annotation, *Racial, Religious, Economic, Social, or Political Prejudice of Proposed Juror as Proper Subject of Inquiry or Ground of Challenge on Voir Dire in Civil Case,* 72 ALR2d 905, 913-14 §7(a) (1960).

[261] Leath v Smith, 240 Ala 639, 200 So 623 (1941).

[262] Rose v Magro, 220 Ala 120, 124 So 296 (1929).

[263] *Id* at 124, 124 So at 299.

all unclear.[264] Despite the juror's assertion that he would be guided only by the evidence and the court's instructions, denial of the challenge for cause was held improper.

Thus, even where union membership or a union itself is not the subject matter of a lawsuit, if the suit is brought by a worker against a company or corporation, union membership is probably a legitimate matter for inquiry. A juror who is a union member is much more likely to identify with a union member plaintiff than with an employer defendant. There is a realistic possibility of bias, and the defendant should be permitted to explore this possibility.

§7.39 —Intoxicants and Gambling

Some civil cases have held it proper to not permit inquiry into juror prejudice against intoxicants or the liquor industry.[265] On the other hand, there is authority that a juror may properly be questioned about his or her attitude toward the use or sale of liquor.[266] Jurors have been held not disqualified despite a prejudice against intoxicants where it appeared that the juror could give the parties a fair trial.[267] Where a juror's prejudice for or against intoxicants is so strong that it is likely to affect the juror's impartiality, however, the juror is properly subject to challenge.[268]

Criminal prosecutions can directly or indirectly involve use of intoxicants or violations of liquor laws. In these cases inquiry into the prospective juror's attitudes toward the use of alcohol is permitted.[269] A prospective juror who may have a prejudice against liquor but not a prejudice against the defendant will not, however, be disqualified for cause.[270] Only when the prejudice will

---

264 Metallic Gold Mining Co v Watson, 51 Colo 278, 117 P 609 (1911).

265 *E.g.*, Carpenter v Hyman, 67 W Va 4, 66 SE 1078 (1910); *See generally* Annotation, *Racial, Religious, Social, or Political Prejudice of Proposed Juror as Proper Subject of Inquiry or Ground of Challenge on Voir Dire in Civil Case,* 72 ALR2d 905, 917-18 §9(a) (1960).

266 *E.g.*, United States v Ible, 630 F2d 389 (5th Cir 1980); Theisen v Johns, 72 Mich 285, 40 NW 727 (1888). *See also* City Transp Co v Sisson, 365 SW2d 216 (Tex Civ App 1963) (permitting questioning re bias against narcotics use).

267 *E.g.*, Robinson v Randall, 82 Ill 521 (1876); Scott v Shope, 33 Neb 41, 49 NW 940 (1891). *Contra* Fletcher v Crist, 38 NE 472 (Ind 1894).

268 Albrecht v Walker, 73 Ill 69 (1874); Theisen v Johns, 72 Mich 285, 40 NW 727 (1888). *See generally* Annotation, *Racial, Religious, Economic, Social, or Political Prejudice of Proposed Juror as Proper Subject of Inquiry or Ground of Challenge on Voir Dire in Civil Case,* 72 ALR2d 905, 918-20 §9(b) (1960).

269 *E.g.*, State v Miller, 60 Idaho 79, 88 P2d 526 (1939); State v Carson, 131 SC 42, 126 SE 757 (1925). *See generally* Annotation, *Racial, Religious, Economic, Social, or Political Prejudice of Proposed Juror as Proper Subject of Inquiry or Ground of Challenge on Voir Dire in Criminal Case,* 54 ALR2d 1204, 1221-23 §9(a) (1957).

270 *See* State v Davis, 371 SW2d 270 (1963); State v Wideman, 218 La 860, 51 So 2d 96 (1951).

interfere with the juror's ability to give the defendant a fair trial will it lead to disqualification.[271]

Where in a civil suit, such as one for damages arising from an automobile collision, there is evidence that a party had been drinking, a juror's attitude toward liquor is a proper subject of inquiry. A juror adamantly opposed to the use or sale of alcohol will be properly subject to challenge for cause.

Prejudice against gambling will usually not disqualify a juror. In states where gambling is illegal, courts reason that such a prejudice is one merely in favor of enforcing the laws.[272] Thus, in a prosecution for depositing a lottery ticket in the United States Mail, it was held that the trial court did not commit error in refusing to grant the defendant's challenge to a juror who stated that, if there were a conflict in testimony, he would be inclined to give more weight to the testimony of a witness against the defendant. The court said that all good citizens should be prejudiced against crime, and that if this bias were to be regarded as disqualifying, no juror could ever be obtained to try anyone accused of crime.[273] The troublesome aspect of the court's analysis is that it seems to have proceeded on the assumption that the defendant was guilty. In any event, a contrary result would presumably be required in the increasing number of states in which lotteries are legal.

§7.40 —Religion

An otherwise competent juror cannot be disqualified on the basis of religious belief or lack thereof.[274] Indeed, exclusion of persons from jury service because of their religious beliefs implicates federal constitutional rights. Requiring an oath as to a juror's belief in God has been held to violate the fourteenth amendment,[275] and jurors who do not believe in God may affirm rather than take an oath.[276] In a case without religious issues or where no special circumstances raise the possibility of religious prejudice, inquiry into a juror's religious beliefs

---

[271] *See* Stoots v State, 108 Ind 415, 9 NE 380 (1886); Gonzales v State, 331 SW2d 748 (Tex Crim App 1960).

[272] *See* United States v Noelke, 1 F 426, 434 (NY Cir 1880); *see also* United States v Duff, 6 F 45 (NY Cir 1881).

[273] United States v Borger, 7 F 193, 198 (NY Cir 1881); *but see* Lurding v United States, 179 F2d 419 (6th Cir 1950) (held in a prosecution for income tax evasion that existence of a prejudice against gambling was a proper subject of inquiry, since some veniremen might have been prejudiced against bookmaking operations, whether or not prohibited by law).

[274] Coleman v United States, 379 A2d 951 (DC 1977); *In re* Malvasi's Estate, 96 Cal App 204, 273 P 1097 (1929); State v Jackson, 156 Iowa 588, 137 NW 1034 (1912); Smith v Sisters of Good Shepherd, 27 Ky L Rptr 1107, 87 SW 1083 (1905). *See generally* Annotation, *Religious Beliefs, Affiliation, or Prejudice of Prospective Juror as Proper Subject of Inquiry or Ground for Challenge on Voir Dire,* 95 ALR3d 172 (1979); Annotation, *Voir Dire Examination of Prospective Jurors Under Rule 24(a) of Federal Rules of Criminal Procedure,* 28 ALR Fed 79-82 §§14-15 (1976).

[275] Schowgurow v State, 240 Md 121, 213 A2d 475 (1965).

[276] *See* Jones v State, 585 P2d 1340 (Nev 1978).

is improper.[277] Nor is a juror disqualified for being of the same religion as a party.[278]

On the other hand, religious beliefs are an appropriate subject of voir dire where religion is an issue in the case or where a religious organization is a party.[279] A California decision seems to stretch this principle to its limits. In the case, a divorced wife sought to recover amounts unpaid under the terms of a property settlement. The court held that questions concerning jurors' religious beliefs on divorce and remarriage were proper.[280] Although the holding is questionable, the court's observation that even though no person should be rendered incompetent as a juror because of religious belief, a prospective juror might be unable to try a particular case impartially because of a religious belief[281] is eminently sound. It has also been held that a juror's predisposition to unduly credit the testimony of a person with religious status (e.g., a priest) is a proper grounds for challenge.[282]

In a jurisdiction that allows voir dire in order to facilitate the intelligent exercise of peremptory challenges, questioning about religion is more likely to be allowed.[283] In *Wasy v State,*[284] for example, an abortion prosecution, refusal to permit inquiry into a juror's religious faith was held to be error on the grounds that without such information the defendant could not intelligently exercise her peremptory challenges. The court arguably could have also justified the questioning to identify jurors subject to challenge for cause, as one's views on abortion and one's views on religion tend to be linked.[285]

Where no religious issues appear to be involved in a case, religious questions are generally not allowed. Thus, a Missouri court held that a plaintiff's counsel was properly prohibited from examining jurors about membership in particular churches.[286] The case neither related to religion nor involved a religious organization, and the plaintiff's lawyer provided no justification for the questions. The court observed quite rightly that religious affiliations in themselves are

---

[277] United States v Barnes, 604 F2d 121 (2d Cir 1979), *cert denied,* 446 US 907 (1980); Yarborough v United States, 230 F2d 56 (4th Cir), *cert denied,* 351 US 969 (1956); People v Velarde, 616 P2d 104 (Colo 1980); State v Huff, 14 NJ 240, 102 A2d 8 (1954).

[278] Birmingham Baptist Hosp v Orange, 284 Ala 160, 223 So 2d 279 (1969); Smith v Sisters of Good Shepherd, 27 Ky L Rptr 1107, 87 SW 1083 (1905); Coleman v United States, 379 A2d 951 (1977).

[279] United States v Ible, 630 F2d 389 (5th Cir 1980); United States v Clancy, 276 F2d 617 (7th Cir 1960); Coleman v United States, 379 A2d 951 (DC 1977).

[280] Smith v Smith, 7 Cal App 2d 271, 46 P2d 232 (1935).

[281] *Id* at 274, 46 P2d at 233.

[282] Coleman v United States, 379 A2d 951 (DC 1977). *See also* Casey v Roman Catholic Archbishop, 217 Md 595, 143 A2d 627 (1958).

[283] Wasy v State, 234 Ind 52, 123 NE2d 462 (1955); Young v State, 41 Okla Crim 226, 271 P 426 (1928); Coleman v United States, 379 A2d 951 (DC 1977).

[284] 234 Ind 52, 123 NE2d 462 (1955).

[285] *See* State v Barnett, 251 Or 234, 445 P2d 124 (1968).

[286] Rose v Sheedy, 345 Mo 610, 134 SW2d 18 (1939).

neither a qualification nor a disqualification for jury service.[287] Likewise, in a malpractice action against physicians which had nothing to do with religion, it was held that the trial court acted properly in preventing the plaintiff's counsel from asking about jurors' membership in religious societies.[288]

Voir dire questioning about religious beliefs and affiliations is a sensitive matter requiring great delicacy and tact on the part of counsel. Questions regarding religion can cause discomfort to many jurors, and therefore should be avoided unless thought to be absolutely necessary. If such questioning is necessary, counsel should explain to the jury the purpose behind the questioning and stress that it is not counsel's purpose to embarrass any individual or denigrate any religion. Jurors who are nonetheless offended by the questioning may need to be challenged peremptorily.

§7.41 —Race Generally

Many persons hold conscious or subconscious racial prejudices. A defendant in a criminal case or a party in a civil case cannot receive a fair trial where there is a juror whose vote will be based on the color of the party's skin. Race rarely, if ever, has any relevance to the merits of a case.

In *Aldridge v United States,*[289] the United States Supreme Court held it to be reversible error for a trial judge not to permit the defendant's counsel to inquire about racial prejudice in a case where a black defendant was charged with the murder of a white victim. The Court, in an opinion by Chief Justice Hughes, explained the rationale for such questioning:

> The argument is advanced on behalf of the Government that it would be detrimental to the administration of the law in the courts of the United States to allow questions to jurors as to racial or religious prejudices. We think that it would be far more injurious to permit it to be thought that persons entertaining a disqualifying prejudice were allowed to serve as jurors and that inquiries designed to elicit the fact of disqualification were barred. No surer way could be devised to bring the processes of justice into disrepute.[290]

Prejudice against races or nationalities other than blacks may also be a proper subject of inquiry and basis for challenge.[291]

---

[287] *Id* 19. *Accord* State v Betts, 646 SW2d 94 (Mo 1983).

[288] Van Skike v Potter, 53 Neb 28, 73 NW 295 (1897).

[289] 283 US 308 (1931).

[290] *Id* 314-15.

[291] *See, e.g.,* People v Car Soy, 57 Cal 102 (1880) (prejudice against Chinese); Potter v State, 86 Tex Crim 380, 216 SW 886 (1919) (anti-Semitism). *But see* Commonwealth v De Palma, 268 Pa 25, 110 A 756 (1920) (refusing to sustain challenge to juror who admitted bias against Italians); Romeo v State, 107 Tex Crim 70, 294 SW 857 (1927) (refusing to sustain challenge to juror who admitted bias against Mexicans). In both *De Palma* and *Romero,* the jurors claimed they could be impartial despite their prejudice,

Quite probing voir dire may be necessary both because racial prejudice has become so unacceptable in modern society that few will admit to it and because much racial prejudice exists on a subconscious level. It is usually not productive to ask jurors if they are prejudiced against blacks; a negative answer will be semi-automatic. An approach more likely to elicit revealing information is to ask an open-ended question about the juror's experiences with blacks.

Many of the legal issues relating to exclusion of persons based on race from the jury are addressed elsewhere in this book. The systematic exclusion of blacks and other minorities from the venire is constitutionally impermissible and can give rise to a challenge to the array; the relevant law was examined in the preceding chapter. The use of peremptory challenges to exclude blacks from jury panels also has constitutional implications; this topic will be examined in the next chapter. The following sections are concerned with voir dire of individual jurors in order to reveal racial prejudice.

§7.42 —Supreme Court Development on Race Prejudice

In *Ham v South Carolina,*[292] a bearded, black civil rights worker was convicted of possession of marijuana. The defendant claimed that he had been framed in retaliation for his civil rights activities. On voir dire he sought to question jurors about their racial prejudice, as well as their prejudice against persons with beards. The trial court refused to allow questioning on either topic. The United States Supreme Court, although rejecting petitioner's contentions regarding persons with beards,[293] held that the refusal to allow inquiry as to racial bias denied the petitioner a fair trial in violation of the due process clause of the fourteenth amendment:

> [O]ne of the purposes of the Due Process Clause of the Fourteenth Amendment is to insure these "essential demands of fairness," . . . and since a principal purpose of the adoption of the Fourteenth Amendment was to prohibit the States from invidiously discriminating on the basis of race, . . . we think that the Fourteenth Amendment required the judge in this case to interrogate the jurors upon the subject of racial prejudice. South Carolina law permits challenges for cause, and authorizes the trial judge to conduct voir dire examination of potential jurors. The State having created this statutory framework for the selection of juries, the

---

and the judge believed them. The holdings are questionable. On the general topic of racial prejudice of jurors as a proper subject of voir dire, see Annotation, *Racial or Ethnic Prejudice of Prospective Jurors as Proper Subject of Inquiry or Ground of Challenge on Voir Dire in State Criminal Case,* 94 ALR3d 15 (1979).

[292] 409 US 524 (1973).

[293] *Id* 528. The Court said that given its "inability to constitutionally distinguish possible prejudice against beards from a host of other possible similar prejudices, we do not believe the petitioner's constitutional rights were violated when the trial judge refused to permit this question." *Id.*

> essential fairness required by the Due Process Clause of the Fourteenth Amendment requires that under the facts shown by this record the petitioner be permitted to have the jurors interrogated on the issue of racial bias.[294]

Subsequent to *Ham* the Supreme Court was again presented with the opportunity to address the issue of voir dire questioning regarding racial prejudice in *Ristaino v Ross.*[295] The case involved similar yet distinguishable facts. A black defendant was tried and convicted of violent crimes against a white security guard. Although state law required a general inquiry into prejudice, the trial court declined to make a specific inquiry into racial prejudice. The United States Supreme Court held that in the absence of the kinds of circumstances present in *Ham,* which the Court found not to be present, examination of jurors regarding racial prejudice was not *constitutionally* required. Thus, there was no error of constitutional dimension when the state trial judge questioned jurors about general bias but declined to question them about racial bias. The Supreme Court indicated that it was not prepared to require voir dire examination on racial prejudice in all cases:

> The Constitution does not always entitle a defendant to have questions posed during voir dire specifically directed to matters that conceivably might prejudice veniremen against him. Voir dire "is conducted under the supervision of the court, and a great deal must, of necessity, be left to its sound discretion." . . .
>
> In *Ham,* we recognized that some cases may present circumstances in which an impermissible threat to the fair trial guaranteed by due process is posed by a trial court's refusal to question prospective jurors specifically about racial prejudice during voir dire. *Ham* involved a Negro tried in South Carolina courts for possession of marihuana. He was well known in the locale of his trial as a civil rights activist, and his defense was that law enforcement officials had framed him on the narcotics charge to "get him" for those activities. Despite the circumstances, the trial judge denied Ham's request that the court-conducted voir dire include questions specifically directed to racial prejudice. We reversed the judgment of conviction because "the essential fairness required by the Due Process Clause of the Fourteenth Amendment requires that under the facts shown by this record the [defendant] be permitted to have the jurors interrogated [during voir dire] on the issue of racial bias." 409 U.S., at 527.
>
> By its terms *Ham* did not announce a requirement of universal applicability. Rather, it reflected an assessment of whether under all of the circumstances presented there was a constitutionally significant likelihood that, absent questioning about racial prejudice, the jurors would not be as "indifferent as [they stand] unsworn."[296]

---

[294] *Id* 526-27.

[295] 424 US 589 (1976).

[296] *Id* 594-96 (citations omitted).

In *Rosales-Lopez v United States,*[297] the defendant was convicted for his participation in a campaign to smuggle fellow Mexican-Americans into the country. The issue again was the propriety of voir dire questions dealing with racial prejudice. The trial judge questioned the jurors about prejudice in general and about their attitudes to aliens, but not about their attitude toward persons of Mexican descent. The Supreme Court found no constitutional error. The Court said that absent "special circumstances," voir dire as to racial prejudice was not required. As a nonviolent victimless crime involving fellow Mexicans had been committed, the Court found no special circumstances.

Thus, whether questions on racial prejudice are required is determined by the facts of the case. The mere fact of interracial violence in and of itself is not enough; presumably, the violence will have to have been racially precipitated. If there are unusual circumstances present comparable to those in *Ham,* such questioning may also be required. Otherwise, a defendant will have to show a strong possibility of racial prejudice in order to justify such questioning. The majority in *Rosales-Lopez* specifically left open the possibility of "other circumstances" which would warrant inquiry into racial bias.[298]

Even if not required, it is arguably the better practice to allow questioning on the issue of racial prejudice.[299] One reason is that it will assist counsel in the intelligent exercise of peremptory challenges.[300] Another is that it will serve the long-term interests of the state and its legal system. It is important that both the defendant and members of defendant's race believe that the law has provided fair treatment. Confidence in the jury system and the state responsible for it will suffer if there is even the slightest basis for thinking that a jury's verdict was tainted by racial prejudice. As in the Supreme Court cases discussed, the failure to allow questioning about possible racial prejudice tends to shift the focus from defendant's responsibility for the crime charged to the latent racism in the state's criminal justice system.

§7.43 —Prosecution Questions on Race Prejudice

Questions about racial prejudice are usually raised by a defendant in a criminal case. They have also been held proper when posed by the prosecution. Usually this occurs when the victim is a member of a minority race. In *Lester v*

---

[297] 451 US 182 (1981).

[298] *Id* 192. In Turner v Murray, 476 US 28 (1986), the Supreme Court held that questions about racial prejudice may be required to ensure a defendant an impartial jury at the penalty phase of a capital trial.

[299] *Id* 191. *See also* State v Reed, 629 SW2d 424 (Mo Ct App 1981) (questions calculated to expose prejudice should be liberally permitted; those designed to induce prejudice should be vigorously denied).

[300] *See* Pantos v City & County of San Francisco, 151 Cal App 3d 258, 198 Cal Rptr 489 (1984).

State,[301] for instance, the white defendant was on trial for the murder of a black. The court held that the prosecutor could properly ask whether a juror would return the same verdict against a white defendant charged with the murder of a black that the juror would return if the defendant were charged with the murder of a white. The court said that anyone who believed, morally, socially, politically, or religiously, that it is not murder for a white person to take with malice the life of a black person was unfit to serve as a juror. The court rejected the contention that racial prejudice was not a ground for disqualification because it was not mentioned in the controlling statute. The court reasoned that the statute was not exclusive, and, in any event, mentioned bias and prejudice generally as grounds for disqualification.

§7.44 —Membership in Racially Biased Organizations

Most jurors are conscious of the social disapproval of racial prejudice and will deny such prejudice when questioned directly about it. Indeed, denial would be the expected response from an individual who seeks to be on a jury in order to vent a racial prejudice. Lawyers should therefore approach the issue in a way that does not elicit a perfunctory negative response. The value of open-ended questions regarding the juror's experiences with the racial group in question has already been mentioned.[302] Another tactic is to ask jurors about the organizations to which they belong. Membership in racially restrictive organizations may be telling. Persons who join racially restrictive clubs and societies may do so to avoid contact with the excluded race. Membership alone, however, is usually not sufficient to sustain a challenge for cause.[303] The nature and extent of the juror's commitment to the racial policies of the organization, as well as the juror's willingness to decide the case on the merits, need to be probed.

Although membership in a racially restrictive organization may not by itself be a sufficient grounds for challenge, it is an indication that the juror may be racially prejudiced.[304] Accordingly, courts often will allow inquiry into a juror's

---

[301] 2 Tex App 432 (1877).

[302] *See* **§7.41.** *See generally* **§9.15.**

[303] Malvo v JC Penney Co, 512 P2d 575 (Alaska 1973); State v Square, 257 La 743, 244 So 2d 200 (1971), *vacated on other grounds,* 408 US 938 (1972); State v Rideau, 249 La 1111, 193 So 2d 264 (1966), *cert denied,* 389 US 861 (1967); *but see* People v Reyes, 5 Cal 347 (1855), which suggests that an oath or other obligation required for membership may support a challenge for cause. *See generally* Annotation, *Jury: Membership in Racially Biased or Prejudiced Organization as Proper Subject of Voir Dire Inquiry or Ground for Challenge,* 63 ALR3d 1052 (1975); Annotation, *Voir Dire Examination of Prospective Jurors Under Rule 24(a) of Federal Rules of Criminal Procedure,* 28 ALR Fed 26, 78-79 §13 (1976).

[304] *See* People v Presley, 22 AD2d 151, 254 NYS2d 400 (1964), *affd,* 16 NY2d 738, 209 NE2d 729, 262 NYS2d 113 (1965).

affiliations with such an organization. Jurors may be asked about specific organizations[305] or about organizations of a particular nature.[306]

Some courts appear skeptical about the value of questions relating to memberships in organizations with racially biased policies.[307] They are apparently wary of injecting animosities toward controversial organizations into a case in which they are not proper issues. In most of the cases upholding the refusal to allow questioning about membership in racially restrictive organizations, the trial court had permitted inquiries of a general nature designed to expose racial prejudice.[308] As usual, whether questioning about membership in racially restrictive organizations is to be allowed will ordinarily be left to the discretion of the trial judge, whose decision will not be disturbed absent a showing of clear abuse. Questioning about such membership in order to allow for a more intelligent exercise of peremptory challenges has also been permitted in states which allow voir dire for this purpose.[309]

§7.45 —Politics

A juror's political beliefs or opinions are rarely relevant. They tend to become so, however, when a prominent political figure is either a party or a witness in a case, or where the actions of a party were politically motivated.[310] As a general rule, political prejudice is not a valid basis for disqualification of a juror.[311] Whether to permit inquiry into political prejudice is a matter for the discretion of the court, and refusal to permit inquiry has been held not to constitute an abuse of discretion.[312] It is even less likely in civil than in

---

[305] *See* State v Rideau, 249 La 1111, 193 So 2d 264 (1966), *cert denied,* 389 US 861 (1967); People v Presley, 22 AD2d 151, 254 NYS2d 400 (1964), *affd,* 16 NY2d 738, 209 NE2d 729, 262 NYS2d 113 (1965); Lopez v Allee, 493 SW2d 330 (Tex Ct App 1973).

[306] *See* United States v Bamberger, 456 F2d 1119 (3d Cir), *cert denied,* 406 US 969 (1972), *cert denied,* 413 US 919 (1973); State v Hills, 241 La 345, 129 So 2d 12 (1960).

[307] *E.g.,* Wallace v Kemp, 581 F Supp 1471 (MD Ga 1984), *revd on other grounds,* 757 F2d 1102 (11th Cir 1985); Seals v State, 282 Ala 586, 213 So 2d 645 (1968); Raullerson v People, 157 Colo 462, 404 P2d 149 (1965); Wallace v State, 248 Ga 255, 282 SE2d 325 (1981), *cert denied,* 455 US 977 (1982); State v Chavis, 24 NC App 148, 210 SE2d 555 (1974); State v Sellers, 257 SC 35, 183 SE2d 889 (1971), *cert denied,* 410 US 908 (1973).

[308] *See* Wallace v Kemp, 581 F Supp 1471 (MD Ga 1984), *revd on other grounds,* 757 F2d 1102 (11th Cir 1985); Seals v State, 282 Ala 586, 213 So 2d 645 (1968); State v Chavis, 24 NC App 148, 210 SE2d 555 (1974); State v Rideau, 249 La 1111, 93 So 2d 264 (1966), *cert denied,* 389 US 861 (1967).

[309] *E.g.,* State v Hills, 241 La 345, 129 So 2d 12 (1961).

[310] *See, e.g.,* United States v Chapin, 515 F2d 1274 (DC Cir), *cert denied,* 423 US 1015 (1975).

[311] *See* Commonwealth v Casper, 392 A2d 287 (Pa 1978).

[312] Connors v United States, 158 US 408 (1895); State v Longo, 121 NJL 427, 3 A2d 127 (1938); *see also* Annotation, *Racial, Religious, Economic, Social, or Political Prejudice of Proposed Juror as Proper Subject of Inquiry or Ground of Challenge on Voir Dire in Criminal Case,* 54 ALR2d 1204 (1957).

criminal cases that membership in a political organization will be a valid basis for a challenge for cause.[313] Older cases rationalized a refusal to allow questioning about prejudice against communism or fascism on the ground that the prejudice would be a permissible one, or that such inquiry was not relevant to the particular case.[314]

Unless it appears that a juror could not have given the defendant a fair and impartial trial, refusal to allow counsel to inquire into the politics of a juror is not reversible error.[315] However, there have been a few cases where questions about political prejudice have been held proper.[316] In one, the defendant was charged with disrupting Congress. It was held that the trial court had abused its discretion in not specifically asking jurors whether they felt any prejudice against the defendant because of his political views and affiliations.[317] At the least, said the appellate court, the trial judge should have alerted the jury to the political issues involved and inquired whether the jurors could be impartial.

Individuals whose crimes are designed to be an expression of political protest often seek to question jurors about the political cause which they were espousing. In *United States v Malinowski*[318] the defendant claimed his income tax violations were a protest against the Vietnam War. He sought to question jurors on their views of that conflict, as well as civil disobedience generally. The trial court's refusal to allow this questioning was upheld. Conversely, in *United States v Dellinger*[319] where defendants were tried for activities arising out of their protest demonstration at the 1968 Democratic National Convention, the Seventh Circuit Court of Appeals held that the defendants should have been allowed to question jurors about their views regarding the Vietnam War.[320]

Political prejudices are usually held not to disqualify a juror. However, if it can be shown that the political prejudice could affect the juror's impartiality, the juror should be excused for cause. At the very least, inquiry should be permitted in order to provide an attorney with an informed basis for exercising peremptory challenges.

---

[313] *See* Scott v Chope, 33 Neb 41, 49 NW 940 (1891); Gray v State *ex rel* Langham, 19 Tex Civ App 521, 49 SW 699 (1898). *See generally* Annotation, *Racial, Religious, Economic, Social, or Political Prejudice of Proposed Juror as Proper Subject of Inquiry or Ground of Challenge on Voir Dire in Civil Case,* 72 ALR2d 905, 912-13 §6 (1960).

[314] *See* Ruthenberg v United States, 245 US 480 (1918); Spies v People, 122 Ill 1, 12 NE 865, *error dismissed,* 123 US 131 (1887).

[315] State v Maxwell, 151 Kan 951, 102 P2d 109 (1940).

[316] *E.g.,* United States v Dellinger, 472 F2d 340, 366-70 (7th Cir 1972), *cert denied,* 410 US 970 (1973); Cordero v United States, 456 A2d 837 (DC 1983); People v Fitzgerald, 14 Cal App 2d 180, 58 P2d 718, *cert denied,* 299 US 593 (1936).

[317] Cordero v United States, 456 A2d 837 (DC 1983).

[318] 347 F Supp 347 (ED Pa 1972), *affd,* 472 F2d 850 (3d Cir), *cert denied,* 411 US 970 (1973).

[319] 472 F2d 340 (7th Cir 1972), *cert denied,* 410 US 970 (1973).

[320] *Accord* Cordero v United States, 456 A2d 837 (DC 1983).

§7.46 —Certain Witnesses

Courts are divided on the issue of whether jurors may be questioned about the weight that they would give to the testimony of a particular witness. Many courts have held such questions proper.[321] They reason that the questioning is designed to serve the legitimate purpose of ascertaining whether a juror's respect or disrespect for a particular witness will bias the juror for or against the side for which the witness testifies. Questions usually follow this form:

Q. Mr. Blank may testify in this case. Are any of you acquainted with or know Mr. Blank?

Q. Have you had any dealings with Mr. Blank?

Q. If so, could you tell us about them?

Q. Do you have an opinion of Mr. Blank?

Q. If so could you tell us what it is?

Q. Given this opinion, if Mr. Blank were to testify, could you give his testimony the same weight as the testimony of any other witness, under the same circumstances?

or:

If Mr. Blank testified in this case, would you give his testimony such weight as it is entitled to under the law?

or:

If Mr. Blank testified in this case, would you be prejudiced or unduly influenced against (or in favor) of his testimony, or would you give his testimony less (or more) weight than the testimony of other witnesses, simply because of the fact that he is a (description of position held by witness)?

Some courts, however, have held it improper to ask (or at least have held it not an abuse of discretion not to allow) questions concerning the weight jurors would give to testimony of a particular witness.[322] These courts are concerned that the questioning is designed to entrap jurors into committing themselves in advance to the side for which the witness testifies.

Defense attorneys in criminal cases are concerned that jurors will not give proper weight to a defendant's testimony, particularly where the defendant has a record of previous convictions. The trial judge has a broad range of

---

[321] Sellers v United States, 271 F2d 475 (DC Cir 1959). Stoots v State, 108 Ind 415, 9 NE 380 (1886); People v O'Neill, 109 NY 251, 16 NE 68 (1888).

[322] Fredrick v United States, 163 F2d 536 (9th Cir), *cert denied,* 332 US 775 (1947); People v Warner, 147 Cal 546, 82 P 196 (1905); State v McKeever, 339 Mo 1066, 101 SW2d 22 (1936).

discretion as to whether to allow voir dire on this topic. Refusals to permit inquiry as to the weight which a juror will give to the accused's testimony have been upheld,[323] but so have decisions to allow such questions.[324]

The juror's prejudice may relate not to the defendant's status as a defendant but to some distinct aspect of the defendant's character. In one case the defendant had misled his superiors in the course of an investigation. It was held error to refuse to question jurors about their moral or ethical repugnance to lying.[325]

Questions as to how jurors would weigh testimony of particular types of witnesses can arise in as many contexts as there are types of witnesses. Among those types of witnesses which have proved particularly troublesome are accomplices of a criminal accused, informers, and prostitutes and their procurers.[326] In *State v Edwards,*[327] the Louisiana Supreme Court found no error in excusing a juror who said she would be unable to credit the testimony of a five-year-old. The court cited approvingly *State v Murray,*[328] in which the court upheld a challenge for cause to jurors who stated that under no circumstances would they believe the testimony of a homosexual.

The focus is often on law enforcement officials, with defense counsel concerned that jurors will give the testimony of police undue weight. In an illustrative Texas case, it was held that the trial court committed reversible error when it refused to allow the defense to ask whether jurors could conceive of the possibility that police officers might lie on the witness stand.[329] Similarly, federal courts have held that a trial judge's refusal to ask whether jurors would give undue weight to the testimony of law enforcement officers where the case against the accused rested primarily on officers' testimony can constitute reversible error.[330] A Louisiana court stated that a juror who unquestioningly would credit the testimony of law enforcement officers over that of defense

---

[323] *E.g.*, Fredrick v United States, 163 F2d 536 (9th Cir), *cert denied,* 332 US 775 (1947); People v Fowler, 178 Cal 657, 174 P 892 (1918); German v State, 159 Ga App 638, 284 SE2d 654 (1981).

[324] *E.g.*, United States v Napoleone, 349 F2d 350 (7th Cir 1965); State v Ramirez, 116 Ariz 259, 569 P2d 201 (1977). Stoots v State, 108 Ind 415, 9 NE 380 (1886). *See generally* Annotation, *Propriety, on Voir Dire in Criminal Case, of Inquiries as to Juror's Possible Prejudice if Informed of Defendant's Prior Convictions,* 43 ALR3d 1081 (1972).

[325] United States v Napoleone, 349 F2d 350 (7th Cir 1965).

[326] *See generally* Annotation, *Propriety and Effect of Asking Prospective Jurors Hypothetical Questions, on Voir Dire, as to How They Would Decide Issues in Case,* 99 ALR2d 7, 59-76 §5 (1965).

[327] 419 So 2d 881 (La 1982).

[328] 375 So 2d 80 (La 1979).

[329] Hernandez v State, 508 SW2d 853 (Tex Crim App 1974). *But compare* Kennard v State, 649 SW2d 752 (Tex Ct App 1983) (statement by juror that he would put testimony of a police officer above that of another not a basis for challenge for cause).

[330] Sellers v United States, 271 F2d 475 (DC Cir 1959); United States v Spaar, 748 F2d 1249 (8th Cir 1984); United States v Espinosa, 771 F2d 1382 (10th Cir 1985). *But see* United States v Golden, 532 F2d 1244 (9th Cir 1976).

witnesses was not competent to serve, and should have been excused for cause.[331]

Some courts are not enthusiastic about this general line of questioning. In *State v Williams*,[332] the court stated that it was improper to ask jurors to speculate about testimony which they had yet to hear.

It is useful to question jurors not simply about their relationships with specific witnesses but more generally about their experiences with persons of the same background or occupation as a witness. Thus, for example, it is quite common for defense attorneys in criminal cases to question jurors about their relationships and friendships with persons involved in law enforcement.[333]

§7.47 —Certain Types of Litigation and Defenses

In addition to prejudices against certain types of persons or organizations, prospective jurors may have prejudices against certain types of litigation. In most instances these prejudices are superficial and abstract;[334] in others they are deeply engrained and rigidly fixed.[335] A superficial prejudice which is not likely to affect the juror's thinking will usually not result in disqualification;[336] a prejudice which is deep-seated, of long standing, and firmly held may.

In a California wrongful death action, for example, it was held error to deny challenges for cause to jurors who stated that they were prejudiced against suits for personal injuries, felt that many such suits were without merit, and believed that the number of such suits was constantly increasing.[337] Similarly, in an action based on an employer's alleged negligence, the Texas Court of Appeals upheld the trial court's ruling sustaining the plaintiff's challenges for cause to jurors who were prejudiced against suits of that nature.[338] The court explained its rationale:

> [P]rejudice against a class of litigation under which the plaintiff's cause of action comes, is tantamount to a prejudice against the law which gives him the right to recover in his suit. And its existence in the mind of a juror, in the trial of the case, might work a greater injury than actual prejudice against him personally by the juror would cause him.[339]

---

[331] State v Nolan, 341 So 2d 885 (La 1977). *But compare* State v Allen, 380 So 2d 28 (La 1980) (distinguishing *Nolan*). *See also* State v Riley, 605 P2d 765 (Utah 1980) (where juror indicates that he would give police testimony greater credence than that of other witnesses, trial judge should either inquire further or excuse juror).

[332] 617 SW2d 98 (Mo Ct App 1981).

[333] *See* State v Jackson, 43 NJ 148, 203 A2d 1 (1964), *cert denied*, 379 US 982 (1965).

[334] *See, e.g.*, Ramirez v Wood, 577 SW2d 278 (Tex Civ App 1978).

[335] *See, e.g.*, Ellison v National By-Prods Inc, 153 Ga App 475, 265 SE2d 829 (1980).

[336] *E.g.*, Capeland v Gulf Oil Corp, 672 F2d 867 (11th Cir 1982); Ramirez v Wood, 577 SW2d 278 (Tex Civ App 1978).

[337] Quill v Southern Pac Co, 140 Cal 268, 73 P 991 (1903). *Accord* Henrie v Compton, 357 SW2d 589 (Tex Civ App 1962).

[338] Galveston, H & SA Ry v Manns, 37 Tex Civ App 356, 84 SW 254 (1904).

[339] *Id* at 360, 84 SW at 255.

Where the prejudice will not influence the juror's verdict, however, the juror will not be disqualified.[340]

Many personal injury lawyers are hired on a contingent fee basis. It has been held that a juror who is adamantly opposed to contingent fee arrangements is unqualified to sit on a case in which the attorney is employed on that basis.[341]

There have also been cases where the prejudice has worked the other way, in which prospective jurors are highly in favor of certain actions. In these instances it is the defendant whose fair trial is at risk. In one such case, an action by a miner against his employer for negligence, it was held to be error for the trial judge to deny a challenge to a juror who declared that he had a natural sympathy for the working man such that it would require perfectly clear evidence for him to find for the defendant.[342]

Membership in an organization whose goals favor a particular side of a litigation can also give rise to an inference that the juror is not free from bias. Counsel representing a defendant charged with drunk driving, for example, would want to challenge a juror who belonged to an organization which condemned the drinking of alcohol. Without knowing the extent of the juror's commitment to the principles of the organization, however, it would be inappropriate for a court to sustain a challenge for cause to the juror.[343] Membership alone is usually not a basis for disqualification, particularly if the juror pledges to decide the case on the evidence and not on his or her personal views.[344] The attorney who disbelieves the juror retains, as always, the option to exercise a peremptory challenge against the juror.

Some jurors are reluctant to accept certain defenses permitted by law.[345] Perhaps the prime example is the insanity defense. There are persons who believe in total personal accountability for one's actions and will not accept a defense that attempts to shift responsibility to a mental condition; others who accept the concept of mental illness will balk at acquitting a dangerous defendant on that grounds for fear that the defendant will be returned to the community. A juror who is unable to accept a defense, such as insanity, which is recognized by law is subject to challenge for cause.[346] In relevant cases, for a court to refuse to permit voir dire on attitudes toward the defense is reversible error.[347] In one case, however, the failure to allow such questions was held not to be error

---

[340] *See, e.g.*, McCarthy v Cass Ave & Fair Grounds Ry, 92 Mo 356, 4 SW 516 (1887); Denham v Washington Power Co, 38 Wash 354, 80 P 546 (1905).

[341] Rhoades v El Paso & SW Ry, 248 SW 1064 (Comm App Tex 1923).

[342] Metallic Gold Mining Co v Watson, 51 Colo 278, 117 P 609 (1911).

[343] *See* United States v Salamone, 800 F2d 1216 (3d Cir 1986).

[344] *Id. See also* State v Square, 257 La 743, 244 So 2d 200 (1971), *vacated on other grounds,* 408 US 938 (1972). *See generally* Annotation, *Competency of Juror As Affected By His Membership in Co-operative Association Interested in the Case,* 69 ALR3d 1296 (1976).

[345] *See, e.g.*, State v Sylvester, 400 So 2d 640 (La 1981) (juror who refused to accept defense of self-defense properly excused).

[346] State v Leonard, 296 NC 58, 248 SE2d 853 (1978). *See also* **§7.09.**

[347] *See* United States v Allsup, 566 F2d 68 (9th Cir 1977); People v Robinson, 102 Ill App 3d 884, 429 NE2d 1356 (1981).

because the appellate court concluded, somewhat speculatively, that the finding of the defendant's guilt would not have changed if the suggested questions had been asked.[348] The scope of the inquiry in insanity cases may be quite far-ranging and include personal psychiatric treatment experiences of the juror or a family member, relevant readings on the subject, willingness to listen to expert opinion with an open mind, and friends and acquaintances in the psychiatric profession.[349]

§7.48 Attitudes on Damages—Compensatory

In some personal injury cases large damages are sought, and plaintiff's counsel must determine the attitudes of jurors towards such awards generally. Many a juror will balk at awarding an injured party a sum which exceeds the amount of money the juror can personally expect to earn in a lifetime. Possible prejudice against large verdicts is generally held to be a proper subject for voir dire; but courts will draw the line at an attempt by plaintiff's counsel to obtain a pledge from the jury to return a verdict in a particular amount.[350]

The trial judge has broad discretion to control the scope of voir dire as to jurors' attitudes toward the amount of damages sought. The judge's ruling will be reversed on appeal only for an abuse of discretion and only if the ruling resulted in prejudice. Thus, in *Murphy v Lindahl*[351] it was held that there was no abuse of discretion in allowing the plaintiff's attorney to question prospective jurors about their attitudes toward returning a verdict of $300,000. The court pointed out that some prospective jurors have fixed objections to large verdicts, which might not readily yield to proper evidence. The court qualified its decision by stating that attempts to obtain a commitment from jurors as to how they would decide the case or to elicit an indication of which party they would favor on a hypothesized state of the evidence were improper.[352]

In another case plaintiff's counsel asked each juror whether, if the proof were to show that plaintiff had been severely damaged, it would be embarrassing to return the large verdict which was being sought. The court said that although this examination was unusual, defendant's counsel could have put the converse proposition to the jurors, and asked whether, since a large amount was being sought, the jurors would be embarrassed to return nothing if they found the defendant not liable.[353]

---

[348] People v Pitts, 104 Ill App 3d 451, 432 NE2d 1062 (1982). The court did add that the better practice would have been for the trial court to ask the requested questions. *Id* at 457, 432 NE2d at 1067.

[349] *See* United States v Jackson, 542 F2d 403, 413 (7th Cir 1976).

[350] Atlantic Joint Terminal v Knight, 98 Ga App 482, 106 SE2d 417 (1958); Murphy v Lindahl, 24 Ill App 2d 461, 165 NE2d 340 (1960); Morgan v Liberty Mut Ins Co, 323 So 2d 855 (La Ct App 1975); Dehn v Otter Tail Power Co, 251 NW2d 404 (ND 1977).

[351] 24 Ill App 2d 461, 165 NE2d 340 (1960).

[352] *Id* at 470, 165 NE2d at 345.

[353] Curry & Turner Constr Co v Bryan, 184 Miss 44, 185 So 256 (1939).

Many courts disapprove any mention of a specific figure or any attempt to commit the jury to return a verdict for a certain amount.[354] In *Henthorn v Long,*[355] for instance, it was held that the trial court properly refused to allow counsel to ask the following question:

> If the plaintiff proves by a preponderance of the evidence that the defendant's fault caused the death of . . . Henthorn and that the distributees of his estate . . . suffered pecuniary damages or financial loss in the amount of $20,000, would you be willing to return a verdict for said amount?[356]

The court said that the proposed question appeared designed to induce the jurors to return a specific verdict. If the question were answered in the affirmative, it could lead to an argument by counsel at the close of trial that the jurors had already promised to return a verdict for the amount specified.

Arguably, an attorney should be allowed to inform prospective jurors that a significant amount of damages is being sought in the case, and that counsel needs to know if any juror is so opposed to the recovery of such a sum that it would not be possible to return a verdict for that amount. Counsel, however, should avoid the appearance of attempting to commit the jury to return a verdict for a specified amount. The following prefatory remarks may prove helpful:

> Now, ladies and gentleman of the jury, as I have previously told you, Mr. Smith has been seriously injured as a result of the defendant's negligence. He has suffered untold physical and mental pain and anguish, and he has incurred huge medical bills. We have sued in this case for the amount of one million dollars, which is admittedly a huge sum of money. We would not ask for this amount unless we were absolutely convinced that it was justified. We believe that the evidence will prove that Mr. Smith is entitled to this recovery. Now, ladies and gentlemen, what I need to know is this: Are there any of you on this panel who, for any reason at all, have such a prejudice or feeling against damage suits or against the award of huge sums of money in damage suits, that you could not under any circumstances return a verdict in a case like this for a large amount of money? Are there any of you on this panel who, regardless of the evidence put on during the trial, would say: "Nobody is deserving of a million dollar damage award?" Could all of you sit on the jury, listen carefully to the evidence adduced, and then return a verdict in a large amount, even the amount I have mentioned, if you felt, after listening to the evidence, that the plaintiff was entitled to it?

---

[354] *See supra,* note 350, and cases cited therein.

[355] 122 SE2d 186 (W Va 1961).

[356] *Id* 196.

§7.49 —Punitive

In some actions, such as those in which the defendant is found to have acted willfully or maliciously, the plaintiff may be entitled to exemplary or punitive damages in addition to compensatory damages. Many jurors, however, while prepared to compensate a plaintiff, are not prepared to punish a defendant. Plaintiff's lawyer needs to explain that the punitive damages are not only to compensate the plaintiff for flagrant and grievous injuries, but also to deter the defendant and others from committing similar wrongs in the future.

There are several points to be made on voir dire. Plaintiff's lawyer should, in asking prospective jurors about their willingness to award punitive damages, stress that the jurors must first be convinced that defendant has acted maliciously (or whatever the standard is in the jurisdiction to warrant punitive damages). Second, it should be stressed that the law provides for punitive damages, and that the purpose is not to punish defendant for the sake of punishment, but to prevent egregious wrongs such as the one committed by the defendant. The plaintiff's lawyer should attempt to commit each member of the panel to return a substantial award for exemplary damages if, but only if, warranted by the evidence.

The defendant's lawyer also wants to screen the jurors. Some persons tend, for whatever reason, to be overly susceptible to an appeal for large punitive damages. Defense counsel must attempt to identify and challenge jurors who indicate an overeagerness to punish. Where it is clear that the defendant did commit a wilful and perhaps malicious act and the only issue is the amount of damages, counsel should concede the wrongfulness of the defendant's conduct, stress the defendant's sincere regret, and do everything possible to commit the jury to base its verdict on reason rather than passion.

A juror who declares an unalterable opposition to punitive damages is in effect declaring that he or she intends to follow a personal conception of the law rather than that set forth in the judge's instructions. As in other cases where jurors indicate an intent not to be bound by the judge's instructions, the juror can be challenged for cause.[357]

§7.50 Physical Condition and Intellectual Functioning

Physical infirmity may render an individual incapable of serving as a juror.[358] Courts are careful, however, to distinguish between those infirmities which render a juror incapable of serving and those which just make it more difficult to serve.[359] In the latter situation, courts will attempt to see if a reasonable accommodation can be made so that the juror will be able to serve.

---

[357] *See* **§7.09.**

[358] *See* State v Tauzier, 397 So 2d 494 (La 1981).

[359] Where physical infirmity makes it difficult to serve, the juror may be able to obtain an excuse on hardship grounds. *See generally* **§6.06.**

Illustrative are cases involving jurors with hearing impairments. In one case it was held that no abuse of discretion occurred when the trial judge rejected a challenge for cause to a juror who admitted to a hearing defect but said that she would be able to hear if the parties and witnesses spoke up.[360] Similarly, it was held that a juror with a hearing problem who would be able to hear adequately if seated in the front row was not subject to challenge for cause.[361] In still another case where a hearing impaired juror was held qualified, the juror indicated that he would raise his hand during the proceedings if he failed to hear what a witness said.[362]

On the other hand, there have been cases where the juror's hearing disability justified a disqualification. In one such case where it was found that the juror's disability was so acute that he might not have heard material testimony, the court held that the defendant was denied a fair trial.[363]

Sometimes a certain physical capacity is required to understand critical issues at trial, and jurors who lack that capacity are properly subject to challenge for cause. *Commonwealth v Susi*[364] provides a good example. The defendant was charged with armed robbery and assault. The key issue was identification. Jurors were going to have to be able to view and compare drawing and photographic evidence, as well as the appearance of the defendant at trial with his appearance in a composite drawing. Under the circumstances the Massachusetts Supreme Judicial Court ruled that the trial judge abused her discretion in denying the defendant's challenge for cause to a blind juror.

The fact that the juror's infirmity is self-induced will not prevent the juror's disqualification. In *People v Lieberman,*[365] it was held that the trial judge acted properly in discharging a juror who had become intoxicated during trial, even though the juror's drinking may have been attributable to her indecision in the case. Likewise it has been held not to be an abuse of discretion to discharge a juror caught sleeping during trial.[366]

If a juror is capable of understanding the testimony of witness and the issues in the case, the mere fact that the juror's intellectual functioning, education, or reading skills are deficient is not cause for disqualification.[367] A juror need only meet the statutory minimum qualifications for service.[368] On the other

---

[360] United States v Tegzes, 715 F2d 505 (11th Cir 1983).

[361] State v Parry, 684 SW2d 441 (Mo Ct App 1984).

[362] State v King, 311 NC 603, 320 SE2d 1 (1984).

[363] Commonwealth v Greiner, 309 Pa Super 291, 455 A2d 164 (1983).

[364] 394 Mass 784, 477 NE2d 995 (1985).

[365] 107 Ill App 3d 949, 438 NE2d 516 (Ill Ct App 1982).

[366] United States v Warner, 690 F2d 545 (6th Cir 1982). People v Russell, 112 AD2d 451, 492 NYS2d 420 (1985).

[367] *E.g.*, Strauss v Allstate Ins Co, 417 So 2d 60 (La Ct App 1982).

[368] *See* People v Guzman, 125 Misc 2d 457, 478 NYS2d 455 (Sup Ct 1984). *See generally* **§6.04.**

hand, a juror who cannot understand the nature of the proceedings or basic questions propounded by counsel will be excused for cause.[369]

§7.51 Nervous or Emotional Condition

A few cases have recognized a nervous or emotional condition as a proper ground of challenge for cause.[370] In *People v Kurth,*[371] for instance, it was revealed to the trial judge that a juror suffered from claustrophobia. The judge questioned the juror, who admitted that she became nervous when confined to a room for any length of time. The juror nevertheless maintained that she could perform jury duty with the court's cooperation. Counsel for defendants moved unsuccessfully for a mistrial on the ground that they did not receive a fair and impartial trial because of the condition of that juror. On appeal the conviction was reversed. The court explained:

> The trial was lengthy and the issues were complicated. . . . While we are unable to determine whether the deliberation of the juror in question was, in fact, influenced by her fear of confinement, in a case of this magnitude, where of necessity lengthy deliberation would normally be required to consider the evidence and the instructions of the court, the possibility of prejudice is high. The difficulty which the parties encountered in selecting a jury who had no preconceived notions concerning the case has already been related. To accept a juror who acknowledged a longstanding fear of closed places and to deny counsel the right to interrogate this juror, or even disclose her name, was, under the circumstances, prejudicial error. Although we are reluctant to reverse these convictions for an error which occurred even prior to the reception of the voluminous testimony, we are of the opinion that the interests of justice require that a new trial be granted.[372]

Several cases, on the other hand, have found an emotional or nervous condition of a juror insufficient grounds for a new trial.[373] In *United States v Ross,*[374] the defendant was convicted of conspiring to transfer counterfeit notes. After the trial, a juror asked the trial judge to excuse her for the three remaining days of her jury duty because her husband had been in an automobile accident.

---

[369] High v State, 247 Ga 289, 276 SE2d 5 (1981). *See also* United States v Rucker, 557 F2d 1046 (4th Cir 1977).

[370] *E.g.*, State v Haislip, 237 Kan 461, 701 P2d 909 (1985); State v Skipper, 285 SC 42, 328 SE2d 58 (1985); People v Kurth, 34 Ill 2d 387, 216 NE2d 154 (1966). *See generally* Annotation, *Claustrophobia or Other Neurosis of Juror As Subject of Inquiry on Voir Dire or of Disqualification of Juror,* 20 ALR3d 1420 (1968).

[371] 34 Ill 2d 387, 216 NE2d 154 (1966).

[372] *Id* at 390-91, 216 NE2d at 156.

[373] *E.g.*, United States v Marchant, 774 F2d 888 (8th Cir 1985); United States v Ross, 203 F Supp 100 (ED Pa 1962); People v Butler, 104 Cal App 3d 868, 162 Cal Rptr 913 (1980).

[374] 203 F Supp 100 (ED Pa 1962).

The defendant's counsel in *Ross* then moved for a new trial, arguing that the juror may have been upset by her husband's condition and unable to exercise her best judgment as a juror. The trial court examined the juror and concluded that the juror's husband had not been seriously injured and that the juror's deliberations in the case had not been affected.[375]

§7.52 Connection with Law Enforcement

Accuseds in criminal cases are understandably anxious about jurors who are involved in law enforcement or connected with persons involved in law enforcement. The views of such jurors may be jaded by criminal types about whom they have heard or with whom they have come in contact. Often law enforcement personnel are disqualified or exempted by statute.[376] When they are not, or when their friends and relatives are called for jury duty, they need to be carefully questioned on voir dire.[377] In some cases disqualification has been held appropriate.[378] More commonly, courts say that mere association with law enforcement or persons involved in law enforcement is not per se a basis for challenge,[379] particularly where the juror claims to be able to be impartial.[380] In *State v Beckett,*[381] the court drew a distinction between jurors who were employees of law enforcement or prosecutorial agencies, who were subject to a per se disqualification for cause if challenged, and jurors with a consanguinous, marital, or social relationship with such employees, who were not subject to a per se disqualification unless the employee was actively involved in the case.

In the typical case, there is not a disproportionate number of law enforcement officers and their relatives in the jury pool. In one highly unusual murder case, however, 12 members of a 39-member jury pool were either police officers or related by blood or marriage to police officers. The defendant, after exhausting all his peremptory challenges, was forced to accept six jurors connected with law enforcement. The Mississippi Supreme Court held that because of the disproportionate number of law enforcement officers and their

---

[375] *See also* Barney v State, 698 SW2d 114 (Tex Crim App 1985).

[376] *See* **§§6.04-6.05.** *See generally* Annotation, *Law Enforcement Officers As Qualified Jurors in Criminal Cases,* 72 ALR3d 895 (1976).

[377] State v Sylvester, 400 So 2d 640 (La 1981).

[378] *E.g.,* State v Sylvester, 400 So 2d 640 (La 1981); State v Kayser, 637 SW2d 836 (Mo Ct App 1982). *See also* State v Jackson, 43 NJ 148, 203 A2d 1 (1964), *cert denied,* 379 US 982 (1965); Commonwealth v Colon, 223 Pa Super 202, 299 A2d 326 (1972) (police commissioner should have been removed from jury in trial of defendant for attempted shooting of police officers, but error was harmless).

[379] *See, e.g.,* United States v Daly, 716 F2d 1499 (9th Cir 1983); State v Taylor, 669 SW2d 694 (Tenn Crim App 1983); State v Benson, 40 Wash App 729, 700 P2d 758 (1985).

[380] *See, e.g.,* United States v McCord, 695 F2d 823 (5th Cir 1983); Wilson v State, 250 Ga 630, 300 SE2d 640 (1983); State v Dees, 639 SW2d 149 (Mo Ct App 1982).

[381] 310 SE2d 883 (W Va 1983).

relatives in the jury pool, the defendant was denied his constitutional right to an impartial jury.[382] The court advised that the trial judge could have ameliorated the situation by increasing the size of the venire, granting the defendant additional peremptory challenges, or sustaining more of the defendant's challenges for cause.[383]

Former and future law enforcement personnel raise problems, too. In one case it was held that the trial court did not commit reversible error in denying a challenge for cause to a juror who was attending school preparatory to going to work as a law enforcement officer, and was at the time a reserve police officer. This decision was reached despite the fact that the juror conceded the "possibility" of prejudice.[384] Past law enforcement personnel have also been held not subject to challenges on that basis alone.[385] On the other hand, where the present, past, or future employment has so biased the juror that he or she is incapable of being impartial, the juror must be excused. Regardless of whether a challenge for cause to a juror associated in some way with law enforcement is successful, defense attorneys remain free to challenge such jurors peremptorily, and frequently do so.

§7.53 Qualification in Death Penalty Cases

Criminal cases in which a defendant faces a potential death penalty if convicted pose a unique problem in the law of challenges for cause. Prosecutors commonly seek to remove from the jury those persons who are unwilling to impose the death penalty. They fear that such jurors will opt to set a guilty defendant free rather than incur responsibility for the death of another human being. On the other hand, defense attorneys are concerned that a jury from which persons opposed to capital punishment have been culled will be unduly prone to convict. Both prosecutors and defense attorneys have sought to challenge jurors because of their views on the death penalty. The issue has come before the United States Supreme Court on several occasions.

In *Witherspoon v Illinois*[386] the Supreme Court examined an Illinois statute that allowed a challenge for cause to jurors who were opposed to or had "conscientious scruples" against capital punishment. Under the authority of the statute, the prosecutor had eliminated nearly half the venire. The Court found that while there had been no showing that the jury had been biased on the issue of guilt, it was self-evident that the jury lacked the impartiality required

---

[382] Mhoon v State, 464 So 2d 77 (Miss 1985).

[383] *Id* 81.

[384] Skipper v State, 400 So 2d 797 (Fla Dist Ct App 1981).

[385] *E.g.*, Hill v State, 250 Ga 277, 295 SE2d 518 (1982) (retired supervisor at penitentiary); State v Williams, 650 SW2d 642 (Mo Ct App 1983) (retired police officer). *But see* State v Clark, 164 Conn 224, 319 A2d 398 (1973) (not error for trial judge to disqualify former law enforcement officer). *See generally* Annotation, *Former Law Enforcement Officers As Jurors in Criminal Cases,* 72 ALR3d 958 (1976).

[386] 391 US 510 (1968).

by the Constitution on the issue of punishment.[387] Speaking for the majority, Justice Stewart said that "a jury composed of [those favoring the death penalty] cannot speak for the community."[388] Such a jury would be one "uncommonly willing to condemn a man to die."[389] The Court held that a sentence of death could not be carried out if imposed by a jury from which persons opposed to capital punishment had been excluded.[390] Although the Court's decision technically related only to the imposition of the death penalty, the implication was that a juror should not be subject to challenge for cause in a capital case solely because of a philosophical, moral, or religious objection to the death penalty.

On the other hand, the *Witherspoon* Court did identify two classes of jurors who were properly subject to challenge for cause: those who would automatically vote against the imposition of the death penalty regardless of the evidence; and those whose views on the death penalty would prevent them from making an impartial decision on the issue of guilt.[391] In order to be subject to disqualification, however, the juror would have to make his position in this regard "unmistakably clear."[392]

The Supreme Court appeared to retreat from its *Witherspoon* position in *Wainwright v Witt.*[393] The Court there said that a juror whose views on capital punishment would "prevent or substantially impair the performance of his duties as a juror in accordance with his instructions and his oath" could properly be challenged.[394] The Court expounded on its reasoning:

> [T]he quest is for jurors who will conscientiously apply the law and find the facts. That is what an "impartial" jury consists of and we do not think, simply because a defendant is being tried for a capital crime, that he is entitled to a legal presumption or standard that allows jurors to be seated who will quite likely be biased in his favor.[395]

The Court in *Witt* also rejected the "unmistakably clear" test of *Witherspoon.* Such a standard, said the Court, was unrealistic; jurors rarely could be asked sufficient questions to flesh out their bias with unmistakable clarity.[396]

The Court's reasoning in *Witt* is questionable at best. The presumption of innocence demands that jurors be biased in a defendant's favor at the outset of the trial, and the fact that they are so should not be cause for disqualification. The Court's concern, however, was presumably with jurors whose anti-capital

---

[387] *Id* 518.

[388] *Id* 520.

[389] *Id* 521.

[390] *Id* 522. The Court has since indicated that violations of *Witherspoon* are not subject to harmless error analysis. Gray v Mississippi, 481 US 648 (1987).

[391] 391 US 522, n 21.

[392] *Id.*

[393] 469 US 412 (1985).

[394] *Id* 424 (quoting from Adams v Texas, 448 US 38, 43 (1980)).

[395] *Id* 423.

[396] *Id* 424-25.

punishment, pro-defendant biases were not amenable to change in response to the evidence.

Even so, the Court's reasoning in *Witt* is at odds with the long recognized (albeit not uncontroversial) doctrine of jury nullification.[397] This doctrine permits jurors to acquit a defendant even though the strict application of controlling legal principles to the evidence would logically require a conviction. It is a doctrine that allows the jury to temper the rigors of the law with a community sense of mercy, and partially explains why a judge may direct a verdict in favor of, but never against, a defendant. Sometimes, as in the case of the acquittal of a defendant who commits a mercy killing, jury nullification allows the result that the legislature would have desired had the legislators been able to foresee the precise factual situation. Other times, as when juries refused to convict for violation of prohibition laws, the jurors were expressing the public's disapproval of the law in question. Finally, and most ironically in light of the Supreme Court's statements in *Witt,* jury nullification occurred when jurors disagreed not with the law whose violation was charged or the application of that law to the defendant on trial, but with the penalty for the violation of that law. In nineteenth century England, where innumerable crimes carried an automatic death penalty, jury acquittals often reflected not the defendant's innocence but the jury's belief that the penalty was disproportionate to the offense. The Supreme Court's decision in *Witt* deprives a defendant of those jurors most likely to be willing to exercise their nullification prerogative.

In *Witherspoon* the Supreme Court rejected the petitioner's argument that jurors who were not opposed to the death penalty were more likely to favor the prosecution; the Court found the evidence in support of this contention "too tentative and fragmentary."[398] Following *Witherspoon,* substantial empirical evidence was accumulated to demonstrate that death qualified juries were in fact significantly more likely to convict a defendant of the underlying murder charge than were juries whose members were not subject to death qualification.[399] On the basis of this evidence, it was argued that a death qualified jury deprived a defendant of the right to an impartial jury drawn from a cross-section of the community[400] and, ultimately, the right to a fair trial. In *Lockhart v McCree*[401] the Supreme Court disagreed.

---

[397] *See generally* **§§2.20-2.21.**

[398] 391 US at 517.

[399] *E.g.*, Cowan, Thompson, & Ellsworth, *The Effects of Death Qualification on Jurors' Predisposition to Convict and on The Quality of Deliberation,* 8 Law & Hum Behav 53 (1984); Goldberg, *Toward Expansion of Witherspoon; Capital Scruples, Jury Bias, and Use of Psychological Data to Raise Presumptions in the Law,* 5 Harv CR-CL L Rev 53 (1970); Jurow, *New Data on the Effect of a "Death Qualified" Jury on the Guilt Determination Process,* 84 Harv L Rev 567 (1971). These and other studies are reviewed in depth in Hovey v Superior Court, 28 Cal 3d 1, 616 P2d 1301, 168 Cal Rptr 128 (1980). *See also* Grigsby v Mabry, 569 F Supp 1273 (ED Ark 1983), *affd,* 785 F2d 226 (8th Cir 1985), *revd sub nom* Lockhart v McCree, 476 US 162 (1986).

[400] *See generally* **§6.13.**

[401] 476 US 162 (1986).

Although expressing considerable skepticism about the validity and reliability of the studies upon which the defendant's arguments were premised,[402] the Court in *McCree* proceeded on the assumption that they were correct.[403] The Court ruled, however, that a death qualified jury did not offend constitutional guarantees, even if it were somewhat more prone to convict.[404] Cross-section representation, the Court stated, applied only to the venire and not to the petit jury and, in any event, did not apply to groups defined in terms of shared attitudes when the attitude in question would prevent or substantially impair the jurors' ability to perform their function.[405] The Court also rejected the defendant's claim that he had been denied the right to an impartial jury. The Court reasoned that the removal of *Witherspoon*-excludables served the state's "entirely proper interest in obtaining a single jury that could impartially decide all of the issues in [the case]."[406]

---

[402] *Id* 168-73.

[403] *Id* 173.

[404] *Id* 173-77.

[405] *Id* 180. *See also* Darden v Wainwright, 477 US 168 (1986). The Supreme Court's opinions for all practical purposes foreclose further *federal* constitutional arguments against death qualification. They do not, however, foreclose arguments that death qualification violates guaranties of a *state* constitution. *See, e.g.,* Hovey v Superior Court, 28 Cal 3d 1, 616 P2d 1301, 168 Cal Rptr 128 (1980).

[406] 476 US at 180.

8 Peremptory Challenges

§8.01 Introduction

The peremptory challenge permits a party to excuse a juror for any reason that the party sees fit, or for no reason at all. Historically, peremptory challenges were available in both civil and criminal trials.[1] Unlike in the case of

[1] There is some question as to whether peremptory challenges were available in civil cases at common law. *See* Kobatchnick v Hanover-Building Corp, 331 Mass 397, 119 NE2d 169, 172 (1954).

a challenge for cause, an attorney ordinarily does not have to provide an explanation for a peremptory challenge.[2]

At early common law jurors were chosen by the Crown, and it in effect had an unlimited number of peremptory challenges. The prosecutor's right of peremptory challenge, however, was rescinded by statute in 1305.[3] In its stead, there developed the right to ask jurors to stand aside. No reason for the request had to be provided unless, after the defense had exercised its peremptory challenges, there was an insufficient number of jurors to compose a jury.[4] The defendant's right of peremptory challenge, on the other hand, was unquestioned. According to Blackstone, it reflected "that tenderness and humanity for which . . . English laws are justly famous."[5] At common law a defendant was entitled to 35 peremptory challenges.[6]

In the United States, an early congressional act permitted a defendant 35 peremptory challenges in trials for treason and twenty in trials for other felonies punishable by death.[7] Allowing peremptory challenges to a defendant was relatively uncontroversial; allowing them to a prosecutor was more controversial, but its permissibility was accepted by the United States Supreme Court in *Hayes v Missouri.*[8] Present federal law grants both prosecution and defense twenty peremptory challenges in cases where a capital crime is charged and three in cases where a misdemeanor is charged.[9] In a felony prosecution the defendant is entitled to ten peremptory changes and the prosecution to six.[10] The peremptory challenge is of such importance that its denial or impairment is reversible error without a showing of prejudice.[11]

State laws, too, recognize the right of peremptory challenge. Initially the general practice was to allot the same number of challenges to the defense as was permitted at common law in England.[12] Prosecutors were often also conceded

---

[2] The one exception to this general rule occurs when a defendant in a criminal prosecution establishes a prima facie case that the prosecutor has exercised peremptory challenges so as to exclude minority jurors of the same race as the defendant. *See* Batson v Kentucky, 476 US 79 (1986) *discussed at* **§§8.05-8.11.**

[3] 33 Edw 1, stat 4 (1305).

[4] *See* Hayes v Missouri, 120 US 68, 70-71 (1887). Apparently this right was liberally exercised. *See* Swain v Alabama, 380 US 202, 213 n 11 (1965).

[5] 4 W. Blackstone, Commentaries 353, *quoted in* Lewis v United States, 146 US 370, 376 (1892). It might be noted in passing that in England the peremptory challenge was abolished in the Criminal Justice Act 1988. *See generally,* Gobert, *The Peremptory Challenge—An Obituary,* [1989] Crim L Rev 528.

[6] *See* Swain v Alabama 380 US 202, 212 (1965).

[7] 1 Stat 119, ch 30 (1790), cited in Swain v Alabama, 380 US 202, 214 (1965).

[8] 120 US 68, 70-71 (1887).

[9] Fed R Crim P 24(b).

[10] *Id.*

[11] *See* Swain v Alabama, 380 US 202, 219 (1965); Gulf & Santa Fe Ry Co v Shane, 157 US 348 (1895). *But compare* Ross v Oklahoma, 487 US 81 (1988) (no reversible error where defendant required to exercise peremptory challenge to remove juror who should have been excluded for cause).

[12] *See* Swain v Alabama, 380 US 202, 215-16 (1965).

to retain the common law right to have jurors "stand aside."[13] State statutes subsequently codified the prosecutor's right of peremptory challenge. The number of challenges allotted to the prosecutor ranged from a number of one-half that allotted to the defendant up to, in many states, an equal number.[14]

The United States Supreme Court has rejected the position that there is a constitutional right of peremptory challenge.[15] More recently, the Court has ruled that the loss of a statutorily created right of peremptory challenge is not unconstitutional.[16]

There are numerous purposes served by the peremptory challenge. From the perspective of the legal system, the challenge provides a ready corrective for errors by a judge in refusing to grant a challenge for cause. The party who believes that the judge has made an incorrect ruling can remove the juror in question through a peremptory challenge.[17] This corrective function in turn permits judges greater latitude in accepting juror claims of impartiality.

From the perspective of the parties, the peremptory challenge allows counsel to remove from the jury individuals whom the attorney suspects are biased (or not favorably inclined to the client's cause) where there is not the overt manifestation of bias necessary to justify a challenge for cause. The peremptory challenge thus allows the attorney to give full vent to that intuition, judgment, and experience developed over the course of a legal practice. By permitting the removal of jurors whose impartiality is suspect, the peremptory challenge furthers society's interest in a fair and impartial jury.[18]

Beyond the issue of bias, peremptory challenges permit parties to remove jurors they, for whatever reason, dislike. As a result, parties are tried by jurors of their choice, and are consequently more likely to be accepting of the jury's verdict. In this way the peremptory challenge furthers the state's interest in the acceptance of decisions of its legal system.

Because the basis for a peremptory challenge does not have to be articulated, the challenge, as one author put it, avoids having to traffic in the "core of truth in most common stereotypes"; it allows "the covert expression of what we dare not say but know is true more often than not."[19] Human experience, common sense, and public opinion polls tell us that certain classes of persons have psychological predispositions that will interfere with their ability to be impartial in certain types of cases. These deeply ingrained, often unconscious, often class-based biases are generally not proper grounds for challenge unless the juror will admit to them. But the juror will often be unaware of the bias, or,

---

[13] *See* United States v Marchant, 25 US (12 Wheat) 297, 299-300 (1827); Commonwealth v Eisenhower, 181 Pa 470, 37 A 521 (1897).

[14] *See* Swain v Alabama, 380 US 202, 216 (1965).

[15] Stilson v United States, 250 US 583, 586 (1919).

[16] Ross v Oklahoma, 487 US 81 (1988).

[17] *Id* (upholding state requirement that peremptory challenges be used to cure incorrect refusal by judge to excuse a juror for cause).

[18] *See* Hayes v Missouri, 128 US 68, 70 (1887).

[19] Babcock, *Voir Dire: Preserving "Its Wonderful Power,"* 27 Stan L Rev 545, 553-54 (1975).

if aware, reluctant to concede it because of the social disapproval involved. Although one might decry reliance on stereotypes, it must be remembered that all too often lawyers lack sufficient information about jurors to make a truly informed selection. This is particularly so when a trial judge restricts the time allotted for voir dire, limits the scope of voir dire, or prohibits pretrial investigation of jurors.

Finally, peremptory challenges permit attorneys to choose jurors about whom they feel comfortable. Attorneys are more likely to be effective in presenting their client's case before such jurors than before jurors perceived as hostile. The result will be, as envisioned by the adversary system, that each side will be able to present its case in the strongest possible light.

For attorneys who have integrated into their jury selection strategy those social science methodologies advocated in Part II, including the construction of favorable and unfavorable juror profiles,[20] or who have investigated the members of the venire prior to trial,[21] the peremptory challenge is especially important. It allows them to reap the harvest of their pretrial labors. It is through the peremptory challenge that an attorney may remove a juror whose potential partiality is indicated by an unfavorable socio-psychological profile or by a pretrial investigation when the juror's responses to voir dire questions do not themselves indicate bias. In this connection, the peremptory challenge protects a party from the juror whose voir dire answers are untruthful or misleading.

Despite its constructive functions, the peremptory challenge has not escaped criticism. Its detractors point to its tendency to produce homogenized and unrepresentative juries.[22] Peremptory challenges are designed to "eliminate extremes of partiality on both sides"[23] but are perhaps used to eliminate persons on the extremes. With which extreme one is concerned depends, of course, on which side one represents. A law of opposites is at work: a juror perceived as extremely favorable by one side will very likely be perceived as extremely unfavorable by the other. As such, the juror will be a prime candidate for a peremptory challenge. If both attorneys pursue this strategy, the resulting jury will not be reflective of the community—absent from its midst will be those on the far left or right wings of politics, the destitute poor and the affluent rich, and persons whose life styles are unconventional or idiosyncratic.[24] Also likely to be removed are persons of strong will; attorneys generally do not want the fate of the client resting in the hands of a single individual, and a strong-willed juror may be able to convert others to his or her position. Some attorneys go farther and strike jurors who appear to be intelligent and discerning. Their objective is a jury of malleable minds which they can then mold.

---

[20] *See* **§3.08.**

[21] *See* **ch 4.**

[22] *See* J. Van Dyke, Jury Selection Procedures: Our Uncertain Commitment to Representative Panels 154 (1977).

[23] Swain v Alabama, 380 US 202, 219 (1965).

[24] *Id.*

Criticism has been particularly virulent of the prosecutorial practice of using peremptory challenges to strike minority jurors in criminal cases out of fear that they will be overly sympathetic to black defendants.[25] When this occurs, the black defendant may be denied a jury of his or her peers[26] and society may be denied its interest in a jury which is representative of a cross-section of the community.[27] Jurors who are excluded as a result of unexplained peremptory challenges may resent both the attorney responsible for the challenge and the legal system which permits it. In *Batson v Kentucky*,[28] a decision which will be examined in depth in this chapter,[29] the United States Supreme Court addressed the problem of the discriminatory use of peremptory challenges.

Batson can be viewed as part of a larger picture. Over the past decade both state and federal courts have begun to recognize that the exercise of peremptory challenges has implications for several constitutional rights: the right of equal protection, the right of cross-section representation, and the right to an impartial jury. Although not itself of constitutional stature, the peremptory challenge, because it affects other constitutional rights, needs to be analyzed in constitutional terms.

§8.02 Number of Peremptory Challenges

The number of peremptory challenges allotted to each side is usually fixed by statute.[30] In a federal *civil* case, each side is allowed three peremptory challenges.[31] In a federal prosecution for a capital offense, each side is allowed twenty peremptory challenges.[32] If the prosecution is for a misdemeanor, the number of challenges is reduced to three.[33] Symmetry ends when the prosecution is for a felony—the defense is entitled to ten peremptory challenges and the prosecution to six.[34] If alternate jurors are to be seated, the number of peremptory challenges may be increased.[35]

---

[25] While this stratagem is most often employed by prosecutors, it will occasionally be used by defense counsel. For instance, a white defendant charged with a crime against a black victim may attempt to eliminate all blacks from the jury.

[26] *See* **§§2.07-2.08.**

[27] *See* **§6.13.**

[28] 476 US 79 (1986).

[29] *See* **§§8.05-8.11.**

[30] In comparison, the number of challenges for cause is unlimited.

[31] 28 USC §1870.

[32] Fed R Crim P 24(b). *See generally* Annotation, *Number of, and Manner of Exercising, Peremptory Challenges in Federal Criminal Trials Subsequent to Promulgation of Rule 24(b) of Federal Rules of Criminal Procedure,* 11 ALR Fed 713 (1972).

[33] Fed R Crim P 24(b).

[34] *Id.*

[35] Fed R Civ P 47(b); Fed R Crim P 24(c). *See also* Annotation, *Alternate Jurors in Federal Trials Under Rule 24(c) of Federal Rules of Criminal Procedure or Rule 47(b) of Federal Rules of Civil Procedure,* 10 ALR Fed 185 (1972).

A similar pattern exists in state courts. The number of peremptory challenges allowed in civil cases is usually less than the number allowed in criminal cases.[36] The more serious the crime, the greater the number of peremptory challenges allowed to each side.[37] The fact that a defendant is charged with multiple offenses in a single trial will not, however, usually lead to an increase in the number of peremptory challenges; in such circumstances the number of peremptory challenges generally will be the number available for the most serious of the offenses charged.[38] If the number of a defendant's peremptory challenges is increased due to multiple charges, it will not necessarily follow that the prosecutor's will be also.[39]

The number of peremptory challenges available to the prosecutor will not be more, but may be less, and is most often the same as the number available to the defense.[40] The fact that the prosecution may turn out to have more peremptory challenges than the defense is not constitutionally fatal. In *Ross v Oklahoma*[41] the defendant was required by state law to use peremptory challenges to cure erroneous refusals by the trial judge to excuse jurors for cause. Defendant in fact had to do so. Although the net result was that the defendant wound up with one less peremptory challenge then the prosecutor, the United States Supreme Court found no constitutional violation.[42]

Each state may determine for itself the number of peremptory challenges to permit each side. There is no constitutional minimum.[43] The optimal number of challenges to allow is a matter upon which reasonable minds can differ. Conflicting policies need to be balanced. On the one hand, the greater the number of challenges, the greater the likelihood of removing all persons who are biased from the jury and impaneling a truly impartial jury. On the other hand, peremptory challenges systematically exercised on the basis of race, sex, occupation, education, socio-economic class, or any other single variable can

---

[36] *See* Swain v Alabama, 380 US 202, 217 (1965).

[37] In some states the number of peremptory challenges will depend on whether the offense is a felony or misdemeanor. *See, e.g.,* Commonwealth v McColl, 376 NE2d 562 (Mass 1978); People v Turner, 27 Ill App 3d 236, 326 NE2d 425 (1975). In others it will turn on the sentence provided for the offense charged. *See, e.g.,* Freeman v People, 4 Denio 9 (NY 1847). *See also* Annotation, *Validity and Construction of Statute or Court Rule Prescribing Number of Peremptory Challenges in Criminal Cases According to Nature of Offense or Extent of Punishment,* 8 ALR4th 149 (1981).

[38] Additional peremptory challenges may be authorized by statute. *See* Sanders v State, 328 So 2d 268 (Fla Dist Ct App 1976). *See generally* Annotation, *Additional Premeptory Challenges Because of Multiple Criminal Charges,* 5 ALR4th 533 (1981).

[39] *See, e.g.,* Sanders v State, 328 So 2d 268 (Fla Dist Ct App 1976).

[40] *See* Swain v Alabama, 380 US 202, 216 (1965).

[41] 487 US 81 (1988).

[42] *Id.*

[43] This follows from the fact that there is no constitutional right to any peremptory challenges. *See* Stilson v United States, 250 US 583, 586 (1919). The degree of latitude allowed the legislature is indicated by *Hayes v Missouri,* 120 US 68 (1887), where the Supreme Court upheld as a valid exercise of legislative discretion a statute permitting 15 peremptory challenges in capital cases in cities of over 100,000 inhabitants and 8 peremptory challenges in other parts of the state.

lead to a jury that is not reflective of a cross-section of the community; the greater the number of peremptory challenges, the greater the potential deviation.

A criminal prosecution in which there is more than one defendant raises the question of whether the number of peremptory challenges should be cumulated to equal the number that would have been available if the defendants had been tried separately. Some jurisdictions will cumulate peremptory challenges;[44] others require that defendants share the number of peremptories that would be available to a single defendant;[45] and still others have adopted some in-between policy.[46] Requiring the sharing of peremptory challenges should be strenuously resisted by defense counsel. Multiple defendants will often seek to vindicate different interests in exercising their peremptory challenges. One, for example, may be concerned with racial prejudice; a codefendant may be more concerned with the effects of pretrial publicity. No two defendants are completely alike, and each must be sensitive to the particular prejudices arising from individual circumstances. This fact notwithstanding, in many joint trials common interests predominate and the defendants can be expected to exercise their peremptory challenges for much the same reasons and against the same jurors. In this situation cumulating defense peremptories puts the prosecution, whose number of peremptories may not be increased, at an unfair disadvantage. Perhaps the most sensible solution is to leave to the trial judge's discretion whether to grant additional peremptory challenges to multiple defendants in a joint prosecution.[47] If so, the judge will have to determine how many additional challenges to grant and whether to grant additional challenges to the state as well.[48]

---

[44] *See* United States v Marchant, 25 US (12 Wheat) 297, 300 (1827); Kunk v Howell, 40 Tenn App 183, 289 SW2d 874 (1956); People v Caruso, 170 Mich 137, 135 NW 168 (1912).

[45] *See* Stilson v United States, 250 US 583 (1919); United States v Franklin, 471 F2d 1299 (5th Cir 1973); United States v Williams, 463 F2d 393 (10th Cir 1972); State v Brown, 45 RI 9, 119 A 324 (1923). *See generally* Annotation, *Jury: Number of Peremptory Challenges Allowed in Criminal Case Where There are Two or More Defendants Tried Together* 21 ALR3d 725 (1968).

[46] *See, e.g.*, United States v Bascaro, 742 F2d 1335, 1349 (11th Cir 1984), *cert denied,* 417 US 1017 (1985) (permitting codefendants the 10 peremptory challenges allowed by federal law plus an additional five); People v King, 240 Cal App 2d 389, 49 Cal Rptr 562, *cert denied,* 385 US 923 (1966). *See generally* ABA Standards for Criminal Justice, Standard 15-64 (2d ed 1980); Annotation, *Additional Peremptory Challenges Because of Multiple Criminal Charges* 5ALR4th 533.

[47] *See* Fed R Crim P 24(b). *See also* Annotation, *Jury: Number of Peremptory Challenges Allowed in Criminal Case Where There are Two or more defendants tried together.* 21 ALR3d 725 (1968). A similar approach is warranted in civil cases. *See* 28 USC §1870. *See generally* Annotation, *Jury: Number of Peremptory Challenges Allowable in Civil Cases Where There are More Than Two Parties Involved* 32ALR3d 747; Annotation, *Distribution and Exercise of Peremptory Challenges in Federal Civil Cases under 28 USC §1870,* 50 ALR Fed 350 (1980).

[48] *See, e.g.,* Maddox v State, 145 Ga App 363, 243 SE2d 740 (1978). *Compare* R E Gaddie, Inc v Evans, 394 SW2d 118 (Ky 1965) (grant to defendants of additional peremptory challenges justified by their antagonistic interests, but error to also grant additional peremptory challenges to plaintiffs whose interests were not antagonistic).

The discretion to permit multiple defendants additional peremptory challenges is in fact part of a larger judicial discretion to increase the number of peremptory challenges in any case, regardless of the number of defendants. Thus, in a prosecution where the seating of an impartial jury may be difficult, counsel can and should move for additional peremptory challenges. Cases involving extensive pretrial publicity are prime candidates for such a motion.[49] The judge may increase proportionately the number of peremptory challenges allowed to each side or may increase only the number available to one side. In a case in which there has been prejudicial pretrial publicity, the judge may choose to allow additional peremptory challenges only to the side damaged by the publicity.

A party who plans to challenge the number of peremptory challenges allowed must generally exhaust the number available; otherwise, the party may encounter difficulty showing prejudice.[50] This rule is akin to that requiring that a defendant to exhaust peremptory challenges in order to be able to claim to have been prejudiced by an erroneous rejection of a challenge for cause.[51]

§8.03 Procedures

The procedure by which attorneys exercise their peremptory challenges is of strategic significance. The matter, unless controlled by statute, lies within the discretion of the trial judge.[52] The United States Supreme Court has held that a criminal defendant has no right to have the prosecution exercise its peremptory challenges first in order to save the defendant from having to challenge a juror unacceptable to both sides.[53] The diligent attorney will review the procedures whereby challenges are exercised in a given court, and, if that practice is too restrictive, should move the court to adopt a system that gives greater flexibility and room for judgment.

The system that least achieves these goals is one in which each side is required to decide whether to challenge a particular juror immediately after the juror has been passed for cause.[54] The problem with this approach is that it does not permit a comparative assessment of jurors.[55] As a general proposition, attorneys make relative rather than absolute judgments about jurors. An attorney may decide to retain a not particularly sympathetic juror if the attorney

---

[49] *See, e.g.*, United States v Blanton, 719 F2d 815 (6th Cir 1983), *cert denied*, 465 US 1099 (1984).

[50] *See, e.g.*, Meridian City Lines v Baker, 206 Miss 58, 39 So 2d 541 (1949).

[51] *See, e.g.*, People v Durrant, 116 Cal 179, 48 P 75 (1897). *But see* State v Reynolds, 619 SW2d 741, 749 (Mo 1981). *See generally* **§7.05.**

[52] *See* Pointer v United States, 151 US 396 (1894); United States v Morris, 623 F2d 145 (10th Cir 1980).

[53] Pointer v United States, 151 US 396 (1894).

[54] *See* St Clair v United States, 154 US 134, 147-48 (1894); Jeffries v State, 255 Ark 501, 501 SW2d 600 (1973), *cert denied*, 417 US 920 (1974); Foraker v State, 394 A2d 208 (Del 1978).

[55] *See* Lewis v United States, 146 US 370, 378 (1892).

believes that the remaining members of the panel are even less sympathetic. Conversely, an attorney may strike an unobjectionable juror if the attorney believes that the other members of the panel are likely to be more favorable. This type of comparative assessment is not possible where peremptory challenges must be made immediately after a juror has been passed for cause. Of course, the attorney who has conducted a pretrial investigation of the venire[56] and who has compared members of the venire against preconstructed socio-psychological demographic profiles of favorable and unfavorable jurors[57] is better placed to make judgments under a system that requires noncomparative exercise of peremptory challenges.

A somewhat better, and more common, practice is to conduct voir dire in groups, usually of twelve. The prosecution will question a group, make challenges for cause, and exercise its peremptory challenges. Excused jurors will be replaced with others. At the end of this process, the prosecution tenders a panel with which it is satisfied to the defendant. The defendant then proceeds similarly. The process continues until a jury acceptable to both sides is seated or until both sides have exhausted their peremptory challenges.

The most advantageous system from an attorney's perspective is the "struck" system. Under this system jurors are first questioned and challenged for cause. This process continues until there remains in the jury box a panel whose size equals the number of persons who will sit on the jury[58] augmented by a number equal to the combined number of peremptory challenges available to each side. The parties then alternately exercise peremptory challenges until each is satisfied with the panel or until all challenges are exhausted.[59] Extra jurors are either excused or seated as alternates. While the struck system may be more time-consuming than other methods and may entail some unnecessary voir dire, it permits attorneys to make a meaningful comparison among the prospective panel members and to strike those jurors whom the attorneys believe to be the most objectionable. If a state provides such a large number of peremptory challenges that a struck system is deemed too inefficient, a modified struck system can be devised. As the matter lies within a judge's discretion, an attorney should not feel constrained to propose innovative approaches provided they are well-reasoned.

Peremptory challenges must usually be exercised before a juror is sworn.[60] However, this rule may be relaxed for good cause, as where a juror admits to

---

[56] *See generally* **ch 4.**

[57] *See* **§3.08.**

[58] Usually this number will be twelve but it is constitutionally permissible both in civil and criminal cases to have juries of fewer than twelve. *See* **§§2.13, 2.14.**

[59] If the defense is permitted more peremptory challenges than the prosecution, this ratio can be taken into account. Assume, for example, that the defense is allotted twice as many challenges as the prosecution. At the stage at which the challenges are exercised in a "struck" system, the defendant can be called upon to exercise two of its challenges for every one of the prosecutor's. See the description of the Alabama "struck" system in Swain v Alabama, 380 US 202, 210 (1965).

[60] *E.g.*, State v Grillo, 16 NJ, 103, 106 A2d 294, 298 (1954).

a mistaken response to a voir dire question at a point in time after the juror is sworn but before evidence is introduced.[61] Whether to permit a party to amend or change a peremptory challenge lies in the discretion of the trial court.[62]

§8.04 Discriminatory Peremptory Challenges: The Pre-*Batson* State of the Law

Historically, the peremptory challenge could be exercised on any basis that a challenging party saw fit. No reason for the challenge had to be provided. The first major United States Supreme Court case in which this unfettered discretion was called into question was *Swain v Alabama.*[63]

The defendant in *Swain,* a black youth, was indicted for the rape of a seventeen-year-old white girl in Talledaga County, Alabama. At trial the prosecution used its peremptory challenges to strike all prospective black jurors. The result was that the defendant was tried and convicted by an all-white jury. Defense counsel moved to strike the jury on the ground that it had been selected in a racially discriminatory manner in violation of the equal protection clause, but the trial court denied the motion.

The Supreme Court's opinion began by noting the history, tradition, and function of the peremptory challenge in the Anglo-American legal system. The court said that to permit an examination of the prosecutor's reasons for exercising peremptory challenges in a given case or to subject the challenge to the demands of the equal protection clause would undercut the historic purposes of the challenge[64] and entail a "radical change in the nature and operation of the challenge."[65] The Court approved all peremptory challenges made in a particular case by the prosecutor for the purpose of prevailing in that case.

Rather than probe the prosecutor's motives in exercising peremptory challenges, the *Swain* majority presumed that the prosecutor's goal was the seating of a fair and impartial jury.[66] This presumption was not rebutted by the mere fact that there were no blacks on the jury which convicted the defendant or the allegation that all blacks were removed because of their race.[67] In any given case, observed the Court, any race, not just blacks, could find itself inordinately subject to challenge.[68]

---

[61] *E.g.,* State v Jackson, 43 NJ 148, 203 A2d 1, *cert denied,* 379 US 982 (1964). *See also In re* Mendes, 23 Cal 3d 847, 592 P2d 318, 153 Cal Rptr 831 (1979); State v McLamb, 313 NC 572, 330 SE2d 476 (1985) (defendant's motion, after jury impaneled, to exercise peremptory challenge against juror recently discovered to be a receptionist at dental office where state's chief witness was a patient held to have been improperly refused).

[62] State v Williams, 606 SW2d 777 (Mo 1980).

[63] 380 US 202 (1965).

[64] *Id* 221-22.

[65] *Id.*

[66] *Id* 222.

[67] *Id.*

[68] *Id* 221.

How, then, could the presumption be rebutted? The Supreme Court stated that for a prosecutor consistently to exercise peremptory challenges to prevent blacks from serving on any jury, "whatever the circumstances, whatever the crime, and whoever the defendant or the victim,"[69] would constitute a perversion of the peremptory challenge and would rebut the presumption.[70] The difficulty of rebuttal, however, is reflected by the facts of *Swain:* the Supreme Court found no constitutional violation despite the undisputed fact that no black had served on a jury in Tallegada County in fifteen years.[71] The Court reasoned that, standing alone, this fact did not establish the prosecutor's responsibility for the absence of black jurors. More to the point, it did not prove that peremptory challenges had been exercised in a racially discriminatory manner.

The *Swain* decision was criticized by courts[72] and commentators[73] alike. Many pointed out the virtually insurmountable burden in rebutting the presumption of good faith.[74] The burden can be seen as even heavier in light of the fact that the defendant raising an equal protection claim is unlikely to have been a participant in any, and certainly not all, of the previous trials in which there may have been a discriminatory exercise of peremptory challenges. The defendant might be hard pressed to discover what had happened in those trials, especially in jurisdictions that did not keep records of voir dire. Even where records were kept, they might not reveal the race of excluded or selected jurors. *Swain* was also of no use in the not atypical situation where a prosecutor engaged in the discriminatory use of peremptory challenges only in exceptional cases. Nor would it help the first defendant subject to discrimination.

---

69 *Id* 223.

70 *Id* 224.

71 *Id* 205.

72 *See, e.g.*, Booker v Jabe, 775 F2d 762, 767 (6th Cir), *vacated & remanded,* 478 US 1001 (1985), *opinion reinstated,* 801 F2d 871 (6th Cir 1986), *cert denied,* 479 US 1046 (1987); McCray v Abrams, 750 F2d 1113, 1120-122 (2d Cir 1984); *vacated on other grounds,* 478 US 1001 (1986); People v Wheeler, 22 Cal 3d 258, 583 P2d 748, 148 Cal Rptr 890 (1978).

73 *See, e.g.*, Brown, McGuire, & Winters, *The Peremptory Challenge as a Manipulative Device in Criminal Trials: Traditional Use or Abuse,* 14 NE L Rev 192 (1978); Comment, *A Case Study of the Peremptory Challenge: A Subtle Strike at Equal Protection and Due Process,* 18 St Louis U LJ 662 (1974); Note, *Limiting the Peremptory Challenge: Representation of Groups on Petit Juries,* 86 Yale LJ 1715 (1977); Comment, *Swain v Alabama: A Constitutional Blueprint for the Perpetuation of the All-White Jury,* 52 Va L Rev 1157 (1966).

74 The court in United States v Childress, 715 F2d 1313 (8th Cir 1983) indicated that its research had disclosed only two cases in which a defendant had been able to establish a violation under the *Swain* test. *Id* 1316. *See also* McCray v Abrams, 750 F2d 1113, 1120-121 (2d Cir 1984), *vacated on other grounds,* 478 US 1001 (1986). For a compilation of cases, *see* Annotation, *Use of Peremptory Challenge to Exclude from Jury Persons Belonging to a Class or Race,* 79 ALR3d 14 (1977).

The Supreme Court's opinion in *Swain* indicated that both blacks and whites could be subject to arbitrary challenge.[75] Although true in theory, the reality is quite different. As a practical matter, an attorney would be hard pressed to eliminate all whites from a jury because there would be an inadequate number of peremptory challenges for the task compared to the number of white jurors. On the other hand, it is quite feasible to eliminate a relatively small minority.

In light of its practical and theoretical limitations, it is perhaps not surprising that the *Swain* decision failed to curb the use of peremptory challenges to exclude blacks from serving on juries. Justice Marshall, concurring in *Batson v Kentucky,*[76] cited the example of Dallas County, Texas, where, in 1983-84, prosecutors had exercised peremptory challenges to strike 405 out of 467 eligible black jurors.[77] Thus, despite (or perhaps because of) *Swain,* black defendants continued to be subject to the conscious and subconscious biases of all-white juries. Both because of its theoretical weaknesses and its practical shortcomings, *Swain* was ripe for reconsideration.

§8.05 *Batson v Kentucky*

The decision of the United States Supreme Court in *Batson v Kentucky*[78] is of potentially revolutionary importance in regard to the law of peremptory challenges, even if it is still too soon to say what its ultimate reach will be. What can be said is that *Batson* represents the Supreme Court's most significant statement to date on the subject. This section will introduce the Court's decision. Subsequent sections will examine in depth issues raised by it, as well as its long-term implications.

The petitioner in *Batson,* a black male, had been charged with second-degree burglary and the receipt of stolen goods. After the judge had conducted voir dire, the prosecutor used his peremptory challenges to strike all black jurors on the panel. Defense counsel moved to discharge the jury on the ground that the prosecution's exercise of its peremptory challenges violated both the defendant's right of equal protection and his right to a jury drawn from a cross-section of the community.

The trial judge denied the defense motion. The judge stated that the parties were entitled to exercise their peremptory challenges in whatever way they saw fit. The judge further ruled that the requirement of cross-section representation applied only to the venire and not to the petit jury. The defendant was subsequently convicted of both charges by an all-white jury.

In a brief, one-paragraph opinion, the Kentucky Supreme Court affirmed. It declined to follow decisions from other jurisdictions[79] which, under similar

---

[75] 380 US at 221.

[76] 476 US 79, 104 (1986) (Marshall J, concurring).

[77] *See generally* Johnson, *Black Innocence and the White Jury,* 83 Mich L Rev 1611 (1985).

[78] 476 US 79 (1986).

[79] *E.g.,* People v Wheeler, 22 Cal 3d 258, 583 P2d 748, 148 Cal Rptr 890 (1978); Commonwealth v Soares, 377 Mass 461, 387 NE2d 499, *cert denied,* 444 US 881 (1979), *discussed* at **§8.12.**

circumstances, had found violations of state constitutional provisions guaranteeing a jury drawn from a representative cross-section of the community. Defense counsel in *Batson* similarly had argued that the prosecutor's challenges violated the Kentucky constitution. The Kentucky Supreme Court paid short shrift to the state constitutional arguments. Instead, it looked to *Swain v Alabama*[80] where the United States Supreme Court had held that, although a prosecutor could not arbitrarily exclude all blacks from serving on juries, a petitioner had to establish a pattern of discrimination over time. The fact that all blacks were removed from a jury in a given case as a result of a prosecutor's exercise of peremptory challenges was not sufficient to satisfy the *Swain* standard.

In the United States Supreme Court, the *Batson* decision was reversed. The Court began by reaffirming two settled principles which might be thought to be in philosophical conflict. The first is that when a state tries a defendant before a jury from which all members of the defendant's race have been purposefully excluded from the venire, it violates the defendant's right to equal protection of the laws.[81] The second is that a defendant has no right to be tried by a "petit jury composed in whole or part of persons of his race."[82]

The Court's task in *Batson* was to reconcile these principles with the historic prerogative of the peremptory challenge, which allowed a lawyer to challenge a juror for any reason that counsel saw fit, or for no reason at all. The Court held that the "Equal Protection Clause forbids the prosecutor to challenge potential jurors solely on account of their race or on the assumption that black jurors as a group will be unable impartially to consider the State's case against a black defendant."[83]

It was inevitable that the Supreme Court would have to reexamine *Swain v Alabama.* It conceded that Swain's requirement that a defendant show a systematic pattern of prosecutorial challenges to blacks over a series of cases imposed a "crippling burden of proof."[84] The burden could in fact be impossible if jurors' races were not recorded or voir dire records were not kept.[85] Because this burden of proof in effect immunized racially discriminatory practices from constitutional scrutiny, the Court rejected it as inconsistent with equal

---

[80] 380 US 202 (1965), *discussed* at **§8.04.**

[81] Batson v Kentucky, 476 US 79, 85 (1986).

[82] *Id.* The conflict lies in the fact that part of the purpose of not excluding members of defendant's race from the venire is defeated if no member of defendant's race serves on the actual jury. Defendant is in no better position than if all members of his race had been excluded from the venire. The practical problem lies in including all races and nationalities in a jury which consists of at most twelve members.

[83] *Id.* 476 US at 89. It is noteworthy that the Court decided the case on equal protection grounds. The defendant had argued that his sixth and fourteenth amendment rights to a jury representative of a cross-section of the community had been violated. The majority, however, chose not to express an opinion on the merits of this contention (*Id* 90, n 14). Chief Justice Burger criticized the majority for ruling on an issue not raised by the defendant. *Id* 112-16 (Burger, CJ, dissenting). In a concurring opinion, Justice Stevens responded to this criticism. *Id* 108-10 (Stevens, J, concurring).

[84] *Id* 92.

[85] *Id* n 17.

protection standards developed since *Swain*. The Court had in mind a number of decisions which had allowed a defendant to challenge a venire on the basis of racial discrimination in an individual case.[86]

The Court stated that in order to establish a prima facie case of racial discrimination, a defendant had first to show that he belonged to a cognizable racial group whose members had been removed from the panel by the prosecutor's exercise of peremptory challenges.[87] In making this showing, the defendant was allowed to rely on the fact that peremptory challenges permit "those to discriminate who are of a mind to discriminate."[88] The trial court ultimately had to be persuaded that, given this inference in conjunction with the facts and all "relevant circumstances," the prosecutor had exercised peremptory challenges to exclude jurors on the basis of race.[89] The Court cited as examples of "relevant circumstances" a pattern of strikes against black jurors and the prosecutor's questions and statements during voir dire and in making challenges.[90]

After a prima facie showing of discrimination, the burden shifts to the prosecutor. The prosecutor must provide a neutral explanation for the challenges of the black jurors.[91] The explanation does not have to rise to the level justifying a challenge for cause.[92] On the other hand, an assumption by the prosecutor that black jurors will be partial to black defendants because of their shared race will not suffice.[93] Nor will a violation be excused by a declaration of good faith or a lack of intent to discriminate. What is required is a case-specific neutral explanation for the challenges.[94]

In a concurring opinion, Justice Marshall expressed the view that the evils masked in the racially discriminatory exercise of peremptory challenges could be eliminated only by eliminating the peremptory challenge itself.[95] He pointed out that under the majority's approach, the defense would often find it difficult to establish a prima facie case. This would be particularly true in those jurisdictions where there were few blacks on the venire.[96] If so, in many predominantly white districts *Batson* would have little effect. Justice Marshall also noted the problems involved in assessing a prosecutor's motives for purposes of rebuttal. He asserted that any competent prosecutor could fabricate racially neutral

---

[86] *See, e.g.*, Castaneda v Partida, 430 US 482, 494 (1977); Alexander v Louisiana, 405 US 625, 629-30 (1972); Whitus v Georgia, 385 US 545, 552 (1967).

[87] 476 US at 96.

[88] *Id* (quoting Avery v Georgia, 345 US 559, 562 (1953)).

[89] *Id* 96-97.

[90] *Id* 97. The elements of a prima facie case are explored in depth at **§8.06.**

[91] 476 US at 97.

[92] *Id.*

[93] *Id.*

[94] *Id* 98. The issue of rebuttal is examined in depth at **§8.07.**

[95] *Id* 105-08.

[96] *Id* 105.

reasons for striking a black juror.[97] Indeed, the reasons might not be so much a fabrication as a rationalization; prosecutors, because of their own conscious or subconscious racism, might want to believe and actually believe their neutral explanations.[98] The *Batson* holding places the trial judge in the unenviable position of having to assess whether the prosecutor is a liar or a closet racist. To avoid this dilemma, or because of the judge's own conscious or subconscious racism, the judge also may prefer to accept the proffered neutral explanation.[99] For all these reasons, Justice Marshall concluded that the soundest course would be to ban peremptory challenges altogether, both for the prosecution and the defense.

Chief Justice Burger and Justice Rehnquist dissented. The Chief Justice first traced the long and venerable history of the peremptory challenge and the functions it serves.[100] He then drew a critical distinction between cases, such as *Strauder v West Virginia,*[101] involving racial exclusion in the compilation of the venire, and cases involving the racially discriminatory exercise of peremptory challenges: Exclusion from the venire constitutes a *declaration by the state* that a class of persons is unfit to serve as jurors in *any* case; a peremptory challenge represents the *opinion* of a *single, admittedly partisan, attorney* that a class of persons might be unsuited to serve on a *particular* case.[102] There is a far greater and altogether different stigma attached to the former proposition than the latter. An exclusionary statute implies a group's inferiority. No such inference arises from the exercise of a peremptory challenge. Even if it did, it would express the opinion only of the attorney who made the challenge. The Chief Justice also pointed out the inherent inconsistency of applying a rational basis test of equal protection to a prerogative whose raison d'être permitted its exercise on irrational grounds.[103] The majority's concession that a lesser justification would be required to sustain a peremptory challenge than a challenge for cause struck the Chief Justice as somewhat fanciful, the equivalent of saying that peremptory challenges would be permitted if they were "just a little bit arbitrary—but not too much."[104] The Chief Justice noted the practical difficulties in applying equal protection analysis in the jury context, as virtually every juror will have some combination of characteristics (race, sex, age, religion, etc.) not shared by other members of the panel.[105] Finally, he took to task the majority for not more carefully considering the state interest in impartial juries

---

[97] *Id* 105-06.

[98] *Id* 106.

[99] *Id.*

[100] *Id* 118-21. *See generally* **§8.01.**

[101] 100 US 303 (1880), *see* **§6.12.**

[102] 476 US at 122-23. The Chief Justice quoted from United States v Leslie, 783 F2d 541, 554 (5th Cir 1986).

[103] 476 US at 123.

[104] *Id* 128.

[105] *Id* 124.

furthered by the peremptory challenge,[106] and whether this interest was of sufficient magnitude to overcome the equal protection objection.[107]

Justice Rehnquist (as he was then) joined the Chief Justice's dissent but also wrote separately. Basically, he saw little reason not to continue to adhere to *Swain.* In his view there was

> nothing "unequal" about the State's using its peremptory challenges to strike blacks from the jury in cases involving black defendants, so long as such challenges are also used to exclude whites in cases involving white defendants, Hispanics in cases involving Hispanic defendants, Asians in cases involving Asian defendants, and so on.[108]

Thus he was not opposed to the use of racial stereotypes, only to their selective use. Given the inherent limitations of voir dire, exercising peremptory challenges on the theory that members of a distinct group are likely to favor defendants of that same group seemed sensible to Justice Rehnquist.

§8.06 —Establishing a Prima Facie Case

The Supreme Court set forth a three-step process by which a defendant could establish a prima facie case of a *Batson* violation:

> [T]he defendant first must show that he is a member of a cognizable racial group, and that the prosecutor has exercised peremptory challenges to remove from the venire members of the defendant's race. Second, the defendant is entitled to rely on the fact, as to which there can be no dispute, that peremptory challenges constitute a jury selection practice that permits "those to discriminate who are of a mind to discriminate". Finally, the defendant must show that these facts and any other relevant circumstances raise an inference that the prosecutor used that practice to exclude the veniremen from the petit jury on account of their race.[109]

It would seem that, as a preliminary matter, a defendant has to make a timely objection to a prosecutor's discriminatory use of peremptory challenges.[110] Defense counsel in *Batson* had moved to strike the jury before it was sworn, and this appeared to satisfy the timeliness requirement.[111] As a tactical matter, the defense should object as soon as it suspects prosecutorial misconduct, perhaps even as soon as the first black juror is challenged. Besides avoiding any

---

[106] The tension in this context between the constitutional right to equal protection and the constitutional right to an impartial jury is explored in **§8.13.**

[107] For more on the relationship between peremptory challenges and impartial juries, see **§8.13.**

[108] 476 US at 137-38.

[109] *Id* 96 (citations omitted).

[110] *Id* 99.

[111] *Id* 100.

subsequent claim of waiver, an early objection may have two salutary effects: first, it may alert the trial judge to possible discriminatory tactics by the prosecution; and second, it may cause the prosecutor to be more circumspect in exercising peremptory challenges against blacks.

The first part of the required prima facie showing has two branches. The first amounts to a requirement of standing. The defendant must show that he or she is a member of a cognizable racial group. In one sense, this requirement is meaningless. Every person belongs to some racial group. The Court, however, doubtless had in mind those minority groups which have historically been discriminated against. In the context of exclusion of minority groups from the venire, the Court has defined a cognizable group as one which has been subject to widespread community prejudice.[112] It is not clear, however, that *Batson* extends to groups other than blacks.[113]

It is arguable that the Court did not intend to impose a formal standing requirement. In cases where it has been alleged that blacks have been discriminately excluded from the venire, the Court has permitted white defendants to raise the constitutional issue.[114] In *Batson* itself, the Court acknowledged that the rights of those denied the opportunity to serve on the jury are implicated by the discriminatory exercise of peremptory challenges.[115] The failure to accord standing to defendants who are not members of the excluded class would allow prosecutors to continue to discriminate in cases involving such defendants. Although the Court seems to have assumed that prosecutors excuse black jurors because they are likely to be sympathetic to black defendants because of their common race, in fact prosecutors may excuse black jurors because personal experiences with police have made many blacks suspicious of state authority.[116] Prosecutors may be more concerned with antiauthoritarian bias than a pro-black defendant bias. The *Batson* decision does nothing to eliminate peremptory challenges based on this type of stereotypic thinking in cases where the defendant is not black. One would have thought that the Court would have been concerned about all discrimination against blacks in juror selection.[117]

The second branch of the Court's first prong requires a showing that the prosecutor exercised peremptory challenges so as to exclude members of the defendant's race. Thus, a defendant has to establish for the record that he or she belongs to the same race as the excluded jurors. A two-step process is called for. First, the defendant will have to make a showing for the record of his or her race. Second, the defendant will have to make an inquiry for the record

---

[112] Hernandez v Texas, 347 US 475 (1954) (equal protection challenges to composition of venire not limited to blacks but any identifiable group subject to community prejudice). *See generally* **§6.16.**

[113] This issue will be examined at **§8.08.**

[114] *See, e.g.*, Peters v Kiff, 407 US 493 (1972).

[115] 476 US at 87.

[116] *See* Bueno-Hernandez v State, 724 P2d 1132, 1135 (Wyo 1986).

[117] *See* State v Superior Court, 157 Ariz 541, 760 P2d 541 (1988) (white defendant may challenge use of peremptories against blacks).

into the race of each juror. This inquiry will have to extend to the race of jurors who are not challenged as well as those who are in order to show a discriminatory pattern of challenges. Unfortunately, many jurors may resent being questioned about their race. To avoid any backlash, counsel should petition the trial judge to ascertain this information in a pre-voir dire questionnaire. Some appellate courts may permit an inadequate record relating to race of jurors to be supplemented by affidavits.[118] It is important to observe that the true racial identity of a juror is not as important as the apparent racial identity, for a prosecutor bent on eliminating blacks from a jury will discriminate against those who appear to be black. The prosecutor's actions should not be excused by the fortuitous discovery that some of those excused were not black.[119]

It should again be noted that a literal approach to the Supreme Court's test can lead to results at odds with the Court's stated goals. Under the Court's test there is no constitutional violation unless both the defendant and the excused jurors belong to the *same* cognizable racial group. Thus, if a prosecutor challenges all black jurors in a case involving an Hispanic defendant on the theory that blacks are likely to empathize with the plight of Hispanics, there is no *Batson* violation. Again, it is debatable whether the Supreme Court intended such a result.

It is unclear from the Court's holding in *Batson* how many or how few members of a defendant's race must be struck before a prima facie case is established. To illustrate, assume that on a venire of thirty there are two blacks. The prosecutor by state law is entitled to eight peremptory challenges. Among the eight jurors struck are the two blacks. Is this sufficient to establish a prima facie case?[120] The fact that white jurors are also challenged is arguably irrelevant; otherwise the prosecution would be able to insulate itself from the finding of a *Batson* violation by the simple expedient of striking a few token white jurors, who might in any event be objectionable.

Consider the converse case where there are ten blacks on the venire and the prosecutor has only eight peremptory challenges. The prosecutor uses all eight challenges to strike blacks. Two blacks still remain on the jury. Given that the

---

[118] *See, e.g.*, People v Motton, 39 Cal 3d 596, 704 P2d 176, 180, 217 Cal Rptr 416 (1985). *Compare* Bueno-Hernandez v State, 724 P2d 1132, 1133 (Wyo 1986) (where voir dire not recorded and race of jurors not established, defendant failed to establish a prima facie case by showing that three challenged jurors had Spanish surnames).

[119] *See* People v Motton, 39 Cal 3d 596, 704 P2d 176, 180, 217 Cal Rptr 416 (1985).

[120] *Compare* Commonwealth v Robinson, 382 Mass 189, 415 NE2d 805 (1981) and People v Rousseau, 129 Cal App 3d 526, 179 Cal Rptr 892 (1982) (mere fact that prosecutor struck all blacks insufficient to establish a prima facie case) *with* United States v Chalan, 812 F2d 1302 (10th Cir 1987) (where three of four Indian jurors removed for cause and prosecutor peremptorily challenged last Indian juror, prima facie case established); People v Clay, 153 Cal App 3d 433, 200 Cal Rptr 269 (1984) (prima facie case established where prosecutor exercised four of ten peremptory challenges against blacks and no blacks ultimately sat on jury); and Commonwealth v Brown, 11 Mass App Ct 288, 416 NE2d 218, 223 (1981) (prima facie case established where prosecutors struck all black jurors).

jury is integrated, is it possible to claim a *Batson* violation?[121] On the one hand, it seems likely that the prosecutor's actions have been promoted by a racially discriminatory animus. On the other, it is not clear that the defendant has been harmed as there are blacks on the jury. A defendant is not entitled to any specific number or percentage of members of his or her race on the jury. The *Batson* Court, however, gave no indication that the doctrine of harmless error should apply in this context. The irony may be that although the Court has repeatedly stated that a defendant has no constitutional right to members of his race on the jury that tries him,[122] there may be a constitutional violation even when members of a defendant's race are on the jury that tries him.[123]

Similarly, should it matter that, despite the fact that most but not all of the prosecutor's peremptory challenges have been used to exclude black jurors, the prosecutor has not challenged some black jurors? In this situation a court must be sensitive to the possibility that a prosecutor is allowing a token member of the defendant's race to serve in order to avoid a finding of a *Batson* violation.[124] As the Massachusetts Supreme Judicial Court observed in *Commonwealth v Soares:*[125]

> One need not eliminate 100% of minority jurors to achieve an impermissible purpose. If the minority's representation is reduced to impotence as, for example, by the disproportionate challenge of group members, and the failure to challenge only a minority member who can reasonably be relied on as safe, the majority identified biases are likely to meet little resistance. . . .[126]

Token representation should be particularly scrutinized in those jurisdictions that permit less than unanimous verdicts in criminal cases.[127]

Finally, consider the in-between case in which the venire is half-black but the prosecutor uses 75 per cent of the allotted peremptory challenges to strike blacks. Where the percentage of black jurors struck is higher than that to be

---

[121] *See* United States v Williams, 822 F2d 512 (5th Cir 1987) (no violation found); United States v Woods, 812 F2d 1483 (4th Cir 1987) (same). State v Vincent, 755 SW2d 400 (Mo Ct App 1988) (same).

[122] 476 US at 85.

[123] *See, e.g.,* Commonwealth v Soares, 377 Mass 461, 387 NE2d 499, *cert denied,* 444 US 881 (1979).

[124] *See, e.g.,* People v Motton, 39 Cal 3d 596, 704 P2d 176, 183, 217 Cal Rptr 416 (1985).

[125] 377 Mass 461, 387 NE2d 499, *cert denied,* 444 US 881 (1979).

[126] 387 NE2d at 516, n 32. *See also* United States v Clemons, 843 F2d 741 (3d Cir), *cert denied,* 109 S Ct 97 (1988); United States v Battle, 836 F2d 1084 (8th Cir 1987); Fleming v Kemp, 794 F2d 1478 (11th Cir 1986). *But see* United States v David, 662 F Supp 246 (ND Ga 1987), *affd,* 844 F2d 767 (11th Cir 1988) (prosecution's challenges of blacks upheld where jury ultimately selected contained one black member).

[127] *See* **§§2.17-2.19.**

mathematically expected, is a prima facie case of discrimination established?[128] If so, how great must the disparity be? Defense counsel should be prepared to prove that, as a matter of probabilities, the differential is statistically significant. An expert witness may be required to testify. The greater the disparity, the stronger the inference of discrimination.

The second prong of the *Batson* test establishes no evidentiary burden whatsoever. The Supreme Court simply takes judicial notice of the fact that peremptory challenges permit those who are of a mind to discriminate to discriminate. The Court's gratuitous observation that this is a reality regarding which there can be no dispute[129] implies that the Supreme Court has created an irrebuttable presumption which, in a given case, a trial court may not decline to accept. How much this presumption actually reduces a petitioner's burden in establishing a prima facie case is problematic.

The third requirement of a prima facie case is that the defendant show that the facts and relevant circumstances give rise to an inference that the prosecutor has used peremptory challenges to exclude members of the venire because of their race. The negative implication of this third prong is that a mere showing that the prosecutor has excluded members of the defendant's race from the panel is insufficient to discharge a defendant's burden. The defendant must further show that the exclusion was *on account of* the jurors' race. This latter requirement seems both to undercut the Court's presumption that peremptory challenges provide the opportunity to discriminate for those inclined to discriminate, and to blur the line between the defendant's obligation to establish a prima facie case and the prosecutor's burden, after a prima facie case is established, to provide a neutral explanation for the challenge of the black jurors.[130]

How can a defendant discharge this third requirement? The Court, somewhat summarily, suggested looking at the prosecutor's "pattern" of strikes.[131] Presumably the Court had in mind the number of strikes of black jurors compared to the number of strikes over all. The Court also suggested examining the prosecutor's statements on voir dire and in exercising peremptory challenges.[132]

The strongest evidence of discrimination would be a prosecutor's admission that race was a factor in determining whom to challenge.[133] Barring such an unlikely occurrence, a strong inference of discrimination would arise if the prosecutor excused black jurors after asking them no questions on voir dire.[134]

---

[128] *See* Commonwealth v Soares, 377 Mass 461, 387 NE2d 499, *cert denied,* 444 US 881 (1979).

[129] 476 US at 96.

[130] *See* **§8.07.**

[131] 476 US at 96-97.

[132] *Id* 97.

[133] *See, e.g.,* State v Washington, 375 So 2d 1162 (La 1979). A defense attorney is of course not permitted to cross-examine a prosecutor to extract such an admission.

[134] *See* Booker v Jabe, 775 F2d 762, 764 (6th Cir 1985); People v Wheeler, 22 Cal 3d 258, 583 P2d 748, 764, 184 Cal Rptr 890 (1978).

Similarly, a few desultory questions yielding no basis for a challenge for cause followed by a peremptory challenge would raise an inference of an intent to discriminate.[135]

A potentially profitable exercise for defense counsel is to examine the responses to voir dire given by challenged black jurors, both separately and in comparison with those given by unchallenged non-black jurors. Often prosecutors fall into a pattern of questioning. If the answers of the non-black and black jurors are virtually indistinguishable, yet only the black jurors are challenged, an intent to discriminate may be inferred.[136] In this same vein, an attorney should be sensitive to the questions asked of black but not white jurors; a prosecutor bent on eliminating blacks may refrain from asking whites potentially disqualifying questions.

It is possible for defense counsel to lay the groundwork for an argument along these lines. The attorney should attempt to have the court call on the prosecutor for a neutral explanation of peremptory challenges of black jurors as early as possible. After the neutral explanation is on record, the defense attorney can question non-black jurors to see if they, too, have the characteristic that the prosecutor found objectionable. If they do, and if the prosecutor does not challenge these non-black jurors, the inference of discrimination is strengthened.

Likewise, the voir dire responses of all challenged black jurors should be compared. If the only common denominator among the struck jurors is their race, their background and answers to voir dire displaying a wide heterogeneity, an inference of discriminatory intent would again arise.[137]

Also of relevance would be a showing that the prosecutor had engaged in the discriminatory exercise of peremptory challenges in the past. Although this evidentiary requirement of *Swain v Alabama*[138] was discarded in *Batson,* a defense attorney should not be precluded from introducing such evidence in furtherance of the establishment of a prima facie case.

Defense counsel should be aware that a peremptory challenge of a black juror by the defense could potentially compromise its claim of a *Batson* violation. In *State v Moore*[139] the defendant had peremptorily challenged a black juror whom the prosecutor had accepted. The court of appeals held that this combination of circumstances defeated the defendant's prima facie claim.[140] The result is questionable, since it forces the defense to accept an objectionable juror, in effect a compelled albeit limited waiver of its right of peremptory

---

135 People v Wheeler, 22 Cal 3d 258, 583 P2d 748, 764, 148 Cal Rptr 890 (1978).

136 *See, e.g.,* United States v Wilson, 853 F2d 606 (8th Cir 1988); Slappy v State, 503 So 2d 350 (Fla Dist Ct App 1987), *cert denied,* 108 S Ct 2273 (1988) (black teachers challenged but not white teachers).

137 People v Wheeler, 22 Cal 3d 258, 583 P2d 748, 764, 184 Cal Rptr 890 (1978).

138 380 US 202 (1965), *discussed* at **§8.04.**

139 490 So 2d 556 (La Ct App 1986).

140 *Id.*

challenge, in order to preserve its *Batson* rights. The proper focus under *Batson* should be on the prosecutor's challenges and motives and not those of the defense.[141]

Although the Supreme Court in *Batson* indicated the qualitative elements of a prima facie case, it did not shed light on the quantitative burden involved. Must a defendant merely present some evidence of discrimination, or sufficient evidence to make the claim of discrimination more likely than not? In this respect the requirement that the trial court take judicial notice of the fact that peremptory challenges allow those who are of a mind to discriminate to do so should lighten the petitioner's burden of proof. The Supreme Court expressed confidence that "trial judges, experienced in supervising voir dire, will be able to decide if the circumstances concerning the prosecutor's use of peremptory challenges [create] a prima facie case of discrimination against black jurors."[142] This statement suggests that the matter will lie within the sound discretion of the trial judge,[143] and that the trial judge's ruling will not be overturned absent a showing of abuse of that discretion.[144] In light of this standard, defense counsel should alert the court as soon as prosecutorial abuse of the peremptory challenge is suspected. The judge is then more likely to pay careful attention to the prosecutor's voir dire questions and challenges for evidence of improper motive. An early motion may also have the salutary effect of deterring the prosecutor from continuing on a course of discriminatory peremptory challenges.

§8.07 —Rebutting a Prima Facie Claim

After a defendant has made the prima facie showing of discrimination required by *Batson,* the burden shifts to the prosecutor to come forward with a "neutral explanation" for the peremptory challenges.[145] This requirement is perhaps the most remarkable aspect of a remarkable holding, for it represents the first time that a court has ever called for the basis of a peremptory challenge to be articulated. The hallmark of the peremptory challenge has always been that it did not have to be explained.

Unfortunately, the *Batson* Court provided only limited guidance regarding the nature of the explanation required. The Court stated that the explanation "need not rise to the level justifying exercise of a challenge for cause,"[146] but went on to say that the prosecutor "may not rebut the defendant's prima facie case of discrimination by stating merely that he challenged jurors of the defen-

---

[141] Of course, if it is alleged that the defense has itself violated *Batson,* examination of its challenges would be appropriate. *See* **§8.09.**

[142] 476 US at 97.

[143] *See also id* 99 n 21.

[144] *See* Commonwealth v DiMatteo, 12 Mass App 547, 551-53, 427 NE2d 754, 758 (1981) (any support in trial record for judge's decision will preclude the appellate court from substituting its judgment for that of the trial court).

[145] Batson v Kentucky, 476 US 79, 97 (1986).

[146] *Id.*

dant's race on the assumption—or his intuitive judgment—that they would be partial to the defendant because of their shared race."[147] Nor could a prosecutor rebut a prima facie case simply by denying a discriminatory motive or affirming good faith.[148] The task of implementing these broad and somewhat conflicting guidelines was left to the trial judge.

In a concurring opinion in which he urged the abolition of the peremptory challenge as the only viable means of eliminating its discriminatory exercise, Justice Marshall pointed out the difficulties involved in attempting to determine whether a prosecutor has acted upon an impermissible discriminatory motive:

> Any prosecutor can easily assert facially neutral reasons for striking a juror, and trial courts are ill-equipped to second-guess those reasons. How is the court to treat a prosecutor's statement that he struck a juror because the juror had a son about the same age as the defendant, see *People v Hall,* 35 Cal 3d 161, 197 Cal Rptr 71, 672 P2d 854 (1983) or seemed "uncommunicative," *King v County of Nassau,* 581 F. Supp. 493, 498 (EDNY 1984), or "never cracked a smile" and, therefore "did not possess the sensitivities necessary to realistically look at the issues and decide the facts in this case," *Hall,* supra, at 165, 197 Cal. Rptr. at 73, 672 P.2d, at 856? If such easily generated explanations are sufficient to discharge the prosecutor's obligation to justify his strikes on nonracial grounds, then the protection erected by the Court today may be illusory.[149]

Justice Marshall recognized that often the problem is not prosecutorial dissembling. Like others, prosecutors may be the product of a racist society.[150] A prosecutor may want to believe and may actually believe a nonracist explanation for the challenges. The explanation, however, may be but a rationalization for a subconscious racism which neither the prosecutor nor the court will be able to discern. Furthermore, "a judge's own conscious or subconscious racism" may lead to the inappropriate acceptance of a purported neutral explanation.[151] Justice Marshall concluded that "[e]ven if all parties approach the Court's mandate with the best of conscious intentions, that mandate requires them to confront and overcome their own racism on all levels—a challenge I doubt all of them can meet."[152]

There are several traditional uses of the peremptory challenge whose continuing viability seems threatened by the Court's rebuttal standards. For example, attorneys often will excuse jurors whom they have closely questioned on voir dire and then unsuccessfully challenged for cause. The fear is that such jurors

---

147 *Id.*

148 *Id* 98.

149 *Id* 106.

150 *Id.*

151 *Id.*

152 *Id.*

will have become alienated by the process.[153] But what if a prosecutor strikes black jurors on this rationale? If this "neutral explanation" is not deemed acceptable, the prosecutor's legitimate pursuit of grounds for challenges for cause may be unfairly chilled. If it is deemed acceptable, the prosecutor may be able to evade the requirements of *Batson* by hostile questioning of black jurors. In these circumstances, a court might look to whether the prosecutor restricted the hostile questioning to black jurors and whether, if non-black jurors were also subject to hostile questioning, they, too, were challenged peremptorily. This approach, while providing some objective support of discriminatory intent, is still not altogether fair to the prosecutor: It is logical for a prosecutor to probe more searchingly a black juror than a non-black juror for evidence of bias toward a black defendant.

Another traditional basis for an attorney's exercise of a peremptory challenge which may be at risk as a result of *Batson* is the attorney's personal sense of discomfort in trying a case before a particular juror. Arguably such discomfort will affect the attorney's performance to the detriment of the client. To allow such an explanation for a prosecutor's exercise of peremptory challenges of black jurors, however, would render *Batson* a nullity. It would indirectly approve the racism that the Supreme Court sought to eliminate by its holding.

It is not completely clear what sort of "neutral explanation" for the peremptory challenge of blacks will satisfy the prosecutor's burden of rebuttal. Suppose that a prosecutor states that a black juror was peremptorily challenged because of a suspicion that the juror would be partial to a black defendant not because of their common race but because of similar values and life styles. Will this satisfy the prosecutor's burden of rebuttal? If so, *Batson* may prove as easy to evade as was *Swain*[154] before it.

Post-Batson decisions have not necessarily calmed these fears. In several cases, perceived hostility to the prosecution was deemed sufficient to justify facially racial peremptory challenges.[155] Similar are those cases where the peremptory challenges of jurors who appeared "defense oriented" were sustained.[156]

The Supreme Court in *Batson* provided some examples of purported justifications which would not suffice; it failed to provide examples of justifications which would suffice. The tenor of the Court's discussion suggests some guidelines. The prosecutor's explanation will have to be (a) case-specific and (b) race-neutral. Thus a prosecutor cannot rebut a prima facie case by introducing empirical evidence to support the validity of racial stereotypes.[157] A related "scientific" explanation that will probably be rejected is one premised on a

---

[153] *See* Lewis v United States, 146 US 370, 376 (1892).

[154] Swain v Alabama, 380 US 202 (1965), *discussed at* **§8.04.**

[155] *E.g.*, United States v Forbes, 816 F2d 1006 (5th Cir 1987); United States v Matthews, 803 F2d 325 (7th Cir 1986), *revd on other grounds,* 485 US 58 (1988); United States v Biaggi, 673 F Supp 96 (EDNY 1986), *affd,* 853 F2d 89 (2d Cir 1988).

[156] *E.g.*, People v Chambie, 189 Cal App 3d 149, 234 Cal Rptr 308 (1987).

[157] *See* 476 US at 125, n 5 (Burger, CJ, dissenting) (citing Saltzburg & Powers, *Peremptory Challenges and the Clash between Impartiality and Group Representation,* 41 Md L Rev 337, 365 and n 124 (1982)).

juror's body language and paralinquistic cues. While these indicia are often valuable aids in determining a juror's true feelings toward parties, witnesses, and attorneys,[158] they may be inappropriate considerations in a *Batson* context.[159] The danger is that when these factors lead a prosecutor to exclude all blacks, they may simply be subconscious (or conscious) proxies for racism.

Batson seems to imply that a prosecutor's explanation for allegedly discriminatory peremptory challenges will be judged by an objective rather than a subjective standard. Furthermore, a mere conclusory statement that the prosecutor suspects that a juror will not be impartial will not suffice. Supporting reasons for the conclusion will be required. As the Supreme Court indicated that all relevant circumstances should be considered in evaluating a prima facie case, so, too, should all relevant circumstances be considered in determining whether the stated reasons for a peremptory challenge accord with objective facts. Reasons that are illogical or not supported by objective facts should not be effective.[160]

If the purported reasons should logically have led to the challenge of non-black jurors similarly situated, but who were not challenged, the explanation should also not be accepted.[161] Thus, for instance, if a prosecutor attempted to justify the peremptory challenge of a young black female juror on the basis of her youth, the court should look to whether young white jurors were challenged. If the proffered justification related to the juror's sex, the court should look to whether non-black females were challenged.

To effect a successful rebuttal, a prosecutor should be prepared to show that similar questions were asked of blacks and non-blacks on voir dire (or, if not, the reason for the different questioning), different responses were received, and the responses of the blacks, unlike those of the non-blacks, indicated that they were not likely to be able to be impartial in the given case. It would also help the prosecutor to show that not all blacks were eliminated, although this was possible given the number of peremptory challenges available,[162] and that non-blacks who were situated similarly to the excluded blacks were also

---

[158] *See* **§§12.09-12.12.**

[159] *See* People v Trevino, 39 Cal 3d 667, 692, 704 P2d 719, 733, 217 Cal Rptr 652, 666 (1985). *But see* United States v Forbes, 816 F2d 1006 (5th Cir 1987) (posture and demeanor indicated hostility to prosecution).

[160] *See, e.g.*, United States v Brown, 817 F2d 674 (10th Cir 1987) (state may not presume black jurors will be unduly influenced by black defense attorney); State v Butler, 731 SW2d 265 (Mo Ct App 1987) (challenge to nurse).

[161] *See, e.g.*, Garrett v Morris, 815 F2d 509 (8th Cir), *cert denied,* 108 S Ct 233 (1987); Slappy v State, 503 So 2d 350 (Fla Dist Ct App 1987), *cert denied,* 108 S Ct 2273 (1988).

[162] *See* Evans v Cabana, 821 F2d 1065 (5th Cir), *cert denied,* 483 US 1035 (1987); United States v Montgomery, 819 F2d 847 (8th Cir 1987); United States v Hawkins, 781 F2d 1483 (11th Cir 1986); United States v Jackson, 696 F2d 578, 593 (8th Cir 1982), *cert denied,* 460 US 1073 (1983); United States v David, 662 F Supp 244 (ND Ga 1987), *affd,* 844 F2d 767 (11th Cir 1988).

challenged.[163] In sum, the prosecutor should be prepared to show a consistent pattern of challenges and the logic behind that pattern.

The majority in *Batson* does not make clear whether the prosecutor, once a prima facie case is established, must rebut the challenge of every black juror or whether it is sufficient to rebut some lesser number. A case can be made that the prosecutor who has come forth with a neutral explanation for the overwhelming majority of peremptory challenges has rebutted the inference of purposeful discrimination. To further disallow remaining challenges of blacks based on an explanation, such as intuition, which would not justify a pattern of such challenges, would be to interpret *Batson* with an unnecessary degree of strictness. On the other hand, if the United States Supreme Court's unarticulated goal in *Batson* was peer representation on a black defendant's jury wherever possible, a more compelling argument can be made that the prosecutor must rebut every challenge of a black. A particularly strong case can be made for this proposition if the result would otherwise be an all-white jury.

In traditional equal protection analysis, unrebutted proof of discrimination does not end the inquiry. A state is permitted to establish that the discrimination serves a state interest of sufficient magnitude to outweigh the harm caused by the discrimination. In cases involving fundamental rights or suspect classifications, the justification must rise to the level of a compelling state interest.[164] In cases of gender discrimination, the government interest must be an important one.[165] In other cases, a legitimate state interest will suffice.[166] In *Batson,* however, the Court in discussing the prosecutor's burden of rebuttal did not indicate that a discriminatory exercise of peremptory challenges could be justified by any state interest, no matter how strong. The negative implication may be that it cannot. If so, a prosecutor's failure to provide a neutral explanation for the allegedly discriminatory exercise of peremptory challenges both confirms the discrimination and forecloses further inquiry into competing state interests.

One issue not addressed in *Batson* related to the timing of objections and rebuttals. The majority seemed to indicate that an objection would have to be timely[167] and that defense counsel's motion at trial to discharge the jury before it was sworn satisfied this requirement.[168] For tactical reasons a defense attorney may choose to raise a *Batson* claim as soon as the first black juror is challenged.[169] To require a prosecutor to rebut a claimed violation at this point in time, however, would be unfair. It would compel the prosecutor to provide for the record a neutral explanation for a challenge before a pattern

---

[163] *See, e.g.,* United States v McCoy, 848 F2d 743 (6th Cir 1988) (challenge to young black female and young white male, both of whom were unemployed).

[164] *See* Roe v Wade, 410 US 113, 155-56 (1973).

[165] *See* Orr v Orr, 440 US 268, 279 (1979).

[166] *See, e.g.,* Massachusetts Bd of Retirement v Murgia, 427 US 307 (1976).

[167] 476 US at 99-100.

[168] *Id* 100.

[169] See **§8.06,** notes 110, 111 and accompanying text.

of purposeful discrimination was established. The effect would be to force disclosure of the prosecutor's peremptory challenge strategy.

Because so much turns on the credibility of the prosecutor's explanation and because the trial court is in the best position to judge credibility, great deference will ordinarily be given to the trial court in this matter.[170] For its part, the trial should not scrutinize the prosecutor's explanations overcritically, lest it in effect take on the role of defense counsel.[171] Yet Justice Marshall's admonitions, discussed previously in this section, should not be lost sight of.[172]

§8.08 —Applicability to Groups Other than Blacks

It is difficult to determine from a reading of *Batson* whether the Supreme Court intended its decision to apply to groups other than blacks and, if so, to which groups. The specific holding of *Batson* is that a prosecutor cannot use peremptory challenges to exclude blacks from a jury that is to try a black defendant solely on account of their race or the assumption that black jurors cannot impartially try a black defendant.[173] In discussing the prima facie burden of a petitioner in such a case, however, the Court spoke in broader terms. A defendant, according to the Court, had to show that "he is a member of a cognizable racial group . . . and that the prosecutor has exercised peremptory challenges to remove from the venire members of the defendant's race."[174] This language raises the question of what constitutes a cognizable racial group and which racial groups will qualify as cognizable.

Cognizability should be determined in terms of function. In referring to the related concept of a *distinctive group,* the Supreme Court in *Lockhart v McCree*[175] stated:

> We have never attempted to precisely define the term "distinctive group" and we do not undertake to do so today. But we think it obvious that the concept of "distinctiveness" must be linked to the purposes of the fair cross-section requirement. In *Taylor* (Taylor v Louisiana, 419 US 522 (1975)), we identified those purposes as (1) "guard[ing] against the exercise of arbitrary power" and ensuring that the "commonsense judgment of the community" will act as "a hedge against the overzealous or mistaken prosecutor," (2) preserving "public confidence in the fairness of the criminal justice system," and (3) implementing our belief that "sharing in

---

170 Batson v Kentucky, 476 US 79, 98 n 21 (1986). *See also* United States v Garrison, 849 F2d 103 (4th Cir 1988); United States v Davis, 809 F2d 1194 (6th Cir 1987).

171 *See* United States v Thompson, 827 F2d 1254, 1260 (9th Cir 1987).

172 *See* Batson v Kentucky, 476 US 79, 105 (1986) (Marshall, J, concurring).

173 Batson v Kentucky, 476 US 79 (1986).

174 *Id* 96.

175 476 US 162 (1986).

the administration of justice is a phase of civic responsibility." *Id*, 419 U.S., at 530-31.[176]

To qualify as cognizable, a group must have characteristics that set it apart from other groups. In the jury context, furthermore, the group should share a perspective, attitude, and/or experience that would not otherwise be represented on the jury. The group must, of course, be competent to serve, even though historically it may have been prevented from serving by discriminatory laws. (Indeed, the cognizable groups with which the Court has mostly been concerned have historically been the victims of discrimination in society and the legal system.) Continued disqualification of such a group should be such as to give rise to an "appearance of unfairness" and deprive members of the group of their right to serve on juries.[177]

Under these criteria it is obvious that *Batson* applies to blacks. It is equally obvious, however, that racial groups other than blacks and, indeed, groups defined in terms of characteristics other than race will also be able to meet these criteria. The Supreme Court has interpreted the equal protection clause to forbid discrimination based on, among other characteristics, sex,[178] age,[179] and alienage.[180] In his dissent in *Batson,* Chief Justice Burger cited additional characteristics which have been used to define classes protected by equal protection.[181]

Whether *Batson* will be applied to any, or all, of these groups is unclear from the Court's decision. On the one hand, none of the groups fall within the Court's category of cognizable *racial* groups. On the other, all come within the protective ambit of the equal protection clause. More significantly, none of the characteristics, any more than race, bears on a person's competence to be a juror.

The Supreme Court may be concerned that a pervasive application of equal protection standards to a group as small as a jury will prove unmanageable. The Court had previously suggested that in order to be deemed cognizable, a group might have to meet a minimum albeit unspecified size.[182] If *Batson* were to be extended, for example, to groups defined in political, educational, or occupational terms, or some combination of these, there would be innumerable groups on a venire which would consist of one member. Every peremptory challenge might be subject to attack as an attempt to exclude the group with the excluded juror's characteristics. If there were no other juror with identical char-

---

[176] *Id* 174-75.

[177] *Id* 175.

[178] *See, e.g.*, Mississippi Univ for Women v Hogan, 458 US 718 (1982); Craig v Boren, 429 US 19 (1976); Frontiero v Richardson, 411 US 677 (1973).

[179] *See, e.g.*, Massachusetts Bd of Retirement v Murgia, 427 US 307 (1976).

[180] *See, e.g.*, Plyer v Doe, 457 US 202 (1982); Graham v Richardson, 403 US 365 (1971).

[181] 476 US at 124 (Burger, CJ, dissenting).

[182] *See* Duren v Missouri, 439 US 357, 364 (1979). Whether a group which meets the size requirement in the population at large but not in the district of trial will be deemed cognizable is unclear.

acteristics, the charge of discrimination would be difficult to rebut. It is one thing to ferret out discrimination in the population at large and quite another in a group as small as that typically subjected to voir dire in order to select a jury.

There are other options available to the Court, however, if it wanted to extend *Batson* beyond blacks or cognizable racial groups. One would be to apply the decision to all so-called suspect classifications, those based on race, religion, or national origin.[183] Lower federal courts have applied *Batson* to, among others, American Indians[184] and Italian-Americans.[185] Alternatively, the Court might extend *Batson* to groups whose members are identifiable by immutable characteristics of birth.[186] Unlike such characteristics as occupation or education, which may in a particular case bias all members of the relevant group, immutable characteristics such as race, national origin, and gender have no inherent relation to one's competence as a juror.[187] Still another possibility would be to limit *Batson* to discrete and insular minorities who have been historically underrepresented in the political process.[188] Ironically, while most attorneys will strike a juror on the basis of their perception of the juror's values and beliefs, the Supreme Court has rejected an analytical approach to cognizable groups which would define cognizability in terms of shared attitudes and beliefs, at least where the shared attitude is opposition to the death penalty.[189] Perhaps the critical distinction is that attitudes and beliefs, unlike other potential distinguishing characteristics of cognizable groups, are subject to change.

State courts which have held that the discriminatory exercise of peremptory challenges violates *state* constitutional provisions requiring cross-section representation on juries[190] have extended the rationale of their decisions to groups other than blacks.[191] Of course, where the rationale is that the jury resulting from a prosecutor's exercise of peremptory challenges to exclude all persons of a given class runs afoul of a constitutional requirement that the jury be

---

[183] *E.g.*, McLaughlin v Florida, 379 US 184 (1964) (race); Graham v Richardson, 403 US 365 (1971) (alienage); Sherbert v Verner, 374 US 398 (1963) (religion).

[184] United States v Chalan, 812 F2d 1302 (10th Cir 1987).

[185] United States v Biaggi, 673 F Supp 96 (EDNY 1986), *affd,* 853 F2d 89 (2d Cir 1988). *But see* United States v Bucci, 839 F2d 825 (1st Cir), *cert denied,* 109 S Ct 117 (1988).

[186] *See* Lockhart v McCree, 476 US 162, 175 (1986).

[187] *Id.* Courts, however, have generally refused to extend *Batson* to peremptory challenges based on gender. *See, e.g.*, United States v Hamilton, 850 F2d 1038 (4th Cir 1988).

[188] *See* Plyer v Doe, 457 US 202 (1982); United States v Carolene Prods Co, 304 US 144, 152-53 n 4 (1938).

[189] Lockhart v McCree, 476 US 162 (1986).

[190] *E.g.*, People v Wheeler, 22 Cal 3d 258, 583 P2d 748, 148 Cal Rptr 830 (1978); Commonwealth v Soares, 377 Mass 461, 387 NE2d 499, *cert denied,* 444 US 881 (1979). *See generally* **§8.12.**

[191] *See, e.g.*, People v Trevino, 39 Cal 3d 667, 704 P2d 719, 217 Cal Rptr 656 (1985) (Hispanics); Commonwealth v Reid, 384 Mass 247, 424 NE2d 495, 498 (1981) (men). A California appellate court, however, rejected the extension of *Wheeler* to peremptory challenges to women. People v Macioce, 197 Cal App 3d 362, 242 Cal Rptr 771 (1987).

representative of a cross-section of the community, it follows logically that the decision should be extended to any cognizable group in that community. Where the basis for the decision is a violation of equal protection, as it is in *Batson,* logic does not dictate a similar extension, although policy considerations may.

§8.09 —Applicability to Defense Counsel

The majority in *Batson* limited itself to the propriety of peremptory challenges against blacks by *prosecutors.* The majority specifically declined to express a view as to whether the Constitution imposed any limits on the exercise of peremptory challenges by the defense.[192] Neither Justice Marshall, in a concurring opinion, nor Chief Justice Burger, in a dissent, felt a similar compunction.

Justice Marshall advocated the abolition of peremptory challenges as the only viable means of accomplishing the majority's objective of eliminating the racially discriminatory use of peremptory challenges. At the same time, Justice Marshall recognized that a critical balance between prosecution and defense needed to be maintained:

> Our criminal justice system "requires not only freedom from any bias against the accused, but also from any prejudice against his prosecution. Between him and the state the scales are to be evenly held." Hayes v. Missouri, 120 US 68, 70, 7 S. Ct. 350, 353, 30 L Ed 578 (1897). We can maintain that balance, not by permitting both prosecutor and defendant to engage in racial discrimination in jury selection, but by banning the use of peremptory challenges by prosecutors and by allowing the states to eliminate the defendant's peremptory as well.[193]

The negative implication in the last sentence of the quotation appears to be that Justice Marshall might find no *constitutional* violation if a state chose to preserve peremptory challenges by the defense. His position seems rather to be based on policy.

Chief Justice Burger appeared to go farther. He apparently thought that the constitutional restrictions imposed by the majority had to be extended to the defense:

> [T]he clear and inescapable import of this novel holding will inevitably be to limit the use of this valuable tool to both prosecutors and defense attorneys alike. Once the Court has held that *prosecutors* are limited in their use of peremptory challenges, could we rationally hold that defendants are not?[194]

The answer to the Chief Justice's rhetorical question is that the constitutional basis for restricting the prosecutor's use of peremptory challenges is

---

[192] Batson v Kentucky, 476 US 79, 89 n 12 (1986).

[193] *Id* 107-08 (Marshall, J, concurring).

[194] *Id* 125-26 (emphasis in original) (Burger, CJ, dissenting).

much stronger than that for restricting the corresponding use of peremptory challenges by the defense. The *Batson* holding is grounded in a violation of equal protection. The equal protection clause applies only to state officials and state entities; as a prerequisite to an equal protection analysis, a court must find "state action." Peremptory challenges made by a prosecutor, appointed by the state and acting in its behalf in a criminal prosecution brought in the state's name, indisputably qualify as state action. The holding of *Batson* is implicitly premised on acceptance of this proposition, and no Justice questioned it. On the other hand, it is far less obvious that the exercise of peremptory challenges by a private defense attorney representing a client involuntarily haled into court constitutes state action.[195]

There are at least four possible bases for extending *Batson* to defense counsel. First, a court might take cognizance of the fact that peremptory challenges are created by statute.[196] As the Supreme Court recognized in *Batson,* there is no *constitutional* right of peremptory challenge.[197] The statute authorizing peremptory challenges could constitute the requisite state action for constitutional analysis.[198] The unconstitutionality of the statute would lie in its potential for discrimination. This analysis would differ from that in *Batson.* The Court there was concerned only with the discriminatory use of peremptory challenges; it did not address the underlying constitutionality of the statute which authorized peremptory challenges.

A second and related basis for extending *Batson* to defense counsel would find the requisite state action in the acceptance by the trial court, a state-created entity, of the peremptory challenge. In *Shelly v Kraemer,*[199] a decision which is still good law despite heavy criticism of its reasoning[200] and a failure of the Supreme Court to accept the logical implications of its rationale in other contexts,[201] the Supreme Court found state action in the judicial enforcement of

---

[195] See Goldwasser, *Limiting a Criminal Defendant's Use of Peremptory Challenges: On Symmetry and the Jury in a Criminal Trial,* 102 Harv L Rev 808 (1989). *But compare* Note, *Discrimination by the Defense: Peremptory Challenges After Batson v Kentucky,* 88 Colum L Rev 355 (1988).

[196] Where the right of peremptory challenge has been created by the judiciary, the power to limit or abolish it would lie within a court's supervisory power. *See* United States v Jackson, 696 F2d 578, 592-93 (8th Cir 1982), *cert denied,* 460 US 1073 (1983).

[197] 476 US at 91.

[198] *But see* Flagg Bros v Brooks, 436 US 149 (1978) (proposed sale of debtor's goods by warehouseman not state action despite fact warehouseman acting pursuant to state statute).

[199] 334 US 1 (1948).

[200] *See, e.g.,* Wechsler, *Toward Neutral Principles of Constitutional Law,* 73 Harv L Rev 1, 29-31 (1959). The basic criticism is that state action becomes a meaningless concept if the bringing of a case to court for resolution and the court's subsequent decision, including dismissal for lack of state action, satisfies the state action requirement. *See also* Pollak, *Racial Discrimination and Judicial Integrity: A Reply to Professor Wechsler,* 108 U Pa L Rev 1 (1959).

[201] Any case which a court dismissed for lack of state action would have state action at the appellate stage by virtue of the court's dismissal. Yet the Supreme Court has upheld dismissals for lack of state action. *See, e.g.,* Patrick v Burget, 486 US 94 (1988).

a racially restrictive covenant. A like argument could be applied to the judicial acceptance of a racially inspired series of peremptory challenges.[202]

A third line of analysis which would permit the holding in *Batson* to be extended to the defense would require a shift in focus from equal protection to the constitutional right to a fair and impartial jury.[203] This sixth amendment guarantee has been incorporated into the fourteenth amendment.[204] The state, as well as the defense, is entitled to an impartial jury.[205] A defense attorney who challenges black jurors perceived to identify with the prosecution (as perhaps where a white defendant is on trial for a crime committed against a black victim) undermines the constitutional right to a fair and impartial jury every bit as much as a prosecutor who challenges black jurors perceived to identify with a black defendant.[206]

Finally, it should be borne in mind that there is no constitutional right of peremptory challenge.[207] Thus, if a state should elect to abolish peremptory challenges altogether, neither prosecutors nor defense attorneys would have a constitutional basis of complaint. A state might choose to abolish peremptory challenges in order to protect the interests of the excluded jurors. The *Batson* majority recognized, as had the Supreme Court on other occasions,[208] that the intentional exclusion of minorities from jury service both stigmatizes and violates the rights of the excluded jurors. It is the exclusion and not the source of the exclusion which arguably causes the stigma. Thus, whether it stems from a peremptory challenge by the prosecution or the defense is largely irrelevant. Furthermore, in both instances the peremptory challenge is in effect sanctioned by the court by its acceptance of it. To vindicate the rights of the excluded jurors, who are unlikely to be in a position to be able to bring suit to vindicate their own rights,[209] a state could decide to eliminate the source of the problem—the peremptory challenge.

---

[202] *See also* Lugar v Edmondson Oil Co, 457 US 922 (1982) (court aid in enforcement of action by private creditor satisfied requirement of state action).

[203] *See generally* **§§2.09-2.12**

[204] Duncan v Louisiana, 391 US 145 (1968).

[205] *See* Singer v United States, 380 US 24, 36 (1965); Chicago Council of Lawyers v Bauer, 371 F Supp 689, 691 (CD Ill 1974), *revd,* 522 F2d 242 (7th Cir 1975), *cert denied,* 427 US 912 (1976) ("the right to a fair and impartial adjudication extends not only to criminal defendants but also to the government, and through it, to society").

[206] *See* Booker v Jabe, 775 F2d 762, 772 (6th Cir), *vacated & remanded,* 478 US 1001 (1985), *opinion reinstated,* 801 F2d 871 (6th Cir 1986), *cert denied,* 479 US 1046 (1987).

[207] *See* Stilson v United States, 250 US 583, 586 (1919).

[208] *See* Carter v Jury Commn, 396 US 320 (1970); Turner v Fouche, 396 US 346 (1970).

[209] It is doubtful that any individual juror would be likely to be aware that the challenge to him or her was part of a larger discriminatory pattern. Even if the juror was so aware, it is doubtful that the juror would be willing to invest the time and expense required to challenge the prosecutor's actions. The juror would have to bring the challenge as a representative of the excluded class, and a court would have to determine whether to grant the juror standing for the suit. *Batson* accorded standing only to the defendant whose racial compatriots were struck. Finally, it is not clear what relief, if any, the juror would be entitled to in such a case. The wrong to the juror from wrongful exclusion in the particular case could not be righted, injunctive relief would not benefit

§8.10 —Application to Civil Cases

Batson was concerned with the rights of a defendant in a criminal case. The applicability of the court's decision to civil cases was not commented upon. One difficulty in applying *Batson* in a civil context stems from the fact that the case was decided on equal protection grounds. The equal protection clause applies to state officials and entities. As a prerequisite to an equal protection analysis, a court must find "state action." In *Batson,* this finding was obvious, for the individual who had engaged in the discrimination was a state official, the prosecutor, acting as the state's representative in a criminal prosecution brought in the state's name. In a civil case involving private parties, it is far less clear that there is any state action.

The issue is not unlike that which arises in determining whether *Batson* applies to defense counsel in a criminal case. This issue was discussed in the preceding section.[210] As was suggested there, the requisite state action might be found either in the state statute which creates the right of peremptory challenges or in the acceptance by the trial judge, a state official, of a racially based peremptory challenge. A court could also find that the discriminatory exercise of peremptory challenges violates the constitutional right to an impartial jury[211] or a jury drawn from a fair cross-section of the community.[212]

Courts have recognized the importance of nondiscrimination in the civil jury context, albeit not specifically in relation to the discriminatory exercise of peremptory challenges. The Supreme Court has disapproved of discrimination in the selection of a civil venire.[213] State courts which have held that the state constitutional requirement of fair cross-section representation is abridged when peremptory challenges are exercised so as to exclude a cognizable group have extended their decisions to civil cases.[214]

A state is, of course, free to eliminate peremptory challenges, as they have no constitutional basis.[215] Less drastically, it could choose to forbid the discriminatory exercise of peremptory challenges in civil cases. Sound policy considerations would support such legislation. As the vice in *Batson* was in part the stigma attached to those excluded from jury service, a state legislature could conclude that a similar stigma arises in civil cases and is equally deserving of redress. A state legislature could also logically decide that its civil court system would receive more widespread popular support if juries actually represented a fair cross-section of the community. The discriminatory exercise of peremptory challenges defeats cross-section representation.

---

the excluded jurors, and prosecutors are immune from damages. *See* Imbler v Pachtman, 424 US 409 (1976).

210 *See* **§8.09.**

211 *See generally* **§§2.09-2.12.**

212 *See generally* **§6.13**

213 *See* Thiel v Southern Pac Co, 328 US 217, 220 (1945).

214 *See, e.g.,* Holley v J&S Sweeping Co, 143 Cal App 3d 588, 192 Cal Rptr 74 (1983); Miami v Cornett, 463 So 2d 399 (Fla 1985).

215 *See* Stilson v United States, 250 US 583, 586 (1919).

§8.11 —Remedies

In *Batson* the trial court had rejected the defendant's motion to discharge the jury because of the prosecutor's discriminatory exercise of peremptory challenges. It therefore never reached the question of whether there was a neutral explanation for the prosecutor's challenges. Accordingly, it was sufficient for the Supreme Court to remand the case for further proceedings.[216] The Court did, however, add that "[i]f the trial court decides that the facts establish, prima facie, purposeful discrimination and the prosecutor does not come forward with a neutral explanation for his action, our precedents require that petitioner's conviction be reversed."[217] Reversal of a conviction would also appear to be the appropriate remedy where, on appeal from a conviction, an appellate court determined that a prosecutor's explanation did not rebut a defendant's prima facie case.

But what should a trial court do if it determines prior to the swearing in of the jury that there has been a *Batson* violation? In *Batson* the Supreme Court declined to endorse any specific remedy. It did, however, suggest two possible alternatives.[218] One would be to discharge the venire and select a new jury from a panel not previously associated with the case. This remedy is the one most commonly chosen by courts which have found that the discriminatory exercise of peremptory challenges violates a constitutional requirement that the jury be drawn from a fair cross-section of the community.[219]

There are, however, several objections to this remedy. First, it is both expensive and time-consuming, for voir dire would have to be begun anew. Second, it provides no redress for those jurors who have been the subject of the discrimination. Indeed, the remedy itself creates an additional injustice, denying those jurors already selected their right to serve on the jury. Third, in some instances it can make the discriminatory exercise of peremptory challenges a cost-free and attractive option. If dissatisfied with the entire original venire, both its black and white members, the prosecutor can simply strike all blacks. The defendant is then left with the choice of retaining the favorable white jurors or insisting upon his or her *Batson* rights.

Where a court subscribes to the remedy of summoning a new venire, counsel should carefully consider what its composition will look like before making a claim of a *Batson* violation. If the new venire, even with a full complement of prospective black jurors, will be less favorable than the first venire, even when stripped of its black jurors, the attorney would be ill-advised to lodge an objection. The attorney who has made a pretrial demographic and attitudinal

---

[216] Batson v Kentucky, 476 US 79, 100 (1986).

[217] *Id.*

[218] *Id* 99 n 24.

[219] *See, e.g.*, Booker v Jabe, 775 F2d 762, 773 (6th Cir), *vacated & remanded*, 478 US 1001 (1985), *opinion reinstated*, 801 F2d 871 (6th Cir 1986), *cert denied*, 479 US 1046 (1987); Commonwealth v Soares, 377 Mass 461, 387 NE2d 499, *cert denied*, 444 US 881 (1979); People v Wheeler, 22 Cal 3d 258, 583 P2d 748, 184 Cal Rptr 890 (1978). *See generally* **§8.12**.

survey of the community[220] is in a good position to make this comparative judgment.

A related remedy would be to summon additional black jurors.[221] This would be less time-consuming than selecting a new panel, would preserve the right of already selected jurors to serve, and would allow the defendant to retain previously selected jurors thought to be favorable. It is not clear, however, that many states have a mechanism for summoning jurors of a particular race. More significantly, this remedy would have the practical effect of creating a quota of blacks on the jury. The Supreme Court has repeatedly maintained that a defendant in a criminal prosecution is not constitutionally entitled to members of his race on the jury.[222] Finally, this remedy, like that of summoning a new venire, suffers from the defect of not vindicating the rights of those jurors who have been improperly excluded.

An alternative remedy suggested by the Supreme Court in *Batson* is to disallow the challenges and reinstate the improperly excluded black jurors.[223] This option is advantageous to the defense, for it permits the retention of unchallenged non-black jurors thought to be favorable as well as the reinstatement of the improperly challenged black jurors. The prosecution would be expected to object, however, on the ground that it saddles the state with jurors who may well resent having been challenged. To allow the prosecutor to challenge the reseated jurors because of this perceived antagonism would result in a bootstrap avoidance of *Batson*. Although reinstatement might appear unfair to a prosecutor, especially one who may have acted in good faith, it must be remembered that the prosecutor is responsible for the predicament. Moreover, this approach is the only one which vindicates the rights of the improperly excluded jurors. Also eliminated is the cost in time inherent in impaneling a new jury. The potential for hostility to the prosecutor from the unsuccessful peremptory challenge can be avoided by having both sides register challenges outside the presence of the jurors[224] pursuant to a "struck" system.[225] If a claimed *Batson* violation is also heard and adjudicated at this time, and is upheld, no juror will be aware of having been challenged.

If challenged black jurors are reinstated, it would seem to follow that the peremptory challenges exercised by the prosecutor in excluding the jurors should also be reinstated. A policy argument, however, could be made for not reinstating the peremptory challenges of prosecutors who have acted in bad faith as a form of punishment and as a deterrent to future violations of *Batson*.

---

[220] *See generally* **ch 3.**

[221] *See* Note, Batson v Kentucky: *The New and Improved Peremptory Challenge*, 38 Hastings LJ 1195, 1220-221 (1987).

[222] *See* Batson v Kentucky, 476 US 79, 85 (1986).

[223] *Id* 99 n 24 (citing United States v Robinson, 421 F Supp 467, 474 (D Conn 1976), *mandamus granted sub nom* United States v Newman, 549 F2d 240 (2d Cir 1977)).

[224] This mode of challenging has the additional advantage of not alienating friends of the juror who is successfully challenged, for the friend will not know which side made the challenge.

[225] *See* **§8.03.**

If the challenges were reinstated, the question would then arise whether the reinstated challenges could be exercised against jurors whom the prosecutor had previously passed. Some courts hold that the failure to exercise a peremptory challenge against a juror at the appropriate time constitutes a waiver of the right to challenge the juror.[226] The rule should be relaxed in a *Batson* context, however, for the prosecutor's failure to challenge may not so much have reflected the acceptability of the juror as the fact that at the time the prosecutor found other jurors more objectionable. The power to permit a prosecutor to challenge a juror previously accepted would most likely fall within the trial judge's general discretion to control procedures relating to challenges.[227]

§8.12 Peremptory Challenges and the Right to a Jury Drawn from a Fair Cross-Section of the Community

The sixth amendment to the United States Constitution guarantees a jury from "the State and district wherein the crime shall have been committed. . . ."[228] In the past half-century, the Supreme Court has apparently either transformed this provision into a mandate that jurors be drawn from a fair cross-section of the community or found an independent fair cross-section requirement implicit in the sixth amendment.

The first seeds seem to have been planted in *Smith v Texas,*[229] where the Court stated: "It is part of the established tradition in the use of juries as instruments of public justice that the jury be a body truly representative of the community."[230] The nurturing process continued in *Glasser v United States*[231] and *Ballard v United States.*[232] In *Taylor v Louisiana,*[233] the Court harvested its crop: "We accept the fair cross-section requirement as fundamental to the jury trial guaranteed by the Sixth Amendment."[234]

In *Batson* the Supreme Court approached the problem of discrimination in the exercise of peremptory challenges from a perspective of equal protection. The Court held that "the Equal Protection Clause forbids the prosecutor to challenge potential jurors solely on account of their race or on the assumption that black jurors as a group will be unable impartially to consider the State's

---

[226] *E.g.,* Le Gro v Moore, 51 Del 116, 138 A2d 644 (1958). *But see* United States v Turner, 558 F2d 535 (9th Cir 1977) (acceptance of juror should not be deemed to constitute a corresponding waiver of a peremptory challenge).

[227] *See* Pointer v United States, 151 US 396, 409-11 (1984).

[228] US Const amend VI.

[229] 311 US 128 (1940).

[230] *Id* 130.

[231] 315 US 60, 85-86 (1942).

[232] 329 US 187, 191 (1946). *See also* Thiel v Southern Pac Co, 328 US 217 (1946).

[233] 419 US 522 (1975).

[234] *Id* 530. More in-depth discussion is provided in **§6.13.**

case against a black defendant."[235] Although the defendant had claimed that the prosecutor's actions had violated his sixth and fourteenth amendment rights to a jury drawn from a fair cross-section of the community, the Court expressly chose not to address the merits of this argument.[236]

At least two federal appellate courts had found merit in the sixth amendment argument.[237] In a case handed down one week after *Batson,* however, the Supreme Court appeared to suggest that it would not be receptive to such an argument.[238] The defendant in *Lockhart v McCree*[239] contended, among other things, that permitting the prosecutor to challenge for cause persons who could not vote for the death penalty if they determined that the defendant was guilty of murder violated the fair cross-section requirement of the sixth amendment. The defense had introduced social science studies which tended to show that the removal of jurors opposed to capital punishment produced a jury that was more conviction prone than a "non-death qualified" jury. Even assuming the accuracy of these studies (about which it expressed considerable doubt), a majority of the Supreme Court found no constitutional violation. In responding to the argument that defendant's sixth amendment rights had been violated, the Court said:

> We have never invoked the fair cross-section principle to invalidate the use of either for-cause or peremptory challenges to prospective jurors, or to require petit juries, as opposed to jury panels or venires, to reflect the composition of the community at large. See *Duren v Missouri,* 439 U.S. 357, 363-364, 99 S. Ct. 664, 668, 58 L Ed. 2d 579 (1979); *Taylor v Louisiana,* 419 U.S. 522, 538, 95 S. Ct. 692, 701-702, 42 L. Ed.2d 690 (1975) ("[W]e impose no requirement that petit juries actually chosen must mirror the community and reflect the various distinctive groups in the population"); cf. *Batson v Kentucky.* __ U.S. __, __, n.4, 106 S. Ct. 1712, 1716, n. 4, 89 L. Ed.2d _ (1986) (expressly declining to address "fair cross-section" challenge to discriminatory use of peremptory challenges). The limited scope of the fair cross-section requirement is a direct and inevitable consequence of the practical impossibility of providing each criminal defendant with a truly "representative" petit jury, see id., at _, n. 6, 106 S. Ct. at 1717, n. 6, a basic truth that the Court of Appeals acknowledged for many years prior to its decision in the instant case. See *United States v. Childress,* 715 F.2d 1313, (CA8 1983 (en banc), cert. denied, 464 U.S.

---

[235] Batson v Kentucky, 476 US 79, 89 (1986).

[236] *Id* 84 n 4.

[237] Booker v Jabe, 775 F2d 762 (6th Cir), *vacated & remanded,* 478 US 1001 (1985), *opinion reinstated,* 801 F2d 871 (6th Cir 1986), *cert denied,* 479 US 1046 (1987); McCray v Abrams, 750 F2d 1113 (2d Cir 1984), *vacated on other grounds,* 478 US 1001 (1986). The *McCray* test was affirmed in Roman v Abrams, 822 F2d 214 (2d Cir 1987). *But see* Teague v Lane, 820 F2d 832 (7th Cir 1987), *cert denied,* 108 S Ct 1106 (1988); United States v Hamilton, 850 F2d 1038 (4th Cir 1988).

[238] Lockhart v McCree, 476 US 162 (1986).

[239] *Id.*

> 1063, 104 S. Ct. 744, 79 L. Ed.2d 202 (1984); *Pope v. United States,* 372 F.2d 710, 725 (CA8 1967) (Blackmun, J.) ("The point at which an accused is entitled to a fair cross-section of the community is when the names are put in the box from which the panels are drawn"), vacated on other grounds, 392 U.S. 651, 88 S. Ct. 2145, 20 L.Ed.2d 1317 (1968). We remain convinced that an extension of the fair cross-section requirement to petit juries would be unworkable and unsound. . . .[240]

This language strongly suggests that the Court would not be receptive to a fair cross-section argument in a case involving the use of peremptory challenges to exclude blacks or other groups in the community from a petit jury, as opposed to the venire.

State supreme courts have not shared the United States Supreme Court's reservations. Perhaps because of the uncertain status of the federal constitutional claim, state courts have preferred to rely upon state constitutional provisions construed to guarantee a jury drawn from a cross-section of the community. The first and leading decision is that of the California Supreme Court in *People v Wheeler.*[241] In *Wheeler* two black defendants were charged with the murder of a white victim. The prosecution used its peremptory challenges to strike all black jurors, with the result that the defendants were convicted by an all-white jury.

The California Supreme Court accepted that the fair cross-section requirement was guaranteed by both the federal Constitution and article 1, §16 of the California state constitution.[242] The court identified three stages at which the right might be compromised: (1) in the initial compilation of the roll of eligible jurors; (2) in the process by which jurors were excused or disqualified prior to trial; and (3) in the process of challenging individual jurors.[243] The *Wheeler* case involved the third of these situations.

The California Supreme Court drew a critical distinction between a specific bias—a bias relating to the particular case, the parties, or the witnesses—and a group bias—a bias against persons because of their membership in an identifiable group distinguished on racial, religious, ethnic, or similar grounds.[244] Specific biases are neutral with respect to the various groups which are represented on the venire; by definition group biases are not. When peremptory challenges are exercised on the basis of group bias, they distort the demographic balance of the venire.[245] They also frustrate one major purpose of the cross-section requirement—to allow the interaction on the jury of persons with diverse val-

---

[240] *Id* 173-74.

[241] 22 Cal 3d 258, 583 P2d 748, 184 Cal Rptr 890 (1978).

[242] 583 P2d at 758.

[243] *Id* 758-59.

[244] *Id* 760-61.

[245] *Id* 761.

ues and beliefs.[246] On the basis of this reasoning, the California Supreme Court ruled that the use of peremptory challenges to remove jurors for group bias violated the right to a jury drawn from a representative cross-section of the community and guaranteed by the California constitution.[247]

Procedurally, the approach of the California Supreme Court in *Wheeler* resembled that of the United States Supreme Court in *Batson.* The starting point is a presumption that peremptory challenges are being exercised in a constitutionally permissible fashion.[248] A party who believes that the opposing party is exercising peremptory challenges in an impermissible fashion must make a timely objection and establish a prima facie case of a constitutional violation.[249] A prima facie case consists of a showing both that the excluded jurors belong to a cognizable group and that the reason for their being challenged is their membership in that group.[250] Once this showing is made, the burden shifts to the opposing party to demonstrate that the peremptory challenges were made for reasons of specific bias. The rebuttal does not have to rise to the level required to justify a challenge for cause. If the rebuttal is ineffective, the court is required to dismiss the jurors so far selected, quash the remaining venire, and convene a new venire.[251]

One year after *Wheeler,* the Massachusetts Supreme Judicial Court decided *Commonwealth v Soares.*[252] In that case the prosecutor had excluded 97 per cent of the available black jurors but only 34 per cent of the available white jurors. The resultant jury which convicted the defendants had one black member. On appeal, the Massachusetts Supreme Judicial Court attempted to strike a balance among the goals of diffused impartiality (furthered by cross-section representation), the limitations inherent in any attempt to impanel a jury truly representative of the community, and the historic and legitimate role of the peremptory challenge. The court began with the observation that, because of the numbers involved, it is far easier to remove members of a minority group from a panel than members of a majority group. The danger which the court envisioned was "a jury in which the subtle group biases of the majority are permitted to operate, while those of the minority have been silenced."[253] The court held that the use of peremptory challenges to exclude jurors solely because of their membership in, or affiliation with, a defined group violated the Massachusetts Declaration of Rights provision guaranteeing a jury drawn from a representative cross-section of the community.[254] The Massachusetts court delineated those characteristics which were impermissible bases for jury exclusion—sex,

---

[246] *Id.*

[247] *Id* 761-62.

[248] *Id* 762.

[249] *Id* 763.

[250] *Id* 764.

[251] *Id* 765. For a critical evaluation of this remedy, see **§8.11.**

[252] 377 Mass 461, 387 NE2d 499, *cert denied,* 444 US 881 (1979).

[253] 387 NE2d at 516.

[254] *Id* 515-16.

race, color, creed, or national origin.[255] The procedures adopted by the Massachusetts court were similar to those of *Wheeler* and *Batson*—a presumption of proper use of peremptory challenges which had to be rebutted by the party alleging abuse, with the opportunity for rebuttal once a prima facie case was established.[256] The Massachusetts court adopted the *Wheeler* remedy of dismissing the jurors previously selected, quashing the remaining venire, and summoning a new venire.[257]

Several state courts, including those of Florida,[258] New Jersey,[259] and Delaware,[260] have adopted the reasoning of *Wheeler* and *Soares.*[261] Others have declined to do so.[262] Whether *Batson* will cause the latter courts to reconsider their pre-*Batson* decisions, or influence courts which have yet to address the issue to prefer an equal protection analysis to a fair cross-section analysis, remains to be seen.

An exclusive focus on equal protection would be unfortunate. Many of the problematic issues raised by *Batson* can be clarified by consideration of the fair cross-section representation dimensions of the controversy. More specifically, a fair cross-section analysis would allow a court to address discrimination against groups other than blacks. Moreover, under a cross-section analysis, it would not matter whether the defendant was a member of the excluded group. There would also be a more compelling argument for extending a court's prohibition to both prosecutor and defense, and to attorneys in civil cases as well, for the question of state action would be less critical. Of course, the equal protection and cross-section representation claims are not mutually exclusive, and a diligent attorney will doubtless consider the viability of each.

§8.13 Peremptory Challenges and the Right to an Impartial Jury

Arguably the most critical of the constitutional rights pertaining to the jury is that which guarantees an impartial jury.[263] Jury deliberations take place in secret. A jury is not required to provide reasons for its decisions or an explana-

---

[255] *Id* 516.

[256] *Id* 516-17.

[257] *Id* 518. For a critical evaluation of this remedy, see **§8.11.**

[258] State v Neil, 457 So 2d 481 (Fla 1984).

[259] State v Gilmore, 103 NJ 508, 511 A2d 1150 (1986).

[260] Riley v State, 496 A2d 997, 1012 (Del 1985), *cert denied,* 478 US 1022 (1986).

[261] *See also* Fields v People, 732 P2d 1145 (Colo 1987); State v Crispin, 94 NM 486, 612 P2d 716 (NM Ct App 1980).

[262] *See, e.g.,* People v McCray, 57 NY2d 542, 443 NE2d 915, 457 NYS2d 441 (1982), *cert denied,* 461 US 961 (1983); People v Davis, 95 Ill 2d 1, 447 NE2d 353 (1983); State v Raymond, 446 A2d 743 (RI 1982).

[263] US Const amend VI. *See* **§§2.09-2.12.** *See generally* Gobert, *In Search of the Impartial Jury,* 79 J Crim & Criminology 289 (1988).

tion of its decision-making processes.[264] An individual juror may not impeach the verdict of the jury.[265] A verdict of acquittal is virtually unreviewable by an appellate court,[266] and a verdict of guilty only slightly less so.[267] Jurors cannot be punished or otherwise held legally responsible for their verdicts.[268] In light of this lack of accountability, the requirement that jurors be impartial stands as one of the few and prime safeguards that a fair and just verdict will be reached.

In the search for an impartial jury, the peremptory challenge is one of the attorney's most valuable tools. It permits the removal of a juror whose impartiality is suspect, even though the juror's responses to voir dire do not conclusively establish a basis for a challenge for cause. But what happens when the peremptory challenge, employed in the pursuit of impaneling an impartial jury, leads a party to excuse members of a cognizable racial group or an identifiable segment of the community? Stated in constitutional terms, which gives way when there is a clash between the right to an impartial jury and the guarantees of equal protection and cross-section representation?

In answering this question it is instructive to compare *Batson* with *Ross v Oklahoma.*[269] In *Ross* the trial judge erroneously refused to remove a juror who declared that he would automatically vote for the death penalty if the defendant was found guilty of murder. Under *Witherspoon v Illinois*[270] such a juror should have been excused for cause. The improperly seated juror, however, did not hear the case. Under state law the defendant was required to, and did, use a peremptory challenge to strike the juror.[271] On appeal the defendant argued that he had been denied his sixth and fourteenth amendment rights to an impartial jury, as well as his due process right to a full complement of peremptory challenges. The Supreme Court rejected both claims.

In addressing the petitioner's contention that his right to an impartial jury had been abridged, the Court stated that the critical question was whether the jury which had heard the defendant's case was impartial.[272] Since the tainted juror did not in fact serve, and since there was no showing that the jurors who did serve were not impartial, the Court found no constitutional violation. The

---

[264] *See* United States v Lee, 532 F2d 911 (3d Cir), *cert denied,* 429 US 838 (1976).

[265] McDonald v Pless, 238 US 264 (1915).

[266] This result is the byproduct of the constitutional guarantee against double jeopardy. US Const amend VIII; 28 USC §3731 (government may not appeal where prosecution would be barred by double jeopardy).

[267] *See* Jackson v Virginia, 443 US 307, 319 (1979) (verdict of guilty cannot be overturned on appeal if, "after viewing the evidence in the light most favorable to the prosecution, *any* rational trier of fact could have found the essential elements of the crime beyond a reasonable doubt").

[268] *See* Butz v Economou, 438 US 478, 509 (1978); Bushell's Case, 124 Eng Rep 1006 (CP 1670).

[269] 487 US 81 (1988).

[270] 391 US 510 (1968).

[271] State law required that peremptory challenges be used to cure incorrect refusals to excuse a juror for cause.

[272] 487 US 81.

Supreme Court also rejected defendant's due process claim, based on the fact that he had been required unnecessarily to use a peremptory challenge to excuse the improperly seated juror. The Court pointed out that peremptory challenges were not of constitutional dimension and could be made subservient to the goal of impaneling an impartial jury.[273]

In contrast to *Batson,* where the spotlight was on the jurors who had been excused, the spotlight in *Ross* was on the jurors who had been seated. The Court in *Batson* never addressed the issue of whether the jury that sat in judgment of Batson was impartial. Of course, the defendant in *Batson* did not contend that the jury which tried him had not been impartial, and the defendant in *Ross* did not claim that he had been denied equal protection.[274] Beyond this surface distinction, however, a different philosophical approach can be discerned between the two cases. The *Ross* Court viewed the peremptory challenge in instrumental terms, as a means to the end of selecting an impartial jury. As long as the defendant had received a fair trial by an impartial jury there was no constitutional violation. The *Batson* Court found the nondiscriminatory exercise of peremptory challenges to be an end in itself. It did not ask whether the defendant had received a fair trial. This focus implies that it was the rights of the excluded jurors and not those of the defendant which were of primary concern to the *Batson* Court. If so, however there is little justification for the restriction in *Batson* that the defendant be of the same race as the excluded juror.

Both *Batson* and *Ross* illustrate the close connection between the peremptory challenge, not itself of constitutional stature, and other constitutional rights. While the peremptory challenge can be a means of securing the constitutional right to an impartial jury, it can also be a means of subverting the constitutional right of equal protection. The questions both asked and unasked by the *Batson* Court seem to suggest that when peremptory challenges used to select an impartial jury have the effect of discriminating against a cognizable racial group of which the defendant is a member, equal protection claims prevail over impartial jury defenses.

§8.14 Implications for the Future

In his concurring opinion in *Batson,* Justice Marshall advocated the elimination of the peremptory challenge as the only viable means of eliminating the evils masked in its racially discriminatory exercise. Clearly the majority, not to mention the dissent, was not prepared to go this far. Nonetheless, the *Batson* decision, along with those state court decisions prohibiting discriminatory use

---

[273] *Id.*

[274] In fact, the defendant in *Ross* did object at trial to the fact that there were no blacks on the jury which tried him, but the objection was overruled and the claim was not further pressed. *Id.*

of peremptory challenges on fair cross-section representation grounds,[275] threatens to dramatically alter the nature of voir dire and the exercise of peremptory challenges. This will be true even if few constitutional violations are actually found.

There are several variables which will determine the ultimate effect of these decisions. Perhaps the most critical will be the burden of rebuttal placed on the party alleged to have engaged in the discriminatory exercise of peremptory challenges and the standards used by the trial court in determining whether a *Batson* violation has occurred. The *Batson* Court stated that the neutral explanation required to rebut a prima facie case did not have to rise to the level which would be required for a challenge for cause.[276] But the Court also said that mere protestations of good faith and a lack of intent to discriminate would not discharge the prosecutor's burden.[277] The Court allocated to trial judges the task of steering a course through these straits.

The line separating the two is a thin one indeed. If the trial judge requires a neutral explanation that demands a rigor which is only slightly less than that required to justify a challenge for cause, a prosecutor may conclude that the risks of making peremptory challenges to blacks outweigh the benefits, as unsuccessful peremptory challenges may alienate the jurors challenged. As a consequence, the prosecutor's exercise of peremptory challenges may be chilled. A similar effect may be expected on defense attorneys if, as suggested by Chief Justice Burger, Justice Marshall, and some state courts they, too, are bound by the restrictions of *Batson.* The more trial courts rigorously scrutinize "neutral explanations" for race- or class-based peremptory challenges, the more probing the voir dire will have to be in order to lay a foundation for a peremptory challenge. The more probing the voir dire, the greater the risk of antagonizing a juror. Many attorneys will reluctantly conclude that the effort to determine whether a juror is impartial is not worth the risk of alienating the juror, particularly if the likelihood of a successful challenge for cause or sustainable peremptory challenge is slight.

A trial judge can minimize some of the negative effects by hearing peremptory challenges and *Batson* motions out of the presence of the jury. Jurors will then not be aware of the fact that they have been challenged. Nevertheless, the chilling effect on attorneys will not altogether be avoided. One saving grace of the peremptory challenge has always been its finality. An attorney, whether prosecutor or defense, in a civil or criminal case, has always been able to engage in searching and even embarrassing voir dire examination secure in the knowledge that if the questioning failed to elicit a basis for a challenge for cause, the attorney could exercise a peremptory challenge against the juror. There was no risk that a juror who was offended by the questioning would serve on the jury if the attorney who caused the offense did not want the juror to serve. *Batson* and its state court counterparts remove this safety net. As a result, they may inhibit the vigor of voir dire questioning generally.

---

[275] *See* **§8.12.**

[276] Batson v Kentucky, 476 US 79, 97 (1986).

[277] *Id* 98.

The resulting chilling effect on voir dire and the exercise of peremptory challenges may not be in the best interests of the legal system. The search for an impartial jury may be detrimentally affected by the reluctance of attorneys to engage in probing voir dire.[278] Verdicts may not be as readily accepted in the community if the jury that returned the verdict is perceived as biased. Litigants denied the right to challenge jurors whom they think but cannot prove are partial are also less likely to be accepting of the jury's verdict.

In order to avoid these adverse effects, it may be necessary to ease existing limitations on challenges for cause. Such a solution has its costs. In addition to the fact that voir dire may become more time-consuming, the trial judge will be called upon to rule on more challenges for cause. No longer will the judge be able to accept uncritically juror declarations of impartiality, relying on the attorney who does not believe them to exercise a peremptory challenge.

A judge's disqualification of a juror for cause, moreover, may have greater repercussions than an attorney's peremptory challenge. When a judge allows a challenge for cause, the judge in effect declares that, from the state's perspective, the juror is unfit to serve on that case. When a judge discounts a juror's claim of impartiality, the judge implies that the juror is at best mistaken[279] and at worst a liar. A juror is likely to resent these insinuations, especially when made by a supposedly unbiased state official with the stature of a judge. A peremptory challenge, on the other hand, can always be rationalized as the product of an attorney's unquestioned partisanship. The resentment stemming from a challenge for cause is likely to be generalized to the legal system; the resentment stemming from a peremptory challenge is likely to be restricted to the attorney responsible. In any event, there is no particular reason to believe that judges are either equipped to or want to be placed in the role of having to analyze a juror's subconscious biases and conscious credibility.

The United States Supreme Court and the state supreme courts which have addressed the discriminatory use of peremptory challenges have had to choose between constitutional values in conflict. Although the peremptory challenge is not of constitutional dimension, the right to an impartial jury is. Without peremptory challenges, jurors who are biased, but not so blatantly as to justify a challenge for cause, cannot be removed from the jury. The impartiality of the resulting jury becomes more suspect. The various courts which have restricted the use of the peremptory challenge, however, have been persuaded that the threat posed by its discriminatory exercise is a greater evil.

The ultimate legacy of *Batson* may be to force attorneys to think through their jury selection decisions more carefully. Reliance on racial stereotypes is the lazy lawyer's way of avoiding difficult choices. Clearly blacks, or members of any cognizable group, are not indistinguishable in their values and beliefs. In its conception of the proper relationship between the individual and the state, the black viewpoint is not monolithic. Attorneys who indiscriminately strike

---

[278] *See* Hayes v Missouri, 120 US 68, 82 (1887).

[279] Jurors may not be aware of their subconscious biases, or, if they are aware, may be reluctant to admit them. *See* Broeder, *Voir Dire Examination: an Empirical Study,* 38 S Cal L Rev 503, 510-15, 528 (1965).

blacks on the assumption that all blacks share a common bias do a disservice not only to blacks but also to their clients, squandering the few precious peremptory challenges that the law allows. If *Batson* does nothing more than compel attorneys to think more critically about the attributes that make for a desirable and undesirable juror and to make juror selection decisions on an individual rather than on a class basis, it will have accomplished quite a bit. The peremptory challenge will survive, but in a form which not only will advance the cause of equality but will benefit attorneys and parties as well.

But *Batson* should do more. In concluding this chapter, it is perhaps useful to ask, as the *Batson* Court did not, how the tawdry state of affairs which *Batson* sought to rectify came into being. To some extent the legal system must share the blame for the tendency of lawyers to rely on racial stereotypes. Judge-conducted voir dire, the requirement that lawyers examine the jury panel en masse rather than individually, and limitations on the scope and time allotted for voir dire[280] fail to provide attorneys with the detailed information that they need in order to make individualized jury selection decisions. While pretrial community surveys,[281] mock trials,[282] and investigation of jurors prior to trial[283] can help fill the void, many parties cannot afford these aids.[284] Their attorneys must continue to rely on voir dire. It is unfortunate but not surprising that these attorneys fall back on racial stereotypes. If the Supreme Court is to decry decision making based on racial stereotypes, it must also encourage a more liberal approach to voir dire.[285] In recent years the Court has in fact gone in the opposite direction.

In *Ham v South Carolina,*[286] a bearded black man, active in the civil rights movement, was convicted of possession of marijuana. The trial court refused the defendant's request that jurors be questioned regarding their prejudices against blacks and persons with beards. The Supreme Court found that the failure to make inquiry on voir dire regarding racial bias denied the defendant due process. However, it upheld the judge's refusal to permit questioning regarding prejudice against persons with beards. That the latter part of the Court's opinion has broader implications was indicated by the Court's statement that, given "our inability to constitutionally distinguish possible prejudice against beards from a host of other possible similar prejudices, we do not believe the petitioner's constitutional rights were violated when the trial judge

---

[280] *See* **§§9.05-9.08, 9.11.** *See generally* Babcock, *Voir Dire: Preserving "Its Wonderful Power,"* 27 Stan L Rev 545 (1975).

[281] *See* **§§3.02-3.10.**

[282] *See* **§§5.02-5.06.**

[283] *See* **ch 4.**

[284] *But see* **§§3.15-3.18.**

[285] *See* Note, *Voir Dire: Establishing Minimum Standards to Facilitate the Exercise of Peremptory Challenges,* 27 Stan L Rev 1443 (1975).

[286] 409 US 524 (1973).

refused to put this question."[287] The same premise (the inability to constitutionally distinguish prejudice against persons with beards from other prejudices) could have justified the opposite conclusion: the right to a wide-ranging voir dire on *all* possible grounds of prejudice. Only in such a way can the right to an impartial jury be vindicated. If time is a consideration, much of the questioning can be done through a pre-voir dire questionaire.[288]

In *Ristaino v Ross*[289] the Supreme Court cut back on that part of its holding in *Ham* relating to voir dire questioning as to racial prejudice. The defendant, a black man, was charged with crimes of violence against a white security guard. The trial judge denied the defendant's motion to specifically question jurors regarding racial prejudice. The Supreme Court affirmed the trial court's ruling, holding that inquiry into racial prejudice had to be justified by a showing of specialized circumstances suggesting the possibility of racial prejudice. The Court distinguished *Ham* on the basis that racial prejudice was inextricably bound up with the defendant's claim to his civil rights activities. The mere fact that a black man is charged with a crime of violence against a white victim, however, was, according to the Court, an insufficiently specialized circumstance to suggest that racial prejudice would infect the trial and that voir dire questioning regarding racial prejudice was constitutionally required.[290] In a footnote, the Court did concede that it would have been preferable for the trial judge to propound the requested question, and that, if the case had arisen in federal court, it would have required the questioning under its supervisory power.[291]

Ham and *Ristaino*, seen as part of a larger trend toward restricted voir dire in the name of expediency and efficiency, need to be rethought. *Batson* provides the impetus for both the Court and the states to reconsider the conditions under which voir dire is conducted.

---

[287] *Id* 528.

[288] *See* **§9.01.**

[289] 424 US 589 (1976).

[290] *Id* 597-98.

[291] *Id* 597 n 9. *See also* Aldridge v United States, 283 US 308 (1931).

Part IV

Voire Dire

Overview

Voir dire is undoubtedly a critical stage of jury selection. It is the only time when the lawyer has the right to talk directly to jurors and to require them to answer questions. At the same time, voir dire provides a unique opportunity to establish rapport with the jurors and to get to know them as persons. It will be the jury's first introduction to the case, and to the legal principles which will govern it. Both because of the obligation to the client and the opportunity for the lawyer, voir dire should rarely, if ever, be waived.

The goals of an attorney during voir dire may vary depending on the degree to which the attorney has conducted mock trials and undertaken the types of pretrial surveys and investigations recommended in Part II of this book. Where, as a result of community analyses and mock trials, the attorney has constructed profiles of favorable and unfavorable jurors, the primary aim in voir dire will be to match the jurors against the profiles. Questioning will to a large extent reflect those matters which made a significant difference to the participants in the mock trials and community surveys.

The lawyer who has engaged in mock trials, community surveys, and pretrial investigations should not, however, lose sight of the other potential uses of voir dire. These include the establishment of rapport with jurors, the previewing of the party's theory of the case, and the education of the jury in regard to applicable legal principles.

The attorney who has not engaged in mock trials, community surveys, or pretrial investigations has more to accomplish in voir dire. In addition to the objectives already mentioned, the attorney must learn enough about each juror to be able to make an enlightened decision about which jurors to challenge.

The extent to which the lawyer will be able to accomplish these myriad goals will depend in part on the lawyer's abilities and in part on the time and scope allotted to voir dire by the trial judge. It will also depend on whether the trial judge conducts the voir dire or permits the lawyer to conduct it.

The three chapters in this section explore issues relating to voir dire. Chapter 9 examines general matters unrelated to the type of case involved. Chapter

10 focuses on voir dire in civil cases and Chapter 11 on voir dire in criminal cases. Both Chapters 10 and 11 touch upon and in some instances expand on the general matters raised in Chapter 9. Throughout all three chapters, but particularly in Chapters 10 and 11, sample questions are presented on particular topics. These are intended to be illustrative rather than definitive. The final 11 sections of Chapter 11 present a fairly lengthy excerpt from a voir dire examination conducted by a prominent criminal defense attorney, Richard "Racehorse" Haynes.

The discussion in these chapters is designed to be both practical and theoretical. Legal theory can be used to support arguments for improved voir dire conditions in a particular case. Policy considerations, as well as legal arguments, are presented which might sway the trial judge in an area (the conducting of voir dire) which has repeatedly been held to lie within the judge's discretion. The practical discussion is designed to provide insight into strategy and tactics in general, not just in regard to the particular examples presented.

9 Voir Dire Generally

§9.01 Pre-Voir Dire Questionnaires

The criticism one increasingly hears of voir dire is that it takes too long. In *Press-Enterprise Co v Superior Court,*[1] the voir dire lasted for six weeks. Chief Justice Burger commented that such lengthy voir dire undermined confidence in the courts and the legal profession.[2] The Chief Justice further noted that the length of the voir dire in the case was not that exceptional; counsel had indicated in response to a question that it was not unknown for jury selection in California to take six months.[3]

The problem is that voir dire is used to accomplish too much.[4] Lawyers want to establish rapport with jurors, preview the main features of their case, and acquaint jurors with the applicable principles of law in a way that is most consistent with their theory of the case. At the same time, the lawyer must learn enough about each juror to be able to determine whether the juror will be impartial.

One solution is to obtain as much information as possible through pre-voir dire questionnaires. These differ from the pretrial questionnaires sent to jurors in the federal system and some state systems.[5] The pretrial questionnaires are standardized and not designed with any particular case in mind. They seek to determine whether a prospective juror is willing to serve and is not subject to disqualification, exemption, or excuse. The pre-voir dire questionnaire is more detailed and keyed to the particular case. The questionnaire is jointly prepared by the lawyers for each side, and covers the major areas which each attorney would like to explore on voir dire.

A proposal for a pre-voir dire questionnaire should appeal to a judge, for it can save valuable court time.[6] In court voir dire can be limited to questions designed to clarify or follow up on a questionnaire response. The need to repeat routine background questions to jurors is obviated.

---

[1] 464 US 501 (1984).

[2] *Id* 510 n 9.

[3] *Id. See also* Chambers, *Who Should Pick Jurors, Attorneys or the Judge,* NY Times, June 13, 1983, at B4 (in 20% of cases in study, voir dire took longer than the trial, and on average voir dire consumed 40% of total trial time).

[4] *See generally* **§9.04.**

[5] *See* 28 USC §1864(a). *See generally* **§6.10.**

[6] *See* Hittner, *Federal Voir Dire and Jury Selection: An Alternative View,* 25 Trial 85 (Mar 1989). The gain in court time, moreover, is generally not at the expense of juror time.

The benefit for the attorneys is that, because in-court time is not at stake, the judge may permit greater latitude in the range of questions. A pre-voir dire is particularly advantageous where the alternative is perfunctory questioning by the judge; in the pre-voir dire questionnaire, the lawyer chooses the subjects to be explored and frames the questions to be asked.

More honest and candid responses from the jurors may also be received. Some jurors may be willing to write in private what they are reluctant to say in public. Furthermore, since jurors need not know which side prepared which questions (indeed, some questions may be submitted by the judge), sensitive topics can be probed without the risk of alienating the juror from the side asking the questions.

The pre-voir dire questionnaire should be considered a supplement to, rather than a substitute for, voir dire. Follow-up questions will be needed to explore areas of bias suggested by a questionnaire response. Moreover, one of the weaknesses of questionnaires is that they do not allow an attorney to observe a juror's nonverbal responses to questions, which are often as enlightening as the juror's words; some in-court questioning will allow this observation. Finally, no experienced trial attorney would agree to forgo voir dire altogether because the attorney would still want the opportunity to establish rapport with the jurors, preview the main features of the case, and discuss applicable legal doctrines in the light most consistent with the attorney's theory of the case.

§9.02 Initial Conditioning of the Panel

Many of those summoned for jury duty will not have previously served on a jury. They will usually know nothing about legal procedures in general or the law as it relates to the particular case. The courtroom is a strange and unfamiliar world. The task of the trial judge and the lawyers is to put the jurors at ease, enlighten them regarding all pertinent legal matters, and determine which of them shall hear the case.

When the jury panel is first brought into the courtroom, the trial judge will usually take control of the proceedings. The judge will greet the jurors and make them feel welcome. The judge should introduce himself or herself, the lawyers, and the parties.

The judge might also explain to the jurors the basis on which they were selected, their role in the proceedings, and the likely duration of their service. The respective functions of court and counsel should be delineated, and in particular jurors should be instructed that rulings of law are for the court and not for the attorneys. Jurors should be assured that they are not expected to know the law.

At this point the judge may say a few general words about the nature of the case to be tried, without going into detail regarding the facts. The judge will

---

As many jurors are too well aware, considerable time is spent sitting waiting to be summoned. This time could be profitably used in filling out the pre-voir dire questionnaire.

explain that the lawyers may choose to provide greater factual detail during voir dire as well as setting out their respective positions.

The court should then move on to an explanation of the nature and function of voir dire. Its purpose, the jury should be told, is to help the lawyers and the judge select a fair and impartial jury. What is meant by a fair and impartial jury should be explained and the need for absolute honesty and candor in response to voir dire questions should be stressed. The judge must impress upon the jurors that truthfulness and frankness are essential to the fair operation of the legal system, even though this might result in some jurors not being selected to serve on the case. The judge should underscore that the fact that some members of the panel are not selected for the particular case does not mean that they are not fair persons or that they are incompetent to sit on other cases.

Voir dire can be analogized to a job interview: the job is that of juror in the case; the applicants are members of the panel. Voir dire provides jurors with a general understanding of the nature of the job for which they are being interviewed, allows them and their employers the opportunity to learn something about each other, and provides sufficient background information to enable the identification of those who are unsuited for the job. Just as some very competent persons are not suited for particular jobs, so, too, the jury should be told, some jurors are not suited for particular cases, which is not to say they would not be eminently suitable for others.

To avoid backlash to the attorneys, the judge should point out that they also have a job to do. The attorneys' job is to adequately represent their clients. It is the lawyer's legal and ethical duty to ensure that the jury which hears the case is impartial. To this end, the judge should explain, the lawyer may ask the jurors what seem to be prying questions. But it is not the lawyer's aim to pry; rather, the aim is to learn enough about the jurors to ensure that the jury will be impartial. Every effort should be made to assure jurors that each of them is in the courtroom not to be embarrassed or mistreated, but to carry out a very important civic responsibility.

Typically the next step in the preliminary conditioning is for the judge to instruct panel members not to discuss the case with anybody, including their families and acquaintances, until after the trial is over. The judge will emphasize that this prohibition extends to discussion of the case with other members of the jury before it retires to consider its verdict. Another common admonition is that jurors are prohibited from having any contact or communication whatever with anyone involved in the trial, including the parties, witnesses, and attorneys. Thus a juror should not feel slighted when a friendly or casual comment to one of the lawyers in the hallway seems to be ignored. Similarly, jurors will be told not to give to, nor receive from, anyone involved in the trial any favors, regardless of how trivial these might seem.

At this point the judge will often provide a procedural outline of the trial and advise the panel regarding the burden of proof (which will differ depending on whether the case is civil or criminal). The judge will explain that the party having the burden of proof will be allowed to speak first both on voir dire and in introducing evidence. If a case involves multiple parties, the judge may announce the order in which the parties will speak. The judge may also note that at times the trial may be interrupted by conferences between the judge and the lawyers at the bench, out of the hearing of the jury; and that the aim is not to keep from the jurors matters which they are properly entitled to know.

Prior to turning the proceedings over to counsel, the judge may choose to discuss with panel members their function as jurors. The judge will explain in some detail that the jurors' task is to consider all the evidence, to evaluate it, and to use what evidence they find credible in reaching their verdict. The judge will often observe that in determining the facts jurors are free to reject all or part of any witness's testimony, and to accept one witness's version of the facts over that of another, although of course they must not do so arbitrarily. Furthermore, while the determination of factual issues is for the jury, rulings and instructions on issues of law are for the court and it is not for the jurors to assume the role of judge. The panel should be informed that before it retires to deliberate on its verdict, the court will prepare a charge containing a statement of the law which governs the case.

Although this preliminary conditioning may be time-consuming, it is generally time well spent. The quality of jurors' service is likely to be in direct proportion to the jurors' understanding of their role.

§9.03 —Observation by Counsel

While the judge is conditioning the panel, and even before, counsel should pay careful attention to each of the prospective jurors. The observation process begins as the jurors walk to their seats, with the bearing and gait of each being noted. Does the juror strut in an aggressive manner, or shuffle into the courtroom? Dress and accessories (earrings, wrist watches, etc) which reflect the juror's status (or desired status) should also be noted. The walk, posture, dress, and demeanor of a juror may provide clues to the juror's general attitudes.

The observation process should continue during recesses, when jurors tend to congregate in the hall, and during lunch breaks. The lawyer wants to know which jurors are friendly to each other. This information is valuable, for such jurors may be allies on a divided jury. Also, if a lawyer decides to challenge a particular juror, the lawyer may need to challenge the juror's friends on the panel, for they may resent the challenge of their colleague.

In like vein, if the voir dire extends beyond one day, counsel should arrange to have a confederate arrive early on the following day to observe jurors as they arrive for the day's session. Note should be made of the jurors' automobiles, and any bumper stickers on their cars. Is the juror carrying a newspaper—is it the *New York Times* or the *National Inquirer?* Particularly important is whether more than one juror arrive in the same car, a clear sign of friendship.

All jurors should be observed during the judge's initial conditioning, as well as during voir dire, for glances, frowns, or other expressions which may indicate favor or disfavor toward either party. Signs of boredom or lack of interest are also noteworthy. The information obtained by this type of observation is not foolproof, but it is certainly relevant and forms part of the lawyer's total picture of each juror. In close cases, it may tip the balance in favor of the peremptory challenge of one or more jurors.

§9.04 Purposes of Voir Dire

The theoretical purpose of voir dire is to determine the state of the jurors' minds so that a fair and impartial jury can be chosen. For counsel to be able to exercise an informed challenge to a juror, either for cause or peremptorily, it is essential to have as much knowledge as possible of all matters which might compromise the juror's impartiality. The voir dire examination also provides the judge with the information needed to make a proper ruling on whether an individual is qualified to serve as a juror.

While the theoretical purpose of voir dire may be to ascertain sufficient information to be able to select a fair and impartial jury, many attorneys use it for other purposes.[7] Some, recognizing the value of first impressions, strive to impress jurors with the merits of their cause. Their voir dire tends to become the functional equivalent of an opening statement. Their goal is to preview their case for the jurors, hoping to condition the jurors' expectations.

Other lawyers, convinced that jurors try the attorneys as much as the facts, use voir dire to establish rapport with the jurors. The first step in this process is to establish one's credibility and the second is to cultivate the jurors' favor. The lawyer wants to identify those jurors whom the lawyer likes and those jurors who like the lawyer. The lawyer must take care, however, that the attempt to establish rapport is not perceived as a feeble attempt at ingratiation.

Still other lawyers see voir dire as a time for education and indoctrination. If permitted by the court, they will explain to the jurors the applicable principles of law and why those principles will inevitably compel the jury to find in favor of their client. Questions asked by these attorneys tend not to be questions at all, but rather statements preceded by, "I am sure that you agree, do you not, with the proposition of law which states . . ." The perfunctory response of the juror is largely irrelevant.

The various purposes of voir dire so far identified are not mutually exclusive. In a well integrated voir dire the lawyer will educate the jurors, establish rapport, preview the case, *and* uncover enough information to exercise challenges intelligently.

The agenda of the attorney who has conducted mock trials and engaged in pretrial investigation of the community and the venire (as advocated in Part II of this book) may be somewhat different. Where the attorney has constructed profiles of favorable and unfavorable jurors from the results of community surveys and mock trials, part of the goal in voir dire is to match the members of the panel with the juror profiles. The attorney accomplishes this by asking the jurors the same background questions asked of the persons in the mock trials

---

[7] *See generally* Broeder, *Voir Dire Examinations: An Empirical Study,* 38 S Cal L Rev 503 (1965); Campbell, *The Multiple Functions of the Criminal Defense Voir Dire in Texas,* 1 Am J Crim L 255 (1972).

and community surveys. The lawyer wants to ascertain which prospective jurors have the same demographic, attitudinal, and socio-psychological characteristics as the favorable jurors in the mock trials and community surveys.

The attorney who has conducted a pretrial investigation of the venire will often be able to omit areas of questioning altogether. In particular, the attorney need not go into sensitive matters which might embarrass the juror. Some questioning may still be necessary in order to confirm the results of the investigation, and some may be necessary to explore areas which were not covered in the investigation, but the questioning can often be less direct and more tactful. If the pretrial investigation suggests that a certain juror is likely to be very favorable, the attorney may choose to ask only perfunctory, closed-ended questions which will prevent the juror from making a disqualifying slip or saying anything which might alert opposing counsel to the desirability of challenging the juror. The attorney can also concentrate on establishing rapport with the favorable juror.

The lawyer who has undertaken mock trials, pretrial surveys, and investigations of the venire, however, should not lose sight of the other purposes of voir dire. As indicated, these include the establishment of rapport, the previewing of the party's theory of the case, the education of the jury with regard to applicable legal principles, and the conditioning of the jurors' expectations. Because of these multiple functions of voir dire, it should hardly ever, if ever, be waived.

§9.05 Judge- or Counsel-Conducted Voir Dire

In federal court, the Federal Rules of Civil Procedure permit the court to conduct the voir dire or to allow counsel to do so.[8] If the court elects to conduct the voir dire, as it usually does, it may permit the attorneys to ask additional questions. In criminal cases, the same rule applies: the court may conduct the voir dire itself or it may permit the lawyers to conduct it; if the court is of the view that additional voir dire is desirable, following its own examination, it may solicit further questions from counsel or permit counsel to ask further questions.[9] Voir dire examinations conducted by trial judges under these federal rule provisions have been consistently upheld.[10]

In practically every federal court, the judge does conduct most, if not all, of the voir dire. Typically the judge will briefly describe the lawsuit to be tried and then ask the jurors as a group general questions regarding their knowledge of the case or acquaintance with the parties, witnesses, or attorneys, together with other general questions directed to possible grounds of disqualification. This portion of voir dire is often rather brief. The attorneys will then be offered

---

[8] Fed R Civ P 47(a).

[9] Fed R Crim P 24(a).

[10] *E.g.*, United States v White, 750 F2d 726 (8th Cir 1983); United States v Ainsworth, 716 F2d 769 (10th Cir 1983); Hamer v United States, 259 F2d 274 (9th Cir 1958), *cert denied*, 359 US 916 (1959). *See generally* Annotation, *Right of Counsel in Criminal Case to Conduct the Voir Dire Examination of Prospective jurors*, 73 ALR2d 1187 (1960).

the opportunity to supplement the court's questions with questions of their own. If it is the practice of the judge to pose these supplemental questions to the jurors rather than allowing the attorneys to do so, the attorneys may have to prepare the questions in writing and submit them in advance of trial.[11]

Most state jurisdictions also permit the trial judge the option of conducting the voir dire personally or allowing counsel to do so.[12] It is the responsibility of the trial court to satisfy itself that each member of the jury panel is qualified and unbiased, and in discharging this responsibility the judge has considerable discretionary power.[13] Individual practices vary: some state court judges follow the federal example and conduct most of the voir dire themselves; others ask a few general questions and leave the case-specific questioning to counsel; and still others permit counsel to conduct the entire voir dire.

§9.06 —Arguments for Questioning by Judge

The factor most cited in favor of court-conducted voir dire is the saving in time. Court-conducted voir dire avoids lengthy, repetitious, and unnecessary questioning of the panel by the lawyers. (The response to this argument, of course, is, as one court said with respect to individual questioning of jurors: "The time required for individual examination is small when compared with the possibility of a new trial."[14]) Perhaps more compelling arguments in support of judge-conducted voir dire are the following: (1) judges will be more even handed, and will not mislead the jurors by their questions; (2) judges can ask questions which need to be asked but which might prove embarrassing to jurors—whatever offense is taken by a juror will be visited on the court, and not on the attorney who would otherwise be forced to ask the question; and (3) judges will not spend time, as might attorneys, in efforts to indoctrinate or cultivate the favor of jurors.[15]

The United States Supreme Court has held that in a criminal case the trial court must not abuse its discretion in conducting the voir dire examination and that restrictions upon inquiries by counsel must satisfy the essential demands of fairness. Thus in *Aldridge v United States,*[16] and *Turner v Murray,*[17] the failure to question jurors on racial prejudice was held to be prejudicial

---

[11] *See* United States v Dellinger, 472 F2d 340 (7th Cir 1972), *cert denied,* 410 US 970 (1973).

[12] *See, e.g.,* Connor v State, 225 Md 543, 171 A2d 699, *cert denied,* 368 US 906 (1961); Commonwealth v Spencer, 212 Mass 438, 99 NE 266 (1912).

[13] *See generally* Annotation, *Right of Counsel in Criminal Case to Conduct the Voir Dire Examination of Prospective Jurors,* 73 ALR2d 1187 (1960).

[14] United States v Starks, 515 F2d 112, 125 (3d Cir 1975), *affd in part, revd in part,* 431 US 651 (1977).

[15] *See generally* Stanley, *Who Should Conduct Voir Dire? The Judge,* 61 Judicature 70 (1977).

[16] 283 US 308 (1931).

[17] 476 US 28 (1986).

error.[18] *Aldridge* was concerned with racial prejudice in respect to verdict and *Turner* in respect to penalty, but the basic principle was the same—the trial judge's discretion relating to voir dire questions is bounded by legal and constitutional constraints.

§9.07 —Arguments for Questioning by Counsel

Most trial lawyers are convinced that voir dire examination should be conducted by counsel.[19] It is the *only* phase of a trial where the attorneys have the opportunity for give-and-take contact with prospective jurors. It gives the attorneys the opportunity to confront jurors personally, asking pertinent questions to unearth prejudices which would make particular panel members undesirable or unacceptable. It also allows the jurors the opportunity to get to know the attorneys and to see if there is any reason why they cannot be fair to them, as well as to their clients.

The primary objective of the court in jury selection is to ensure a fair and impartial jury. Although this concern may be uppermost in a judge's mind, the judge may also be sensitive, consciously or subconsciously, to a crowded docket. A judge is more inclined than counsel to want to end the preliminaries quickly and to proceed to the actual trial.

Another criticism frequently made by attorneys of judge-conducted voir dire is that the phrasing of the judge's questions and the judge's demeanor often suggest to the jurors the appropriate answers. The jurors, anxious to please the judge, will readily give the "correct" response. This lack of candor may promote efficiency, but it will not help identify jurors who are not impartial.

The trial attorney has the same basic goal of fairness as a judge, but is often more demanding than the judge. While a judge tends to search for jurors who meet the minimum standard of impartiality that the law requires, an attorney seeks the best jurors available for the particular case. In addition, the attorney desires that those who are selected start in an appropriate frame of mind, and with a knowledge of the theories on which recovery or its denial is sought.

The attorney believes that these objectives can best be reached by an examination of the jury panel, preferably individually, by the lawyer. The lawyer is more familiar with the facts of the case and more cognizant of the types of jurors best suited to serve on the case. The judge, though experienced in litigation generally, is rarely sufficiently knowledgeable about the nuances of the particular case to pinpoint all the potential biases that may exist in a juror's mind.[20] The judge is unlikely to have given the same thought and preparation to the case as the lawyer. Finally, questioning by the judge will not elicit possible hostility to an attorney.

---

[18] *See also* Ham v South Carolina, 409 US 524 (1973). *But see* Ristaino v Ross, 424 US 589 (1976). *See generally* **§9.12.**

[19] *See, e.g.,* Gutman, *The Attorney-Conducted Voir Dire of Jurors: A Constitutional Right,* 39 Brooklyn L Rev 290 (1972).

[20] *See* United States v Ible, 630 F2d 385, 395 (5th Cir 1980); United States v Ledee, 549 F2d 990, 993 (5th Cir), *cert denied,* 434 US 902 (1977).

An argument for voir dire examination by counsel is not an argument for examination which is unlimited or uncontrolled. The trial judge has the discretion to regulate the inquiry.[21] This discretion gives the court the right to restrict the extent, scope, and duration of the examination. Redundant or inflammatory questioning can be halted, as can questioning designed to curry favor or commit jurors to a particular verdict. The judge's discretion, however, is restricted by the essential demands of fairness.[22]

§9.08 Group, Individual, and In Camera Questioning

Panel members may be interrogated as a whole, in small groups, individually, or both as a group and as individuals. Some jurisdictions specify that each juror be examined individually,[23] but in most, panel members tend to be examined either collectively or in small groups (usually groups of four). Appellate courts have considered whether the right to examine jurors (if such a right exists) is improperly abridged by a trial judge's refusal to allow individual questioning. In most instances, they have decided that the matter properly lay within the trial judge's discretion.[24]

On a policy level there are both advantages and disadvantages to the various approaches. Group questioning is efficient but is least likely to elicit a response from an individual juror. The implicit group pressure for conformity will likely dissuade a juror from raising his hand when the panel is asked, for example, whether any member would be biased against a party because of the party's occupation. Individual questioning is more likely to reveal such prejudice but asking the same questions of each juror can be repetitive, time-consuming, and tedious. Moreover, the judge's or the lawyer's response to an early answer to a question may educate other jurors as to what to respond in order to stay on or to be excused from the jury. Once a lawyer embarks on individual questioning, the lawyer may become committed to asking the same questions of all jurors lest any juror feel slighted by not being asked a particular question.

The most appropriate manner of proceeding depends in part on the nature of the questions to be asked. Routine questions, such as whether any member of the panel knows any of the parties, lawyers, or witnesses, are best addressed to the panel as a whole, with individual questioning of any juror who gives an affirmative answer. Other questions, such as those relating to personal experiences and prejudices, need to be put to jurors individually. Alternating between questions to the panel as a whole and to individual jurors, even in a somewhat

---

[21] *See* Aldridge v United States, 283 US 308 (1931).

[22] *Id;* Sellers v United States, 271 F2d 475 (DC Cir 1959).

[23] *See, e.g.,* Springdale Park, Inc v Andriotis, 30 NJ Super 257, 104 A2d 327 (1954).

[24] *E.g.,* Fredericks v United States, 292 F 856 (9th Cir 1923); Connor v State, 225 Md 543, 171 A2d 699, *cert denied,* 368 US 906 (1961). *But see* United States v Dansker, 537 F2d 40 (3d Cir 1976), *cert denied,* 429 US 1038 (1977). *See generally* Annotation, *Right of Counsel in Criminal Case to Conduct the Voir Dire Examination of Prospective Jurors,* 73 ALR2d 1187, 1203 §7 (1960).

random fashion, has the advantage of variety, and will require the jurors to stay alert, as they will never be quite sure when they will next be called upon to participate.

In some cases it is desirable to conduct an *in camera* voir dire.[25] There are several advantages. One is to avoid embarrassing jurors on subjects which are personal and controversial. Jurors may also be more candid if questioned out of the presence of others, and the potential for peer group pressure affecting a juror's responses will be lessened.[26] In camera questioning will also prevent the corrupting of all members of the panel by the response of a single juror. In addition, in camera questioning has the advantage of preventing jurors from learning (by observing the questioning of another juror) what is an acceptable and what an unacceptable response to a question.

Despite the advantages of in camera voir dire, it is doubtful that it will be constitutionally required. Indeed, it may be constitutionally prohibited. In *Press-Enterprise Co v Superior Court,*[27] the United States Supreme Court stated that the interests of the press and public required voir dire in open court unless closure was "essential to preserve higher values and [was] narrowly tailored to serve that interest.[28]

Whether or not voir dire is conducted in camera, there is much to be said for allowing all challenges to be made in camera or at least out of the presence of the jury. Jurors will then not know which side is responsible for the challenge. Otherwise, jurors challenged unsuccessfully for cause may resent the attorney who made the challenge, as may friends of jurors who are successfully challenged. As a practical matter, however, jurors will be able to make an educated guess as to which side challenged a juror; it will usually be the side which most vigorously questioned the juror.

Challenges made in the presence of the jury must be handled tactfully. The juror should be thanked by the lawyer, and the court told that the juror's services will not be needed. If a challenge for cause to a particular juror is rejected, the standard advice is to use a peremptory challenge to strike that juror. The theory is that the juror is likely to have become alienated by the challenge. This should not be considered an iron-clad rule, however, for in some instances voir dire may have so sensitized the juror to the danger of prejudice that the juror will bend over backwards to be fair to the lawyer who made the challenge. The juror may want to prove that the lawyer was wrong to have challenged him or her.

---

[25] *See* United States v Colabella, 448 F2d 1299 (2d Cir 1971), *cert denied,* 405 US 929 (1972).

[26] *See* Irvin v Dowd, 366 US 717, 728 (1961) ("No doubt each juror was sincere when he said he would be fair and impartial, . . . but the psychological impact of requiring such a declaration before one's fellows is often its father").

[27] 464 US 501 (1984).

[28] *Id* 510.

§9.09 Attitudes and Demeanor of Counsel

Counsel must be sensitive to his or her demeanor during voir dire.[29] The view of the typical trial lawyer, probably correct, is that the lawyer is a salesperson. Counsel is selling a product—the client's side of the story—whether it be the cause of action of a plaintiff in a personal injury suit, the defense of an accused in a criminal case, or the defense of a corporation in a products liability case. The attorney is trying to convince the jury of the superiority of counsel's product (cause of action) over the product being offered by the other side. Counsel should have, and must display, confidence in that product. Counsel should take on the personality traits of a good salesperson—generally warm, pleasant and friendly; never bullying, antagonistic or overbearing (although it must be conceded that some attorneys, like some salespersons, use the disapproved tactics to good advantage).

Judge Jordan, the author of the first edition of this book, told of a trial in which one of the lawyers was extremely abrasive. During the lawyer's examination of the jury, one panel member, when asked if there was any reason why he could not be impartial, replied: "Yes—I find you very obnoxious and insulting, and I could not be a fair juror in any case in which you are involved." Needless to say, this outburst caused some embarrassment to the lawyer, if to no one else. The juror was excused, and the remaining panel members were instructed that they should disregard the juror's comments. Many a juror, however, no doubt secretly harbors the sentiments to which this particular juror was so bold as to give expression.

Although the lawyer is a salesperson, the lawyer does well to remember that in the eyes of many, salespersons have acquired a reputation for sleaziness. The lawyer, unlike the salesperson, is also a professional, and should act professionally. The lawyer's dress, speech, and manner should at all times be that of a professional. Just as a lawyer should respect the jurors, the lawyer should behave in a manner that will cause the jurors to respect him or her.

One of the best ways of showing respect for a juror, as well as establishing rapport, is to take a genuine interest in what the juror has to say. Maintain eye contact while the juror is speaking. Provide encouragement, perhaps with a gentle head nod. Reinforce through repetition favorable responses. Try not to leave too great a physical distance between yourself and the juror, but do not tower over the juror (three to six feet is probably the appropriate distance of separation). And never ignore the juror who is answering your question by scribbling, talking to the client or a colleague, or turning your back to the juror.

---

[29] *See generally* 1 M. Belli, Modern Trials §§112-121 (1954); F. Bailey & H. Rothblatt, Successful Techniques for Criminal Trials §§78-98 (1971); I. Goldstein, Trial Techniques §§9.33-.75 (2d ed 1969); 1 S. Schweitzer, Cyclopedia of Trial Practice §§144-146 (2d ed 1954).

§9.10 Juror's Duty of Full Disclosure

There is a right not to be arbitrarily or discriminatorily excluded by law from jury service,[30] but there is arguably a correlative duty not to serve on a jury if one is not able to do so fairly and impartially. In order to be able to exercise challenges in an intelligent manner, a lawyer must know everything which could disqualify a juror or cast doubt on the juror's impartiality. Jury selection is difficult under the best of circumstances, but it is more difficult if the lawyer does not have all the information concerning a juror's views on matters relevant to the case at hand or is denied insight into the juror's prejudices. It is therefore a juror's duty, undertaken under oath,[31] to answer truthfully and in full all questions asked on voir dire. A juror must not falsely state any fact, conceal any relevant matter, or mislead counsel in any way. The judge should, in the strongest possible terms, emphasize the need for juror honesty and candor in responding to voir dire questions.[32] The lawyer at the outset of voir dire should reinforce this message.

A juror's failure to properly respond to voir dire questions does not automatically entitle a party to a reversal or a new trial. If the misstatement is relatively insignificant, or only remotely suggestive of a lack of impartiality, it will most likely be deemed harmless. Prejudice must be shown before a litigant will be entitled to a new trial because of misleading or inaccurate statements by a prospective juror, and the trial judge is usually deemed to be in the best position to decide whether a party has suffered prejudice.[33]

The constitutional demensions of this issue were explored by the United States Supreme Court in *McDonough Power Equipment v Greenwood.*[34] The Court held that a juror's honest but mistaken response to a voir dire question would not warrant a new trial unless the juror's failure to disclose denied a party its right to an impartial jury. Citing the practical necessities of judicial management, the Court said that an aggrieved party had to establish: (1) that a juror had failed to honestly answer a *material* question on voir dire; and (2) that a correct answer would have established a basis for a challenge for cause. That a correct response would have led to the exercise of a peremptory challenge was not enough to override the interest of the judicial system in finality.

A few state courts have taken the position that a juror's false or incomplete answer to a question on voir dire can itself be the basis for a new trial. In a

---

30 *See generally* **ch 6.**

31 The language used may vary from state to state, but in general the trial judge gives the entire jury panel the following oath, or something very similar: "Do each of you solemnly swear that you will give true and complete answers to all questions concerning your qualifications and service as a juror, so help you God?" The juror who violates that oath not only commits perjury, but undermines the right to an impartial jury.

32 *See* **§9.02.**

33 McDonough Power Equip v Greenwood, 464 US 548 (1984); Reich v Thompson, 346 Mo 577, 142 SW2d 486 (1940); Firestone v Freiling, 22 Ohio Op 2d 356, 188 NE2d 91 (1963); *see also* Annotation, *Effect of Juror's False or Erroneous Answer on Voir Dire as to Previous Claims or Actions Against Himself or His Family,* 63 ALR2d 1061, 1063 §2 (1959).

34 464 US 548 (1984).

Kentucky case, *Drury v Franke,*[35] the court stated that when it appears that a juror has given false information on voir dire, and the information is relied upon, the right of the aggrieved party to a new trial follows as a matter of law. The court's opinion was based on the following chain of reasoning:

1. The right to challenge a juror peremptorily is one of the rights which assure a party a fair trial
2. The right to challenge need not be exercised until the party has an opportunity to examine a prospective juror
3. The right to challenge includes the incidental right to truth in information elicited from the juror, and if a party is misled by erroneous information, the right of challenge is impaired
4. If false information prevents a challenge, the party's right so loses its efficacy as to amount to its deprivation
5. The fact that a juror who is disqualified has served on the panel is a sufficient ground for setting aside the verdict, even without an affirmative showing that this fact accounts for the verdict
6. The fact that the false information was unintentional is irrelevant, as the harm lies in the falsity of the information, regardless of the informant's knowledge of its falsity[36]

The rule in *Drury* is arguably too draconian. Indisputably jurors should give full and accurate answers to questions propounded on voir dire. The fact, however, is that sometimes they do not. Jurors are thrust into unfamiliar circumstances, and in many cases give incomplete or inaccurate answers unintentionally. Sometimes a juror does not understand the import of a question; other times the juror believes that a complete answer would be so long and involved that nobody would want to hear it. Before a false or incomplete answer of a prospective juror should be held to warrant a new trial, it should have to be shown that a party was in effect deprived of the right to question that particular juror or that the juror in question was biased against the complaining party.

The holding in *Drury* was subsequently qualified in another Kentucky case, *Crutcher v Hicks.*[37] The court said that false or misleading statements on voir dire should not invariably result in reversal:

> If the false information is of such character as to indicate probable bias on the part of the juror, it may be presumed that a free exercise of the right of peremptory challenge has been so restricted as to result in prejudice to the party affected; [but] if information innocently withheld or

---

[35] 247 Ky 758, 57 SW2d 969 (1933).

[36] *See also* Stillwell v Johnson, 272 P2d 365 (Okla 1954).

[37] 257 SW2d 539 (Ky Ct App 1953).

given, although false, is so insignificant or trifling as to indicate only a remote or speculative influence on the jury, the right of peremptory challenge has not been affected.[38]

In order to obtain a reversal based on a juror's false or misleading answers to voir dire questions, a party should not be required to establish that the verdict would have been different. This inquiry is too speculative. It would require examination of a particular juror's role in the verdict. Given prevailing rules prohibiting juror impeachment of verdicts or disclosure of the deliberations,[39] such an examination is neither possible nor desirable.

§9.11 Court's Duty and Discretion

As essential and vital as voir dire is, it must be kept within reasonable limits. Probably the major criticism of voir dire is the amount of time expended on it. Questioning of prospective jurors has not infrequently taken longer than the trial itself.[40] In part this is attributable to a tendency by some lawyers to unduly prolong examination in an effort to ingratiate themselves with the panel and to indoctrinate jurors with their theory of the case.

The responsibility for keeping voir dire within bounds lies with the trial judge. No matter who conducts voir dire, the trial judge must oversee the examination, using discretion wisely in controlling the extent and scope of inquiries made. The exercise of this discretion is constitutionally constrained by the essential demands of fairness.[41]

The trial court of necessity has broad discretion as to the scope of voir dire, the form and number of questions permitted, and the length of time allocated to the process.[42] In one illustrative case it was held that a trial court's denial of extra time beyond the 30 minutes allowed for voir dire was not error.[43] The party seeking the extra time gave no reason for the request; nor did counsel's loosely organized questions provide a basis for the request. In light of this and comparable decisions, a lawyer seeking extended time for voir dire is well-advised to place on record the reasons why such time is needed.

An abuse of the trial court's discretion was found in *United States v Segal,*[44] a case of alleged bribery of an internal revenue agent. It was held that the trial court erred in refusing to ask, or permit defense counsel to ask, if anyone on the jury or any juror's immediate family member was employed by the Internal

---

[38] *Id* 540. *See generally* Annotation, *supra* note 33.

[39] *See* Tanner v United States, 483 US 107 (1987). *See also* Fed R Evid 606(b).

[40] *See* Chambers, *Who Should Pick Jurors, Attorneys or the Judge,* NY Times, (June 13, 1983), at B4 (in 20% of cases in New York study, voir dire exceeded trial).

[41] Aldridge v United States, 283 US 308 (1931); Moore v Atchison, T & SF Ry, 28 Ill App 2d 340, 171 NE2d 393 (1960); Commonwealth v Ricard, 355 Mass 509, 246 NE2d 433 (1969).

[42] *See* Ham v South Carolina, 409 US 524 (1973).

[43] Barrett v State, 516 SW2d 181 (Tex Crim App 1974), *cert denied,* 420 US 938 (1975).

[44] 534 F2d 578 (3d Cir 1976).

Revenue Service. The judge also refused to ask about specific employment activities of some jurors who had intimated that they were employed by the federal government. A new trial was ordered.

The trial court's exercise of discretion in conducting voir dire will not generally be reversed unless a petitioner can show not only that there has been a clear abuse of discretion but also that the party suffered prejudice as a result.[45] One federal court put it this way: "We recognize that there is no generally accepted formula for determining the appropriate breadth and depth of the voir dire, except that the court's discretion is subject to the essential demands of fairness.[46]

§9.12 Example: Racial Prejudice Questions

The trial court's discretion is limited only by the demands of essential fairness and is reviewable only for abuse.[47] Two United States Supreme Court decisions illustrate the application of these principles in cases where trial courts had refused questions relating to racial prejudice. In *Ham v South Carolina,*[48] a bearded black civil rights worker charged with possession of marijuana claimed that the police had framed him. Although issues of racial prejudice seemed likely to arise, the trial judge denied a defense request to question prospective jurors about racial prejudice, as well as about prejudice against people with beards.

The Supreme Court held that the failure to allow questioning on racial prejudice was in violation of the fourteenth amendment. The Court's holding was premised not on the constitutional guaranty of an impartial jury, but on the idea that "a principal purpose of the adoption of the Fourteenth Amendment was to prohibit the states from invidiously discriminating on the basis of race. . . ."[49]

In contrast, the Court held that the refusal to permit questioning with respect to prejudice against persons with beards was not error. The Court stated that it could not "constitutionally distinguish possible similar prejudices. . . ."[50] This aspect of the Court's holding seems to ignore the fundamental purpose of voir dire—discovery of any prejudice that might affect the impartiality of the jury.

---

[45] Mercer v Commonwealth, 330 SW2d 734 (Ky Ct App 1959); Bullock v Sklar, 349 SW2d 381 (Mo Ct App 1961); Tellefsen v Key Sys Transit Lines, 158 Cal App 2d 243, 322 P2d 469 (1958).

[46] United States v Dellinger, 472 F2d 340, 367 (7th Cir 1972), *cert denied,* 410 US 970 (1973).

[47] Ham v South Carolina, 409 US 524 (1973); Aldridge v United States, 283 US 308, 310 (1931); United States v DePugh, 452 F2d 915 (10th Cir 1971), *cert denied,* 407 US 920 (1972).

[48] 409 US 524 (1973).

[49] *Id* 526-27.

[50] *Id* 528.

In the 1976 case of Ristaino v Ross,[51] a black defendant was charged with the assault of a white security guard. The trial court refused to permit inquiry into racial bias, limiting the questioning to a general inquiry into prejudice. The Supreme Court distinguished *Ham* on its facts. The Court stated that in *Ham,* because of the defendant's civil rights activity and his defense that he was being framed, "racial issues . . . were inextricably bound up with the conduct of the trial".[52] The Court found a critical difference in *Ross:*

> The mere fact that the victim of the crimes alleged was a white man and the defendants were Negroes was less likely to distort the trial than were the special factors involved in *Ham.* . . . The circumstances thus did not suggest a significant likelihood that racial prejudice might infect Ross' trial.[53]

The Court held that the constitutional demands of due process could be satisfied by a "generalized but thorough inquiry into the impartiality of the veniremen".[54] The Court did, however, suggest that while its holding defined minimum constitutional requirements, the better practice would be to allow such questioning: "Under our supervisory power we would have required as much [i.e., mandating inquiry] of a federal court faced with the circumstances here. The states are also free to follow or require questions not demanded by the constitution".[55]

Ross seems to imply that before questioning on racial prejudice will be *constitutionally* required there must be some nexus between the prejudice feared and the issues likely to arise in the trial. This test seems to be a strong reaffirmation of the role of the trial judge in determining the limits of voir dire.

§9.13 Scope of Examination

The scope of voir dire examination should encompass any matter which would disclose prejudice against any party, witness, or attorney, or on any issue. The inquiry, however, must directly relate to the issues involved in the case and to the existence of bias. In suit on a promissory note, for instance, inquiry into possible prejudice against banks or lending institutions or questions dealing with an individual juror's experience with repayment of loans would be proper; inquiry into a juror's politics or religion would not. To illustrate the case-specific nature of the inquiry, however, questions on a juror's political views might be proper where the defendant's reason for not repaying the promissory note was a Marxist conviction that all members of a society were equally entitled to share in the society's wealth.

---

[51] 424 US 589 (1976).

[52] Ristaino v Ross, 424 US 589, 597 (1976).

[53] *Id* 597-98.

[54] *Id* 598.

[55] *Id* 597 n 9 (citations omitted).

Because of the all-embracing nature of prejudice, and because prejudices often exist on a subconscious level and are difficult to root out, great latitude should be allowed in voir dire.[56] Unfortunately, most courts tend to take a restrictive approach,[57] most likely for reasons of efficiency. Arguably, an examination is proper so long as it aims directly at discovering a juror's state of mind with respect to the case itself or any collateral matter reasonably likely to have an undue influence in the case.[58] Some sense of the potential range of topics which might be covered in a case can be gathered by looking into the various grounds of challenge for cause discussed in Chapter 7.

As a general proposition, courts will not allow counsel to inquire into extrinsic, collateral matters which have no bearing on the case. A resourceful attorney however, may be able to persuade a court of the merits of asking jurors their views of highly publicized incidents unconnected to the case as a means of indirectly discovering a juror's prejudices. Thus, in the prosecution of a political activist, defense counsel might ask the jurors' views on the Vietnam War; if the defendant is a military officer, the jurors' views of a well-publicized defense department scandal; and if the defendant is black, the jurors' views on a recent urban riot.

Matters which are not proper subjects for trial will not be permitted on voir dire. Whether a party is insured, whether there have been settlement negotiations, and whether a defendant has a criminal record may, depending on the jurisdiction, not be gone into at trial. Their insertion on voir dire, by means subtle, surreptitious, or otherwise, will likewise be improper and can lead to a mistrial.[59]

In most jurisdictions attorneys for both sides are permitted on voir dire to explain the general nature of the case to the jury, to set forth their respective positions, and to briefly state what they expect the evidence to show. This introductory statement is sometimes overdone to the extent that a lawyer will actually make two opening statements: one on voir dire, and the other at the time reserved for opening statements. This arguably improper tactic poses a dilemma for opposing counsel, forced to either object, risking the alienation of jurors interested in what the lawyer has to say, or remain silent, risking the opposing lawyer's gaining an unfair advantage.

The situation should be controlled by the trial court. The judge should explain to the jury that counsel are permitted to state their positions and to explain briefly what they expect the evidence to show, but that they are not permitted to go into detail with respect to the evidence. This explanation

---

[56] *See* United States v Peterson, 483 F2d 1222 (DC Cir), *cert denied,* 414 US 1007 (1973); Delaney v United States, 199 F2d 107 (1st Cir 1952).

[57] *See generally* Annotation, *Racial, Religious, Economic, Social, or Political Prejudice of Proposed Juror as Proper Subject of Inquiry or Ground of Challenge on Voir Dire in Civil Case,* 72 ALR2d 905, 907 (1960).

[58] *See* Loveland v Nieters, 79 ND 1, 54 NW2d 533 (1952); Parker v Hoefer, 118 Vt 1, 100 A2d 434 (1953).

[59] *See* Tellefsen v Key Sys Transit Lines, 158 Cal App 2d 243, 322 P2d 469 (1958); Stehura v Short, 39 Ohio App 2d 68, 315 NE2d 492 (1974).

should be given both during the preconditioning[60] and if counsel exceeds permissible bounds.

Greater latitude should be allowed on voir dire in criminal cases than in civil cases. The reason is that the opportunity to demonstrate actual bias is arguably an integral part of the defendant's sixth amendment right to an impartial jury.[61] It is therefore commonly held that a defendant in a criminal case should be allowed to make relevant inquiries of a prospective juror not only for the purpose of establishing a basis for a challenge for cause but also for the purpose of determining whether to exercise a peremptory challenge.[62] In a Kansas case, for example, where the defendant was charged with abortion, the court stated that counsel's attempt to uncover bias justified questioning on the moral attitudes of jurors to abortion, even though such attitudes were technically immaterial.[63]

§9.14 Jurors' Privacy Rights

A 1979 federal court case, *United States v Barnes*,[64] illustrates the broad discretion of the trial judge in the matter of the extent and scope of voir dire examination generally and how it can be exercised to insure juror privacy. The case involved alleged violations of federal narcotics laws. The trial court conducted the voir dire, and announced that it planned to withhold the names and addresses of prospective jurors from counsel. It also refused to inquire into the religious and ethnic backgrounds of the jurors.

Eleven of the fifteen defendants were convicted. On appeal they contended that they were denied the opportunity to intelligently exercise their peremptory challenges by the actions of the trial judge. The appellate court held that the trial judge had the authority to withhold the names and addresses of jurors in a criminal trial in the interest of their safety, and could prohibit questioning about religion and ethnicity in order to preserve their privacy.

The appellate court observed that the trial judge has broad discretion in conducting voir dire, and that this discretion will generally be upheld unless the defendant has been prevented from obtaining an impartial jury. The court concluded that defense counsel had not demonstrated a need to go into the religious and ethnic background of the jurors. It also found that there was no evidence that any particular group would be biased on the issues, and that the trial judge's questioning would have brought to light any racial prejudice against the black or Hispanic defendants. The unlikelihood that the questions would uncover bias made the proposed intrusion into private beliefs even less

---

[60] See **§9.02.**

[61] Morford v United States, 339 US 258 (1950); Dennis v United States, 339 US 162 (1950).

[62] *See, e.g.*, United States v Bear Runner, 502 F2d 908 (8th Cir 1974); United States v Dellinger, 472 F2d 340 (7th Cir 1972), *cert denied*, 410 US 970 (1973); People v Williams, 29 Cal 3d 392, 628 P2d 869, 174 Cal Rptr 317 (1981).

[63] State v Darling, 208 Kan 469, 493 P2d 216 (1972).

[64] 604 F2d 121 (2d Cir 1979), *cert denied*, 446 US 907 (1980).

defensible. The court opined that the possibility of having their private affairs unnecessarily exposed might make citizens less willing to serve on juries.

The appellate court's finding on the reasonableness of the trial judge's action in keeping names and addresses secret was based on several factors peculiar to *Barnes:* the overall "sordid history" of narcotics prosecutions in the district; the fact that one witness had already been threatened; and the considerable pretrial publicity given to the case. Less extreme facts may warrant less drastic restrictions. *Barnes,* however, does indicate the trial judge's authority to protect juror privacy.[65]

§9.15 Open- & Closed-Ended Questions

Traditional voir dire tends to resemble cross-examination, with lawyers asking jurors a series of closed-ended questions calling for either a yes-no or a short answer response. Why this should be so is unclear. In cross-examination the lawyer is attempting to either make a very narrow point or discredit a witness. The lawyer does not want to give the witness the leeway to make a potentially damaging response. In voir dire the lawyer is trying to discover sufficient information about the juror to make an enlightened decision as to whether to challenge the juror. The lawyer should want to give the juror as much leeway as possible. A damaging response will indicate the unsuitability of the juror. To this end, open-ended questions are often apt to be more illuminating than closed-ended questions.

An open-ended question is like a Rorschach ink blot test. There is no right or wrong answer. Rather, the respondent, be it psychiatric patient or prospective juror, is put in an ambiguous situation where the answer will reveal the respondent's inner thoughts. As in a Rorschach test, an open-ended question may elicit an unanticipated response and suggest a line of inquiry not previously considered. The open-ended question, because it more often results in an extended response, will also be more revealing of the juror's personality, articulateness, and leadership potential on the jury.

Take the common case where an attorney represents a black defendant and is concerned about racial bias. To ask a juror a closed-ended question such as, "Would you be prejudiced against the defendant because he is black?," will avail nothing. A negative answer will be semi-automatic. It will be the rare juror who will openly admit to being a racist. Indeed, the lawyer's question itself suggests the answer; the juror knows that the "correct" response is "no." Moreover, the juror may actually believe that the true answer is no; the juror may be unaware of his or her own prejudice.

Much more likely to flush out bias is an open-ended question: "Would you please describe to us your experience with blacks." No particular answer is expected, and the juror's response will be revealing of the juror's character. The juror must choose which incidents to relate, and the juror must choose what words to use in relating those incidents. The attorney may come at the

---

[65] *See also* Press-Enter Co v Superior Court, 464 US 501 (1984).

issue even more indirectly. For example: "Mrs. Williams, you have said that your husband works in the construction industry. There has been considerable publicity recently about the government's affirmative action policies in the construction industry. I would imagine that you and your husband have had occasion to talk about these policies and their effects. If so, could you please tell us about those discussions?" Similarly, questions about interracial marriage or urban riots may lead a juror to reveal latent racial prejudice.

Another illustration can be drawn with respect to the burden of proof in a criminal case. A question of whether a juror understands that the state must prove its case beyond a reasonable doubt will invariably yield an affirmative answer. Instead, the lawyer might profitably ask what the phrase *beyond a reasonable doubt* means to the juror. The latter question forces the juror to think about the concept and to articulate those thoughts.

This is not to say that all voir dire questioning should be open-ended. Closed-ended questions may be needed to pin down ambiguous answers or to avoid potential responses that may prejudice other members of the panel. There are also jurors who feel too nervous to respond to open-ended questions; closed-ended questions may be necessary to draw them out. Sometimes, as in cross-examination, where the goal is to discredit a witness, the lawyer's goal is to disqualify a juror. The lawyer may know from the response to a previous question or from pretrial investigation that a prospective juror will be unfavorable. A series of closed-ended questions aimed at exposing the juror's bias is needed to lay the basis for a challenge for cause. Conversely, where pretrial investigation suggests that a juror is likely to be favorable, a series of close-ended questions will prevent the juror from making a disqualifying slip and at the same time not alert opposing counsel to the need to challenge the juror peremptorily.

Closed-ended questions are also useful in introducing jurors to principles of law. The lawyer will typically state the relevant principle, and ask the jurors whether they agree with it. The perfunctory affirmative response is largely irrelevant, for the lawyer has already made the point with the panel. The response may, however, commit the jurors to following the law, and the lawyer's phrasing of the question (you do agree, I am sure, with the legal doctrine which holds that . . .) expresses the lawyer's confidence in the jurors' ability to follow the judge's instructions. A negative answer to the attorney's question, of course, will pave the way for a successful challenge for cause.

A combination of open-ended and closed-ended questions is often productive. Open-ended questions may help a juror to relax and become acclimated to the idea of being questioned. An initial open-ended question on a subject can be followed by a series of closed-ended question aimed at clarifying or fleshing out aspects of the juror's response. The open-ended question often may begin with, "Tell us about . . . ;" for example, "Tell us, please, about what you have heard (or read) about this case." The follow-up may be another open-ended question: "And what was your reaction when you heard (or read) what you did?," or a closed-ended question: "And what you heard (or read) made you think that the defendant was probably guilty, is that not so?" The latter closed-ended question may ultimately be necessary to lay the basis for a successful challenge for cause.

If the lawyer feels that the juror is not being totally forthcoming in responding to an open-ended question, a simple "uh-huh" combined with an expectant look may encourage the juror to continue talking. Silence may be used to the same effect. Television interviewers frequently employ a technique of sticking a microphone in an interviewee's face, asking a question, and leaving the microphone there until the victim gives a newsworthy response.

§9.16 Hypothetical Questions

Hypothetical questions are sometimes used by lawyers to determine prejudice or bias of prospective jurors. Hypothetical questions can also be misused to attempt to build sympathy for a party's cause. In the same improper vein, hypothetical questions are sometimes designed to commit a juror, before the introduction of evidence, to a particular position.

Jurors should not be made to commit in advance to a point of view by asking them to make a decision, even a hypothetical one, based on evidence which may or may not later be adduced at trial.[66] Hypothetical questions which ask a juror to make such a commitment are therefore generally disallowed. The matter, however, lies within the broad discretion of the trial judge.[67]

The law regarding hypothetical questions is in a confused state, as appellate courts have affirmed dissimilar treatment of similar questions. The following types of questions are illustrative of those which have been allowed in some cases and disallowed in others:

1. Questions asking how a juror would be affected if certain demonstrative evidence were presented
2. Questions asking how a juror would be affected if evidence were presented of a particular person's prior conviction of a crime or immoral behavior
3. Questions asking how a juror would be affected if a particular party were not to present any evidence, testify, or call a certain witness[68]

Questions as to whether prospective jurors would be influenced by other jurors if there were disagreement as to the appropriate verdict have been held

---

[66] State v Henry, 197 La 999, 3 So 2d 104 (1941); State v Huffman, 86 Ohio St 229, 99 NE 295 (1912); *see generally* Annotation, *Propriety and Effect of Asking Prospective Jurors Hypothetical Questions, on Voir Dire, as to How They Would Decide Issues in Case,* 99 ALR2d 7 (1965).

[67] State v Henry, 197 La 999, 3 So 2d 104 (1941).

[68] *See generally* Annotation, *supra* note 66, at 82-84.

improper.[69] The courts reason that this type of inquiry encourages jurors to disregard the opinions of their fellow jurors, and discourages them from reaching a unanimous verdict.[70] In some cases, however, it has been held proper for counsel to ask jurors whether they would be influenced by other jurors,[71] and it is a question often asked by defense counsel in criminal trials.

Hypothetical questions asking what a juror's verdict would be if the evidence at trial were evenly balanced have also had a mixed reception. Some courts have held them improper,[72] but other courts have allowed them.[73] Arguably such a question is simply another way of testing a juror's understanding of the burden of proof, a permissible topic of inquiry.

Hypothetical questions can create problems, and they should be sparingly used. If a particular hypothetical question does not misstate any fact, and if it is designed to discover prejudice, it probably will be permitted. On the other hand, the trial court must be certain that no juror is made to commit to a particular position before trial. The jury's eventual verdict must be based on the evidence adduced at trial and not on commitments made pretrial.

Hypothetical questions need to be framed with great care. Sometimes, in an effort to include all relevant facts in the hypothetical, an attorney will make the question so long and convoluted that the juror becomes confused. The juror's response under such circumstances may be meaningless.

§9.17 *Dos* and *Don'ts*

Although they are not supposed to, jurors often try the lawyers instead of the facts. Every trial lawyer can tell of cases which have been decided in favor of a particular party because some jurors thought that one lawyer was more deserving than the other. Cases have been lost because of the jurors' dislike of a lawyer.

Voir dire is the first contact between counsel and jury. It is the first opportunity a lawyer has to talk to the jurors and to make a favorable impression. The preliminary questioning should be conducted in an open and friendly manner, and a judgmental or domineering attitude should be avoided. Counsel should strive to create an impression of fairness and sincerity.[74] Each juror should feel that the lawyer is genuinely interested in him or her, and in what the juror has to say.

---

[69] State v Talley, 22 SW2d 787 (Mo 1929); State v Morgan, 192 Wash 425, 73 P2d 745 (1937); Caesar v State, 135 Tex Crim 5, 117 SW2d 66 (1938).

[70] *See* State v Morgan, 192 Wash 425, 73 P2d 745 (1937); Caesar v State, 135 Tex Crim 5, 117 SW2d 66 (1938).

[71] *E.g.*, Temperly v Sarrington's Admr, 293 SW2d 863 (Ky Ct App 1956); State v Boyer, 342 Mo 64, 112 SW2d 575 (1938).

[72] *E.g.*, Kurczak v United States, 14 F2d 109 (6th Cir 1926); Chicago & AR Co v Fisher, 141 Ill 614, 31 NE 406 (1892).

[73] *E.g.*, People v Peck, 139 Mich 680, 103 NW 178 (1905); Monaghan v Agricultural Fire Ins Co, 53 Mich 238, 18 NW 797 (1884).

[74] See also **§9.09.** *See generally* 1 S. Schweitzer, Cyclopedia of Trial Practice §145 (2d

The fact that lawyers must be personable and sell themselves as well as their cases does not mean that they should be weak or indecisive. It does mean that they should bear in mind that they are on constant display to the jurors and, therefore, should not gratuitously antagonize them. With this goal in mind, the following sections offer some constructive suggestions.

§9.18 —Prepare Your Questions

Unless counsel is a seasoned veteran, and even then, it is sound advice to prepare voir dire questions in advance. Advance preparation will assure coverage of all important matters, help guarantee that the particular nuances of the case are taken into account, and avoid some topic that the panel should be asked about from being overlooked. Preparation for voir dire forces the lawyer to be thoroughly familiar with the facts and law of the case, and to construct a theory of the case.

Advance preparation of voir dire questions will also free counsel's mind to study and evaluate the jurors as they respond. Undue time needs not to be spent thinking of one's next question. Advance preparation is particularly helpful in those courts where the judge, after questioning the jury panel, asks counsel for additional questions and expects an immediate response.

At a minimum, it is advisable to write out in advance a list of the topics one plans to cover on voir dire, checking them off as they are covered. If a lawyer has difficulty formulating questions on the spur of the moment, specific questions can also be written out in advance. In some jurisdictions, by statute or local rule, questions on certain topics have to be put in a particular form; an improper form of the question may have been disapproved by a higher court. The lawyer should be familiar with such requirements and should in advance of trial work out the proper phrasing of the question.

Advance preparation should also entail alternative formulations of the same question (in case the form of the question is successfully objected to) and alternative ways of getting at the same information (in case the juror does not understand the lawyer's original question or is evasive in responding to it). Alternative phrasings will also help prevent the jury from becoming bored or allowing a juror to be educated about the correct response to a question as a result of the lawyer's voir dire of another juror.

Voir dire questions will be of two types. First, there are the general background information questions which will be asked in all cases—age, occupation, residence, marital status, etc. A list of such topics is all that is needed; one is provided in **§9.35.** Second, there are the case-specific questions which require advance preparation. The community surveys, mock trials, and juror investigations recommended in Part II of this book will point the way to case-specific lines of inquiry. Common sense and social science research will suggest others. In Chapters 10 and 11, examples of specific questions in various types of civil and criminal cases will be presented.

---

ed 1954); I. Goldstein, Trial Techniques §9.34 (2d ed 1969); F. Bailey & H. Rothblatt, Successful Techniques for Criminal Trials ch 3, §85 (1971).

§9.19 —Use Jurors' Names

Counsel should have a jury list with the names and addresses of the panel members. A first step in establishing rapport with the jury is to refer to jurors by name during the course of the questioning. Referring to a juror by name indicates the lawyer's interest in the juror as an individual. Counsel should address male jurors as Mr. ______. It is more difficult to know the proper form of address for a female juror. Ms. is acceptable in modern society, but may be resented by some female jurors. A lawyer may solicit the female juror's help in determining the appropriate form of address: "It is Miss or Mrs. ______?" Use of a juror's first name, however, is more likely to be seen as patronizing than friendly.

As an aid in remembering juror names, as well as for other purposes, it is useful to construct a chart of the jury box and enter each juror's name in the appropriate box as the juror is called and seated. By noting the juror's name before the juror enters the box, the lawyer is in a position to begin voir dire by addressing the juror by name. Each box on the chart should be sufficiently large to allow for the possibility that several jurors may be challenged. In each juror's box the lawyer should note key facts about the juror as they come to light.[75] This information will be invaluable when it comes to exercising peremptory challenges.

The attorney who is second to conduct voir dire should attempt to commit to memory the names of the jurors while the opposing side is questioning the jurors. When it is the attorney's turn to address the panel, he or she will be able to call jurors by their correct names. Jurors may be impressed not only by the keen memory of the lawyer, but, more importantly, by the fact that the lawyer has enough of a personal interest in the jurors to learn their names.

§9.20 Avoid Unfairness

A trial lawyer should studiously avoid any hint of unfairness to an opponent. Without giving ground, a lawyer should be polite and courteous. The lawyer should always strive to create an impression of fairness. In jury selection, the lawyer should stress that it is an impartial jury which is being sought, not a partisan one.

As will be discussed in a subsequent section, a lawyer should disclose to the jury on voir dire the weaknesses in the client's case.[76] Besides defusing potentially damaging issues while presenting them in their best light, such disclosure enhances the lawyer's image of fairness. Similarly, in telling jurors that they are to abide by the judge's instructions on the law and not by what the lawyers say about the law, the lawyer builds on the image of fairness. As the judge will tell them this anyway, the lawyer's statement is cost-free. In the same category is a lawyer's statement that the jury's verdict should be based on the jurors'

---

[75] If counsel has investigated members of the panel, as recommended in **ch 4,** relevant information about the juror should also be noted.

[76] *See* **§9.29.**

and not counsel's, recollection of the evidence. Again, as the jury will do this anyway, and the judge will instruct the jury to do so, for the lawyer to also tell this to the jury projects fairness at no cost.

Opportunities for reinforcing one's image of fairness often arise in the course of voir dire. If, for instance, it becomes obvious that a juror is for some reason disqualified or subject to challenge for cause by opposing counsel, the lawyer can demonstrate fairness by stipulating that the juror may be excused.

Fairness enhances credibility. A jury will accept a partisan argument from a lawyer perceived as fair. It may reject an argument based on fairness from a lawyer perceived as partisan.

§9.21 —Be Courteous and Sympathetic

Jurors perform a vital public service, often at considerable expense to themselves. A lawyer should not forget this fact, and should not bypass the opportunity to let the jury know that the lawyer appreciates that jurors are "special people" doing a "special job." It follows that the lawyer should treat these "special people" with respect and dignity. The words *please* and *thank you* should be sprinkled liberally throughout the examination. This is not only a good display of common courtesy and politeness, but a signal of the respect that the lawyer has for the juror. On the other hand, counsel should be careful not to appear fawning.

A juror is often in a strange and uncomfortable position. It may be the first case on which the juror has sat. All eyes in the courtroom are on the juror. Lawyers and court officials appear to hang on the juror's every word. It is an awkward situation, and an attorney should try to put the juror at ease: "I realize this may be difficult. I, too, often have trouble talking about . . . , but could you please tell us . . ." Sympathy for the juror's plight may be repaid with sympathy for the lawyer's position.

A lawyer should never be consciously discourteous to a juror. One should not interrupt a juror, turn one's back on the juror, or talk to a third party while the juror is speaking. To do so risks alienating the juror for no good reason. A lawyer should be interested in what the juror is saying; and, equally important, should appear to the juror to be interested. Eye contact is important but, as anyone who has ever been stared at knows, should not be overdone.

Positive feedback is also useful. Most persons respond positively to a subtle nod of the head. The repeating or paraphrasing of key favorable responses of the juror both indicates that the lawyer has been paying attention and reinforces the response. Positive feedback works to establish rapport with the individual juror. At the same time repetition of a juror's statement allows the lawyer to emphasize a point to the entire panel. Like eye contact, however, it can be counterproductive if overdone.

§9.22 —Do Not Be Brilliant

Successful trial lawyers rarely attempt to impress the jury with their brilliance. Some trial lawyers, some of whom actually are brilliant, try to make opposing counsel look the fool. Such a lawyer, when successful, often succeeds only in inducing sympathy for opposing counsel; when unsuccessful, the lawyer generates a well deserved and self-inflicted dislike among the jurors.

All the world loves an underdog, and a jury is no exception. The jury which feels sorry for a lawyer because it thinks the lawyer is outmatched may bend over backwards to construct theories and arguments that will allow it to find in that lawyer's favor. For partly this reason, many attorneys try to portray themselves as the intellectual inferior of opposing counsel. Rather than pointing to their own brilliance, these lawyers will point to the handicap they suffer from being matched against so brilliant an adversary. They will solicit the help of the jurors in overcoming this handicap and in seeing through the "clever" arguments of opposing counsel. More often than not, they will receive it.

§9.23 —Never Consciously Embarrass a Prospective Juror

A lawyer should phrase questions in a way which will minimize embarrassment to a prospective juror. The lawyer should not ask questions which bring out the juror's ignorance or lack of education. Lawyers should not use voir dire to display their impressive vocabulary; a juror who does not understand the words used by the attorney will be embarrassed. At the other extreme, the lawyer should not speak as if to a class of seven-year-olds; the lawyer will be perceived as condescending. Neither image is likely to cultivate the jury's good will.

A lawyer should not draw attention to a physical deformity or disability of a juror in a manner that will cause the juror discomfiture. At times it may be necessary to inquire whether an impairment, such as a hearing defect, will make it difficult for a juror to serve. Tact and discretion, however, must be used. Never should a lawyer make jokes at a juror's expense.

A lawyer's questions which are perceived as contemptuous or condescending may alienate not only the juror being questioned, but others on the panel as well. While the embarrassed juror can be eliminated by peremptory challenge, the remaining jurors may remember the slight. As the lawyer may be unable to identify who these jurors are, the wiser course is to avoid embarrassing any juror in the first place.

Counsel should consciously refrain from asking questions in an accusatory tone or in a manner indicating disbelief in the juror's replies. Voir dire should not be confused with cross-examination. A sarcastic or judgmental tone will work at cross-purposes to the lawyer's goal of establishing rapport with the jurors.

Sometimes during voir dire, despite counsel's best efforts, situations arise which do embarrass a prospective juror. When they do, counsel should apologize both to the juror and the jury. As a general rule, the lawyer should take responsibility for matters which would otherwise cause a juror embarrassment. If, for instance, a juror does not seem to understand the lawyer's questions, the lawyer should apologize for asking the questions in a confusing form, even if the questions are completely clear. Likewise, if the juror mumbles his or her responses, the lawyer should preface a request for the juror to speak up with an apology for not hearing very well. Sparing the juror embarrassment will be no hardship to the lawyer, and will be appreciated by the juror.

§9.24 —Don't Bore the Jury

Many voir dire examinations are of necessity long and tedious, at least to those not at the moment being questioned. After several hours of listening to repetitious questioning, some jurors may become restless and irritated. To avoid this reaction, counsel should consider in camera individual questioning[77] and eliciting as much information as possible in a pre-voir dire questionnaire.[78] Counsel should also ask as many questions as possible to the panel as a whole.

Some questions will need to be directed to each member of the panel individually. It may be that the lawyer desires an individual response; or it may be that the lawyer wants to emphasize a point through repetition. There should, however, be a purpose to the lawyer's repeating of questions. A lawyer must constantly draw a fine line between being thorough and not being boring.

Compromises are possible. In some instances, counsel might ask one or two jurors a question and then ask the other members of the panel if their answers would be different if the question were put to them individually. This approach saves time and is less wearing on the panel. It also has the effect of keeping the jurors' attention fixed on the attorney as the jurors come to appreciate that they may also be called upon to respond to the attorney's questions to another juror.

In preparing for voir dire a lawyer should develop various ways of asking the same question and different approaches for eliciting the same information.[79] This advance preparation will help to avoid boring the jury with the same questions and may circumvent an objection to the phrasing of a question or to a particular line of inquiry. Alternative phrasings of the same question will also prove useful in the case of the juror who does not comprehend the lawyer's original question or is evasive in answering it.

§9.25 —Avoid Legalese and Other Complex Language

An attorney should speak simply in conducting voir dire. Counsel should make all statements and ask all questions in as plain, simple, and everyday language as possible. It is important to remember that a jury may contain persons who have not had the benefit of a college education and who, accordingly, may not possess the knowledge and vocabulary of the questioning attorney. Legal terms, the meaning of which even an educated lay person could not be expected to know, should in particular be avoided. Use of complex language or legalese

---

[77] *See* **§9.08.**

[78] *See* **§9.01.**

[79] *See* **§9.18.**

may not only confuse but irritate the jurors. In any event, if the jurors do not understand the lawyer's terminology and, as a consequence, the lawyer's questions, their answers will be neither meaningful nor informative.

An instructive illustration appears in *Successful Techniques for Criminal Trials* by F. Lee Bailey and Henry Rothblatt.[80] The authors ask their readers to place themselves in the position of an attorney defending a person charged with assault. The defendant seeks to raise a claim of self-defense. A not uncommon voir dire question might be: "Do you believe that a person is justified in injuring his attacker if, by the exercise of ordinary discretion and care, he has reasonable ground to believe that he is in imminent danger of losing life or of incurring great bodily harm:"[81] Bailey and Rothblatt point out that while the accuracy of the law in the question is not to be doubted, its value as a question is. The problem is that the lay mind is likely to have difficulty grasping the attorney's point. If so, the juror's response may be unenlightening at best and misleading at worst.

Bailey and Rothblatt suggest a more simplified question along the following lines: "Do you believe that a person is justified in injuring another if he honestly believes that he is in actual danger of being harmed by his attacker?"[82] This question is less complex, uses simpler language, but still explains to the jury the rudiments of the law of self-defense.

§9.26 —Advise Jurors of Prying Questions

A lawyer may avoid unnecessary resentment by explaining to jurors at the outset why it may be necessary to ask questions which delve into a juror's personal affairs. The lawyer should explain that a failure to make this inquiry would be a breach of the lawyer's legal, ethical, and moral duty to the client. Further, jurors should be educated by counsel about the reasons for certain lines of questioning, and why certain experiences, occupations, and beliefs may render a juror unsuitable to serve in the case. It should be emphasized that the attorney is not trying to pry or meddle in the juror's personal business. Sometimes the court will explain all this to the jury,[83] but otherwise counsel should.

§9.27 —Mention Trial Objections

Jurors tend to be suspicious of attorneys who object to the introduction of evidence, particularly on what seem to be technical grounds. They think (often correctly) that the lawyer is trying to keep the evidence from them. Nonetheless, such objections are legally permissible and the judge should so inform the jury.

---

[80] F. Bailey & H. Rothblatt, Successful Techniques for Criminal Trials §84 (1971).

[81] *Id.*

[82] *Id.*

[83] *See* **§9.02.**

During voir dire, the lawyer should reinforce this message, particularly where the lawyer anticipates having to make many such objections. Counsel should explain that the rules of evidence must be followed by all parties, and that there will be times when one of the lawyers will feel that some rule of evidence is being violated and will make an objection which the judge will rule on. The jury should be told that it should not view such actions as an attempt on the part of the lawyer to slow down the trial or to hide anything from the jurors. It should be made clear that once an objection has been made, the trial court will rule on it. A judge who agrees with the lawyer making the objection will sustain the objection; a judge who disagrees will overrule the objection, which will mean that the evidence is proper and may be considered by the jury.

The lawyer should ask the panel if they understand this procedure. If a juror has a question about the procedure, the lawyer should attempt to answer it. The lawyer should extract from the jury a pledge not to hold an objection against the side which raises it.

§9.28 —Explain Burden of Proof

It is critical that counsel discuss with the jury the burden of proof in the case. Some jurors in a civil case may have previously served in a criminal case, or vice versa. Other jurors who have never served on either a civil or criminal jury may have an inaccurate impression of the burden of proof based on fictionalized drama.

In a criminal case, the panel should be advised that it is the state's burden to prove the guilt of the accused beyond a reasonable doubt; it should receive an explanation of what reasonable doubt entails. In a civil case, the panel should understand that the burden rests on the plaintiff to prove the case as a whole by a preponderance of the evidence. Preponderance of the evidence can be explained as the greater weight of the credible evidence admitted in the trial. It is important to explore the difference between these two burdens, emphasizing that the burden of proof in a criminal case is an onerous one, while the burden of proof in a civil case is significantly lighter but still formidable.[84]

Visual demonstrations may prove helpful, and some lawyers use their hands to represent scales of justice, elevating one to indicate how much the scales must be tipped to meet the burden of proof. Other lawyers prefer sports analogies, equating the burden of proof in a civil trial with the crossing of the 50-yard line in a football game, but with close to scoring a touchdown in a criminal case. Sports analogies, however, may not be understood by jurors who are not interested in sports.

---

[84] There are a few causes of actions, such as civil commitment, where the burden of proof falls in between the criminal/civil standards. These cases are generally characterized as requiring proof by "clear and convincing" evidence. In such cases the lawyer should accordingly modify the explanations and examples used.

§9.29 —Admit the Weaknesses of Your Case

If there are weaknesses in a case, which there often are, they should be brought to the jury's attention during voir dire. It is tactically advisable for counsel whose case has weaknesses to admit them. Since the weakness will ultimately be disclosed anyway, it is better for counsel, who can put the weakness in the best possible light, to do so. Otherwise, the weakness will be revealed during trial, usually with more devastating effect. Admission of a weakness in one's case has the ancillary benefit of reinforcing the image of fairness which the lawyer seeks to project.[85]

Consider, for example, the witness with a questionable past which is bound to come out on cross-examination. Counsel would be well advised to divulge that fact on voir dire, and to ask jurors whether they would disbelieve the witness solely because of the witness's background. Presented in this form, and wanting to appear to be fair-minded, most jurors will answer no. During closing argument, counsel can remind them of this answer.

§9.30 —Discuss Handicaps of Client or Witness

Some clients and witnesses suffer from speech, language, or physical defects. The attorney should disclose these defects at the voir dire stage, in order to avoid surprise or even shock during trial. The lawyer wants to make the point that such a disability is irrelevant in determining whether a witness is being truthful.

Suppose counsel plans to introduce a witness who stutters. The attorney should question jurors about their experiences with persons who stutter. Invariably there will be a juror who knows a stutterer. The juror should be asked whether that acquaintance was nonetheless a fair and honest individual. Hopefully the juror will answer yes. Having made the point, the lawyer should address the entire panel and ask whether they would let the fact that a witness stutters influence their judgment of the witness's credibility. Assuming that the jurors answer the latter question in the negative, the lawyer can seek from them a commitment to that effect, about which they can be reminded on closing argument. The juror who will allow the fact that a witness stutters affect his or her assessment of the witness's truthfulness can be challenged for cause.

§9.31 —Commit Jurors to Law as Given by Court

In most jurisdictions, counsel is restricted in discussing the law with the jury, whether on voir dire, during trial, or on summation. Most judges will sustain an objection to any attempt on the part of counsel to go into the law of the case with the jury. The jury's concern is with the facts, and it is in theory bound to follow the law as given by the court.

Knowing that a judge will instruct the jury to this effect, a lawyer can turn this duty of the jury to his or her advantage. On voir dire the lawyer can extract

---

[85] *See* **§9.20.**

from all jurors a commitment to follow the instructions of the court. The jurors can be further told that it is their duty not to substitute their own opinions of the law for the instructions in the judge's charge. The court will tell them this anyway. For the attorney to do it first on voir dire will impress the jury with the lawyer's fairness.[86]

A lawyer, however, should carefully consider how to phrase the questioning. Counsel should not ask whether a juror will take the law from the court or follow a personal conception of the law if the juror's idea differs from the one given by the court. Such a question may embarrass the juror who out of ignorance announces an intent to follow a personal conception of the law. The juror may be rebuked by the judge and informed that all jurors have a responsibility to follow the law given by the court. The better procedure is to inform jurors that it is the duty of all citizens, including jurors, to abide by the law. It can be explained that laws are made by the legislature and construed by the court, and that as a general rule it is the juror's duty to follow the law even though an individual member of the panel might feel that the law either is or should be to the contrary. The juror can then be asked whether he or she will have any problem following the instructions of the judge.

The degree to which a lawyer stresses the jury's duty to follow the law will be in direct proportion to the extent that the lawyer believes that the law favors the client's position. If in a given case the lawyer plans to appeal to the jury to exercise its power of nullification,[87] the lawyer might attempt to explain that prerogative to the jury during voir dire. The lawyer might remind the jury of its role as the conscience of the community, and note that throughout history jurors have returned the verdict that they thought was fair and just under the circumstances. It would not be surprising, however, for a judge to sustain an objection to this line of inquiry.

§9.32 —Don't Take the First 12 Jurors

Some, usually inexperienced, lawyers may see nothing to be gained from voir dire. These lawyers naively believe that the merits of their cause and the eloquence of their pleading will persuade any twelve jurors. More experienced attorneys appreciate that all persons have deeply ingrained values, attitudes, and biases which will resist certain claims and arguments. Voir dire provides a unique opportunity to learn about such matters. Even if this were not so, even if all jurors responded to evidence in a logical and predictable fashion, voir dire provides the opportunity to establish rapport with the jury and condition their expectations regarding the case. *It should not be waived.*

Occasionally, after the jury panel has been instructed by the trial judge, opposing counsel may declare, "If the court please, all the jurors look fair to me, and I'll just take the first twelve." If this happens, one must be wary. While opposing counsel may mistakenly think that this show of confidence will ingra-

---

[86] *Id.*

[87] *See* **§§2.20-2.21.**

tiate the lawyer with the jurors, he or she may also recognize a client or a close personal friend on the panel and prefer that this fact not be brought out on voir dire. Sometimes opposing counsel may have investigated the venire[88] and have concluded that the first twelve jurors called are the best that could be hoped for from the client's perspective. In short, unless inexperienced or lazy, a lawyer who avows the intention to "take the first twelve jurors" probably has a good reason for this display of confidence.

The lawyer faced with this situation should not feel pressured to accede to opposing counsel's attempted tour de force. The lawyer should assure the jury that, while personally confident that the jurors are all qualified and fair, a lawyer owes certain obligations to a client, one of which is to ask a few questions to familiarize the jury with the case. The lawyer might also point out that voir dire provides jurors and counsel the opportunity to become better acquainted.

§9.33 —Have Voir Dire Reported

A lawyer who can envision the possibility of an appeal will see the obvious value of having the voir dire reported. In criminal cases involving life or liberty of an accused, and in civil cases where important property rights or large amounts of money are at stake, the voir dire examination should certainly be reported. Any error of opposing counsel in asking improper questions or making prejudicial remarks, as well as any error of the trial judge in ruling on challenges, will be preserved.

Suppose the trial judge refuses to excuse a juror challenged for cause, and counsel can show prejudice from being forced to accept the unwanted juror. If the voir dire is reported, the complete record is before the appellate court. If counsel on appeal can show that the client was compelled to accept a prejudiced juror because of the court's erroneous refusal to excuse the juror for cause, it may be possible to obtain a new trial. Although the lawyer may have to show that the juror gave a false or misleading answer to a material question on voir dire, a correct answer to which would have established a basis for a challenge for cause,[89] and although this burden might be quite difficult to meet, the lawyer will not get out of the starting blocks unless the juror's answers appear on the record.

§9.34 —One Last Question

When counsel is permitted to either conduct voir dire or ask supplemental questions, the examination should conclude with the emphasis on the need for a fair and impartial jury and on voir dire as the means of meeting this need. Counsel's final question should be whether there is any reason, already men-

---

[88] *See* **ch 4.**

[89] *See* McDonough Power Equip v Greenwood, 464 US 548 (1984). *See also* **§9.10.**

tioned or not, why any juror could not be totally fair and impartial.[90] This question sums up the whole purpose behind both voir dire and having a jury. It provides jurors with a final opportunity to disclose a ground of prejudice not previously brought out, while gently reminding them of their duty in the case. If no juror says anything in response to this final question, the lawyer should then thank the jurors for their time and patience, and sit down.

§9.35 General Topics for Introductory Questioning

Every case is different, and in each there will be case-specific issues to be explored. Some insight into the range of possible subjects which might be explored on voir dire can be gained by reexamining the topics covered in Chapter 7 dealing with challenges for cause. Nonetheless, there is a core of basic information which it is useful for the lawyer to have, regardless of the type of case. There follows a list of such general topics. The topics are not in any particular order, as their importance may vary depending on the nature of the case. Also, depending on the nature of the case, the list of topics can often be pruned. Questioning on these relatively nonthreatening topics will help break the ice between lawyer and juror, assist in establishing rapport, and in many instances provide a lead-in to questioning in more sensitive areas:

Marital status and children

Present and former residences; nature of neighborhoods; reasons for moving

Ancestry and cultural heritage of juror (many times, like age, these will be obvious and will not require inquiry)

Occupation, present and past, of juror, juror's spouse (if married), juror's adult children, and juror's parents

Juror's responsibilities and duties at workplace

Present and former employers

Education, schools and colleges attended, and subjects studied, with particular emphasis on study of law-related subjects (same questions can be asked in respect to juror's spouse and children)

Formalized special training (including short seminars, self-help courses, nonacademic courses, etc.)

Military service; positions held (with particular concern for whether juror served with military police)

Property interests

Attitudes toward the legal system

---

[90] Another way of eliciting this same information is to ask the juror whether he or she would have any hesitance in being tried by a jury composed of persons with the same frame of mind as the juror.

Previous involvements with the legal system

Knowledge of the English language (again, this will usually be obvious and unnecessary to inquire into)

State of health and condition of juror's faculties

Previous jury service, the verdicts of the juries on which the juror served, and the juror's reactions to those verdicts and past jury duty generally

Membership on a previous jury that heard the same or related evidence to that to be offered in the case

Membership on a previous jury that heard any of the witnesses who will testify in the case

Relationship to a party, attorney, or witness

Membership in any organization to which one of the parties, attorneys, or witnesses belongs

Social, religious, fraternal, labor, and political affiliations (and whether juror is "active member" or member in name only)

Religion (including whether church attendance is regular)

Hobbies and spare-time activities

Whether the prospective juror or member of juror's family or close friend has been in a position similar to that of any of the parties

Whether the prospective juror has been engaged in litigation and, if so, its nature and outcome

Knowledge of the facts of the case

Acquaintance with or knowledge of any of the parties, attorneys, or witnesses

Exposure to pretrial publicity

Friendship, animosity, prejudice, or bias against or in favor of a party, attorney, or witness

Prejudice against the race, nationality, political affiliation, or religion of a party, attorney, or witness

Prejudice against a party's occupation

Prejudice against particular types of actions or defenses

Burden of proof and order of proceeding

Juror's description of self (strengths and weakness)

As can be seen, the list of topics is quite extensive, a fact which reinforces the argument made in the first section of this chapter for the use of pre-voir dire questionnaires.

10 Voir Dire in Civil Cases

§10.01 Introduction and Preliminary Comments

The preceding chapter examined general principles of voir dire. The present chapter explores voir dire in the more specific context of various types of civil cases, with examples of suggested questions. Experienced trial lawyers will appreciate the impossibility of covering all questions that might be appropriate in a particular case. These will depend on the facts of the case, the parties and witnesses involved, and a host of other variables. The sample questions presented in this chapter are designed to be illustrative rather than exhaustive.

Voir dire questioning and style inevitably will reflect the personality of the attorney doing the questioning. Every trial lawyer tends to have an individualistic approach to voir dire, born in part of the lawyer's experiences. Every lawyer also has unique abilities; a style that is effective for one attorney may not be effective for another. In the final analysis, a lawyer's approach to voir dire will be a combination of what the lawyer feels comfortable with and what works for that lawyer. It is hoped that some of the suggestions that emerge from this chapter and the next can be integrated into that approach or will at least stimulate a lawyer's thinking on the subject.

Some preliminary comments on basic principles of voir dire in civil cases should precede discussion of voir dire in specific types of cases. It must always be remembered that jurors are human beings, and that all human beings, as a result of their life experiences, have beliefs, values, and prejudices which make impartiality in the tabula rasa sense impossible. The lawyer's task is to discover those biases which would affect a juror's thinking to the detriment of the client's case.

Voir dire is an intimidating experience for many jurors, unlike any other that the juror may have ever had. The atmosphere of the courtroom is itself intimidating. The judge sits in a black robe behind a massive bench, elevated above everyone else. Jurors are formally sworn to tell the truth, as if the law otherwise would expect them to lie. Lawyers stare intently at jurors, sometimes writing feverish notes when a juror speaks. Questions are asked by total strangers and required to be answered in the presence of total strangers. And the questions are often of a highly personal nature, asking for information that one might not reveal to one's closest friend.

An attorney should be aware of the jurors' discomfort and do everything possible to put them at ease. A brief explanation of the purpose of voir dire, along the following lines, might prove helpful:

> Please understand that it is necessary for me as a lawyer, in order to adequately represent my client, to ask questions of all members of the jury panel with regard to your qualifications to serve as jurors in this case. The purpose is not to embarrass any of you, or to delve into your personal affairs. Rather, my questions are asked so that His Honor, the judge, and the attorneys can assess whether there is anything in any juror's background or experience that might possibly affect that person's fairness and impartiality to both sides in this case. If you are excused, you should understand that it represents not a judgment about you as a person, or your competence to be a juror in other cases, but our best guess, and it is only that, that something in your background makes it inappropriate for you to serve in this particular case.

§10.02 Commitments

After explaining briefly the nature of the case, and after asking some general questions of the panel, the lawyer reaches the commitment stage. Jurors, of course, cannot be committed to return a specific verdict for a particular party.

It is necessary, however, that the jurors feel some obligation to accept and follow certain principles.

For instance, each member of the panel should be committed to answer candidly and truthfully all questions on voir dire. Jurors should also be committed to following the law as given to them by the judge.[1] Promises should be extracted to decide the case only on the evidence presented in court, and not on personal prejudice or personal values.

A lawyer will often remind jurors on summation of promises made on voir dire. This reminder can evoke a strong sense of duty on the part of the jurors to keep their word. In a personal injury case where the injured party is a child, for example, defense counsel might say in summation:

> You will recall that at the beginning of this trial, I asked each of you if you would enter a verdict for this defendant if the plaintiffs failed to prove their case by a greater weight of the evidence, and you assured me that you would. You also assured me that you would do this in spite of your natural feelings of sympathy for this child and his parents. Her Honor, the judge, will instruct you that before plaintiff can recover for injuries, no matter how serious, the law requires that he prove that he is entitled to damages from this defendant. As this trial comes to a close, I want to remind all of you of your promise to follow the law and the judge's instructions, and to decide this case on the evidence alone, and not on sympathy.

Jurors should be committed to set aside any prejudices they may have. If the lawyer's case is complicated by legal irrelevancies, the jurors should be committed to not let them influence their verdict. Suppose, by way of illustration, that a lawyer is representing a plaintiff who speaks with a foreign accent. Some jurors may resent immigrants, particularly those who do not speak good English. The jurors should be committed not to let this type of resentment or prejudice affect their verdict:

> Now, ladies and gentlemen, Mr. Papendropelis, my client, has just recently moved to this country and to this state. He is, in other words, a foreigner. Is there anyone on this panel who would hold this fact against him—anyone who, because he is a foreigner, could not give him a fair and impartial trial?
>
> I'm sure it's true that some people do have prejudices against immigrants. However, jurors have a duty to decide a case fairly on the evidence, setting aside any such feelings that they may have. Will you promise me that you will give Mr. Papendropelis the same fair trial that you would give any other American?

---

[1] This commitment might not be so emphasized if the lawyer plans to ask the jurors to exercise their power of nullification. *See* **§§2.20-2.21.**

§10.03 Form of Questions

Voir dire questions will depend on many factors, including the law and customs in the jurisdiction, the attitudes and preferences of the trial judge, the nature of the case, the personalities of the attorneys, and the amount of time an attorney desires and the judge is willing to allot to voir dire. Any of these can determine the form of questions in a particular case. Some general questions will always be permissible, but the remainder will vary with the type of case and its precise issues.

Trial counsel must elicit as much information as possible about a juror's character in a very short time. One of the best ways to do this is to ask open-ended questions that will get the juror to talk, which call for an extended response.[2] Key questions should generally be asked in this form. In a case involving a cervical sprain injury, for example, a question might be phrased as follows: "Could you please tell us your thoughts, if you have any, about people who sue for injuries to the neck as a result of a rear-end automobile collision?" A juror is more likely to reveal important personal information in response to the proposed question than to one which asks: "Do you have any prejudice against a person who sues for injury to his neck as a result of a rear-end automobile collision?"

Sometimes closed-ended leading questions may be more desirable than questions which call for an extended response.[3] A rhetorical question such as the following has the advantage of saving time: "I am sure that you are not prejudiced against people who, as the law allows them to do, sue for injuries they have received, are you?" In addition to shortening the examination, this question expresses the attorney's confidence in the juror's impartiality, informs the juror of the governing legal principle, and elicits a commitment, albeit a somewhat perfunctory one, on the juror's part not to be influenced by prejudice. Closed-ended questions are also useful in pinning a juror down, especially when the attorney seeks to establish a basis for a challenge for cause.

§10.04 Automobile Collisions

Automobile collisions have long been a fertile source of litigation. These can range from the minor fender-bender to the crash in which a person has incurred catastrophic injuries.

For the purpose of a sample voir dire, assume the following hypothetical facts. Plaintiff, Ed Williams, 25 years of age, was injured about 11:30 p.m., while returning from a bachelor party at which he had "two beers." His late-model automobile collided with a truck owned by the XYZ Corporation. The truck was driven by an employee of the XYZ Corporation, Jack Smith. The collision between the two vehicles was virtually head-on, the vehicles having approached each other from opposite directions. The point of the impact was between the front end of the plaintiff's vehicle and the left front wheel of the defendant's

---

[2] *See* **§9.15.**

[3] *Id.*

truck, on the far edge of the shoulder on the defendant's side of the road. As a result of the accident, the plaintiff sustained fractures of the spine, broken ribs, a punctured lung, serious internal injuries, and deep lacerations on both legs. The truck driver, while not as seriously injured, sustained a compound fracture of his left arm, a concussion, and numerous bruises and contusions on various parts of his body. The plaintiff filed suit against both the driver of the truck and the XYZ Corporation for $1,000,000 damages.The plaintiff maintains that while he was driving in his own lane on a two-lane state highway, the defendant, approaching from the opposite direction, crossed over the center line into the plaintiff's lane, about 500 feet from impact. The plaintiff then veered into the defendant's lane in order to avoid colliding with the defendant's truck. At this point the truck driver also veered suddenly, about 200 feet from the plaintiff's vehicle, and came back onto his own side of the road. The two vehicles collided, after skidding, on the far edge of the shoulder on the defendant's side of the road.

The defendant claims that he was at all times in his own lane, that the plaintiff suddenly and without warning veered across the center line into the defendant's lane, and that the truck driver did everything possible to avoid the collision. The defendant contends that the plaintiff lost control of his car, in all likelihood due to his inebriated condition.

Plaintiff's Voir Dire

Ladies and gentlemen of the jury, you have heard me briefly describe the facts of this collision and our contentions with respect to that collision. I have described the extremely serious injuries suffered by Mr. Williams as a result of that collision. I have several questions I would like to ask each of you, some individually and some to the panel as a whole. Please understand that it is necessary, in order to assist the court as well as to properly represent my client, that I ask these questions. I am not trying to be tedious, I am not trying to make things difficult, and I am not attempting to pry into your personal affairs. I am simply trying, to the best of my ability, to make sure that the jurors who decide this case can be fair and impartial to both sides. Please, if you will, bear with me and answer each of my questions as best you can.

Q. Do any of you know Mr. Jack Smith, the driver of the truck involved in this collision? [If any juror does know Mr. Smith, follow-up questions should focus on the nature of the relationship, its duration, its closeness, and the effect it would have on the juror's impartiality. The same type of follow-up should be used if any of the general questions posed in this and subsequent sample voir dire examinations should yield an affirmative response.]

Q. Do any of you know Mrs. Brown, the attorney representing the defendants in this case?

Q. Do any of you know anyone who works or has worked for the XYZ Corporation, or any officers or executives of that company?

Q. Does anyone on this jury panel own any stock in the XYZ Corporation or have any of you ever owned any stock in that company? Has any member of your family ever owned, or do any of them presently own, any stock in that corporation?

Q. There are some very intelligent people who believe that persons injured by someone else's conduct should not sue for damages as a result of those injuries, that such persons should just bear their own losses. Is there anyone on the panel who thinks that way? [By prefacing her question with the observation that there are "very intelligent" people who have this belief, the lawyer makes it easier for a juror to admit the bias which is the subject of the questioning.]

Q. Do any of you just not like lawyers, particularly lawyers who try personal injury cases? I have met many people who feel that way, and while everyone has that right, I need to know, to protect my client, if there is anyone on this panel with that type of feeling. I am sure that you can appreciate that it is not fair to Mr. Williams to punish him because you do not like me. [Again, the lawyer makes it relatively easy to admit to the particular bias, while at the time explaining to the jurors why the bias is disqualifying.]

Q. Have any of you, or has any member of your family, ever been involved in an automobile collision which resulted in the filing of any type of claim either by or against you or some member of your family?

Q. Have any of you, or has any member of your family, ever been involved in an automobile collision which resulted in a lawsuit filed either by or against you or some member of your family?

Q. Have any of you ever served on a jury? [If a juror has served on a criminal case, the lawyer should seize the opportunity to explain the differences between the burden of proof in a civil and criminal case. This is a topic which the plaintiff's lawyer wants to discuss with the jury anyway, as some jurors may have the misimpression that plaintiff must establish his case by proof beyond a reasonable doubt.]

Q. Have any of you ever been on a jury which tried an automobile collision case?

Q. Do any of you have any personal convictions or fixed opinions that might make it difficult for you to award fair and adequate damages to Mr. Williams for the injuries he has suffered, if the evidence during this trial supports such damages?

Q. Mr. Williams is seeking $1,000,000 in damages for the injuries and pain and suffering he has incurred. I appreciate that is a lot of money, and it is important that I ask each of you individually how you would feel about awarding anybody such a large sum of money? [After exploring with each juror his or her views as to the damages asked, the lawyer might wrap up the discussion with a question such as the following:] Am I correct, then, in assuming that there is nobody on this panel who would say: "No injuries are worth $1,000,000?"

Q. The evidence will show that Mr. Williams' car struck the defendant's truck on the defendant's side of the road, in fact on the shoulder of the defendant's side of the road. Will any of you be prejudiced against Mr. Williams because of this fact, if the evidence also indicates that Mr. Williams was in fact trying to avoid a head-on collision in every way possible? [Note that the lawyer refers to her client by name and to the truck driver as the defendant. The purpose is to personalize one's client and to depersonalize one's opponent.]

Q. I also assume, and again please correct me if I am wrong, that all of you will be able to dismiss from your minds any sympathy you may feel for the truck driver who was injured in this collision, just as you dismiss any feeling of sympathy for Mr. Williams. [The lawyer seeks to establish her fairness and objectivity, while defusing possible sympathy for the defendant.]

Q. There will be evidence that Mr. Williams was at a party shortly before this collision and that at that party he drank two bottles of beer. How do you [turning toward a particular juror], Mrs. Brock, feel about persons who drive an automobile after consuming an alcoholic beverage? [This is obviously a key issue in the case, and should be probed individually with each juror.]

Q. Is anyone on this panel presently or has anyone been in the past employed as a truck driver?

Q. Regardless of whether any of you are employed as truck drivers, is there anyone on the panel who regularly drives any kind of truck, either for business or pleasure? [Truck-driving jurors are obviously likely to identify with a defendant who is a truck driver.]

Q. Have any of you ever been involved, or has any close friend or member of your immediate family ever been involved, in an automobile collision where the other driver had anything alcoholic to drink before the collision? [The lawyer returns to the drink-driving issue. Any juror who has had a friend or relative injured in an accident with a drunk driver is unlikely to be sympathetic to the plaintiff.]

Q. Is there anyone on this panel who, for religious or any other reasons, does not believe in medicine or in doctors.

Q. Is there anyone on this panel who does not believe that mental pain and anguish can be just as real and hurt just as much as physical pain? [The lawyer returns to the issue of damages, trying to help the jury understand why $1,000,000 in damages is being asked for.]

Q. Is there any reason whatever why any member of this panel can't sit and listen to the evidence in this case for several days, paying close and careful attention to it? Any reason, whether physical, mental, or other, why any of you can't do that?

Q. Will all of you promise me that you will listen to all of the evidence, and to the judge's instructions on the law, and decide this case fairly and impartially on the evidence and in accord with the instructions? [The lawyer tries to reinforce her image of fairness.]

Q. Is there any reason whatever, whether I have mentioned it or not, why any of you feel you cannot be fair and impartial jurors in this case?

The above questions are illustrative and not exhaustive. Note that the two most critical questions—relating to the jurors' feelings about persons who drink and drive and relating to the jurors' feelings about awarding damages of $1,000,000—are asked individually to each juror and through an open-ended question. Plaintiff's counsel, if for no other reason than to establish some degree of rapport with the jurors, will want to ask a few background questions of each juror, primarily in connection with the juror's employment, the juror's spouse's employment, the juror's residence, the number of children in the juror's family (if pertinent), and other relevant matters.[4] Any of the general questions which elicit an affirmative response, such as, for example, whether a juror has ever been involved in an automobile accident, will, of course, require detailed, individual follow-up questioning. In addition to the sample questions, plaintiff's counsel should check local law to determine whether it is proper to question jurors about connections with insurance companies, insurance adjusters, or claims services. Counsel should also be familiar with any other pertinent aspects of the law in the case which might call for other questions to the jury panel.

Defendant's Voir Dire

Q. Does anyone on this panel know or have any acquaintance with the plaintiff in this case, Mr. Williams, or any member of his family?

Q. Do any of you know Mrs. Jones, the attorney representing the plaintiff in this case, or have any of you ever been represented in any matter by her or any member of her law firm?

Q. Is there anyone on this panel who has ever received some type of injury to his or her body as a result of an accident of any kind, whether an on-the-job accident, an automobile collision, or some other type of occurrence?

Q. Is there anyone who, as a result of any type of personal injury received by him or her, has sued anyone else, an individual or a company, for those personal injuries? [Jurors who have themselves been plaintiffs are likely to identify with the plaintiff. If their suit was unsuccessful, they may take out their frustration on the defendant.]

Q. Have any of you ever filed a lawsuit of any kind against either an individual or a corporation, partnership, or other type of company?

Q. Have any of you ever worked for the XYZ Corporation or for a similar type of company, or for any other corporation?

---

[4] *See generally* **§9.35.**

Q. If so, were any of you ever terminated by the company or corporation under circumstances where you thought the termination was unjustified and that you were mistreated?

Q. Could each of you tell me something about your experiences with and feelings toward big corporations or companies in general? [The lawyer with this open-ended question is seeking to identify jurors with an anti-big business bias, whether the product of general philosophy or personal experience.]

Q. I am sure all of you realize that the XYZ Corporation is very successful and prosperous. Is there anyone on this panel who feels that just because the XYZ Corporation is in a better financial position than the plaintiff that it should pay for plaintiff's injuries regardless of who was at fault in causing the collision? [The lawyer makes her point more directly . . .] You understand, I am sure, that the law does not require one person to pay for another's injuries unless that person was in some way at fault. [And indicates that the law agrees with her.]

Q. Could you please tell us about your experiences with truck drivers and your feelings about big trucks in general. [Again, an open-ended question designed this time to unearth a not uncommon prejudice against truck drivers.]

Q. Could you set those feelings aside and give the defendants in this case a fair and impartial trial based on the evidence presented to you?

Q. In other words, you all do agree with me, don't you, that these defendants, including the XYZ Corporation, are entitled to the same kind of fair and impartial trial that the plaintiff in this case is entitled to?

Q. Now, another thing, ladies and gentlemen, all of us have a natural sympathy with anyone who is injured, with anyone who is hurt and has suffered pain and anguish, but will each of you promise me that you will not let that natural feeling of sympathy decide this case against my clients and deprive them of that fair trial on the evidence which our legal system entitles them to? [The lawyer seeks to defuse the issue of sympathy, indicating that as a human being she understands, but that as an officer of the court she, as well as the jurors, has a duty to uphold the law in a fair and impartial manner. She seeks a commitment from the jurors on the issue which she can remind them of in summation.]

Q. Is there anyone on the panel who does not drive an automobile?

Q. Do any of you feel that just because a plaintiff files a lawsuit, he is entitled to something? Is there any feeling among you that the mere act of filing suit indicates that there is some merit in the plaintiff's claim? [Many jurors will think that "where there is smoke, there is fire." A defense attorney wants to disabuse the jury of the idea that when there is a lawsuit, there is the basis for the lawsuit.]

Q. Are any of you acquainted with, or have you ever been treated by, Dr. Blank, the physician who treated and cared for the plaintiff in this case?

Q. Is there anyone on the panel who has ever studied law or medicine to any extent?

Q. Is there any reason, whether I've mentioned it or not, why any of you could not give both of these defendants a completely fair and impartial trial?

§10.05 Child-Pedestrian Accidents

Many tort suits involve personal injuries suffered by children hit by automobiles. Typically these are the result of a child darting into the street from between parked cars or from the curb and being struck by a moving vehicle. Young children in particular are unpredictable because their reasoning has not yet matured, and the foolish and unexpected things they do often result in injury.

In the past many courts were willing to absolve drivers of liability because of either the contributory negligence of the child in running into the roadway or the contributory negligence of the parent in not supervising the child properly. Increasingly, however, the trend seems to be in the other direction. The modern theory is that since it is foreseeable that children may suddenly dart into a roadway, motorists must be on the lookout for them and drive accordingly, particularly in residential areas.

Most everyone has sympathy for an injured child and its parents. It is less commonly appreciated that many jurors identify with the defendant-driver. Most jurors drive, and fear that they might one day be involved in a similar type of accident. Some may have had near-accidents when a child darted in front of them. This subconscious identification with the driver needs to be borne in mind by a plaintiff's attorney. Plaintiff's counsel should be loathe to dismiss a nondriver, the only person with whom it will not be necessary to overcome a built-in identification with the defendant driver. Parents of young children also tend to be plaintiff's jurors, women perhaps more so than men. They are familiar with the unpredictable actions of children, and will empathize with the child's parents.

Single men, who are not parents, and childless career women usually are inclined toward the defendant-driver. Taxi drivers, truck drivers, commercial vehicle operators, and others who drive for a living may be particularly unsympathetic to the plaintiff's case. At some point in their careers, they most likely have had to slam on their brakes to avoid hitting a child. They constantly have to worry about a young child running out in front of their vehicle.

During voir dire plaintiff's counsel should stress that children are to be expected on residential streets, that the movements of children at play are unpredictable, and that it is not unusual for a child to suddenly dash into the street and in front of a vehicle. Counsel should emphasize that a motorist driving on a residential street has to be constantly alert for children and drive accordingly.

Plaintiff's counsel must be familiar with the applicability in the jurisdiction of contributory negligence principles to children of tender years. As a general rule, the law does not equate the standard of care for a child with the standard of care for an adult. In some jurisdictions a child under a certain age is incapable of being contributorily negligent as a matter of law. Counsel for the plaintiff might also remind jurors that at some time they, too, have probably been in similar situations, and that on those occasions they managed to avoid hitting the child. This is a delicate argument, however, for the juror may decide that the difference in result between the juror's experience and the defendant's experience was a matter of fortuity.

The attorney for the plaintiff must be sure that prospective jurors consider the child's age *at the time of the accident.* This is extremely important, because the trial may be held years after the event. The child will almost always be more mature, mentally and physically, at the time of the trial than at the time of the accident.

Following is a list of sample questions that might be asked in a child-pedestrian accident case.

Plaintiff's Voir Dire

Q. Is there anyone on the panel who knows either young Billy (the child), Mr. and Mrs. Edwards (parents of the child), the defendant, Mr. Sneed, Mr. Jackson (defendant's attorney), or any member of Mr. Jackson's law firm? [The term used to refer to the child—young Billy—itself induces sympathy in a way that an impersonal reference to "the plaintiff and his family" would not.]

Q. Is there anyone on the panel who does not drive an automobile or other vehicle?

Q. Have any of you ever been involved, as a driver of a vehicle, in an accident involving a child?

Q. Is there anyone on the panel who has ever narrowly missed hitting a child on a residential, or any other, street. [If so, the juror should be asked to relate the experience and how he or she felt about it. The lawyer should express sympathy for the juror's experience, but poignantly observe that in fact the juror was able to take action to avoid hitting the child.]

Q. Have any of you, while driving, ever had a child dart out unexpectedly from a curb or from behind a parked car, right in front of you?

Q. Is there anyone on the panel who does not slow down and drive very cautiously on residential streets or around a school? [The lawyer seeks to point out that in their everyday driving jurors routinely consider the possible presence of children.]

Q. Now, the court, in its charge, will instruct you as follows with respect to *ordinary care* and *negligence* of a child of this age:

Ordinarily care, when used with respect to the conduct of a child, means that degree of care which an ordinary, prudent child of the same age, experience, intelligence, and capacity would have used under the same or similar circumstances. You are further instructed that negligence, when used with respect to the conduct of a child, means failure to do that which an ordinary, prudent child of the same age, experience, intelligence, and capacity would have done under the same or similar circumstances, or doing that which such a child would not have done under the same or similar circumstances.

Now, my question, ladies and gentlemen, is whether you will be able to follow that instruction, follow the law, and not hold the child in this case to any higher or more stringent degree of care? [In this question and the next the lawyer impresses the jury with his knowledge of the law and seeks to commit the jurors to following the law.]

Q. The court will also instruct you that the driver of a vehicle has a duty to exercise the same degree of reasonable care that an ordinarily reasonable and prudent person would exercise under the same or similar circumstances. Can you all apply that law to the defendant-driver in this case?

Q. Are there any among you who feel that a motorist on a residential street where children are present should not be required to look out for their safety? That it is the child's responsibility to look out for himself?

Q. Is there anyone on this panel who believes that a motorist should not be held responsible for striking a child who has run out from behind parked cars, if the evidence establishes that the motorist should have foreseen the child's presence? [The lawyer wants to place the focus on the motorist's responsibilities and not those of the child.]

Q. Under the law, the father of a child is responsible for his child's medical bills and support. The father is permitted by law to sue to recover any medical expenses or support which he may have lost in the past or incur in the future, from any person whose negligence caused injuries to the child. My question, now, is whether there is any member of this panel who feels it is wrong or improper for a father to bring such an action, despite what the law says?

Q. Also, under our law, minor children cannot sue in their own right; a court-appointed guardian or *next friend* must bring the suit in a child's behalf. This is what has been done in this case. Billy's father has brought this suit in his own behalf, to recover his expenses, and also in behalf of his son, to recover damages for the injuries sustained by Billy. Does anyone on the panel believe that regardless of the law, a father should not act on behalf of his child and bring such a suit?

Q. Is there anyone on the panel who feels that he or she will not be able to remember throughout this trial, that Billy at the time of the accident was only seven years old, and not ten years old, as he is at the present time?

Q. Are any of you parents of elementary school children?

Q. I am sure that all of you realize that children of seven are sometimes unpredictable and even careless. Have any of you had such experiences with seven-year-olds? [It is useful to ask jurors to relate their experiences in this regard.]

Q. Is there anyone who would expect the child in this case to exercise the same degree of care that an adult would exercise?

Q. Do all of you agree that drivers need to be prepared for the unexpected when young children are about?

Q. Do any of you feel that at least one parent of a child should watch for and be with that child at all times?

Q. Is there anyone on the panel who is of the opinion that a child should not be allowed to recover for injuries incurred while a parent was not with the child?

Q. Would any of you hold Billy to the same understanding of the need for care that you would expect of a person 35 years of age, or would you hold him to the standard of conduct of children of similar age, education, and understanding? [A rhetorical question designed to reinforce the point that the lawyer has been trying to make—that a child is not to be held to the same standard of care as an adult.]

Q. Now the evidence in this case will show that the speed limit on Spruce Street at the time of this accident was 30 miles per hour. The evidence may further show that defendant at the time of the accident was proceeding at 30 miles per hour. Is there anyone who feels that regardless of the circumstances or conditions, a motorist who was driving within the speed limit should not be held liable for injuries he causes? [The lawyer will want to follow this question with an explanation or illustration to show how a driver can be negligent even when abiding by the speed limit.]

Q. The court will explain and define proximate cause to you. In order to recover damages, plaintiff need only show that the defendant's conduct was *a* proximate cause of the accident, not the *only* cause. Do any of you feel that, in spite of this instruction, the defendant's negligence must appear to be the sole cause of the accident that resulted in these injuries?

Q. Have any of you ever been sued, or had some other manner of claim filed against you or a close friend or any member of your family, as a result of an automobile collision?

Q. Have any of you ever been sued, or had a claim of any kind filed against you, as a result of an accident involving a child? What about members of your families or close friends?

Q. Now, we all have some sympathy for a driver of an automobile involved in a collision with a child. We know that no one would purposely hit a child, and we are therefore understanding of the feelings of someone who has, regardless of the circumstances, struck a small child. However, will all of you promise me that you will not let that natural feeling of sympathy enter into your verdict if you feel from the evidence that this defendant was responsible for this accident? [The lawyer tackles the driver-identification issue head on, while indicating that a driver does not have to have intended to hit his victim in order to be held liable.]

Q. Now many of you have watched lawyer shows like Perry Mason on television, and you have probably heard the phrase "proof beyond a reasonable doubt." Do all of you understand that that is the standard of proof in a criminal case and that this is a civil case? In a civil case, as the judge will instruct you, a plaintiff must only establish proof by a preponderance of the evidence, that is, that it was more likely than not. [The lawyer may, using his hands to resemble scales, illustrate the difference between the burdens of proof in civil and criminal cases.]

Q. Is there any reason, whether I have mentioned it or not, why any of you feel that you should not sit on this jury, why you could not make a totally fair and impartial juror to both sides?

Defendant's Voir Dire

Because motorists are more likely than nonmotorists to empathize with the defendant in a child accident case, defendant's counsel will be trying to obtain as many jurors who drive as possible. Defense counsel will constantly try to remind jurors of the difficult position a driver is in when a child unexpectedly runs in front of a car. The defendant's lawyer will also want to emphasize that before the jury can hold the defendant liable, it must find that he was guilty of negligence. The defendant's strategy is to convince the jury that what happened was an unfortunate but unavoidable accident.

It is important for defense counsel to be aware of the natural tendency for jurors to sympathize with the injured child and his parents. Counsel should stress the jurors' duty to return a verdict based on the law and not their quite understandable sympathy for the child and his parents.

The following questions might be asked by defense counsel:

Q. Is there anyone on this panel who knows either of the plaintiffs in the case, any members of their family, or the plaintiff's lawyer or any member of the lawyer's family or law firm? [Note the use of the impersonal term "plaintiff," as compared to plaintiff's attorney's reference to her client as "young Billy."]

Q. Is there anyone on this panel who does not drive?

Q. Have any of you ever been involved in any type of automobile or other vehicle collision which resulted in a claim or lawsuit filed by you against another party?

Q. Have any of you ever incurred injuries as a result of an automobile accident or any other type of accident?

Q. How many of you have very young children, children of elementary school age or younger?

Q. To those of you with children of that age, has your child ever been injured as a result of any type of accident? [Parents in general, and parents of young children who have been injured in an accident in particular, are likely to identify with the plaintiffs.]

Q. Have any of you ever known a child, of any age, involved in a child-pedestrian automobile accident?

Q. Now, all of us have a natural feeling of sympathy for this injured child and his parents, but the law tells us that sympathy is not to enter into your verdict in this case in any way. Is there anyone who, for any reason, thinks this is wrong? Is there anyone who cannot or will not follow this principle? [Defense counsel should at this point pick several jurors at random, and, addressing them by name, ask if they can follow this principle.]

Q. The court will instruct you that a motorist is only liable for an accident in case of failure to exercise that degree of care which an ordinarily reasonable, prudent person would have exercised under the same or similar circumstances. My question is, will each of you follow the court's instructions on that point, and return a verdict for the defendant if you find that he acted in accord with the law? [Again, the lawyer wants to extract this commitment from individual jurors. The defense counsel wants to commit the jurors to deciding the case on the law, and not to let sympathy for the plaintiff affect their verdict.]

Q. Is there anyone here who lives in a neighborhood or on a street where no children at all reside or play, as a general rule?

Q. Is there anyone on the panel who has ever filed a claim or a lawsuit against anyone else for injuries to a child resulting from any type of accident, particularly one similar to that involved in this case?

Q. Do any of you believe that just because a person, particularly a child, files a lawsuit, that person is entitled to recover some damages, or that there is bound to be some merit to the claim?

Q. Does anyone on this panel feel that regardless of the facts and evidence as to the defendant's responsibility for this unfortunate accident, that the young child in this case is entitled to some recovery? [Defense counsel seeks to get at the sympathy issue from another angle.]

Q. Have any of you ever worked on or been involved in a campaign urging motorists to watch out for children?

Q. I have this question for those on the panel who have very young children. Do each of you make it a practice to warn your children about the dangers of running blindly out into the streets? Do you not instruct them to look both ways before crossing a street? [Defense counsel wants to remind jurors of the parents' responsibilities for their children's actions.]

Q. Is there any reason, whether I have mentioned it or not, why any of you could not give to all the parties the benefit of the fair and impartial trial which the law guarantees to them?

§10.06 Legal Malpractice Actions

Many unsuccessful litigants prefer to blame their in-court losses on the weaknesses of their attorneys rather than on the weaknesses of their case. Many prospective jurors have also had unpleasant or unprofitable experiences with attorneys. This volatile combination has produced a proliferation of plaintiffs willing to sue lawyers and a large core of prospective jurors willing to return verdicts against lawyers. In this mushrooming climate of malpractice litigation, the task of choosing a fair and impartial jury is a difficult one.

Even jurors who have not had unsatisfactory personal experiences with lawyers may dislike or distrust them as a class. Opinion polls consistently show that lawyers are held in low esteem by the public. These results should not be surprising. Lawyers are called in times of trouble, and, in enforcing their clients' legal rights, cause trouble for other persons. Criminal defense attorneys often represent individuals accused of heinous crimes; many of the public identify these lawyers with the clients they represent, regardless of whether this identification is justifiable. Many lawyers are perceived as greedy and unscrupulous, others as stuffy and arrogant. Those who dislike lawyers for whatever reason may be delighted to be provided the opportunity to return a verdict against a lawyer sued by a disgruntled client. A juror will almost invariably identify with the client rather than with the lawyer.

To illustrate a typical voir dire in a legal malpractice case, consider the following fact situation. The defendant lawyer, Mr. Taylor, a sole practitioner, was hired by a person injured in an automobile collision to sue the other party to the collision. Negotiations between the parties were entered into, but proved unsuccessful. Meanwhile, Mr. Taylor had failed to timely file the lawsuit, with the result that the client's claim for $100,000 damages was barred by the statute of limitations. The former client has sued Mr. Taylor for malpractice.

Plaintiff's Voir Dire

Q. Does anyone on the panel know, or has anyone on the panel had business dealings with, Mr. Taylor, the defendant in this case?

Q. Is there anyone on the panel who feels that lawyers should not be sued, whatever the circumstances?

Q. Many intelligent persons, lawyers among them, think that all lawsuits are a bit of a gamble, and that a litigant should gracefully accept whatever is the result of the suit? Is there anyone on the panel who shares this feeling?

Q. Are there any lawyers on this panel or anyone who has ever studied law at any time? [Lawyers, even if not disqualified from jury service, will identify with other lawyers. Those who have studied law are likely to have great respect for lawyers.]

Q. Is there anyone on the panel with a family member who is a lawyer or law student?

Q. Do any of you have close friends or business associates who are lawyers?

Q. How many of you have your own personal lawyer?

Q. How many of you, who have your own personal lawyers, have a special feeling of respect and admiration for that lawyer?

Q. All of you, I am sure, realize that lawyers can make mistakes like everybody else? [Plaintiff's counsel seeks to disabuse jurors of the notion that lawyers are special persons who do not make mistakes.]

Q. Do all of you believe that lawyers should be held accountable for their mistakes, just as you and I are? [Plaintiff's counsel continues her effort to bring lawyers to the level of ordinary persons.]

Q. Have any of you ever been represented by a lawyer in a personal injury suit?

Q. If any of you have been represented by a lawyer in a suit to recover damages for personal injuries, were the results of that suit satisfactory or unsatisfactory to you?

Q. Now, this suit against the defendant is based on his alleged negligence in failing to timely file a lawsuit against a person who collided with the plaintiff's automobile and caused him severe injuries. It involves issues of negligence and proximate cause. The judge will define negligence and proximate cause for you. Can each of you listen to the evidence in this case, consider the definitions of negligence and proximate cause, and base your verdict entirely on the evidence you hear and see in this case, and on the law as applied to those facts?

Q. Will each of you promise to return a verdict awarding damages against this lawyer if you feel, at the conclusion of the case, that we have proved by a preponderance of the evidence that the defendant's negligence was a proximate cause, as Her Honor, the judge, will define that term to you, of loss and damages to the plaintiff?

Q. Is there any reason at all, whether I've mentioned it or not, why any of you feel that you cannot be completely fair and impartial in this case?

Defendant's Voir Dire

The defendant's lawyer in a legal malpractice case will want to challenge, either for cause or peremptorily, jurors who dislike lawyers or who may have had a bad experience with a lawyer. Following are some voir dire questions which might identify such jurors:

Q. Does anybody on the panel know the plaintiff in this case or any member of his family?

Q. Do any of you know Miss Corso, the plaintiff's lawyer in this case? Have any of you had any dealings with the lawyers in Miss Corso's firm?

Q. Now the defendant in this case, Richard Taylor, as you are aware, is a lawyer. What I would like is for each of you to tell me a little bit about your experience with lawyers, particularly those experiences which made a lasting impression on you. The experiences could be those of a close friend or relative, if they made a significant impression on you. [With this open-ended question, defense counsel seeks to have jurors, by their own words and choices of memorable experiences, indicate their feelings about lawyers.]

Q. We have all seen lawyers portrayed on television and in the theater. Perhaps in addition you have read books where a lawyer was one of the principal characters. Based on these portrayals of lawyers, as well as your own personal experiences, do you have an opinion of lawyers? If so, I would appreciate your sharing that opinion with us.

Q. Is there anyone on the panel who at some stage of his or her life thought seriously about becoming a lawyer but didn't? Could you please tell us what caused you to change your mind? [The reasons why a juror might have rejected a career in law will provide insight into the juror's attitude toward lawyers. Those who had the choice imposed on them (e.g., by rejection of their application to law school) may harbor a resentment at those who were not denied the opportunity to practice law.]

Q. Are any of you on the panel currently lawyers or law students?

Q. Do any of you have family members or close friends who are lawyers or law students?

Q. How many of you have your own personal attorney or one you regularly consult?

Q. Have any of you ever been represented by a lawyer in any lawsuit?

Q. (to jurors who answered the preceding question affirmatively) Could you please tell us how you felt about the quality of the representation provided by your attorney in the case, and whether you were satisfied with the results of the suit?

Q. Have any of you ever had a bad or unpleasant experience with a lawyer whom you hired to represent you in any capacity, in a lawsuit or otherwise?

Q. Have any of your relatives or close friends ever had a bad or unpleasant experience with a lawyer whom they hired to represent them in any capacity, in a lawsuit or otherwise?

Q. Is there anyone here who has ever felt misrepresented or harmed by his or her lawyer in any way?

Q. Have any of you ever felt that your lawyer was negligent or careless in the handling of your law business, whatever it was?

Q. Have any of you ever felt that your lawyer "sold out" to the other side?

Q. Have any of you ever felt that a lawyer dealt unfairly with you in a legal matter?

Q. Is there anyone on the panel who simply dislikes and mistrusts lawyers as a class?

Q. Some famous writer once said that following the revolution the first thing to do was kill all the lawyers. What do each of you think about that statement? [Another open-ended question, to which there is no "correct" response. Defense counsel keeps returning to this issue because of its critical importance.]

Q. Do any of you feel that lawyers are overpaid for what they do? That they charge too much?

Q. Now, this may seem harsh and blunt to you, but it is important that I ask all of you, do any of you feel that lawyers, or most lawyers, are just plain crooks or cheats? [While it is unlikely that this earthy form of the question will elicit a yes answer, a juror may, by an unconscious head nod or wry smile, indicate agreement. The lawyer may then choose to direct specific questions to such jurors with an aim to eliciting a disqualifying bias.]

Q. In opinion polls taken at different times and in different parts of this country, lawyers are not rated very highly. Would that be your opinion as well? Would that fact alone give you any problems if you were a juror in this case? Would knowledge of these polls, which I'm sure most of you have seen, make it difficult for you to be fair and impartial to Mr. Taylor, who is a lawyer?

Q. Would each of you be able to give Mr. Taylor the same fair and impartial trial you would give anyone else? [Like plaintiff's attorney, defense counsel wants to place the lawyer on the same footing as ordinary citizens, but in respect to the right to a fair and impartial trial.]

Q. Would each of you be able to give Mr. Taylor the same fair and impartial trial you would want from a jury if you were a party to a lawsuit? [The personalized form of the question reinforces the lawyer's point.]

Q. Have any of you ever sued a lawyer for anything?

Q. Have any of you ever sued a lawyer who has represented you in a lawsuit?

Q. Has anyone on the panel ever threatened to sue a lawyer, or had a claim for negligence against a lawyer which was settled?

Q. Will each of you promise me that you will listen to both sides here, listen to all of the evidence, and not make up your minds on this case until you have heard all the evidence?

Q. Would each of you look Mr. Taylor in the eye and promise him that you will give him a totally fair and impartial trial and not return a verdict against him unless you are thoroughly convinced by a preponderance of the evidence that he was guilty of negligence which proximately caused damage to the plaintiff? [Establishing eye contact with the defendant is generally important but perhaps particularly so in this case. A juror who is biased against the lawyer may experience difficulty looking the defendant in the eye. Eye contact may cause the jurors to see Mr. Taylor as a person rather than as "a lawyer."]

Q. Is there any reason at all, whether I've mentioned it or not, why any of you feel that you could not be totally fair and impartial jurors in this case?

§10.07 Medical Malpractice Actions

The litigious trend in the United States is perhaps most noticeable in the field of medicine. The threat of a malpractice suit has become a fact of life for the physician practicing in the United States today. American doctors face possible suits not just for surgery that goes awry, but for mistakes in judgment which result in disability or injury to a patient. To many doctors it seems as if mere bad results or the failure to totally cure a patient, or even serious disappointment with the result of treatment, will lead to a lawsuit, with little concern for whether the doctor has been negligent.

One of the byproducts of this litigation boom has been a skyrocketing increase in the price of malpractice insurance, with much of the cost passed on to patients in the form of higher fees. Another effect is the increasing tendency on the part of doctors to practice defensive medicine, ordering tests and examinations to cover remote contingencies, again with the cost being passed on to the patient.

Several general considerations should be kept in mind by attorneys in selecting a jury to try a medical malpractice case. The first of these relates to the changing image of the modern doctor. The growing number of malpractice suits has generated much discussion in the media. Often commentators will point out differences between the caring family doctor of yesteryear and the modern physician who neither sees patients at home nor gets to know them as individuals.

As a result of this unfavorable publicity, many doctors, particularly surgeons, fear a jury trial in a malpractice case. They think that the average juror is prejudiced against them. Actually, the reverse may be true. On balance, the jury may start out with sympathy for the defendant physician, which will be maintained throughout the trial unless changed by the evidence. Many experienced trial lawyers believe that the average citizen tends to be more favorably inclined toward the defendant doctor, and toward a hospital defendant, than toward the plaintiff in a malpractice case.

There are several reasons for this sympathy for the doctor. It is not uncommon to feel that one owes one's life or good health to a doctor's care. Many persons also have a well-nurtured, almost inbred respect toward physicians and surgeons. Many parents hope that their children will become doctors.

This respect toward physicians is a factor which affects the voir dire strategy of both sides in a malpractice case. The defendant's attorney will recognize it as an advantage if skillfully handled and not overdone. The plaintiff's attorney needs to diagnose whether any jurors have such veneration for physicians that it would be impossible for them to conceive of a doctor being guilty of negligence.

The converse may also be true, however. While many jurors are sympathetic to doctors, some have no faith in them. Such an attitude, whether based on ignorance or insight, must be ferreted out by the defendant's attorney. Past unpleasant experiences with doctors need to be explored. Many patients have received real or imagined unsatisfactory treatment from a physician. Those who admit to such an experience should be asked whether it would make it difficult to decide the case only on the evidence. A juror who has had an unsatisfactory past experience with doctors or hospitals is not likely to make a good defendant's juror.

Jurors should be questioned about whether they have their own doctors and whether they are satisfied with the medical care they receive. A juror's general attitude toward doctors will usually reflect the degree of satisfaction with the juror's own doctor.

Religious attitudes also need to be explored. This is a delicate area and should be handled with sensitivity and tact, as some jurors may be offended by any probing of their religious beliefs. Some individuals, however, reject accepted principles of medicine on religious grounds; to varying degrees, they neither believe in nor rely on physicians for medical care for themselves or their families.

Occupations of jurors and their spouses are always an important area of inquiry, but particularly so in a medical malpractice case. Persons who have worked in a hospital, a doctor's office, a pharmacy, or for a drug company will usually favor the defense, although sometimes their first-hand exposure to shoddy medical practice may bias them against doctors. Spouses of physicians obviously must be challenged. Less obvious are spouses of other professionals. These, too, may tend to favor the defense. In personal injury suits, workers are generally considered to be favorable to a plaintiff, but this may not be the case in malpractice actions. Some lawyers feel that working-class persons and their families are more likely than upper-income earners to be impressed by doctors. Those in the higher socio-economic strata may have witnessed doctors leave cocktail parties to go to the hospital. It is also important that the lawyer determine how long a worker has been with the same employer; stable employment usually indicates a stable personality, and such a person will be more likely to favor the "establishment," of which the medical profession is a part.

Past jury service, particularly in a malpractice case, is a factor of vital concern. If a prospective juror has served previously in a malpractice case, counsel should attempt to learn the disposition of that other case and the juror's reaction to his or her service. It is critical to ascertain any possible effect that the prior service may have on the juror.

§10.08 —Illustrative Fact Pattern and Voir Dire in a Medical Malpractice Case

For purposes of a sample voir dire in a medical malpractice case, consider the following facts. Plaintiff, Frank Smith, a truck driver, was involved in an accident in which he received multiple injuries. The injuries included cuts and bruises on the top of his head, a sprained back, and damage to his shoulders and neck. Following the accident, Smith was taken to the emergency room of a nearby hospital for treatment. Subsequently he complained of severe headaches, and was referred by his family doctor to an orthopedist, Dr. Jones. Dr. Jones saw Smith approximately seven times and provided him with physical therapy. Smith complained of severe headaches while under treatment, but continued to work as a truck driver. Sometimes the headaches would be so bad that he would have to pull off the road and rest until the pain subsided.

Finally Dr. Jones referred Smith to Dr. Black, a neurosurgeon. Dr. Black conducted only a brief examination of Smith, and did not carry out any neurological tests (such as an electroencephalogram, spinal tap, or brain scan). The day after his examination by Dr. Black, Smith passed out while driving on an interstate highway. He lost control of his truck, and the truck crashed into a bridge abutment.

Smith is now completely paralyzed from the neck down. He has filed suit against both doctors. Smith contends that the defendants failed to diagnose and treat the structural lesion of the brain which was responsible for the symptoms which caused the accident which paralyzed him. Dr. Black was allegedly negligent for failing to employ appropriate laboratory tests which would have detected the lesion, and Dr. Jones for not referring Smith sooner to a specialist. Both defendants were allegedly negligent in failing to warn the plaintiff not to drive his tractor-trailer rig until his symptoms could be more thoroughly analyzed.

Plaintiff's Voir Dire

Q. Is anyone on the panel related to or acquainted with either of the defendants, Dr. Jones or Dr. Black?

Q. Do any of you know anyone who works for either of these doctors?

Q. Has anyone ever been treated by, or been a patient of, either of the defendants?

Q. Do any of you know Mr. Johnson, the attorney representing Dr. Jones, or Mrs. Gans, the attorney representing Dr. Black? Or any member of their law firm?

Q. Could each of you tell us whether you, or any member of your family or a close friend, has ever been seriously injured?

Q. If you, a member of your family, or a close friend were ever so injured, and received medical treatment, could you please tell us about the quality of the medical treatment that was received?

Q. Do all of you have a family physician, or at least a doctor you regularly use when you or the members of your family are ill?

Q. How do you feel about the quality of the medical service that your doctor provides?

Q. Have you ever sought out a second opinion, after receiving the opinion of your family doctor? A third opinion? [This is a very enlightening question, for jurors who seek out second and third opinions recognize that doctors are not infallible.]

Q. Do any of you feel indebted to a physician or surgeon who rendered services which saved your life or that of a close friend or a member of your family?

Q. Those of you on this panel who feel that way, would it be possible for you to weigh the evidence in this case carefully, and if it is proven to you, find negligence on the part of either or both of these doctors? Could you, in other words, give this plaintiff a fair and impartial trial based solely on the evidence in this case?

Q. How many of you have children? If so, did you ever want any of your children to study medicine or become a doctor?

Q. Now, I am sure we all have great respect for the medical profession, I know I do, but is there anyone here who just feels that doctors as a class are special, or that they can do no wrong?

Q. Each of you, I am sure, recognizes that doctors are human beings, and can make mistakes and errors in judgment like any human being, is that not so? [The lawyer seeks to bring doctors down to the level of ordinary mortals.]

Q. Will each of you promise me that if a preponderance of the evidence shows that the care and treatment rendered by either of these doctors was not up to the skill and care required of doctors with their respective specialties in this community, you will return a verdict in favor of Mr. Smith? [This question incorporates a common legal standard in medical malpractice cases. If the standard in a particular jurisdiction is different, the question should be adjusted accordingly.]

Q. Would it embarrass you in any way to find a doctor negligent?

Q. Now, as has been explained to you, this is a medical malpractice case, a civil case. These doctors are not charged with a crime. [The lawyer at this time will want to explain to the jurors the differences between the burden of proof in a civil and criminal case.]

Q. Do each of you understand that the defendants' license and right to practice medicine is in no way involved in this case? [Some jurors may believe that doctors found liable in a malpractice suit will automatically have their licenses revoked. The lawyer needs to educate the jury lest some of its members be disinclined from returning a verdict for the plaintiff because of a reluctance to see either of the doctors lose their license.]

Q. Do each of you understand that this is just a civil suit for damages suffered by Frank Smith as a result of substandard care by these doctors?

Q. Do each of you understand and agree that a doctor, just like any other professional man or woman, must meet and conform to certain standards and requirements within that doctor's particular field of medicine?

Q. Has anyone on this panel ever studied medicine to any extent?

Q. Are there any nurses on this panel, or did any of you at one time or another study nursing, whether you finished the course or not?

Q. Is there anyone here who either now works or has ever worked for a doctor or a hospital in any capacity?

Q. Do any of you have, or have you ever had, a doctor or nurse in your family?

Q. Have any of you ever been sued for damages for personal injuries because of some conduct on your part?

Q. I would like to talk to each of you individually for a moment and I would appreciate it if we could begin by your telling me your occupation, where you work, and how long you have worked there, and the precise nature of your job responsibilities. If you are married or have adult children, could you please also provide me with the same information about your spouse and your children. [At this point, the plaintiff's lawyer is looking particularly for spouses of doctors, lawyers, accountants, engineers, and other professionals.]

Q. Is there any reason at all, whether it concerns something I have mentioned or not, why any of you feel that you could not be impartial and fair jurors for all parties in this case, basing your decision on the evidence alone and not on any bias or prejudice?

Defendant's Voir Dire

Q. Is anyone on the panel acquainted in any way with Mr. Smith, the plaintiff in this case?

Q. Has anyone ever been employed in any capacity by the ABC Corporation, the trucking company which employed Mr. Smith?

Q. Have any of you ever been employed, or are you now employed, by any trucking company, or by a bus company, or by any company or individual whose business it is to transport or haul people, freight, or merchandise of any kind? [Jurors who are themselves truck drivers will empathize with a plaintiff who is a truck driver, particularly one who will never again be able to work in that capacity.]

Q. Do any of you know anyone who works for the ABC Corporation or have you ever had any relatives who worked for that company?

Q. If any of you have ever been involved in any kind of vehicle collision which resulted in personal injuries to you or to any member of your family, could you please tell me about that experience.

Q. Have any of you ever been employed as a truck driver?

Q. Have any of you who have been involved in vehicle collisions ever filed a lawsuit against the other party as a result of injuries you sustained?

Q. How many of you have ever sat on a jury before?

Q. Have any of you ever sat on a jury which tried a medical malpractice case?

Q. For those of you who have been on a jury which tried a medical malpractice case, could you tell me about the verdict and how you felt about your service on the case? Was there anything about that other case, and about your jury service on that case, which may in any way affect your thinking in this case?

Q. Have any of you at some time been treated for some ailment by a doctor of any kind?

Q. Have any of you had any unpleasant or unfortunate experience with a doctor? If you have, could you please tell me about it, what it involved?

Q. Will that experience in any way affect your decision in this suit, will it, in other words, in any way prevent you from being a totally fair and impartial juror in this case?

Q. Do any of you believe that a doctor in effect guarantees or, given the money that doctors charge, should guarantee that patients will get well, and should be held responsible when they don't? [Defense counsel wants to disabuse jurors of any idea that a doctor is a guarantor of a patient's health.]

Q. Is there anyone on this panel who, for any reason, just does not like doctors? That question may seem strange to you, but there are many intelligent people who feel this way, and I need to know if there are any of them on this panel. [The reference to "intelligent people" makes it easier for a juror to admit to a dislike of doctors.]

Q. Has anyone ever studied medicine to any extent? By that I mean, have you ever enrolled in medical school, or have you ever taken a course in medicine, pathology, first aid, or anything of that nature?

Q. Now, ladies and gentlemen, I am going into a rather sensitive area, and in doing so I certainly don't mean to pry or embarrass anyone. However, in order to properly represent my client, it is necessary that I learn about attitudes that might prevent any of you from being fair and impartial in this case. Is there anyone on this panel who, because of religious beliefs, does not believe in medical doctors, nurses, hospitals, or the use of medication? [It is important that the lawyer explain why the inquiry regarding religion is being made, as jurors might otherwise see it as irrelevant and an invasion of their privacy.]

Q. Is there anyone who, because of religious beliefs, simply will not use a doctor for any reason, or will not take medication for any purpose? As I have said, I do not want to embarrass anyone on this panel, but some people do have those beliefs, and it is necessary, in order to fulfill my responsibility to my client, for me to learn about them.

Q. Is there anyone here who for any reason would refuse medical treatment? [The answer to this and the following question may be more telling than questions about general attitudes toward doctors.]

Q. Is there anyone who does not now use, or who has never used, medical doctors for any purpose, regardless of the occasion?

Q. Have any of you ever studied law, whether you went to law school or simply took some law courses at one time?

Q. Is there anyone here who has ever worked for a lawyer in any capacity, that is, as a secretary, file clerk, or assistant?

Q. Have any of you read any articles about the so-called explosion in medical malpractice claims? [The lawyer will follow up an affirmative response to this question with an inquiry into the nature of the article and the effect it had on the juror.]

Q. Has anyone here ever worked in any capacity for a doctor or in a hospital?

Q. Has anyone ever been employed as a medical assistant of any kind, or as a lab technician?

Q. Are any of you now or have you in the past been employed in any way in a pharmacy or drugstore?

Q. Have any of you ever been employed in any capacity where drugs or medicines, and the handling of them, was a part of your work or business?

Q. Do any of you know any reason, whether or not I have referred to it, why, if chosen for this jury, you could not listen to the evidence, and decide this case fairly and impartially?

§10.09 Slip and Fall Cases

Many suits arise as a result of injuries on allegedly defective premises. Commonly referred to as *slip and fall* cases, the phrase covers a multitude of types of accidents. The basis of liability in these cases generally is negligence. The negligence may consist of a defect in design, a failure to repair, improper repairs or maintenance, a failure to warn of dangerous conditions, or the placing of foreign substances on, or failure to remove them from, the floor of a building. In some jurisdictions liability may also depend on the legal status of the injured person—whether the person is an invitee, licensee, or trespasser.

Typically, the defendant in these actions is the corporate or individual owner of the premises. Often the building manager, rental agent, or person responsible for the maintenance of the premises will be joined as a defendant. Some slip and fall cases are filed against municipalities or other governmental entities; these usually follow a fall on a sidewalk or street, or in a building owned by or under the control of the governmental entity.

There are certain types of jurors either plaintiff or defendant will want to exclude. A juror's occupation may have considerable bearing on the juror's perspective. Homemakers tend to be good plaintiff's jurors, particularly in a grocery store slip and fall case. Homemakers can identify with the plaintiff who has fallen on a slippery floor. Persons who live in substandard housing, especially members of minority groups, may have a deep-seated resentment of landlords. Many tenants, in fact, whether they live in substandard housing or not, may dislike landlords, property owners, or building managers in general. Many tenants believe that landlords, particularly absentee owners of apartment units, are more interested in the size of their profit than in the welfare of their tenants.

Building owners and managers, store owners and proprietors, and owners and managers of real property are likely to be unsympathetic to plaintiffs in slip and fall cases. Such people realize the practical difficulties of maintaining 100 per cent safe premises at all times. They will not want to participate in the establishment of a precedent for liability which may later be applied to them. They may also fear the possibility of an increase in their insurance rates should the plaintiff prevail.

§10.10 —Illustrative Fact Pattern and Voir Dire in a Slip and Fall Case

To illustrate a typical voir dire in a slip and fall case, assume the following facts. One evening, Mrs. Smith, 46 years old, while attempting to leave her apartment, tripped and fell on the stairway maintained for the use of tenants. The incident occurred at about 8:30 p.m., well after dark. Mrs. Smith, who was severely injured, alleged that the corporate owner of the apartment complex was negligent in three respects:

1. The defendant corporation failed to properly light the stairway
2. The defendant corporation failed to cause the lights which were to illuminate the stairway to be lit at the time Mrs. Smith fell
3. The defendant corporation failed to provide a stairway which was safe

Plaintiff sued for pain and suffering, permanent disabilities, and doctor and hospital bills. The defendant maintained that Mrs. Smith was contributorily negligent in not looking where she was going, in descending the stairs in the dark when she obviously could not see, and in not waiting until more light could be provided.

Plaintiff's Voir Dire

Q. Do any of you know any of the officers, directors, or employees of the Apartment Beautiful Complex, Inc.? Do any of you own stock or have any other financial interest in ABC, Inc.?

Q. Do any of you know, or have you ever been represented by, Miss Law, the attorney representing the defendant in this case, or any other member of her law firm?

Q. Is there anyone on the panel who is now or has ever been engaged in any phase of the real estate business either as a real estate broker, agent, or owner of rental property? [These, and the following two questions, seek to identify jurors who will be likely to identify with the defendant.]

Q. Have any of you ever been involved in the business of owning, managing, or renting real property?

Q. Have any of you ever owned, operated, or managed a hotel, motel, or other kind of hostelry?

Q. Has any member of the jury panel ever been sued as a defendant in any type of personal injury case?

Q. Have any of you ever been sued because of some accident on your property? [An affirmative answer should be followed up with questions on the nature of the suit, disposition of the suit, and the effect the suit might have on the particular juror.]

Q. Are any of you or have any of you ever been a tenant in an apartment unit or complex? [Most jurors will answer affirmatively. The attorney will then want to question each juror individually about his or her experience as a tenant.]

Q. If so, where is the apartment located and how long did you or have you lived there?

Q. Tell us if you could, a little bit about your relationship with your landlord? [The answer to this open-ended question is likely to provide important insight into whether the juror will be sympathetic to the plaintiff.]

Q. Have you or has any member of your family ever had any type of accident which caused personal injury which occurred in the apartment where you live? If so, could you please tell us about it?

Q. So far as you know, has any other tenant of your apartment complex ever suffered any type of injury in or around the apartment complex?

Q. Is there anyone on this panel who feels it is wrong or improper for a tenant to sue a landlord for damages as a result of an accident occurring in or about an apartment?

Q. Is there anyone here who feels that owners or managers of rental property have the right to run their businesses and operate their property as they please, and that they should not be responsible for any accidents which occur on or about their property? [The lawyer anticipates an argument that might be persuasive to some jurors.]

Q. What do you believe is the responsibility of an owner or manager of an apartment building, to maintain the premises in a safe condition?

Q. Do any of you believe that it is solely or primarily the responsibility of the tenants in an apartment building to look out for their own safety? [Obviously a juror who answers affirmatively is likely to be a poor juror for the plaintiff.]

Q. I appreciate this may be a difficult question to answer but where do you believe the responsibility of the owner or manager ends and the responsibility of the tenant begins?

Q. Do any of you work or have any of you worked at night in places which were not well lit?

Q. Is anyone employed in the electric supply business, or in a light fixture store or business?

Q. Do any of you have relatives or close friends who either own, operate, maintain, or manage rental property of any kind?

Q. Do any of you live in an area which is not well lighted and where it is difficult to walk or get around at night?

Q. Do any of you have relatives or close friends who are handicapped to the extent that they need help to get around, particularly at night?

Q. Do any of you work in the construction, maintenance, or repair business, particularly as it involves real property?

Q. Has anyone on this panel ever had any medical or legal education or training of any kind?

Q. Can and will each of you follow the law in this case as given by the court?

Q. Can and will each of you promise that you will listen carefully to the evidence, and decide this case solely on the law given you by the court and on the evidence you hear and see in this courtroom during this trial?

Q. Is there any reason at all, whether it concerns something I've mentioned or not, why any of you feel that you could not be completely unbiased, fair, and impartial jurors?

Defendant's Voir Dire

Q. Do any of you know the plaintiff in this case, Mrs. Smith, or any member of her family?

Q. Do any of you know her attorney in this case, Mr. Clear?

Q. Have any of you ever been involved in any accident which resulted in personal injuries of any kind to you?

Q. Has any member of your family ever suffered any personal injury because of an accident of any kind?

Q. Have any of you, or has any member of your family, ever fallen in a grocery or department store, office or apartment building, or any other kind of building? If so, did that fall result in personal injuries?

Q. Has anyone on this panel ever filed a lawsuit for damages for personal injuries of any kind? If so, could you tell us something about that suit and its disposition?

Q. How many of you live or have lived in a multi-story apartment complex?

Q. How many of you who live or did live in such an apartment complex have to travel up and down stairs at night to get to and from your apartment?

Q. Do any of you live in governmental housing or apartments of any kind? [Those jurors who do are likely to be poor, and unsympathetic to the defendants. Persons who are in apartments by choice are more likely to be satisfied with their accommodations than persons who have had such housing arrangements imposed on them.]

Q. Those who do live in apartments, whether governmentally or privately owned, could you please tell me where that apartment or apartment complex is located, i.e., what part of town is it in? What is the surrounding area like? [Another question designed to learn about the juror's socioeconomic status. Apartments in the poorer part of town are less likely to be well kept up, and consequently more likely to have led to injuries.]

Q. For those of you who live in apartments, could you tell us about the experience which you best remember, whether pleasant or unpleasant, involving the owner, manager, or rental agent of your apartment? [Like the plaintiff's lawyer, defense counsel is vitally interested in the juror's relationship with those in charge of the juror's apartment. Defense counsel employs a somewhat different technique, however, to ascertain this information, asking about the juror's most memorable relevant experiences.]

Q. Have any of you ever had occasion to complain to a landlord or a manager of a building about the maintenance of the building or the surrounding premises?

Q. Do any of you, for any reason, feel opposed to or resentful of, or simply dislike, anyone who owns, manages, maintains, or rents apartments?

Q. Do any of you have relatives or close friends who, because of some physical disability, have difficulty walking or getting around?

Q. Do any of you have vision problems?

Q. We all feel sorry for Mrs. Smith, but the court will instruct you that you are not to let your natural feeling of sympathy for an injured plaintiff play any part in your deliberations. Can you follow this instruction, and will each of you promise me that you will not let sympathy affect your verdict in any way? [The lawyer seeks to commit the jurors to resist natural feelings of sympathy.]

Q. Will each of you assure me that you will listen to the evidence and decide this case solely on that evidence, and on nothing else?

Q. Do any of you have any problems with your balance or equilibrium, that is, with staying upright?

Q. Do each of you agree that people should look where they are going, and be careful and cautious in all their movements? [Without mentioning her specifically, the lawyer subtly insinuates that the plaintiff may have been responsible for her injuries.]

Q. Now, finally, ladies and gentlemen, is there any reason, whether it concerns something I have mentioned or not, why any of you could not be a fair and impartial juror?

§10.11 Products Liability Suits

A products liability case differs from the usual personal injury or property damage case in its technical content. The plaintiff's attorney must know as much about the product in question as the manufacturer of the product.

Voir dire may be more important in a products liability case than in other tort cases, as the evidence in the case may be particularly difficult to understand. The lawyer must educate the jury on the subject matter of the suit while at the same time determining which jurors will be undesirable. Where a products case will involve a specialized field such as engineering, physics, or electronics, it is imperative to question each juror about any technical background that the juror may have in that field.

It is often a good tactic for the plaintiff's lawyer to relate the accident to a common experience the jurors may have had and the product to one the jurors are likely to have used. The attorney can often analogize the technical failure involved in the case to a common failure relating to a household, office, or shop product. The analogy can be referred to when counsel is examining the plaintiff's expert, so that the jury will pick up on the connection between the technical proof and the everyday experience.

The plaintiff's lawyer should impress on jurors that an ordinary consumer who purchases a product assumes that the product was properly manufactured, that it will do what it is supposed to do, and that it is not dangerous. Through voir dire questions to jurors about their own expectations when they purchase a product and about their reliance on the manufacturer of the product, counsel lays the groundwork for final argument.

If the case is based on a manufacturer's inadequate directions or failure to warn of the dangers of a product, the jurors should be asked about their personal practice in regard to directions which accompany the products they buy.

Few consumers pay much attention to directions or warnings unless they are prominently displayed; they do not read between the lines to discover danger. By questions about their own practices in dealing with products they buy, jurors can be conditioned to use their personal experiences as a reference point in determining the adequacy and reasonableness of the directions or warnings which accompanied the product involved in the suit.

Homemakers tend to make excellent jurors for the plaintiff in cases involving household products. They are likely to empathize with the person injured. Married men, on the other hand, who for the most part do not shop in supermarkets and who may be impressed with the manufacturer's technology and testing of its product, are less likely to be plaintiff's jurors.

Engineers and others who work in technical fields present problems for both plaintiff's and defendant's attorneys in products liability cases. Sometimes an engineer will make an excellent plaintiff's juror—the engineer understands the technology involved and the evidence relating to the defects in the product. The engineer will be able to explain this evidence to other members of the jury. If the product is one among millions manufactured, however, the engineer may sympathize with the plight of the manufacturer in producing a foolproof product. If evidence of the manufacturer's claims experience with the particular product is admissible and favorable to the manufacturer, the engineer may conclude that a mere handful of injuries out of several million products manufactured is an acceptable record.

Retailers who operate small businesses are conservative by nature, and are generally poor plaintiff's jurors. They are often impressed by large corporate entities. They may also be concerned that the costs of successful products liability suits will be passed on to them in the form of higher wholesale prices.

Plaintiff's counsel should ask about the prospective juror's familiarity with the defendant's product, and the extent of the juror's use of that product. Jurors should also be asked about their understanding of the operation and function of the product. By such questions, counsel can acquaint jurors with the product and the problem in the particular case. If the product failed during normal use, jurors who have themselves used the product are more likely to identify with the plaintiff.

§10.12 —Illustrative Fact Pattern and Voir Dire in a Products Liability Suit

For the purpose of looking at a typical voir dire in a products liability case, assume the following fact situation, taken from an actual case. In 1989 Mr. Anderson purchased from the Square Deal Automobile Company a new 1989 Supremo automobile, manufactured by Automobiles Supreme, a Michigan automaker. One of the accessories in the car was an automobile jack, made by the Best Jack Company and distributed by Automobiles Supreme.

On September 14, 1989, Mr. Anderson attempted to change a tire on his car. Using the jack that had come with the car, he raised the automobile off the ground. He blocked the remaining three wheels of the automobile so that the car could not move and proceeded to remove the tire from the car. He then noticed a leak near the oil pan and crawled part way under the car to examine it more closely. At this point the jack collapsed and the automobile fell on him.

The plaintiff alleges that the jack was in a defective condition at the time it left the manufacturer, Best Jack Company; at the time it was installed in the car by Automobiles Supreme; at the time it was delivered to the Square Deal Automobile Company; and at the time the car was sold to him. The plaintiff maintains that the defendant Best Jack Company was negligent in the design or manufacture of the jack and that the defendants Automobile Supreme and the Square Deal Automobile Company were negligent in failing to inspect the jack and discover the defect. The negligence of the respective defendants, the plaintiff alleges, was the proximate cause of his injuries. The plaintiff seeks damages for the injuries suffered as a result of his accident, including pain and suffering, medical expenses, lost earnings, and loss of future earnings.

Plaintiff's Voir Dire

Q. Do any of you know anyone connected with any of the defendants in this case? By that I mean, any officer, director, stockholder, or employee of any one of the three corporate defendants?

Q. So far as you know, do any of you know any member of the family of any officer, director, stockholder, or employee of any one of these defendants?

Q. Do any of you know, or have you ever been represented by, Mr. Nelson, Miss Goldman, or Mrs. O'Hara, the attorneys representing these defendants or any members of their law firms?

Q. Do any of you not drive an automobile?

Q. Has anyone on the panel not, at some time, bought a new car from an automobile dealer? Were you satisfied with your purchase?

Q. How many of you have ever changed a tire on an automobile?

Q. Is anyone on this panel involved in any way in the new or used car business? In the tire business?

Q. Is anyone employed, either independently or by someone else, as an automobile mechanic?

Q. Have any of you ever been so employed or engaged?

Q. Have any of you, or has your employer, ever been sued in a products liability case as a result of the sale or lease of any product?

Q. If any of you have answered "yes" to this question, could you please tell me about the suit and its disposition?

Q. Has anyone here ever been injured as a result of an incident involving an automobile? If so, I'd appreciate your telling me about your experience.

Q. Have any of you ever either purchased or used the type of jack involved in this lawsuit?

Q. Has anyone on the panel ever had any type of mechanical, technical, or engineering schooling or training?

Q. Are any of you involved in the manufacture of a product?

Q. If so, do you ever purchase component parts of your product from third parties or delegate responsibility for the manufacture or construction of part of your product to third parties?

Q. Are any of you engaged in any way in the retail sales business? If you are, could you please tell me about that business?

Q. Let me ask you this question, ladies and gentlemen. When you purchase any product from a store or any other place of business, do you expect it to work properly and safely? [The lawyer suggests that jurors should look to their own expectations in regard to products.]

Q. There is an old Latin saying, *caveat emptor,* which means "Let the buyer beware." What do you think about such a philosophy, which, I should hasten to tell you, is no longer the law in this state? [A key open-ended question, designed to learn the juror's views regarding the appropriate allocation of risk between buyer and seller.]

Q. Have any of you ever had any accident involving an automobile jack?

Q. Have any of you ever owned or operated the same make of automobile which was owned by the plaintiff in this case, that is, a Supreme Automobile?

Q. [The lawyer at this point explains the mechanical operation of the jack.] Now, I have explained to you briefly how the jack which is involved in this case works and operates. Do all of you understand, at least generally, how it is supposed to work?

Q. There will be considerable technical testimony, some of it rather complicated and difficult. Do each of you feel that you can listen carefully to that testimony, understand it, and decide from it what happened in this case and why?

Q. The court will instruct you, at the conclusion of the trial, on the law in this case. Do each of you feel that you can listen to those instructions on the law and follow them, even though they may differ in some way from your own ideas of what the law is or should be?

Q. Have any of you ever sat on a jury in a products liability case? If so, I would like you to tell me about that experience, and whether you think it will affect or influence in any way your decision in this case?

Q. Do any of you feel that it is simply wrong to sue a company or individual that has either manufactured or sold any type of commercial product? That it just shouldn't be done?

Q. How many of you, when you buy a product, carefully read all the instructions or warnings that come with it? [The lawyer again tries to get the jurors to consider their own, usually rather slipshod, practices in reading instructions.]

Q. Do all of you believe that a company which manufactures a product or a company or individual who sells a product should stand behind it?

Q. Now, I have asked you a lot of questions, and I have mentioned many subjects, but I obviously cannot look into your hearts and minds, so please answer this last question. Is there any reason at all, whether it concerns something I've mentioned or asked you about or not, why anyone here feels he or she could not make a completely fair and impartial juror in this case?

Defendant's Voir Dire

Q. Does anyone on this panel know Mr. Anderson, the plaintiff in this case, his wife, or any member of their family?

Q. Do any of you know Mr. Olsen, the attorney for the plaintiff, or any member of his law firm, or have any of you ever been represented by Mr. Olsen or his firm?

Q. Have any of you ever sued for damages any individual, partnership, or company, whether a corporation or not, for personal injuries of any sort?

Q. Have any of you ever suffered personal injuries because of an accident of any kind, an automobile collision injury, an on-the-job injury, or any other type of injury, particularly one received as a result of any defective product? If so, I would appreciate it if you would tell me about it.

Q. Have any of you ever had any unpleasantness or disagreement with a manufacturer, seller, or distributor of any product, as a result of your purchase of that product?

Q. Have any of you ever owned, rented, or operated, or do any of you presently own, rent, or operate a Supremo car?

Q. Have any of you ever had a claim, or filed a lawsuit, because of what you felt was a defective product of any kind which caused personal injuries to you or to any member of your family?

Q. Have any of you ever purchased, or do you now own, an automobile jack, the same as or similar to the one in this case?

Q. Have any of you ever been injured as a result of an accident with an automobile jack?

Q. Have any of you, or any of your close friends or members of your families, ever been involved in any way in the new or used car business? In the tire or automobile appliance business?

Q. Are any of you employed, either on your own or by someone else, as a mechanic?

Q. How many of you have ever changed a tire on an automobile?

Q. How many of you, while changing a tire, have ever crawled under an automobile while it was jacked up?

Q. Some people say that they don't make things, particularly automobiles, the way they used to. What do you think? [A key open-ended question, the defense lawyer's counterpart to plaintiff's question asking jurors their views of the doctrine of "caveat emptor."]

Q. All of you realize, I am sure, that this corporation, just like the plaintiff in this case or any individual, is entitled to a fair trial. Will each of you promise me that you will give these corporate defendants the same kind of fair trial that you would want as an individual, and that you would expect to give any other individual?

Q. I am sure that we all have, I know that I have, a natural feeling of sympathy for anyone who has been severely injured. But if the judge instructs you that feelings of sympathy should not lead you to return a verdict in favor of the plaintiff if the defendants are not legally liable, will each of you promise to follow the judge's instructions and not let your natural feelings of sympathy for the plaintiff affect your verdict? [Defense counsel seeks a useful commitment.]

Q. Do any of you feel that some corporations, especially some car manufacturing companies, are just too big, or are too greedy and money hungry? Do any of you feel that just because car manufacturers make a lot of money, they should compensate persons who were injured when using their product, regardless of whose fault caused the injury? [When large wealthy corporations are being sued, defense counsel must make sure that there are not persons on the jury who are prepared to return a verdict for the plaintiff simply because the defendant is large and wealthy, and in a better financial position to bear the loss.]

Q. Does anyone on the panel feel that just because the plaintiff has brought this lawsuit against these defendants, he is entitled to some damages?

Q. How many of you on this panel, when you buy a product with instructions or warnings of some type on it or in it, simply ignore them?

Q. Do any of you feel that generally it is not necessary for consumers who purchase products to read and follow the instructions, advice, or warnings which may accompany a product? [Defense counsel seeks to place the jurors on record as recognizing that consumers should read instructions, labels, and warnings, regardless of their own personal practices.]

Q. Have any of you ever heard or read anything about this lawsuit?

Q. From what Mr. Olson, plaintiff's attorney, and I have told you about this case, and about the evidence you are going to hear, do any of you feel that you might have difficulty understanding the technical evidence in this type of case, and that for this reason you would prefer not to sit on this jury?

Q. Both sides in this case will be presenting expert witnesses. Do any of you feel that you probably know more about this type of thing than any expert?

Q. Now ladies and gentlemen, is there any reason at all, whether it concerns something we have mentioned or not, why any of you feel that you could not be fair and impartial jurors in this case?

§10.13 Commercial and Consumer Protection Cases

Each prospective juror in a business, consumer protection, or commercial case should be questioned about educational, business, and work background. Jurors should be asked about their experiences with the type of company which is a party in the case as well as with the type of product involved in the case. Similarly, there should be inquiries into whether any member of the jury panel, or a close friend or relative, has ever been involved in a business transaction similar to the one in the suit at hand. If there are such jurors, they must be examined closely about their experiences.

If a party in a commercial, contract, or consumer protection case is a corporation or large business, jurors should be questioned as to their feelings about big business generally. They should be specifically asked by defense counsel whether they would be able to give the same fair and impartial trial to a corporate or business party that they would to an individual. Many persons are hostile to big business and large corporations, and obviously would be poor defendant's jurors.

The plaintiff who sues a business contractor for breach of contract or fraud will usually be looking for nonbusiness, blue-collar types of jurors. Renters are more likely than property owners to favor the plaintiff. The plaintiff will also be looking for jurors who have had experiences similar to the experience of the plaintiff, and who as a result might be able to identify with the plaintiff. On the other hand, the defendant will generally prefer persons who regularly engage in business deals. Property owners and investors, as well as professional persons, tend to be good jurors for the defendant.

§10.14 —Illustrative Fact Pattern and Voir Dire in a Commercial-Consumer Case

Consider the following example of a commercial-consumer case. In 1988 Mr. Hirschkoff purchased a new automobile, manufactured by a large national automobile manufacturer, from a local dealer. The car turned out to be a "lemon." Each week something new seemed to go amiss. Door handles would fall off, the trunk would not open, the car stalled incessantly, and a dozen other small things went wrong. Each time Mr. Hirschkoff would return the car to the dealer from whom he purchased it. The dealer was courteous and cooperative and would fix each defect as it was brought to his attention. Nevertheless, often the plaintiff had to leave the car overnight, because the dealer could not repair it immediately. The plaintiff had to take several days off work in order to bring in the car for repairs. Finally, Mr. Hirschkoff demanded that he be given a replacement vehicle or be refunded the purchase price. The dealer refused his request. Likewise, appeals to the manufacturer were unavailing. Mr. Hirschkoff has sued the auto maker and the local dealer, claiming fraud, misrepresentation, and breach of express and implied warranties.

Plaintiff's Voir Dire

Q. Do any of you know either party, or either lawyer, or any member of the family of either of the parties or lawyers?

Q. Have any of you ever been represented by the defendant's lawyer or by anyone in that firm?

Q. Has anyone on the panel ever purchased a new automobile?

Q. If so, was it purchased on credit or paid for in cash?

Q. Are there any of you who have had the pleasant experience of purchasing a car with which you have been perfectly satisfied, with which you have never had any complaints whatever?

Q. On the other hand, are there any of you or any members of your family who have purchased a car and been quite dissatisfied with it? If so, I would appreciate it if you would share with us your experience. [Jurors who have had unsatisfactory past experiences with manufacturers and dealers will obviously be likely to favor the plaintiff. Identification of such persons is, however, a mixed blessing. They will probably be challenged peremptorily by the defense. Nevertheless, by asking them on voir dire to recount their experiences, the plaintiff's lawyer in effect conscripts them to be an unwitting witness for the plaintiff.]

Q. Do any of you own your own business, or have you ever been self-employed?

Q. Have any of you ever been engaged in the automobile business, new or used, as an executive, salesperson, service department employee, or in any other capacity?

Q. Have any of you ever been accused of fraud or misrepresentation in your business dealings?

Q. Have any of you ever been sued or had any kind of claim filed against you as a result of a sale or business transaction?

Q. Is there anyone who has never purchased or leased an automobile, new or used, from an individual or company?

Q. Is there anyone on the panel who does not drive, and who has never driven, an automobile? [Nondrivers will be less likely to identify with the plaintiff's specific experience. However, there may be some nondrivers who have chosen this status because of a distrust of car manufacturers.]

Q. Have any of you ever been sued, or had any kind of claim filed against you, as a result of sale of an automobile?

Q. Have any of you served on a jury in a similar case? If so, I would appreciate it if you would please tell us a bit about that case, the verdict, and your feelings about your experience.

Q. Many of you may have heard the expression "let the buyer beware." What does that expression mean to you? [A key open-ended question.]

Q. If the judge instructs you that this is not the law in this state, would any of you have trouble following the judge's instruction?

Q. Some people, including some leading economists, believe that a person who makes a deal should accept it, good, bad, or indifferent, and not sue the other party in the deal. Do you agree? [The lawyer, by the reference to leading economists, makes it more acceptable for a juror to admit to a pro-business bias.]

Q. Is there anyone who feels that the law allowing the award of damages for fraud or misrepresentation, or double or treble damages for certain types of fraud and misrepresentation, is not sound policy? If any of you do feel this way, will you promise to follow the law as given by the court rather than your own sense of what the law should be, and decide the case in accord with the law of this state and based on the evidence presented at trial? [The lawyer might well at this point, explain the social policies served by the law allowing the recovery of damages in excess of those strictly required for compensation.]

Q. Is there any reason, whether it has been mentioned or not, why any of you feel you cannot be completely fair and impartial jurors?

Defendant's Voir Dire

Q. Is there anyone on the panel who is acquainted with Mr. Hirschkoff, the plaintiff, or any member of plaintiff's family, or with Mr. McGowan, the attorney for plaintiff, or any member of his family or law firm?

Q. Has anyone on the panel ever filed a lawsuit of any kind?

Q. Have any of you ever purchased a new or used automobile? What was your experience with that automobile?

Q. If your experience with the automobile was not satisfactory, did you complain to the dealer or manufacturer? If so, was your complaint resolved to your satisfaction?

Q. Did you wind up having to file a lawsuit, against either the manufacturer, dealer, or anybody else? How was it resolved? Were you satisfied with this resolution?

Q. Is there anyone who has never purchased or leased an automobile of any kind, new or used?

Q. Is there anyone who does not now drive, or who has never driven, an automobile?

Q. Has anyone on the panel ever had any type of sales training?

Q. Have any of you ever had any schooling or training as automobile mechanics?

Q. Has anyone here ever worked as an automobile mechanic?

Q. Has anyone ever worked for an automobile agency, either as an office employee or as a service department employer? If so, what were your impressions of the company?

Q. Have any of you ever had any disagreement with the owner, manager, or supervisory personnel of a new or used automobile agency?

Q. Has anyone ever been fired or terminated as an employee by an automobile agency?

Q. Do any of you just plain dislike or mistrust automobile dealers in general, for any reason, whether on general principles or because of some specific experience? [The lawyer will be looking not only for verbal agreement, which is unlikely to be forthcoming, but also for kinesic cues (*see* **§§12.08, 12.09, 12.11**) which reveal agreement.]

Q. How many of you read consumer-oriented magazines, such as *Consumer Reports*? [Jurors who read such magazines tend to be anti-big business, and pro-consumer. The lawyer, however, should look into the matter more deeply, as he does in the next series of questions.]

Q. How many of you have read some of the present-day criticisms of car manufacturers and their products? What, can you recall, did you read? And what was your reaction to what you read? Did you think: "By George, they've got it absolutely right;" or did you say "Well, wait a minute. . . .?" [A key series of questions. The lawyer seeks to identify the articles which made the greatest impression on the juror and to ascertain the juror's reaction to those articles, whether positive or negative.]

Q. For those of you who have heard or read such criticism, is there anyone who, because of reading or hearing such material, would not be able to give the defendant here a fair and impartial trial?

Q. How many of you read magazines such as *Motor Trend* which are primarily devoted to articles about automobiles? [In contrast to jurors who read consumer-oriented magazines, those who read car magazines tend to be impressed by the quality of the products of automobile manufacturers]

Q. I'm sure that you have heard the expression, "They don't make them like they used to." Do any of you feel that is an appropriate expression to apply to today's manufacturers? Could you tell us a bit about your feelings in this regard?

Q. The defendants in this case are large automobile corporations. They make large profits each year. Do any of you feel that just because they make a lot of money they should pay damages to any dissatisfied customers?

Q. Does anyone feel that if a customer does get a defective car, that the manufacturer of that car, or the dealer who sold it, or both, should be punished in any way? [Note the use of the term "punished." Plaintiff's lawyer spoke of double and treble damages without using this highly evocative term. Defense counsel seeks to put the matter in a different light. Most jurors in a civil case are reluctant to "punish" a defendant.]

Q. Is there anyone on this panel whose work involves penalty or punishment of any kind, corporal, penal, or other? [Defense counsel, following on his previous question, seeks to identify jurors who are comfortable with imposing punishment.]

Q. Is there any reason, whether it has been mentioned so far or not, why any of you feel that you could not be a fair and impartial juror in this case?

§10.15 Divorce and Child Custody Cases

In most states, domestic relations actions are heard by the court without a jury. In some, however, parties to a contested divorce proceeding are entitled to a trial by jury on contested issues of fact,[5] including whether there are grounds for divorce. Similarly, in some state custody proceedings, the jury will find the facts and will determine which parent, or other person, is entitled to custody. Depending on the law of the jurisdiction, this finding may be only advisory on the trial court.[6]

Even in those few states where the parties are entitled to a jury trial in a divorce case, only child custody matters are usually submitted to the jury. As virtually all states have adopted some form of no-fault divorce laws, the question of divorce is rarely an issue. In some states, however, traditional fault-based grounds, such as adultery, cruelty, and abandonment, coexist with the no-fault ground. If such a state also allows for a jury trial, a party could demand a jury to determine if grounds for divorce existed.

A suit involving child custody tends to be very emotional. Usually, the contest is between the natural parents of the child, although exceptionally, child custody may be awarded to a nonparent. The controlling consideration is always the best interest of the child. The interests of the parents, or others seeking custody, are secondary to the interests of the child.

A jury which is to decide the custody of a child should ideally be composed of persons who either are raising or have raised children. Mature, married individuals are usually to be preferred over young, single individuals. Professional child raisers or academics who teach child psychology, however, may be inclined to follow their own views rather than to accept the law of the jurisdiction.

There are many values and beliefs to be explored on voir dire. Religion can be a critical consideration. Some religions are opposed to divorce. "True believers" in these religions tend to be closed-minded and judgmental.

Some people think that custody of small children should always, regardless of circumstances, be awarded to the mother. There are others who believe just the contrary, and are predisposed to award custody to the father. A trial is wasted on jurors with either philosophy, as their decisions will be based not on the evidence, but on the sex of the contestants. People with arbitrary, fixed views on the subject should be removed from the jury.

Also to be avoided are jurors who would punish a parent for any kind of improper or immoral conduct. For instance, there are persons so opposed to extramarital sex that they could not vote to award custody to a parent shown

---

[5] *See generally* 24 Am Jur 2d *Divorce and Separation* §335 (1966).

[6] *Id* §791.

to have engaged in an extramarital affair, regardless of the reason. Such jurors will be unable to implement a "best interests of the child" standard. Jurors who have been divorced, or whose parents have been divorced, or who may themselves have been the subject of a child custody contest, should be questioned closely to determine their fitness to serve as jurors in a custody case. Often they will be too emotionally scarred by their own experiences to be objective.

What follows is an example of a voir dire examination by a plaintiff's attorney in a divorce case where the wife is seeking custody of the couple's child. The lawyer might begin with the following prefatory remarks:

Q. You have been told that this is a child custody case. You are going to have to decide the question of which parent should have the care, custody, and control of this child. It will be your task, after hearing the evidence, to decide which of these parties will be entitled to custody of this child. This is an awesome responsibility, and, in representing Mrs. Shaw in this case, I must ask you some probing and, in some instances, rather personal questions. I don't do this to pry or embarrass anyone, but simply to fulfill my responsibility to my client and the court to make sure that the jury which hears this case is fair and impartial.

Typical voir dire questions might include:

Q. Does anyone know either of the parties, Mr. and Mrs. Shaw, or the child, Jenny, whose custody is the subject of this suit?

Q. Is there anyone here who does not believe in divorce, for any reason?

Q. Is there anyone who does not believe that parents of children should ever sue for divorce? That the parents should stay together for the sake of the child, no matter how bad the marriage?

Q. Would anyone on the panel hold against Mrs. Shaw the fact that she is seeking a divorce?

Q. Is anyone here a member of the Catholic Church, or of any other religious group which does not approve of divorce?

Q. Have any of you ever been divorced? [An affirmative answer will generate a very delicate and tactful probing of the juror's experience, and if it has left the juror embittered in any way.]

Q. Have any of you ever been involved, as litigants, in a suit which involved the custody of a child? If so, could you tell us what happened in the case and how you felt about it? I appreciate that this may be a very difficult subject to discuss, and I certainly don't want to embarrass you, but I'm sure that you understand that it is necessary to examine this matter to ensure the parties in this case a fair trial. [It is important, particularly in this type of case, that the lawyer constantly explain why personal questions need to be asked.]

Q. Have any of you ever had a member of your own family, or a very close personal friend, involved as a litigant in a child custody case? If so, would that experience affect your deliberations or decision in this particular case? Could you cast aside someone else's experience and decide this case only on the facts you hear in this courtroom, or is that asking too much? [With the last question, the lawyer offers a juror a graceful way out.]

Q. Are there any persons on this panel who were themselves, as children, the subjects of a child custody dispute? Any of you who, as children, were placed in the care, custody, and control of one of your parents, after a court battle? If so, do you remember your feelings at the time; and could you describe them to us?

Q. Would that experience color, in any way, your thinking and your conduct as a juror in this case?

Q. If you were involved as a child in a custody case, do you think that you will be able to distance yourself from that personal experience, and decide this case only on what you hear and see in this courtroom during this trial?

Q. Now, the real question in this case, as the judge will tell you, is what is in the best interests of this child. Will each of you keep that question in mind, and determine this case based strictly on what you decide, after hearing the evidence, is in the best interests of Jenny?

Q. Will you promise me that you will determine custody here based on what is best for the child, Jenny, not on what is best for either or both parents? [The lawyer wants to impress the jury with his fairness and the fact that his concern is more with what is best for the child than what is best for his client.]

Q. We all know that it is a terrible thing for a parent, any parent, no matter how bad a person, to lose custody of his or her child, but can each of you decide this case, not on sympathy for either parent, but strictly on what, under the facts of this case, is best for this child, disregarding the feelings of the parent who may lose custody?

Q. The awesome task of deciding which parent will get custody of this child will place a heavy and unpleasant burden on each of you who is selected. My question to you, ladies and gentlemen, is this: Can each of you shoulder this heavy burden, take on the responsibility, and decide, on the evidence you hear and see in this courtroom, which parent should have the management, care, and control of this child?

Q. Now, the child involved here is a five-year-old girl. Some people very strongly feel that mothers should always have custody of small children, regardless of the circumstances. Is there anyone on this panel who feels that way, that, regardless of the circumstances and the facts in this case, this little girl should be placed in the custody of her mother?

Q. Is there anyone on this panel who feels just the opposite, that custody of small children should be awarded to the father? That fathers have been shortchanged by courts in the past when it came to child custody and that it is time for juries to make it up to them?

Q. Now, the father in this case has alleged, and will attempt to prove, that my client, Mrs. Shaw, sometimes drank alcoholic beverages to excess, and that on one or more occasions she was involved in some extramarital sexual activity. My *very important* question to each of you is this: Supposing that the evidence in this case does reveal some excessive drinking and even some sexual conduct with one or more other men, would those facts, if proven, by themselves persuade you to grant custody of this small child to the father? If you hear such evidence, and if you believe that it is true, could you ignore that evidence and award custody to the mother if you were persuaded that it was in the best interest of the child to do so?

Q. Stated another way, ladies and gentlemen, would the mere fact that there was occasional excessive drinking and extramarital sexual activity so influence and affect you, that you would automatically, without further consideration, award custody of this child to her father? If that is the case, it is necessary that you tell me, and Mrs. Shaw, and the judge about your feelings. You are certainly entitled to believe what you want and nobody will try to tell you that your beliefs are wrong. All we are trying to do is to secure a fair and impartial jury for the parties in this case.

Q. Does everyone here understand and agree that is possible for a parent, either mother or father, to make some mistakes and even engage in immoral conduct, or at least in conduct not condoned by many people, and still be a very stable, capable, and desirable parent and custodian of a small child? Do any of you disagree with that proposition? [The lawyer explains why sexual or other misconduct is legally irrelevant. It is a mistake to simply leave the matter in the form of: "It is irrelevant because the law says it is irrelevant."]

Q. Would any of you punish my client for her immoral conduct, if you were in fact convinced she had engaged in immoral conduct, by denying her custody of her child? [The lawyer uses the evocative term "punishment" to characterize a decision denying his client custody solely because of her immoral conduct.]

Q. Has anyone on the panel ever previously been involved, either as a party or a witness, in a child custody case?

Q. Have any of you, regardless of whether you have been a party to a child custody case, ever had any interest in the outcome of such a case?

Q. Has anyone on this panel ever served previously as a juror in a child custody case? Could you please describe that experience to us? Would that experience have any effect on your service in this case?

Q. Is there anything about the facts of this case, as I have related them, or anything about the nature of the case which simply repels or disgusts you to the point where you would be unable to be a fair and impartial juror?

Q. Is there any reason, whether I've mentioned it or not, why any of you could not serve as jurors in this case? Would any of you be uncomfortable or upset if asked to serve as a juror in this case?

11 Voir Dire in Criminal Cases

§11.01 Introduction

Chapter 9 dealt with voir dire generally and Chapter 10 with voir dire in civil cases. The present chapter focuses on voir dire in criminal cases. Specific topics will be examined and the voir dire in a highly publicized trial where the charge was solicitation of murder will be presented to illustrate the effective integration of the different parts of voir dire.

Voir dire is always important but particularly so in a criminal trial. The typical civil case involves money or property; the typical criminal case involves an individual's freedom, and sometimes the individual's life. Juror attitudes toward crime are likely to be stronger than their attitudes toward torts, and their feelings about criminals stronger than their feelings about tortfeasors. For society, voir dire and the selection of an impartial jury in a criminal case help ensure that justice is done, and that justice is seen to have been done.

Most of the general suggestions for voir dire contained in Chapter 9 apply to criminal as well as civil cases. There are, however, obvious differences between the voir dire in a civil and a criminal case, which this chapter will explore. The chapter begins with a discussion of general principles and then goes on to cover specific aspects of voir dire in criminal cases.

§11.02 Making a Good Impression

The adage that first impressions are lasting impressions is particularly true of a jury trial. While attorneys are conducting voir dire and evaluating the jurors, the jurors are listening to the attorneys' questions and evaluating the attorneys. If a lawyer makes a good first impression, that impression is likely to last throughout the trial.

The criminal trial lawyer's basic theme in jury selection should be that the lawyer is only seeking a fair and impartial jury, one which will try the case on the law and the evidence. The jury panel should be impressed that the lawyer's objective is to see that justice is done, and not simply to win.

A defense lawyer starts with a handicap. Some jurors identify the criminal defense lawyer with the person he or she represents. Counsel's task is to replace this initial unfavorable impression with a favorable one. A genuine effort to understand and relate to the jurors' problems will help. Counsel for defendants charged with particularly heinous crimes should stress that the rightness of the law against murder or rape, for example, is not on trial, but only the issue of whether the defendant is guilty of the crime charged.

§11.03 Putting Jurors at Ease

A lawyer *should* be interested, and *must* appear to the jury to be interested, in what a juror has to say. Eye contact is essential. Many lawyers will talk to the panel as a whole, or even to individual members, without ever looking the jurors in the eye. Eye contact demonstrates the lawyer's interest in and respect for the jurors. It also allows the attorney to observe body movements and gestures that may be more revealing of the jurors' true feelings than the jurors' verbal answers. In addition to eye contact, the gentle head nod, the occasional uh-huh, and the repetition of key responses of a juror all indicate that the lawyer is paying attention and is interested in the juror as an individual.

Sometimes defense counsel may find it helpful to inject a little levity into the voir dire proceedings. This must never be at the expense of an individual juror, and should not be overdone. Counsel must approach the use of humor with caution, and be particularly sensitive as to timing.[1] It is nevertheless valuable to identify jurors with a sense of humor, for they are more likely to be understanding of the foibles of human nature than persons who are stern and unsmiling. Moreover, prospective jurors who are relaxed are more likely to be forthcoming on voir dire than jurors who are stiff or tense. Informative and truthful answers are easier to come by when jurors feel as if they are participating in a conversation rather than undergoing an inquisition. Judicious use of humor can help create the right atmosphere.

Counsel should recognize that jurors are giving of their time and energy in serving on the case, and should tell the jurors how appreciative the lawyer is of their sacrifice. Jurors should be told that they are "special persons" occupying a special position.

During voir dire it is important to be calm and diplomatic, remaining unruffled regardless of a juror's response to questions. Counsel should never argue with a juror whose answers indicate bias. The unfavorable comments which might emerge from such an exchange could poison the minds of the other jurors. It is better simply to wind up the voir dire quickly with a few innocuous, bland questions, and subsequently challenge the biased juror.

§11.04 Explanations to Jurors

The lawyer should explain as much as possible to the jury. Jurors should be told that the purpose of voir dire is to select a fair and impartial jury, and that in order to achieve this goal jurors need to answer all questions truthfully and candidly. It should be explained that every juror is entitled to his or her own opinion, and that the issue is not whether a juror's opinion is right or wrong, but whether the opinion will impair the juror's ability to be fair and impartial in the case. Further, it should be explained that the fact that a particular juror may be excused does not mean that the juror is in any way unfit gener-

---

[1] *See* **§11.06** for an example of the use of humor.

ally; the juror may be perfectly competent to serve on other cases. The judge will probably tell the jury all of this,[2] but counsel should reinforce the message.

Before beginning the formal questioning, counsel should provide a clear exposition of the nature of the case and a simple statement of the defenses. Concepts such as reasonable doubt, circumstantial evidence, and burden of proof should be explained in ordinary language. While counsel does not want to use abstruse or legalistic language, it is also important not to insult jurors' intelligence. The goal should be to strike a happy medium—simple, easy-to-understand language, but not language which will sound as if the lawyer is talking to a group of elementary school children. To help ensure that counsel's explanations are clear, it is useful to tell jurors at the outset that they should feel free to interrupt and ask questions if they do not understand the lawyer. Most jurors are reluctant to ask questions for fear of showing their ignorance. They should be put at ease and encouraged to inquire if anything is not clear to them:

> As we conduct this inquiry, it will be necessary to explain to you some principles of law that may arise in the trial of this case with which you may not be familiar. Most, if not all, of you have never studied law or been involved in the trial of a criminal case such as this, and accordingly you could not be expected to be aware of all the complexities of the law. I plan to discuss a few legal concepts with you, and explain to you how common things that we've all heard about, such as self-defense and burden of proof, are treated by the law. We've all heard of the term *self-defense,* but only lawyers and judges actually have had the luxury of being able to dissect that term in the comfort of their own offices. If, while I am trying to explain self-defense to you, there is something about the concept that you don't understand, perhaps because I have not made myself clear or have spoken too fast, simply hold up your hand, and make me make sure that you do understand it. In that way, when I am ready to ask you some questions about your views on the law of self-defense or some other matter, you and I will be on the same wave length. Here again, let me encourage each of you not to be bashful about asking questions. There is no such thing as a stupid question when it comes to a jury trial. There may be stupid answers, but not stupid questions. I hope my answers to your questions will not be stupid, but will help you to understand these things we'll be talking about, not only during this voir dire examination, but during the course of the trial. If you're accepted as a juror in this case, I know that each of you will want to know as much as you possibly can, not only about the facts of this case, but about the law that is involved, so that you can do your best as jurors.

Counsel should then explain the applicable legal principles in a way that the average juror can grasp. Examples are often easier to understand than technical definitions. Analogies between the law and everyday experiences are particu-

---

[2] *See* **§9.02.**

larly helpful in allowing the jury to understand the application of complex legal concepts.

Lawyers should try not to unduly drag out voir dire. Jurors get bored after a certain length of time. The lawyer who goes second should listen carefully to the voir dire of opposing counsel, and not repeat questions already asked and answered unless necessary for emphasis or to clarify some matter. It is important that counsel capture and retain prospective jurors' interest in the voir dire process. If the jurors lose interest in counsel's questions, they may also have lost interest in counsel's side of the case.

§11.05 Juror Silence

Silence of panel members in response to a general question can mask a multitude of meanings. If counsel asks whether anyone on the panel knows the defendant or the prosecuting attorney and there is silence, it is usually safe to assume that no one knows these individuals. However, if counsel asks whether any panel members will expect the defendant to testify during trial and there is silence, it does not necessarily follow that there is no one on the panel who might not expect the defendant to testify.

If an important question, such as that relating to the defendant's testifying, is asked of the panel generally and greeted with silence, it should be rephrased and repeated to an individual juror. The lawyer might indicate his own puzzlement: "I know that if I were a juror and Mr. Williams, the defendant, didn't take the stand to testify, I'd be asking myself why, if he has nothing to hide, he wouldn't testify and tell us that he was innocent. Now [turning to a particular juror] is that not what you are thinking as well?" If one juror opens up and expresses his or her feelings, it will encourage other jurors to do the same. It will also allow counsel to explain why an innocent defendant might choose not to take the stand.

Often an attorney will ask a question with the aim of using the juror's answer, no matter what it is, to make a point about the concept in question. Take the issue of probation. Some states permit the jury to recommend probation, and jurors should be examined on their attitudes toward probation under particular conditions. Defense counsel should not ask panel members generally if they believe in probation and whether they would fairly consider it as an alternative to imprisonment. The question might well be met with silence, but this by no means precludes the possibility that someone on the panel might be opposed to probation under any circumstances. Counsel should ask one or more individual jurors, either by an open-ended question or a hypothetical fact situation, for their thoughts on probation. This will encourage jurors to respond. The response will give the attorney the entré to explain the rationale and purposes of probation.

§11.06 Educative Questions

In all criminal trials certain matters need to be brought home forcefully to jurors to prevent prejudice to the defendant. When highlighting such a point, defense counsel should use a juror who appears favorable or at least neutral toward the defendant's position. It is important not to illustrate the point using a juror who gives an indication of being unfavorable to the defendant; that juror may respond to counsel's questions with answers that could hurt the defendant's cause and poison other jurors' minds.

The meaning of an indictment provides a good example. An indictment is no evidence of a defendant's guilt, and cannot be so considered by the jury. Many persons who are not familiar with the law, however, believe that an indictment means there must be at least some basis for believing a defendant is guilty. It is often difficult to convince the average layperson that an indictment only indicates that in the opinion of the grand jury a person should be tried for a particular offense.

Counsel can make this point using a single juror, perhaps taking an approach such as the following:

> "Mr. Jones, you understand, do you not, that a grand jury is not obligated to consider both sides of a matter or dispute in deciding whether or not an indictment should be returned?"

The juror will answer *yes* or *no* to that question. Regardless of the answer, counsel will continue:

> As a matter of fact, Mr. Jones, more often than not the grand jury only hears the prosecution's theory of a case. The law does not require that the defendant be given an opportunity to come before the grand jury or present witnesses. He may be called by the grand jury, if the grand jury decides to hear him, but it is not necessary that the grand jury summon him. On the other hand, he has no right to present his side of the case to the grand jury, and no right to testify before the grand jury.

At this point, counsel will probably see looks of incredulity on the faces of some jurors, because most people do not know much about the grand jury. They assume that the grand jury hears all the evidence and then makes its decision. Counsel should go on to point out the differences between a trial jury, which hears evidence from both sides, and a grand jury, which generally hears only one side. The attorney might drive home the point in this manner:

> As a matter of fact, Mr. Jones, let's suppose that at the next recess here, you leave this courtroom, walk out in the hall, and discover that your watch is missing. Do you realize that you could, if you desired, go to the grand jury, tell them that you had your watch when you came into this courtroom, but that it was gone when you went out into the hall, and there is no one who could have taken it except Mr. Smith, here, who was sitting on your left. You could tell them that your watch was on your left wrist, right next to Mr. Smith. The grand jury could, if it thought proper, return a true bill against Mr. Smith here, based only on what you told them about your watch being missing.

Counsel can then turn to Mr. Smith:

> Mr. Smith, can you now see why the mere return of an indictment must not be considered as any evidence of guilt?

Smith will immediately agree, since he had nothing to do with Jones's missing watch. The lawyer may then end this exchange with a bit of levity, if it seems appropriate under the circumstances, by looking directly at Mr. Smith and saying:

> By the way, Mr. Smith, you didn't take Mr. Jones's watch, did you?

Most jurors will chuckle, and the point will have been made.

§11.07 Areas of Voir Dire Requiring Tact and Delicacy

There are many sensitive areas that need to be probed in voir dire in a criminal case. In doing so, the lawyer must take care not to unnecessarily embarrass a juror. The lawyer must constantly bear in mind that jurors are giving of their time to help the legal system, not to be subjected to harassment. To ask a juror embarrassing questions works at cross purposes to the lawyer's goal of establishing rapport. Not only will such questions be resented by the juror of whom they are asked, but also by others on the panel as well. While the embarrassed juror can be challenged peremptorily, those others who are offended by the lawyer's questions may not even be able to be identified. The potential for embarrassment is particularly great when the questioning turns to areas such as religion, politics, divorce, and prior criminal difficulties and arrests. The lawyer should approach the jury panel, particularly in these sensitive areas, with the *in-group—out-group* concept in mind. Prospective jurors are the in-group and the lawyer is part of the out-group. Counsel who embarrasses a member of the in-group risks alienating other members of the in-group, i.e., the jury.

When questioning on sensitive topics is necessary, as it often is, the lawyer should preface the questioning with an explanation of why the questions are being asked. The lawyer should assure the jury that the goal is not to pry or to embarrass anybody, but to determine whether the juror can try the case fairly and impartially. Explanations of the purpose behind a line of questions will not only help obviate resentment, but also may lead to more candid responses.

§11.08 —Religion

In questioning jurors on the subject of religion, a lawyer should not assume that all jurors attend church regularly, nor should the lawyer assume the contrary. Some jurors do and some do not, but many of the latter are reluctant and somewhat embarrassed to say so in front of strangers. Nevertheless, it is important in many criminal cases for defense counsel to determine the strength of a juror's religious beliefs in order to gauge the rigidity of that juror's concepts of right and wrong. A regular churchgoer, active in religious circles, is likely to take a more moralistic, more dogmatic view of right and wrong. Such a juror will tend to favor the prosecution.

In inquiring about a juror's religion, the lawyer might consider using the more neutral term *preference.* Instead of asking the juror directly about church attendance, counsel might try this approach:

> Now, Mr. Hardin, you've indicated that you are a Methodist by preference. Let me ask you whether or not you hold any office in your church or in your Sunday school structure?

If Mr. Hardin answers that he does hold office, the lawyer can assume that he is regular in his church attendance, and it is unnecessary to pursue the matter further. If he answers that he does not hold office in his church or Sunday school, the lawyer may obtain some insight from the manner of his answer, perhaps an indication that he does not attend regularly, but is a Methodist in name only. This is true of many people who serve on juries. If it is necessary to pursue the matter further, the juror might be asked this question:

> Mr. Hardin, would you characterize your attendance as regular, or occasional, or neither of these?

The juror who is somewhat religious but not a regular churchgoer will reply that he would classify himself as an occasional churchgoer. The third option is unlikely to be chosen by those who consider themselves at all religious.

§11.09 —Divorce

In a case involving domestic violence jurors tend to identify with the principal, either the defendant or the victim, on the basis of the person's sex. This is particularly so in the case of divorced jurors. In a prosecution where a husband is charged with assaulting his wife, the prosecutor will be inclined to challenge divorced male jurors; and the defendant, divorced female jurors. Voir dire on what is likely to be a sensitive topic—the juror's marital relations—will be necessary. In some jurisdictions, a juror information sheet may supply the desired information, and render unnecessary a public inquiry into the juror's marital situation. The attorney who has investigated the venire prior to trial[3] is also likely to already know the answer. Where the required information is not available, counsel might join in a request to distribute a pre-voir dire questionnaire[4] so that such questions can be asked without putting the juror through the possible embarrassment of having to answer in open court.

If a juror does mention a prior divorce, the lawyer must continue inquiries, but with tact and delicacy. This type of question might be asked:

---

[3] *See* **ch 4.**

[4] *See* **§9.01.**

Q. Now, Mr. Harrison, you have indicated that you have had an unfortunate experience during your life which resulted in a divorce. Without going into any of the details of that matter, which, of course, is none of my business, let me ask you if you personally feel that you were treated fairly in those proceedings?

If the juror's verbal or nonverbal response is to be taken aback at the use of the word *fairness,* the lawyer may suspect that the juror still harbors some bitterness toward the former spouse.

§11.10 —Use of the Term *Prejudice*

Counsel should try to avoid the use of the term *prejudice.* Most jurors appreciate that there is a pejorative connotation to being prejudiced, and will tend to semi-automatically deny it. For instance, if a black man stands accused of an assault with a deadly weapon, his attorney should not ask if a juror "would be prejudiced against the accused because he is black." The *no* answer counsel would receive would be meaningless, as few people will admit to being racist. Instead, counsel should ask an open-ended question like:

> Could you please describe what experiences you have had with black persons?

The answer to this question will give counsel greater insight into the juror's attitudes.

Suppose the defendant has a criminal record and counsel has decided it will be necessary to put her on the witness stand. Counsel should not ask a juror about *prejudice* against the defendant because of her criminal record. Again, the *no* will be unenlightening. Instead, it should be put this way:

> We will admit that Miss Kline has been previously convicted. She has paid the penalty for her crimes. Do you think that the fact that Miss Kline has a record will affect your judgment of her credibility or your verdict?

If the term *prejudice* is used, and sometimes it is hard to avoid it, the lawyer should explain that prejudice is not necessarily evil. The lawyer might give the following explanation to soften the use of the term:

> Mrs. Jones, I have used the word *prejudice.* I do not mean by that that there is anything wrong or bad about being prejudiced against certain things. I am personally prejudiced against eggplant. I have tried it. I do not like it. I will not like it, and I will not eat it. Consequently, I have a strong feeling against, a prejudice against, eggplant. When I use the term prejudice, I do not mean that it is wrong or shameful. So, in asking you some questions, if I use the word prejudice, I would appreciate it if you would remember, then, that I am using it in the sense of a strong feeling or opinion.

An effort to remove the pejorative content of the term *prejudice* may evoke more open and honest responses from jurors. It will help counteract the common juror impression that the attorney is judgmental.

§11.11 Relationship with the Court

Counsel should try to avoid confrontation with the trial court. Many judges have set ideas about voir dire, and these may be rather rigid. In most jurisdictions, the scope and extent of voir dire is discretionary, and the court's rulings on voir dire matters are not reversed except for an abuse of discretion. Accordingly, an argument with the court over a voir dire ruling is often pointless. It can also be counterproductive. Jurors usually have an inbred respect for a judge, a respect which the legal system promotes by the judge's dress (black robe) and physical position in the courtroom (elevated). If a lawyer argues with a judge, the jury will be disposed to side with the judge. There is the further point that the lawyer who offends the judge with time-consuming arguments on voir dire matters may find the judge less receptive to arguments on evidentiary and other rulings which lie in the judge's discretion.

Defense counsel in an appropriate case should not, however, be deterred from moving for more time and an extended scope to voir dire. Nor should counsel be deterred from moving for additional peremptory challenges if warranted by the circumstances. In pursuit of these objectives, however, the attorney should educate, not argue with, the judge. Both in regard to such motions and challenges for cause, the lawyer also needs to protect the record for possible appeal, but in doing so the lawyer should be courteous and respectful to the court. If the court makes a ruling that is particularly frustrating, the best approach is for counsel to approach the bench and discuss the matter outside the hearing of the jury. The reporter should be at the bench to record what is said.

When a judge is disinclined to allow a particular line of inquiry on voir dire, counsel must be prepared to show the relevance of the questions in dispute either to a possible challenge for cause or to the intelligent exercise of peremptory challenges. The constitutional dimensions of the ruling should not be ignored; the defendant's rights to a fair trial, an impartial jury, and the effective assistance of counsel under the sixth and fourteenth amendments of the United States Constitution and under appropriate state constitutions may all be at stake. The lawyer should also be familiar with and be prepared to cite relevant statutory authority.

§11.12 Protecting Favorable Jurors

There may be members of the panel who, based on the juror's fit with a favorable juror profile,[5] the lawyer's pretrial investigation of the venire,[6] or the juror's response to voir dire questions, counsel will decide are likely to be inclined toward defendant's side of the case. Counsel will want to do everything possible to make sure that such panel members are not challenged. It is important to ask questions which will not eliminate the juror from the panel. The questions should be asked in such a way that the juror's answers will not be disqualifying, and yet will not alert opposing counsel to the need to strike the juror. The best questions will be closed-ended, somewhat leading, and quickly answerable in the affirmative.[7] The lawyer should make some brief statements about matters involved in the case, then follow with a positive rather than a negative question. Often the questions may verge on the rhetorical. For example:

Q. Mr. Willis, I am sure that you can listen to the law the court gives you on the matter of the presumption of innocence, and then follow that law to the letter; isn't that correct?

Q. Mr. Willis, we all know that, whatever the crime charged, under our American system of justice every defendant charged with a crime is entitled to a fair and impartial trial. You won't have any problem giving Ms. Griscomb that kind of trial, will you?

Q. Mr. Willis, you have heard me talk about the law in this country which says that no one can be convicted of a crime unless the jury is satisfied beyond a reasonable doubt that that person is guilty of the crime charged. You certainly don't have any problem or question about that principle of law, do you? You would never vote to convict a person of a crime unless you were satisfied beyond a reasonable doubt of his or her guilt, would you?

Defense counsel's confidence in particular jurors should not be too obvious to the rest of the jury or the prosecution. Otherwise, the prosecution may peremptorily challenge the jurors in question. The prosecution may not even know why it should be challenging the jurors, only that for some reason the defense wants to retain the jurors, and what is good for the defense is rarely good for the state.

If counsel should observe a particularly strong-willed person, with obvious leadership qualities, who appears reasonably responsive to defendant's position, every effort should be made to keep that person from being challenged. He or she could be the eventual foreman, or at least would not hesitate to take a leading role in the deliberations. Persons who are likely to influence other jurors, or who have the strength of character to hold out against a majority who disagree with them, are, if they believe in a defendant's innocence, defendant's most valued members of the jury.

---

[5] *See* **§§3.08, 5.05.**

[6] *See* **ch 4.**

[7] *See* **§9.15.**

§11.13 Applicable Legal Principles

If permitted by the judge, defense counsel should discuss relevant points of law with the jury on voir dire rather than waiting for the points to be raised by the judge in the course of the trial. Counsel can place the point in context, as well as in the light most favorable to the accused. When the point of law is again made by the court, the jury may be impressed with counsel's knowledge of the law and fairness in stating the point of law accurately. Points of law should be explained in clear, nontechnical language. Examples to which the jurors can relate can help illuminate what might otherwise seem a technical concept.

Often criminal trials are the focal point for a television or theatrical drama. Liberties may be taken for the sake of dramatic effect. The result is that many jurors who have seen the shows have a misunderstanding of courtroom procedures and legal concepts. The lawyer should confront these problems directly and correct whatever wrong impressions exist. For example, as part of counsel's discussion of the burden of proof, the following point might be made:

> Now I realize that all of you may have seen shows like Perry Mason where an innocent defendant is charged with murder and under brilliant cross-examination by Perry somebody else confesses. I am sure that all of you are aware that that is fiction and this is reality. In the real world, the prosecution must prove defendant's guilt beyond a reasonable doubt. It is not, and the judge, His Honor, will tell you this, defendant's responsibility to prove his innocence. I take it, then, that the fact that some other person does not come forward to confess to this crime with which Charles Reynolds is charged would not prevent you from returning a verdict of not guilty if you were persuaded that the prosecution had not carried its burden of proof?

It is a good tactic to involve individual jurors in the explanation of a point of law. Through one juror, counsel can educate the other members of the panel in regard to the point under discussion. The principle of law can be summarized for the next juror and a question rephrased so as to reinforce counsel's point. For example, the first juror might be asked whether she agreed with the point of law, the second whether he would change it if he could. No more than one point of law, however, should generally be covered with any one juror.

Following is a checklist of some of the more common principles of law likely to arise in a criminal case:

Presumption of innocence
Burden of proof
Reasonable doubt
Significance of indictment
Circumstantial evidence
Confessions and admissions
Right not to testify

Search and seizure
Accomplice testimony
Conspiracy
Character evidence
Expert witnesses
Insanity
Irresistible impulse
Diminished capacity, whether from alcohol or drugs
Assault and battery
Self-defense and defense of others
Alibi
Abduction and kidnapping
First-degree murder, second-degree murder, and manslaughter (voluntary and involuntary)
Malice aforethought
Specific intent
Provocation and heat of passion
Justifiable and excusable homicide
Attempt and preparation

In the following eight sections, the approach to several of these topics will be specifically discussed.

§11.14 Specific Topics—Reasonable Doubt

Criminal defense counsel must at all times avoid the trap of appearing to favor crime. Many prospective jurors have a poor impression of criminal defense lawyers and many identify the lawyer with his or her client. The lawyer must reassure the panel that this is not the case, that the lawyer does not favor crime. In a murder case, for example, the lawyer might early in voir dire make the following statement:

Q. Now, all of us, I am sure, are in agreement that the law against murder is a good and necessary law. Certainly, we would not want to live in a society where people could run around indiscriminately killing other people. But remember that we are not here to decide whether the law of murder is a good law or a bad law. We are here to decide whether Edward Lee Marshall has violated that law. This question cannot be decided without twelve of you people hearing all of the facts in this case. Can you, then, Mrs. Gray, assure me that if you are chosen on this jury, that you will not decide the case on whether murder is a good or evil thing, but rather on whether the state has proven beyond a reasonable doubt that

Mr. Marshall has intentionally and without justification caused the death of William Reddy?

Defense counsel in a criminal case must impress on each juror that an individual is presumed innocent until proven guilty beyond a reasonable doubt. Most everyone has heard this phrase, *reasonable doubt,* but few have thought about it and even fewer understand its full significance. It may therefore be useful to ask some jurors:

Q. What does the phrase *reasonable doubt* mean to you?

Whatever the response, the lawyer can expand on the legal parameters of the concept:

Q. Now, Mrs. Gray, suppose that after you have heard all the evidence, you were convinced that Edward Marshall *probably* was responsible for killing Mr. Reddy. But you still had some doubts, some reasonable doubts. Would you be prepared under those circumstances, even though you thought he was probably guilty, to return a verdict of not guilty? For that is what the law requires, and that is what the concept of reasonable doubt is all about.

The lawyer might also usefully explain why the criminal law uses a reasonable doubt standard, and why it is thought better that ten guilty defendants go free than one innocent defendant go to jail.

Each juror should be individually made to promise that he or she will abide by the reasonable doubt standard. Counsel's task, after the inevitable affirmative response, is to determine which jurors are genuinely committed to the reasonable doubt standard and which are paying mere lip service to it.

At the end of voir dire, counsel might reinforce the point about voir dire with the following question:

Q. If at the conclusion of all the evidence, you harbor a doubt which is based on reason, would each of you now look at Mr. Edward Lee Marshall and promise him that you will resolve that doubt in his favor?

While the importance of juror-lawyer eye contact is generally appreciated, it is less widely appreciated but equally important to bring about eye contact between the jurors and the defendant. Psychologically, it is more difficult to take an action that will cause harm to another human being if one must look that person in the eye while causing the harm.

§11.15 —Right Not to Testify

Another topic which should be thoroughly explored with the jury is the defendant's right not to testify. If a lawyer knows or suspects that the defendant will not testify, counsel should prepare the panel by discussing with them the defendant's *absolute right not to testify.* Most jurors will expect defendants to tell their side of a story. They are inclined to believe that a defendant who does not testify has something to hide. Defense counsel should explain that a defendant is not obligated to testify, that the decision whether to testify is usually made by the attorney and not by the defendant, and that there are valid reasons why a lawyer might decide not to have the defendant testify. Use of a hypothetical may help to elicit any reservations jurors may have about this right not to testify:

Q. Now, Mrs. Williams, in any criminal case the state has the burden of proving the guilt of the defendant beyond a reasonable doubt. The defendant does not have any burden to prove anything. He is not obligated even to offer evidence or to produce witnesses. Many times, in trying to resolve disputes or conflicts, we obtain statements, first of one side of the conflict, then of the other. In other words, both sides, more or less, are expected to produce evidence in a criminal case. Let me pose this hypothetical situation: suppose that in the trial of a criminal case, the state put on some evidence and then rested. The defendant would then have the *opportunity* to present evidence if desired. But let's suppose, for whatever reason, the defendant were to choose not to offer any evidence nor to testify. Now, the law would require you at this point to analyze the case of the prosecution and decide based only on that evidence whether the defendant was guilty beyond a reasonable doubt. Let's suppose further that you felt that the defendant was probably guilty, although you were not clearly convinced. Would you be willing to examine the prosecution's case under the microscope, without regard to whether the defendant testified or offered any evidence? Would you be prepared to return a verdict of not guilty even though you thought the defendant was probably guilty if you still had some reasonable doubts on the matter?

Following the juror's response, counsel might go on:

Q. Would you be willing to make a decision based on this evidence even though you might *wish* the defendant had testified or even perhaps might have wanted him to testify?

If the juror responds in the affirmative, he or she can be further reinforced:

Q. Now, if you have agreed to look at the evidence without regard to the total absence of defense testimony, could you tell the court and this defendant Mr. Golding here and now that if you had any thoughts in your mind while in the jury room as to why he didn't testify, that you would immediately put those thoughts aside and say to yourself, "Wait a minute. I understand the law does not permit me to consider that, so I will not consider it for any purpose in making a decision as to whether the state has brought evidence which convinces me beyond a reasonable doubt on the issues in this case."

Some prosecutors questioning the panel on the defendant's right not to testify will observe that the right finds its basis in the fifth amendment. The term *fifth amendment* may connote something sinister to the panel. Fifth amendment is a term which has come to be associated with organized crime figures. It is a term which has received bad press in the newspapers and magazines, and one which suggests that somebody has something to hide. The result is that a great many prospective jurors equate taking the fifth with an admission of guilt.

Defense counsel must dispel this conception of the fifth amendment. Counsel should explain that the right of silence was one of the rights held most dear by the founding fathers of the country; that these founding fathers had witnessed firsthand the kinds of injustices which could occur when the government was permitted to badger a suspect until the suspect made an admission capable of being interpreted as a confession, often simply to stop the badgering; and that they had decided that they preferred a system in which the government had to shoulder the burden of proving guilt, without being able to call upon the accused to help it.

§11.16 —Public Opinion

In a case which has received extensive publicity, public opinion can run either for or against a defendant, although more often than not it runs against the defendant. What the jurors have heard or read about a case needs to be thoroughly explored on voir dire. It is often advisable in such cases to move the court to conduct individual voir dire *in camera,* out of the presence of other jurors. This will prevent the utterance of a damaging statement about what one juror has seen or read from corrupting the minds of those members of the panel who may not have been exposed to the story.

If a juror claims that, despite exposure to adverse pretrial publicity, he or she has no opinion on the guilt or innocence of the defendant or that it will be possible to cast aside what that juror has heard or read about the case, defense counsel should generally not accept the claim at face value but should pursue the matter further. Counsel should ask what, specifically, the prospective juror has read or heard. The words chosen to describe what was read or heard may be revealing of the juror's attitude, perhaps more so than the juror's statements of attitude. The juror should be asked whether, as a result of what was heard or read, the juror has formed any *impressions* about the defendant or the case. Use of the word *impression* gives the juror a graceful mode of self-description. It avoids the insinuation that the juror may be biased. Open-ended questions about a juror's reactions, what the juror thought at the moment when the article in question was read, will be more informative than closed-ended questions asking the juror whether he or she will be prejudiced by what was heard or read. Ultimately, however, in order to establish a basis for a challenge for cause, defense counsel will have to extract from the juror an admission that what was read or heard could cause the juror to be prejudiced against the defendant.

§11.17 —Inflammatory Evidence

The prosecution will sometimes plan to introduce evidence, usually photographs, which may be shocking or gruesome. If such exhibits are likely to be introduced during the trial, counsel should prepare the jury as early as possible. This is particularly true in a homicide case where it is anticipated that bloody photographs or evocative physical evidence will be admitted. If the evidence is described during voir dire, jurors will be better prepared for it. The shock effect will be less than if the evidence is introduced without forewarning.

Where photographs of a dead or severely injured victim are to be introduced, defense counsel might point out that there is no dispute that a shocking crime has occurred. The dispute is over who committed the crime. The pictures do not in and of themselves prove the guilt of anyone. Counsel might also observe that to convict the wrong person out of a feeling that somebody should pay for the crime only compounds the tragedy which has already occurred.

§11.18 —Insanity Defense

A person who is legally insane at the time of committing a crime cannot be convicted of that crime. The standard of legal insanity varies from state to state, and the law of the particular state should, of course, be checked. The applicable law of insanity must be explained to the jury panel. Jurors should be individually questioned about their attitudes toward the defense.

Although statistically not a frequent defense in criminal cases, insanity has received considerable negative publicity in the media with the result that many prospective jurors are opposed to the defense. Some persons are opposed in principle, believing that it constitutes an abdication of personal responsibility for one's actions. Others are opposed because they envision the effect of an acquittal being the loosing of a deranged criminal on the community. Counsel might, after explaining the relevant law, probe jurors' attitudes with the following questions:

Q. Have any of you ever had a close friend or relative who was mentally ill? Could you, and I don't mean to pry, tell us about your relationship with that person, and how his or her mental illness made you feel?

Q. Have any of you had occasion to work with mentally ill persons?

Q. Miss Krepps, the defendant in this case, admits she shot the victim, but claims that she was legally insane at the time that she pulled the trigger. Do you understand that the law does not hold a person responsible for an action if she was insane at the time that she committed the action?

Q. Do you have any difficulty with that principle of law? Does it not seem odd that the law allows a person who has caused the death of another to go free just because that person was insane at the time of the crime? [The lawyer is concerned not only that the juror knows the law, but also understands the reasons for the law. Whatever the juror's response to the question, the lawyer will follow it up with an explanation of the rationale behind the insanity defense.]

Q. Would you experience any difficulty in following the law and finding not guilty a person who had caused the death of another?

Q. I am sure that you realize that not all mentally ill persons are confined to mental institutions. Some live in homes, like you or I; others, unfortunately, have no home—park benches and back alleys are their home. Will the fact that Miss Krepps was not in a mental institution at the time of the alleged crime prevent you from returning a verdict of not guilty should you determine that she was insane?

Q. Have you or any member of your family, or a close friend, ever been the victim of a crime?

Q. Have you ever read any books or articles about the insanity defense? If so, what do you remember about the book or article?

Q. Could you please, and I realize this may be difficult, tell us your personal feelings about whether insanity should be a defense?

Q. If you had the power to rewrite the law, would you abolish it as a defense?

Q. The judge will instruct you that if you find the defendant, at the time that she committed the crime, was acting under such a defect of reason from a disease of the mind as not to know the nature and quality of her act, she is legally insane and must be acquitted. Can you accept this legal definition of insanity and not apply one that might make more sense to you?

Q. If you find that Miss Krepps was legally insane when she committed the crime, will you promise to follow the court's instructions and return a verdict of not guilty? [The lawyer seeks a commitment to follow the law.]

Q. Would it cause you unease or discomfort knowing that you had acquitted a person you knew had caused the death of another? [A key question, attempting to move from a discussion of the defense in the abstract to the personal impact that recognition of the defense might have on the juror. Hesitance in responding to the question may be telling.]

Q. Would you have any difficulty returning to your home and telling your friends and neighbors that you had acquitted Miss Krepps in this case? [A question similar in purpose to the preceding one.]

In most, if not all, jurisdictions, a person found not guilty by reason of insanity will be automatically committed to a mental institution. If permitted in the jurisdiction, this fact should be told to the jurors, lest they be left with the impression that an acquittal will mean that a deranged criminal will be returned to their neighborhood.

§11.19 —Identification

In many cases identification is a critical issue. In an assault case, for instance, the complainant may not have had a good look at the attacker's face, or may only have seen him in the dark. Especially in a case involving a sudden and unexpected crime of violence such as rape, murder, or armed robbery, a witness who was present or involved may have been so confused, or even hysterical, that his or her ability to identify the culprit may be seriously suspect.

The ability to identify another person varies greatly; some people are very observant and others are not at all. This point should be made on voir dire by counsel in any case where the question of identification is likely to be raised. Six people who see the same incident, whether that incident is a murder or an automobile accident, are likely to come up with six different versions of the incident. Furthermore, it is not unheard of for a witness to falsely identify a person as the perpetrator of a crime for personal reasons. Voir dire on this subject is as much educative as anything else.

Following are some voir dire questions which might be asked where identification is going to be an issue in the case. The perfunctory affirmative answers which are likely to be forthcoming are to an extent secondary. Defense counsel is primarily attempting to point out to jurors all the reasons why eyewitness testimony may not be reliable.

Q. If, during this trial, any witness identifies my client, Stephen Harris, as the person who committed this crime, will you listen carefully to that testimony, and decide for yourself, after hearing it, whether it is believable or not?

Q. Will you evaluate the testimony of that witness and his ability to have actually observed what he says he observed on the occasion in question?

Q. Will you consider all the testimony, both on direct and cross-examination, about his ability to observe, where he was when he supposedly saw what he says he saw, and under what circumstances he saw it?

Q. Will you take into consideration, from the evidence, the witness's capacity and ability to remember what he saw or thinks he saw?

Q. Will you consider whether he had previously known Mr. Harris or not, and what his relationship, if any, with him was or had been?

Q. Will you listen to and carefully consider any testimony as to why this witness may be identifying Mr. Harris as the perpetrator of this crime?

Q. Will you consider whether this witness might have some personal motive or reason to identify Mr. Harris?

Q. Will you also consider, in judging the credibility of this identification witness, the time of day or night when this crime occurred and whether the witness actually was in a position to see what he says he saw?

Q. Will you also consider, in evaluating such testimony, whether the witness appeared to be interested in making a correct identification, or whether he simply did not seem to want it to appear that he may have made a mistake?

Q. Do you agree, Mr. Perkins, that if a witness were to observe a person for only a few seconds and then later identify that person from a photograph claimed to be that of the person he had seen, that in court the witness actually might be identifying the photograph rather than the person he has previously seen?

Q. Have you ever been mistaken in identifying someone, that is, have you ever thought you saw a person whom you recognized, and later discovered that it was someone else, and that you had been mistaken? [Almost every juror will have had this experience. By linking formal issues of courtroom identification with everyday experiences to which jurors can personally relate the lawyer brings home the point being made.]

Although framed as questions, the lawyer's queries are designed to alert the jurors to the possibility of misidentification. The lawyer has identified a number of reasons why misidentifications occur, without impugning the character of any particular witness. In closing argument, the lawyer can return to the most salient of the themes touched upon in voir dire.

§11.20 —Police Procedure

In some cases, an attorney plans to call into question the procedures followed by the police. Many jurors are suspicious of attacks on police. "What do the police stand to gain by lying?" is the question they ask themselves. The corollary is "What does the defendant stand to gain by lying?" The answer to the latter question is far more obvious than the answer to the former: the defendant hopes to gain his or her freedom. The issue needs to be addressed and the following questions are suggested for use by defense attorneys in cases where police procedures are to be challenged:

Ladies and gentlemen, in the case on trial it may become necessary for me as the attorney for Allan Ingrams to raise some questions with regard to the manner in which the police handled the investigation of this case.

Q. If the police in fact did act inappropriately, do each of you understand that I would not be doing my duty if I did not challenge the police actions?

Q. Is there anyone on the panel who feels that an attorney should not, in doing her duty to her client, call into question the actions of police or law enforcement agencies? [Chances are that the above questions will meet with silence, but they can be used as a predicate for the following questions:]

Q. Have any of you ever heard of or participated in a "support your local police" campaign? What, might I ask, are your views on supporting your local police?

Q. Is there anyone on the panel who would tend to believe a policeman's version of how some act or event occurred just because he was a policeman?

Q. In other words, if a civilian witness testified that something occurred one way, and a police witness testified it occurred a different way, would you believe the policeman over the civilian just because of his status or because he was wearing an official uniform? Many persons feel this way, and their right to that opinion is not in question. If you do feel that way, however, it is important that you tell me and Mr. Ingrams and the judge that you feel that way.

Q. Have any of you ever run across a rude policeman or in any way taken abuse from a policeman which you felt was unwarranted or unjustified? [The lawyer tries to relate the issue to a personal experience with which the juror can identify.]

Q. Have any of you on the jury panel ever received a traffic citation which you did not feel was justified? [A few hands will probably show at this point; select one and propound the following question:]

Q. Now, Mr. Sullivan, without going into the details of the traffic citation, let me ask you, sir, whether or not you paid the ticket or contested it in municipal court? [If he paid the ticket he probably has resented it ever since. If he tried the case in traffic court, the chances are he was found guilty anyway and has harbored some resentment against the judicial system as well as against the policeman. Follow it up with a closing question to make a point:]

Q. Mr. Sullivan, since you've indicated that you did receive a ticket which you felt was unjustified, I take it that you agree that policemen, like everyone else, are human beings and capable of making mistakes? [This question is a two-edged sword. An affirmative answer will make an important point with the jury, but may lead the prosecutor to challenge a juror who would be favorable to the defense.]

Q. If you are selected as a member of this jury, would you be willing to keep in mind the fact that policemen are human, and can and do make mistakes in their daily lives, and weigh the testimony of a policeman in light of all of the evidence of the case, not giving it any more or less weight than that of any other witness?

§11.21 —Lesser Included Offenses

In many cases defense counsel may hope for an acquittal but be willing to settle for a conviction on a lesser charge. If the attorney believes that the jury, given the choice between convicting the defendant of a somewhat questionable serious offense or releasing the defendant outright, will vote to convict, then the lawyer wants to bring to the jury's attention the possibility of conviction on a lesser offense. Consider the defendant who is clearly guilty of assault but who has been charged with the more serious offense of assault with intent to commit murder. Defense counsel may want to use voir dire to open jurors' minds to the possibility of conviction of the lesser included offense:

Q. Now, Miss Gold, the defendant, Ernest Claude, is charged in this case with the offense of assault with intent to commit murder. It may well be that at the conclusion of the case, you might believe beyond a reasonable doubt that an assault was committed on the injured person, but you have some reasonable doubt as to whether Mr. Claude intended to murder him. In that situation, the law requires that you find Mr. Claude not guilty of assault with intent to murder. The law does, however, permit you to find him guilty of a lesser offense such as simple assault. It may be that you are not aware of this portion of our law. Did you know that this was a possible jury verdict in a case such as this? [Chances are the juror will say no.]

Q. Let me continue a bit further. In most criminal cases, the state will charge the most serious crime it possibly can under the circumstances. In other words, the prosecution wants to take as big a bite of the apple as it possibly can. Do you understand that merely because the state chooses to try to take a big bite of the apple, this does not mean that you as a juror are required to limit your choice of verdicts to either the more serious crime or nothing at all.

Q. Do you understand that the state is obligated to prove beyond a reasonable doubt each and every element of the charge brought against the defendant? In other words, if the state successfully proves that an assault was committed, but does not successfully prove beyond a reasonable doubt that there was an intent to kill, then you as a juror would not only be permitted, but would in fact be obligated under our law to find the defendant not guilty of assault with intent to commit murder.

Q. If you were taken as a juror, Miss Gold, would you, as the evidence unfolded, keep in your mind not only the charge brought against the defendant of assault with intent to commit murder, but also at the same time the charge of simple assault?

Q. Miss Gold, it may well be that as the evidence develops, you will want to ask yourself this question: "If Mr. Claude had intended to kill the injured party, why didn't he do so?" [It is to be hoped that this lingering question will now be planted in the jurors' minds and that they will consider this possibility as the facts of the altercation are developed.]

Q. Would it in any way embarrass you, Miss Gold, if at the conclusion of the evidence you felt that the state had not proven beyond a reasonable doubt that the offense as charged has been committed, but you did feel that some violation of law had occurred, to return into court with a verdict which was somewhat less than what the prosecutors had sought?

§11.22 General Questions

The object of voir dire is to educate the jurors, to establish rapport with them, and, most importantly, to determine whether any juror is so biased as to make him or her unsuitable to serve on the case. Bias may be either implied in law or actual. Examples of bias implied in law occur where the prospective juror is related to a party or attorney, where the juror served on the grand jury that indicted the defendant, or where the prospective juror had a prior civil suit against the defendant. Actual bias is a state of mind that will prevent the juror from giving the defendant a fair trial.

Defense counsel should preface questioning with a disclaimer of any intent to pry into the personal lives or affairs of the jurors, or to embarrass them in any way. Prospective jurors should understand that the duty counsel owes to the client compels the making of such inquiries. Counsel should begin voir dire with questions about the juror's background—whether the juror is married or single, the number and ages of any children, the juror's employment, and the residence of the juror.[8] These general questions are unlikely to cause discomfort, will acclimate the juror to the idea of being questioned, and will help to establish rapport.

The good trial attorney will adapt questions to the individual case and to the prospective juror being questioned. The questions that follow are intended to give some sense of the kinds of general questions typically asked by defense counsel in a criminal case:

Q. Have you, or has any member of your immediate family, ever been the victim of a crime? [An affirmative answer will require follow-up questioning as to the type of crime, the disposition of the case, and the juror's reactions to the experience. Any juror who has been the victim of a crime, however, is likely to favor the prosecution and is unlikely to be sympathetic to the defendant.]

Q. Have you, or has any member of your immediate family, ever been a complainant or witness in a criminal investigation, grand jury proceeding, or trial?

Q. How many of you have previously sat as jurors in any case? [If a juror has previously served on a civil case, defense counsel should seize the opportunity to explain the difference between the burdens of proof in civil and criminal cases. The lawyer plans to discuss burden of proof at some point but the answer to this question may provide a natural lead-in to the topic.]

Q. How do you perceive the crime problem in this community? Do you think it is getting worse or better? What leads you to that conclusion?

Q. Do you think society (and the courts) have been "soft" on crime? [This question and the previous one are designed to gain insight into whether a juror is liberal (likely to favor the defense) or conservative (likely to favor the prosecution).]

Q. Are any of you acquainted with, or related to, anyone who works in any capacity in the prosecutor's office, the police department, the sheriff's department, or any law enforcement agency?

Q. Were any of you ever members of a law enforcement agency, either in civilian or military life?

Q. The following persons will appear as witnesses in this case. Are any of you acquainted with, or related to, any of these persons?

[If not supplied with names of prosecution witnesses, counsel might ask the following question:]

---

[8] *See generally* **§9.35.**

Q. Since the prosecutor has refused to disclose the names of the state's witnesses, I cannot ask you if you know them. If it develops that any of you are acquainted with one or more of them, will you promise me that you will cast aside any feeling of friendship with the witness, and consider his or her testimony as you would that of a total stranger? I know this will be difficult to do, particularly if you are well acquainted with the witness, but it is important that I have your solemn promise that you will not let your friendship influence your weighing of the evidence in this case. [The defense lawyer has turned a disadvantage, not being supplied with the names of witnesses, to an advantage, being able to suggest that the prosecutor is not being fair.]

Q. Do or did any of you know the complaining witness in this case [or in a homicide case, the deceased] or do you know any members of the complaining witness's family?

Q. Have any of you read or heard anything about this case, whether in the press, or on radio or television, or do any of you have any knowledge of this case, or of the defendant? [If there are any affirmative answers to this question, counsel should ask the juror what was seen or heard, and the juror's reactions at the time. Counsel needs to determine whether the juror's opinions are firm and fixed or only lightly held, and whether a juror holding such opinion is likely to compel the defendant to offer proof to change or remove it.]

Q. Do each of you understand that the prosecutor and I are both lawyers, equal in the eyes of the law, and both doing our best to represent clients? [In some jurisdictions the practice is to refer to the prosecutor by the formal title of attorney general or just simply "general." This designation may give the prosecutor an artificially high stature in the eyes of the jury. Defense counsel attempts to counteract this effect by referring to the State's lawyer as the prosecutor, which does not perhaps carry as positive connotations.]

Q. Will each of you promise me that you will not give more weight to the prosecutor's arguments than you give to mine, merely because she holds a formal title?

Q. Do each of you realize that the indictment in this case is merely a formal legal pleading, a piece of paper which starts the ball rolling, and which has no evidentiary weight whatsoever?[9]

Q. All of you, I am sure, have heard the saying that where there's smoke, there's fire. That saying may be true in some situations, but it has no applicability in a criminal trial, where the prosecution must prove guilt beyond a reasonable doubt. Do all of you understand, and accept, that an indictment is no evidence of guilt? Do each of you understand that the grand jury that returned this indictment, this piece of paper, heard

---

[9] *See also* **§11.06.**

only the prosecutor's side of the case, and that neither I nor my client were allowed to appear before that grand jury?

Q. Do all of you accept and believe in the principle of American justice that all persons are presumed innocent until proven guilty? [The lawyer might then ask individual jurors what that principle means to them.]

Q. Will each of you follow the court's instruction that the defendant must be presumed innocent until guilt is proved beyond a reasonable doubt,[10] and that this presumption continues in effect throughout this entire trial?

Q. As each of you sit there now, without having heard a word of testimony, do you in fact presume that the defendant is innocent of the crime charged?

Q. If you were asked to vote at this very moment about whether defendant was guilty or innocent, would you all vote innocent or would you say "Well, I just don't know?" [The lawyer will want to emphasize that before any evidence is presented, the presumption of innocence demands that the jury deem the defendant not guilty.]

Q. Do all of you understand that under our law and system of justice, the burden of proving a case beyond a reasonable doubt is always on the prosecution, and remains there during the entire trial?

Q. Will all of you follow the law and compel the district attorney to prove beyond any reasonable doubt that my client is guilty as charged?

Q. Do you also understand that under the law the defendant has no obligation to prove or disprove any fact, or anything whatsoever, but may remain silent?[11] That the defendant does not have to prove his innocence or rebut the prosecutor's allegations? Do any of you have any reservations about these principles? [Defense counsel who senses any doubt on any of the propositions should explain the rationale behind them to the jurors.] Will you have any problems following them?

Q. If, in my sound legal judgment, I deem it advisable not to put my client on the stand to testify, will each of you follow the court's instruction that you may draw no inference of guilt from that failure to testify?[12]

Q. Will each of you follow the court's instructions on the applicable law, in each instance, whether you agree with that law or not? [This line of questioning should not be pursued if the lawyer intends to ask the jury to exercise its power of nullification.[13]]

Q. Will each of you follow the court's instructions as to what constitutes reasonable doubt?

Q. Will each of you promise me that, after hearing all the evidence and listening to the court's charge on the law, if you have a reasonable doubt as

---

[10] *See also* **§11.14.**

[11] *See also* **§11.15.**

[12] *Id.*

[13] *See* **§2.20.**

to my client's guilt, you will vote for acquittal because of that reasonable doubt, even if you think that, more likely than not, the defendant committed the crime charged?[14]

§11.23 Illustrative Voir Dire in a Rape Case

For purposes of this discussion, assume that a 20-year-old female, Claudia Pappas, was forcibly raped by a man who broke into her apartment, through a window, at about 3:00 A.M. The rape was accomplished by both physical force and threats of physical harm to Miss Pappas if she did not submit. Edward Fox, an unemployed farm worker who had two weeks earlier been released from prison, was charged with the crime. The case received extensive coverage in the local papers, particularly the *Sun Valley News.*

The crime of rape, particularly forcible rape, is generally regarded as especially heinous. Defense counsel should in no way trivialize the harm to the victim. Usually, however, the issue is identification. Counsel's emphasis on voir dire will be on the prosecutor's burden of proof beyond reasonable doubt and the jury's role in weighing the credibility of witnesses. The following general and specific questions might be asked:

Q. Have any of you, or has any member of your family or a close friend, ever been the victim of a sex crime?

Q. Have any of you, or has any member of your family or a close friend, ever been the victim of a crime of violence?

Q. Have any of you, or has any member of your family or a close friend, ever been the victim of any kind of crime?

Q. Have any of you ever testified in a criminal case? [If a juror has been involved in a criminal case, whether as a victim or witness, or if any member of the juror's family or a close friend of the juror has been the victim of a crime, the lawyer needs to probe more deeply to discover what effect the experience will have on the juror.]

Q. Do any of you know or are you related to any person employed in the district attorney's office, the police department, the sheriff's office, or any other law enforcement agency?

Q. Do any of you know Miss Pappas, the victim in this case, or any member of her family?

Q. Do any of you know Mr. Lee, the prosecutor, or any of the assistant prosecutors in Mr. Lee's office, or any other person who works for Mr. Lee or in his office?

Q. Have any of you ever been a civilian or military policeman?

Q. Have any of you ever been employed by, or otherwise connected with, any other type of law enforcement agency, including the military police?

---

[14] *See also* **§11.14.**

Q. Has anyone on the panel ever had any legal training of any kind?

Q. Do any of you know any of the witnesses who will testify in this trial, either for the prosecution or for the defense?

Q. Have any of you ever before served as a juror in a criminal case? [If the answer is in the affirmative, the nature of the case and the verdict of the jury should be ascertained, if possible, as well as the juror's reactions to the experience.]

Q. Have any of you ever served as a juror in a civil case? [When a juror answers affirmatively to this question, counsel should explain the difference between the burden of proof in civil and criminal cases.]

Q. Do you understand that the indictment in this case charging Mr. Edward Fox with forcible rape is no evidence whatever of his guilt of that crime? [Defense counsel should refer to the defendant by name rather than by "the defendant" or "the accused." It is important that the jurors perceive him as an individual human being, not as an impersonal "defendant."]

Q. Will you promise me that you will not regard the fact that the grand jury has returned an indictment, which is nothing more than a piece of paper, actually the state's pleading in this case, as any evidence or proof of Edward Fox's guilt of that crime?

Q. As you sit here now, do you regard Mr. Fox as innocent of this crime until he is proven guilty beyond any reasonable doubt?

Q. Will you regard him as totally innocent, without any mental reservations, until the opposite is shown beyond a reasonable doubt?

Q. Mr. James, there is no question that Miss Pappas was mistreated sexually. Do you believe that this fact alone will tend in any way to make you want to convict Mr. Fox?

Q. Will this fact, that she was sexually mistreated, tend in any way to make you want to obtain revenge on her behalf?

Q. Do you have any children? If so, what are their ages and sexes? [Jurors who have female children or grandchildren of the same age as the complainant are likely to identify with the victim. Those with male children or grandchildren of the same age as the defendant are more apt to identify with the defendant.]

Q. In order to prove that Mr. Fox is guilty of rape, the prosecution must prove various facts. It must prove, for instance, that he engaged in sexual intercourse with the complainant; and that this was accomplished by means of forcible coercion. That is, they must prove that he either used physical force to overcome her resistance or made an express or implied threat which placed her in fear of immediate death or serious physical injury. Do you promise, Mr. James, to vote not guilty to the charge of rape in the first degree if you are not satisfied beyond a reasonable doubt that the prosecutor has established each and every one of these elements, even if you should happen to believe that the prosecutor has established some of them? [This question is more appropriate in a case where the defendant claims that the sexual relations were consensual than in a case where defendant claims he did not have sexual intercourse with the victim. Even where a defendant is legally permitted to raise inconsistent defenses (e.g., I did not have sex with the victim, but, if I did, it was with her consent), it is tactically inadvisable to do so. Jurors quite understandably are skeptical of a defendant who raises inconsistent claims.]

Q. Do you believe that a defendant in a case like this should be required to offer some proof of his innocence before he is entitled to a verdict of acquittal? [This question can be used as an opportunity to again emphasize the burden of proof and the fact that the defendant is not required to prove anything.]

Q. Are you aware that the laws of this state and this country say that a defendant is not required to testify, that a defendant is not required to offer any proof or to take the witness stand, and that a defendant's failure to testify cannot be taken as an indication of his guilt? Do you agree with those laws? Would you have any difficulty following them?

Q. Had you read or heard anything about this case before you arrived here today? If so, could you please tell us what you heard and what were the sources of this information, or these rumors, as the case may be?

Q. Do you recall your thoughts or feelings at the time you received this information? Could you please tell us about them?

[Where there has been very damaging or prejudicial publicity in any particular publication or on any particular radio or television program, direct and specific questions, rather than general ones, should be asked of each juror. For instance:

Q. Mr. James, do you ever read the *Sun Valley News?* Have you read anything in that paper written by Mr. Sam Mengle? If so, do you recall what you read? Have you, from reading this paper, formed any opinion of the guilt or innocence of Mr. Fox? If you have an opinion of guilt, based on what you have read, will it take evidence to remove that opinion?]

Q. Have you ever discussed this case, or anything about it, with anyone? Could you describe these discussions?

Q. I suppose, Mr. James, that you have formed some opinion, from what you have heard or read, as to the guilt or innocence of Mr. Fox?

Q. I suppose, also, that you expect Mr. Fox to produce some evidence at trial in order to change your opinion? [Either the prosecutor, for purpose of rehabilitating the juror, or the court is likely to ask the juror whether he will be able to set aside any opinions he holds and decide the case solely on the evidence he hears and sees in this courtroom, giving the defendant the full benefit of the presumption of innocence. If defense counsel wants to retain the particular juror, he might do the same.]

Q. Considering your present frame of mind, if you were charged with a crime like this, would you want to be tried by a jury composed of persons with a similar frame of mind? [Defense counsel tries to make the jurors think what it would be like to be in the defendant's shoes, and the type of jury they would want if they were to be so unfortunate.]

Q. Do you think, given the amount of publicity this case has generated, that you will be able to decide this case without fearing any criticism of your verdict by friends, relatives, or associates who may disagree with it?

Q. If you were one of a minority of jurors, or the only juror, who believed that the prosecution had not established every element of its case beyond a reasonable doubt, would you be apt to change your vote just because you were in the minority? Would you let the fact that you were in the minority affect your vote?

Q. Now, Miss Pappas will testify about her experience. All of us have a natural sympathy for her. She has undergone a truly horrible experience. But the question in this case is not whether Miss Pappas has been raped, but whether Mr. Fox is the person who raped her. Will each of you promise not to say: "Well somebody ought to pay for what happened to Miss Pappas, and since it is Mr. Fox who is charged with this crime, he should be the one to pay?" [Defense counsel tries to place the issue of sympathy in proper perspective, and to nip any urge to convict for the sake of revenge.]

Q. Do you understand that nothing I or the prosecutor say in this case is evidence? Will each of you be able to disregard our remarks and return a verdict solely on the evidence you hear and see in this courtroom, from witnesses who are sworn to tell the truth and from exhibits admitted by the court?

Q. If a witness, such as Miss Pappas, identifies the defendant, will you, as you evaluate her testimony, consider her opportunity and ability to have made the observation to which she testifies, her capacity for memory, her prior familiarity or unfamiliarity with the defendant, and her possible bias or prejudice? [In this question and the next, the lawyer tries to educate the jurors as to the reasons why an incorrect identification can occur.]

Q. Will you also consider, in evaluating such identification testimony, whether the witness was more interested in making a correct identification or simply in not having it appear that she might have made a mistake?

Q. Have you ever thought you recognized a person and later discovered that you were mistaken, that it was someone else whom you had seen? [A question designed to bring home the possibility of a misidentification, as all jurors will have had this experience at some time or another.]

Q. Each of you realize, I assume, that if convicted of this offense, Mr. Fox could lose his liberty for a very long time?

Q. Now, none of you, I am sure, would want any person to lose his liberty on the basis of the testimony of a witness who might, just might, be mistaken, would you?

[If the case is based on circumstantial evidence, explain or define the term *circumstantial evidence* to the entire panel, then ask:]

Q. Do you understand the meaning of the term *circumstantial evidence?*

Q. Do you understand that circumstantial evidence is like a chain, and that it is only as strong as its weakest link?

Q. You will be instructed, ladies and gentlemen, that you may not convict Edward Fox on circumstantial evidence unless that evidence is wholly consistent with guilt and wholly inconsistent with innocence. If you decide, on the basis of circumstantial evidence, that Mr. Fox is probably guilty, but that there are also inferences which may be drawn which suggest his innocence, are you prepared to vote not guilty, in spite of the likelihood of his guilt? Will each of you look Edward Fox in the eye and promise him that in those circumstances you will vote not guilty?

Q. In his past, Mr. Fox has admittedly made mistakes. These mistakes led to his conviction for certain crimes. He has paid the penalty for those crimes. Will you promise not to regard those convictions as any evidence or proof, whatsoever, of his commission of the crime here charged, but only for the purposes the court, in its instructions, designates? [Defense counsel discloses a major weakness in the case that would otherwise have been revealed during the course of the trial and, by explaining that the defendant has paid the penalty for his previous crimes, hopes to minimize its effect.]

Q. Is there anything in your background, your past experience, anything at all, which will make it difficult for you to sit as a juror in this rape case? Is there any reason at all why you cannot give this defendant the fair and impartial trial to which the law entitles him?

Q. Is there anything about the crime of rape which so repels you, so disgusts and affects you, that you just could not be a fair and impartial juror in a rape case?

Q. Is there any reason, whether I have mentioned it or not, why you should not serve on this jury, or why, if seated, you could not be completely fair and impartial?

§11.24 Illustrative Voir Dire in a White Collar Crime Case

White collar crime is a generic term used to refer to nonviolent crimes such as embezzlement, forgery, and writing checks without sufficient funds. White collar crimes are usually committed by those in a position of financial responsibility, hence the name. What follows are some suggested questions in an embezzlement prosecution, to illustrate voir dire in a typical white collar crime case. These questions should be preceded by appropriate general questions.[15]

Q. We lawyers have a tendency to assume that jurors are familiar with terms that we use all the time and take for granted. There is no reason why

---

15 *See also* §§9.35, 11.22.

you should be familiar with these terms. So let me ask you, are any of you at all unclear about what the term *embezzlement* means? [If there is an affirmative answer or quizzical looks, the attorney should explain embezzlement. Even if there aren't, the lawyer might choose to discuss the crime generally, as some jurors might be embarrassed to admit their ignorance, while others, who think they understand the crime, may be laboring under misapprehensions.]

Q. You realize, of course, that the indictment against the defendant, Arthur Mathews, is no evidence of the crime at all; that the indictment is merely a piece of paper used to bring the defendant into court, just like a petition in a civil case?

Q. You also realize, I am sure, that a person is presumed innocent until proven guilty beyond a reasonable doubt?

Q. And do you realize that you must give the benefit of this presumption of innocence without any mental reservations whatever?

Q. Will you promise me and Mr. Mathews that you will give him the full benefit of that presumption of innocence?

Q. Do you understand that all the elements of the crime charged must be proven beyond a reasonable doubt, and that if one element of this crime is not proven, you must find Mr. Mathews not guilty?

Q. Do you understand that the burden of proving guilt beyond a reasonable doubt is on the prosecution, and that Mr. Mathews is not required to introduce any evidence at all?

Q. Knowing that, would you be inclined at all to require, in your own mind, that Mr. Mathews satisfy you that he is not guilty?

Q. Do you feel that, regardless of the law, a defendant charged with embezzlement ought to say something in his own behalf?

Q. Would you consider a defendant's failure to testify as any indication of guilt?

Q. Now, as you have been told, Mr. Mathews has been charged with embezzling one million dollars. Could you give him the same fair trial that you would give him if he were charged with taking a lesser amount?

Q. In other words, would you let the magnitude of the crime affect your thinking on whether he committed the crime?

Q. Are you familiar at all with any of the facts of this case, other than what you have been told here today?

Q. Have you read anything about this case in the newspapers or heard anything about it over the radio or television?

Q. Most of us are influenced by what we read in the papers. Have you formed any opinion as to the guilt or innocence of Arthur Mathews, or the merits of this case, from what you have read in the newspapers?

Q. Would it require some evidence to remove or change your opinion? [If the juror says *yes* to this, the juror should be challenged for cause.]

Q. With what you know about this case and any opinion you have formed from reading about it, would you, if you were on trial, be satisfied to be tried by a jury having your frame of mind?

Q. Mr. Mathews works for the Last National Savings Bank here in town. Have any of you ever had any dealings with that bank?

[In the next series of questions, the lawyer seeks to identify jurors who might hold a grudge against bankers.]

Q. Mr. Mathews, as you know, is a banker. I would appreciate it if you would tell me a bit about your experiences with bankers.

Q. Have you ever applied for a loan or a mortgage from a bank and been refused?

Q. If your loan or mortgage was granted, did you feel that the amount of interest that you were required to pay was excessive or exorbitant?

Q. Do you think banks, in charging interest on loans, make an unfair profit?

Q. Do you have any feeling that the crime of embezzlement is a particularly bad crime, perhaps worse than some other crimes?

Q. Have you ever had any association with anyone who was accused of embezzlement?

Q. Have you yourself ever worked in a bank, savings and loan association, insurance company, or other such financial institution?

Q. If you no longer work for that employer, could you tell us the circumstances under which that employment ended?

Q. Will you be able to judge this case solely on the evidence introduced during trial, setting aside any opinion you may have about banks, bankers, or financial institutions?

Q. If you have the feeling, after all the evidence is in, that Arthur Mathews is probably guilty, but that guilt has not been proven beyond a reasonable doubt, would you be prepared to return a verdict of not guilty, as the law requires?

Q. As the judge will tell you, you, the jurors, are the judges of the credibility of the witnesses. In evaluating the credibility of any of the witnesses, will you consider the demeanor of the witness, the opportunity and ability of the witness to observe, the possibility of bias or prejudice, and the likelihood of the witness's story being true?

Q. Some of the witnesses who will testify in Mr. Mathews's behalf will be bankers and bank personnel. Will you judge their testimony by the same standards which you would use in judging any other witness's testimony?

Q. Is there any reason, whether I have mentioned it or not, why you cannot be a fair and impartial juror in this case?

§11.25 Sample Voir Dire: Solicitation of Capital Murder Case

In this and the preceding chapter, examples of voir dire questions on selected and representative topics have been presented. What has not been presented is a voir dire examination in its entirety. The fact that a complete voir dire in a given case may be far lengthier than this book militates against such a presentation. Nonetheless, it is valuable to have a sense of how voir dire develops in the hands of a skilled trial lawyer. Accordingly, the remaining sections of this chapter will present significant excerpts from the voir dire conducted by Richard "Racehorse" Haynes, one of America's most well known defense attorneys, in the trial of Thomas Cullen Davis, one of Texas's wealthiest citizens, for the solicitation of the murder of his wife. The trial from which the voir dire is taken resulted in a hung jury; a second trial resulted in an acquittal. The two trials, particularly the first one, which took place in Houston, Texas pursuant to a change of venue, received nationwide publicity.

In order that the reader be better placed to follow the voir dire, a brief summary of the facts is presented. Sometime in 1974, Davis and his wife, Priscilla, began what turned out to be the longest pending divorce case in Texas history. It was complicated primarily by Mr. Davis's vast holdings and complex property ownership. Davis had inherited tremendous wealth from his father. At the time of his marriage to Priscilla in 1968, he owned, as separate property, many interests in many different businesses throughout the world. Mr. Davis and his wife were residents of Forth Worth, Texas, and the divorce suit was filed in a Fort Worth district court presided over by Judge Joe Eidson, Jr.

In August 1976, an assailant shot and seriously wounded Priscilla Davis at the multi-million dollar Davis residence in Fort Worth. On the same evening, also at the Davis home, Mrs. Davis's 12-year-old daughter and Mrs. Davis's male companion were killed, and a young man who was bringing his girl friend to the mansion to spend the night with Priscilla Davis's teen-age daughter was wounded.

Cullen Davis was arrested the next day, and subsequently indicted on two counts of capital murder. He was also charged with the shootings of Priscilla Davis and the young man who was bringing his date to the Davis residence. He was tried in Amarillo, Texas, in 1977, on a change of venue because of the great and unrelenting publicity given the case, on the charge of murdering Priscilla Davis's 12-year-old daughter by a former marriage. In the trial he was represented by Richard "Racehorse" Haynes, a widely known and successful criminal defense attorney from Houston, Texas, and by Phil Burleson, also a well known, capable, and successful lawyer from Dallas, Texas. Joe Shannon, a young but experienced assistant district attorney, took the lead for the state. After many weeks the trial resulted in Davis's acquittal.

Meanwhile, the Davis divorce case was still pending in Fort Worth. It was delayed following the August 1976 shootings and the 1977 trial, but several different hearings took place in the course of 1978. Early in that year, Davis's lawyers moved to disqualify Judge Eidson in the divorce case. One of the grounds for this motion was that Judge Eidson had testified at the Amarillo murder trial. This motion, heard by a visiting judge, was denied.

In mid-August of 1978 there was another hearing on the divorce case in Judge Eidson's court. The court ordered Davis to pay some of his wife's bills and increased the amount of temporary alimony. On August 20, 1978, Cullen Davis was again arrested; this time charged with attempting to hire a professional killer to murder Judge Eidson. Davis allegedly had paid a friend, an employee of one of his many companies, to hire a gunman to kill the judge. The friend, David McCrory, had contacted the FBI. The FBI set up a meeting on Sunday, August 20, 1978, between McCrory and Davis. At this meeting, Davis allegedly paid McCrory $25,000 for the murder of Judge Eidson. The conversation between McCrory and Davis was taped by the FBI.

The solicitation of murder trial was moved to Houston on a change of venue because of the extensive pretrial publicity. The trial took over three months, beginning in late 1978, and ended with a hung jury in January 1979. Davis was represented on this trial by several attorneys, including "Racehorse" Haynes and Phil Burleson.

§11.26 —Introduction

It is from the Houston solicitation trial that the following excerpts from the voir dire of "Racehorse" Haynes are taken. The voir dire is noteworthy for its lengthy and thorough introductory remarks to the jury. Haynes prepares the jurors for the topics which he plans to discuss with them, at the same time educating them as to why these are matters of concern:

> May it please the Court, ladies and gentlemen, as His Honor has told you, my name is Richard Haynes and I am a practicing attorney here in Houston, Texas, representing Mr. Thomas Cullen Davis, who is the citizen accused here today. You are now involved and understand how we go through this business of selecting jurors; the effort, as those of you who are in the sciences can now perceive, is indeed not a very scientific one at all. It really is more a matter of an educated guesswork on the part of the lawyers who are entrusted with the responsibility of endeavoring to select from fifty people, twelve people who are qualified to serve on this jury and from my point of view to sit in judgment on Thomas Cullen Davis.
>
> We have rules that have been handed to us by older lawyers. Whether they are accurate or not, I am not certain. We are told to take in things such as occupation and don't take this one because he is too tall, and don't take that one because he is too fat or don't take that one because he has long hair or short hair or a mustache or no mustache.
>
> When you get right down to it, it is not very scientific. What we are really relegated to and what you as citizens are relegated to because you are part of the system, is total reliance upon your candor in the responses that you make. Absolute total reliance. All of the lawyers, the prosecution and the defense, alike, are members of the system. We are part of the system. We are officers of this court. We are endeavoring, both sides,

to ask these questions. We are permitted, by law, to impose upon you and your time and to trespass upon your time with these questions.

As the Court has told you it is no lawyer's desire to intrude into an area that is private. That is unto you yourself. Here perhaps is the last vestige of voluntary service to the community that a citizen can provide, now that they have the abolition of the draft, and you have answered the summons to be here and give us your time and be away from your work and your families and to participate in the system.

Without you it does not work and the lawyers on both sides recognize that we trespass on your time but I can assure you, as you must certainly know, it is so vital and so important that we get twelve citizens who are qualified to serve on this jury. It may be that a citizen is qualified in every way to serve . . . in any other kind of case . . ., but for some reason known to that person they are not qualified to serve on this jury and I am confident that each of you will agree with me that we will have no system at all—we would have no jury system if the citizens who came up to serve on this jury had some preconceived notion that dictated a little bit to that citizen the end result that is sought by this system.

If we have any citizen at all serving on this jury that has some preconceived notion, some bias, however slight it may be, that would keep them from being totally fair and impartial, then I am sure you will agree with me that we'd need to know about it.

Now, likewise, there is no lawyer in the system on either side of this docket who would not champion your right to have an opinion or the right to have an opinion of anything that you wanted to. As citizens you are entitled to an opinion about anything. Likewise, if you have an opinion about any aspect of this lawsuit, then the litigants on both sides are entitled to know something about that opinion.

Now, let me say this to you right at the very beginning. There is no right or wrong answer to these questions asked of you. The only requirement is as much candor as you can muster, and there is another step because as Judge Moore told you earlier, no citizen forgoes the right to privacy and . . . each of you will not be required to answer any question if you think even for an instant that I am infringing upon your right to privacy and if I decided to ask you a question and I can assure you it will not be in an effort to pry into some area of your life, that ought to be private to you, but if I ask you a question and you feel that that question impinges upon your right of privacy, please call it to my attention and we will ask the Court's permission to go before the Court and ask the question again to the Court and the Court will make a decision as to whether you are obligated to answer that question or not or whether I am entitled to ask it or not.

So you are protected in that regard and you do not have to give any answers to any questions that you don't feel right about in your own mind, and that you could give without impinging upon your right to privacy, even to the slightest extent, and I want to assure you of this.

§11.27 —Trial Procedures

Let me just first talk about some of the fundamentals that are related to the trial of a criminal case, and that is what this is. Those of you who have before served know these things, and to those of you who do know of it, I apologize in advance for the repetition, but it is vitally important that we have some understanding right up front about the fundamentals.

His Honor has told you that the burden of proof is upon the prosecution which you know and have known since time one, since we were grade school children. We learned that all persons are presumed innocent until their guilt is established by legal and by competent evidence beyond a reasonable doubt.

And, one of the few times in the course of a trial that I will agree with the prosecution, I do agree that the Court will not charge this jury or instruct this jury on what reasonable doubt means, but will leave it to you and each one of you to decide in your minds, after having heard all of the evidence, what reasonable doubt means. It has been defined as being that doubt which would cause a reasonably prudent person to hesitate—in the conduct of his or her own most important personal business. I like that definition. [This definition was objected to, but was permitted by the court.]

Now, because it is not defined and because it's incumbent upon each of you if selected to serve on this jury and from my vantage point it's important if you sit in judgment on Thomas Cullen Davis, it's important, it's vitally important that you and each of those, those of you who are finally selected, start off in neutral with no preconceived notions that would keep you from being totally fair and impartial.

I want you to think, if you will, about how you feel. For example, isn't the prospect of sitting in judgment on another human being where a serious criminal accusation, the sort of four-pronged accusation—first, the prosecution will endeavor to prove solicitation of capital murder. If they do not prove that alternatively they will prove attempt—they will endeavor to prove attempted solicitation of capital murder and failing to do that, they will attempt to prove it is a different date and finally, if there is no proof the prosecution will endeavor to demonstrate . . . conspiracy to commit the offense . . . . [E]ven though the prosecution has pled it in the alternative . . . we have four accusations.

But, it is pled in that fact and you would be permitted as jurors to take it with you back into the jury room when you commence your deliberations, the indictment in the lawsuit to read along with the Charge on the law that will be given to you by His Honor.

No juror is expected to remember those observations or comments made by the lawyer about the law at this juncture because the truth of it is what we say about the law . . . may be the law [but the] only law that applies to a lawsuit . . . is the law that the Judge gives you when you finally go back to the jury deliberation room . . . .

§11.28 —Prejudice

I would like to ask you to think about this so that I can talk to you a little bit further when I come to you individually. How you would feel about sitting in judgment on a person in this serious offense—a person of immense wealth and that may seem at first blush facetious, but I can assure you, you examine your thoughts you will recognize and know that many times an intelligent sensitive person or people are feeling things against those of great wealth.

If one has a feeling, however slight it might be, against a person of great wealth one would be entitled to that feeling. You have a right to any feeling that you have. You have a right to feel any way that you want to feel, but if, indeed, you do feel something in your mind and in your heart, however slight, against a person of great wealth and I can tell you that the evidence will determine straight out that Mr. Davis is a person of immense wealth, but if that preempts your ability to be a fair and impartial juror, however slight it may be, then you need to let me know about it and more importantly you need to let Thomas Cullen Davis know about it, and I will talk to you, with your permission, a little more about it personally when it comes time to talk to you individually.

I would like to ask you to reflect upon this. There are a number of lawyers representing the prosecution and a number of lawyers, three at the table, and Mr. Sumner will be here, I expect, at the end of the week, or the first of next week, representing Mr. Davis. The number of lawyers that appear in a litigation should not, in and of itself, be a fact that would cause any citizen to have a feeling prejudicial or some preconceived notion against the citizen on trial, and yet, if one reads the papers and from the juror cards that you citizens sent back to us, that information sheet, we know on both sides that you read the newspapers and we know that lawyers for the most part are classed, at least unfortunately are not held in great repute.

We enhance our problem or maybe it is more difficult for us, but one should not see it as any admission of guilt as far as Thomas Cullen Davis is concerned, because he has three lawyers and will have four, then you should draw a similar finding that the prosecution has four lawyers representing the prosecution.

§11.29 —Objections

Likewise, as you know, in the course of a trial lawyers on either side will make whatever objections they deem are proper. You have seen some brief examples of this during this period of time [while] we have been discussing your prospect as jurors as to your serving on this jury, to sit in judgment of Thomas Cullen Davis.

When a lawyer makes an objection, His Honor will make a ruling. Sometimes the objection of the lawyer has a way of irritating the citizens who serve on juries because objections do interrupt. But, I want to caution you this and question of you this, that you are not permitted any aggravation you have with reference to the lawyer to prevent you from being a fair—a totally fair person, and if indeed you have had experience and have had some aggravation towards lawyers for the objections that they air at the time that they deem proper, you are entitled to feel that way, but please permit that aggravation to extend only to the lawyer, not to the citizen accused.

§11.30 —Probation Application

His Honor has told you that in this litigation there has been an application for probation made. You were told, and this is repetitious, but so vitally important, that the law requires those who are eligible to make that eligibility known to the Court and to the prosecution in advance of the trial before the trial commences. Each of you, myself, and all of you who are eligible, and that is because we have never before been convicted in this or any other state of a felony, are eligible to make an application, myself, you, any one of you who are on trial would be eligible to make that known to the jury. You have got to make that application in advance, under oath. You have to swear to this Court, to the clerk of this Court, you have never before been convicted of a felony in this state or any other state of the United States.

Now, this puts the prosecution on notice, if indeed one should make such an oath to God that they have never been before convicted of a felony in this or any other state and the prosecution had evidence to the contrary that certainly would be demonstrated to the jury because a person who has before been convicted of a felony in this or any other state is not eligible.

Now, what concerns the lawyers, what concerns me and my colleagues representing Thomas Cullen Davis is the paradox of having to make this application in advance and the paradox is one comes into the court and enters a plea of not guilty, and I tell you now that the plea of Thomas Cullen Davis in this case will be not guilty, and we will persist in that plea throughout this trial, but a citizen comes into court and enters a plea of not guilty in response to the questions asked by the Court. "Not guilty, Your Honor." And at any time concerning this filing of this application for probation says in the event that you find me guilty, I ask that you please consider probation and I would not want, nor should you want, as a member of the system, any citizen who would think that following the law to make that eligibility known is any sort of concession.

The concern by the jury is to determine whether or not the citizen accused is guilty or not guilty. If they find that the State has not met its burden of proof, if they have a reasonable doubt after considering all of the evidence that has been presented and after considering what was not presented, the omission on the part of the prosecutorial teams, anything that is before them properly that is logically inferred they can draw from what is presented to them and after considering all of this there remains in the mind of a juror, reasonable doubt, they are obliged by their oaths as jurors and by the law to find this citizen not guilty.

So they simply say not guilty, in which case the trial is over. But in the event, in a case where a jury considering all of the evidence is persuaded beyond a reasonable doubt that the citizen on trial is guilty, then they are obliged to decide what punishment is proper under the facts and circumstances. Under the law adult probation, as we call it, which is the application to this court, it is sort of a case and you need to search your minds and hearts so that when I talk to you individually you can tell me how you feel about the law of probation.

Remember this, you have a right as citizens, to disagree with any part of the law. You can do it now. If you have a disagreement with the law you can simply say: "Lawyer, I disagree with the law," and we can talk about it. And if you have a disagreement on the law perhaps it is that you should not serve on this jury because part of the law that would be involved even though it is no concession that the law of probation is involved, we have the right to know now how you feel about that the same way as the prosecution has a right and did ask how you felt about the maximum punishment. You need to ask yourselves in your own minds and in your own hearts how you feel about the law so that when I talk to you individually you can tell me how you feel and what concerns you may have.

I would want, and that is what you should want—no citizen who has ever gone to trial imposed upon him or her a jury who would dodge that first obligation, that first obligation to insist that the prosecution prove to you beyond a reasonable doubt guilt as accused.

I get a recurring nightmare of those who are in the system, and a citizen having heard evidence, of course, you don't hear evidence in criminal cases without there being what could be called some smoke and we have all known that story that where there's smoke there's fire, but the law is more sophisticated than that and you don't convict people on smoke. They must prove the allegations.

But, suppose you had—just suppose for a moment, for the purpose of a juror, who, after having heard all of the evidence still has that reasonable doubt in his mind, but thought, I know this citizen made an application for probation and so, well, I still have a doubt and I know I ought to find this person not guilty but I will go ahead and find him guilty because I would not want a guilty person to be around but then when it comes time to deliberate on punishment you would put him on probation.

That would be hedging the system does not need or want; nor should you as citizens, and you should insist on full compliance with the law.

So, I ask you, yourselves, how you feel about the law of probation in your minds and in your hearts as to what it is and when it comes my turn to talk to your individually, we can talk about that for a moment.

§11.31 —Nature of Questions to Be Asked

> I do not intend to ask you about your political affiliations. That is private to you and the sanctity of the ballot box and I am a champion of the law on both sides, but I would like to ask you individually whether you have been active in politics other than at the ballot box or have you participated in grass roots politics or been present or active in campaigns for the candidate of your choice.
>
> I will ask you when I get to you individually about your outside interests and hobbies, and I will ask you individually if you have any prior union affiliations and if so whether or not you have been active in the union and you are entitled if you think that my questions are transcending out of the bounds of propriety in that area to call it to my attention so that we can petition the Court.

At this juncture, counsel asked if any prospective jurors or any members of their families had ever previously sat on a federal grand jury or a grand jury in Texas or any other state. He asked those who had so served if there was anything about that service that would in any way affect their service in the Davis case.

§11.32 —Credibility of Witnesses

Haynes's opening voir dire comments then turned to the credibility of witnesses.

> The jurors' function, those of you who have served would know this, is to be the judges of the facts presented. You get all the law from the Court but, as jurors, those of you who are ultimately selected to serve on this jury, to sit in judgment of Thomas Cullen Davis, will be the exclusive judges of the facts, the credibility of the witnesses, and the weight to be given their testimony. Essentially what that means is this: As a juror you know, those of you who served, you have a right to believe all of what a witness says or part of what a witness says or none of what a witness says. That is your prerogative and your obligation as jurors.
>
> You judge the credibility of the witnesses and curiously enough, for the most part, the law does not give to jurors criteria by which they may judge credibility. The law envisions and contemplates that you will call upon your own life experiences, your own logic, your own intellect in deciding credibility of a particular witness in a case.
>
> The law gives no special credibility to any particular witness. No one gets special credibility at time one. The theory is that all witnesses are under oath and the mere fact that a witness is a police officer or a deputy sheriff or an FBI agent, a law enforcement agent of any kind, does not give that witness special credibility at time one.
>
> But there are those, and I know people who feel this way, and I'm confident either some here do or may know people who are intelligent, sensi-

tive people, literate people, concerned people, and they feel in their own minds and hearts that a police officer or an FBI agent ought to be entitled to special credibility because of their jobs and their profession of law enforcement and they honestly feel that way.

Well, if you honestly feel that way about it, you are entitled to it. You are entitled to the way you feel. What I would like to know, what the system requires and what Cullen Davis desperately needs as a citizen and is entitled to, are citizens who will tell us that candidly, if you feel in any way, however slight it may be, that a police officer is to be believed, his testimony is to be believed before the testimony of some other citizen, simply because he is a police officer and for no other reason, if you really feel that way, I want to know about that and please tell me when I talk to you individually. There are those who feel that way.

But, no witness is entitled under the law to special credibility simply because of their position in life. The fact they wear a uniform or are in law enforcement, or any other, such as lawyers, judges, nobody gets special credibility under the law.

You judge credibility of each witness exactly like you do every other witness. Of course, you could take into consideration all of the factors that are permitted by the Court's rulings to be demonstrated for you.

§11.33 —Length of Trial

There is another factor with reference to this case that I think important to talk to you about now. I know it directly affects several of the citizens who are here assembled on a commission basis. I cannot represent to you as a lawyer representing—one of the lawyers representing Thomas Cullen Davis how long the lawsuit will last. Because the truth of it is the lawyers don't know. Lawyers for both sides, the prosecution and the defense, have represented to the Court who was interested because of the schedule problems and so forth and in obtaining this courtroom in how long this case would last, and the suggestions from both sides were to the effect that four weeks, five weeks, something in that area and that's not a guarantee, that any lawyer on either side can give you. Those were the representations made on both sides.

Now, the reason I say that to you is this: If in fact a perfectly qualified citizen, qualified to serve not only on other jury cases, but on this jury case is in a situation where a protracted trial works a financial hardship, and it will if you are on commission or if your source of income is curtailed to a being—by your being at this courthouse from nine to five, if it works a financial hardship we all regret that part. Here is the key and here is what I want you to think about and only you know if it is indeed a personal concern, because we are all concerned about our families and our obligations and our jobs and so forth, if a personal concern about the deprivation that occurs, financial deprivation, such that it would be keeping you from being the same sort of fair and impartial juror you would want to be, you have only one opportunity to talk about it and it is now. The lawyers on either side as you have already seen demonstrated will take into consideration those things and present the same to the Court and the ultimate ruling will be from the Court because everybody knows that jury service does work hardships on all persons who serve.

But, if the preoccupation concern about the deprivation would keep you from being the same fair and impartial juror you would otherwise be, then it would be time now, now is the time to talk about it. Again, I am not representing to you the case will last that long. It may last less or it could conceivably go longer. I don't know. You think about it and let the lawyers now know and more importantly you let the Court know.

§11.34 —Basis of Verdict

Now, as you know, those of you who have before served, and perhaps all of you know, that in a lawsuit, the prosecution, because it has the burden of proof, goes first, pretty much the same as they were permitted to first inquire of the prospective jurors, they likewise are permitted first to put on evidence because they have the burden of proof. They get to make the last argument because they, the prosecution, have the burden of proof. What we ask those conscientious people who are ultimately selected to sit in judgment on Thomas Cullen Davis, that you not finalize in your conclusions until such time as or in your opinion until such time as you have heard all of the case and all of the evidence and it is submitted to you by the Court.

Now, everyone realizes that as we go along people tend to form opinions about things as the prosecution mentioned to you yesterday. You are obliged as you sit as jurors to listen to fellow jurors. You are obliged as jurors to exchange ideas and concepts with fellow jurors, but the ultimate obligation on the part of the jurors, is to vote his or her own personal conscience. The final vote must be unanimous, but it requires individual judgment of each person who serves on the jury taking into consideration what everyone else has to say.

You come to this courtroom, strangers to each other. Those of you who are selected to serve on this jury will be instructed by the Court that at the time you are not actually in the courtroom together as a group, you are not to discuss the case even with each other. You don't deliberate on the case until such time as you have heard all of the case. You have been given all of the law that applies and you go back in the jury room and what that does is that it permits the jurors, because you can't talk about the case, to talk to each other and you are traditionally learning something about the backgrounds of some of the jurors and their homes and their ideas and their dreams and their trips and their children and all of those things that human beings talk about as jurors because they can't talk about the case.

As a consequence, jurors traditionally find that of twelve people selected, they're a cross-section of the community, they will find members of the jury for whom they have the greatest respect possible in selecting character and integrity and personal habits and traits and fast friendships live long. Friendships can be accomplished in the course of jury duty.

When you get down to voting as jurors, despite the fact that you have formed a friendship with some juror, despite the fact that you have fellow jurors, you have great confidence in the integrity and intellect of a fellow juror, you must vote your own conscience, how you personally feel after a fair consideration of all the evidence.

As to a fair consideration of what fellow jurors have to say, it is the personal obligation of each juror to vote his or her own conviction. I am sure all of you know that.

§11.35 —Selected Questions

The actual voir dire questions asked by Mr. Haynes took several days. A sampling of some of the more important questions are presented for illustrative purposes. Some of the questions have been paraphrased:

Q. Does anyone on the panel have or has anyone had a close friend or relative engaged in law enforcement, either now or in the past? [To those answering affirmatively, questions concerning the nature of the relationship were asked, as well as questions about any discussion between the juror and the person engaged in law enforcement.]

Q. Do you know from any source whether I have ever represented police officers, police officers who have been accused of criminal activity?

Q. Do you know, or have you heard about, from newspapers, television, or radio, any of the prosecutorial team from Tarrant County?

Q. Have any of you heard of the lawyers representing Mr. Davis?

Q. Do any of you have any feelings about me [Haynes]? [This last question was preceded by this statement: Let me say this. I would have to be green as grass to think . . . that everyone who has ever heard of me . . . would like to have me come to dinner with them on Sunday evening. I get some mail that indicates to me that some people would not like me to come to dinner. I know that. And I feel the same is true with reference to my colleagues. . . . I would like to discuss them with you because if you have any feelings, however slight they might be, whatever it is based upon, that would keep you from being the same sort of fair and impartial juror you would otherwise be in some other case. Don't you all agree with me it's necessary to talk about it? . . . I would like to think I'm a grown man, and if you have something to say, I can handle it. I might cry and suck my thumb later on about it, but I can handle it. It's so important that we know, because it shouldn't ever be, and I think you would agree with me on this, it shouldn't be a trial of the lawyers. The defense lawyer versus the prosecution or the prosecution versus the defense lawyer. Or the defense lawyer versus the witness. It's not a contest in that sense. And yet I know as they read the media, people I don't fault them, I don't fault the media. I have represented them in the past for accusations about those things, it tends to pitch in terms of a contest and it is not. And I am sure you would agree with me. For any citizen accused of a crime to have a person on his or her jury who has some special feelings in their mind or heart against the lawyer that would keep that juror from being the same sort of fair and impartial human being that that juror would be in any other case or where that lawyer is not involved. So, don't hold back. Feel free to discuss it as openly with me as humanly possible. I know it's a crowded courtroom but this is a special circumstance and you are special people. You are called here and sworn for the possibility of serving on a jury, sitting in judgment on another human being, and it is important.] [Several follow-up questions were asked jurors who did know or had heard of Mr. Haynes. If the jurors had heard about him they were asked about the effect of that knowledge, and whether it would influence them as jurors.]

Q. Have you read, seen, or heard any news reports about what purport to be the facts made the basis of the indictment in this case?

Q. Can you tell me, Mrs. __________, how long you have been aware of the name Cullen Davis, when is the first time you heard something on the radio or on television about Cullen Davis? [This last question was to a panel member who had heard something about the case. All of these next questions were directed to different, individual jurors.]

Q. Do you recall any particulars that you remember seeing on television, or the television newscast?

Q. Do you subscribe to newspapers every day?

Q. Which paper, may I ask?

Q. At the time of the first discussion in the media, did you have any casual conversation with any adult friend, over coffee or socially, about the fact that the case had been moved here to Houston from Fort Worth, Tarrant County?

Q. Have you at any time up to right now had any conversation, however casual, about this case?

Q. May I ask you, Mrs. __________, what your outside interests and hobbies are, if you have time for them?

Q. Do you have any outside interests or activities other than sports as a spectator?

Q. May I ask you, since you said you have lived in Houston all your life, what high school or other schools here you have attended?

Q. Long ago, I had the nickname Racehorse tacked on to me, and the press favors me with it daily. That wouldn't make any difference to you would it?

Q. Do you have any objection to the right of a human being to own firearms or have possession of firearms?

Q. Let me ask you this, Mrs. ________, have you before as a child or young adult or adult ever been accused of something that you were in fact not guilty of—something serious?

Q. Have you ever taken an active interest in politics, that is, other than voting? Have you supported a particular candidate?

[In response to a question about whether she knew when she reported for jury duty she would be on the Davis case, a juror said she gathered that she would because of all the camera people around. She also indicated that she figured it would be a long trial, because of the other trial (the Amarillo murder trial), about which she had heard. Haynes then asked this question:]

Q. Did you before ever follow the news media accounts of Mr. Davis? Ever see it in the papers or read about it or heard about it? You can tell me about how you became aware.

Q. Knowing about that what you call the other case [the Amarillo murder trial], would that make any difference in this case?

Q. Do you have any feeling about what you call the other case?

Q. Did it give you any opinion at all to reflect upon the other case, however slight it was?

Q. Other than the fact that it was a long case, did you know how it came out?

Q. Do you know to this day how it came out?

Q. Was there anything about that case, other than the fact that it was a long trial, other than that, that gave you any special feeling in your mind or heart with reference to this case?

Q. In hearing about this case [the solicitation of murder case] on the television and on the radio, and from reading the newspapers, do you have any feeling or have you formed any opinion, however slight it might be, as to the guilt or innocence of Thomas Cullen Davis?

[After some discussion of news reports of this case which were heard by one juror, this question:]

Q. Was there anything in the newscasts which you listened to, and I think you can accurately analyze, to indicate whether Mr. Davis was more guilty or innocent, which made any impression that could, even to the slightest extent, affect you in your thinking if you were selected on this jury and sat in judgment on Mr. Davis?

Q. Have you had any occasion, as an executive secretary, Mrs. ________, to become familiar with recording tapes or recording words?

Q. Do you use some sort of dictating equipment?

Q. Do you have any individual hobbies, such as photography, or have you had a relative or close friend who dabbles in any way in photography?

Q. Do any of you have close friends or relatives who are engaged in law enforcement—any relative or close friend who works for the Houston

Police Department, the sheriff's department, the FBI, or any other law enforcement agency?

Q. You have told me that your parents are presently still living. Let me ask you what business your father is engaged in, or was engaged in, if he is retired?

Q. Now, Mrs. ________, I don't want to know the name of your best friend, but tell me, please, what period or era of your life did your best friend come from? Childhood, young adult, co-worker, co-employee, high school, college, or what period of your life?

Q. Do you belong to any charity organizations or sororities, business or professional?

Q. Have you been active in your church other than by attendance, and by that I mean, do you have an office in your church?

Q. And, may I ask you what church that is?

Q. Does the accusation against Cullen Davis create any special feelings in your mind on your part against him? [This last question came after a discussion of how sometimes, in the minds of many people, the accusation, alone, particularly of a heinous crime, can create feelings against the accused.]

Q. Did you know that Mr. Davis is married? And did you know that marriage is in the process of being dissolved by divorce?

Q. Did you know that the accusation in this case has to do with the presiding judge in that divorce case?

Q. You knew that from just the newspaper or the newscasts, did you not?

Q. Does the fact of divorce in and of itself create any hostilities, maybe hostilities is not the word, any special feelings at all against Mr. Davis?

Q. Now, the evidence in this case will show that Mr. Davis, in the process of a divorce, is now living with a woman to whom he is not married. Would that fact bother you at all, influence in any way your thinking or your decision in this case?

Q. Does the fact that the allegations here refer to the Judge in the divorce case as being "one of the 15 victims," does that fact in and of itself create any hostility in your mind or heart against Cullen Davis?

Q. Now, if you were selected on this jury, Mrs. ________, it would be a case of a woman sitting in judgment on a man. From experience, I know some women that could never give a man a fair trial, and vice versa. Do you agree that any human beings, once they take the oath as jurors, should not permit that fact alone to make them less fair persons than they would otherwise be? That fact alone, that you're a woman and Mr. Davis is a man, that fact alone wouldn't bother you, or affect your verdict in any way, would it?

Q. Now, Mr. ________, I want you, please, to take a good look at the citizen accused, Mr. Davis, here. Is there anything about his looks, anything at all, anything you don't like about his looks, that would keep you from being a fair and impartial juror if you were to be on this jury?

Q. Can you think of any reason at all, Mr. ________, why you would hesitate to serve on this jury and sit in judgment on Thomas Cullen Davis?

Q. Can you think of anything at all that you think would help me and my colleagues in deciding whether you are one of the persons who should sit in judgment on this man as I discussed with you?

[To a nurse on the panel who had worked in a psychiatric hospital, the following questions:]

Q. Has any part of your professional responsibility ever been dealing with people who were mentally ill, who also had some problem relating to criminal accusations? People who were not only mentally ill, but also had some accusation pending against them for antisocial behavior and general conduct? As a consequence of that have you ever before been called on to give any testimony in any court about some patient? Have you ever had occasion to be interviewed by any law enforcement people with reference to patients that you had under your care as a registered nurse? Have you had occasion as the nurse to listen to the recitations or conversations of those people under your care, mentally ill people, concerning their problems with the law, did they ever endeavor to talk to you about those problems from time to time? As a consequence of your work, have you ever had occasion to come in contact with any members of the legal profession, either those who prosecute or those who defend those people against allegations or charges involving mental illness?

Q. Have any of you ever had any medical or nursing training or education of any kind?

Q. Mrs. ________, do you subscribe to any magazines of any sort?

Q. Do you have any friends or relatives in the Dallas-Fort Worth area with whom you have any contact, either by mail or telephone, or in person?

Q. I have told the panel as a whole that the evidence will reveal that Mr. Davis is a very wealthy man. Now, Mrs. ________, would that fact make any difference to you if you were called upon as a juror to sit in judgment on him?

Q. Does it create any feeling in your mind one way or the other, however slight that feeling may be, that he is able to have three or four lawyers to represent him in this case? Does that make any difference?

Q. Now, we all know that there are many people who have criminal accusations brought against them who do not have the money to engage counsel to defend them? You've heard of that, Mrs. ________, haven't you? Is there anything about that situation, the fact that there are people who cannot afford to defend themselves, and here we are, representing a very wealthy man who can afford to defend himself—does that fact in and of itself create any feelings in your mind or in your heart against him?

Q. Do you have any feelings in your own mind about the law of probation, whether it's appropriate, whether it ought to be the law that applies only to young people, or do you think it should be across the board? Any feelings whatsoever about the law of probation?

Q. Do you understand, as I explained to the whole panel, why we have to go into probation now, that the law compels that, and that it is in no way any admission of guilt or any concession?

Q. You don't feel that you would be one who would say to yourself "No, I could never do that," with regard to probation?

Q. And if the facts, the law and the circumstances warranted it, you could give due and fair consideration to probation, could you not?

Q. Do you, Mr. ________, have any feelings about a police officer, that a police officer ought to be believed before some other witness just because he is a police officer and for no other reason?

Q. How would you answer that question with respect to the FBI, or any other law enforcement agency?

Q. Would you endeavor in every way, if selected to serve on this jury, to be fair and impartial and wait until you have heard all of the evidence and gotten the Court's charge on the law, and go in the jury room before you make up your mind?

Q. And endeavor in every way humanly possible to judge this case strictly on the facts and the evidence presented to you?

Q. Have you, Mr. ________, ever been personally interested in the outcome of a criminal case as a friend or relative of a person who is the defendant or a witness or a complainant in a criminal case?

Q. Do you know whether or not your husband has ever made an application of any kind to be a police officer?

Q. Do you understand that the prosecution has the burden of proof, that the citizen accused doesn't have to prove anything?

Q. Also, do you understand the citizen accused does not have to testify if that citizen does not want to?

Q. Have you ever thought of yourself as being a person who wants to hear both sides of the story? And are you in fact that kind of person?

Q. So, while you may be a person who wants to hear both sides of the story, the law says Mr. Davis doesn't have to testify if he doesn't want to, and do you have any quarrel with that law? Would you change it if you could?

Q. You understand that a person accused has the right not to testify? If you were selected as a juror, would you respect that right?

Q. Do you read any magazines or books?

Q. Is there anything you have ever read that you think may in some way keep you from being a totally fair and impartial person in this case if you are selected?

Q. Have you, Mr. ________, ever had any kind of formal legal training or education?

Part V

Choosing the Jury

Overview

Chess games are divided into openings, middle games, and end positions. If jury selection were to be similarly trifurcated, the opening phase would consist of community surveys, mock trials, and investigations of the venire. The early middle game might include motions for a change in venue and challenges to the array, on the basis of either statutory or constitutional grounds. In the late middle game, at trial, there would be voir dire and, if permitted, pre-voir dire questionnaires. The end position would center on the actual choosing of the jury. As in chess, all that has preceded the end game has a bearing on how it is played; and, yet, as in a chess game, it has an identity all its own.

The actual selection of the jury brings into active play the lawyer's knowledge and research. It is when the lawyer's understanding of the role of the jury and law of challenges assume practical importance. It is the stage at which the lawyer's information about individual jurors acquired from pretrial investigations, pre-voir dire questionnaires, and voir dire must be transformed into decisions about which jurors should and should not hear the case. Jury selection also requires the lawyer to apply abstract profiles of favorable and unfavorable jurors to live human beings. The selection process tests not only the lawyer's empirical research and theoretical knowledge, but also the lawyer's experience, judgment, and intuition.

The selection of the jury can affect the course of the trial. Regardless of the persuasiveness of the lawyer's evidence and arguments, they may be lost on the wrong jury. As comedians have recognized that some audiences are more receptive to their jokes than others, so too have lawyers recognized that some jurors are more receptive to their arguments than others. Some jurors respond to logic; others, to emotional appeals. To the extent that the jury tries the lawyers as well as the facts, as many veteran trial lawyers believe, counsel needs to know what types of jurors will respond favorably to him or her. The challenge facing the attorney is to identify the right type of juror for the particular case, given the parties, witnesses, issues, and lawyers; and then to determine which of the prospective jurors fit the desired mold.

To set the stage for the chapter which follows, the assumption is made that the lawyer has decided to opt for a jury trial, that the decision whether to move for a change in venue or to challenge the array has been made and resolved, and that those prospective jurors who are properly subject to challenge for cause have been removed from the panel. The lawyer's task is then to determine which of the remaining jurors to challenge peremptorily.

In Chapters 10 and 11 some general observations regarding this issue of whom to challenge peremptorily were made based on the subject matter of the litigation. It was suggested, for example, that homemakers are apt to be favorably inclined to the plaintiff in a products liability case involving a common household appliance. Conversely, persons who have been victims of a serious crime are unlikely to be sympathetic to a defendant charged with the same crime.

In Chapter 12 an attempt will be made to further probe this issue of which jurors to challenge, but in cases where the subject matter of the suit is less defining of the characteristics of a favorable juror. In these more murky situations, on what basis should a lawyer decide on whom to expend scarce peremptory challenges? Intuition, experience, judgment, stereotypes, social science studies, voir dire responses (both verbal and nonverbal), community surveys, mock trials, juror investigations, pre-voir dire questionnaires, authoritarian ratings, and juror philosophical perspectives all come into play in answering this question. As the preceding smorgasbord of factors may suggest, the question is quite complex. Yet the verdict in the case may depend on the ability to answer it well. Chapter 12 makes an attempt to sort out these variables. The reader should not expect universal truth; the more modest goal is to provide food for thought.

12 Approaches to Jury Selection

§12.01 Introduction

The ultimate end to which the various strategies discussed in this book are directed is the selection of a suitable jury. An understanding of the history and function of the jury, community demographic surveys, juror investigations, mock trials, voir dire, a knowledge of the law of challenges, and the intelligent exercise of challenges are all means to this end.

A suitable jury is a case-specific concept—what will constitute a suitable jury in one case may not in another. It is also a relative concept—a lawyer seeks the best jury possible as opposed to the best possible jury. From the vantage point of the practicing attorney, a suitable jury is one which is emotionally, psychologically, and philosophically receptive to the client's case. A suitable jury is obtained by removing from the jury those persons whose presence would contribute to an adverse verdict and by including on the jury those whose presence will contribute to a favorable verdict. If both lawyers are equally skilled, and each has access to the same information regarding prospective jurors, the result should be a stand-off, in that the jury will not be slanted in favor of either side. What will emerge is the neutral and impartial jury which the law envisions.

The term *jury selection* is a misnomer. A lawyer cannot choose the jurors who will hear a case. All the lawyer can do is to reject, through challenges for cause and peremptory challenges, those persons whom the lawyer believes are unsuitable to hear the case.

The burden falls most squarely on the peremptory challenge, for most judges are quite chary in granting challenges for cause. Even when a lawyer establishes a viable claim of prejudice, the judge will often simply ask the juror some appropriate variation of the following question: "Do you think that you can set aside your prejudice and decide this case fairly on its merits, on the basis of the evidence that is presented in court?" Human nature being what it is, it will be the rare juror who will answer in the negative, and the rare judge who, having received an affirmative answer, will excuse the juror for cause. However, the number of jurors who can be eliminated through peremptory challenges is limited by the relatively small number of such challenges available in most jurisdictions.[1]

The selection of jurors is both an art and a science. Sometimes it is more one than the other. But it is an error to think that judgment and scientific method are mutually exclusive; the most effective trial lawyers recognize that there is room for both. In this chapter a number of different approaches to jury selection, ranging from the intuitive to the scientific, will be canvassed.

Sometimes the choice of approach is foisted upon the lawyer by external circumstances beyond the lawyer's control. A judge may set unduly strict time and scope limits on voir dire. The judge may be disinclined to grant challenges for cause. Local rules may bar pretrial investigation of jurors. The client's resources may not permit pretrial surveys, mock trials, and juror investigations. Where the attorney is appointed by the court, there may be insufficient time to conduct these studies unless the trial judge will grant a continuance and many trial judges will not. Most commonly, the case is simply not worth it; it is in neither the lawyer's nor the client's interest to spend significant amounts of time, energy, and money on the case.

Because lawyers find themselves in positions where they must make selection decisions with a widely varying amount of available information, this chapter examines the different selection techniques used by lawyers under different conditions. In general terms, the progression is from the simple to the complex; from where the attorney has a paucity of information at his or her disposal, to where the attorney has all the information that one could desire. The more

---

[1] *See* **§8.02.**

information the lawyer has, the more informed and accurate the selection process can be. Thus it is important to try, to the extent realistically possible, to engage in the pretrial preparation advocated in Part II of this book. It is also important to attempt to persuade the trial judge to adopt a flexible and liberal attitude to voir dire, and to err on the side of granting rather than denying challenges for cause.

§12.02 Choosing Jurors versus Choosing a Jury

The tendency in selecting a jury is to consider each juror on his or her individual merits. There is much to be said for this approach. Obviously, a lawyer who succeeds in packing a jury with twelve persons favorably disposed to the client's position is likely to receive a favorable verdict. Unfortunately, one's adversary will rarely accede to this strategy.

Moreover, the situation is not so simple. In theory, and usually in practice as well, the jury's verdict will be the product of group deliberation and not just a count of twelve individual votes. It therefore behooves the lawyer to attempt to assess the group dynamics likely to occur in the jury room, as well as individual juror proclivities.

Leaders and Followers

One critical dimension to this analysis lies in discerning which jurors are likely to take an active role and which a passive role in the deliberations. Who will be the leaders and who the followers? Research indicates that on most juries the three most active jurors, or one-fourth of the jury, account for over one-half of all juror statements during deliberations.[2] A lawyer's final argument is often predicated on persuading those persons whom the lawyer predicts will be the leaders in the jury room.

High-status, well-educated persons are often looked to for leadership. Also, persons who exercise supervisory authority at work or who hold elected positions in social organizations are likely to be leaders; they are used to directing others and will probably continue to do so in the jury room. Background information relevant to leadership potential, such as the juror's education, employment responsibilities, and offices in social organizations, are typically inquired about on voir dire. A pretrial investigation may have already supplied the answers. The articulateness and forcefulness of a juror's responses to voir dire questions may also indicate the juror's leadership abilities.

Some lawyers instinctively challenge persons whom they perceive to be leaders; they reason that it is better to have the case tried by a jury of twelve than by a jury of one. This theory is subject to an obvious qualification: it is acceptable, indeed desirable, to have a jury of one if that one is strongly supportive of the client's position. The general appeal of the client's case to the average juror is an important factor. Where the client's position is likely to have widespread appeal, the lawyer would prefer not to have strong-willed leaders on

---

[2] *See* Call, *Psychology in Litigation,* 21 Trial 48, 50 (Mar 1958).

the jury. It may be wiser to exercise a peremptory challenge than to run the risk that one juror will lead the jury to an adverse verdict. In cases where the client's position is unlikely to appeal to most jurors, on the other hand, it may be an acceptable risk to take a chance on a strong leader whose leanings are unknown but who may be inclined to be sympathetic.

A lawyer can enhance a potential leader's stature on the jury by in effect nominating the juror for foreperson. On voir dire the lawyer might say: "Now, Mr. Cohen, it may turn our that you will be elected foreman of this jury. If so, could you and would you be fair to both sides?" The juror will inevitably answer yes, and the lawyer will have planted the seed for the juror's subsequent election as foreman.

In some criminal cases, where defense counsel can at best hope for a hung jury, it may be in a defendant's interest to have not simply one but many leader types on the jury. Sometimes strong-willed individuals have difficulty agreeing with each other. Each wants to be in control. Hostility may develop between these persons, with the result that they will experience difficulty agreeing on anything, let alone a verdict.

The prospects for a hung jury will also increase with an increase in the number of jurors who are strong-willed and independent, even if not necessarily leaders. Iconoclasts are not likely to compromise their principles for the sake of a consensus. They are less likely to be uncomfortable with the role of the holdout. A criminal defense attorney often consciously seeks such individuals, particularly in jurisdictions where a unanimous verdict is required.

A lawyer with a strong case, on the other hand, may not want strong jurors. Such jurors may not be amenable to persuasion. Their opinions may be fixed and unshakeable. Better to have jurors with open minds who are sufficiently intelligent to follow the lawyer's arguments.

Open-mindedness may be lacking in a juror with an expertise in the subject matter which lies at the heart of the litigation. That juror, by dint of experience, may already have settled opinions, which might not be those of the lawyer. Moreover, such a juror, because of his or her expertise, is likely to be a leader on the jury. Either one side or the other is likely to challenge the "expert" on the jury.

Subgroups and Alliances

It is valuable to assess the probable subgroups and alliances likely to form on the jury. Observation of jurors before entering the courtroom, during voir dire, and during recesses provides potential clues. Which jurors talk to each other before court begins and during breaks? Which exchange knowing glances during voir dire? Common backgrounds and interests may also suggest future alliances. As jurors are forbidden to discuss the case during trial, idle time is generally spent in getting to know each other. One can expect that persons who have interests in common will become friendly and, as friends, will influence each other's thinking during deliberations. Conversely, jurors who seem hostile or cold to each other may be dismissive of each other's arguments and may experience difficulty agreeing on a verdict.

The importance of identifying subgroups and their leaders should not be underestimated. If one member of a subgroup must be challenged peremptorily, it may become necessary to challenge the other members as well, lest they resent the lawyer responsible for the removal of their friend. If the leaders of the subgroups can be identified, the lawyer can shape arguments in terms likely to appeal to these individuals, with the reasonable expectation that they in turn will carry the lawyer's case to their constituents. It may also be sound strategy to refrain from challenging a problematic juror with whom a favorable juror who is likely to be a leader in the jury room appears friendly. It is sound strategy to provide a leader with followers. It is also easier to be a holdout, even for a strong-willed person, if one has an ally.

In these tasks, as in many others, the assistance of a social scientist can be invaluable. Unlike most lawyers, social scientists have commonly received training in the analysis of group dynamics. Moreover, during voir dire, a lawyer's attention is often focused on other matters—the response of the juror to the lawyer's questions, the lawyer's next question, etc. The lawyer has neither the time nor the opportunity to observe the subgroups and alliances which are forming on the jury. The social scientist is better placed to evaluate these developments.[3]

§12.03 Jury Selection Where Minimal Information Is Available

Informed jury selection requires thorough preparation. Community surveys,[4] juror investigations,[5] and mock trials[6] are an integral part of that preparation. Extensive and probing voir dire also helps lay the groundwork for an informed selection process. Jurors with both specific and nonspecific biases are removed through challenges for cause. Jurors whose bias is suggested by their responses but not established to the satisfaction of the court are removed through peremptory challenges. So goes the theory.

The reality may be altogether different. Often the defendant in a criminal case is indigent and counsel is appointed by the court. Such clients, and many civil litigants as well, cannot afford the cost of pretrial community surveys, juror investigations, and mock trials. In many civil suits the cost may be more than the value of the suit; to win a lawsuit where full recovery does not cover one's litigation costs is a pyrrhic victory indeed. Judges are understandably reluctant to commit limited financial resources to these endeavors.

Often the disadvantage of not being able to engage in pretrial jury screening can be compensated for by a thorough and probing voir dire. A judge, however, may be unwilling to expend valuable court time on voir dire. Many judges take the view that jurors are basically fungible except for those with a direct personal

---

[3] *See also* **§12.13.**

[4] *See* **ch 3.**

[5] *See* **ch 4.**

[6] *See* **ch 5.**

or pecuniary interest in the outcome of the case. Such judges are reluctant to allot significant time for voir dire and are sparing in their grant of challenges for cause. If they themselves conduct the voir dire, their questions are perfunctory. In this situation the lawyer should attempt to persuade the judge that there are means of ascertaining the relevant information about prospective jurors without costs in court time (such as by the use of pre-voir dire questionnaires[7]), that an investment of time at the jury selection stage will be offset by a savings in time at the appellate stage (for unnecessary appeals will be obviated), and that the constitutional right to a fair and impartial jury demands that the task of jury selection not be sacrificed to considerations of efficiency and expediency. The judge, however, may not be convinced.

The lawyer may ultimately choose to appeal the judge's decisions (although the likelihood of a successful appeal is slight, given the generally prevalent "abuse of discretion" standard of reversal), but in the meantime the lawyer must proceed with the task of selecting a jury. Despite having relatively little information to go on, the lawyer must decide which jurors to challenge peremptorily. The following four sections will offer some suggestions.

§12.04 —Intuition and Personal Experience

When information about prospective jurors is scarce, the lawyer is often best guided by intuition and experience. Intuition is commonly derided as the voice of ignorance, but often it is the product of a powerful internal computer whose rational workings have simply yet to be memorialized in a printout. A lawyer's brain, perhaps subconsciously, constantly internalizes bits of information, including the characteristics of jurors who have sat on past cases where the outcome was better or worse than anticipated. On the next occasion when the lawyer confronts a juror with similar characteristics, the lawyer may experience an intuitive like or dislike of the juror. The tendency is to dismiss this visceral reaction as unscientific, and not the proper basis for the exercise of a peremptory challenge. To do so may be a mistake; the fact that the lawyer cannot articulate the basis of the visceral reaction does not mean that there is not a basis for it. Often in these murky situations, where information is minimal, the lawyer's intuition is the best guide available. Indeed, if the lawyer feels uncomfortable with certain jurors, no matter what the reason, the lawyer may not be as effective in presenting the client's case as the lawyer would be before a jury composed of persons with whom he or she felt more comfortable.

Experience is said to be the best teacher, and a lawyer's experience should play a prominent role in jury selection. A lawyer who has lived and practiced in a community will know the people of that community, and what can realistically be expected of prospective jurors. Equally importantly, the lawyer will know himself or herself. A middle-aged male attorney, for example, may be most effective before a jury consisting of other middle-aged males, or young females, or the elderly. Only the lawyer, as a result of experience, can supply

---

[7] *See* **§9.01.**

the formula. The lawyer's experiences in similar situations will often be replicated in new but comparable circumstances. The lawyer who fails to learn from past experience does the present client a disservice.

§12.05 —Experience of Other Lawyers

Trial experience is an invaluable aid in selecting a jury when there is minimal information about prospective jurors available, but the trial experience need not be the lawyer's personal experience, a fact which should be of comfort to the neophyte attorney. Many successful lawyers have succumbed to the urge to set down their memoirs for posterity. Often this recordation includes the lawyer's thoughts on jury selection. Clarence Darrow, for instance, cautioned criminal defense attorneys against selecting Germans because "they are bullheaded"; Swedes because "they are stubborn"; Presbyterians because "they know right from wrong but seldom find anything right"; and Lutherans, prohibitionists, and the wealthy because they are prone to convict. Conversely, Darrow favored Irishmen and Jews, because "they are easiest to move to emotional sympathy"; old men, because "they are generally more charitable and kindly disposed than young men"; and persons who laugh, because they are loathe to find anyone guilty.[8]

Henry Rothblatt and F. Lee Bailey similarly provide advice to criminal defense counsel based on generalizations about human nature:

> Generally speaking, the heavy, roundfaced, jovial-looking person is the most desirable. The undesirable juror is quite often the slight, underweight and delicate type. His features are sharp and fragile, with that lean "Cassius" look. The athletic-looking juror is hard to categorize. Usually he is hard to convince; but once convinced he will usually go all the way with you.[9]

Bailey and Rothblatt, along with other successful attorneys, favor female jurors where the client or the lawyer is handsome, jurors between the age of 28 and 55, and persons, such as salesmen, actors, and writers, who have enjoyed wide and varied life experiences.[10] They are disinclined toward jurors who have been trained either to give or take orders.[11] The first time juror is considered more desirable than the experienced juror for he or she is less likely to be jaded and more likely to be open to suggestion.[12]

The temptation may be to dismiss any such stereotypical thinking about jurors as ill-informed and unfashionable. Before doing so, however, one should not forget the reason why stereotypes develop in the first place. Often the stereotype represents not the observation of a lone cynic but the shared perspec-

---

[8] *See* Darrow, *Attorney for the Defense,* 8 Esquire 35 (1936).

[9] F. Bailey & H. Rothblatt, Successful Techniques for Criminal Trials 104-05 (1971).

[10] *Id* 106-07.

[11] *Id* 107.

[12] *Id.*

tive of many observers that certain views and attitudes are common to persons with certain background characteristics. The truth of yesterday's stereotype is often confirmed by a subsequent "scientific" study. Assuming that the lawyer recognizes that not all individuals will conform to their stereotypic image, reliance on this accumulated wisdom of the ages can be of assistance in jury selection, particularly where there is little else to go on: "The limited time available for appraisal of individuals on the panel makes it necessary to rely to a great extent upon the assumption that attitudes of particular individuals conform to those usually held by persons of similar backgrounds."[13]

A different and less obvious cautionary note about stereotypes should be sounded, however: stereotypic reasoning is abstract reasoning, and fails to take context into account. The Lutheran of German descent whom Darrow would predict would be prone to convict may not conform to character in a criminal trial where the defendant, the defendant's witnesses, and the defendant's attorney are all German Lutherans. Similarly, while retired military officers are generally considered poor defense jurors in a criminal case, they may be eminently desirable in a case where the defendant is a decorated veteran. Often the critical factor in determining a juror's subconscious leanings is the juror's ability to identify with a key figure, be it party, witness, or lawyer, in the case.[14]

There is an additional caveat about relying on the experience of others. Few attorneys have the skill of a Clarence Darrow, and methods that served Darrow well may ill serve an attorney with lesser talents. An attempt to mirror the style of another may leave jurors with the impression that the lawyer is insincere and disingenuous. Thus, while the advice of more experienced counsel can be valuable, it must be made to fit within the lawyer's own personal style. If the advice of a Darrow regarding jury selection will lead to a jury with which the lawyer does not feel comfortable, the fact that Darrow would have been able to extract a favorable verdict from that jury will be of little solace when an unfavorable verdict is returned.

§12.06 —Social Science Research

In addition to looking to one's personal experiences and the experiences of prominent trial lawyers in making jury selection decisions where minimal information about jurors is available, there is the jury research of social scientists to consider. The value of having social scientists participate in pretrial community surveys and mock trials has been previously discussed.[15] Many lawyers also use social scientists in the courtroom to evaluate juror nonverbal responses to voir dire questioning[16] and to identify the likely group dynamics of the jury.[17]

---

[13] R. Keeton, Trial Tactics and Methods 239 (1954).

[14] *See* **§12.07.**

[15] *See* **chs 4, 6.**

[16] *See* **§§12.09-12.15.**

[17] *See* **§7.02.**

But the teachings of social scientists are not the exclusive domain of those who can afford their services. For years social scientists have been studying the relationship between personal variables and juror decision making. To the potential benefit of attorneys who can spare a trip to the library, they often have published their findings. Their studies examine, for example, the relationship between juror attitudes and such variables as occupation, sex, and socio-economic status.[18] Like the courtroom experiences of the veteran trial lawyer, the laboratory experiences of the trained social scientist can assist the attorney in making jury selection decisions in cases where not much information about the actual jurors is available. A juror's sex and race will be obvious, juror forms will generally list occupation, and dress and demeanor will indicate socio-economic status.

As in respect to the courtroom experience of other lawyers, the attorney should not blithely transpose the abstract findings of the social scientists to a case without taking into account the contextual setting of the case. While, for example, jurors of high socio-economic status may generally favor the state in a criminal trial, they may be pro-defense in certain cases of white collar crime.

§12.07 Identification

In addition to intuition, personal experience, the experiences of other trial lawyers, and the published studies of social scientists, the lawyer should not neglect the teachings of common sense. A thoughtful criminal defense lawyer does not need to consult a renowned expert, whether an attorney or a social scientist, to predict that bank presidents will not be sympathetic jurors in a case where the defendant is charged with robbery; or that ex-police officers are more likely to believe the testimony of a policeman than that of an accused; or that minority jurors will not be receptive to the self-defense claim of a Ku Klux Klansman charged with assaulting a black. These are matters of common sense.

The common denominator in the hypotheticals is identification. The bank president will identify with the bank and not the robber, the ex-police officer with the police witness and not the defendant, and the minority juror with the black victim and not the Ku Klux Klansman.

---

[18] *See, e.g.*, Broeder, *Occupational Expertise and Bias as Affecting Juror Behavior: A Preliminary Look,* 40 NYUL Rev 1079 (1965); Hermann, *Occupations of Jurors as an Influence on Their Verdict,* 5 Forum 150 (1970); Snyder, *Sex Role Differential and Juror Decisions,* 55 Soc & Social Res 442 (1971); Stephan, *Sex Prejudice in Jury Simulation,* 88 J Psychology 305 (1974); Strodtbeck & Mann, *Sex Role Differentiation in Jury Deliberations,* 19 Sociometry 3 (1956); Adler, *Socioeconomic Factors Influencing Jury Verdicts,* 3 NYU Rev L & Soc Change 1 (1973); Rose & Prell, *Does the Punishment Fit the Crime? A Study in Social Valuation,* 61 Am J Soc 247 (1955); Strodtbeck, James, & Hawkins, *Social Status in Jury Deliberations,* 22 Am Soc Rev 713 (1957). *See generally* Frederick, *Jury Behavior: A Psychologist Examines Jury Selection,* 5 Ohio NUL Rev 571 (1978).

In cases where the lawyer has minimal information about prospective jurors, the lawyer should seek jurors who are likely to identify with one of the dominant figures in the trial. That figure may be the victim in a criminal case; or a party, a key witness, or the attorney in either a civil or criminal case. In order to determine with whom jurors are likely to identify, the attorney needs to find the common links between jurors and trial participants.

Identification may be the product of a similar occupation, education, or upbringing. It may result from a shared experience, or a common socio-economic status. It may simply reflect similar attitudes. One means of verifying the potential for identification is to ask one's client and key witnesses the questions which one plans to ask the jury; jurors who respond the same as the client or the witness may well identify with them. Identification may also result from having had a similar experience to that of one of the principals, in which case the juror's attitude to the experience needs to be probed. Identification, it should be noted, does not necessarily mean identity; parents of young children can be expected to identify with an injured plaintiff who is a minor.

Many times the potential for identification will be obvious. A common age, sex, and ethnic background will strongly suggest this potential. A young male Hispanic juror, for example, can be expected to identify with a young male Hispanic defendant. Besides the common age, sex, and ethnic background, the two will very likely have been raised in similar environments, have undergone similar life experiences, and have been taught similar values. It is likely that their attitudes and aspirations will also be similar.

In other cases some rudimentary information will need to be discovered about the juror in order to determine the potential for identification. A common religion, hobby, or social or political affiliation may provide common ground between a juror and the client or key witness. If this information about the client or witness will come to light during the trial, comparable information about the jurors should be discovered on voir dire.

Often juror lists will note juror occupation; a juror with the same occupation as a party or witness may identify with that party or witness. The two may speak a common jargon, and their economic position and social status will probably be similar. (The same observations may hold true for a juror whose spouse is engaged in the same occupation as the client or witness.)

To actualize the potential for identification, the lawyer should present the client and the client's witnesses in human and personal terms. In voir dire the client should be referred to by name, and the opposing side by position in the lawsuit, either as plaintiff or defendant. The lawyer should also be aware of his or her own image, and project one that is warm, friendly, positive, and professional.

While one should not ignore common sense, it is not always a reliable guide. Often the logic of common sense is belied by experience or the findings of social science research. For example, while common sense might suggest that women will identify with other women, many women are apparently distrustful of other women, particularly when they are attractive.[19] For this reason, some defense attorneys will actively seek women jurors in rape cases, although common sense might suggest otherwise.

Surface similarities can also be misleading. An upwardly mobile juror may resent the false stereotype perpetuated by a rebellious youth of the same ethnicity. An ethical doctor may want to vindicate the stain on the image of physicians created by a doctor charged with fraud.

Beyond these cases, there are persons who can readily identify with another yet not like that other. Many persons do not like themselves, but are not in a position to change their lives. To direct their frustration and anger inward may lead to an unacceptable level of internal turmoil. Still, the anger and frustration may need to be relieved. An often convenient target is a person with similar characteristics. In these situations jurors may project outwardly toward persons who are similar to themselves that anger and frustration which they feel about their own lives. We tend to fault others most harshly for the faults that we see in ourselves. If so, identification with a party or witness may be not a positive but a negative factor. This analysis suggests a refinement of the "identification" hypothesis: jurors who appear satisfied or pleased with their position in life, or, although dissatisfied, appear to blame others for their plight, are likely to be favorably inclined to a party or witness with whom they can identify; jurors who are dissatisfied with their lot in life, and who blame themselves for their situation, may well be unsympathetic to a party or witness with whom they identify.

§12.08 Jury Selection Based Primarily on Voir Dire

Typically lawyers are not as bereft of information about prospective jurors as in the extreme cases discussed in the preceding sections. On the other hand, rarely do lawyers engage in the kind of extensive pretrial preparation advocated in Part II of this book. Community surveys, juror investigations, and mock trials are still beyond the financial reach of most litigants. As an empirical matter, most jury selection decisions are based on information discovered in voir dire.

While most lawyers rely on voir dire for information about jurors, few extract the full amount of information to be gained from voir dire. The problem is that lawyers tend to evaluate jurors on the basis of their verbal responses to voir dire questions. Obviously, what the juror says is not to be ignored. But often a juror's verbal statements are incomplete, misleading, or false.[20]

Some prospective jurors, anxious to please or eager to serve, will give what they perceive to be the "acceptable" response. The juror may want to serve either for the experience or out of a sense of civic responsibility, neither of

---

[19] *See* Blinder, *Picking Juries,* 1 Trial Dipl 8 (1978); Smith, Keating, Hester, & Mitchell, *Role and Justice Considerations in the Attribution of Responsibility to a Rape Victim,* 10 J of Res in Personality 346 (1976).

[20] *See* Broeder, *Voir Dire Examinations: An Empirical Study,* 38 S Cal L Rev 503 (1965).

which is an ignoble motive, or for the more base opportunity to vent a personal prejudice. Those in the latter category will not readily disclose their bias upon questioning for to do so would defeat their goal. Other jurors may not disclose their bias in order to avoid the public disapproval which they anticipate would follow an admission. Few jurors, for example, are likely to admit to racial prejudice. Still other jurors may not admit bias because they are unaware of the bias; they may honestly believe that they are fair and impartial. But many prejudices exist on a subconscious level. Many have been beaten into subconsciousness because of their social unacceptability. In order to discover such biases, a lawyer must construct voir dire in a way that will cause the juror to reveal the bias, and be sensitive to nonverbal responses, particularly kinesic and paralinguistic cues, which reveal the bias.

The latter cues are especially important. It is not difficult for prospective jurors who wish to conceal their biases to lie; it is far more difficult for them to control their facial and bodily movements, which may be involuntary, or their manner of response. Few even appreciate that their nonverbal responses can betray their verbal falsehoods. Fewer still would know how to control their bodies even if they were aware of the need to do so. The lawyer who is attuned to nonverbal, as well as verbal, responses is accordingly better placed to discern a juror's true leanings.

Unfortunately, most attorneys are not aware of the benefit to be gained, and few have received any systematic training in this area. While an overview of the subject and some specific examples will be presented in the following sections, an in-depth analysis of this topic is beyond the scope of this book and the discussion here presented should not be seen as a substitute for comprehensive study. To help in deciphering nonverbal cues, an attorney might also choose to enlist the assistance of a trained social scientist.[21]

In order to record a juror's voir dire responses, both verbal and nonverbal, a seating chart of the jury should be prepared.

[21] *See* §12.13.

The chart should be sufficiently large to take into account the fact that several jurors may be removed through challenge. On the chart should be recorded: (a) demographic information about each juror; (b) the juror's answers to key questions; and (c) nonverbal cues given by the juror. The chart will facilitate association of names and faces with information relevant to the exercise of challenges. During voir dire it will help the lawyer to address jurors by name, and when the time comes to exercise peremptory challenges, it will allow for a comparative evaluation of jurors. The chart may also prove useful on summation when the lawyer wishes to address a point to a juror for whom the point may have particular relevance.

§12.09 —Verbal and Nonverbal Responses

A prospective juror's inner feelings are communicated not only verbally, but nonverbally. Few persons remain motionless while speaking (rigidity may itself be telling), and the expressions, gestures, and body movements of jurors during voir dire should be carefully observed. Likewise, a lawyer should be sensitive not only to what a juror says, but to how the juror says it. It is nonverbal cues that betray verbal deceptions and provide insight into a juror's true feelings.[22]

Often there is no contradiction between a juror's verbal and nonverbal responses. In the case of a juror who answers a question affirmatively while shaking her head up and down, for example, verbal and nonverbal responses are consistent. The juror is simply reinforcing the affirmative response with an appropriate gesture, although the fact of the gesture may indicate the depth of the juror's feeling on the subject. On the other hand, the juror who gives an affirmative response while imperceptibly shaking her head from side to side conveys a mixed message. The verbal response indicates agreement with the questioner; the nonverbal response indicates disagreement. It is this kind of incongruity or dissonance for which the lawyer must be alert. It may not be clear which of the two responses, the verbal or the nonverbal one, accurately reflects the juror's true position, but the lawyer should be aware that something is amiss, and that the juror's verbal response should not necessarily be taken at face value.[23]

§12.10 —Eye Contact

One of the most critical of kinesic cues, and one to which most lawyers are already rightly sensitive, is eye contact. It is difficult to look in the eye a person to whom one is lying. The juror who avoids eye contact with the lawyer may

---

[22] *See* Ekman & Friesen, *Nonverbal Leakage and Clues to Deception,* 32 Psychology 88 (1968).

[23] *See* Mehrabian & Wiener, *Decoding of Inconsistent Communications,* 6 J Personality & Soc Psychology 109 (1967).

not be entirely truthful in his or her verbal response. Conversely, increased eye contact may indicate a positive feeling toward the lawyer to whom the juror is speaking.[24]

Observations about eye contact must be taken advisedly, however. Many shy persons have difficulty looking others in the eye, and many chronic liars are able to maintain eye contact while practicing their deceit. Lack of eye contact may also simply indicate anxiety, brought on by the unfamiliar surroundings of the courtroom or the voir dire "interrogation." In such circumstances, however, one would expect the juror to avoid eye contact with both lawyers; lack of eye contact with only one may reflect a lack of sympathy with that lawyer's position.

The last point can be generalized. The comparative amount of eye contact that a juror has with the respective lawyers is significant. Social science research suggests that people maintain eye contact with those from whom they seek approval.[25] In the voir dire context, approval often is sought from the examining attorneys. Comparisons of the juror's eye contact during voir dire with the lawyers on each side may indicate the side from whom the juror wants approval and with whom the juror desires a positive relationship.

Of particular significance may be a juror's quick glance at opposing counsel after responding to a voir dire question, as if to ask whether the juror got the answer right. A defiant look toward opposing counsel, or the defendant in a criminal case, is another matter. Glares commonly indicate hostility,

Eye contact with the client may be as important as eye contact with the lawyer. A defense attorney in a criminal case should, at some point in the voir dire require the jurors to make eye contact with the defendant. A question such as the following might be posed: "Now, Mr. Boyd, will you look the defendant, Thomas Lee Jones, in the eye and promise him that you will give him the benefit of the presumption of innocence to which he is entitled." Jurors who are unable to do so, or whose gaze falters, may well be hostile.

§12.11 —Facial and Body Cues

Facial cues during voir dire convey their own meaning. Frowns, smiles, grimaces, and other facial expressions may reflect a juror's attitude toward the lawyer and the lawyer's questions more accurately than the juror's words.[26] Most persons are aware, for instance, that a sudden facial blush usually suggests that an embarrassing or sensitive subject has been touched upon. Frowns, grimaces, and smiles are equally self-explanatory. The important point for the attorney is not to ignore these facial cues. In this regard, it has been suggested

---

[24] *See* Argyle & Dean, *Eye Contact, Distance, and Affiliation,* 28 Sociometry 289 (1965).

[25] *See* Effran, *Looking for Approval: Effects on Visual Behavior of Approbation from Persons Differing in Importance,* 10 J Personality & Soc Psychology 21 (1968).

[26] *See* Mehrabian, *Nonverbal Communication,* 19 Neb Symp on Motivation 107 (1971).

that facial cues indicate what emotion an individual is feeling, while body cues indicate the intensity of that feeling.[27]

Just as there can be dissonance between verbal responses and facial expressions, sometimes there is dissonance between facial expressions and body movements. In these circumstances body movements may be a more accurate indicator of true feelings. The reason is that many persons are aware of their facial expressions, and have learned to control them. Fewer are aware of their bodies, and how body posture and movements can be revealing. It also may be more difficult to control the reactions of one's body.

Many body postures and movements are idiosyncratic, and one must be wary in drawing inferences from them. Others are more standard. A juror who leans forward and directly faces the lawyer in answering a question displays a positive interest in that lawyer, particularly if the juror also maintains eye contact during the response.[28] Another positive indicator is the fact that the juror is relaxed. A sideways or slightly reclining lean, head and neck muscles which are not tense, and arm and leg symmetry are all signs of relaxation.[29] Other indicia of a relaxed attitude include an unbuttoned jacket, uncrossed legs, open hands, and a warm smile.[30] All of these body signals point to a juror who feels comfortable with the lawyer, and, therefore, may feel comfortable with (at least not hostile to) the lawyer's position. It might also be observed that the lawyer who conveys a relaxed, somewhat informal attitude to the jurors is likely to elicit a comparable response in return. Most auspicious may be the juror who starts unconsciously mirroring the lawyer's own style and gestures.

Excessive or agitated body movements, on the other hand, such as hand wringing and finger tapping, are signs of anxiety[31] and may indicate hostility or deception.[32] Such movements are inconsistent with the relaxed attitude which accompanies a positive feeling toward the questioner. Often, moreover, these body movements are the outward manifestation of the inner conflict experienced by the juror who is saying one thing but meaning another.

The inner turmoil which accompanies deceit may alternatively be reflected in tenseness or rigidity. Crossed legs, tightened neck muscles, folded arms, and clenched fists may signify hostility. A sudden buttoning of a coat or the thrusting of hands into one's pockets may indicate that the juror feels threatened and has decided to resist. Similarly, an extreme backward arching may constitute a symbolic effort on the part of the juror to get as far away as possible from the interrogating lawyer.

---

[27] *See* Ekman & Friesen, *Head and Body Cues in the Judgment of Emotion: A Reformulation,* 24 Perceptual & Motor Skills 711 (1967); Ekman, *Differential Communication of Affect by Head and Body Cues,* 2 J Personality & Soc Psychology 726 (1965).

[28] *See,* Mehrabian, *Significance of Posture and Position in the Communication of Attitude and Status Relationships,* 71 Psychology Bull 359 (1969).

[29] *Id.*

[30] *See* Blinder, *Picking Juries,* 1 Trial Dipl 12-13 (1978).

[31] *See* Ekman & Friesen, *Hand Movements,* 22 J Comm 353 (1972).

[32] Suggs & Sales, *Using Communication Cues to Evaluate Prospective Jurors During the Voir Dire,* 20 Ariz L Rev 629 (1978).

Body language should not be evaluated in isolation; it needs to be examined in context. Is the body movement in question appropriate in the particular context? If the answer is no, then an explanation for the incongruity should be sought. Tenseness, for example, is natural when sensitive subjects are being probed, but unnatural when the juror is asked a perfunctory question such as whether he can give the defendant a fair trial. Tenseness accompanying a positive verbal response in the latter situation may indicate that the juror is in fact not prepared to give the defendant a fair trial.

Contextual analysis also requires a determination of whether a particular juror body movement is normal or abnormal for that juror. A lawyer needs to know whether the juror's facial expression or body movement is a response to the lawyer's questions or part of the juror's natural character. To this end, the juror should be observed while engaged in casual conversation (perhaps during recesses or out of court), and when asked routine, nonthreatening questions at the outset of voir dire. It is the departures from normal responses which indicate situational anxiety brought on by the lawyer's questioning. It is the atypical responses which are significant.

Body language must also be evaluated comparatively: do the juror's body movements differ depending on which side is asking the questions? The side with which the juror appears more at ease as indicated by general posture, body movements, and physical reactions is likely to be the side which the juror will favor in deliberations. To fail to do a comparative analysis, however, could lead to the inappropriate challenge of a naturally fidgety juror.

§12.12 —Paralinguistic and Verbal Cues

In addition to observing the body language of the juror during voir dire, the lawyer should be sensitive to paralinguistic cues. The juror's verbal response refers to *what* the juror says; paralinguistic cues refer to *how* the juror says it. Paralinguistic cues include pauses, silences, syntax, choice of words and phrases, and sudden changes in pitch and tone of voice.

Everyone's speech patterns are distinctive, and the lawyer must have a sense of the particular pattern of the individual juror. There are numerous reasons for beginning voir dire with innocuous, nonsensitive questioning. Such questions put the juror at ease, acclimate the juror to the idea of questioning, and help develop a rapport between the attorney and the juror. The responses to such questioning also establish a base line of the juror's paralinguistic patterns. The lawyer who has an accurate sense of a juror's speech rhythms and standard speech patterns is in a position to note variances between the base line response and the response to particular questions.

For example, the fact that a juror talks slowly or stutters may not in itself be significant. If this is not the juror's standard mode of response, however, and appears only when certain topics are mentioned, then the lawyer should conclude that there is something about the topic which causes a disruption from the normal pattern. This is the easy part; the hard part is determining what inferences should be drawn from the nonstandard response pattern.

A silence or pause before answering a question may have many meanings. If the question is complex, difficult, or unexpected, it is natural to stop to gather one's thoughts before answering. No particular significance should be attached to a hesitation between question and answer. (Indeed, a too quick response to a complex question may indicate impulsiveness or that the juror has already considered the issue at length and has a quite firm opinion on the subject.) A pause before answering a fairly straightforward question, on the other hand, may reflect doubt about the juror's answer. Say that in a criminal case the defense lawyer asks a juror whether she is prepared to accord the defendant the presumption of innocence guaranteed by law. The juror hesitates before answering yes. The lawyer can infer that the juror has some reservations about the presumption of innocence, either as a general matter or in the context of the particular case. (Another possibility, of course, is that the juror was daydreaming and not paying attention to the question. The alert attorney, however, will be able to recognize the difference.) Other paralinguistic cues indicating a response which may not be entirely truthful include a drying of the mouth, a licking of the lips, a sudden intake of breath, inappropriate laughter, or visible gulping or swallowing during the response. A rise in the pitch of a juror's voice may also be an indication of disingenuousness.

Inadvertent malapropisms, or Freudian slips as they are popularly known, can likewise be revealing. In a criminal trial the juror who, when referring to the state's case, unwittingly says "persecution" instead of "prosecution" may be an excellent juror for the defense. The tendency is to dismiss such slips of the tongue as meaningless, but many who have spent their lives analyzing human behavior are inclined to believe that they may be more meaningful than most verbal statements of position.

Speech disturbances are very often associated with situational anxiety. Unfinished sentences, repeating words, stuttering, inappropriate laughter, voice changes, and unusual pauses and hesitations all tend to be manifestations of anxiety. To determine whether the anxiety is situational or simply a reflection of the juror's natural personality, the lawyer needs to compare the response to the base line pattern established by the juror's responses to the nonthreatening questions with which the lawyer began voir dire.

Not only are speech disturbances more common when a juror experiences anxiety, but the juror's speech patterns and modes of response vary. It has been found, for example, that the speech of an interviewee who feels anxious tends to become more stilted and stereotyped, with less differentiated word usage.[33] In the voir dire context, a juror who has been answering questions in a casual manner, who abruptly switches to a more formal style when questioned about a particular subject, may be indicating anxiety about the subject being examined. The response may well be deceptive or untruthful.[34]

---

[33] *See* Eldred & Price, *A Linguistic Evaluation of Feeling States in Psychotherapy,* 21 Psychology 115 (1958).

[34] *See* Suggs & Sales, *Using Communication Cues to Evaluate Prospective Jurors During the Voir Dire,* 20 Ariz L Rev 629, 633 (1979).

In a similar vein is the juror's choice of words in answering a question. Take two jurors who are asked whether they are prejudiced against blacks. One responds: "I am not prejudiced against blacks"; the other responds: "I am not prejudiced against those people." Both responses purport to deny prejudice, but the distancing use of "those people" suggests that the second juror may be attempting to conceal his or her true feelings.[35]

Another paralinguistic phenomenon is that persons tend to talk longer to those toward whom they have positive feelings.[36] If so, a lawyer can make a tentative preliminary determination as to which side a juror favors by comparing the length of the juror's answers to the questions asked by each side, making allowance for the amount of response required to answer the questions. If a juror responds to one side's questions with lengthy disquisitions while providing short, pithy answers to the other side's questions, it is not unreasonable to infer that the juror is more favorably inclined to the first side.

In addition to the length of the juror's response, the rapidity with which the juror delivers the response may be significant.[37] Persons who are anxious tend to talk faster. Again, a comparison of the speed of the juror's base line responses with the speed of the juror's responses to particular questions may be revealing of anxiety; and a comparison of the quickness of the juror's delivery of response to the questioning of each side may indicate which side the juror feels most comfortable with.

§12.13 —A Team Approach

Few lawyers have been trained to be aware of kinesic and paralinguistic cues. Neither law schools nor bar courses customarily teach such skills. Many lawyers, however, instinctively sense juror hostility or unease even without being able to pinpoint the specific cues which cause their instincts to be aroused (which is one reason why one's intuitive feel about jurors should not be discounted).[38] But intuition is rarely a substitute for systematic training; and systematic training, in any event, can fine tune a lawyer's intuition.

The lawyer who recognizes the desirability of taking into account a juror's kinesic and paralinguistic cues faces other obstacles besides lack of training. One is finding a method to ensure that these cues are accurately recorded for later analysis. During the voir dire the lawyer is often either considering the content of a juror's last answer or thinking about his or her next question. Even the lawyer attuned to kinesic and paralinguistic cues cannot afford to take the time to record them, for to do so would interrupt the flow of the questioning.

Furthermore, the lawyer's attention during voir dire will be focused on the juror being questioned; it is as important for the lawyer to maintain eye contact with the juror as it is significant that the juror maintains eye contact with the

---

[35] *Id* 638.

[36] *Id* 633-34.

[37] *Id.*

[38] *See* **§12.04.**

lawyer.[39] This preoccupation with the juror being questioned means that the lawyer may not see the reactions of a different juror. It is important, however, to observe the reactions of all the jurors to a particular question or response. A juror may respond emotionlessly when, say, asked whether he believes that an indictment is evidence of guilt. The juror realizes the answer expected of him, and also realizes that his responses are being observed by the questioner. But when another juror is asked the same question, the first juror may shake his head from side to side or give some other indication of disapproval. The juror has in effect let his guard down, believing that he is no longer being scrutinized.

The preceding considerations suggest the value of a team approach to jury selection. Ideally the trial attorney would prefer the assistance of one or more trained social scientists with experience in analyzing kinesic and paralinguistic cues. One observer could watch the juror being questioned, while another could focus on the reactions of the other members of the panel. Each observer would independently record relevant verbal, kinesic and paralinguistic responses on a seating chart clued to the juror's position in the jury box.[40] Key demographic data would have previously been entered on the chart.

These observers should be strategically placed so that they will have a frontal view of the jurors. The optimal observation post would be counsel table, but jurors may resent an army of observers watching their every move and frantically scribbling notes. In response to a dozen or more watchful eyes they may alter their normal behavior patterns. Too many persons at counsel table may also induce sympathy for the opposing side, which the jurors may conclude is outmanned. (For this reason many prominent criminal defense attorneys prefer that only the client sit with them at counsel table.) Consequently, it is preferable if the observers can be placed in the gallery, assuming that their vantage point will not be unduly compromised.

If the client is unable to afford or recruit professional social scientists, there are other possibilities for gathering information relating to nonverbal juror responses. With training, a secretary or associate of the trial lawyer can generally do the job competently. Research indicates that most lay observers are perfectly capable of decoding nonverbal cues.[41] In large firms it is in the firm's interest to designate one member of staff to become expert in these matters, available to assist whichever of the firm's lawyers is trying a case.

Another option is to charge the client with the responsibility of observation. Even if the client is unable to decode the nonverbal cues, he or she is capable of recording the relevant factual data (e.g., juror shrugged shoulders when denying having read anything about the case; juror paused before agreeing with importance of presumption of innocence). The lawyer can later decide what inferences to draw from the client's factual observations. An ancillary benefit of involving the client in this way is the positive psychological effect that

---

[39] *See* **§12.10.**

[40] *See* **§12.08.**

[41] *See* Suggs & Sales, *Juror Self-Disclosure in the Voir Dire: A Social Science Analysis,* 26 Ind LJ 245, 257 (1981).

it will have on the client. (The client should, however, be directed not to speak to the lawyer while the voir dire is being conducted.)

Social scientists and others who are involved in the juror observation should also have input in determining which jurors to challenge. The client in particular should be consulted; the client is the person who has to bear the weight of the jury's verdict, and being consulted about the choice of jurors may make that verdict more palatable. The reactions of the client and the observers, however, must be carefully balanced against those of the lawyer. The lawyer has to present the client's case to the jury, and may not be able to do so as effectively before a jury with whom the lawyer feels uncomfortable as before one with whom the lawyer feels at ease. Prime candidates for challenge will always be jurors whom the attorney may have offended in an unsuccessful attempt to have them removed for cause.

Time will be needed to consult regarding selection decisions. If jury selection requires more than one day, consultation can occur during the evenings. Otherwise, time may have to be snatched from recesses or lunch. If additional time is needed, an appropriate request should be made to the trial judge. The consultation process can be expedited if, before discussion, each observer assigns each juror a rating based on a scale previously agreed upon. (One possibility is a five-point scale wherein a five indicates a highly desirable juror and one a highly undesirable juror. Three would be a neutral rating.) Discussion can then focus on jurors about whom there is disagreement.

§12.14 Jury Selection Based on Juror Profiles and Investigations

Although voir dire continues to be the primary source of information used in jury selection, attorneys are increasingly becoming aware of its limitations. One shortcoming is that voir dire does not always provide the right information. Sometimes the lawyer asks the wrong questions. It is often difficult to anticipate all elements of a juror's background that could affect the juror's perception of a particular case.

Even if the lawyer does ask the right questions, jurors may not be entirely truthful or candid in their answers.[42] Many jurors are reluctant to admit prejudices, because of either an overriding desire to serve on the jury or a fear of the public disapproval that they believe will follow an admission. In other instances jurors will not admit to prejudice because they are not aware of it. Juror reluctance to admit bias may be particularly pronounced when the jury is questioned as a group; it is difficult to speak up when everyone else remains silent.

Voir dire, even if theoretically suited to the discovery of juror prejudice, often falters because of constraints imposed by the trial judge. The time required to conduct an effective voir dire is more than most judges are willing to allot. Even if not limited to a fixed time period, voir dire questioning will

---

[42] *See* Broeder, *Voir Dire Examinations: An Empirical Study*, 38 S Cal L Rev 503 (1965).

try a judge's patience when carried beyond what the judge deems to be a reasonable period. Many lawyers are reluctant to risk the loss of the judge's good will. Judges may also unduly restrict the scope of voir dire.

An even more inhibiting constraint is the tendency of trial judges, particularly in federal court, to assume responsibility for voir dire questioning. Judicial voir dire is rarely as effective as lawyer voir dire. The trial judge is not as familiar with the nuances of the case, and is unable to foresee all areas of potential prejudice. Nor are trial judges as motivated to do so. Furthermore, because of the judge's stature, some jurors may be hesitant to admit bias in response to a judge's question.[43] Judicial voir dire also precludes effective follow-up questions suggested by a juror's initial response, as well as follow-up questions necessary to clarify the initial response; while follow-up questions after the completion of the judge's questioning may be permitted, by that time the thread of the inquiry may be lost. Finally, judicial voir dire prevents the lawyer from ascertaining a juror's reactions to the lawyer.

Even assuming counsel is permitted to conduct voir dire, and that voir dire is a theoretical and practical method for discovering juror bias, many attorneys question whether the time could not be put to better use.[44] The probing and time-consuming voir dire necessary to uncover prejudices may be resented by many jurors. What may be gained in terms of juror information may be lost in terms of juror good will. Some attorneys accordingly prefer to spend voir dire in establishing rapport and ingratiating themselves to the jury. Some seek to impress the jury with their fairness; others, with their expertise; still others, with their personal charm. Another strategy is to use voir dire to indoctrinate the jury to the lawyer's view of the controlling legal principles. While none of these goals is necessarily inconsistent with the use of voir dire to discover juror prejudices, time limitations imposed by the court may force the attorney to prioritize these functions. Many attorneys will opt for purposes other than the ascertainment of information, which may at best be incomplete and inaccurate.

If voir dire is used for purposes other than determining bias, the issue becomes on what bases does the lawyer make informed jury selection decisions. The value of intuition, experience, and social science literature has already been discussed.[45] In addition, or as an alternative for lawyers who seek the harbor of greater scientific precision, is a methodology based on community surveys, mock trials, and juror investigations. These methodologies were discussed in Part II of this book. Without repeating in detail the substance of that discussion, the recommendation was made that the lawyer commission a pretrial survey to determine community attitudes toward the parties, witnesses, and issues in the case. The survey might indicate that a change in venue is desirable or, indeed, that a jury trial is inadvisable. Survey opinions relating to the case can be correlated with demographic, attitudinal, and socio-psychological

---

[43] Suggs & Sales, *Juror Self-Disclosure in the Voir Dire: A Social Science Analysis,* 56 Ind LJ 245 (1981).

[44] *See also* **§9.04.**

[45] *See* **§§12.04-12.06.**

data obtained from the respondents, and used to construct profiles of desirable and undesirable jurors.

Further, the lawyer was advised of the advantages of mock trials. In the mock trial a random sample of jury-eligible members of the community is assembled to hear the opposing sides of the case, as best it can be anticipated they would be presented in court. Following the presentation of each side's case, the mock jurors are instructed regarding the controlling law. They then retire to deliberate. The deliberations are observed or videotaped for replay. By correlating juror positions during the deliberations with demographic, attitudinal, and socio-psychological data obtained from the mock jurors, the lawyer adds to the accuracy of the juror profiles.

The next step, once juror profiles are constructed, is to investigate each member of the venire in order to ascertain the extent to which the prospective juror matches the favorable or unfavorable profile. The investigations should be carried out discreetly and in a professional manner, whether or not performed by professional investigators, and with due respect for a juror's privacy. On the basis of these investigations, each juror can be assigned a rating reflecting the juror's predisposition to each side. The rating can be adjusted to incorporate further information which comes to light during voir dire.

Juror selection decisions can then be made on the basis of these ratings. The underlying and not unreasonable assumption is that jurors with the same profiles as participants in the community surveys and mock trials will have similar views to those of the participants. A prospective juror with an unfavorable rating can be challenged peremptorily, assuming that it is reasonable to expect the juror's replacement to have a more favorable rating. If most of the remainder of the panel have less favorable ratings, on the other hand, the attorney will obviously not be inclined to challenge the juror. Such relative considerations become particularly critical as the number of peremptory challenges remaining dwindles. Lawyers are customarily advised to jealously guard their last peremptory challenge, and it is sound advice. The lawyer armed with juror ratings is particularly well situated to benefit from the advice.

The juror profile approach to jury selection has many advantages. It avoids the need to ask jurors embarrassing questions on voir dire. It lessens the risk of being misled by untruthful juror responses to voir dire questions, and circumvents time and scope restrictions placed on voir dire by the trial judge. The lawyer who has constructed juror profiles needs only to obtain general background and demographic information, the kind of information about which judges are most willing to allow inquiry, and the kind of information about which jurors are least likely to lie. Finally, the juror profile approach to jury selection frees the attorney to use voir dire for other purposes, such as establishing rapport or educating jurors regarding applicable legal principles.

The merit of such an approach to jury selection is supported by empirical research. Studies which have compared decision making by trained professionals with decision making by mathematical models have shown that the mathematical models consistently outperform their human counterparts.[46] Human judgment may be vastly overrated.

Many lawyers, however, are uncomfortable with this scientific approach to jury selection, and to some extent this discomfort is justified. Juror profiles are based on statistical averages, and there will inevitably be exceptions. A prospective juror who, based on a demographic profile, is predicted to be favorable may be anything but. The lawyer's best opportunity to determine whether this is so is during voir dire. For this reason, no matter what one's other goals for voir dire, it is unwise not to explore juror attitudes and biases.

Another difficulty with juror profiles is that the personality characteristics of the lawyer tend to be left out of the equation. To maximize a lawyer's effectiveness, the lawyer should feel at ease with the persons on the jury. Fortunately, determining whether the jury meets the necessary comfort level does not require the expenditure of significant amounts of time in voir dire. As long as the lawyer is permitted some opportunity to personally address the panel, the lawyer should be in a position to temper the rigid dictates of the juror profiles with his or her personal impressions of the jurors. Indeed, reliance on juror profiles frees the attorney to concentrate on building rapport with the jurors.

Another valid criticism of juror profiles is that they focus on jurors as individuals rather than the jury as a whole. For reasons previously discussed, it is important to attempt to discern what subgroups and alliances are likely to form on the jury.[47] It is important to try to identify the leaders of these subgroups. This information will usually not be available until it is seen which members of the venire are called to the box. Juror profiles will not usually reflect this parameter of jury selection.

§12.15 Authoritarianism Ratings

The best method of determining the characteristics of favorable and unfavorable jurors in a given case is, as outlined in the preceding section, by conducting community surveys and mock trials. The positions of the participants can then be correlated with their demographic, attitudinal, and socio-psychological characteristics. Juror profiles fitted to the parties, witnesses, lawyers, and issues in the particular case, as well as the community in which the trial is to take place, can be constructed.

Often, however, community surveys and mock trials are beyond the client's limited resources and the primary source of information for jury selection is voir dire. The attorney may nonetheless be reluctant to base jury selection

---

[46] *See* Saks, *Social Scientists Can't Rig Juries, in* L. Wrightsman, S. Kassin & C. Willis, In the Jury Box 48, 52-53 (1987).

[47] *See* **§12.02.**

decisions on subjective judgments. The lawyer may prefer a more "scientific" approach based on authoritarianism ratings.[48]

The concept of the authoritarian personality, originally developed by psychologists to explain susceptibility to fascist ideologies,[49] has proved useful in evaluating jurors. Psychologists have found that persons with high authoritarian ratings tend to be politically conservative, highly punitive, overly rigid, and generally intolerant. They tend to be hostile toward persons of lower status and deferential toward persons of higher status. Anti-authoritarians, on the other hand, are more tolerant of dissent and deviance, and more sympathetic and forgiving of those who have strayed. They are more likely to see the roots of evil in social injustice, while high authoritarians are more likely to subscribe to a philosophy of personal accountability.

Quite obviously, high authoritarians, because of their respect for authority, will rarely be good jurors for a defendant in a criminal case. They are more likely to accept the testimony of a police officer (a relatively high-status government official) over that of a criminal accused (a low-status "deviant"). They may give undue weight to an "official" indictment. They are less likely to accept excuses for a defendant's actions, and overall more likely to convict. If given a role in sentencing, they are prone to harsh penalties;[50] in capital cases, they will be more willing to impose the death penalty. High authoritarians may be particularly poor jurors in cases where the defense attorney plans to urge the jurors to exercise their power of nullification.[51]

In certain types of criminal cases, however, high authoritarians may be desirable jurors for the defense. They may be willing to accept a legal defense which is unpopular with the public and with which they personally disagree if they are convinced that the defense is mandated by law. They may also be favorably disposed to high-status defendants, such as government officials charged with abuse of power, with whom they can identity. Interestingly, there is research that suggests that low authoritarians are less inclined to base their verdicts on identification with a defendant.[52]

Anti-authoritarians, as one might expect, display the opposite tendencies. They are more likely to be distrustful of the prosecution. They will be less disposed to accept the testimony of a police officer over that of an accused. They will be more tolerant of deviance, more willing to overlook minor offenses. If given a role in sentencing, they will be more receptive to probation; in capital cases, less predisposed to the death penalty. Over all, they will be less inclined to convict and more amenable to exercising their nullification power.

---

[48] *See generally* Boehm, *Mr. Prejudice, Miss Sympathy, and the Authoritarian Personality: An Application of Psychological Measuring Techniques to the Problem of Jury Bias,* 1968 Wis L Rev 734; Note, *Juror Bias—A Practical Screening Device and the Case for Permitting Its Use,* 64 Minn L Rev 987 (1980).

[49] *See generally* T. Adorno, E. Frenkel-Brunswick, D. Levision & R. Sanford, The Authoritarian Personality (1950).

[50] *See* Bray & Noble, *Authoritarianism and Decisions of Mock Juries: Evidence of Jury Bias and Group Polarization, in* L. Wrightsman, S. Kassin, & C. Willis, In the Jury Box 83 (1987).

[51] *See* **§2.20.**

[52] *See* Mitchell & Byrne, *The Defendant's Dilemma: Effects of Jurors' Attitudes and Authoritarianism on Judicial Decisions,* 25 J Personality & Soc Psychology 123 (1973).

In civil cases high authoritarians make poor jurors for low-status plaintiffs suing high-status defendants, such as wealthy corporations, landlords, and the government. In jurisdictions which have adopted a comparative negligence approach to tort, high authoritarians are not good jurors in cases where the attorney wants the jury to apportion fault; high authoritarians tend to see matters in black and white. Low authoritarians, on the other hand, are likely to sympathize with the plight of a severely injured plaintiff, particularly where compensation will be paid by a corporation or an insurance company. In determining which side a high or anti-authoritarian will favor in a civil suit, it is important to take into account the relative status of not only the parties, but also the key witnesses who will testify for each side; high authoritarians are most likely to accept the testimony of a high-status witness.

§12.16 —Evaluating a Juror's Authoritarianism

Psychologists have devised scales to determine an individual's authoritarian rating. The laboratory procedure is to ask the subject a battery of questions, the answers to which will allow the researcher to place the subject along an authoritarian continuum. The subject can then be given a rating reflecting his or her place on the continuum.

The transposition of this methodology to the courtroom is fairly straightforward. The advantages of a pre-voir dire questionnaire have been previously espoused.[53] If a pre-voir dire questionnaire is permitted by the trial judge, and trial judges should be fairly receptive to these questionnaires because court time is not expended in securing the answers, the questions necessary to determine a juror's authoritarian rating can be interspersed with others exploring for case-specific bias. The relevant questions should be refined, as much as possible, to relate to the legal proceeding.

In fact, a questionnaire designed to test for juror authoritarianism has been devised for use in criminal trials.[54] The Legal Attitudes Questionnaire consists of ten sets of three statements. Within each set the jurors are instructed to mark the statement with which they are most in agreement and the one with which they are least in agreement. The third statement is left blank. Of the three questions, there is one to which a high authoritarian will be predisposed, one to which an anti-authoritarian will be predisposed, and one designed to appeal to a person with equalitarian characteristics. The responses are scored by assigning a rating of three to the response with which the juror most agrees, two to the response left blank, and one to the response with which the juror least agrees. The scores for authoritarian, anti-authoritarian, and equalitarian statements are tabulated separately. The higher the juror's score on a particular scale, the more likely the juror will react as one would predict of such a personality. Thus, for example, the higher the juror's score on authoritarian

---

53 *See* **§9.01.**

54 *See* Boehm, *Mr. Prejudice, Miss Sympathy, and the Authoritarian Personality: An Application of Psychological Measuring Techniques to the Problem of Jury Bias,* 1968 Wis L Rev 734.

statements, the greater the likelihood that the juror will have the tendencies predicted of a high authoritarian.

The Legal Attitudes Questionnaire (LAQ) which follows is reprinted from the appendix of the Boehm[55] article cited in the previous footnote. A subsequent field study reported in the Minnesota Law Review confirmed the LAQ's effectiveness.[56]

LEGAL ATTITUDES QUESTIONNAIRE (FORM II)

On the following pages are ten groups of statements, each expressing a commonly held opinion about law enforcement, legal procedures and other things connected with the judicial system. There are three statements in each group.

Please put a plus (+) on the line next to the statement in a group that you agree with most, and a minus (−) mark next to the statement you agree with the least. [The statements are not true or false in any sense and you should not try to judge any of them as true or false. They are opinions and you merely mark the one you agree with the most and the one you agree with the least.]

An example of a set of statements might be:

__+__ A. The failure of a defendant to testify in his own behalf should not be taken as an indication of guilt.

_____ B. The majority of persons arrested are innocent of any crime.

__−__ C. Giving an obviously guilty criminal a long drawn-out trial is a waste of the taxpayer's money.

In this example, the person answering has agreed most with statement A and least with statement C.

Work carefully, choosing the item you agree with most and the one you agree with least in each set of statements. There is no time limit on this questionnaire, but do not spend too much time on any set of statements. Some sets are more difficult than others, but please do not omit any set of statements. [NOTE TO READER: THE ANSWER TO BE EXPECTED OF A HIGH AUTHORITARIAN IS INDICATED BY "A"; THAT TO BE EXPECTED OF AN ANTI-AUTHORITARIAN, "AA"; AND THAT OF AN EQUALITARIAN, "E."]

Set 1

"AA" A. Unfair treatment of underprivileged groups and classes is the chief cause of crime.

"A" B. Too many obviously guilty persons escape punishment because of legal technicalities.

"E" C. The Supreme Court is, by and large, an effective guardian of the Constitution.

---

[55] *Id.* © University of Wisconsin. Reprinted with permission.

[56] *See* Note, *Juror Bias—A Practical Screening Device and the Case for Permitting Its Use,* 64 Minn L Rev 987, 1018-020 (1980).

Set II

"A" A. Evidence illegally obtained should be admissible in court if such evidence is the only way of obtaining a conviction.

"AA" B. Most prosecuting attorneys have a strong sadistic streak.

"E" C. Search warrants should clearly specify the persons or things to be seized.

Set III

"AA" A. No one should be convicted of a crime on the basis of circumstantial evidence, no matter how strong such evidence is.

"E" B. There is no need in a criminal case for the accused to prove his innocence beyond a reasonable doubt.

"A" C. Any person who resists arrest commits a crime.

Set IV

"E" A. When determining a person's guilt or innocence, the evidence of a prior arrest should not be considered.

"AA" B. Wiretapping by anyone and for any reason should be completely illegal.

"A" C. A lot of recent Supreme Court decisions sound suspiciously Communistic.

Set V

"AA" A. Treachery and deceit are common tools of prosecutors.

"A" B. Defendants in a criminal case should be required to take the witness stand.

"E" C. All too often, minority group members do not get fair trials.

Set VI

"AA" A. Because of the oppression and persecution minority group members suffer, they deserve leniency and special treatment in the courts.

"E" B. Citizens need to be protected against excess police power as well as against criminals.

"A" C. Persons who testify in court against underworld characters should be allowed to do so anonymously to protect themselves from retaliation.

Set VII

"E" A. It is better for society that several guilty men be freed than one innocent wrongfully imprisoned.

"A" B. Accused persons should be required to take lie-detector tests.

"AA" C. When there is a "hung" jury in a criminal case, the defendant should always be freed and the indictment dismissed.

Set VIII

"AA" A. A society with true freedom and equality for all would have very little crime.

"E" B. It is moral and ethical for a lawyer to represent a defendant in a criminal case even when he believes his client is guilty.

"A" C. Police should be allowed to arrest and question suspicious looking persons to determine whether they have been up to something illegal.

Set IX

"A" A. The law coddles criminals to the detriment of society.

"AA" B. A lot of judges have connections in the underworld.

"E" C. The freedom of society is endangered as much by overzealous law enforcement as by the acts of individual criminals.

Set X

"AA" A. There is just about no such thing as an honest cop.

"E" B. In the long run, liberty is more important than order.

"A" C. Upstanding citizens have nothing to fear from the police.

Whether or not the judge is receptive to a pre-voir dire questionnaire, the search to identify high authoritarians can continue during voir dire. The lawyer needs to integrate into the voir dire questions which will indicate the juror's degree of authoritarianism. Although the precise methodology of the LAQ, asking for the relative ranking of attitudinal statements, may not be feasible, consider the following questions:

> Which do you consider to be the chief cause of crime—inadequate attention to the needs of the poor or judges who are too soft on crime? (the high authoritarian will likely say the latter; the anti-authoritarian, the former)
>
> What do you personally think: should a defendant be required to testify in his own behalf? (the high authoritarian will answer affirmatively; the anti-authoritarian, negatively); if the defendant does not take the stand, will you say to yourself: "Well, he must have something to hide or else he would testify and tell us that he is innocent?" (The high authoritarian will be inclined to agree)
>
> Some people think that in order to catch criminals, the police are justified in using illegal wiretaps and arrest without warrants—do you agree? (the high authoritarian will likely agree; the anti-authoritarian will disagree)

The significance of the answers to most of these questions will appear a matter of common sense to most practicing attorneys. Indeed, it should be so. There is no magic in psychology; most of it is formalized common sense. It is for this reason, perhaps, that many trial attorneys resist the suggestion that there is something to be learned from social scientists. Nonetheless, it is reassuring to learn that one's instinctive reactions have been empirically validated; and sometimes the discoveries of the social scientists are not what a layperson would have predicted.

One advantage of seeking to discover a juror's degree of authoritarianism in voir dire rather than in a pre-voir dire questionnaire is that the lawyer is able to observe the reactions of the jurors to the relevant questions. Many prospective jurors are not entirely truthful in answering questions;[57] they appreciate that their answers may be disapproved of by society (or by other members of the jury).[58] In the case of high authoritarians, they may be concerned about the disapproval of the judge, a high-status figure. By introducing questions designed to reveal authoritarianism into the voir dire, a lawyer can scrutinize the juror for telltale kinesic and paralinguistic cues that indicate the juror's true feelings.[59]

Because high authoritarians tend to be deferential toward authority, a juror's attitude toward the judge may provide a further clue to the juror's authoritarianism. High authoritarians will be respectful to the judge, probably overly so. They will be attentive when the judge speaks; they may even nod their heads imperceptibly in agreement. Anti-authoritarians, on the other hand, will be less obviously deferential. They may show signs of restlessness or boredom when the judge speaks. While the high authoritarian may spring to attention when the judge enters the courtroom, the anti-authoritarian may rise only grudgingly.

Another indicator of a juror's authoritarianism is the manner in which the juror responds to the lawyer's questions. The high authoritarian is more likely to respond "Yes, sir" and "No, sir." The words chosen by the anti-authoritarian are likely to be less formal, and he or she is less likely to address the attorney as "sir."

Although a juror's authoritarian rating provides a useful tool for assessing a juror's leanings, a lawyer should not be seduced into forgoing other questioning designed to reveal bias. A juror's authoritarian rating will not necessarily reveal a case-specific bias. For example, while anti-authoritarians generally may be favorable to defendants charged with criminal offenses, a particular anti-authoritarian juror may, because of past experience, detest truck drivers. The juror's anti-authoritarian rating will not reflect this bias, yet it may be critical in a case where the lawyer is representing a trucker charged with reckless driving.

---

57 *See* **§12.14.**

58 *Id.*

59 *See* **§§12.09-12.12.**

§12.17 Free Will and Determinist Perspectives

Another rough but useful dimension on which to evaluate jurors involves the extent to which the juror believes that the source of events is the product of individual choice or the result of predetermined forces. A continuum can be constructed. At one end are persons who believe that events are due to circumstances beyond an individual's control. The force which causes the event may be deemed to be external, such as fate or the environment, or internal, such as the actor's genetic constitution or life history. The particular force to which the juror attributes the event is largely irrelevant. Either way the juror is inclined not to accept the principle of personal responsibility.

At the other end of the continuum are persons who believe in free will. Their philosophy is that man is the master of his destiny, and that individuals must assume responsibility for what befalls them. The free will response to the argument that external circumstances control events is that people control external circumstances.

The issue is not who is right or who is wrong. The debate has gone on for millenia and will continue to do so. The point, rather, is to be to able to identify which jurors fall into each of these categories, and to recognize the implications to be drawn from the juror's philosophy. In doing so, the lawyer should appreciate that the extreme cases are rare, that most persons fall somewhere in the middle of the free will-determinist continuum: they accept that there must be a degree of personal responsibility for events, but also recognize that there can be forces at work beyond the individual's control.

In criminal cases, jurors who subscribe to the concept of free will are more likely to hold a defendant legally (and morally) responsible for his or her criminal acts. They are less likely to accept a defense such as insanity or duress. If given a role in sentencing, they will punish perceived transgressors more harshly. Psychological research in fact confirms these common sense predictions.[60] Conversely, those who adhere to a determinist philosophy will be more likely to accept that a defendant can be the victim of circumstances. They tend to think of crime as the product of social conditions. The logical extension of this thinking is that, in the case of guilty defendants, the response should be not to punish the unfortunate souls who committed the crimes but to rectify the social and environmental ills that drove them to it. Such jurors may be more accepting of a defense such as insanity or premenstrual syndrome, if permitted in the jurisdiction. The determinist who is allowed a voice in sentencing will be unlikely to favor harsh penalties.

In tort cases, free will jurors may or may not be poor plaintiffs' jurors. They are likely to want to place blame squarely on one of the parties. Defendant's attorney will want to convince them that the plaintiff must take personal responsibility for his or her misfortune, while plaintiff's attorney will argue that

---

[60] *See* Phares & Wilson, *Responsibility Attribution: Role of Outcome Severity, Situational Ambiguity, and Internal-External Control,* 40 J of Personality 392 (1972). *But see* Saks, *Social Scientists Can't Rig Juries, in* L. Wrightsman, S. Kassin, & C. Willis, In the Jury Box 48, 58 (1987).

defendant bears sole responsibility for the harm.[61] Determinists are more likely to come to the conclusion that both or, more likely, neither of the parties should be held responsible for the mishap, and that therefore damages should be apportioned. Free will jurors are not likely to allow sympathy to override the legal significance of a plaintiff's contributory negligence; determinists will be more responsive to pleas for sympathy.

When it comes to the amount of damages, free will theorists again may or may not be inclined to return a large award. If convinced that the plaintiff must take responsibility for his or her misfortune, they are likely to conclude that the plaintiff should underwrite the recovery process as well. However, if persuaded that the defendant is responsible for the accident, they may be willing to award significant damages. In any event, what they are unlikely to award are damages for pain and suffering: these are usually seen as inconveniences which each of us must put up with.

Astute questions in a pre-voir dire questionnaire[62] or on voir dire should allow the attorney to determine whether a juror subscribes to a free will or determinist philosophy. In a criminal case, for example, the juror could be asked a straightforward question about the role social conditions play in fostering crime. In a civil case, questions about no fault insurance, unemployment compensation, and government sponsored medical programs should reveal the juror's ideology. The juror's personal experiences in overcoming adversity will also be relevant and should be inquired about.

§12.18 An Integrated Approach to Jury Selection

In the best of all possible worlds, where the lawyer has adequate time and resources to thoroughly prepare, and where the trial judge facilitates rather than frustrates the selection process, jury selection reaches its apex as both an art and a science. The totality of the techniques discussed in the previous sections are brought into play. Although a discussion of them will to some extent repeat what has been said previously, it is nonetheless valuable in order to present an integrated approach to jury selection.

The lawyer must first analyze the nature of the lawsuit and the factual and legal issues that it will raise, and develop a cohesive theory of the case. The importance of such preparation is well understood by most lawyers. The lawyer who seeks to make informed jury selection decisions, however, will also analyze the strengths, weaknesses, and general characteristics of the respective parties to the litigation, the witnesses who will testify, and the attorneys who will be trying the case. The lawyer understands that juror reactions to these human dimensions of the case will affect their reactions to the legal issues in the case.

The lawyer's next step is to determine the characteristics of persons who will respond favorably and unfavorably to the persons and issues involved in

---

[61] *See generally* Sosis, *Internal-External Control and the Perception of Responsibility of Another for an Accident,* 30 J Personality & Soc Psychology 393 (1974).

[62] *See* **§9.01.**

the litigation. A trained social scientist can construct a questionnaire to be administered to members of the community in which the trial is to take place (other communities as well if the lawyer suspects community bias). The questionnaire will seek two basic types of data: the demographic, attitudinal, and socio-psychological characteristics of the respondents to the questionnaire; and the respondents' perspectives of the people and issues in the case. The goal is to correlate these two sets of variables in order to construct profiles of favorable and unfavorable jurors. Basically, the lawyer is trying to learn whether a jury trial is advisable, where the trial should be held, and what are the characteristics of favorable and unfavorable jurors. The results of the survey can be used to support a change in venue or venire, and may convince the attorney to waive a jury altogether.

The juror profiles developed from the community surveys can be refined by integrating information obtained from one or preferably more mock trials. In the mock trial the attorney presents the client's case to a random sample of jury-eligible members of the community, just as would be done at trial. An associate of the lawyer presents the opposition's case, as best it can be anticipated. Both sides are presented as persuasively as possible, but without revealing to the mock jurors which side is responsible for commissioning them. At the completion of the presentation of each side's case, the mock jurors receive instructions of law and are left to deliberate. The deliberations are observed through a one-way mirror by the lawyer-social scientist team. The deliberations are also videotaped for later analysis. The objective is to correlate each juror's position during the deliberations with demographic, attitudinal, and socio-psychological data obtained from the juror. The information yielded by the mock trials can be integrated with that obtained in the community surveys to refine the profiles of favorable and unfavorable jurors.

After juror profiles have been constructed, the lawyer must determine the extent to which those persons who have been summoned for jury duty match the profiles. The lawyer must also identify the exceptions: those jurors who, although matching a particular profile, will not vote in the predicted manner. There are three primary points at which the critical information for making these determinations can be ascertained.

First, pretrial investigations can be carried out as soon as a list of members of the venire becomes available. These investigations should be conducted discreetly and professionally (whether by professional or amateur investigators), and with due respect to juror privacy. With the results of these investigations, a preliminary rating can be assigned to each prospective juror indicating the degree to which the juror is favorable or unfavorable. As further information comes to light, these preliminary ratings can be modified accordingly.

Second, the lawyer can seek information at trial but prior to voir dire. The lawyer should attempt to persuade the trial judge to allow the distribution of a pre-voir dire questionnaire, containing questions prepared by the attorneys for each side. The side which has conducted the community surveys and mock trials can, in addition to making case-specific inquiries, ask about demographic, attitudinal, and socio-psychological traits found to correlate with either a favorable or unfavorable juror. Futhermore, the questionnaire can include questions designed to enable the lawyer-social scientist team to give each juror a rating on an authoritarianism scale.[63]

Third, the lawyer can obtain information during voir dire. To maximize the benefit of voir dire, the lawyer should seek voir dire conditions which will facilitate the discovery of juror bias. Arguments should be made to the judge for attorney-conducted voir dire, individual questioning of jurors in camera, and allowance of a wide-ranging scope to voir dire. The constitutional rights to an impartial jury, the effective assistance of counsel, and a fair trial can be cited in support of appropriate motions.

In analyzing juror responses to voir dire questions, verbal assertions should not be taken at face value. Many jurors, for many reasons, are not entirely honest and forthcoming during voir dire. To help determine whether a juror is being truthful, the lawyer should enlist trained social scientists who can observe, record, and interpret the kinesic and paralinguistic cues of the juror.[64] The client should also be actively involved in the process. Verbal responses which are not consistent with nonverbal responses should be carefully analyzed, if not discounted altogether.

Each of these stages for acquisition of juror information has its own advantages and disadvantages. The pretrial investigation will not be restricted by time and scope limitations imposed by the judge on voir dire. It can be as wide-ranging as the lawyer desires. Information can (and, indeed, must) be obtained from third parties; such information may be more candid and reliable than that which the juror may be prepared to admit in court. The information obtained, moreover, need not be shared with opposing counsel, as perforce is the case with respect to answers to voir dire questions. The downside is that because the investigating team cannot speak directly to jurors, it may be unable to verify the accuracy of the information or to ascertain relevant information relating to a case-specific issue. Nor is the information given under oath. Juror reaction to the lawyers in the case also cannot be measured.

Pre-voir dire questionnaires can seek more case-specific information. The jurors respond personally. But the truth of the jurors' responses is difficult to gauge. Immediate follow-up questioning is not possible, and the lawyer is not present to observe the juror who is filling in the questionnaire for kinesic and other cues that may suggest that the juror is not being entirely honest or forthcoming. Third parties who could speak to the truth of the juror's statements are not available for examination. Furthermore, as in the case of pretrial investigations, the lawyer cannot ascertain the juror's response to him or her as a person.

It is only voir dire that allows the lawyer to obtain these reactions. Here, also, the lawyer can best learn whether an individual juror who fits a particular profile in fact has the attitudes predicted by the profile. Follow-up questions designed to clarify a juror's response or test the truthfulness of it can be employed. Juror deceit may be discerned from kinesic and paralinguistic cues.

---

[63] *See* **§§12.15-12.16.**

[64] *See* **§§12.09-12.12.**

While voir dire can be most valuable, its scope is likely to be far more restricted than the scope of either pretrial investigations or pre-voir dire questionnaires. The judge will be more sensitive to considerations of time. Furthermore the verbal and nonverbal responses which indicate a juror's desirability for one side will also be available to the other, which may challenge the juror.

Because of their respective advantages and disadvantages, the three techniques should be viewed as complementary to each other, and not as a substitute for one another.

With the information obtained from community surveys, mock trials, pretrial investigations, pre-voir dire questionnaires, and voir dire, the lawyer is in position to evaluate the extent to which each juror is prejudiced for or against the client's cause. The information obtained about each juror can be matched against the ideal favorable or unfavorable juror profile, as well as being independently evaluated. Each prospective juror can be assigned a rating indicating the degree to which the juror is favorable.

Each juror can also be given an authoritarian rating. As previously discussed,[65] high authoritarians tend to be politically conservative, deferential to authority and high-status individuals, highly punitive, and generally inflexible and rigid. In criminal cases they are likely to side with the prosecution. The opposite is true of anti-authoritarians. The social scientist can advise whether a high authoritarian or anti-authoritarian will be receptive to the client's case. The authoritarian rating can then be factored into the rating yielded by the juror profile.

Armed with an overall rating of each juror, the lawyer is in a position to attempt to have struck for cause jurors projected as unfavorable. The lawyer will need to make a legally cognizable challenge, which requires a thorough knowledge of the law of challenges. The groundwork for the challenge will have to be laid during voir dire by rigorous questioning of jurors predicted to be unfavorable; conversely, the voir dire questioning of jurors predicted to be favorable can be aimed at immunizing the juror from a challenge for cause from the opposing side. All of this questioning must, of course, be done in a way that does not alert the opposing side to one's strategy. If the challenge for cause to the unfavorable juror is denied, the lawyer can (and usually should) challenge the juror peremptorily, for the juror will most likely have been alienated by the hostile questioning.

Peremptory challenges are the lawyer's ultimate weapon in jury selection. They can be exercised without explanation, and can be used to excuse jurors with unfavorable ratings where the lawyer has been unable to convince the judge to excuse the jurors for cause. The number of peremptory challenges available, however, is generally limited, and the lawyer must exercise them with care. In appropriate cases, where, perhaps, the lawyer's community survey indicates an abnormal amount of bias against a party, a motion for additional peremptory challenges should be made.

Before expending a peremptory challenge, the lawyer should determine the impact that the unfavorable juror is likely to have in the jury room. The more

---

[65] *See* **§12.15.**

active a role the unfavorable juror is likely to take, and the more likely the unfavorable juror is to be a leader in the jury room, the more compelling the case for challenging the juror. On the other hand, if the unfavorable juror is likely to assume a passive role in the deliberations, and is likely to be influenced by a favorable juror, then the lawyer may decide not to challenge the juror. To determine whether the juror is likely to lead or be led, and by whom, the lawyer, usually with the help of a trained social scientist, needs to evaluate the subgroups and alliances which are likely to form on the jury and to identify which jurors are likely to be the leaders of the subgroups. The probable group dynamics of the jury must be analyzed. It is the unfavorable leader whom the lawyer should be most anxious to remove, preferably by a challenge for cause but, if necessary, by a peremptory challenge.

Judgments about jurors are relative matters. Consider the juror whose rating is neither positive nor negative to the client's position. When the venire is composed predominantly of persons with negative ratings, the juror with a neutral rating becomes a favorable juror; the lawyer should be reluctant to challenge the juror who would probably be replaced by a juror who was less inclined to the client's position. Conversely, when the venire is composed of persons with highly positive ratings, the juror with a neutral rating becomes an unfavorable juror, and there is a stronger case for challenging the juror in the expectation that the replacement will be more inclined in favor of the client's case. Also, the more favorable the general composition of the venire, the less willing the attorney should be to have a strong leader on the jury; the less favorable the composition, the more there is to be said for taking a chance on a strong-willed leader.

In deciding which jurors to challenge peremptorily, the lawyer must constantly have regard for the remaining members of the pool. This tactical consideration becomes acute as the lawyer exhausts the number of peremptory challenges permitted in the jurisdiction. In some instances, where the number of remaining jurors has dwindled to just a few, the lawyer may be in a position to predict with precision whether the replacement for a challenged juror will be more or less favorable, and by how much. In rare circumstances the attorney may even be in a position to challenge a favorable juror with confidence that the juror's replacement will be even more favorable.

In determining which jurors to challenge, the lawyer should seek the input of as many of those as possible who have been involved in the process to that point. If the lawyer is going to enlist the aid of social scientists, trained investigators, and the client in compiling the relevant data upon which decisions are to be made, it makes sense that the lawyer should listen to their views as to the decisions themselves. While consensus judgments tend to be more accurate, the experienced trial lawyer will not ignore his or her intuition. Although one's "feel" may not be quantifiable or as scientifically precise as a juror rating, it is an important factor to be taken into account. It represents the internalized repository of learning that the lawyer has acquired over a lifetime in and out of the courtroom. It allows for the integration of the lawyer's own strengths and weaknesses, and unique personality, into the jury selection equation. Lawyers ignore intuition and experience at their peril, for a lawyer will not be as effective before jurors with whom the lawyer feels uncomfortable as before jurors with whom the lawyer feels at ease. If the lawyer is not as effective in the presentation of the case, it will be to the client's disadvantage.

The client's preferences should always be taken into account.[66] At the end of the day, it is the client, and not the client's lawyer, who must live with the jury's verdict. The lawyer will proceed to a new case. The client does not enjoy this luxury; the jury's verdict is likely to end the matter. The client will not only appreciate being consulted, but is more likely to be accepting of whatever verdict comes from a jury regarding whose makeup he or she was consulted.

---

[66] However, for a contrary view by a noted lawyer opposed to the involvement of the client in jury selection, *see* Corboy, *Structuring the Presentation of Proof or Evidence,* 1 Trial Dipl J 20, 22-23 (Summer 1978).

Epilogue

The purpose of this book has been to present various approaches to jury selection. Particular emphasis has been placed on the use of social science methodologies. The rules, both legal and ethical, of the contest have been taken as given, as has the adversary system within which jury selection occurs. In a nonadversary system, the rules might be different. Some thoughtful critics have suggested that the increased use of social science methodologies may force lawyers and judges to reconsider the rules of jury selection. Indeed, it may prompt reconsideration of the jury system itself.

The jury selection techniques presented in this book are a bit like nuclear power. In and of itself, nuclear power is neither good nor bad. It all depends on the use to which it is put. It can be harnessed to supply a safe, efficient, and inexpensive source of energy which will benefit humanity; or it can be fashioned into a bomb which can destroy the world. Similarly, jury selection techniques can be used to promote or defeat the goals of the jury system.

The primary goal of a jury trial—indeed, any trial—is to see that justice is done. But every attorney swept up in the trial of a case knows that this goal can too easily be lost sight of and replaced by the goal of winning. Each side wants to prevail over the other, and what is just may become of secondary importance. Perhaps that is inevitable. Perhaps it is to the good—arguably what makes the adversary system operate effectively is two evenly matched lawyers doing their utmost to present the position of their client in the most favorable light, to convince the decision maker that truth and justice lie on their side.

The theory tends to break down to the extent that the two sides are not evenly matched. Often one side has access to resources that the other does not. In a civil case, the side with more money has always been able to hire the best attorneys, the most skilled investigators, and the most articulate and well-informed experts. Money was not always the determining factor, however, as some parties were able to attract able volunteers to their cause.

In a criminal case, the balance usually lay with the prosecutor. At the prosecutor's disposal were the state's police force for investigation, the state's laboratories and computer systems for analysis, and often a large staff of deputy attorneys general to help try the case. Even where the defendant was able to match the resources of the prosecution, tax, criminal, and other governmental records might not be available for the defendant's perusal.

In the past the jury has been a partial corrective for any imbalance. The resources available to each side were unlikely to affect the composition of the jury. Jurors were selected on the basis of voir dire conducted in open court, where both sides had an equal opportunity to ask questions and observe responses. Within the jury room, rich and poor were equal; neither had access. Cases were decided on their merits.

Social science threatens to sabotage this corrective. Critical to the jury's fulfillment of its role is the constitutional requirement that it be impartial. Impartiality does not require that jurors ignore their values, experiences, and training—these are indispensable qualities of the impartial juror. It does require that a juror be free from bias, receptive to arguments from both sides, and prepared to reach a verdict on the basis of the evidence.

Social science methodologies may be used to undermine the impartiality of the jury. Attorneys challenge jurors biased in favor of the opposing side; they are under no obligation to challenge jurors favorable to their own position. Fair enough, as long as each side has an equal opportunity to identify jurors partial to the opposition. Through demographic analyses, the construction of juror profiles, the conducting of mock trials, the pretrial investigations of the venire, and the analysis of the jurors' kinesic and paralinguistic cues on voir dire, one side's lawyer may be better positioned to identify jurors with subconscious biases. Opposing counsel, without the resources to hire social scientists and investigators, may not be privy to these insights. The danger is that the verdict of such a jury may reflect more the psychological predispositions of the jurors than the credibility of the evidence.

Some may dismiss these fears as catastrophic fantasizing. Social science methodologies have not yet developed to the point where the threat is serious. Jurors do not always conform to their profiles or to the hearsay reports of their leanings. Kinesic and paralinguistic cues may be subject to more than one interpretation. There are too many imponderables.

But the future is visible. As jury selection becomes more science than art, those with access to social science methodologies will gain an undue advantage. Impartiality is not an absolute but a relative concept: some juries may be more impartial than others. The jury which results when only one side has access to jury consultants may not be as impartial as that which is impaneled when both sides have access to such experts. Even now, in close cases, those which are most likely to wind up in court, social science may tip the scales of justice, and in a way which does not necessarily reflect the merits of the case. While in any given suit the scientific jury selectors may not prevail, over the long run they will win more than their fair share of cases. As the techniques improve, and with the insights of practical experience and further empirical research, the advantage to the scientific jury selector will increase.

Is the answer then to withhold from lawyers the names of jurors until immediately prior to trial, or to abolish the peremptory challenge which makes implementation of a social science-based jury selection strategy possible, or to make it unethical for an attorney to conduct community surveys, mock trials, or juror investigations? Any of these remedies would be likely to counteract the potential adverse effects of social science methodologies.

The difficulty is that any of these remedies would also defeat the potential benefits to be gained from social science methodologies. The previously stated premise was that jury selection, like nuclear energy, can be used for good or evil. If the goal is a biased jury, then the case for curbing scientific jury selection is strong. But the same techniques which can be used to defeat impartiality can be used to further its achievement. The subtle, internalized biases which may not be revealed by straightforward voir dire may be unearthed by social science. The end product may be an impartial jury in its truest sense—objective, open-minded, and fair to both sides. The verdict of such a jury may capture the justice for which the system strives.

The answer is therefore not to retreat from the brave new world of jury selection; rather, it is to harness its potential. One key step would be to require the sharing of information gathered in community surveys and juror investigations, much as discovery rules presently require that certain evidentiary-related information be disclosed. Court-appointed analysts would further help to alleviate the problem of resource imbalance. With the implementation of these two steps both sides would be in a position to identify subconscious biases and select impartial jurors.

Another approach would be to give greater control over jury selection to the judge. Much to the dismay of most attorneys, judges have already usurped the traditional lawyer role in the conducting of voir dire. A social scientist could be added to the judge's staff to help construct a case-specific pre-voir dire questionnaire designed to reveal subconscious bias. The social scientist could also analyze the kinesic and paralinguistic cues of the jurors during voir dire, identify high and low authoritarians and predict what effect they will have on the jury, and generally assist the court in the exercise of its discretion to excuse jurors. Increased judicial involvement in the detection of bias would reduce the inherent disadvantages facing the indigent litigant or minority defendant in court. It would further still the search for the impartial jury, the true goal of jury selection.

Cases

A

Abbott v Mines, 411 F2d 353 (6th Cir 1969) **§6.02**

Adams v Texas, 448 US 38 (1980) **§7.53**

Adamson v California, 332 US 46 (1947) **§1.11**

Akins v Texas, 325 US 398 (1945) **§6.15**

Alabama Power Co v Bonner, 459 So 2d 827 (Ala 1984) **§7.01**

Albrecht v Walker, 73 Ill 69 (1874) **§7.39**

Aldridge v United States, 283 US 308 (1931) **§§7.41, 8.14, 9.06, 9.07, 9.11**

Alexander v Louisiana, 405 US 524 (1972) **§§6.01, 6.12, 6.17, 6.18, 6.19, 8.05**

Allen v Snow, 635 F2d 12 (1st Cir 1980) **§§4.02, 4.06**

Alston v Manson, 791 F2d 255 (2d Cir 1986) **§6.17**

American Creosote Works v Harp, 215 Miss 5, 60 So 2d 514 (1952) **§7.24**

American Publishing Co v Fisher, 166 US 464 (1897) **§2.18**

Apodaca v Oregon, 406 US 402 (1972) **§§1.19, 2.17**

Archuletta, *In re,* 432 F Supp 583 (SDNY 1977) **§6.11**

Arctic Enter v Plastics, Inc, 292 Minn 16, 192 NW2d 822 (1971) **§2.06**

Arkansas State Highway Commn v Young, 241 Ark 765, 410 SW2d 120 **§7.30**

Atlantic Coast R Co v Mead, 22 Ga App 70, 95 SE 476 (1918) **§7.30**

Atlantic Joint Terminal v Knight, 98 Ga App 482, 106 SE2d 417 (1958) **§7.48**

Atlas Roofing Co v Occupational Safety & Health Review Commn 430 US 442 (1977) **§1.14**

Avery v Georgia, 345 US 559 (1953) **§§6.14, 6.18, 6.19, 8.05**

B

Bailey v McLeod, 143 Kan 638, 56 P2d 460 (1936) **§§7.27, 7.28**

Baldwin v New York, 399 US 66 (1970) **§§1.06, 1.07**

Ballard v United States, 329 US 187 (1946) **§§6.15, 8.12**

Ballew v Georgia, 435 US 223 (1978) **§2.13**

Bandy v United States, 296 F2d 882 (8th Cir 1961) **§3.16**

Barber v Ponte, 772 F2d 982 (1st Cir 1985), *cert denied,* 475 US 1050 (1986) **§6.16**

Barney v State, 698 SW2d 114 (Tex Crim App 1985) **§7.51**

Barrett v State, 516 SW2d 181 (Tex Crim App 1974), *cert denied,* 420 US 938 (1975) **§9.11**

Barron v Baltimore, 32 US (7 Pet) 243 (1833) **§§1.04, 1.09**

Basin Elec Power Coop v Miller, 310 NW2d 715 (ND 1981) **§7.25**

Bass v Dehner, 103 F2d 28 (10th Cir), *cert denied,* 308 US 580 (1939) **§7.33**

Batson v Kentucky, 476 US 79 (1986) **§§2.16, 2.19, 4.01, 6.13, 8.01, 8.04, 8.05, 8.06, 8.07, 8.08, 8.09, 8.11, 8.12, 8.14**

Beacon Theatres, Inc v Westover, 359 US 500 (1959) **§1.15**

Benton v Maryland, 395 US 784 (1969) **§1.03**

Berry v Cooper, 577 F2d 322 (5th Cir 1978) **§6.08**

Best v United States, 184 F2d 131 (1st Cir 1950) **§4.10**

Bethel v State, 162 Ark 76, 257 SW 740 (1924) **§7.24**

Beyer v City of Dubuque, 258 Iowa 476, 139 NW2d 428 (1966) **§§7.04, 7.32**

Billington v United States, 15 F2d 359 (6th Cir 1926) **§7.28**

Birmingham Baptist Hosp v Orange, 284 Ala 160, 223 So 2d 279 (1969) **§7.40**

Birmingham Elec Co v Driver, 323 Ala 36, 166 So 701 (1936) **§7.38**

Black v State, 100 Ind 357 (1884) **§§7.04, 7.27**

Blanton v City of North Las Vegas, 109 S Ct 1289 (1989) **§1.07**

Bloom v Illinois, 391 US 194 (1968) **§1.08**

Bolling v Sharpe, 347 US 497 (1954) **§§3.16, 6.12**

Bonaparte v Smith, 362 F Supp 1315 (SD Ga), *affd,* 484 F2d 956 (5th Cir 1973), *cert denied,* 415 US 918 (1974) **§6.10**

Bonner v State, 180 Ga App 239, 348 SE2d 903 (1986) **§7.19**

Booker v Jabe, 775 F2d 762 (6th Cir), *vacated & remanded,* 478 US 1001 (1985), *opinion restated,* 801 F2d 871 (6th Cir 1986), *cert denied,* 479 US 1046 (1987) **§§8.04, 8.06, 8.11, 8.12**

Borkoski v Yost, 182 Mont 28, 594 P2d 688 (1979) **§7.34**

Boykin v Alabama, 395 US 238 (1969) **§1.21**

Brady v Maryland, 373 US 83 (1963) **§4.10**

Braman v Wiley, 119 F2d 991 (7th Cir 1941) **§7.33**

Broadway v Culpepper, 439 F2d 1253 (5th Cir 1971) **§§6.08, 6.10, 6.11**

Broadway Mfg Co v Leavenworth Terminal Ry & Bridge Co, 81 Kan 616, 106 P 1034 (1910) **§7.32**

Brockett v Tice, 445 SW2d 20 (Tex 1969) **§7.34**

Brown v Harris, 666 F2d 782 (2d Cir 1981), *cert denied*, 456 US 948 (1982) **§6.16**

Brown v Oklahoma Transp Co, 588 P2d 595 (Okla Ct App 1978) **§7.14**

Brown v Woolverton, 219 Ala 112, 121 So 404 (1928) **§§7.02, 7.28**

Bryson v United States, 238 F2d 657 (9th Cir 1956) **§3.14**

Bueno-Hernandez v State, 724 P2d 1132 (Wyo 1986) **§8.06**

Bullock v Sklar, 349 SW2d 381 (Mo Ct App 1961) **§9.11**

Bumpus v Uniroyal Tire Co, 392 F Supp 1405 (ED Pa 1975) **§6.04**

Burch v Louisiana, 441 US 130 (1979) **§2.17**

Burch v Southern Pac Co, 32 Nev 75, 104 P 225 (1909) **§7.35**

Burke v McKenzie, 313 P2d 1090 (Okla 1957) **§§7.05, 7.18**

Burns v State, 145 Wis 373, 128 NW 987 (1910) **§7.08**

Bushell's Case, 124 Eng Rep 1006 (CP 1670) **§§1.02, 2.20, 8.13**

Butz v Economou, 438 US 478 (1978) **§8.13**

C

Caesar v State, 135 Tex Crim 5, 117 SW2d 66 (1938) **§9.15**

Caldwell v Commonwealth, 634 SW2d 405 (Ky 1982) **§7.05**

California v Murtishaw, 29 Cal 3d 733, 631 P2d 446, 175 Cal Rptr 738 (1981), *cert denied*, 455 US 922 (1982) **§4.10**

Callan v Wilson, 127 US 540 (1888) **§1.20**

Camp v United States, 413 F2d 419 (5th Cir), *cert denied*, 396 US 968 (1969) **§6.08**

Capeland v Gulf Oil Corp, 672 F2d 867 (11th Cir 1982) **§7.47**

Capital Traction Co v Hof, 174 US 1 (1899) **§2.14**

Carpenter v Hyman, 67 W Va 4, 66 SE 1078 (1910) **§7.39**

Carter v Jury Commn, 396 US 320 (1970) **§§2.07, 6.02, 6.11, 6.12, 6.15, 8.09**

Carter v Texas, 177 US 422 (1900) **§6.12**

Casey v Roman Catholic Archbishop, 217 Md 595, 143 A2d 627 (1958) **§7.40**

Cassell v Texas, 339 US 282 (1950) **§6.12**

Castaneda v Partida, 430 US 482 (1977) **§§6.09, 6.12, 6.16, 6.17, 6.18, 6.19, 8.05**

Chatterton v State, 221 Ga 424, 144 SE2d 726, *cert denied*, 384 US 1015 (1965) **§7.10**

Chicago & AR Co v Fisher, 141 Ill 614, 31 NE 406 (1892) **§9.16**

Chicago Council of Lawyers v Bauer, 371 F Supp 689 (CD Ill 1974), *revd on other grounds*, 522 F2d 242 (7th Cir 1975), *cert denied*, 427 US 912 (1976) **§§2.03, 2.09, 4.10, 8.09**

Christiancy v State, 106 Neb 822, 184 NW 948 (1921) **§7.28**

Cisneros v Cities Serv Oil Co, 334 F2d 232 (2d Cir 1964) **§7.26**

City Transp Co v Sisson, 365 SW2d 216 (Tex Civ App 1963) **§7.39**

Coca Cola Bottling Co v Jones, 74 Ariz 393, 250 P2d 586 (1952) **§7.17**

Codispoti v Pennsylvania, 418 US 506 (1979) **§1.08**

Coleman v United States, 379 A2d 951 (DC 1977) **§7.40**

Colgrove v Battin, 413 US 149 (1973) **§2.14**

Commonwealth v Brown, 11 Mass App Ct 288, 416 NE2d 218 (1981) **§8.06**

Commonwealth v Casper, 392 A2d 287 (Pa 1978) **§7.45**

Commonwealth v Colon, 223 Pa Super 202, 299 A2d 326 (1972) **§7.52**

Commonwealth v DePalma, 268 Pa 25, 110 A 756 (1920) **§7.41**

Commonwealth v DiMatteo, 12 Mass App 547, 427 NE2d 754 (1981) **§8.06**

Commonwealth v Di Stasio, 297 Mass 347, 8 NE2d 923 (1937) **§7.17**

Commonwealth v Eisenhower, 181 Pa 470, 37 A 521 (1897) **§8.01**

Commonwealth v Galloway, 231 Pa Super 69, 352 A2d 518 (1975) **§4.10**

Commonwealth v Greiner, 309 Pa Super 291, 455 A2d 164 (1983) **§7.50**

Commonwealth v Johnson, 299 Pa Super 172, 445 A2d 509 (1982) **§7.22**

Commonwealth v McColl, 376 NE2d 562 (Mass 1978) **§8.02**

Commonwealth v McGrew, 375 Pa 518, 100 A2d 467 (1953) **§7.10**

Commonwealth v Reid, 384 Mass 247, 424 NE2d 495 (1981) **§8.08**

Commonwealth v Ricard, 355 Mass 509, 246 NE2d 433 (1969) **§9.11**

Commonwealth v Robinson, 382 Mass 189, 415 NE2d 805 (1981) **§8.06**

Commonwealth v Soares, 377 Mass 461, 287 NE2d 499, *cert denied,* 444 US 881 (1979) **§§2.19, 8.05, 8.06, 8.08, 8.11, 8.12**

Commonwealth v Spencer, 212 Mass 438, 99 NE 266 (1912) **§9.05**

Commonwealth v Susi, 394 Mass 784, 477 NE2d 995 (1985) **§7.50**

Commonwealth v Webster, 59 Mass (5 Cush) 295 (1850) **§7.35**

Connor v State, 225 Md 543, 171 A2d 699, *cert denied,* 368 US 906 (1961) **§9.05**

Connors v United States, 158 US 408 (1895) **§7.45**

Cook v Kansas City, 358 Mo 296, 214 SW2d 430 (1948) **§7.16**

Cordera v United States, 456 A2d 837 (DC 1983) **§7.45**

Coughlin v People, 144 Ill 140, 33 NE 1 (1893) **§§7.02, 7.08**

Cox v Roberts, 248 Ala 372, 27 So 2d 617 (1946) **§7.33**

Craig v Boren, 429 US 19 (1976) **§8.08**

Crawley v State, 151 Ga 818, 108 SE 238 (1921) **§7.29**

Cromwell v Benson, 285 US 22 (1932) **§1.14**

Crutcher v Hicks, 257 SW2d 539 (Ky Ct App 1953) **§9.10**

Curry & Turner Constr Co v Bryan, 184 Miss 44, 185 So 256 (1939) **§7.48**

D

Dairy Queen, Inc v Wood, 369 US 469 (1962) **§1.15**

Darden v Wainwright, 477 US 168 (1986) **§7.53**

Davis v State, 594 SW2d 47 (Ark Ct App 1980) **§7.05**

Dehn v Otter Tail Power Co, 251 NW2d 404 (ND 1977) **§7.48**

Delaney v United States, 199 F2d 107 (1st Cir 1952) **§§7.05, 9.13**

Denham v Washington Power Co, 38 Wash 354, 80 P 546 (1905) **§7.47**

Dennis v United States, 339 US 162 (1950) **§§7.25, 9.13**

Dimick v Schiedt, 293 US 474 (1935) **§1.14**

District of Columbia v Clawans, 300 US 617 (1937) **§1.06**

District of Columbia v Colts, 282 US 63 (1930) **§1.06**

Donavon v Davis, 558 F2d 201 (4th Cir 1977) **§7.18**

Douglas v California, 372 US 353 (1963) **§3.16**

Douglas v First Natl Realty Corp, 543 F2d 894 (DC Cir 1976) **§1.07**

Dow v Carnegie-Illinois Steel Corp, 224 F2d 414 (3d Cir 1955) **§§4.01, 4.02**

Duncan v Louisiana, 391 US 145 (1968) **§§1.03, 1.04, 1.06, 1.12, 1.13, 1.19, 2.01, 2.04, 2.09, 2.17, 2.20, 4.10, 6.12, 6.13, 8.09**

Dunn v Blumstein, 405 US 330 (1972) **§6.04**

Duren v Missouri, 439 US 357 (1979) **§§6.05, 6.06, 6.13, 6.16, 6.17, 6.19, 8.08**

Dyke v Taylor Implement Mfg Co, 391 US 194 (1968) **§1.08**

E

Elder v Metropolitan Atlanta Rapid Transit Auth, 160 Ga App, 286 SE2d 315 (1981) **§7.23**

Ellison v National By-Prods Inc, 153 Ga App 475, 265 SE2d 829 (1980) **§7.47**

Enriquez v Texas, 429 SW2d 141 (Tex Crim App 1968) **§4.10**

Estes v Texas, 381 US 532 (1965) **§2.04**

Evans v Cabana, 821 F2d 1065 (5th Cir), *cert denied*, 483 US 1035 (1987) **§8.07**

F

Farar v Commonwealth, 201 Va 5, 109 SE2d 112 (1959) **§7.19**

Farmer v Pearl, 415 SW2d 358 (Ky 1967) **§7.34**

Fay v New York, 332 US 261 (1947) **§§6.13, 7.10**

Fedorinchik v Stewart, 289 Mich 436, 286 NW 673 (1939) **§7.33**

Fields v People, 732 P2d 1145 (Colo 1987) **§8.12**

Firestone v Freiling, 188 NE2d 91 (Ohio CP 1963) **§9.10**

Fitts v Southern Pac Co, 149 Cal 310, 86 P 710 (1906) **§7.08**

Flagg Bros v Brooks, 436 US 149 (1978) **§8.09**

Flemming v Kemp, 794 F2d 1478 (11th Cir 1986) **§8.06**

Fletcher v Crist, 38 NE 472 (Ind 1894) **§7.39**

Florida v Crawford, 257 So 2d 898 (Fla 1972) **§4.10**

Frontiero v Richardson, 411 US 677 (1973) **§8.08**

Foraker v State, 394 A2d 208 (Del 1978) **§8.03**

Foster v Sparks, 506 F2d 805 (5th Cir 1975) **§6.08**

Frazier v United States, 335 US 497 (1948) **§7.25**

Fredericks v United States, 292 F 856 (9th Cir 1923) **§9.08**

Fredrick v United States, 164 F2d 536 (9th Cir), *cert denied,* 332 US 775 (1947) **§7.46**

Freeman v People, 4 Denio 9 (NY 1847) **§8.02**

Fulgate v State, 169 Neb 420, 99 NW2d 868 (1959) **§7.32**

G

Gadd v Commonwealth, 305 Ky 318, 204 SW2d 215 (Ct App 1947) **§7.10**

Galveston, H & SA Ry v Manns, 37 Tex Civ App 356, 84 SW 254 (1904) **§7.47**

Garrett v Morris, 815 F2d 509 (8th Cir), *cert denied,* 108 S Ct 233 (1987) **§8.07**

Gatzow v Buening, 106 Wis 1, 81 NW 1003 (1900) **§7.38**

Genova v Kansas City, 254 SW2d 38 (Mo Ct App 1953) **§7.16**

Georgia v Brailsford, 3 US 1 (1794) **§1.03**

German v State, 159 Ga App 638, 284 SE2d 654 (1981) **§7.46**

Gideon v Wainwright, 372 US 333 (1963) **§3.16**

Gilbreath v Wallace, 292 Ala 267, 292 So 2d 651 (1974) **§2.15**

Glasser v United States, 315 US 60 (1942) **§§6.13, 7.10, 8.12**

Glick v Arink, 58 SW2d 714 (Mo 1932) **§7.33**

Gold v United States, 352 US 985 (1957) **§4.01**

Goldsby v State, 240 Miss 647, 123 So 2d 429 (1960), *cert denied,* 365 US 861 (1961) **§7.25**

Gonzales v State, 331 SW2d 748 (Tex Crim App 1960) **§7.39**

Goshen, City of v England, 119 Ind 368, 21 NE 977 (1889) **§7.17**

Government of the Virgin Islands v Parrott, 551 F2d 553 (3d Cir 1977) **§7.18**

Graham v Richardson, 403 US 365 (1971) **§§6.04, 8.08**

Graham v Waite, 23 AD2d 628, 257 NYS2d 629 (1965) **§7.34**

Granfinaciera v Nordberg, 109 S Ct 2782 (1989) **§§1.14, 1.15**

Gray v Mississippi, 481 US 648 (1987) **§7.53**

Gray v Sherwood, 436 So 2d 836 (Ala 1983) **§7.22**

Gray v State *ex rel* Langham, 19 Tex Civ App 521, 49 SW 699 (1898) **§7.45**

Green v Ligon, 190 SW2d 742 (Tex 1945) **§7.33**

Griffin v Illinois, 351 US 12 (1956) **§3.16**

Grigsby v Mabry, 569 F Supp 1273 (ED Ark 1983), *affd,* 785 F2d 226 (8th Cir 1985), *revd sub nom* Lockhart v McCree, 476 US 162 (1986) **§7.53**

Grimes v United States, 371 F2d 709 (5th Cir), *cert denied,* 393 US 825 (1968) **§6.08**

Groppi v Wisconsin, 400 US 505 (1971) **§2.04**

Gulf & Santa Fe Ry Co v Shane, 157 US 348 (1895) **§8.01**

Gulf Oil Corp v Gilbert, 330 US 501 (1947) **§2.06**

H

Hagans v State, 77 Ga App 513, 48 SE2d 700 (1948) **§7.02**

Ham v South Carolina, 409 US 524 (1973) **§§7.42, 8.14, 9.06, 9.11, 9.12**

Hamer v United States, 259 F2d 274 (9th Cir 1958), *cert denied,* 359 US 916 (1959) **§§4.05, 4.10, 9.05**

Harris v People, 113 Colo 511, 160 P2d 372 (1945) **§7.17**

Harvey v State, 341 So 2d 187 (Ala Crim App 1977) **§7.09**

Hayes v Missouri, 120 US 68 (1887) **§§8.01, 8.02**

Haymes v Catholic Bishop, 41 Ill 2d 236, 243 NE2d 203 (1968) **§7.33**

Haynes v County of Missoula, 163 Mont 270, 517 P2d 370 (1973) **§7.33**

Helber v State, 37 Ohio App 333, 174 NE 804 (1930) **§7.19**

Henderson v Morgan, 426 US 637 (1976) **§1.21**

Henrie v Compton, 357 SW2d 589 (Tex Civ App 1962) **§7.47**

Henthorn v Long, 122 SE2d 186 (W Va 1961) **§7.48**

Hernandez v State, 508 SW2d 853 (Tex Crim App 1974) **§7.46**

Hernandez v Texas, 347 US 475 (1954) **§§2.07, 6.15, 6.16, 6.19, 8.06**

Herring v State, 302 SW2d 428 (Tex Crim App 1957) **§7.06**

Herron v State, 409 So 2d 991 (Ala Crim App 1982) **§7.28**

Hickman v Taylor, 329 US 495 (1947) **§4.08**

High v State, 247 Ga 289, 276 SE2d 5 (1981) **§7.50**

Hill v State, 250 Ga 277, 295 SE2d 518 (1982) **§7.52**

Hoffman v Perucci, 117 F Supp 38 (ED Pa 1953), *appeal dismissed,* 222 F2d 709 (3d Cir 1955) **§7.34**

Hoffman v Royer, 359 NW2d 387 (SD 1984) **§7.33**

Holley v J&S Sweeping Co, 143 Cal App 3d 588, 192 Cal Rptr 74 (1983) **§8.10**

Holt v United States, 218 US 245 (1910) **§7.10**

Hopt v Utah, 120 US 430 (1887) **§§7.05, 7.08**

Houston N Hosp Properties v Telco Leasing, Inc, 688 F2d 408 (5th Cir 1982) **§1.17**

Hovey v Superior Court, 28 Cal 3d 1, 616 P2d 1301, 168 Cal Rptr 128, (1980) **§§2.12, 6.13, 7.53**

Howard v State, 420 So 2d 828 (Ala Crim App 1982) **§7.30**

Hurst v State, 469 So 2d 720 (Ala Crim App 1985) **§7.22**

Hurtado v California, 110 US 516 (1884) **§1.10**

Hyde v United States, 225 US 347 (1912) **§3.12**

I

Imbler v Pachtman, 424 US 409 (1976) **§8.09**

Irvin v Dowd, 366 US 717 (1961) **§§2.04, 2.11, 2.12, 7.03, 7.06, 7.08, 7.10, 9.08**

J

Jackson v Prestage, 204 Va 481, 132 SE2d 501 (1963) **§7.24**

Jackson v Virginia, 443 US 307 (1979) **§8.13**

Japanese Elec Prods Antitrust Litig, *In re,* 631 F2d 1069 (3d Cir 1980) **§1.16**

Jeffries v State, 255 Ark 501, 501 SW2d 600 (1973), *cert denied,* 417 US 920 (1974) **§8.03**

Jenkins v Chase, 53 SW2d 21 (Mo 1932) **§7.33**

Johnson v Louisiana, 406 US 356 (1972) **§1.19**

Johnson v Missouri-K-T RR, 374 SW2d 1 (Mo 1964) **§§7.01, 7.04**

Johnson v State, 311 A2d 873 (Del 1973) **§7.22**

Johnson v State, 1 Okla Crim 321, 97 P 1059 (1908) **§7.19**

Johnston v State, 239 Ind 77, 155 NE2d 129 (1958) **§7.29**

Jones v Ford, 154 Iowa 549, 134 NW 569 (1912) **§§7.04, 7.28**

Jones v State, 230 Ark 18, 320 SW2d 645 (1959) **§7.30**

Jones v State, 585 P2d 1340 (Nev 1978) **§7.40**

Justus v Commonwealth, 266 SE2d 87 (Va 1980) **§7.05**

K

Kalley v Huntley, 88 SW2d 200 (Mo 1935) **§7.33**

Kearney v Case, 79 US (12 Wall) 395 (1871) **§§1.20, 1.22**

Kelly v Gulf Oil Corp, 28 F Supp 205 (ED Pa 1938), *affd,* 105 F2d 1018 (3d Cir 1939) **§7.26**

Kelly v State, 371 So 2d 162 (Fla Dist Ct App 1979) **§7.18**

Kennard v State, 649 SW2d 752 (Tex Ct App 1983) **§7.46**

Kennedy v Raby, 174 Okla 332, 50 P2d 716 (1935) **§7.33**

Kiel v Mahan, 214 SW2d 865 (Tex Civ App 1948) **§7.23**

Kiernan v Van Schaik, 347 F2d 775 (3d Cir 1975) **§2.09**

King v Westlake, 264 Ark 555, 572 SW2d 841 (1978) **§7.34**

Klinck v State, 203 Ind 647, 179 NE 549 (1932) **§§7.04, 7.28**

Kobatchnick v Hanover Building Corp, 331 Mass 397, 119 NE2d 169 (1954) **§8.01**

Kuhnke v Fisher, 210 Mont 114, 683 P2d 916 (1984) **§7.25**

Kujawa v Baltimore Transit Co, 224 Md 195, 167 A2d 96 (1961) **§§7.06, 7.07, 7.11, 7.32, 7.34**

Kunk v Howell, 40 Tenn App 183, 289 SW2d 874 (1956) **§7.16**

Kuntz v Spence, 67 SW2d 254 (Tex Comm App 1934) **§7.33**

Kurczak v United States, 14 F2d 109 (6th Cir 1926) **§9.16**

L

Ladner v State, 148 Miss 243, 114 So 341 (1927) **§7.19**

Langston v State, 129 Miss 394, 92 So 554 (1922) **§7.19**

Leach v State, 47 Md App 611, 425 A2d 234 (1981) **§7.23**

Leath v Smith, 240 Ala 639, 200 So 623 (1941) **§7.38**

Le Gro v Moore, 51 Del 116, 138 A2d 644 (1958) **§8.11**

Leng Wing Chaw v Nagai, 44 Haw 290, 353 P2d 998 (1960) **§1.17**

Leon v State, 396 So 2d 203 (Fla Dist Ct App 1981) **§7.12**

Lester v State, 2 Tex App 434 (1877) **§7.43**

Lett v United States, 15 F2d 690 (8th Cir 1926) **§7.19**

Lewis v State, 469 So 2d 1291 (Ala Crim App 1984), *affd,* 469 So 2d 1301 (Ala 1985) **§7.29**

Lewis v State, 260 Ala 368, 70 So 2d 790 (1954) **§§7.04, 7.16**

Lewis v United States, 146 US 370 (1892) **§§8.03, 8.07**

Liquori v New York, NH & HR Co, 26 FRD 565 (1961) **§1.17**

Livingston v Moore, 32 US (7 Pet) 469 (1883) **§1.18**

Lockhart v McCree, 476 US 162 (1986) **§§2.13, 2.20, 2.22, 6.16, 7.53, 8.08, 8.12**

Lockhart v State, 145 Md 602, 124 A 829 (1924) **§7.25**

Loda v Raines, 193 Ark 513, 100 SW2d 973 (1937) **§7.33**

Lollar v State, 422 So 2d 809 (Ala Crim App 1982) **§7.12**

Lopez v Allee, 493 SW2d 330 (Tex Ct App 1973) **§7.44**

Losavio v Mayber, 178 Colo 184, 496 P2d 1032 (1972) **§4.10**

Loveland v Nieters, 79 ND 1, 54 NW2d 533 (1952) **§9.13**

Lowell v Daly, 148 Conn 266, 169 A2d 888 (1961) **§7.34**

Lugar v Edmondson Oil Co, 457 US 922 (1982) **§8.09**

Lurding v United States, 179 F2d 419 (6th Cir 1950) **§7.39**

M

Maddox v State, 145 Ga App 363, 243 SE2d 740 (1978) **§8.02**

Malvasi's Estate, *In re,* 96 Cal App 204, 273 P 1097 (1929) **§7.40**

Malvo v JC Penney Co, 512 P2d 575 (Alaska 1973) **§§7.05, 7.44**

M&A Elec Power Coop v Georger, 480 SW2d 868 (Mo 1972) **§7.32**

Maness v Bullins, 19 NC App 386, 198 SE2d 752 (1973) **§7.34**

Marshall v United States, 360 US 310 (1959) **§7.10**

Mason v State, 504 F2d 1345 (9th Cir 1974), *cert denied,* 420 US 936 (1975) **§3.16**

Massachusetts Bd of Retirement v Murgia, 427 US 307 (1976) **§§8.07, 8.08**

Mattox v United States, 146 US 140 (1892) **§3.12**

Maxwell v Dow, 176 US 581 (1900) **§§1.09, 2.14**

McCarthy v Cass Ave & Fair Grounds Ry, 92 Mo 356, 4 SW 516 (1887) **§7.47**

McClendon v United States, 587 F2d 384 (8th Cir 1978), *cert denied,* 440 US 983 (1979) **§6.07**

McClesky v Kemp, 481 US 279 (1987) **§2.20**

McCorkle v Mallory, 30 Wash 632, 71 P 186 (1903) **§7.27**

McCray v Abrams, 750 F2d 1113 (2d Cir 1984), *vacated on other grounds,* 478 US 1001 (1986) **§8.04**

McCrosky v Proctor, 332 SE2d 646 (W Va 1985) **§§7.33, 7.34**

McDonald v Pless, 238 US 284 (1915) **§§2.09, 3.12, 8.13**

McDonough Power Equip, Inc v Greenwood, 464 US 548 (1984) **§§2.09, 2.11, 4.01, 4.05, 9.10, 9.33**

McGinnis v ML Harris, Inc, 486 F Supp 750 (ND Tex 1980) **§6.11**

McKiever v Pennsylvania, 403 US 528 (1971) **§1.08**

McLaughlin v Florida, 379 US 184 (1964) **§8.08**

McMann v Richardson, 397 US 759 (1970) **§3.16**

Melbourne v State, 51 Fla 69, 40 So 189 (1906) **§7.31**

Mellinger v Prudential Ins Co, 322 Mich 596, 34 NW2d 450 (1948) **§7.05**

Mendes, *In re,* 23 Cal 3d 847, 592 P2d 318, 153 Cal Rptr 831 (1979) **§8.03**

Mercer v Commonwealth, 330 SW2d 734 (Ky Ct App 1959) **§9.11**

Meridian City Lines v Baker, 206 Miss 58, 39 So 2d 541 (1949) **§8.02**

Metallic Gold Mining Co v Watson, 51 Colo 278, 117 P 609 (1911) **§§7.38, 7.47**

Mhoon v State, 464 So 2d 77 (Miss 1985) **§7.52**

Miami v Cornett, 463 So 2d 399 (Fla 1985) **§8.10**

Miller v California, 413 US 15 (1973) **§6.13**

Miller v Kooker, 208 Iowa 687, 224 NW 46 (1929) **§7.33**

Miller Trucking Co v Wood, 474 SW2d 763 (Tex Civ App 1971) **§7.33**

Miracle v Commonwealth, 646 SW2d 720 (Ky 1983) **§7.19**

Mississippi Univ for Women v Hogan, 458 US 718 (1982) **§8.08**

Missouri Pac Transp Co v Talley, 199 Ark 835, 136 SW2d 688 (1940) **§7.33**

Monaghan v Agricultural Fire Ins Co, 53 Mich 238, 18 NW 797 (1884) **§9.16**

Mono County v Flanigan, 130 Cal 105, 62 P 293 (1900) **§7.31**

Montanick v McMillan, 225 Iowa 442, 280 NW 608 (1938) **§7.33**

Montgomery v State, 277 Ark 95, 640 SW2d 108 (1982) **§§7.05, 7.13, 7.28**

Moore v Atchison, T & SF Ry, Ill App 2d 340, 171 NE2d 393 (1960) **§9.11**

Morford v United States, 339 US 258 (1950) **§9.13**

Morgan v Liberty Mut Ins Co, 323 So 2d 855 (La Ct App 1975) **§7.48**

Morissette v United States, 342 US 246 (1952) **§2.20**

Morris v McClellan, 169 Ala 90, 53 So 155 (1910) **§7.20**

Moss v Fidelity & Cas Co, 439 SW2d 734 (Tex Civ App 1969) **§7.04**

Mottram v Murch, 458 F2d 626 (1st Cir), *revd on other grounds,* 409 US 41 (1972) **§7.18**

Mount v Welsh, 118 Or 568, 247 P 815 (1926) **§§7.01, 7.04, 7.05**

Moya v State, 691 SW2d (Tex Crim App 1985) **§7.18**

Muniz v Hoffman, 422 US 454 (1975) **§1.07**

Murphy v Florida, 421 US 794 (1975) **§§2.11, 7.08, 7.10**

Murphy v Lindahl, 24 Ill App 2d 461, 165 NE2d 340 (1960) **§7.48**

N

Nailor v People, 612 P2d 79 (Colo 1980) **§7.12**

National Bank v Ragland, 51 SW 661 (Tex Civ App 1889) **§7.31**

Neal v Delaware, 103 US 370 (1881) **§§6.12, 6.18**

Nebraska Press Assn v Stuart, 427 US 539 (1976) **§7.10**

Nichols v Oklahoma City, 195 Okla 305, 157 P2d 174 (1945) **§7.32**

Noey v Ukpeagvik Inupiat Corp, 683 P2d 260 (Alaska 1984) **§§7.25, 7.31**

Nolan v Venus Motors, Inc, 64 Wis 2d 215, 218 NW2d 507 (1974) **§7.04**

Norris v Alabama, 294 US 587 (1935) **§§6.12, 6.15, 6.16, 6.18**

North Carolina v Alford, 400 US 25 (1970) **§1.21**

Nuchols v Commonwealth, 312 Ky 171, 226 SW2d 796 (1950) **§7.17**

O

Oborn v State, 143 Wis 249, 126 NW 739 (1910) **§2.03**

Olund v Swarthout, 459 F2d 999 (6th Cir), *cert denied,* 409 US 1008 (1972) **§1.17**

Orr v Orr, 440 US 268 (1979) **§8.07**

Owens-Illinois, Inc v Lake Shore Land Co, 610 F2d 1185 (3d Cir 1979) **§1.14**

Ozark Border Elec Coop v Stacy, 348 SW2d 586 (Mo Ct App 1961) **§§7.25, 7.32**

P

Palko v Connecticut, 302 US 319 (1937) **§1.10**

Pantos v City & County of San Francisco, 151 Cal App 3d, 198 Cal Rptr 489 (1984) **§7.42**

Paper Mach Corp v Nelson Foundry Co, 108 Wis 2d 614, 323 NW2d 160 (1982) **§7.05**

Parker v Gladden, 385 US 363 (1966) **§3.12**

Parker v Hofer, 118 Vt 1, 100 A2d 434 (1953) **§9.13**

Parsons v Bedford, 26 US (3 Pet) 433 (1830) **§1.15**

Paterman v Indian Motorcycle Co, 216 F2d 289 (1st Cir 1954) **§6.11**

Patrick v Burget, 486 US 94 (1988) **§8.09**

Patton v United States, 281 US 276 (1930) **§§1.20, 1.22, 2.13, 2.17**

Patton v Yount, 467 US 1025 (1984) **§§2.10, 7.05, 7.10**

People v Abbott, 47 Cal 2d 362, 303 P2d 730 (1956) **§7.26**

People v Abbott, 690 P2d 1263 (Colo 1984) **§7.12**

People v Aldridge, 47 Mich App 639, 209 NW2d 796 (1973) **§4.10**

People v Boorman, 142 Cal App 2d 85, 297 P2d 741 (1956) **§7.26**

People v Brawley, 1 Cal 3d 277, 461 P2d 361, 82 Cal Rptr 161 (1969) **§4.10**

People v Butler, 104 Cal App 3d 868, 162 Cal Rptr 913 (1980) **§7.51**

People v Carmichael, 198 Cal 534, 246 P 62 (1926) **§2.12**

People v Car Soy, 57 Cal 102 (1880) **§7.41**

People v Chambie, 189 Cal App 3d 149, 234 Cal Rptr 308 (Ct App 1987) **§8.07**

People v Clay, 153 Cal App 3d 433, 200 Cal Rptr 269 (1984) **§8.06**

People v Davis, 95 Ill 2d 1, 447 NE2d 353 (1983) **§8.12**

People v Durant, 116 Cal 179, 48 P 75 (1897) **§8.02**

People v Feagley, 14 Cal 3d 346, 14 P2d 373, 121 Cal Rptr 509 (1975) **§2.15**

People v Fitzgerald, 14 Cal App 2d 180, 58 P2d 718, *cert denied,* 299 US 593 (1936) **§7.45**

People v Fowler, 178 Cal 657, 174 P 892 (1918) **§7.46**

People v Guzman, 125 Misc 2d 457, 478 NYS2d 455 (NY Sup Ct 1984) **§7.50**

People v Harris, 36 Cal 3d 36, 679 P2d 433, 201 Cal Rptr 782, *cert denied,* 469 US 965 (1984) **§6.08**

People v Harris, 84 AD2d, 445 NYS2d 520 (1981), *affd,* 57 NY2d 335, 456 NYS2d 694, 442 NE2d 1205 (1982), *cert denied,* 460 US 1047 (1983) **§7.05**

People v Heard, 58 Mich App 312, 227 NW2d 331 (1975) **§4.10**

People v Horton, 13 Wend 9 (NY 1834) **§7.24**

People v King, 240 Cal App 2d 389, 49 Cal Rptr 562, *cert denied,* 385 US 923 (1966) **§8.02**

People v Kirkpatrick, 70 Ill App 3d 166, 387 NE2d 1284 (1979) **§7.22**

People v Kurth, 34 Ill 2d 387, 216 NE2d 154 (1966) **§7.51**

People v Lieberman, 107 Ill App 3d 949, 438 NE2d 516 (1982) **§7.50**

People v Macioce, 197 Cal App 3d 362, 242 Cal Rptr 771 (1987) **§8.08**

People v Marshall, 82 Mich App 92, 266 NW2d 678 (1979) **§1.08**

People v McCarver, 87 Mich App 12, 273 NW2d 570 (1978) **§7.18**

People v McCray, 57 NY2d 542, 443 NE2d 915, 457 NYS2d 441 (1982), *cert denied,* 461 US 961 (1983) **§8.12**

People v McQuade, 110 NY 284, 18 NE 156 (1888) **§7.27**

People v Motton, 39 Cal 3d 596, 704 P2d 176, 217 Cal Rptr 416 (1985) **§8.06**

People v O'Neill, 109 NY 251, 16 NE 68 (1888) **§7.46**

People v Peck, 139 Mich 680, 103 NW 178 (1905) **§9.15**

People v Pitts, 104 Ill App 3d 451, 432 NE2d 1062 (1982) **§7.47**

People v Presley, 22 AD2d 151, 254 NYS2d 400 (1964), *affd,* 16 NY2d 738, 209 NE2d 729, 262 NYS2d 113 (1965) **§7.44**

People v Provenzano, 70 AD2d 960, 417 NYS2d 317 (1979) **§7.28**

People v Reyes, 5 Cal 347 (1855) **§7.44**

People v Remiro, 89 Cal App 3d 809, 153 Cal Rptr 89 (1979) **§2.05**

People v Robinson, 102 Ill App 3d 884, 429 NE2d 1356 (1981) **§7.47**

People v Rosseau, 129 Cal App 3d 526, 179 Cal Rptr 892 (1982) **§8.06**

People v Russell, 112 AD2d 451, 492 NYS2d 420 (1985) **§7.50**

People v Taylor, 101 Ill 2d 377, 462 NE2d 478 (1984) **§7.16**

People v Trevino, 39 Cal 3d 667, 704 P2d 719, 217 Cal Rptr 652 (1985) **§§8.07, 8.08**

People v Turner, 27 Ill App 3d 236, 326 NE2d 562 (1975) **§8.02**

People v Valardi, 616 P2d 104 (Colo 1980) **§7.40**

People v Warner, 147 Cal 546, 82 P 196 (1905) **§7.46**

People v Wheeler, 22 Cal 3d 258, 583 P2d 748, 148 Cal Rptr 890

(1978) **§§8.04, 8.05, 8.06, 8.08, 8.11, 8.12**

People v Wilkes, 44 Cal 2d 679, 284 P2d 481 (1955) **§§7.27, 7.28**

People v Williams, 29 Cal 3d 392, 628 P2d 869, 174 Cal Rptr 317 (1981) **§§7.01, 9.13**

People *ex rel* Keller v Superior Court, 175 Cal App 2d 830, 1 Cal Rptr 55 (1959) **§4.10**

Perdue v State, 225 Ga 814, 171 SE2d 563 (1969) **§7.06**

Perillo v State, 656 SW2d 78 (Tex Crim App 1983) **§7.05**

Perkins v Smith, 370 F Supp 134 (D Md 1974), *affd,* 426 US 913 (1976) **§6.04**

Petcosky v Bowman, 197 Va 240, 89 SE2d 4 (1955) **§§7.05, 7.30**

Peters v Kiff, 407 US 493 (1972) **§§2.07, 6.11, 6.14, 6.15, 6.19, 8.06**

Pierce v State, 696 SW2d 899 (Tex Crim App 1985) **§7.05**

Plair v State, 453 So 2d 917 (Fla Dist Ct App 1984) **§7.22**

Plyer v Doe, 457 US 202 (1982) **§§6.04, 8.08**

Pointer v United States, 151 US 396 (1894) **§§8.03, 8.11**

Potter v State, 86 Tex Crim 380, 216 SW 886 (1919) **§7.41**

Powell v Alabama, 287 US 45 (1932) **§3.16**

Press-Enterprise Co v Superior Court, 464 US 501 (1984) **§§1.01, 4.05, 4.06, 9.01, 9.08, 9.14**

Preston v Ohio Oil Co, 121 SW2d 1039 (Tex Civ App 1938) **§7.22**

Price v State, 383 So 2d 884 (Ala Crim App 1980) **§7.28**

Privett v St Louis-San Francisco Ry Co, 300 SW 726 (Mo 1927) **§7.27**

Q

Quill v Southern Pac Co, 140 Cal 268, 73 P 991 (1903) **§7.47**

R

R v Shipley, 99 Eng Rep 774 (1784) **§2.20**

Rabinowitz v United States, 366 F2d 34 (5th Cir 1966) **§§6.05, 6.09, 6.10**

Raines v Raines, 97 Colo 19, 46 P2d 740 (1935) **§7.33**

Ramirez v Wood, 577 SW2d 278 (Tex Civ App 1978) **§7.47**

Ramos v United States, 12 F2d 761 (1st Cir 1926) **§7.19**

Raullerson v State, 157 Colo 462, 404 P2d 149 (1965) **§7.44**

Redwine v Fitzhugh, 78 Wyo 107, 329 P2d 257 (1958) **§§7.01, 7.04, 7.27, 7.28**

Reed v Peacock, 123 Mich 244, 82 NW 53 (1900) **§7.24**

RE Gaddie, Inc v Evans, 394 SW2d 118 (Ky 1965) **§8.02**

Reich v Thompson, 346 Mo 577, 142 SW2d 486 (1940) **§9.10**

Remmer v United States, 347 US 227 (1954) **§3.12**

Remser v United States, 350 US 377 (1956) **§4.01**

Reynolds v United States, 98 US 145 (1878) **§§2.11, 7.05, 7.08, 7.10**

Rhoades v El Paso & SW Ry, 248 SW 1064 (Tex Comm App 1923) **§7.47**

Rideau v Louisiana, 373 US 723 (1963) **§§2.04, 2.11, 7.10**

Ridglea v Unified School Dist No 305, Saline County, 206 Kan 111, 476 P2d 601 (1970) **§7.32**

Riley v State, 496 A2d 997 (Del 1985), *cert denied,* 478 US 1022 (1986) **§8.12**

Ristaino v Ross, 424 US 589 (1976) **§§7.42, 8.14, 9.06, 9.12**

Roberts v Roberts, 115 Ga 259, 41 SE 616 (1902) **§7.30**

Robinson v Randall, 82 Ill 521 (1876) **§7.39**

Roe v Wade, 410 US 113 (1973) **§§1.10, 8.07**

Roman v Abrams, 822 F2d 214 (2d Cir 1987) **§8.12**

Romeo v State, 107 Tex Crim 70, 294 SW 857 (1927) **§7.41**

Rosales-Lopez v United States, 451 US 182 (1981) **§7.42**

Rose v Magro, 220 Ala 120, 124 So 296 (1929) **§7.38**

Rose v Mitchell, 443 US 545 (1979) **§6.01**

Rose v Sheedy, 345 Mo 610, 134 SW2d 18 (1939) **§7.40**

Ross v Bernhard, 396 US 531 (1970) **§§1.14, 1.16**

Ross v Oklahoma, 487 US 81 (1988) **§§2.09, 7.05, 8.01, 8.02, 8.13**

Ruthenberg v United States, 245 US 480 (1918) **§7.45**

Ryan v Simeons, 209 Iowa 1090, 229 NW 667 (1930) **§7.33**

S

St Clair v United States, 154 US 134 (1894) **§8.03**

St John v Commercial Union Ins Co, 719 F2d 374 (11th Cir 1983) **§7.20**

Salazar v Ehmann, 505 P2d 387 (Colo Ct App 1972) **§7.33**

Sanders v State, 328 So 2d 268 (Fla Dist Ct App 1976) **§8.02**

Sanford v Hutto, 394 F Supp 1278 (ED Ark), *affd,* 523 F2d 1383 (8th Cir 1975) **§6.10**

Santee v Haggart Const Co, 202 Minn 361, 278 NW 520 (1938) **§7.33**

Schick v United States, 195 US 65 (1904) **§§1.06, 1.22**

Schowgurow v State, 240 Md 121, 213 A2d 475 (1965) **§7.40**

Schwickerath v Mass, 230 Iowa 329, 297 NW 248 (1941) **§§7.04, 7.33**

Scott v Chope, 33 Neb 41, 49 NW 940 (1891) **§7.45**

Scott v State, 473 So 2d 1167 (Ala Crim App 1985) **§7.30**

Scribner v State, 3 Okla Crim 601, 108 P 422 (1910) **§7.08**

Seals v Snow, 123 Kan 88, 254 P 348 (1927) **§7.08**

Seals v State, 282 Ala 586, 213 So 2d 645 (1968) **§7.44**

Sellers v United States, 271 F2d 475 (DC Cir 1959) **§§7.46, 9.07**

Shapiro v Thompson, 394 US 618 (1969) **§6.04**

Shelly v Kraemer, 334 US 1 (1948) **§8.09**

Sheppard v Maxwell, 384 US 333 (1966) **§2.04**

Sherbert v Verner, 374 US 398 (1963) **§8.08**

Sherman v Southern Pac Co, 33 Nev 385, 111 P 416 (1910) **§7.22**

Shon, *In re,* 262 AD 225, 28 NYS2d 872 (1941) **§§2.22, 7.29, 4.04**

Sinclair v United States, 279 US 749 (1929) **§§4.01, 4.05**

Singer v United States, 380 US 24 (1965) **§§1.22, 8.09**

Skinner v Sisters of St Mary's, 686 SW2d 858 (Mo Ct App 1985) **§7.33**

Skipper v State, 400 So 2d 797 (Fla Dist Ct App 1981) **§7.52**

Slappy v State, 503 So 2d 350 (Fla Dist Ct App 1987), *cert denied,* 108 S Ct 2273 (1988) **§8.06, 8.07**

Slinker v State, 344 So 2d 1264 (Ala Crim App 1977) **§4.10**

Smith v German Ins Co, 107 Mich 270, 65 NW 236 (1895) **§7.32**

Smith v Phillips, 455 US 209 (1982) **§7.25**

Smith v Sisters of Good Shepard, 27 Ky L Rptr 1107, 87 SW 1083 (1905) **§7.40**

Smith v Smith, 7 Cal App 2d 271, 46 P2d 232 (1935) **§7.40**

Smith v State, 651 P2d 1067 (Okla Crim App 1982) **§7.18**

Smith v Texas, 311 US 128 (1940) **§§6.13, 8.12**

Snyder v Massachusetts, 291 US 97 (1934) **§1.10**

Sorseleil v Red Lake Milling Co, 111 Minn 275, 126 NW 903 (1910) **§7.27**

Sosna v Iowa, 419 US 393 (1975) **§6.04**

Sparf & Hansen v United States, 156 US 51 (1895) **§§1.03, 2.20**

Spies v Illinois, 123 US 131 (1887) **§§1.09, 7.08, 7.10**

Spies v People, 122 Ill 1, 12 NE 865, *error dismissed,* 123 US 131 (1887) **§7.45**

Spranger v Indiana, 498 NE2d 931 (Ind 1986) **§4.10**

Springdale Park, Inc v Andriotis, 30 NJ Super 257, 104 A2d 327 (1954) **§9.08**

State v Allen, 380 So 2d 28 (La 1980) **§§7.05, 7.46**

State v Alvarez, 93 NM 761, 605 P2d 1160 (1978) **§7.18**

State v Andrews, 29 Conn 100 (1860) **§7.29**

State v Barnett, 251 Or 234, 445 P2d 124 (1968) **§7.40**

State v Beck, 286 SE2d 234 (W Va 1981) **§7.08**

State v Beckett, 310 SE2d 883 (W Va 1983) **§7.52**

State v Berg, 337 Iowa 356, 21 NW2d 777 (1946) **§1.17**

State v Benson, 40 Wash App 729, 700 P2d 758 (1985) **§7.52**

State v Betts, 646 SW2d 94 (Mo 1983) **§7.40**

State v Boyer, 342 Mo 64, 112 SW2d 575 (1938) **§9.15**

State v Brewer, 247 NW2d 205 (Iowa 1976) **§6.16**

State v Brown, 45 RI 9, 119 A 324 (1923) **§8.02**

State v Butler, 221 SW2d 160 (Mo 1949) **§7.06**

State v Butler, 731 SW2d 265 (Mo Ct App 1987) **§8.07**

State v Carson, 131 SC 42, 126 SE 757 (1925) **§7.39**

State v Carter, 121 Iowa 135, 96 NW 710 (1903) **§7.27**

State v Chavis, 24 NC App 148, 210 SE2d 555 (1974) **§7.44**

State v Clark, 164 Conn 224, 319 A2d 398 (1973) **§§7.25, 7.52**

State v Connor, 59 Idaho 695, 89 P2d 197 (1939) **§7.19**

State v Corbett, 309 NC 382, 307 SE2d 139 (1983) **§7.05**

State v Crispin, 94 NM 486, 612 P2d 716 (Ct App 1980) **§8.12**

State v Darling, 208 Kan 469, 493 P2d 216 (1972) **§9.13**

State v Davis, 371 SW2d 270 (1963) **§7.39**

State v Deaner, 334 SE2d 627 (W Va 1985) **§7.05**

State v Dees, 639 SW2d 149 (Mo Ct App 1982) **§7.52**

State v Dickens, 68 Idaho 173, 191 P2d 364 (1948) **§7.26**

State v Eastin, 419 So 2d 933 (La 1982) **§7.28**

State v Edwards, 419 So 2d 881 (La 1982) **§7.46**

State v Forsha, 190 Mo 296, 88 SW 746 (1905) **§7.05**

State v Gates, 131 Mont 78, 307 P2d 248 (1957) **§7.05**

State v Gilmore, 103 NJ 508, 511 A2d 1150 (1986) **§8.12**

State v Glover, 41 SD 465, 113 NW 625 (1907) **§7.28**

State v Golubski, 45 SW2d 873 (Mo Ct App 1932) **§7.26**

State v Grillo, 16 NJ 103, 106 A2d 294 (1954) **§§7.06, 8.03**

State v Guynn, 97 Utah 320, 48 P2d 902 (1935) **§7.26**

State v Haislip, 237 Kan 461, 701 P2d 909 (1985) **§7.51**

State v Hall, 612 SW2d 782 (Mo 1981) **§7.13**

State v Harrell, 637 SW2d 752 (Mo Ct App 1982) **§7.13**

State v Heald, 443 A2d 954 (Me 1982) **§7.13**

State v Henry, 197 La 999, 3 So 2d 104 (1941) **§9.15**

State v Hills, 241 La 345, 129 So 2d 12 (1960) **§7.44**

State v Hitto, 373 NW2d 307 (Minn 1985) **§4.04**

State v Hohman, 138 Vt 502, 420 A2d 852 (1980) **§7.05**

State v Hollingsworth, 11 NC App 674, 182 SE2d 26 (1971) **§7.26**

State v Holmes, 347 So 2d 221 (La 1977) **§4.10**

State v Huff, 14 NJ 240, 102 A2d 8 (1954) **§7.40**

State v Huffman, 86 Ohio St 229, 99 NE 295 (1912) **§9.16**

State v Hutchens, 604 SW2d 26 (Mo Ct App 1980) **§7.19**

State v Jackson, 156 Iowa 588, 137 NW 1034 (1912) **§7.40**

State v Jackson, 43 NJ 148, 203 A2d 1 (1964), *cert denied,* 379 US 982 (1965) **§§7.05, 7.23, 7.46, 7.52, 8.03**

State v Joiner, 163 La 609, 112 So 503 (1927) **§7.23**

State v Kayser, 637 SW2d 836 (Mo Ct App 1982) **§7.52**

State v King, 311 NC 603, 320 SE2d 1 (1984) **§7.50**

State v Kohler, 434 So 2d 1110 (La Ct App 1983) **§7.13**

State v Kuster, 353 NW2d 428 (Iowa 1984) **§7.30**

State v LaFero, 42 NJ 97, 199 A2d 730 (1964) **§3.12**

State v Leonard, 296 NC 58, 248 SE2d 853 (1978) **§§7.01, 7.47**

State v Leslie, 783 F2d 541 (5th Cir 1986) **§8.05**

State v Long, 204 NJ Super 469, 499 A2d 264 (1985) **§6.01**

State v Longo, 121 NJL 427, 3 A2d 127 (1938) **§7.45**

State v Martin, 643 SW2d 63 (Mo Ct App 1982) **§7.22**

State v Maxwell, 151 Kan 951, 102 P2d 109 (1940) **§7.45**

State v McClain, 256 Iowa 175, 125 NW2d 764 (1964) **§7.25**

State v McGraw, 6 Idaho 635, 59 P 178 (1899) **§7.27**

State v McIntyre, 365 So 2d 1348 (La 1979) **§7.23**

State v McKeever, 339 Mo 1066, 101 SW2d 22 (1936) **§7.46**

State v McLamb, 313 NC 572, 330 SE2d 476 (1985) **§8.03**

State v Miller, 60 Idaho 79, 88 P2d 526 (1939) **§7.39**

State v Molasky, 655 SW2d 663 (Mo Ct App 1983) **§7.05**

State v Moore, 490 So 2d 556 (La Ct App 1986) **§8.06**

State v Morgan, 192 Wash 425, 73 P2d 745 (1937) **§9.16**

State v Morse, 35 SD 18, 150 NW 293 (1914) **§7.04**

State v Murray, 375 So 2d 80 (La 1979) **§7.46**

State v Neil, 457 So 2d 481 (Fla 1984) **§8.12**

State v Nolan, 341 So 2d 885 (La 1977) **§7.46**

State v Parry, 684 SW2d 441 (Mo Ct App 1984) **§7.50**

State v Ramirez, 116 Ariz 259, 569 P2d 201 (1977) **§7.46**

State v Raymond, 446 A2d 743 (RI 1982) **§8.12**

State v Reed, 629 SW2d 424 (Mo Ct App 1981) **§§7.01, 7.42**

State v Reynolds, 619 SW2d 741 (Mo 1981) **§8.02**

State v Rideau, 249 La 1111, 193 So 2d 264 (1966), *cert denied,* 389 US 861 (1967) **§7.44**

State v Riley, 151 W Va 364, 151 SE2d 308 (1966) **§7.18**

State v Riley, 605 P2d 765 (Utah 1980) **§7.46**

State v Rowe, 210 Neb 419, 315 SW2d 250 (1982) **§7.09**

State v Russell, 73 Mont 240, 235 P 712 (1925) **§7.19**

State v Sammons, 656 SW2d 862 (Tenn Crim App 1982) **§7.05**

State v Sellers, 257 SC 35, 183 SE2d 1889 (1971), *cert denied,* 410 US 908 (1973) **§7.44**

State v Skipper, 285 SC 42, 328 SE2d 58 (1985) **§7.51**

State v Sommer, 249 Iowa 160, 86 NW2d 115 (1957) **§7.23**

State v Sonnier, 379 So 2d 1336 (La 1979) **§7.31**

State v Square, 257 La 743, 244 So 2d 200 (1971), *vacated on other grounds,* 408 US 938 (1972) **§§7.44, 7.47**

State v Superior Ct, 157 Ariz 541, 760 P2d 541 (1988) **§8.06**

State v Sylvester, 400 So 2d 640 (La 1981) **§§7.13, 7.47, 7.52**

State v Talley, 22 SW2d 787 (Mo 1929) **§9.16**

State v Tauzier, 397 So 2d 494 (La 1981) **§7.50**

State v Taylor, 669 SW2d 694 (Tenn Crim App 1983) **§7.52**

State v Thorne, 41 Utah 414, 126 P 286 (1912) **§§7.06, 7.07**

State v Van Waters, 36 Wash 358, 78 P 897 (1904) **§7.19**

State v Vincent, 755 SW2d 400 (Mo Ct App 1988) **§8.06**

State v Warm, 92 Vt 447, 105 A 244 (1918) **§7.32**

State v Washington, 375 So 2d 1162 (La 1979) **§8.06**

State v West, 200 SE2d 859 (W Va 1973) **§7.05**

State v Wideman, 218 La 860, 51 So 2d 96 (1951) **§7.39**

State v Wilcox, 286 SE2d 257 (W Va 1982) **§7.22**

State v Williams, 650 SW2d 642 (Mo Ct App 1983) **§§7.23, 7.52**

State v Williams, 617 SW2d 98 (Mo Ct App 1981) **§7.46**

State v Williams, 606 SW2d 777 (Mo 1980) **§8.03**

State v Willmoth, 22 Wash App 419, 589 P2d 1270 (1979) **§1.08**

State v Woods, 662 SW2d 527 (Mo Ct App 1983) **§7.05**

State v Young, 643 SW2d 28 (Mo Ct App 1982) **§7.13**

State *ex rel* Douglas County v Sanders, 294 Or 195, 655 P2d 175 (1982) **§7.32**

State *ex rel* Perez v Wall, 41 Fla 463, 26 So 1020 (1899) **§7.29**

Stehura v Short, 39 Ohio App 2d 68, 315 NE2d 492 (1974) **§9.13**

Stephens v Smith, 208 SW2d 689 (Tex Civ App 1948) **§7.25**

Stevens v Burnhart, 412 A2d 1292 (Md Ct Spec App 1980) **§7.23**

Stillwell v Johnson, 272 P2d 365 (Okla 1954) **§9.10**

Stilson v United States, 250 US 583 (1919) **§§8.01, 8.02, 8.10**

Stokes v Delcambre, 710 F2d 1120 (5th Cir 1983) **§7.22**

Stoots v State, 108 Ind 415, 9 NE 380 (1886) **§§7.39, 7.46**

Strauder v West Virginia, 100 US 303 (1880) **§§2.07, 6.12, 6.15, 6.16, 6.18**

Strauss v Allstate Ins Co, 417 So 2d 60 (La Ct App 1982) **§7.50**

Strickland v Washington, 466 US 668 (1984) **§3.16**

Strobles v California, 343 US 181 (1952) **§2.05**

Stroud v United States, 251 US 380 (1920) **§7.05**

Sudds v Maggio, 696 F2d 415 (5th Cir 1983) **§7.13**

Sullins v State, 79 Ark 127, 95 SW 159 (1906) **§7.10**

Swain v Alabama, 380 US 202 (1965) **§§6.02, 6.12, 6.17, 6.19, 7.01, 8.01, 8.02, 8.03, 8.04, 8.05, 8.06, 8.07, 8.12**

Swallow v United States, 307 F2d 81 (10th Cir 1962), *cert denied,* 371 US 950 (1963) **§7.23**

Sydleman v Benson, 463 So 2d 533 (Fla Dist Ct App 1985) **§§7.22, 7.23**

T

Tanner v United States, 483 US 107 (1987) **§§2.09, 3.12**

Tate v People, 125 Colo 527, 247 P2d 665 (1952) **§7.26**

Tayloe v Commonwealth, 335 SW2d 556 (Ky Ct App 1960) **§7.24**

Taylor v Louisiana, 419 US 522 (1975) **§§2.07, 2.19, 6.02, 6.11, 6.13, 6.14, 6.15, 6.16, 6.19, 8.12**

Taylor v State, 243 Ga 222, 253 SE2d 191 (1979) **§7.30**

Teague v Lane, 820 F2d 832 (7th Cir 1987), *cert denied,* 108 S Ct 1106 (1988) **§8.12**

Tellefsen v Key Sys Transit Lines, 158 Cal App 2d 243, 322 P2d 469 (1958) **§§9.11, 9.13**

Temperley v Sarrington's Admr, 293 SW2d 863 (Ky Ct App 1956) **§9.16**

Test v United States, 420 US 28 (1975) **§4.05**

Theisen v Johns, 72 Mich 285, 40 NW 727 (1888) **§7.39**

Thiel v Southern Pac Co, 328 US 217 (1945) **§§2.09, 2.11, 6.02, 6.13, 6.16, 7.10, 8.12**

Thomas v State, 133 Ala 139, 32 So 250 (1902) **§7.31**

Thomas v Union Carbide Agric Prods Co, 473 US 568 (1985) **§1.14**

Thompson v Sawnee Elec Membership Corp, 157 Ga App 561, 278 SE2d 143 (1981) **§§7.25, 7.32**

Thompson v Utah, 170 US 343 (1898) **§2.13**

Thornburg v United States, 574 F2d 33 (1st Cir 1978) **§6.11**

Tidmore v Mills, 33 Ala App 243, 32 So 2d 769, *cert denied,* 249 Ala 648, 32 So 2d 782 (1947) **§7.30**

Tomlin v State, 81 Nev 620, 407 P2d 1020 (1965) **§7.26**

Tracy v Municipal Court, 22 Cal 3d 760, 597 P2d 227, 150 Cal Rptr 785 (1978) **§1.07**

Tubb v State, 109 Tex Crim 455, 5 SW2d 152 (1928) **§7.19**

Tull v United States, 481 US 412 (1983) **§1.14**

Turner v Fouche, 396 US 346 (1970) **§§2.07, 6.11, 6.12, 6.15, 6.19, 8.08**

Turner v Murray, 476 US 28 (1986) **§§7.42, 9.05**

Twitchell v Pennsylvania, 74 US (7 Wall) 321 (1868) **§§1.04, 1.08**

U

United States v Agurs, 427 US 97 (1976) **§4.10**

United States v Ainsworth, 716 F2d 769 (10th Cir 1983) **§9.05**

United States v Allsup, 566 F2d 68 (9th Cir 1977) **§§7.25, 7.47**

United States v Anderson, 509 F2d 312 (DC 1974), *cert denied,* 420 US 991 (1975) **§6.07**

United States v Andrews, 342 F Supp 1261 (D Mass), *revd on other grounds,* 462 F2d 914 (1st Cir 1972) **§6.16**

United States v Armsbury, 408 F Supp 1130 (D Or 1976) **§§6.01, 6.04, 6.08, 6.09, 6.11**

United States v Armstrong, 621 F2d 951 (9th Cir 1980) **§§3.16, 6.11**

United States v Arnett, 342 F Supp 1255 (D Mass 1970) **§6.11**

United States v Bagley, 473 US 667 (1985) **§4.10**

United States v Baldwin, 607 F2d 1295 (9th Cir 1979) **§7.30**

United States v Bamberger, 456 F2d 1119 (3d Cir), *cert denied,* 406 US 969 (1972), *cert denied,* 413 US 919 (1973) **§7.44**

United States v Barnes, 604 F2d 121 (2d Cir 1979), *cert denied,* 446 US 907 (1980) **§§4.05, 9.14**

United States v Barnette, 800 F2d 1558 (11th Cir 1986) **§6.06**

United States v Bascaro, 742 F2d 1335 (11th Cir 1984), *cert denied,* 417 US 1017 (1985) **§8.02**

United States v Battle, 836 F2d 1084 (8th Cir 1987) **§8.06**

United States v Bear Runner, 502 F2d 908 (8th Cir 1974) **§9.13**

United States v Bearden, 659 F2d 590 (5th Cir 1981), *cert denied,* 456 US 936 (1982) **§6.11**

United States v Bennett, 445 F2d 638 (9th Cir 1971), *cert denied,* 404 US 1023 (1972) **§6.08**

United States v Biaggi, 673 F Supp 96 (EDNY 1986), *affd,* 853 F2d 89 (2d Cir 1988) **§§8.07, 8.08**

United States v Blair, 493 F Supp 398 (D Md 1980), *affd,* 665 F2d 500 (4th Cir 1981) **§6.06**

United States v Blanton, 719 F2d 815 (6th Cir 1983), *cert denied,* 465 US 1099 (1984) **§8.02**

United States v Borger, 7 F 193 (NY Cir 1881) **§7.39**

United States v Boyd, 446 F2d 1267 (5th Cir 1971) **§7.25**

United States v Brady, 579 F2d 1121 (9th Cir 1978), *cert denied,* 439 US 1074 (1979) **§6.08**

United States v Briggs, 366 F Supp 1356 (ND Fla 1973) **§6.06**

United States v Brown, 644 F2d 101 (2d Cir), *cert denied,* 454 US 881 (1981) **§7.25**

United States v Brown, 817 F2d 674 (10th Cir 1987) **§8.07**

United States v Brown, 799 F2d 134 (4th Cir 1986) **§7.30**

United States v Brummitt, 665 F2d 521 (5th Cir 1981), *cert denied,* 456 US 977 (1982) **§§6.02, 6.08, 6.11**

United States v Bucci, 839 F2d 825 (1st Cir), *cert denied,* 109 S Ct 117 (1988) **§8.08**

United States v Burkett, 342 F Supp 1264 (D Mass 1972) **§6.08**

United States v Burr, 25 F Cas 49 (CCD Va 1807) (No 14, 692g) **§§2.11, 7.03, 7.06, 7.10**

United States v Butera, 420 F2d 564 (1st Cir 1970) **§6.09**

United States v Butler, 611 F2d 1066 (5th Cir), *cert denied,* 449 US 830 (1980) **§6.05**

United States v Cabrera-Sarmiento, 533 F Supp 799 (SD Fla 1982) **§6.07**

United States v Carolene Prods Co, 304 US 144 (1938) **§8.08**

United States v Caron, 552 F Supp 662 (ED Va 1982), *affd,* 722 F2d 739 (4th Cir 1983), *cert denied,* 465 US 1103 (1984) **§6.11**

United States v Chalan, 812 F2d 1302 (10th Cir 1987) **§§8.06, 8.08**

United States v Chapin, 515 F2d 1274 (DC Cir), *cert denied,* 423 US 1015 (1975) **§7.45**

United States v Childress, 715 F2d 1313 (8th Cir 1983) **§8.04**

United States v Clancy, 276 F2d 617 (7th Cir 1960) **§7.40**

United States v Clemons, 843 F2d 741 (3d Cir), *cert denied,* 109 S Ct 97 (1988) **§8.06**

United States v Coats, 611 F2d 37 (4th Cir 1979), *cert denied,* 446 US 909 (1980) **§6.08**

United States v Colabella, 448 F2d 1299 (2d Cir 1971), *cert denied,* 405 US 929 (1972) **§9.08**

United States v Corey, 625 F2d 704 (5th Cir 1980) **§7.05**

United States v Costello, 255 F2d 876 (2d Cir 1958) **§§4.05, 4.10**

United States v Cotton, No 68-CR-113 (ED Wis Sept 9, 1969) **§§2.03, 3.07, 7.10**

United States v Craner, 652 F2d 23 (9th Cir 1981) **§1.06**

United States v Cronic, 466 US 648 (1984) **§3.16**

United States v Daly, 716 F2d 1499 (9th Cir 1983) **§§7.25, 7.52**

United States v Dangler, 422 F2d 344 (5th Cir 1970) **§6.08**

United States v Danskar, 537 F2d 40 (3d Cir 1976), *cert denied,* 429 US 1038 (1977) **§9.08**

United States v David, 662 F Supp 244 (ND Ga 1987), *affd,* 844 F2d 767 (11th Cir 1988) **§§8.06, 8.07**

United States v Davis, 809 F2d 1194 (6th Cir 1987) **§8.07**

United States v Davis, 546 F2d 583 (5th Cir), *cert denied,* 431 US 906 (1977) **§§6.07, 6.11**

United States v De Alba-Conrado, 481 F2d 1266 (5th Cir 1973) **§6.11**

United States v Dellinger, 472 F2d 340 (7th Cir 1972), *cert denied,* 410 US 970 (1973) **§§6.08, 7.45, 9.05, 9.11, 9.13**

United States v DePugh, 452 F2d 915 (10th Cir 1971), *cert denied,* 407 US 920 (1972) **§9.12**

United States v Dioguardi, 492 F2d 70 (2d Cir), *cert denied,* 419 US 873 (1974) **§6.04**

United States v DiTommaso, 405 F2d 385 (4th Cir 1968), *cert denied,* 394 US 934 (1969) **§6.09**

United States v Dougherty, 473 F2d 1113 (DC Cir 1972) **§2.20**

United States v Driscoll, 276 F Supp 333 (SDNY 1967) **§3.12**

United States v Duff, 6 F 45 (NY Cir 1881) **§7.39**

United States v Duke, 263 F Supp 828 (SD Ind 1967) **§6.09**

United States v Duncan, 456 F2d 1401 (9th Cir 1972) **§6.04**

United States v Durant, 545 F2d 823 (2d Cir 1976) **§3.16**

United States v Eskew, 460 F2d 1028 (9th Cir 1972) **§6.06**

United States v Espinoza, 771 F2d 1382 (10th Cir 1985) **§7.46**

United States v Facchiano, 500 F Supp 896 (SD Fla 1980) **§6.08**

United States v Falange, 426 F2d 930 (2d Cir), *cert denied,* 400 US 906 (1970) **§4.10**

United States v Forbes, 816 F2d 1006 (5th Cir 1987) **§8.07**

United States v Foxworth, 599 F2d 1 (1st Cir 1979) **§§6.04, 6.11, 6.12, 6.13**

United States v Franklin, 700 F2d 1241 (10th Cir 1983) **§7.19**

United States v Franklin, 471 F2d 1299 (5th Cir 1973) **§8.02**

United States v Franks, 511 F2d 25 (6th Cir), *cert denied,* 422 US 1042 (1975) **§3.14**

United States v Freeman, 514 F2d 171 (8th Cir 1975) **§6.08**

United States v Garrison, 849 F2d 103 (4th Cir 1988) **§8.07**

United States v Golden, 532 F2d 1244 (9th Cir 1976) **§7.46**

United States v Gometz, 730 F2d 475 (7th Cir 1984), *cert denied,* 475 US 1124 (1986) **§§6.01, 6.07, 6.09, 6.10**

United States v Goodlow, 597 F2d 159 (9th Cir), *cert denied,* 442 US 913 (1979) **§§6.05, 6.06**

United States v Gordon-Nikkar, 518 F2d 972 (5th Cir 1975) **§6.04**

United States v Graham, 739 F2d 351 (8th Cir 1984) **§7.28**

United States v Green, 742 F2d 918 (11th Cir 1984) **§6.11**

United States v Grey, 355 F Supp 529 (D Okla 1973) **§6.06**

United States v Hafon, 726 F2d 21 (1st Cir), *cert denied,* 466 US 962 (1984) **§6.11**

United States v Haley, 521 F Supp 290 (ND Ga 1981) **§6.11**

United States v Hamdan, 552 F2d 276 (9th Cir 1977) **§1.07**

United States v Hamilton, 850 F2d 1038 (4th Cir 1988) **§§8.08, 8.12**

United States v Hanson, 618 F2d 1261 (8th Cir), *cert denied,* 449 US 854 (1980) **§6.08**

United States v Hanson 472 F Supp 1049 (D Minn 1979) **§§6.01, 6.09**

United States v Harris, 542 F2d 1283 (7th Cir 1976) **§4.10**

United States v Hawkins, 781 F2d 1483 (11th Cir 1986) **§8.07**

United States v Hawkins, 566 F2d 1006 (5th Cir), *cert denied,* 439 US 848 (1978) **§§6.07, 6.11**

United States v Hill, 738 F2d 152 (6th Cir 1984) **§7.09**

United States v Homer, 411 F Supp 972 (WD Pa 1976), *affd,* 545 F2d 864 (3d Cir), *cert denied,* 431 US 954 (1977) **§3.12**

United States v Horton, 526 F2d 884 (5th Cir), *cert denied,* 429 US 820 (1976) **§6.06**

United States v Hyde, 448 F2d 815 (5th Cir 1971), *cert denied,* 404 US 1058 (1972) **§§6.09, 6.10, 6.11**

United States v Ible, 630 F2d 389 (5th Cir 1980) **§§7.39, 7.40, 9.07**

United States v Jackson, 696 F2d 578 (8th Cir 1982), *cert denied,* 460 US 1073 (1983) **§§8.07, 8.09**

United States v Jackson, 542 F2d 403 (7th Cir 1976) **§7.47**

United States v Jenison, 485 F Supp 655 (SD Fla 1979) **§§6.02, 6.11**

United States v Jenkins, 496 F2d 57 (2d Cir 1974), *cert denied,* 420 US 925 (1975) **§6.17**

United States v Jones, 687 F2d 1265 (8th Cir 1982) **§6.11**

United States v Kennedy, 548 F2d 608 (5th Cir), *cert denied,* 434 US 865 (1977) **§6.07, 6.08, 6.11**

United States v King, 492 F2d 895 (8th Cir 1974) **§6.08**

United States v Kronke, 321 F Supp 913 (D Minn 1970) **§§6.01, 6.08**

United States v Kuhn, 441 F2d 179 (5th Cir 1971) **§6.08**

United States v Kyle, 469 F2d 547 (DC Cir 1972), *cert denied,* 409 US 1117 (1973) **§4.04**

United States v La Chance, 788 F2d 856 (5th Cir 1986) **§6.11**

United States v Layton, 519 F Supp 946 (ND Cal 1981) **§6.11**

United States v Ledee, 549 F2d 990 (5th Cir), *cert denied,* 434 US 902 (1977) **§9.07**

United States v Lee, 532 F2d 911 (3d Cir), *cert denied,* 429 US 838 (1976) **§8.13**

United States v Leonetti, 291 F Supp 461 (SDNY 1968) **§6.06**

United States v Lewin, 467 F2d 1132 (7th Cir 1972) **§7.01**

United States v Lewis, 504 F2d 92 (6th Cir 1974), *cert denied,* 421 US 975 (1975) **§§6.06, 6.07**

United States v Liddy, 509 F2d 428 (DC Cir 1974), *cert denied,* 420 US 911 (1975) **§7.01**

United States v Malinowski, 347 F Supp 347 (ED Pa 1972), *affd,* 472 F2d 850 (3d Cir), *cert denied,* 411 US 970 (1973) **§7.45**

United States v Manbeck, 514 F Supp 141 (DSC 1981) **§6.05**

United States v Marcano, 508 F Supp 462 (DPR 1980) **§§6.07, 6.11**

United States v Marcello, 280 F Supp 510 (ED La 1968), *affd,* 423 F2d 983 (5th Cir), *cert denied,* 398 US 959 (1970) **§2.05**

United States v Marchant, 25 US (12 Wheat) 297 (1827) **§§8.01, 8.02**

United States v Marchant, 774 F2d 888 (8th Cir 1985) **§7.51**

United States v Maskeny, 609 F2d 183 (5th Cir 1980) **§6.05**

United States v Mathews, 803 F2d 325 (7th Cir 1986), *revd on other grounds,* 485 US 58 (1988) **§8.07**

United States v Matthews, 350 F Supp 1103 (D Del 1972) **§6.11**

United States v McAlister, 630 F2d 772 (10th Cir 1980) **§1.07**

United States v McCord, 695 F2d 823 (5th Cir 1983) **§7.52**

United States v McCoy, 848 F2d 743 (6th Cir 1988) **§8.07**

United States v McIver, 688 F2d 726 (11th Cir 1982) **§7.19**

United States v McVean, 436 F2d 1120 (5th Cir), *cert denied,* 404 US 822 (1971) **§6.16**

United States v Mesarosh, 116 F Supp 3435 (W D Pa 1953), *affd,* 223 F2d 449 (3d Cir 1955), *revd,* 352 US 1 (1956) **§7.10**

United States v Miller, 284 F Supp 220 (D Conn 1968), *appeal dismissed,* 403 F2d 77 (2d Cir 1968) **§§3.12, 3.14**

United States v Montgomery, 819 F2d 847 (8th Cir 1987) **§8.07**

United States v Morris, 623 F2d 145 (10th Cir 1980) **§8.03**

United States v Musto, 540 F Supp 346 (DNJ 1982), *affd,* 715 F2d 822 (3d Cir 1983), *cert denied,* 468 US 1217 (1984) **§6.11**

United States v Napoleone, 349 F2d 350 (7th Cir 1965) **§7.46**

United States v Nelson, 718 F2d 315 (9th Cir 1983) **§§6.07, 6.11**

United States v Noelke, 1 F 426 (NY Cir 1880) **§7.39**

United States v Okiyama, 521 F2d 601 (9th Cir 1975) **§6.04**

United States v Olson, 473 F2d 686 (8th Cir), *cert denied,* 412 US 905 (1973) **§6.16**

United States v Owen, 492 F2d 1100 (5th Cir), *cert denied,* 419 US 965 (1974) **§6.16**

United States v Parisi, 365 F2d 601 (6th Cir 1966), *vacated on other grounds,* 386 US 345 (1967) **§7.26**

United States v Parker, 428 F2d 488 (9th Cir), *cert denied,* 400 US 910 (1970) **§6.08**

United States v Pellegrini, 441 F Supp 1367 (ED Pa 1977), *affd,* 586 F2d 836 (3d Cir), *cert denied,* 439 US 1050 (1978) **§6.04**

United States v Percival, 756 F2d 600 (7th Cir 1985) **§6.11**

United States v Perez-Hernandez, 672 F2d 1380 (11th Cir 1982) **§6.02**

United States v Perry, 480 F2d 147 (5th Cir 1973) **§§6.04, 6.16**

United States v Peterson, 483 F2d 1222 (DC Cir), *cert denied,* 414 US 1007 (1973) **§9.13**

United States v Phillips, 577 F2d 688 (10th Cir 1978) **§7.19**

United States v Pope, 251 F Supp 234 (D Neb 1966) **§3.16**

United States v Pyle, 518 F Supp 139 (ED Pa 1981) **§1.08**

United States v Raineri, 670 F2d 702 (7th Cir), *cert denied,* 450 US 1035 (1982) **§6.11**

United States v Robinson, 421 F Supp 467 (D Conn 1976), *mandamus granted sub nom* United States v Newman, 549 F2d 240 (2d Cir 1977) **§8.11**

United States v Ross, 468 F2d 1213 (9th Cir 1972), *cert denied,* 410 US 989 (1973) **§§6.04, 6.06, 6.08**

United States v Ross, 203 F Supp 100 (ED Pa 1962) **§7.51**

United States v Rucker, 557 F2d 1046 (4th Cir 1977) **§7.50**

United States v Salamone, 800 F2d 1216 (3d Cir 1986) **§7.47**

United States v Sanchez-Mesa, 547 F2d 461 (9th Cir 1976) **§1.06**

United States v Santos, 588 F2d 1300 (9th Cir), *cert denied,* 441 US 906 (1979) **§§6.10, 6.11**

United States v Savides, 787 F2d 751 (1st Cir 1986) **§§6.02, 6.11**

United States v Scott, 437 US 82 (1978) **§2.20**

United States v Segal, 534 F2d 578 (3d Cir 1976) **§9.11**

United States v Silverman, 449 F2d 1341 (2d Cir 1971), *cert denied,* 405 US 918 (1972) **§6.11**

United States v 662.44 Acres of Land, More or Less, 45 F Supp 895 (DDC 1942) **§7.20**

United States v Spaar, 748 F2d 1249 (8th Cir 1984) **§7.46**

United States v Starks, 515 F2d 112 (3d Cir 1975), *affd in pt, revd in pt,* 431 US 651 (1977) **§9.06**

United States v Tarnowski, 429 F Supp 783 (ED Mich 1977), *affd,* 583 F2d 903 (6th Cir 1978), *cert denied,* 440 US 918 (1979) **§6.11**

United States v Tegzes, 715 F2d 505 (11th Cir 1983) **§7.50**

United States v Test, 550 F2d 577 (10th Cir 1976) **§§6.02, 6.08, 6.11**

United States v Thompson, 827 F2d 1254 (9th Cir 1987) **§8.07**

United States v Tropiano, 418 F2d 1069 (2d Cir 1969), *cert denied,* 397 US 1021 (1970) **§6.09**

United States v Turner, 558 F2d 535 (9th Cir 1977) **§8.11**

United States v Valentine, 472 F2d 164 (9th Cir 1973) **§6.06**

United States v Warlick, 742 F2d 113 (4th Cir 1984) **§4.04**

United States v Warner, 690 F2d 545 (6th Cir 1982) **§7.50**

United States v Wellington, 754 F2d 1457 (9th Cir 1985) **§6.11**

United States v Wesivich, 666 F2d 984 (5th Cir 1982) **§6.08**

United States v White, 750 F2d 726 (8th Cir 1983) **§9.05**

United States v Whiting, 538 F2d 220 (8th Cir 1976) **§4.05**

United States v Whitley, 491 F2d 1248 (8th Cir), *cert denied,* 416 US 990 (1974) **§6.17**

United States v Williams, 822 F2d 512 (5th Cir 1987) **§8.06**

United States v Williams, 463 F2d 393 (10th Cir 1972) **§8.02**

United States v Wilson, 853 F2d 606 (8th Cir 1988) **§8.06**

United States v Wonson, 28 F Cas 745 (CCD Mass 1812) (No 16, 750) **§1.14**

United States v Woods, 812 F2d 1483 (4th Cir 1987) **§8.06**

United States v Woods, 299 US 123 (1936) **§2.07**

United States Fin Sec Litig, *In re,* 609 F2d 411 (9th Cir 1979), *cert denied,* 446 US 929 (1980) **§1.16**

V

Vaise v Delaval, 99 Eng Rep 944 (1785) **§§2.09, 3.12**

Van Dusen v Barrack, 376 US 612 (1964) **§2.06**

Van Skike v Potter, 53 Neb 28, 73 NW 295 (1897) **§7.40**

Vasquez v Hillery, 474 US 254 (1986) **§§6.01, 6.12, 6.19**

Virginia v Rives, 100 US 313 (1879) **§2.07**

W

Wagner Elec Corp v Snowden, 38 F2d 599 (8th Cir 1930) **§7.33**

Wainwright v Witt, 469 US 412 (1985) **§2.22**

Walker v Savinet, 92 US 90 (1876) **§§1.09, 1.18, 2.13**

Wallace v Kemp, 581 F Supp 1471 (MD Ga 1984), *revd on other grounds,* 757 F2d 1102 (11th Cir 1985) **§7.44**

Wallace v State, 248 Ga 255, 282 SE2d 325 (1981), *cert denied,* 455 US 977 (1982) **§7.44**

Ward v Commonwealth, 695 SW2d 404 (Ky 1985) **§7.30**

Warden v State, 214 Tenn 398, 381 SW2d 247 (1964) **§7.18**

Washington v City of Seattle, 170 Wash 371, 16 P2d 597 (1932) **§7.25**

Wasy v State, 234 Ind 52, 123 NE2d 462 (1955) **§7.40**

Welch v City of Birmingham, 389 So 2d 521 (Ala Crim App 1980) **§7.25**

Whitney v Louisville & NR Co, 296 Ky 381, 177 SW2d 139 (1944) **§7.28**

Whitus v Georgia, 385 US 545 (1967) **§§6.18, 6.19, 8.05**

Wilburn v United States, 340 A2d 810 (DC App 1975) **§7.23**

Wilkes v United States, 291 F 988 (6th Cir 1923), *cert denied,* 263 US 719 (1924) **§7.19**

Williams v Florida, 399 US 78 (1970) **§§2.02, 2.13, 2.17, 4.10**

Williams v Layne, 53 Cal App 2d 81, 127 P2d 582 (1942) **§7.33**

Williams v Martin, 618 F2d 1021 (4th Cir 1980) **§3.16**

Williams v State, 682 SW2d 538 (Tex Crim App 1984) **§7.05**

Williams v Texas City Ref, Inc, 617 SW2d 823 (Tex Civ App 1981) **§7.14**

Wilson v State, 250 Ga 630, 300 SE2d 640 (1983) **§7.52**

Winship, *In re,* 397 US 358 (1970) **§§2.10, 2.17**

Witherspoon v Illinois, 391 US 510 (1968) **§§7.53, 8.13**

Witt v Roper, 150 Kan 722, 96 P2d 643 (1939) **§7.33**

Words v State, 367 So 2d 974, *revd,* 367 So 2d 982 (Ala 1978) **§7.22**

Y

Yarborough v United States, 230 F2d 56 (4th Cir), *cert denied,* 351 US 969 (1956) **§7.40**

Young v State, 41 Okla Crim 226, 271 P 426 (1928) **§7.40**

Z

Zarate v Villareal, 155 SW 328 (Tex Civ App 1913) **§7.31**

Zein v Pickel Stone Co, 273 SW 165 (Mo Ct App 1925) **§7.23**

Zimmerer v Prudential Ins Co, 150 Neb 351, 34 NW2d 750 (1948) **§7.29**

Zartman v State, 667 P2d 1256 (Alaska Ct App 1983) **§7.19**

Authorities

Books and Periodicals

A

Adler, *Socioeconomic Factors Influencing Jury Verdicts*, 3 NYU Rev L & Soc Change 1 (1973) **§2.12**

T. Adorno, E. Frenkel-Brunswick, D. Levision & R. Sanford, The Authoritarian Personality (1950) **§12.15**

J. Alexander, A Brief Narration of the Case and Trial of John Peter Zenger (1963) **§§1.03, 2.20**

Alshculer, *The Supreme Court and the Jury: Voir dire, Peremptory Challenges, and the Review of Jury Verdicts*, 56 U Chi L Rev 153 (1989) **§3.12**

American Bar Association Advisory Comm on Fair Trial and Free Press, Standards Relating to Fair Trial and Free Press (1968) **§7.10**

American Bar Association Standards for Criminal Justice (2d ed 1980) **§§1.23, 2.03, 4.05**

47 Am Jur 2d *Jury* §265 (1969) **§7.02**

24 Am Jur 2d *Divorce and Separation* §335 (1966) **§10.15**

Annotation, *Additional Peremptory Challenges Because of Multiple Criminal Charges*, 5 ALR4th 533 (1970) **§8.02**

Annotation, *Alternate Jurors in Federal Trials Under Rule 24(c) of Federal Rules of Criminal Procedure or Rule 47(b) of Federal Rules of Civil Procedure*, 10 ALR Fed 185 (1972) **§8.02**

Annotation, *Claustrophobia or Other Neurosis of Juror as Subject of Inquiry on Voir Dire or of Disqualification of Juror*, 20 ALR3d 1420 (1968) **§7.51**

Annotation, *Competency of Juror as Affected By His Membership in Co-operative Association Interested in the Case*, 69 ALR3d 1296 (1976) **§7.47**

Annotation, *Distribution and Exercise of Peremptory Challenges in Federal Civil Cases Under 28 USC §1870*, 50 ALR Fed 350 (1980) **§8.02**

Annotation, *Effect of Juror's False or Erroneous Answer on Voir Dire as to Previous Claims or Actions Against*

Himself or His Family, 63 ALR2d 1061 (1959) **§9.10**

Annotation, *Effect Upon Accused's Sixth Amendment Right to Impartial Jury of Jurors Having Served on Jury Hearing Matter Arising Out of Same Transaction or Series of Transactions,* 68 ALR Fed 919 (1984) **§7.19**

Annotation, *Failure of Juror in Criminal Case to Disclose His Previous Jury Service Within Disqualifying Period as Ground for Reversal or New Trial,* 13 ALR2d 1482 (1950) **§7.17**

Annotation, *Former Law Enforcement Officers as Qualified Jurors in Criminal Cases,* 72 ALR3d 958 (1976) **§7.52**

Annotation, *Juror's Presence at or Participation in Trial of Criminal Case(or Related Hearing) as Ground for Disqualification in Subsequent Criminal Case Involving Same Defendant,* 6 ALR3d 519 (1966) **§§7.18, 7.20**

Annotation, *Juror's Previous Knowledge of Facts of Civil Case as Disqualification,* 73 ALR2d 1312 (1960) **§7.16**

Annotation, *Juror's Relationship to Witness, in Civil Case, as Ground of Disqualification or for Reversal or New Trial,* 85 ALR2d 851 (1962) **§7.30**

Annotation, *Juror's Voir Dire Denial or Nondisclosure of Acquaintance or Relationship With Attorney in Case, or With Partner or Associate of Such Attorney, as Ground for New Trial or Mistrial,* 64 ALR2d 126 (1975) **§7.27**

Annotation, *Jury: Membership in Racially Biased or Prejudiced Organization as Proper Subject of Voir Dire Inquiry or Ground for Challenge,* 63 ALR3d 1052 (1975) **§7.44**

Annotation, *Jury: Number of Peremptory Challenges Allowable in Civil Case Where There are More Than Two Parties Involved,* 32 ALR3d 747 (1970) **§8.02**

Annotation, *Jury: Number of Peremptory Challenges Allowed in Criminal Case Where There are Two or More Defendants Tried Together,* 21 ALR3d 725 (1968) **§8.02**

Annotation, *Law Enforcement Officers as Qualified Jurors in Criminal Cases,* 72 ALR3d 895 (1976) **§7.52**

Annotation, *Number of, and Manner of Exercising, Peremptory Challenges in Federal Criminal Trials Subsequent to Promulgation of Rule 24(b) of Federal Rules of Criminal Procedure,* 11 ALR Fed 713 (1972) **§8.02**

Annotation, *Prior Jury Service on Grand Jury Which Considered Indictment Against Accused as Disqualification for Service on Petit Jury,* 24 ALR3d 1236 (1969) **§7.18**

Annotation, *Professional or Business Relations Between Proposed Juror and Attorney as Ground for Challenge for Cause,* 52 ALR4th 965 (1987) **§7.27**

Annotation, *Professional or Business Relations Between Proposed Juror and Attorney as Ground for Challenge for Cause,* 72 ALR2d 673 (1960) **§7.27**

Annotation, *Propriety and Effect of Asking Prospective Jurors Hypothetical Questions, on Voir Dire, as to How They Would Decide Issues in Case,* 99 ALR2d 7 (1965) **§§7.46, 9.15**

Annotation, *Propriety, on Voir Dire in Criminal Case, of Inquiries as to Juror's Possible Prejudice If Informed of Defendant's Prior Convictions,* 43 ALR3d 1081 (1972) **§7.46**

Annotation, *Racial or Ethnic Prejudice of Prospective Jurors as Proper Subject of Inquiry or Ground of Challenge on Voir Dire in State Criminal Case,* 94 ALR3d 15 (1979) **§7.41**

Annotation, *Racial, Religious, Economic, Social, or Political Prejudice of Proposed Juror as Proper Subject of Inquiry or ground of challenge on Voir Dire in Civil Case,* 72 ALR2d 905 (1960) **§§7.24, 7.38, 7.39, 7.45**

Annotation, *Racial, Religious, Economic, Social, or Political Prejudice of Proposed Juror as Proper Subject of Inquiry or Ground of Challenge on Voir Dire in Criminal Case,* 54 AR2d 1204 (1957) **§§7.39, 7.45**

Annotation, *Religious Belief, Affiliation, or Prejudice of Prospective Juror as Proper Subject of Inquiry or Ground for Challenge on Voir Dire,* 95 ALR3d 172 (1979) **§7.40**

Annotation, *Right of Counsel in Criminal Case to Conduct the Voir Dire Examination of Prospective Jurors,* 73 ALR2d 1187 (1960) **§§9.05, 9.08**

Annotation, *Similarity of Occupation Between Proposed Juror and Alleged Victim of Crime as Affecting Juror's Competency,* 71 ALR3d 974 (1976) **§7.12**

Annotation, *Social or Business Relationship Between Proposed Juror and Nonparty Witness as Affecting Former's Qualification as Juror,* 11 ALR3d 859 (1967) **§§7.23, 7.26**

Annotation, *Statutory Grounds for Challenge of Jurors for Cause as Exclusive of Common-Law Grounds,* 64 ALR 645 (1929) **§7.04**

Annotation, *Use of Peremptory Challenge to Exclude from Jury Persons Belonging to a Class or Race,* 79 ALR3d 14 (1977) **§8.04**

Annotation, *Validity and Construction of Statute or Court Rule Prescribing Number of Peremptory Challenges in Criminal Cases According to Nature of Offense or Extent of Punishment,* 8 ALR4th 149 (1981) **§8.02**

Annotation, *Voir Dire Examination of Prospective Jurors Under Rule 24(a) Federal Rules of Criminal Procedure,* 28 ALR Fed 26 (1976) **§§7.40, 7.44**

Annotation, *Voir Dire Inquiry, in Personal Injury or Death Case, as to Prospective Jurors' Acquaintance With Literature Dealing With Amounts of Verdicts,* 89 ALR2d 1177 (1963) **§7.11**

Argyle & Dean, *Eye Contact, Distance, and Affiliation,* 28 Sociometry 289 (1965) **§12.10**

Arnold, *A Historical Inquiry into the Right to Trial by Jury in Complex Civil Litigation,* 128 U Pa L Rev 829 (1980) **§1.16**

Asch, *Effects of Group Pressure Upon the Modification and Distortion of Judgments, reprinted in* Groups, Leadership, & Men (H. Guetzkow ed 1951) **§2.16**

B

Babcock, *Voir Dire: Preserving "Its Wonderful Power",* 27 Stan L Rev 545 (1975) **§§8.01, 8.14**

F. Bailey & H. Rothblatt, Successful Techniques for Criminal Trials (1971) **§§9.09, 9.16, 12.05**

M. Belli, Modern Trials (1954) **§9.09**

W. Blackstone, Commentaries **§8.01**

Blinder, *Picking Juries,* 1 Trial Dipl 8 (1978) **§12.07**

M. Bloomstein, Verdict: The Jury System (1968) **§§1.02, 1.20**

Blume, *The Place of Trial of Criminal Cases: Constitutional Vicinage and Venue,* 43 Mich L Rev 59 (1944) **§2.02**

Boehm, *Mr. Prejudice, Miss Sympathy and the Authoritarian Personality: An Application of Psychological Measuring Techniques to the Problem of Jury Bias,* 1968 Wis L Rev 734 **§§2.12, 12.15, 12.16**

Bray & Noble, *Authoritarianism and Decisions of Mock Juries: Evidence of Jury Bias and Group Polarization, in* L. Wrightsman, S. Kassin, & C. Willis, In the Jury Box 83 (1987) **§12.15**

Broeder, *The Negro in Court,* 1965 Duke LJ (1965) **§2.12**

Broeder, *Occupational Expertise and Bias as Affecting Juror Behavior: A Preliminary Look,* 40 NYU L Rev 1079 (1969) **§2.12**

Broeder, *Voir Dire Examinations: An Empirical Study,* 38 S Cal L Rev 503 (1965) **§§8.14, 9.04, 12.08, 12.14**

Brown, McGuire, & Winters, *The Peremptory Challenge as a Manipulative Device in Criminal Trials: Traditional Use or Abuse,* 14 NE L Rev 192 **§8.04**

Buckhout, Licker, Alexander, Gambardella, Eugenio, & Kakoullis, *Discretion in Jury Selection, in* L. Abt & I. Stuart, Social Psychology and Discretionary Law 176 (1979) **§§2.12, 2.21**

C

Call, *Psychology in Litigation,* 21 Trial 48 (Mar 1958) **§12.02**

Campbell & Le Poidwin, *Complex Cases and Jury Trials: A Reply to Professor Arnold,* 128 U Pa L Rev 965 (1980) **§1.16**

Campbell, *The Multiple Functions of the Criminal Defense Voir Dire in Texas,* 1 Am J Crim L 255 (1972) **§9.04**

Chambers, *Who Should Pick Jurors, Attorneys or the Judge,* NY Times, June 13, 1983, at B4 **§9.01**

E. Coke, Commentary Upon Littleton Section 1556 (9th ed London 1832) **§2.10**

Comment, *A Case Study of the Peremptory Challenge: A Subtle Strike at Equal Protection and Due Process,* 18 St Louis U LJ 662 (1974) **§8.04**

Comment, *Constitutional Law: The Complexity Exception and the Seventh Amendment,* 20 Washburn LJ 153 (1980) **§1.16**

Comment, *Swain v Alabama: A Constitutional Blueprint for the Perpetuation of the All-White Jury,* 52 Va L Rev 1157 (1966) **§8.04**

Corboy, *Structuring the Presentation of Proof or Evidence,* Trial Dipl J 20 (Summer 1978) **§12.18**

W. Cornish, The Jury (1968) **§1.01**

Cowan, Thompson, & Ellsworth, *The Effects of Death Qualification on Jurors' Predisposition to Convict and on The Quality of Deliberation,* 8 Law & Hum Behav 53 (1984) **§7.53**

D

Darrow, *Attorney for the Defense,* 8 Esquire 35 (1936) **§12.05**

Davis, *Black Juror,* 30 Guild Prac 112, *quoted in* V. Hans & N. Vidmar, Judging the Jury (1986) **§2.08**

P. DiPerna, Juries on Trial (1984) **§2.16**

Dubois, *Desirability of Blue Ribbon Juries,* 13 Hastings LJ 479 (1962) **§7.10**

E

Eastman, *The History of Trial by Jury,* 3 Natl BJ 87 (1945) **§1.02**

Effran, *Looking for Approval: Effects on Visual Behavior of Approbation From Persons Differing in Importance,* 10 J Personality & Soc Psychology 21 (1968) **§12.10**

Ekman, Differential Communication of Affect by Head and Body Cues, 2 J Personality & Soc Psychology 726 (1965) **§12.11**

Ekman & Friesen, *Hand Movements,* 22 J Comm 353 (1972) **§12.11**

Ekman & Friesen, *Head and Body Cues in the Judgment of Emotion: A Reformation,* 24 Perceptual & Motor Skills 711 (1967) **§12.11**

Ekman & Friesen, *Nonverbal Leakage and Clues to Deception,* 32 Psychology 88 (1968) **§12.09**

Eldred & Price, *A Linguistic Evaluation of Feeling States in Psychotherapy,* 21 Psychology 115 (1958) **§12.12**

H. Ellenberger, The Discovery of the Unconscious (1970) **§2.12**

F

Finkelstein, *The Application of Statistical Decision Theory to Jury Discrimination Cases,* 80 Harv L Rev 338 (1966) **§6.17**

W. Forsyth, The History of Trial by Jury (1852) **§§1.02, 2.07, 2.13**

J. Frank, Courts on Trial (1949) **§§1.01, 2.12**

Frankfurter & Corcoran, *Petty Federal Offenses and the Constitutional Guaranty of Trial by Jury,* 39 Harv L Rev 917 (1926) **§1.06**

Frederick, *Jury Behavior: A Psychologist Examines Jury Selection,* 5 Ohio NUL Rev 571 (1978) **§12.06**

S. Freud, The Psychotherapy of Everyday Life (Brill ed 1948) **§2.12**

L. Frey-Robin, From Freud to Jung: A Comparative Study of the Psychology of the Unconscious (1950) **§2.12**

G

Gidmark, *The Verdict on Surrogate Jury Research,* ABAJ 82 (Mar 1, 1988) **§5.02**

A. Ginger, Jury Selection in Civil & Criminal Trials (2d ed 1984) **§§2.03, 2.21, 3.07, 4.03, 7.10**

Gobert, *The Peremptory Challenge—An Obituary,* 1989 Crim L Rev 528 **§8.01**

Gobert, *In Search of the Impartial Jury,* 79 J Crim L & Criminology 269 (1988) **§§2.09, 2.22, 8.13**

Goldberg, *Toward Expansion of Witherspoon; Capital Scruples, Jury Bias, and Use of Psychological Data to Raise Presumptions in the Law,* 5

Harv CR-CL L Rev 53 (1970) **§7.53**

Goldwasser, *Limiting a Criminal Defendant's Use of Peremptory Challenges: On Symmetry and the Jury in a Criminal Trial,* 102 Harv L Rev 808 (1989) **§8.09**

G. Groddick, Exploring the Unconscious (1950) **§2.12**

Gutman, *The Attorney-Conducted Voir Dire of Jurors: A Constitutional Right,* 39 Brooklyn L Rev 290 (1972) **§9.07**

H

Hatchell, *A View from the Defense Bar: Insurance Advertising—Much Ado About Nothing,* 10 St Mary's LJ 427 (1979) **§7.34**

F. Heller, The Sixth Amendment to the Constitution (1969) **§§1.02, 1.03, 1.09**

Hepburn, *The Objective Reality of Evidence and the Utility of Systematic Jury Selection,* 43 Law & Hum Behav 89 (1980) **§2.12**

Hermann, *Occupations of Jurors as an Influence on Their Verdict,* 5 Forum 150 (1970) **§§2.12, 12.06**

Hittner, *Federal Voir Dire and Jury Selection: An Alternative View,* Trial (March 1989) **§9.01**

Howe, *Juries as Judges of Criminal Law,* 52 Harv L Rev 582 (1939) **§1.03**

Hunt, *Putting Juries on the Couch,* NY Times, Nov 28, 1982 (Magazine) **§5.05**

J

J. Spencer, Jackson's Machinery of Justice (1989) **§1.01**

James, *Status and Competence of Jurors,* 64 Am J Soc 563 (1959) **§2.12**

Johnson, *Black Innocence and the White Jury,* 83 Mich L Rev 1611 (1985) **§8.04**

C. Jung, Psychology of the Unconscious (1950) **§2.12**

Jurow, *New Data on the Effect of a "Death Qualified" Jury on the Guilt Determination Process,* 84 Harv L Rev 567 (1971) **§7.53**

K

Kairys, Kadane, & Lehoczky, *Jury Representativeness: A Mandate for Multiple Source Lists,* 65 Cal L Rev 776 (1977) **§§6.01, 6.07**

H. Kalven & H. Zeisel, The American Jury (1966) **§§1.23, 2.12, 2.16, 2.17**

B. Keeney, Judgement by Peers (1952) **§2.07**

R. Keeton, Trial Tactics and Methods (1954) **§§1.23, 12.05**

Kershen, *Vicinage,* 29 Okla L Rev 803 (1976), 30 Okla L Rev 1 (1977) **§2.02**

Kronzer, *A View from the Plaintiff's Bar: Jury Tampering—1978 Style,* 10 St Mary's LJ 399 (1979) **§7.34**

L

2 W. LaFave & J. Israel, Criminal Procedure (1984) **§§1.23, 4.05**

W. LaFave & A. Scott, Criminal Law (2d ed 1986) **§1.06**

Larue, *A Jury of One's Peers,* 33 Wash & Lee L Rev 841 (1976) **§2.07**

N. Lefstein, Criminal Defense Services for the Poor (1982) **§3.17**

Lempert, *Civil Juries and Complex Cases: Let's Not Rush to Judgment,* 80 Mich L Rev 68 (1981) **§1.16**

M

Margolin, *The Indigent Criminal Defendant and Defense Services: A Search for Constitutional Standards,* 647 Hastings LJ 24 (1973) **§3.16**

Marshall, *The Judgement of One's Peers: Some Aims and Ideals of Jury Trial, in* N. Walker, The British Jury System (1974) **§2.07**

McConahy, Mullin & Frederick, *The Uses of Social Science in Trials with Political Overtones: The Trial of Joan Little,* 41 Law & Contemp Probs 205 (Autumn 1977) **§2.05**

Mehrabian, *Nonverbal Communication,* 19 Neb Symp on Motivation 197 (1971) **§12.11**

Mehrabian, *Significance of Posture and Position in the Communication of Attitude and Status Relationships,* 71 Psychology Bull 359 (1969) **§12.11**

Mehrabian & Wiener, *Decoding of Inconsistent Communications,* 6 J Personality & Soc Psychology 109 (1967) **§12.09**

Mitchell & Byrne, *The Defendant's Dilemma: Effects of Jurors' Attitudes and Authoritarianism on Judicial Decisions,* 25 J Personality & Soc Psychology 123 (1973) **§12.15**

L. Moore, The Jury: Tool of Kings, Palladium of Liberty (1973) **§§1.02, 1.03**

N

National Jury Project, Jurywork (2d ed 1987) **§§2.05, 3.01, 3.03, 3.05, 3.07, 3.16, 3.17, 5.05**

Note, *Batson v Kentucky: The New and Improved Peremptory Challenge,* 38 Hastings LJ 1195 (1987) **§8.11**

Note, *The Blue Ribbon Jury,* 60 Harv L Rev 613 (1947) **§7.10**

Note, *The Case for Black Juries,* 79 Yale LJ 531 (1970) **§2.07**

Note, *Discrimination by the Defense: Peremptory Challenges After* Batson v Kentucky, 88 Colum L Rev 355 (1988) **§8.09**

Note, *Change of Venue in Criminal Cases: The Defendant's Right to Specify the County of Transfer,* 26 Stan L Rev 131 (1973) **§2.05**

Note, *Community Hostility and the Right to an Impartial Jury,* 60 Colo L Rev 349 (1960) **§2.03**

Note, *The Constitutional Need for Discovery of Pre-Voir Dire Juror Studies,* 49 S Calif L Rev 597 (1976) **§§3.08, 4.10**

Note, *Juror Bias—A Practical Screening Device and the Case for Permitting Its Use,* 64 Minn L Rev 987 (1980) **§§2.12, 12.15, 12.16**

Note, *Limiting the Peremptory Challenge: Representation of Groups on Petit Juries,* 86 Yale LJ 1715 (1977) **§8.04**

Note, *The Right of Privacy of Prospective Jurors during Voir Dire,* 70 Calif L Rev 708 (1982) **§4.05**

Note, *Validity of a Statute Granting the State Change of Venue in a Criminal Trial,* 17 Iowa L Rev 399 (1932) **§2.03**

Note, *Voir Dire: Establishing Minimum Standards to Facilitate the Exercise of*

Peremptory Challenges, 27 Stan L Rev 1443 (1975) **§8.14**

O

Okun, *Investigation of Jurors by Counsel: Its Impact on the Decisional Process,* 56 Geo LJ 839 (1968) **§§4.02, 4.09**

P

Padawar, Singer & Burton, *Impact of Pretrial Publicity on Juror's Verdicts, in* The Jury System in America: A Critical Overview (R. Simon ed 1975) **§7.10**

R. Perry, Sources of Our Liberties (1959) **§1.03**

Phares & Wilson, *Responsibility Attribution: Role of Outcome Severity, Situational Ambiguity, and Internal-External Control,* 40 J Personality 392 (1972) **§12.17**

Pollak, Racial Discrimination and Judicial Integrity: A Reply to Professor Wechsler, 108 Pa L Rev 1 (1959) **§8.09**

R

Recent Development-Equal Protection-Refusal to Provide Expert Witness for Indigent Defendant Denies Equal Protection- Williams v Martin, 618 F2d 1021 (4th Cir 1980), 59 Wash U LQ 317 (1981) **§3.17**

Rose & Prell, *Does the Punishment Fit the Crime? A Study in Social Valuation,* 61 Am J Soc 247 (1955) **§§2.12, 12.06**

S

Saks, *Social Scientists Can't Rig Juries,* Psychology Today (1976), *reprinted in* L. Wrightsman, S. Kassin & C. Willis, In The Jury Box (1987) **§§3.08, 12.14, 12.17**

Saltzburg & Powers, *Peremptory Challenges and the Clash Between Impartiality and Group Representation,* 41 Md L Rev 337 (1982) **§8.07**

Schulman, Shaver, Colman, Emrich, & Christie, *Recipe for a Jury,* Psychology Today 37 (May 1973) **§§3.05, 3.08**

1 S. Schweitzer, Cyclopedia of Trial Practice (2d ed 1954) **§§9.09, 9.16**

R. Simon, The Jury and Defense of Insanity (1956) **§2.12**

Snyder, *Sex Role Differential and Juror Decisions,* 55 Soc & Soc Res 442 (1971) **§§2.12, 12.06**

Sosis, *Internal-External Control and the Perception of Responsibility of Another For an Accident,* 30 J of Personality & Soc Psychology 393 (1974) **§12.17**

H. Spencer, Representative Government, In Essays: Moral, Political, and Aesthetic 182 (1968), *quoted in* Hassett, *A Jury's Pre-Trial Knowledge in Historical Perspective: The Distinction between Pre-Trial Publicity and "Prejudicial" Publicity,* 43 Law & Contemp Probs 155 (Autumn 1980) **§§2.11, 7.10**

Sperlich, *The Case for Preserving Trial by Jury in Complex Civil Litigation,* 65 Judicature 397 (1982) **§1.16**

Stanley, *Who Should Conduct Voir Dire? The Judge,* 61 Judicature 70 (1977) **§9.06**

Stephan, *Selective Characteristics of Jurors and Litigants: Their Influence on Juries' Verdicts, in* R. Simon, The Jury System in America: A Critical Overview (1975) **§2.12**

Stephan, *Sex Prejudice in Jury Simulation,* 88 J Psychology 305 (1974) **§§2.12, 12.06**

Strodtbeck, James & Hawkins, *Social Status in Jury Deliberations,* 22 Am Soc Rev 713 (1957) **§2.12**

Strodtbeck & Mann, *Sex Role Differentiation in Jury Deliberations,* 19 Sociometry 3 (1956) **§§2.12, 12.06**

Suggs & Sales, *Juror Self-Disclosure in the Voir Dire: A Social Science Analysis,* 56 Ind LJ 245 (1981) **§§12.13, 12.14**

Suggs & Sales, *Using Communication Cues to Evaluate Prospective Jurors During the Voir Dire,* 20 Ariz L Rev 629 (1978) **§12.11**

T

Thayer, *The Jury and It's Development,* 5 Harv L Rev 249 (1892) **§1.02**

M. Twain, Roughing It (1872) **§7.10**

V

J. Van Dyke, Jury Selection Procedures: Our Uncertain Commitment to Representative Panels (1977) **§§1.18, 2.17, 2.20, 2.21, 8.01**

Vinson, *The Shadow Jury: An Experiment in Litigation Science,* 68 ABAJ 1242 (Oct 1982) **§5.09**

W

Weschler, *Toward Neutral Principles of Constitutional Law,* 73 Harv L Rev 1 (1959) **§8.09**

Wigmore, *A Program for the Trial of a Jury,* 12 Am Jud Socy 166 (1929) **§1.01**

Wolfram, *The Constitutional History of the Seventh Amendment,* 57 Minn L Rev 639 (1973) **§1.14**

Index

B

C

D

E

F

J

K

L

M

N

O

Q

R

T

W